Studies in Jazz

The Institute of Jazz Studies
Rutgers—The State University of New Jersey
General Editors: Dan Morgenstern and Edward Berger

1. BENNY CARTER: A Life in American Music, *by Morroe Berger, Edward Berger, and James Patrick, 2 vols., 1982*
2. ART TATUM: A Guide to His Recorded Music, *by Arnold Laubich and Ray Spencer, 1982*
3. ERROLL GARNER: The Most Happy Piano, *by James M. Doran, 1985*
4. JAMES P. JOHNSON: A Case of Mistaken Identity, *by Scott E. Brown;* Discography 1917–1950, *by Robert Hilbert, 1986*
5. PEE WEE ERWIN: This Horn for Hire, *as told to Warren W. Vaché Sr., 1987*
6. BENNY GOODMAN: Listen to His Legacy, *by D. Russell Connor, 1988*
7. ELLINGTONIA: The Recorded Music of Duke Ellington and His Sidemen, *by W. E. Timner, 1988; 4th ed., 1996*
8. THE GLENN MILLER ARMY AIR FORCE BAND: Sustineo Alas / I Sustain the Wings, *by Edward F. Polic;* Foreword *by George T. Simon, 1989*
9. SWING LEGACY, *by Chip Deffaa, 1989*
10. REMINISCING IN TEMPO: The Life and Times of a Jazz Hustler, *by Teddy Reig, with Edward Berger, 1990*
11. IN THE MAINSTREAM: 18 Portraits in Jazz, *by Chip Deffaa, 1992*
12. BUDDY DeFRANCO: A Biographical Portrait and Discography, *by John Kuehn and Arne Astrup, 1993*
13. PEE WEE SPEAKS: A Discography of Pee Wee Russell, *by Robert Hilbert, with David Niven, 1992*
14. SYLVESTER AHOLA: The Gloucester Gabriel, *by Dick Hill, 1993*
15. THE POLICE CARD DISCORD, *by Maxwell T. Cohen, 1993*
16. TRADITIONALISTS AND REVIVALISTS IN JAZZ, *by Chip Deffaa, 1993*
17. BASSICALLY SPEAKING: An Oral History of George Duvivier, *by Edward Berger;* Musical Analysis *by David Chevan, 1993*
18. TRAM: The Frank Trumbauer Story, *by Philip R. Evans and Larry F. Kiner, with William Trumbauer, 1994*
19. TOMMY DORSEY: On the Side, *by Robert L. Stockdale, 1995*
20. JOHN COLTRANE: A Discography and Musical Biography, *by Yasuhiro Fujioka, with Lewis Porter and Yoh-ichi Hamada, 1995*
21. RED HEAD: A Chronological Survey of "Red" Nichols and His Five Pennies, *by Stephen M. Stroff, 1996*
22. THE RED NICHOLS STORY: After Intermission 1942–1965, *by Philip R. Evans, Stanley Hester, Stephen Hester, and Linda Evans, 1997*
23. BENNY GOODMAN: Wrappin' It Up, *by D. Russell Connor, 1996*

Mr. Trumpet

The Trials, Tribulations, and Triumph of Bunny Berigan

Michael P. Zirpolo

Studies in Jazz, No. 64

THE SCARECROW PRESS, INC.
Lanham • Toronto • Plymouth, UK
2013

Published by Scarecrow Press, Inc.
A wholly owned subsidiary of The Rowman & Littlefield Publishing Group, Inc.
4501 Forbes Boulevard, Suite 200, Lanham, Maryland 20706
www.rowman.com

10 Thornbury Road, Plymouth PL6 7PP, United Kingdom

British Library Cataloguing in Publication Information Available

Library of Congress Cataloging-in-Publication Data Available

The hardback edition of this book was previously catalogued by the Library of Congress as follows:
Zirpolo, Michael P.
    Mr. Trumpet: the trials, tribulations, and triumph of Bunny Berigan / Michael P. Zirpolo
        p. cm. — (Studies in jazz ; No. 64)
Includes bibliographical references and index.
1. Berigan, Bunny, 1908-1942. 2. Jazz musicians—United States—Biography. I. Title.
ML419.B297Z57 2011
784.4'165092—dc22
[B]
                                     2011017359

ISBN: 978-0-8108-8152-5 (cloth : alk paper)
ISBN: 978-0-8108-8874-6 (pbk : alk. paper)
ISBN: 978-0-8108-8153-2 (electronic)

Printed in the United States of America

Contents

Introduction

It has now been more than one hundred years since the birth and more than sixty-nine years since the death of the jazz trumpeter Bunny Berigan. In his short life (November 2, 1908–June 2, 1942), Berigan's trumpet artistry made a deep and lasting impression on almost everyone who heard him play. The body of recorded work he left continues to evoke a wide range of emotions in those who hear it. The outline of Berigan's life resembles an ancient Greek tragedy: a heroic figure rises from obscurity to dizzying heights, touches greatness, becomes ensnared by circumstances, some beyond his control, others of his own making, and comes to a disastrous early end.

My own introduction to the music and mystique of Bunny Berigan came early in my life through my father, Michael P. Zirpolo Sr. In his youth in the 1930s, he collected a number of 78 rpm records by Berigan, and on one memorable occasion saw him perform. Throughout the 1950s, when I was a child, he would occasionally play these 78s, and lament that while he was in the army during World War II, one of his sisters had broken the most prized of his Berigan discs, RCA Victor 36208, a twelve-inch record with "I Can't Get Started" on side A, and "The Prisoner's Song" on side B. In the late 1950s, he began replacing his old, scratchy 78s with new improved-fidelity long-playing records. One of the LPs he got, RCA Victor LPM 2078, which I still have, contains twelve performances by Berigan's big band of the late 1930s.

In December of 1960, I, like most other ten-year-olds in America, was counting down the days until Christmas. As anyone who knows me will attest, I have always had an insatiable curiosity about many things. At that time, my curiosity was focused on what Santa Claus would be bringing me for Christmas. The previous Christmas, I had argued passionately to my older sister that Santa did indeed exist, and that I believed in him. She dismissed this, informing me that Santa Claus was nothing but a mythical character. I was crestfallen, but stubbornly clung to the notion that Santa was real. As Christmas 1960 approached, I began to reevaluate the question of the existence of Santa Claus. I decided to begin looking for gifts in hiding places around the house. If I did not find any hidden gifts, then Santa Claus probably existed. If I found gifts, then Santa did not exist.

In a very short time, I discovered a cache of articles in a remote part of the basement under some summer clothes that had been stored away for the winter. I was ambivalent about sorting through these items. I really didn't want to prove to myself that Santa Claus did not exist. So I picked up the item that was on top of the pile, the sealed dust jacket containing RCA Victor LPM 2078. This must be a gift for my father, I thought, as I read the writing on the front. It said *The Great Dance Bands of the '30s and '40s—Bunny Berigan and His Orchestra.* The color drawing on the dust jacket was of a handsome tuxedo-clad man in front of a band holding a gleaming, gold trumpet, singing into a small overhead microphone on a canopied bandstand. Glamorous couples danced in front of the bandstand. The man had arresting blue eyes.[1] I concluded that this must be Bunny Berigan. I turned the dust jacket over and read the writing on the back. There were six brief paragraphs written by Stewart Williams which summarized the life of Bunny Berigan.

Almost the first thing I read was that Bunny Berigan was dead. At age ten, I knew almost nothing about death. Basically, the only things I knew about death were that it scared me, that I didn't want to die, and that I didn't want anyone or anything else to die. The rest of the story was rather meaningless to me, but I sensed that the life of Bunny Berigan must have been sad. I put the dust jacket back where I had found it, covered it with the summer clothes, and went upstairs. My curiosity had caused me to learn two things that day: that Santa Claus didn't exist, and that Bunny Berigan was dead.

In the house where I lived with my family in 1960 was a cozy, comfortable room on the second floor where my father's record player and records were. I was strictly forbidden from touching either. In order to do anything in that room, I would have to have been more or less invited by my father. One day shortly after Christmas, I knew he was up there because I could hear the most marvelous music wafting down the stairs. What I heard was the sound of a soaring trumpet. I softly climbed the stairs and quietly entered the music room. My father was there, sitting on the edge of a chair, leaning forward with his elbows on his knees, his head in his hands. He was *listening.* The trumpet music had stopped and a man was now singing, "...I've flown around the world in a plane..." I just stood there and said nothing. When the music stopped, my father raised his head, removed the tone arm from the record, turned, and looked at me. There were tears running down his cheeks.

I was confused by this, and very uneasy. My father was not a man who expressed his emotions freely. I had never seen him cry before, and indeed never saw him cry again, though he lived for another forty-three years. This scene took on an almost surreal quality. I really didn't know what to say, so I said the most obvious thing: "Dad, why are you crying?" As he took out his handkerchief and began wiping the tears from his eyes, he said rather forcefully, "Dammit, why did he have to kill himself with the booze?" I had no idea to whom he was referring, so I said, "Who killed himself?" He then replied softly, "Bunny did. Bunny Berigan—the guy who made that record." I then asked him if he had ever seen Bunny Berigan perform. A smile came across his face as he began to recount the one occasion when he had witnessed the full force of Berigan's music and persona. It was a story I was to hear again many times over the next decades, told each time with gusto and joy.

****

I obtained much of the information contained in this book from what is referred to in the endnotes as "the White materials." Cedric Kingsley "Bozy" White (1927–2004) gathered and edited details about Bunny Berigan's life and career for over fifty years, being assisted at various times by others: first by Tom Cullen, and later by Martin L. Kite, Opie Austin, John Grams, Don Wilson, Morton Savada, John Stanton, Ian Crosbie, and others. After White's death, these materials were preserved and edited further by Perry Huntoon and Ed Polic, among others. As this is being written, the White materials are being readied for publication as a Bunny Berigan biodiscography. The White materials contain literally thousands of bits of information about Bunny Berigan and the milieu in which he lived and worked that, when considered individually, are of little significance. They are, however, very much like the small tiles that make up a mosaic. When they are regarded in the context of Berigan's life story, they take on a much greater meaning and provide a deeper understanding of the man. It would have been impossible for me to have written this book without having complete access to the White materials, and for that I thank Perry Huntoon.[2]

I also relied upon Robert Dupuis's biography of Berigan, *Bunny Berigan— Elusive Legend of Jazz*, for much information. This biography contains many recollections of Berigan family members, friends, and musical associates. Unlike most of the White materials, the Dupuis biography includes a narrative. It also contains Mr. Dupuis's judicious opinions. It is certainly possible to find contradictions between the White materials and the Dupuis biography. Indeed, some of the conclusions I reach in this book are not to be found in either of those sources. Nevertheless, to me both sources are absolutely essential pieces of Berigan scholarship, and each of them contributes to a more complete understanding of Bunny Berigan. I must also thank Bob Dupuis for taking the time to answer the many questions I have asked him over many years about Bunny Berigan.

Many of the photos in this book have never been published before. Most were found by me in the Norm Krusinski Berigan archive at the Mills Music Library, University of Wisconsin–Madison. These photos were made available to me by Jeanette L. Casey, director of that library. Other previously unpublished photos were located by me in the Harriet O'Connell Historical Room at the Fox Lake, Wisconsin, Public Library, and were made available to me by Julie Flemming, who for many years was director of that library. She is now retired but a quite active volunteer there. I am most grateful to both of these ladies for allowing me to use those photos in this book, and for patiently assisting me as I rooted through their archival materials and asked an unending series of questions while I was in their libraries and later.

Finally, I often referred to the various writings of jazz trumpeter Richard M. Sudhalter[3] (1938–2008) about Berigan, most notably his liner notes for the

Time-Life *Giants of Jazz* set of LPs covering Berigan's work; the liner notes to the RCA-BMG Bluebird CD entitled *Bunny Berigan—The Pied Piper, 1934–40*; his monumental book *Lost Chords*; and lastly his liner notes for the Mosaic Berigan CD collection: *The Complete Brunswick, Parlophone and Vocalion Bunny Berigan Sessions*. No one has ever written more perceptively and poetically about Bunny Berigan the musician. Unfortunately, illness caused the flow of Mr. Sudhalter's brilliant commentary on Berigan's music to cease shortly after publication of the Mosaic liner notes.

Both Robert Dupuis and Richard M. Sudhalter had access to some or all of the White materials when they were writing about Bunny Berigan.

All photos used in this book are from the author's collection unless otherwise noted in a photo's caption.

Michael P. Zirpolo
Canton, Ohio
August 2011

Notes

[1] This drawing was derived from a photo of Bunny Berigan taken in early 1936 when he was appearing at the Famous Door, a jazz club on Fifty-second Street in Manhattan.
[2] Perry Huntoon is a former president of the International Association of Record Collectors (IAJRC).
[3] Richard M. Sudhalter, born on December 28, 1938, in Boston, was the son of Al Sudhalter, a noted Boston-area saxophonist. He was the unique individual who combined the professional talents of jazz cornetist and writer. In addition to performing with many jazz groups from 1964 to 2003, when he suffered a stroke, he was a correspondent for United Press International in the 1960s, stationed in Europe. He also wrote jazz criticism for the *New York Post* from 1978 to 1984. For his liner notes to *Bunny Berigan: Giants of Jazz* (1982), he received a Grammy Award; and for his book *Lost Chords: White Musicians and Their Contribution to Jazz, 1915–1950* (1999), he received an ASCAP Deems Taylor Special Citation for Excellence. After Sudhalter's stroke, he developed multiple system atrophy, a condition that left him unable to speak, and ultimately led to his death from pneumonia on September 19, 2008, in New York City.

Chapter 1
Beginnings: Home and Family

Roland Bernard[1] Berigan, who will forever be known to those who appreciate his music as "Bunny," was born at 5:30 a.m. on November 2, 1908, in Hilbert, Calumet County, Wisconsin. His parents were William Patrick Berigan and Mary Catherine (Schlitzberg) Berigan. H.E. Luehrs, M.D., was in attendance at his birth, which took place in a rented two-story frame house at 150 North Seventh Street. Hilbert, then also known as Hilbert Junction, had a population of between 300 and 500. The Berigan family was of Irish extraction, tracing their ancestors to Kilkenny and Galway, Ireland. The Schlitzberg family was of German extraction, with their ancestors coming from Hanover, Germany.[2] The Schlitzberg family was notable for its musical talent.

John Schlitzberg Sr. and his wife, Julia Phlipson Schlitzberg, had five children, of whom the oldest, Mary Catherine, was Bunny Berigan's mother. The Schlitzbergs were Protestant; the Phlipsons were Catholic. The Schlitzberg children were raised as Catholics. All of the Schlitzberg children received musical training, and they all played musical instruments, very frequently in bands assembled and led by their father. John Schlitzberg Sr. played violin and cornet; his wife played organ. Their daughter Mary, know to all as "Mayme," played piano and organ from an early age. She received musical training first by studying piano at Downer College in Fox Lake, Wisconsin, and later at Wayland College in nearby Beaver Dam. Later still, she played organ at St. Mary's Catholic Church in Fox Lake for many years. Mayme also carried on the family music tradition by playing in various bands led by her father, performing on alto and baritone horns, both before and shortly after her marriage to William P. Berigan. Due to the circumstances of the first three years of their marriage however, including two pregnancies, the constant care required by her infant sons, and the rather frequent moves occasioned by William's employment, Mayme's musical activities were suspended then. This could not have been pleasant for someone who enjoyed playing music as much as Mayme Berigan.

Both of Bernard Berigan's parents were born in rural Wisconsin, Mayme in Packwaukee in 1875, and William in Fox Lake, in 1872. For that time and place, they were much older than the norm when they married in Fox Lake on October 5, 1904, at St. Mary's Catholic Church. Their first son, Donald, was born in Madison, Wisconsin, on September 3, 1905, where William was then employed by the U.S. Express Company. Soon thereafter, he was transferred to Menominee, then to Hilbert. Mayme was very close to her mother. She visited her at the Schlitzberg homestead in Fox Lake on occasion, and stayed there temporarily shortly after Donald's birth. When her pregnancy with her second child entered its last month, her mother came to Hilbert to stay with her, and help her. Shortly after Bernard's birth, he developed whooping cough, and by the spring of 1909 was living with his mother and brother in the home of his maternal grandparents, 524 West State Street, Fox Lake, where Julia Schlitzberg lavished care on her tiny grandson, and enjoyed the return home of her oldest child.

William Berigan's work kept him in Hilbert until he moved back to Fox Lake to take a job as a traveling salesman with the Badger Candy Company, probably in mid-1909. His new job required him to be away from home five days a week, returning on Friday evenings for the weekend. It was at this time that he started bowling regularly, and became quite good at it. He soon acquired the nickname "Cap" because he was usually the captain of the teams on which he bowled. Previously, William Berigan had been a prominent member of the Fox Lake baseball team, and had excelled at other athletic activities. Later, he was a fine trapshooter. William Berigan was over six feet tall, and a nondrinker. His family still resided in the Schlitzberg house as late as the April 1910 census.[3]

Mayme Berigan was undoubtedly happy to be back in her parents' home and back in Fox Lake. The Schlitzberg house was large and comfortable; her parents were constantly caring and supportive. And the house was filled with music. The Schlitzberg home had a piano in its parlor, and Mayme quickly resumed her piano playing there. She also returned to playing in her father's various bands, and independently for a variety of social gatherings. As a result, from infancy, little Bernard was very often exposed to the performance of music. Mayme's father, John Schlitzberg, was by then a leading Fox Lake businessman, and musician. He was tall and blond, and had inherited his musical talent from his father, Frederick Schlitzberg. He evidently was a man with some business acumen. It was put to good use when he joined his future father-in-law, John Phlipson, first in the operation of his wagon shop, and later in his furniture store and funeral parlor. After Phlipson's death in 1909, John Schlitzberg continued to operate this Fox Lake business successfully for many years. John Schlitzberg, patriarch, businessman, and musician, was a paragon for his entire family, and especially for Mayme's younger son, Bernard, who spent a great deal of time in the Schlitzberg family home while he was growing up.

Cap and Mayme Berigan's younger son never used his given first name, Roland. Almost from the beginning, he was referred to with variations on his middle name, Bernard. As a child in Fox Lake, he was called "Bun." Still, most references to him in the local newspaper, the *Fox Lake Representative*, until the 1930s, were by the name "Bernard Berigan."

Bunny's life progressed in an unremarkable way until he was about eight, at which time he began playing the violin. His first solo in public in February of 1917 was as a singer, however. This event was the basis for the oft-told story of him singing with his mother accompanying him on a piano that was keyed higher than the instrument they had practiced with. Before Mayme could tell

Bunny to wait while she found a lower key, he was off and singing in the higher key. After completing the song successfully, he said to his mother: "Gee, Ma, that was hard, but I got it, didn't I?" Mayme said it was then that she realized that Bunny had a good understanding of music.[4] Shortly thereafter, Bunny was playing alto horn (an instrument his mother also played) in a community children's band organized by his grandfather. This band was quite active through the summer months and into the fall each year. It is this band that is pictured in a photograph of Bunny holding an alto horn.[5] Also in the photo are his brother, three cousins, and John Schlitzberg Sr. By the time this photo was taken (spring 1917) Bunny's haunting good looks had already manifested themselves. The major focal points even then were the blue-gray eyes he inherited from his mother. Bunny finished the third grade around the time this photo was taken.

Some insights into the Berigan side of Bunny's family were provided by Cap's sister Delia Berigan Casey:

> Mayme was the church organist for many years. She was an easy-going type of person, not easily excitable or concerned. Bill, my brother, tended to be more excitable, but the two boys idolized him. He was 6'2" tall, a non-drinker and a sports enthusiast, who was on the road much of the time. Mayme was a very active lady, always on the go, so the kids didn't have much home life until the weekends when dad came home. Bill encouraged the boys' musical interests as the Berigan family also had some musicians. 'Big Bob,' my brother, was a fine drummer, brother John played clarinet, and Leroy played saxophone. Bill had a good voice and was due to sing solo in church one Christmas, but froze when his turn came![6]

Since Bunny's mother was the organist at St. Mary's Catholic Church in Fox Lake, he spent a good deal of time there with her. He was baptized and confirmed in that church, sang in the church choir, and was an altar boy. On special occasions, he would bring his violin to church and play it. In addition, Bunny was involved in other performances in Fox Lake: "The Memorial Day (1918) program in Fox Lake includes the parade, exercises at the cemetery and a program at Odd Fellows Hall by school children, which includes a dialogue by Bernard Berigan and Charles Casey, entitled *We Are the Men of the Coming Years.*"[7] Bunny returned to Odd Fellows Hall a couple of months later, presenting something called *The Farther It Is from Tipperary*, with his cousin Adrian Schlitzberg. The great flu epidemic of 1918 struck Fox Lake in October 1918, causing the closure of all public buildings for a period of time. There were twenty-five cases of flu in Fox Lake then.

World War I ended on November 11, 1918, shortly after Bunny's tenth birthday. In February 1919, the Fox Lake Juvenile Band, including Bunny on alto horn, played at the Fox Lake train depot to welcome home army veterans. A photo of this appeared in the *Fox Lake Representative* on February 20, 1919. By the summer of 1919, Bunny had begun learning how to play the trumpet.

The next event of significance in young Bunny's life occurred in February, 1920, when he almost died from appendicitis.

Bernard Berigan, the young son of Will P. Berigan of this village, was taken with an attack of appendicitis Friday, and on Saturday morning was taken to Portage to the hospital, where Dr. Meacher performed an operation for the removal of his appendix. The operation was successful, the patient got along nicely. He is doing as well as can be expected and will probably be able to be brought home in the course of a few days. His mother has been with him right along and the boy was as brave and courageous as anybody could ask. The father, and John Schlitzberg, grandfather, accompanied him to Portage on Saturday.[8]

"Cully" Schlitzberg, Bunny's aunt whose real name was Cora Angeline, and who was ten years younger than her oldest sister, Mayme, recalled: "When Bunny was 11, his appendix broke and he nearly died at Portage Hospital. Granddad told him to get well, and he'd give him a new instrument, but he looked very pale for some time after he came home." Hattie O'Connell (unofficial Fox Lake historian) said: "Bunny nearly died of peritonitis when he was 11 years old. He'd been in pain at school for three or four days and didn't know what it was. His grandfather promised him a new cornet if he got well. Bunny went to the Portage Hospital."[9] Donald Berigan added:

Bunny practiced violin for about two years, then Granddad gave him a cornet, which he just picked up and played! He never took a lesson that I knew of, and he was also playing alto horn in the kids' band. He was about 10 years old then. We both played baseball in summer and were pitchers on our kids' team. We also did a lot of ice skating in winter, also roller skating at Granddad's roller rink. Bunny was a very good pool player too and although our dad was one of the best at it, Bunny could beat him, and anybody else he played. And this when he was only about 11 years old![10]

The local newspaper continued to follow Bunny's convalescence: "N.H. Berigan spent the day, Friday, at the Portage Hospital with 'Bun' Berigan. W.P. Berigan, and Raymond McCarthy spent Sunday (16th) at Portage, where they visited the former's son, who recently underwent an operation for appendicitis. The boy is getting along fine and will probably be brought home in a short time."[11] Bunny returned home from the hospital on February 26, after having spent nineteen days there. The above is the first reference to Bunny's nickname in the Fox Lake paper, which usually continued to call him Bernard. At about this time, Bunny's grandfather's furniture store began stocking phonographs and records, and Bunny immediately became an enthusiastic listener to the latest releases.

By the summer of 1920, Bunny began to demonstrate his flair for sports, among other endeavors. Adrian Schlitzberg (Bunny's cousin) said: "I remember Bunny for his very erect carriage. He had as hobbies, billiards (was very good), golf and baseball. He was a natural ball player and he could throw a curve ball in the 7th or 8th grade, but his dad (granddad?) made him give it up when he started to take violin lessons. He was level headed and had a quick mind."[12] Bunny also joined the Boy Scouts around this time.

Bunny's aptitude at pool was frequently commented upon by his associates throughout his life. There are myriad references to Bunny's pool playing in the White materials. It appears that he was exceptionally talented at pool, and that he later made the acquaintance of some professional pool players.

In March of 1921, Bunny's maternal grandmother, Julia Phlipson Schlitzberg, died at age sixty-four. This was a traumatic event for Bunny's mother, who had been very close to her mother, and for Bunny, who had spent very much time in his grandmother's house. It appears that Mayme then moved her family into the Schlitzberg home again, and the three generations continued to dwell there under the resolute guidance of John Schlitzberg Sr. The years Bunny spent living in the home of his grandparents were the most secure of his life. In the meantime, Cap Berigan continued to travel constantly with his employment.

That summer, Bunny continued playing in the Fox Lake Juvenile Band, which had been reorganized under new leadership in the wake of the death of John Schlitzberg's wife. Mr. Schlitzberg continued to support the activities of this band however. In due course, he married again, to Mary Casey.[13]

Although Bunny was playing the trumpet by the summer of 1921,[14] and cornets were a part of the Juvenile Band, he continued to play alto horn in that band. He was also studying violin with Clarence H. Wagner in Beaver Dam at that time. Cora Valinske, his seventh-grade teacher recalled the time when Bunny was a pupil in her class:

> Bunny was a bright boy, although school work was not his first interest. I cannot remember that he was impudent, even though he had enough attention and admiration to have become spoiled. He had a reading for a Memorial Day program and had to sing portions of *Annie Laurie*. He didn't get any help from me on the singing part, but his nice voice carried him through that difficult song with credit.[15]

Bunny's development as a musician continued with his performing solos as a singer or violinist at numerous community activities. These performances were sometimes with the Fox Lake Juvenile Band, sometimes with his mother's accompaniment on piano, and often on his own. Kids who grew up with Bunny recall that even though he would join them in various games and other activities, he frequently would leave them to go home to practice his trumpet. In September 1922, Bunny entered high school. It appears that his first public performance on trumpet occurred in 1923, with the Fox Lake Juvenile Band.

Previous reports notwithstanding, available evidence indicates that Bunny continued his musical pursuits in Fox Lake throughout 1922 and into 1923, as he had in the past.[16] His activities that year, aside from music, included campouts with his Boy Scout troop. On November 2, 1923, he celebrated his fifteenth birthday.

By 1924, Bunny was beginning to play his trumpet in public outside of the Fox Lake Juvenile Band. Donald Berigan recalled:

> After Bunny started to play the trumpet, we'd play along with the phonograph records of Paul Whiteman, Red Nichols and bands of that period. I played drums. We also started the *Berigan Three* which was Bunny on the trumpet, mother Mayme on piano and me on drums. I had the nickname of 'Tony' in those days, and we played for dances after card parties, also at the roller skating rink and for our own enjoyment. We'd also play at nights at home and neighbors and others would drop by to listen. Often on waltzes or slow tunes, Bunny would play violin rather than trumpet. We were also known as the *Berigan Orchestra* and my brother was using 'Bunny' as his name by then.[17]

Hattie O'Connell, who knew Bunny's mother well, had these memories of Bunny's early musical development:

> While you'll note that several of Bunny's relatives played a part in the boy's musical development, it always appeared to me that his mother deserved the main credit. She was a completely trained musician, who gave him proper training from the start and was capable of judging his ability. She was, moreover, a calm, dignified personality, who encouraged him to participate in local music events, but never exploited the boy's talent nor boasted of it. In fact, I never heard her mention the subject unless someone else broached it. It was always evident that she was proud and happy over his success, but had the good judgment to understand that everyone was not quite as interested in it as she was. Bunny was always a pleasant, quiet boy; a great deal like his mother in that respect. On his later visits to the old home, he appeared more anxious to forget his public career than to discuss it.[18]

The first public acknowledgment of Bunny's association with the Merrill Owen band appeared in the Fox Lake newspaper on May 8, 1924.[19] The Owen band, a local group out of Beaver Dam, nine miles from Fox Lake, was playing on that evening in Schlitzberg Hall, probably for a dance. This event marked the first step on the road to Bunny Berigan's becoming a professional, touring musician. Like almost all early masters of jazz, Berigan's musical personality was formed in the crucible of popular dance music. Although Bunny had joined the Owen band before the end of the school year, he did indeed finish his second year of high school in early June. In the summer of 1924, he continued playing with the Owen band, frequently staying overnight at the home of fellow band member Hub Keefer, who lived in Beaver Dam and played saxophone and clarinet. The Owen band played one-night engagements throughout the territory surrounding Beaver Dam and Fox Lake during the summer and into the fall. Bunny did not return to school in the fall until the beginning of the second quarter because of his continuing work with the Owen band. During this time, Bunny worked with the Owen band in short pants (knickers) with long stockings. When he returned to Fox Lake, he insisted that he be allowed to wear long pants from then on. He then resumed life as a sixteen-year-old high school student in Fox Lake until the end of the spring quarter of the 1924–1925 school year.

Right after the New Year, Merrill Owen landed a job playing for nightly dancing in Milwaukee at Sam Wah's Chinese Restaurant. The engagement was for fourteen weeks, and Bunny began to travel the sixty miles from Fox Lake to Milwaukee on weekends to play with the band. During part of the gig, the Owen band broadcast over a local radio station, and at some point during that engagement, Bunny took part in his first radio broadcast. Still, he was very much a part of his school's musical activities, participating in its minstrel show in February by playing "cornet" and singing.[20] A photo of the Owen band taken in February 1925 shows a startlingly handsome Bunny holding a trumpet. It is unlikely that he ever played a cornet. He certainly never recorded with a cornet. He also continued appearing at various Fox Lake events in performance with his mother. He participated with a number of family members in St. Patrick's Day festivities at Odd Fellows Hall, this time as an actor in a play called *Kathleen Mavourneen*. But by this time, there was beginning to be tension between Bunny and his parents as a result of his increasing desire to quit school and become a professional musician. At the end of the spring quarter, he left school to work full-time with the Owen band, which had returned to Beaver Dam at the end of the Milwaukee job. But at that time, they were working only sporadically at local venues.

Around the end of May, 1925, Bunny quit the Owen band and joined Si Mahlberg, whose band was from Fond du Lac. He received more money with Mahlberg. As he had been in the Owen band, Bunny was the youngest member of the Mahlberg band. They played in the territory around Fond du Lac throughout the summer until it was time for school to resume around the first of September.

The dispute within the Berigan family over Bunny remaining in school was still very much ongoing in the fall of 1925, just before his seventeenth birthday. His previous year in high school in Fox Lake had been abbreviated with Bunny not attending the fall and spring quarters. Nevertheless, Bunny's Fox Lake High School transcript of grades reveals that he was an above average student. To break the stalemate between the young man and his parents, it was decided that Bunny would go to live with Cap's younger brother, "Big Bob" Berigan, in Madison, and enroll in University (some sources have it Wisconsin) High School there. "Big Bob," who was fifteen years older than Bunny, was a part-time drummer who seemed to have some good musical connections in Madison.[21]

Notes

[1] Berigan's birth certificate states that his name at birth was *Rowland Bernart Berigan.* It also indicates that Bunny's mother was born at Fox Lake, Wisconsin, and that the age of Bunny's father when Bunny was born was thirty-two years. Based on other more reliable information maintained by the Berigan family, Bunny's real birth name was *Roland Bernard;* his mother was born in Packwaukee, Wisconsin; and his father's age at Bunny's birth was thirty-six years.

[2] This information comes from the White materials. Since pagination of the White material was not final when I was reviewing it, I will cite to specific dates contained in the materials, because they are organized chronologically. Henceforth, citations to this source will be as follows: "White materials: date of reference."

[3] White materials: April 1910.

[4] White materials: February 2, 1917.

[5] This photo was initially published in the April Fools edition of *Metronome* magazine in 1938, with a gag caption. Later (1982) it was published in the Time-Life *Giants of Jazz* LP set that was devoted to Bunny Berigan (page 4).

[6] White materials: September 6, 1917.

[7] *Fox Lake Representative:* May 23, 1918, cited in White materials.

[8] *Fox Lake Representative:* February 12, 1920, cited in the White materials.

[9] *Ibid.*

[10] *Ibid.*

[11] *Fox Lake Representative:* February 19, 1920, cited in the White materials.

[12] White materials: August 30, 1920.

[13] White materials: 1913. Note: John Schlitzberg married Mary Casey at least one year after his first wife, Julia Phlipson Schlitzberg, died in March 1921.

[14] There is no evidence that Berigan ever played the cornet.

[15] White materials: May 30, 1921.

[16] The Merrill Owen band, with which he would be connected later, was formed in the spring of 1923. The Owen band first appeared in Fox Lake in August 1923, but nothing suggests that Bunny played with them then.

[17] White materials: February 18, 1924.

[18] White materials: March 25, 1924.

[19] White materials: May 8, 1924.

[20] White materials: February 19–20, 1925.

[21] White materials: September 20, 1925.

Chapter 2
Madison

In reviewing the White materials, I was constantly amazed by the vitality, variety, and sheer size of the music scene in Madison, Wisconsin, in the mid and late 1920s. There was abundant work for musicians there in theaters, restaurants, dance halls and roadhouses, and of course, at the University of Wisconsin. It was in Madison that Bunny Berigan advanced from being a talented youngster to being a professional musician having outstanding ability.

Almost immediately after his arrival in Madison, Bunny's uncle Bob initiated him into the local music scene. He played in a six-piece band Bob co-led with saxophonist Erle Smith, which was booked by the Alvin Thompson Agency. Thompson controlled 90 percent of the band work in Madison. He acted as a broker for musicians, not only finding jobs for them, but forming all kinds of bands for whatever the occasion required. He also led his own band.[1] Erle Smith described the musical environment Bunny found himself a part of in Madison:

I was born on October 30, 1906 in Columbus, Wisconsin, and went to Madison in 1924 to study at the University of Wisconsin, which I left in 1926, but didn't graduate. I got a job in a music store as I wasn't interested in going on the road and there was plenty of work playing in and around Madison. I met Bob Berigan who was playing in student bands, though he wasn't a student himself, around 1925 when the Berigan-Smith band billing began. Bunny joined us that same year and we stayed together as a unit for about two years. Though we were booked by the Al Thompson office, we had no contracts. You'd work when he called, but if you had another commitment he'd get someone else and call you next time. Usually we had no singer, but Bunny would occasionally sing a jazz number. I'd met Bunny a couple of years earlier when he was with Merrill Owen in Beaver Dam. I was playing with a little band out of Columbus, where I was in high school. There were seven or eight good trumpet players in Madison when Bunny arrived, but they couldn't compare with him even then. He was years ahead of them with his ideas, his use of mutes and his jazz style. The Berigan-Smith band played many college dates, usually from 9 p.m. until midnight or later, as the band got into the spirit of the occasion! The dancers wanted fast music like one-steps and the clubs had neither bars nor tables, so you either danced or you sat— if you could get a seat! The Berigan-Smith band and other Thompson units played for fraternity and sorority parties on the University of Wisconsin campus. Each band played a least one party every month, they were normally from 9 p.m. until midnight. Bunny was still in high school when we started the band, but he was never really interested in school, music came first. We used to go down to Bob's house on Doty Street and copy licks from Louis Armstrong records to play on the job, but Bunny went beyond that so he wasn't copying anyone. Our stuff was all improvised. We didn't have any sheet music, and when Bunny played solo, people would often stop dancing to listen—not necessarily every night, but it happened. The band comprised Bunny on trumpet, Jimmy Donahue, piano, Hank Meyers, banjo, Russ Morhoff, bass, Big Bob on drums and me on alto sax. This basic group, sometimes with men added or subbing, did most of Thompson's best work during the 1925–1927 years, and I stuck mainly to alto sax rather than clarinet. Bunny and I used to listen to records by the Dorsey Brothers as well as Louie and perhaps pick out an 8-bar break or solo we particularly liked. In 1928, Bunny and I went into the pit bands of the Madison theaters, before he went east for a time. He was back the following year leading bands for Thompson. I guess I played lead alto in some of those groups, but Big Bob didn't play drums—perhaps he didn't fancy working under his nephew![2]

Lucien "Lou" Hanks, a musician and student at the University of Wisconsin then, added his recollections of the then almost seventeen-year-old Bunny Berigan:

I was born on September 15, 1907, twenty minutes before my twin brother, James J., and I first met Bunny at Wisconsin High School in the fall of 1925, when he'd just come down from Fox Lake. I had been kicked out of the high school where my brother and I were going and that is how I wound up in Wisconsin High. Later I attended the University of Wisconsin, and played 3rd clarinet in the big concert band ca.1930–1932. I used to give a dance every other Friday night at a downtown dance hall for students from the three high schools in Madison. I had a list of all the boys and girls and sent out invitations as well as hiring the hall and an orchestra from the Thompson Agency, which had several bands that serviced high school and college dances. Of course, Bunny persuaded me to hire the Berigan-Smith band whenever I could. He was a mild mannered guy, never extending himself in conversation unless he was drawn into it. He was a year behind me in school, but his main interest was in playing in the band rather than his studies. His entire life was his music and his trumpet was really his best friend. He'd only go out with girls if we were double-dating and I remember going to pick him up at his house on one such occasion and was told he was in his room getting dressed. When I went up, I found him in a closet that was completely lined with pillows, and when I asked Big Bob what that was all about, he told me that if Bunny got an idea for a solo in the middle of the night, he'd shut himself in the closet so his playing wouldn't wake the household! I remember a Frances 'Babe' Weiss was one of the girls Bunny dated around that time, and I guess he liked to impress them with his horn. There was plenty of liquor available then in spite of Prohibition, but I don't recall Bunny drinking and smoking in those days. Whenever I was at a dance where he was playing, he'd always ask me how he sounded and how he went over with the crowd because, although he hadn't developed a great deal of stage presence, he was always concerned with the audience reaction to his playing. We went ice sailing one winter when I was beginning to appreciate how good a player he was. 'Hey Bunny' I asked him 'How come you play the trumpet like you do?' 'The same way you're able to sail this damn ice boat' he replied.[3] (Note: Hanks repeatedly refers to "Wisconsin" High School, as do other persons then in school in Madison. Items about Bunny in his hometown newspaper from this time refer to it as "University" High School.)

In addition to working in the Berigan-Smith band, Bunny's ever-increasing proficiency on trumpet also earned him frequent employment in Alvin Thompson's big band, which played at Thompson's Cameo Room in Madison in the colder months, and at Thompson's Esther Beach Ballroom, on Lake Monona, just outside Madison, in warmer weather. But for both the Thanksgiving and Christmas holidays in 1925, Bunny, who had just recently turned seventeen, was back in Fox Lake to participate in family events.

By mid-January 1926, Bunny's name appeared in a *Madison Capital Times* ad for the Joe Rivers band, which was then playing in the Cameo Room. Between his work with the Berigan-Smith band, the Thompson big band, and other random gigs like the ones he played with Joe Rivers, Bunny kept quite busy in early 1926. He spent some time around Easter at home in Fox Lake. Later that spring, his Fox Lake High School class graduated, without him of course. The Berigan-Smith band played often at the Esther Beach Ballroom in the summer of 1926. As a result of eating large quantities of hamburgers, pie, and cake, after his work at Esther Beach, his weight had gone up to 185 pounds. He now stood over six feet in height. He was back in Fox Lake around Labor Day for about a week, presumably to discuss his school situation with his parents. It appears that he did complete his third year of high school in Madison, but there is not any verification of this in the White materials.[4]

By the fall of 1926, the Berigan-Smith band was playing in the Cameo Room for "official student dances." The enrollment at the University was then 8,000, an all-time high. On Monday, October 25, 1926, just a week before his eighteenth birthday, Bunny Berigan joined Madison Local 166 of the American Federation of Musicians. According to Erle Smith and Bob Berigan: "All of Al Thompson's musicians became members of the Madison branch of the union at the same time. There were about a hundred of them. Before that, we'd get paid around $7.00 a night, afterwards it increased to $8.00 or $9.00, which was pretty good for those days."[5] Once again, Bunny spent the year-end holidays in Fox Lake with his family.

The Berigan-Smith band was appearing at the Cameo Room in early 1927, but now, on occasion, was augmented to ten pieces. Bunny's brother Don, who left high school after the tenth grade, and had been attempting to earn a living as a barber in Fox Lake, moved to Madison about this time. He, Bunny, and their cousin Charles Casey, who had been working as a cartoonist or commercial artist, moved in together with their paternal grandmother, Margaret McMahon Berigan, who also resided in Madison. It is at this time that stories began about Bunny going to Chicago to hear Louis Armstrong.[6] Unfortunately, there is no verification of any of these stories, except one statement by Bunny himself that was published much later in *Down Beat.*[7]

Another Madison musician who worked with Berigan at that time gave some insights as to how the various bands Bunny played with presented their music. Roland Francis Endres (trumpet) recalled:

I did not attend the University of Wisconsin, nor did Bunny, but I knew him and played alongside of him frequently. Although I was considered a pretty competent trumpet player, I played second trumpet when Bunny played first. He was justly considered to be the better performer with his appealing, rolling style and fine technique. All our jobs were for the Al Thompson booking agency, usually 6 or 7 piece bands and always using the same musicians. The library consisted of printed stock charts, no special arrangements. We faked the standards and Bunny's solos were excellent, evoking fervent listener response. Our group would work up certain routines on the standards, which we would memorize. Bunny did no singing with the band, which was usually referred to as Thompson's 1st Band. We usually worked two or three nights a week for about 12 bucks a night. On very rare occasions, we would augment the band to 10 pieces, using 3 brass, 3 reeds and 4 rhythm. All those jobs would pay a premium. Most weekend jobs were 6 or 7 men at fraternities or sororities, privately, but there were frequent public dances at the students' union or some other location. Of course, we played numerous jobs at pavilions or parks, including Thompson's summer pavilion at Esther Beach, and his winter spot, the uptown Cameo Room, a dressy, beautiful dance hall. Bunny and I played many gigs at both spots. Later, I switched to the Cohen booking office.[8] (This reference to "Cohen" is a reference to pianist Jesse Cowan, who went by the name Cohen, and operated a much smaller booking enterprise in Madison than the Thompson office, and also led various bands. There is no evidence that Bunny ever worked for Jesse Cohen.) [9]

Bunny continued working regularly with various Thompson bands, including the Berigan-Smith band, at various locations throughout the summer of 1927. When he was able, he would return home to Fox Lake for visits, usually with his brother and/or cousin. Although there have been assertions that he worked in the pit band at the Ringling Theater in Baraboo, about thirty-five miles from Madison, late in the summer of 1927, there is no verification of this. Nor is there evidence that he took trumpet lessons at this time.

Bunny's grandfather, John Schlitzberg, died in 1927. The cause of death on his death certificate is "sclerosis of the liver."[10] *Sclerosis* appears to be another term to describe "cirrhosis" of the liver. There is no information extant as to whether John Schlitzberg was a drinker. There is however medical evidence that a genetic predisposition to cirrhosis of the liver can be passed from generation to generation. It is among the many ironies in the life of Bunny Berigan that he may have received the genetic predisposition to the disease that killed him from the same person who undoubtedly was a major source of his musical talent, his grandfather, John Schlitzberg.

It appears that Mayme and Bill either returned again or simply continued to live in the Schlitzberg house on West State Street in Fox Lake after John Schlitzberg died. Other members of the Schlitzberg clan may have lived there as well from time to time. The spacious, comfortable home to which Bunny Berigan so frequently returned on his visits to Fox Lake was the place where he had spent so much time while he was growing up.

Around Bunny's nineteenth birthday, November 2, 1927, the Hal Kemp band made some appearances in the Milwaukee-Madison area. In the Kemp band was trombonist Keith "Curly" Roberts, who was from Madison. His brother, Carson Roberts, who was also a musician, was familiar with Bunny's work. The Kemp band was invited to the Roberts family home for dinner, and that same evening Bunny was asked to stop by and play for Kemp. It is this event that is the source of the apocryphal story later told by John Scott Trotter, Kemp's pianist and arranger, that Bunny had "the tiniest, most awful ear-splitting tone I had ever heard." This story gained wide currency over the years because anyone familiar with Berigan's playing was well aware that he was re-nowned for his large, round, full trumpet sound. So there was great irony in this tale. The truth of the matter is that after Kemp heard Bunny play, he invited him to sit in with his band on a gig the very next night, and immediately offered him a job, not seeming to be bothered by the size or quality of Berigan's trumpet tone. Bunny's parents were against him taking the job, presumably because he was still in high school.[11] I have my doubts about the "still in school" reason for Bunny not joining the Kemp band. Big Bob Berigan later recalled: "Bunny was in school in Madison, but by the time his junior year was over both Bill and I realized we weren't going to get anywhere trying to keep him in school. So he never did graduate. I'm not sure exactly when he stopped going to school, but by the end of 1927, he was no longer in my band and I had less and less control."[12] My inference from this is that Bunny's parents simply were not yet prepared to accept the fact that their nineteen-year-old son was now ready, willing, and able to begin touring the nation with a dance band.

By late November 1927, Bunny was working in the pit orchestra at the new Orpheum Theater in Madison, along with Erle Smith, and Curly Roberts, who recently had left the Hal Kemp band to get off the road. This orchestra contained fourteen to eighteen pieces, was under the direction of Joe Lewis, accompanied silent films, and evidently moved onstage but behind a curtain to accompany vaudeville acts. It played shows starting at 2:30, 4:30, 7:00, and 9:00 p.m., Sunday through Wednesday. Rehearsals probably took place on one of the other days for the upcoming week's show and film. This engagement terminated at year's end, after which a number of the musicians, including Bunny and Erle Smith, moved across the street to the pit of the also new Capitol Theater to perform in a similar fashion as they had at the Orpheum. The director at the Capitol was Vernon Bestor, older brother of bandleader Don Bestor. Other conductors were used over the next several months. A photo of the Capitol Theater orchestra, including Bunny, was taken in early February 1928.

On February 4, 1928, the Ben Pollack[13] band played a prom at the capitol building in Madison, with the following probable personnel: Jimmy McPartland, Al Harris, trumpets; Glenn Miller[14] on trombone, Benny Goodman,[15] Gil Rodin,

Larry Binyon, saxophones/clarinets; Vic Briedis, piano; Dick Morgan, banjo/guitar; Harry Goodman, tuba/bass; Ben Pollack, leader/drums/vocal. This item about the Pollack band appeared in the local Madison newspaper:

'I like to make 'em dance', says Ben. It was a toss-up whether to choose Coon-Sanders or Pollack's 10-piece outfit for tonight's prom. Benny Goodman, outstanding on the saxophone and clarinet, is only 19 years old, and alternates between Pollack and Isham Jones. Pollack plays drums and the orchestra features 'Rhapsody in Blue' and 'Tiger Rag.' Pollack's men are all Chicagoans, who strangely enough, started playing together in California. Pollack is only 24 years old and now plays regularly at the new Club Baghdad on the South Side of Chicago at 64th and Cottage Grove.[16]

It is very likely that Bunny would have raced to the nearby capitol building after his work at the Capitol Theater concluded that night to hear the Pollack band, and probably to meet its members.

Even though Bunny Berigan was now working full-time as a professional musician in Madison, and making a good living, he no doubt felt that he had been doing little more than treading water in the months since he had been offered a job by Hal Kemp, but remained in Wisconsin to respect his parents' wishes. He probably expressed these feelings to Curly Roberts, who, after playing alongside Bunny for about four months in the Orpheum and Capitol Theater orchestras, knew what his capabilities were. It was through Curly Roberts that he would make his first attempt to break into the big time in New York. Roberts recalled:

After a couple of months, I moved to New York to study under Charles Randall, a fine trombone teacher, who played with the New York Philharmonic and had been recommended by Frank Cornwell's trombonist, Carl Loeffler. Bunny had indicated that he felt he was ready to try his luck in New York, and asked me to keep an eye open for any possible opening for him. Frank Cornwell was organizing a band for Janssen's new Hofbrau in Philadelphia, which would be led by Speed Young. I was living with Saxie Dowell, Ben Williams and Jim Mullen, who told Ardon Cornwell, Frank's brother, about me. He brought Speed Young to our hotel and offered me the Philly job, which I accepted. Then I told them about Bunny, and what a terrific horn he played, so they told me to go ahead and call him. Well, I finally located him late at night at the Green Circle Inn, and gave him the lowdown on the job. He seemed to like the idea and said he'd be in New York in a couple of days. Ardon and I went down to the railroad station to meet him, but we missed him somehow, and when we got back to the hotel, he was already there. In fact, one of the reasons I joined the band was that I knew Bunny was going to be on hand.[17]

Notes

[1] White materials: October 11, 1925.

[2] *Ibid.*

[3] *Ibid.*

[4] White materials: August 30, 1926.

[5] White materials: October 25, 1926.

[6] Louis Daniel Armstrong, born August 4, 1901, in New Orleans, Louisiana, was a seminal figure in the development of jazz. In addition to his virtuosity as a cornetist/trumpeter, Armstrong's rhythmic approach to music, centered around his superb use of syncopation, moved jazz forward from ragtime and rather (rhythmically) stiff dance music to the flowing loose rhythms of swing. In a very real sense, Louis Armstrong invented swing, as a brilliant series of recordings he made in the late 1920s show. His trumpet playing was passionately dramatic, and he was a dynamic showman and singer. Armstrong's impact on jazz continued throughout his life, though other more technically endowed trumpeters, including Henry "Red" Allen, Rex Stewart, Bunny Berigan, Roy Eldridge, and Cootie Williams began to lead jazz in new directions in the 1930s. The advent of Dizzy Gillespie in the late 1930s began the next seismic shift in jazz, toward what eventually became identified as bebop. Through almost nonstop touring, recording, guest shots on radio and television, and many appearances in feature films from the 1930s to the 1960s, Armstrong remained a potent force on the entertainment scene until shortly before his death on July 6, 1971, in Corona, Queens, New York City.

[7] *Down Beat:* September 1, 1941. See chapter 23, *infra.* In this article, Bunny said: "...when I was a kid in *Chicago* at night I used to sneak down to the Savoy where Louis was playing and listen to him night after night." There is no independent verification that Bunny ever spent any time in Chicago during this period.

[8] White materials: April 29, 1927.

[9] White materials: February 26, 1926.

[10] This information comes from the copy of the death certificate for John Schlitzberg Sr. at the Fox Lake Public Library.

[11] White materials: November 2, 1927.

[12] *Ibid.*

[13] Drummer Ben Pollack was born on June 22, 1903, in Chicago, Illinois. He led one of the first white bands to play jazz-influenced dance music. Pollack was important in the development of the big band era because he discovered so many gifted young musicians who later went on to become either successful leaders of their own bands, or highly regarded jazz artists. Among his discoveries were Benny Goodman, Glenn Miller, Harry James, and Jack Teagarden. Pollack was never able to gain widespread popularity, and this evidently was one of the reasons why he took his own life by hanging in Palm Springs, California, on June 7, 1971.

[14] Alton Glenn Miller was born on March 1, 1904 in Clarinda, Iowa. Although he was a competent trombonist and arranger, his real gifts lay in his ability as an organizer and leader. He effectively began his career as a sideman in Ben Pollack's band in 1926, and arrived in New York with that band in 1928. Once in New York, he was able to earn a living as a trombonist and occasional arranger for several years, but fellow musicians recognized his great ability as an organizer and "straw boss" of bands, and from the early

1930s, he was employed almost constantly to do that for bandleaders Smith Ballew, the Dorsey Brothers, and Ray Noble. He formed his first band in 1937, and led it for about a year, but was forced to disband because of commercial failure. He reorganized in 1938 and again failed to find an audience until a series of successful records and location engagements (with many radio broadcasts) in 1939 finally penetrated the public's consciousness. From 1939 until the fall of 1942, Miller piloted his band to ever greater commercial success. Miller entered the army air force in 1942, formed an excellent service band, and led it both in the United States and in England for the next two years. He was killed, supposedly in an airplane crash on December 15, 1944, though the circumstances surrounding his death are still much disputed.

[15] Clarinetist Benjamin David Goodman was born in Chicago, Illinois, on May 30, 1909. One of twelve children of impoverished Jewish immigrant parents, Goodman learned early that his prodigious musical talent was his ticket out of poverty. He worked continuously during the span of a musical career lasting over sixty years to get ahead in the often brutally competitive music business. Benny Goodman was one of the first true virtuosos to play jazz, and from the mid-1920s until his death, he maintained a level of instrumental facility that was at times astonishing. Goodman's ability as a jazz improviser was great, and he blazed trails as a jazz musician from the 1920s into the mid-1940s. From then until his death, Goodman became increasingly an elder statesman of jazz, playing well always, but no longer in the jazz vanguard. His career was always superbly managed, and he was from the mid-1930s dubbed "The King of Swing" by Music Corporation of America, his booking agency. He died on June 13, 1986, in New York City.

[16] Madison *Capital Times:* February 4, 1928, cited in White materials.

[17] White materials: March 30, 1928.

Chapter 3
First Bite of the Apple

Over the years, I often wondered how Bunny Berigan made the transition from peripatetic midwestern dance band trumpeter to highly paid New York studio musician. The indispensable precondition for that, of course, was his membership in Local 802, the New York branch of the American Federation of Musicians. As will be discussed below, by 1930, New York City was the epicenter of radio and recording activity in the United States. The most plentiful and lucrative work for musicians then was to be found in New York. Good musicians from all over the country knew this and would do almost anything to gain admittance into Local 802 so they might get a shot at that steady and great-paying work. I had previously assumed and later learned that Bunny had joined Local 166 in Madison in the summer of 1926, at age seventeen. But how did he obtain that golden key, his membership in New York Local 802? Union rules then prohibited members of one local from simply transferring their membership to another. To prevent a large influx of musicians into New York, Local 802 instituted a six-month waiting period, to be served between the date a musician applied for membership until the date the coveted membership card was issued by the union. During this six-month period, a musician had to reside within the jurisdiction of Local 802, but could do only casual work there. He could not work in the radio or recording studios or on other jobs where the work was steady or high paying. In this way, Local 802 protected its home turf from interlopers who might take work from members of the local union.

Berigan did not remain permanently in New York the first time he went there. In fact, he did not remain there long enough to fulfill the six-month residency requirement for membership in Local 802. The actual story of how he was able to gain membership in Local 802 can only be partly explained by verifiable facts; the rest of the story can be filled in only by inference and speculation. Bunny left Madison for New York in approximately March of 1928, at the age of nineteen. He went to New York to join a band nominally led by Frank Cornwell, at the behest of Madison trombonist Keith "Curly" Roberts, who had previously worked with Hal Kemp but then returned home briefly to take a rest from touring. The transfer of Bunny's union membership from Madison to New York was noted in *The International Musician*, the union's newspaper, in May 1928. So it is likely that Bunny actually transferred his Local 166 card some time earlier, probably in March, when he arrived in New York. It appears the Cornwell band was formed in Manhattan, and then rehearsed there before opening at Janssen's Hofbrau in Philadelphia (1309 Walnut Street) on April 11,

1928. Cornwell fronted the band only on opening night; thereafter it was led by
the banjo-playing singer Speed Young.[1] During this engagement, the Cornwell
band broadcast over WCAU–Philadelphia. This engagement lasted until late
August or early September. While Bunny played in Philadelphia at Janssen's
Hofbrau with the Cornwell band, he was required to transfer his Madison Local
166 card to Philadelphia Local 77, the result of which was to erase whatever
time he had accrued to satisfy his six-month residency requirement for membership in New York Local 802.

It was during the Philadelphia Hofbrau engagement that Bunny was introduced to marijuana by a saxophonist in the Cornwell band, Julie Towers (Julio
Torres). It does not appear however, that Berigan ever used marijuana very
much.

(Note: The recordings made in late May or early June of 1928 by Jesse Cohen and the Wisconsin University Skyrockets in Chicago for Paramount *do not*
include Bunny Berigan. He was then in Philadelphia with the Cornwell band.)[2]

After the Philadelphia job ended around September 1, this edition of the
Cornwell band apparently broke up.[3] A number of its musicians, including Bunny, returned to New York, where they found little work. Their union cards were
then transferred back to Local 802. Eventually, a few of them, not including
Berigan, landed a job at the China Royal Restaurant in Brooklyn. The band was
billed as Bert Kauff and His Orchestra, but in fact was led by saxophonist Bob
Finley. Finley was friends with Hal Kemp, and Kemp was instrumental in helping the Finley band get the China Royal job. In fact, he sat in with the band on
saxophone at their audition, as did his sidemen drummer Skinnay Ennis and
pianist John Scott Trotter. Bunny joined the band at the China Royal soon thereafter, and was remembered by George Terry, who played banjo and arranged
for the band, as "...a very good-looking guy and a pretty hard drinker by that
time, who also liked the ladies." (There are a number of other recollections from
this period that disagree with this in a very important way. The majority view is
that Bunny had not yet started drinking to any significant degree in 1928 or
1929. The year 1930 was when he was initiated into the culture of Plunkett's by
the Dorsey Brothers, and that would mark the beginning of his use of alcohol
beyond merely social levels.) The Terry/Kauff band opened at the China Royal
on October 20, 1928, and began broadcasting over WLTH–Brooklyn. The hours
at the China Royal were brutal: the band broadcast as early as 12:00 noon, and
as late as 11:00 p.m. In addition to playing trumpet, Bunny sang on the job, and
wrote an occasional arrangement.[4]

By Christmas 1928, he was out of the Terry band and back home in Fox
Lake.[5] He decided to remain in Wisconsin for a while after the holiday season,
but he did not transfer his union card from New York back to Madison. Although the White materials (October 10, 1929) state that it is unclear exactly
when Berigan got his Local 802 card, it is quite clear that by the end of December 1928, he had not spent enough time in New York to have fulfilled the six-
month residency requirement to obtain it, having spent a total of only four con-

secutive months there, from the end of August to the end of December 1928. Further, subsequent events indicate that he had maintained a connection with Frank Cornwell, and undoubtedly planned to return to Manhattan at Cornwell's behest. It is quite possible that Cornwell finessed the balance of Bunny's residency requirement with the union because he had plans as to how he was going to use Berigan in his band for an upcoming important Manhattan engagement. By the time Bunny next went to Manhattan, which would not be until the end of September 1929, he almost certainly had his Local 802 card.

It appears that at least a part of the first two months of 1929 were a layoff period for Berigan. It is likely that he spent the month of January with his family in Fox Lake. Part of the reason, probably, was the severe winter weather in Wisconsin at that time: "It was one of the worst winters for a number of years with great accumulations of snow. With temperatures of 20 to 30 degrees below zero, many highways and railroads were blocked."[6] By March 2, however, Bunny was at the helm of a ten-piece band, a Thompson unit, playing at the Union Great Hall at the University of Wisconsin in Madison. In the band was drummer and pianist Clarence Barto. Barto's wife later recalled the Bunny Berigan of early 1929: "He was such a delightful young man when I knew him. I don't think he drank at all then."[7] The Berigan band played at the Union throughout March, including a St. Patrick's Day dance, and for a military ball on April 5. Bunny was very popular with the University of Wisconsin students. With the arrival of spring, Bunny's band moved to Thompson's Esther Beach Dance Pavilion outside Madison, playing there on Friday and Saturday nights.[8] Drummer Rollo Laylan worked with the Berigan band then at Esther Beach: "At that time, Bunny's three main vices, drink, women, and pool, were, with the possible exception of pool, not yet developed."[9]

Suddenly, on approximately May 15, 1929, Berigan left the band at Esther Beach, and left Madison.[10] The band was then fronted by Jack Mason for the rest of the engagement. (This abrupt exit very likely caused a rupture in the relationship between Bunny and the Thompson booking office. When he returned to Madison the following August, he did not work for Thompson.) Bunny soon turned up in a band called Pete Drum and Paul Beam and Their Apostles of Music, at the Lakeside Pavilion at Champaign-Urbana, Illinois. (It is possible that Berigan stopped in Chicago on his way from Madison to Champaign-Urbana to see and hear his idol, Louis Armstrong. We know that by mid-June 1929, however, Armstrong was in New York, performing with the show *Hot Chocolates*.)[11] Bunny's association with the Apostles of Music did not last long however. Johnny Green, who later composed the great standard and jazz vehicle "Body and Soul," came through the area needing a trumpet player in a band he was leading, and Bunny joined him, being replaced in the Apostles of Music by Benny Goodman's brother Freddy.[12]

Shortly thereafter, Berigan turned up in the Madison-based band of Joe Shoer, a crude and vulgar person, but evidently a capable front man, at Castle Farms, near Cincinnati, Ohio. Bunny played first trumpet and the jazz in Shoer's band. Pianist Tut Soper, who also joined this band then, recalled Castle Farms fondly: "Castle Farms was an enormous place, with a beautiful rock garden, terraced for outdoor dancing, and a ballroom in a hangar type building on a grand scale, with clouds and stars in a phony sky, altogether very glamorous. We wore white suits with blue satin ties."[13] The Shoer band went from Castle Farms to a four-week engagement at Joyland Casino, located in thoroughbred country, outside of Lexington, Kentucky. Soper described it as "...a huge amusement park, with a dance hall, swimming pool, roller coaster, and the usual carnival rides, booths, and sideshows."[14] Soper also recalled that Bunny's drinking then was limited to beer. After the Joyland job ended on July 27, the Shoer band, including Berigan, returned to Madison.

Very soon thereafter, Bunny ended up as leader of what had been the Joe Duren band. This band (not a Thompson unit) was then playing at the Chanticleer Club, seven miles outside of Madison. It included some very talented musicians including Clif Gomon, a trumpet player whose approach to the horn was very similar to Bunny's, and Milt Yaner, who played first alto. (Later, Yaner would play lead alto with many top bands during the swing era, and later yet in the recording studios in New York.) Bunny's leadership of this band continued into mid-September, when the Chanticleer gig ended.

While he was in Madison that summer, Bunny took a ride in what was probably a very primitive airplane, ascending to an altitude of over 3,000 feet, and kept company with Miss Frances Weiss of Madison, with whom he visited his parents in Fox Lake in August.[15]

Some of the musicians who worked with Bunny that summer later commented about him. Clif Gomon said: "...we both played Llewellen model Holton horns. He had good range even then, though he couldn't hit a high F[16] as easily as he could later. Louis Armstrong was the musician Bunny talked about most and tried to copy, although he also had respect for Bix and Red Nichols. He used the lower jaw method of trumpet playing, which caused the horn to be tilted upward for the high notes." Harry Haberkorn (drums) remembered: "He was very ambitious and determined to get to the top."[17]

On September 23, 1929, the *Fox Lake Representative* carried the following item: "Bernard Berigan, cornet *(sic)* virtuoso, who had been playing with an orchestra in Madison all summer, left Saturday morning (21st) for New York City, where he has been engaged to play with Frank Cornwell's orchestra this coming season."[18]

When Bunny returned to New York, he was met at Grand Central Terminal by Frank Cornwell's brother Ardon, who stated: "...he seemed very nervous and apprehensive, saying he had lost his confidence. I assured him that all he needed was a couple of weeks in New York and he'd get it all back, and that was exactly what happened."[19] Soon thereafter, Frank Cornwell's band opened at Janssen's Hofbrau, at Fifty-third and Broadway. Among the other members of this band was pianist Frank Froeba, later a fixture in New York's radio and recording studios, and for about nine months in late 1934 into 1935, a member of Benny Goodman's band, where he worked with Berigan on occasion. Frank Cornwell recalled the scene:

> There were actually two Hofbraus—the first was situated at Thirty-second Street and Broadway, and the second was at Fifty-third and Broadway, where I had Bunny in the band. My brother Ardon did some arrangements for the band and some we exchanged with Fletcher Henderson. We got plenty of airtime over WOR and this band with Bunny was much better than my original group. He was such a good, fast reader and we gave him plenty of solos too. We worked seven days a week, going on the stand around 7.00 p.m., with the first show due at 8.15 p.m. and the final show at midnight. Tommy Dorsey came in quite a lot, Jimmy not so often, but other musicians who hung out there included Jack Purvis, Bob White and Johnny Williams. We used to go up to Harlem to hear the jazz groups, but our favorite hangout was Plunkett's. Bunny and Tommy Dorsey became good friends during that period and he (Bunny) wasn't drinking much in those days. Frank Signorelli played intermission piano during our spell at the Hofbrau.[20]

My educated guess is that Berigan somehow "completed" his six-month NYC residency while he had been back home in the Midwest, from late December 1928 to late September 1929. It seems unlikely that he could have played as a regular member of the Cornwell band in Manhattan at the Hofbrau if he did not have his Local 802 card. Frank Cornwell and/or August Janssen Sr., who was very influential, may have finessed the issue with the union. It is my opinion therefore that Bunny Berigan was a member of Local 802 by the time Frank Cornwell and His Crusaders opened at Janssen's Hofbrau, on October 10, 1929.

Notes

[1] Indeed, the band was known as the Lacy "Speed" Young band, though it was owned by Frank Cornwell and operated for him by his brother Ardon Cornwell, who was a member of the band.

[2] White materials: March to September 1928.

[3] There was another Cornwell band in New York at that time that was actually fronted by Frank Cornwell.

[4] White materials: September–October 1928.

[5] White materials: October 20, 1928, to December 30, 1928.

[6] Fox Lake *Representative:* January 17, 1929, cited in White Materials.

[7] White materials: March 2, 1929.

[8] White materials: April 19, 1929.

[9] White materials: May 10, 1929.

[10] I have not found any explanation as to why Berigan left his band and Madison so suddenly in the spring of 1929. This sort of incautious bridge burning was very uncharacteristic of Berigan.

[11] *Louis Armstrong, An American Genius,* by James Lincoln Collier, Oxford University Press, (1983), 212.

---

[12] White materials: May 24, 1929. Benny Goodman had several siblings who were musicians: Harry Goodman played bass and was a very important influence on Benny during his early years as a professional musician, and especially during the early years of Benny's career as a bandleader. Freddy Goodman, in addition to playing trumpet, worked as road manager for other bandleaders, including Benny's archrival, Artie Shaw. Irving Goodman had a long career as a professional trumpeter, including two years as a member of Bunny Berigan's band.

[13] White materials: June 22, 1929. Chicago pianist Tut Soper's full name was Oro M. Soper.

[14] White materials: July 6, 1929.

[15] White material: August 1929.

[16] High F on the trumpet became Berigan's favorite high note.

[17] *Ibid.*

[18] White materials: September 21, 1929.

[19] White materials: October 10, 1929.

[20] *Ibid.*

Chapter 4
Moving into the Big League

The period from the fall of 1929, when Bunny returned to Manhattan to join Frank Cornwell, until he joined the CBS radio network as a staff musician in early 1931, is the time during which he made the transition from being a very talented young musician to being one of the top musicians in the country. How he made this transition is very much explained by understanding the time he lived in, and the place.

The New York City Bunny Berigan arrived at late in 1929 was in the middle of an explosion of architecture, in addition to the rapid maturation of the Broadway musical stage, and the new mass medium of network radio. The face of modern New York began to appear with the art deco building boom that started in the late 1920s and continued well into the '30s. Among the magnificent structures that leapt skyward downtown then were the Cities Service Building, 40 Wall Street, the City Bank Farmers Trust Building, and One Wall Street, all of which dwarfed the earlier Singer and Woolworth Towers; in midtown were the Empire State Building, for many years the world's tallest, and the Chrysler Building, with its unique stainless steel spire. Overlooking Central Park were the Sherry-Netherland Hotel, Hotel Pierre, from the east, and the San Remo Apartments, the Beresford, and the El Dorado from the west. Just a little south of the park, stood the mammoth Radio City complex. American popular song was in the process of being invented and perfected by Irving Berlin, Jerome Kern, the Gershwins, Cole Porter, Rodgers and Hart, Vincent Youmans, and many others. The Harlem Renaissance was under way. The excitement, the creative ferment, the sense that anything was possible—all of this was a part of the intoxicating atmosphere of New York as the 1930s began.

By the time things got rolling at the Hofbrau with Cornwell, Bunny had set himself up with a room on the twenty-third floor of the Chesterfield Hotel, 130 West Forty-ninth Street. On November 2, 1929, he celebrated his twenty-first birthday. He undoubtedly felt exhilarated to be where he was, doing what he loved and did so very well. He had been a professional musician for four years, perfecting not only his trumpet skills, but also his all-around musicianship. Although Louis Armstrong had been Bunny's idol, and would continue to be an inspiration, the recordings Bunny was soon to begin making show that even at this early date he was no Armstrong clone; he had his own ideas and sound. Also, something else was there: the ineffable "Berigan Magic." That is best understood by listening to the recordings Berigan made in the early 1930s. (See

23

Richard M. Sudhalter's description of Berigan's debut on records, the pop tune "Washin' the Blues from My Soul," *vide infra.*)

The various Hofbraus (there were others in cities other than New York) were operated by the Janssen family,[1] August L. Janssen Sr. being the patriarch. They were well-financed and well-run businesses. When August Sr. died in 1939, his obituary in the *New York Times* described him as one of the best known restaurateurs in the city. The Hofbrau at Fifty-third and Broadway opened in February 1925, with Irving Aaronson's Commanders the featured band. Eventually, Frank Cornwell took over as leader of the band at the Hofbrau for several winter seasons. He would tour with the band in the summers. After trying vaudeville for a time, Cornwell returned to leading a band with the unit he organized to work at the Hofbrau in the fall of 1929, including Bunny Berigan. The band was not a jazz band or even jazz oriented. However, it was playing at a "high class" venue, was broadcasting on radio, was paying pretty well, and was providing Bunny with plenty of solos to show off his rapidly maturing talent. It was also located very near to Plunkett's, then the most famous meeting place and watering hole for musicians in New York.[2]

Jimmy Plunkett's speakeasy was a very friendly place, especially if you were a musician, and many of its most loyal customers were musicians. Eddie Condon recalled:

All sorts of business was transacted at Plunkett's. The telephone rang constantly, bands were organized at the bar and everybody drank. Those who were working bought drinks for those who weren't. One day, Tommy Dorsey came in...he had a radio program in half an hour. 'I'll have to drink in a hurry. I need a shave, but I'll have to skip to the barbershop.' Standing quietly down the bar was Tommy O'Connor, a former wrestler with gnarled fingers and an 18½ inch neck. 'It so happens that I myself am now in the profession you intend to patronize.' O'Connor said and reached into a vest pocket and took out a straight razor. 'It will take but a minute,' he said, 'Jimmy, run some of that draught beer.' Jimmy ran some beer and O'Connor shook some salt into it. A fine head of suds formed. O'Connor scooped the suds off and put them on Dorsey's face. 'Now, Tommy, just lay your head back and relax.' In a few minutes it was over and Dorsey, stunned, bleeding, but shaved, was standing upright with another drink in his hand. 'Just one more thing, Tommy,' O'Connor said. 'Give me a shot of that gin, Jimmy.' He poured the gin over his hands and rubbed Tommy's face. 'Finest after shave lotion in the world!' he said.[3]

'The name of Plunkett's in the telephone book was *The Trombone Club*' said Jimmy Dorsey. 'That was on account of Tommy (Dorsey) was the best customer. He owed the 'til the most money! One time, he owed $850 in cash to Jimmy Plunkett and the barman-philosopher, Gene O'Byrne. Neither of them could afford to be mad at Tommy, he owed them too much money!' 'Plunkett's was a wonderful place with a roster more exclusive than any union league club,' said Tommy Dorsey. 'Late in the afternoon, you'd see Bix and Frank Teschmacher napping in one of the booths after a tough record date. Chances are that Josh Billings, Jack Bland, Eddie Condon and Red McKenzie would be tuning up for an evening's engagement. There was a big icebox, the kind with a door you could open and walk into. Eddie Condon used to keep his entire wardrobe in the icebox, the star's dressing room!' "The Sixth Avenue 'El' turned over to Ninth Avenue, along narrow Fifty-third Street and the premises of 205½ West Fifty-third Street were always in shadow,' said Josh Billings. 'There was the usual metal-sheathed door and the round peep-hole. There were a number of passwords, but the most reliable was 'Tommy Dorsey sent me.' Once inside, you would see hairless Jimmy Plunkett and the silver Sinn Feiner, Gene O'Byrne. Jimmy had lost his locks, his eyebrows and even the hair on his chest through a typhoid attack. It was his everlasting habit to wear a cap and numerous sweaters. The bar at Plunkett's was about ten feet long and on the shelves about it were a half-dozen nondescript beer steins. Tabs represented more of the business than cash. Every day the barreled beer arrived at Plunkett's in a different truck. Sometimes it was a florist's delivery car, sometimes a milk wagon and on one occasion, it was even a hearse! Eddie Condon's 'dressing room,' the icebox, was loaded to the ceiling with thousands of dollars' worth of musical instruments. You could get a haircut or shave from Tommy O'Connor, one time car-pusher in the Scranton coal mines. The camaraderie at Plunkett's was something special!'[4]

Plunkett's was a speakeasy, but it was more than that, it was practically a way of life,' recalled pianist Chummy MacGregor. 'Jimmy Plunkett was a short, cubby little man, approaching middle-age, a very gentle sort of guy, considering the business he was in, in sharp contrast to the cold, gimlet-eyed types usually found in the illicit liquor trade. He had a nice family tucked away in a Brooklyn suburb. His little oasis of good cheer was located on Fifty-third Street in the short block between Broadway and Seventh Avenue under the Elevated. On entering through a nondescript doorway, which was sandwiched in between a shoe repair shop and a tiny hostelry called the Elk Hotel, you found yourself in a little blind entry with another door. When you rapped on this, the usual panel slid open and you were looking into an enquiring eye, to which, if it was your first visit, you addressed the customary 'Benny sent me.' Upon gaining admittance, assuming your credentials were in order, you found yourself in the bar itself, not very large nor very prepossessing to the critical eye, but with the familiarity gained from long-standing membership in this little community of convivial souls, the surroundings took on such a comfortable, clubby atmosphere that you wouldn't have changed a thing for the world. Adjoining the main room was another, a sort of sitting-down room with three or four tables, which had a sliding-panel door leading into the same entry that you encountered on the way in. Many musical contracts of one sort of another were negotiated over these tables. Off this room was a store-room of sorts and the fellows left their instruments and band paraphernalia there. Behind a couple of filing cabinets in the rear was a hidden door, which, on squeezing through, found one in that devious area that lay to the rear of all Manhattan building complexes. This exit was known to only a few of the 'old guard', Jimmy's closest friends. Many a time, if someone had to drive home to Long Island, say, and to Jimmy's experienced eye looked doubtful as to his ability to navigate, he would be unceremoniously and sometimes under violent protest ushered through the rear exit, up the service elevator and put to bed in the Elk. Jimmy would then go down to the lobby, register him, pay the three dollars for the room and put it on his bar tab. His wife would be called at home and told the circumstances. A note would be stuck on his car windshield for the cop on the beat, who were all Jimmy's pals and thus avoid a ticket for overnight parking. Just to show you the insouciant, twinkle-in-the-eye, yet friendly atmosphere of Plunkett's, let me tell you about the priceless work of art that dominated the back wall above the bar. Jimmy, in his quiet way, was something of a wag. At that time, the Goodyear Tire Company had a well-known advertisement in all the magazines. It was a picture of two brontosauruses engaged in a battle to the death and the matter of Tommy and Jimmy Dorsey's endless scrapping was a by-word at the time. So Jimmy Plunkett had this picture blown up and framed. The original caption underneath read: 'When prehistoric monsters fought in Pennsylvania', and Jimmy had the words 'prehistoric monsters' removed and substituted 'The Dorseys.'

Phone calls were meticulously kept track of at Plunkett's. You would get a list of calls, notification of a rehearsal or a record date, etc. You could tell anyone, 'Call me at Plunkett's, if I'm not there, I'll surely pick it up sometime during the day.' You were never hustled for money nor chiseled in any way at Plunkett's. In the morning, when you woke up at the Elk with that king-size hangover, not knowing at first where you were, the Elevated would rush by and you knew. You also knew that your watch was still with you and your wallet was still intact! Another unique feature of Plunkett's was the regular Saturday night soiree. Jimmy was a dyed-in-the-wood Saturday night cat! He could no more get by Saturday night than fly. It was his night to howl! With the joint jumping, the customers lined up five-deep at the bar, our canny, astute James P. would, at the stroke of midnight, set the bottles out on the bar, lock the doors and with owl-like solemnity announce to one and all: 'nobody gets in or out and nobody can buy a drink!'[5]

Since the Hofbrau was so close to Plunkett's, it was only a matter of time until some of Plunkett's regulars, who would on occasion stop by the Hofbrau for dinner and a show, encountered the trumpet playing of Bunny Berigan. Frank Cornwell recalled: "The Hofbrau featured a Saturday lunch session and Bunny was gradually being featured more and more. (I) would bring him 'down front' for his solos. He had no drinking problem then. Bunny played a little violin in addition to some singing, and I was very enthused over his hot choruses on a tin flute. I'm not sure, but I think we worked seven days a week. We certainly kept busy. Bunny had no reputation at all when he first came to New York to join my band. But he sure got one fast! Bunny was truly a musician's musician!"[6] Musicians, including Jimmy Dorsey, were immediately impressed by the young trumpeter in Cornwell's band. Soon Jimmy invited Berigan to Plunkett's. It was there that Bunny got to know Tommy Dorsey.

Tommy Dorsey,[7] then twenty-four years old and in the first flush of his success as a highly paid Manhattan studio musician, was the king of Plunkett's. He was a big, bluff, boisterous, boozing, talented dynamo of a man, and a superb trombonist. He was also the very image of the Irish New York politician and fixer of the day. He was always working some angle, setting something up, negotiating some deal. Tommy wasn't satisfied to be merely one of the best on his instrument; he had to have other irons in the fire too. He led his own bands and he put together ad hoc bands for recording dates and casual jobs, in addition to doing all the radio work he could handle. Tommy was then, and would remain for the rest of his life, a force of nature. One either liked him a great deal, or loathed him; there was no middle ground. From the moment they met, Bunny Berigan liked Tommy Dorsey a great deal, and the feeling was mutual. TD called Bunny "Shanty," presumably a joking reference to Bunny's Irish ancestry. Bunny called Dorsey "Tommy" or "Tom," the latter name being used only by those who knew Tommy very well.

The Cornwell engagement at the Hofbrau ended in the spring of 1930, after which the band broke up. In the early months of that year, Bunny began to work with the Dorsey Brothers on casual jobs, booked through both the Mike Markel booking office, and through Howard Lanin.[8]

One other major event in Bunny's life occurred while he was working at the Hofbrau. It was there that he met Donna McArthur, the woman he eventually would marry.

"Janssen's presented a vaudeville show in which one of the acts was an adagio dance duo called *Darrell and Donna,* wrote Don Wilson, one of the early researchers who worked in association with Bozy White. "Darrell and Donna McArthur were a brother and sister dance team from Syracuse, N.Y. In the adagio ballet sequence, the dancers had a slow duet in which the girl performed balancing feats and in one of them Darrell would support his sister on his shoulders while she would arch slowly backwards and strike a pose. In that suspended upside-down position, she noticed that one of the trumpet players would smile at her. It was Bunny Berigan."[9]

Donna McArthur Berigan remembered:

I was born on April 19, 1912, in Berlin, New Hampshire, but we moved later to Syracuse, New York. It was there that I took dancing lessons before deciding to make it a career. My brother Darrell and I worked together as a dance team, eventually going out on the road with Dan Fitche's Minstrels. When that show closed, we were booked into Janssen's Hofbrau on Broadway, where I first met Bunny, who was playing violin and flute[10] as well as trumpet with the band there. He was too shy to speak for himself and one day after rehearsals, Frank Cornwell told me that Bunny would like to meet me. So, a double date was arranged for Bunny and I to accompany Frank and his wife to the Cotton Club up in Harlem. We had several such dates before Bunny finally left the band to go overseas with Hal Kemp the following summer.[11]

The actual date when Darrell and Donna McArthur opened at Janssen's Hofbrau has not been established. It would appear, however, based on available information, that the McArthurs performed there at the end of 1929 and into early 1930. At that time, Donna McArthur was not yet eighteen years old.

Notes

[1] The White materials state that actor David Janssen, who gained fame in the 1960s on television as *The Fugitive,* was related to August Janssen. This cannot be true because David Janssen was born on March 27, 1931, as David Harold Meyer in Naponee, Nebraska. His father was a banker there. After his parents' marriage failed, young David moved west with his mother, the former Berniece Graf, to Los Angeles, in 1938. There she met and married Eugene Janssen. David took his stepfather's name. August Janssen's son Werner (born June 1, 1900), was a musician who worked in Los Angeles as a conductor. However there is no apparent blood connection between him and David Janssen or Eugene Janssen.

[2] White materials: October 10, 1929.

[3] This passage is contained in the White materials: *ibid.* However there is not a complete citation there as to the source. The full citation is: *We Called It Music—A Generation of Jazz,* by Eddie Condon, with Thomas Sugrue, Da Capo Press edition, (1992), 197–198.

[4] *Esquire Book of Jazz, 1947,* cited in the White materials: *ibid.*

[5] White materials: *ibid.* The quote from pianist John Chalmers "Chummy" MacGregor, (1903–1973), which does not have a complete attribution in the White materials, likely came from MacGregor's unpublished manuscript wherein he recorded his reminiscences as a professional musician. MacGregor bounced around various dance bands from the late 1920s until he joined Glenn Miller's band in the late 1930s. He remained with Miller until Glenn broke up his band in September 1942 to join the army air force. Thereafter, MacGregor was effectively retired as a performer.

[6] White materials: November 2, 1929.

[7] Trombonist Thomas Francis Dorsey Jr. was born in Mahanoy Plain, Pennsylvania, on November 19, 1905. He and his older brother, the saxophonist/clarinetist Jimmy, born on February 29, 1904, shared many experiences as children, the most notable of which was their tuition in music by their father, who instilled in them the discipline necessary to master musical instruments. From early ages, the Dorsey Brothers worked as musicians, becoming professionals while in their midteens. They worked as sidemen in many territory bands in the 1920s, culminating with their membership in Paul Whiteman's orchestra in 1928. After that experience, both Dorseys began careers as freelance broadcast and recording musicians in New York, which continued until 1934, when they formed their own standing band, the Dorsey Brothers Orchestra. In mid-1935, Tommy left the Dorsey Brothers Orchestra and formed his own band, which he continued to lead until his death on November 26, 1956, at Greenwich, Connecticut. Jimmy Dorsey also had a successful career as the leader of his own band, but his insistence on continuing to lead a road band into the early 1950s, when market conditions were very unfavorable, caused him great financial difficulty, which in turn resulted in his joining his brother's band in 1953. Jimmy Dorsey died on June 12, 1957, in New York City.

[8] White materials: April 28, 1930.

[9] White materials: December 31, 1929. White somehow came into possession of a typed document prepared by Don Wilson, who from the late 1950s–early 1960s interviewed Donna McArthur Berigan, as well as a number of people in Fox Lake, about Bunny Berigan.

[10] The "flute" Donna Berigan referred to was a tin flute that Bunny used on novelty tunes, not a regular flute.

[11] *Ibid.*

Chapter 5
The Next Step: Hal Kemp

There had been both good and bad points about Bunny Berigan's association with Frank Cornwell. Although Bunny respected Cornwell, and undoubtedly enjoyed his time with the Crusaders, the hours at the Hofbrau were long, and his work with this essentially commercial band, where he mostly played as a member of the brass section, quickly settled into a numbing, confining routine, especially for someone like Bunny who loved to play improvised solos as frequently as possible. Yes, Bunny was given the opportunity to play solos and sing, but the Cornwell band was really nothing more than a temporary musical unit put together for the specific and limited purpose of "playing the show" at Janssen's Hofbrau. In short, there was not much happening musically in the Cornwell band, and after its reason to exist, the Hofbrau gig, ended, so did the band. Nevertheless, Bunny's membership in this band had allowed him to establish a small beachhead on the ever-shifting sands of Manhattan's highly competitive music scene.

Soon after (or possibly even before) Bunny found himself at liberty from the Hofbrau job, the musical grapevine, always a powerful if indirect method of communication, linked him with bandleader Hal Kemp.[1] Today, if Kemp is remembered at all, it is by aficionados of the music of the big band era, who know his music only as the stylized, somewhat pallid, commercially acceptable fare he served up from the mid-1930s, as one of MCA's most successful road bands, until his untimely death in late 1940, at the age of thirty-six, from injuries he received in an automobile collision while traveling to an engagement. Consequently, one does not think of jazz and Hal Kemp together. Recordings of the Kemp band from the time Bunny was a member, including Berigan's first known recording, suggest a slightly different reality, however.

The Kemp band opened a three-week stand at the Nixon Café, 425 Sixth Avenue, beneath the Nixon Theater, in Pittsburgh, on Monday, April 21, 1930. It was then under contract to record for Brunswick Records. Bunny joined the band shortly after they opened at Nixon's, replacing Holly Humphries, their first trumpeter. T. D. Kemp, (brother of Hal and manager of the Kemp band in its early period) said: "Yes I recall Bunny in the band. He was a quiet, unassuming fellow; real clean cut looking boy in those days. Hal was very careful who he selected for band. First and foremost, all the men were gentlemen; we had no drunks, weed heads, etc. Bunny always seemed to be a 'loner.' I paid the men then and I think Bunny got one hundred dollars a week."[2] A few weeks later, the Nixon's management, which also operated the Willows Ballroom, about fifteen miles up the Allegheny River from Pittsburgh, installed the Kemp band there to play on Friday and Saturday nights, until the full summer season began in late May.[3] After the Pittsburgh jobs ended on May 11, the Kemp band returned to New York. There they prepared for a recording session, which took place on May 14.

The Hal Kemp band with which Bunny Berigan made his first recordings consisted of the following: Milton "Mickey" Bloom, Bunny Berigan, trumpets; Wendell "Gus" Mayhew, trombone; "Jimmy" James, lead alto sax and clarinet; Ben Williams, Saxie Dowell (composer of the immortal swing era opus "Three Little Fishies"), Reggie Merrill, Hal Kemp, saxes and clarinets; John Scott Trotter, piano; J. Paul Weston (not the arranger Paul Wetstein, later known as Paul Weston), bass/tuba; Pinky Kintzel, banjo/guitar; and Skinnay Ennis, drums. The vocalists were Dowell, Ennis, and Smith Ballew, and the arrangers were Trotter and Billy O'Brian. The session took place at the Brunswick studios in New York City. Two tunes were recorded in the morning and two more that afternoon.

No one has written about the music of Bunny Berigan more discerningly than Richard M. Sudhalter, who was a jazz trumpeter himself. Here is his appraisal of Berigan's debut on records:

> 'Washin' the Blues from My Soul' is Bunny Berigan's first solo on record, and by any standard, it's an impressive debut. On both issued takes he uses a straight mute for his opening statement of this minor theme (similar to the better-known Victor Young–Ned Washington 'Got the South in My Soul' of the following year). Even at this early point he's unmistakably Bunny Berigan: the figure-shapes, rhythmic address, attack, and execution—even the sense of swagger in the entrances—are fully formed, recognizable. In a total of twenty-eight solo bars, the young trumpeter has covered two octaves and a fourth, from his instrument's next-to-lowest note, a written G below middle C to its firmly struck high C. Among jazz trumpeters in 1930, only Armstrong and a very few others were working with such a span, and fewer still with such ease.[4]

"Washin' the Blues Away" has a vocal by Skinnay Ennis. The White materials attribute the arrangement to Billy O'Brian. Bunny also has a muted solo on "If I Had a Girl like You," from the same session.

The next day, May 15, 1930, the Kemp band sailed for England aboard the White Star Lines SS *Majestic,* arriving in Southampton on May 21. The band stayed at the Strand Palace Hotel in London. They played initially at the Coliseum Theatre in London, working primarily with the vaudeville review also on the bill, though they did also play a few numbers by themselves. Trumpeter Mickey Bloom (brother of composer Rube Bloom) received praise for his growl-style offerings. Berigan's jazz solos did not register with whoever wrote the review. The band also played at the Café de Paris after the theater job. There they were far less confined and able to play much as they did on dance jobs. Numerous British musicians came in to hear the band, and were immediately impressed by Bunny's playing. The band broadcast over the BBC while at the Café de Paris. In the BBC archives are listings of the titles played by the Kemp band when they were on the air, but no aircheck recordings are known to exist. The Coliseum Theatre engagement ended on May 30, but the Kemp band continued at the Café de Paris. On July 4, they opened for a week at the Plaza Theatre in Picadilly Circus, while continuing to double at the Café de Paris.

On July 7, 1930, Bunny took part in a strictly commercial recording session in London, with a band comprised of mostly British musicians (including Ted Heath[5] on trombone), plus some other members of the Kemp band and Jimmy Dorsey, who (along with Muggsy Spanier) was also in England then with Ted Lewis's band. On July 17, to create a bit of goodwill, the Kemp band played for a hospital charity at Hampton Court. On July 27, they played concerts at the Winter Garden in the afternoon, and at Westbrook Pavilion in the evening. Starting on August 1, the band returned to the Plaza Theatre for two weeks, all the while continuing at the Café de Paris. For four days in early August, the band was tripling, as Kemp accepted a gig at the Dominion Theatre. On August 14, they closed at all three venues.[6]

Saxist Ben Williams roomed with Bunny while the Kemp band was in London. He recalled: "He was a honey and everybody liked him. I guess he smoked a reefer now and then, but I don't recall a drinking problem. He was very well coordinated and did most things well, just like his playing. He could think of a phrase and it would come out right at the ends of his fingers. He was ahead of his time, I guess, always good company and lots of fun."[7]

After the Kemp band closed in London, they were feted. Gus Mayhew said: "We were up all night after closing at the Café de Paris. 'Cookie' Fairchild and 'Whispering' Jack Smith threw a party in the band's honor at La Pontiere, a swank restaurant off Liecester Square (15 Green Street), and afterwards we had to dash off to Liverpool Street to catch the boat-train for Dover. We crossed the English Channel for Ostend, Belgium on very choppy seas which made most of us very sick!"[8]

The band played a ten-day engagement at the Dominion Hotel in Ostend. They then went to Paris for what was supposed to be a long engagement at Les Ambassadeurs Club, opening on August 29. After three weeks, their stay was abruptly terminated by the police, acting at the behest of the Paris Musicians' Union, which by initiating this rather dramatic bit of jingoism, was attempting to draw attention to the problems then being created by sound films throwing French theater pit musicians out of work. Unable to work in Paris, the band then left France from Le Havre on the *Isle de France* on September 24, arriving back in New York on September 30.

Music Corporation of America (MCA), the booking agency representing Kemp, had to find work for the band in a hurry. It eventually came up with a gig at the Daffydill Club in Greenwich Village in New York City, which included radio broadcasts, starting on October 2. It was rumored that vocalist-bandleader Rudy Vallee was an investor in the Daffydill Club. With this location as their base of operations, Kemp set about making records again. He led his band, including Bunny Berigan, at Brunswick recording sessions on October 20 and 30, and November 6. A record date for American Record Company (ARC) on November 7, which featured Kemp sideman Skinnay Ennis singing under the pseudonym "Sid Gary" (the records were issued bearing the names Sleepy Hall and His Collegians/Spec Mason's Orchestra/Mills's Music Makers) did not include Berigan among the backup musicians. Then suddenly on November 8, the Daffydill Club closed.

It appears that the Kemp band, still scrambling for work, then made a series of late-night broadcasts from the studios of WEAF (NBC) in Manhattan from November 10 to the 17th, along with another Brunswick recording session, on November 18. Shortly thereafter, they departed for an engagement in Cleveland at the Golden Pheasant Restaurant, 944 Prospect Avenue. This was to be an eight-week residency, with broadcasts over NBC. The band opened there on November 20, with their first broadcast occurring on the 24th. While the Kemp band was appearing at the Golden Pheasant, various floor shows were also featured there. Kemp also acquired the services of a second pianist who also arranged and sometimes played the vibraphone at this time, a twenty-year-old from Indiana named Claude Thornhill. Thornhill almost immediately formed a friendship with Kemp vocalist Skinnay Ennis, who greatly appreciated his tasteful accompaniment on piano.

Billboard, in its January 17, 1931, issue, provided a concise picture of the microcosm of dance band activity that existed in Cleveland then:

> Long a fertile spot for name bands, Cleveland continues to live up to that reputation. Local night clubs, hotels, and danceterias were facing the toughest competition in years. Hal Kemp and His Orchestra, known to radio listeners throughout the country due to their long run over the NBC system, are on an indefinite contract at the Golden Pheasant. Others currently in Cleveland include Kay Kyser at the College Inn, George Williams at the New China, Ben Pollack at the Hollywood, Stubby Gordon at the Chinese Temple, Ace Brigode at Danceland, Emerson Gill at the Bamboo Inn, and Opie Cates at the Red Lantern.[9]

The Kemp band closed at the Golden Pheasant on January 23, 1931, and then apparently worked a number of one-night stands throughout the Midwest and into Virginia, where they played the "Fancy Dress Ball" at Washington and Lee University in Lexington. This was (and still is) an elaborate costume party/dance, held on January 30. The following night, they played at Virginia Military Institute, also in Lexington. They then resumed playing one-nighters until they returned to New York for a series of Brunswick recording dates, which began on February 13.

The first of these dates produced discs that bore the legend, "Gotham Club Orchestra." The ones that followed, on the 14th ("Hollywood Night Hawks"), the 16th ("Gotham Club Orchestra"), the 18th (numerous pseudonyms including "The Clevelanders" and "The Joy Spreaders"), were all recorded by the regular Kemp band, including Berigan.

Upon the band's return to New York, Bunny gave Kemp his two-week notice. He also resumed his relationship with his many friends in the music business, a number of whom were members of the pools of musicians on salary with the two major radio networks, NBC, the National Broadcasting Company, and CBS, the Columbia Broadcasting System. He wanted to secure steady, lucrative employment, get off the road, and live in New York. He began putting out feelers, hoping to obtain employment on the staff of one of the radio networks.

He also resumed his relationship with Donna McArthur at this time, and began to think about marriage.

Notes

[1] James Harold Kemp was born on March 27, 1905, in Marion, Alabama. He was originally a pianist, later he took up the saxophone and clarinet. In the mid-1920s while at the University of North Carolina, he led a campus band. When he left UNC, he took several key musicians with him and formed a professional touring band. Kay Kyser succeeded Kemp as the leader of the top student band at UNC. Kemp's band was booked by Music Corporation of America, and gained success steadily throughout the late 1920s and 1930s as a middle-of-the-road sweet-styled dance band. While driving from Los Angeles to San Francisco to play an engagement, he was involved in an auto collision on December 19, 1940, and died from the injuries he sustained two days later.

[2] White materials: May 2, 1930.

[3] *Ibid.*

[4] *Lost Chords; White Musicians and Their Contribution to Jazz—1915–1945,* by Richard M. Sudhalter, Oxford University Press (1999), 490-491. Hereafter referred to as *Lost Chords.*

[5] After World War II, Ted Heath (1900–1969) led one of the finest bands in Great Britain for over two decades.

[6] White materials: May 15, 1930, to August 15, 1930.

[7] White materials: May 15, 1930.

[8] White materials: August 14, 1930.

[9] *Billboard:* January 17, 1931, cited in the White materials: January 1931.

Chapter 6
Manhattan Musical Merry-Go-Round

In 1931, the top of the world in Manhattan for a musician was not the New York Philharmonic, or the Metropolitan Opera Orchestra; it was in one of the orchestras then maintained by the two major radio networks, the National Broadcasting Company, NBC, or the Columbia Broadcasting System, CBS. Those two networks sought out, hired, and paid very well, the finest musicians in the country. In exchange, these musicians constituted a sort of musical meritocracy. They were given the opportunity to do as much work as was humanly possible, but were always expected to perform at the top of their ability, no matter what the musical context or situation, morning, noon, or night, seven days a week, 365 days a year, as scheduled.

This rather bizarre work environment had its plusses and minuses for the musicians involved in it. On the plus side, a musician could make unheard-of sums of money, if he simply showed up when scheduled, and played whatever music was required, flawlessly, on the air, after a minimum of rehearsal. On the negative side, the pressure and eventual drudgery of doing this for any period of time was tremendous, and corrosive, especially to the skills required to play jazz. The epitome of the studio musician then, and for the next forty years, first in New York, later in Hollywood, was the trumpeter Emmanuel "Mannie" Klein (1908–1994). He had the uncanny ability to do exactly whatever any conductor in any situation demanded, perfectly, on the first try. He was completely capable of playing first trumpet, straight melodic solos, or quite acceptable jazz solos. As a result, he was the first-call trumpeter for every conductor he ever worked with. He was, for almost his entire professional career, the highest paid studio musician in the nation. He always had much more work than he could handle, and as a result, was required very frequently to send substitutes, almost always for the many rehearsals required by network radio conductors. He would then simply show up later for the live broadcast, play perfectly, and race off to the next broadcast. His subs were kept busy rehearsing, while he was overwhelmed playing live broadcasts. In the early 1930s, Mannie astutely allied himself with the best first trumpeter available in New York, Charlie Margulis (pronounced like "marvelous"), the legendary "Mighty Marg" from Paul Whiteman's orchestra of the 1920s. The two of them played any music in any situation for any conductor under any circumstances, with little or no rehearsal. Margulis played lead, and Mannie played whatever solos were required, including the jazz. In this way, they were able not to exhaust themselves while playing literally dozens of radio broadcasts and studio recording sessions each week. Together, they made an unbeatable duo, and each earned huge sums of money. In late 1937, Mannie moved from New York to Hollywood, where, with his brother Dave Klein, he also began operating as a musical contractor, gathering the musicians required by conductors for thousands of ad hoc recording sessions over the next twenty-five years, in addition to continuing his work as a peerless session man himself. After World War II, he formed a new alliance with the great first trumpeter Conrad Gozzo, and replicated in Hollywood the success of his earlier alliance with Charlie Margulis in New York. Utterly reliable over a professional career spanning more than five decades, alcohol never played a part in Mannie Klein's life.

As great a trumpeter as Mannie Klein was, he was not Bunny Berigan, and he never had the slightest hesitation in pointing out why to anyone who ever asked him about this. Bunny could and did do everything Mannie did—he played any music placed before him flawlessly on the first try; he could and did play lead; he played any solo required of him, be it a straight solo usually played by a first trumpeter, or a jazz solo; and he was a sensitive, inspirational accompanist for singers. The major difference, of course, was in the jazz solos. Mannie's were very good, and were regarded as acceptable jazz by most listeners. Bunny's were on an entirely higher level, in terms of inspiration, excitement, and power. Bunny's playing conveyed excitement and emotion, clearly, strongly, and immediately. Fellow musicians and conductors recognized the difference. Yes, Mannie Klein was on every conductor's "A" list; but Bunny Berigan was everything Mannie was, and a lot more because of the unique jazz excitement he could generate. He alone was on the "A+" list. As a result, Bunny occupied a singular position among New York's studio trumpeters in the early 1930s. During Bunny's tenure at CBS, Mannie Klein and many other fine trumpeters would substitute for him, especially as he began to take more work than he could possibly do, and increase his intake of alcohol. After only a short time in the studios, Bunny Berigan never again substituted for Mannie Klein, or anyone else, unless it was an opportunity he regarded as too good to pass up.

Late in his life, Artie Shaw, reflecting on his own life as a musician, once observed that for him, success had been much harder to handle than failure had been. His career had followed a pattern very similar to Bunny's, the major difference being that Berigan had few if any professional setbacks early in his career. Shaw had at least two of them,[1] and learned a great deal from each. Bunny's career, from its beginning until well into his years as a famous bandleader, would be an uninterrupted upward arc of success. He was the golden boy of the New York music scene in the early and mid-1930s. This skein of solid professional successes began in early 1931, when Bunny suddenly found himself in a professional atmosphere that severely tested his musicianship on an ongoing, daily basis.

From the beginning of his career as a professional musician in 1925 until February of 1931, when he joined the CBS radio network, Bunny Berigan had bounced from job to job, seemingly in the most casual and carefree way, always welcomed by his fellow musicians, always creating pleasure, delight, excitement, and amazement with his trumpet playing for his musical peers, as well as the paying customers. For Bunny, no matter how much had been required of him, playing music had always been fun, not work. The fact that he made others happy by playing was a bonus, as was the money he made. As the clarinetist Johnny Mince,[2] who worked with Bunny on a number of occasions in the 1930s, and worked for Tommy Dorsey for four years (including six months with Berigan in 1940) once explained to me:

> Money was always irrelevant to Bunny. As a young musician, unlike almost everyone else in the profession, he always had more work and money than he needed. He couldn't have cared less about money because ever since he was a boy, he had made money easily by playing music. Early on, this did not cause any problems. Later, when he was a bandleader, and his life became much more complicated, he simply could not adjust. He felt that he should be able to pay someone to worry about his money issues, and forget about them himself. That is possible to a point. But Bunny simply never checked up on those he hired to manage his affairs—he trusted them completely. This is only one way in which he was totally different from Tommy Dorsey. I won't say Tommy was paranoid about money, but he was always checking up on his lawyers, accountants, managers, and booking agents. And if there was even a hint of something being amiss, there would be a violent explosion, meaning Tommy would go after the person in question verbally, and, if necessary, physically. Tommy managed his business affairs in that way—by intimidation.[3]

Berigan's move to CBS was a turning point, not only in his career as a musician, but as a person as well. Yes, as Johnny Mince observed, Bunny had always found work easily. But now, he was on the threshold of being offered the best paying work in the profession. He was no longer simply playing with good musicians: he was playing with musicians who were absolute masters of their instruments, and, professional to the core, were ready to play at the top of their ability all the time, no matter what the situation. They were, for the most part, older men, who had acquired a great deal of personal and professional maturity and sophistication, every bit of which they needed to be successful studio musicians. They had paid their dues. In February of 1931, Bunny Berigan was only twenty-two years old. The CBS orchestra was like the New York Yankees of the time: very talented, very well paid and managed, constantly under pressure to win, and in the World Series almost every year. When the CBS musicians were on the air, live, they had to simply do it— whatever "it" might be at the moment, on-time and without mistakes. There were no excuses or retakes. There was stopwatch discipline and never-ending pressure. Berigan was the rookie on the team, and he had to produce. Probably more significant from Bunny's point of view was the matter of peer group pressure. The veteran musicians whom Bunny joined at CBS undoubtedly were extremely critical of the young *wunderkind* who was suddenly in their midst. Their collective attitude was, if you're so good, prove it!

For the most part, Berigan took these new challenges in stride. His pleasant, easygoing personality allowed him to bend, not break, under the new stresses. He had been well prepared from childhood for these musical challenges: first by his mother, then by his maternal grandfather, later by his constant work in myriad musical situations, playing not only in ensembles, but also as an improvising soloist. The success he had had, and the unstinting praise and approval he had received from fellow musicians and audiences, had given him substantial self-confidence. But Berigan had insecurities as well. The tenor saxophonist Bud Freeman[4] noted that "Bunny wanted everybody to love him. He was terribly insecure."[5] When Bunny joined CBS, he did not know if his playing would receive the praise and approval it had always received, and this bothered him.

Substantial self-confidence is not the same as unlimited self-confidence. The great virtuoso bandleaders who eventually came to fame in the swing era, most notably Benny Goodman, Tommy Dorsey, and Artie Shaw, seemed to possess unlimited self-confidence. They each had, in addition, a colossal ego. They pleased and offended people with little regard for what others thought of them. They each withstood the pressures, problems, and successes of simultaneously being a virtuoso instrumentalist and a bandleader, in their own ways, but self-doubt was simply not present in any of their personalities. Bunny Berigan did not have unlimited self-confidence, nor did he have a giant-sized ego. Instead of reaching within himself and tapping some inner reserve of emotional strength when confronted by major challenges, Bunny began to reach for alcohol to soothe his nerves and bolster his self-confidence. At about the time Bunny joined CBS, Plunkett's became, increasingly, not just a place to relax after work, but a place to go at all hours to obtain the liquid courage he thought he needed to play well, and get through whatever situation he found himself in.[6]

Happily, Bunny Berigan's sterling musicianship enabled him to quickly adjust to the demands of his employment at CBS. He rapidly proved to his new professional colleagues that he was completely capable of doing all that was required for him to be not only a studio musician, but a valuable addition to any musical situation in which he was required to play. Berigan's fellow musicians almost universally had positive recollections about his overall musicianship, as well as his ability as an inspired jazz soloist. In addition to the professional respect Bunny was earning, he was also earning far more money than almost any other musician in New York. That was the good news. The bad news was that he had almost no concept of how to handle this money, and much of it began to pass over the bar at Plunkett's. Although he undoubtedly was using alcohol in 1931 for various purposes, most of them probably social, it does not appear that he immediately began to abuse it. Alcohol had simply taken a place in Bunny Berigan's life; it did not yet rule his life.

Notes

[1] Artie Shaw, born Abraham Isaac Arshawsky on May 23, 1910, in New York City, was one of the greatest clarinetists and most successful bandleaders in the history of jazz. His early career paralleled that of Bunny Berigan. In the mid-1920s, he began working in a succession of dance bands, and (late 1931) became a staff musician at CBS, as well as a freelance recording musician in New York City. In the fall of 1930, Shaw accidentally killed a pedestrian while driving his automobile in Manhattan. This event traumatized him and interrupted his successful career. In early 1937, he was forced to give up his first band, which was built around a string quartet, because it was a commercial failure. He immediately formed a more orthodox swing-styled dance band, and by mid-1938, was one of the most successful bandleaders in America., largely as a result of the spectacular success of his RCA Bluebird recording of Cole Porter's "Begin the Beguine." Numerous other million-selling records followed. His career as a clarinet virtuoso and bandleader lasted into the middle 1950s, when he retired as a performer. Although Shaw permitted his name to be associated with a touring band (starting in 1983), which played music he had recorded, which he sometimes conducted, he never played the clarinet after his retirement. Artie Shaw died on December 30, 2004, in Thousand Oaks, California.

[2] John Henry Muenzenberger, one of the finest jazz clarinetists of the swing era, known professionally as Johnny Mince, was born July 12, 1912, in Chicago Heights, Illinois. He worked in a number of dance bands from the early 1930s until early 1937, when he joined Tommy Dorsey's band as its featured clarinetist. He remained with Dorsey until early 1941, when he entered the army. While in military service, he played in Irving Berlin's wartime show *This Is the Army.* After World War II, Mince began a long tenure on the CBS radio (and sometimes television) network, working regularly in the band that supported entertainer Arthur Godfrey. Starting in the 1960s, Mince returned to playing jazz, principally at jazz parties and festivals, until approximately 1990. He died in Boca Raton, Florida, on December 30, 1994.

[3] Conversation between the author and Johnny Mince: August, 1986.

[4] Lawrence "Bud" Freeman was one of the premier tenor saxophonists in jazz. Born in Chicago on April 13, 1906, he was a member of the "Austin High (School) Gang" of white teenagers who began to experiment with jazz in the early 1920s. He worked in many dance bands and jazz groups throughout the late 1920s and the 1930s. He made some excellent jazz recordings with Bunny Berigan in late 1935, and worked with him again when Berigan was recording and broadcasting with the Tommy Dorsey band in late 1936 into early 1937. Freeman then embarked on a lengthy career as a jazz soloist in 1939. He died on March 15, 1991, in Chicago.

[5] Conversation between the author and Bud Freeman: August 1986.

[6] It was at about this time that Berigan began to wear a moustache. He, along with many other trumpeters, thought that a moustache would strengthen his embouchure (which is made up of the muscles in the lips and mouth that are used when playing the trumpet), and help his playing. There was not universal agreement among trumpeters about this, however. Among the trumpeters who wore a moustache were: Bix Beiderbecke, Cootie Williams, Roy Eldridge, Buck Clayton, Harry James, Dizzy Gillespie, Charlie Shavers, Clark Terry, and Doc Severinsen. Among those who didn't were: Louis Armstrong, Hen-

ry "Red" Allen, Red Nichols, Muggsy Spanier, Ziggy Elman, Clifford Brown, and Chet Baker.

Chapter 7
Building a Reputation

Soon after obtaining a coveted spot as a CBS studio musician, Bunny Berigan began to realize that there were trade-offs to be made if he wanted to maintain his skills as a creative jazz soloist at peak levels. He therefore began to make records whenever possible, to play in various bands in New York, and eventually to take sabbaticals from the stifling confinement of studio work by joining high-profile touring bands. He reasoned quite correctly that these activities would keep his playing fresh, and that they would provide him with some valuable public exposure as well. In 1931, Berigan was very intent on getting ahead in the music business. Four years would pass, however, before he would be featured with the band that would start his rise to national fame.

Never one to pass up an opportunity to play, Bunny began to augment his work at CBS with other employment almost from his first days there. His initial step in supplementing the work he did at CBS was to record in other settings with his frequent boss at CBS, Fred Rich. Rich conducted many programs at CBS, but in addition, he frequently gathered musicians from the CBS staff and elsewhere to make commercial recordings for a number of different companies, using a bewildering array of pseudonyms. The reason why was so that he would not compete against himself in the marketplace. So, on Columbia his band was identified as the Fred Rich Orchestra, or the Columbians; on Brunswick/Melotone, it would be, among others: Ralph Bennett and His Seven Aces, Owen Fallon and His Californians, Sleepy Hall and His Collegians, or Maurice Sherman and His College Inn Orchestra. (Maurice Sherman was a real Chicago bandleader, and the father of the very talented Hollywood studio pianist Ray Sherman.) It was under this last pseudonym that Bunny's first commercial recording with Fred Rich was made, on February 21, 1931, for Brunswick, "Ev'rything That's Nice Belongs to You." The vocal chorus was sung by Smith Ballew, who was either not identified on the label(s), or was identified by using different pseudonyms. This is very typical of most commercial recordings then being made in that the primary purpose was to "sell the song," not the band or the singer. The performance here is first rate: the band is well rehearsed, plays cleanly, and given the time period and purpose of this recording, swings a bit. Bunny plays a brisk, muted sixteen-bar solo at the beginning of the second chorus that is all jazz. It is quintessential Berigan; no one familiar with his playing could possibly mistake him for anyone else. Bunny's first recording with the Dorsey Brothers (they played the pseudonym game too—as the Travelers and the Joy Spreaders), "You Said It," was made five days later, also for Brunswick. It contained a vocal by Scrappy Lambert.

At approximately the same time, Berigan became a part of the revolving group of musicians to be employed by Hit-of-the-Week Records. These records were made in the McGraw-Hill Building on West Forty-second Street, near Ninth Avenue. The story of Hit-of-the-Week Records is told in full in the White materials. Essentially,

> Hit-of-the-Week records were produced by the Durium Products Corporation of 460 West Thirty-fourth Street, New York City. Hit-of-the-Week records were the first flexible, single sided popular hit record to be sold through the medium of mass distribution. Durium began recording in December, 1929, and distribution commenced a couple of months later, via news-stands exclusively. Thursday was selected as release day to coincide with the release of the majority of weekly magazines. It was hoped that people would buy the records at the same time as they purchased their favorite magazines. They were priced at fifteen cents and in order to assure the greatest sales, each news-stand was allotted only five records.[1]

After a fast start and considerable success, HOW became a victim of the ever-deepening economic depression, and after mid-1932, Durium produced only advertising records. But from early 1931 to early 1932, Bunny Berigan worked on a lot of HOW sessions, and increased his professional reputation as a versatile session man, as well as the amount of money he was earning.

On March 14, 1931, Bunny played a one-nighter with the Dorsey Brothers Orchestra at Amherst College in Massachusetts. Also on the date was Bix Beiderbecke.[2] These two titans appeared together with the DBO again at Princeton University on May 8, 1931. On the date with them for that later gig was tenor saxophonist Eddie Miller, who recalled:

> I worked with the Dorsey Brothers for some college dates. I was lucky, being just a kid, to meet these guys so I could work for them. I'd taken Babe Russin's place with Ben Pollack, which was about the only big band that was swinging. The rest of the bands weren't, unless Benny Goodman got a group together to go and play Yale or somewhere. Tommy and Jimmy Dorsey would work the same way. Of course this wasn't regular work, because they normally worked in recording and radio studios, but once in a while a single job would come in at some college or other. The saxophone section was Jimmy Dorsey, Artie Shaw and me. Bix Beiderbecke, right before he passed away, with his lip gone, and Bunny Berigan were there too. Bunny was just a young guy and he was blowing his ass off! I enjoyed Bunny, but for Bix it hurt me to hear him; (Bunny) played so good—not that Bix played that bad—but it was obvious that a young pretender was taking over. Ray Bauduc was on drums and Carl Kress on guitar and it was a great thrill for me, because these were all guys I'd read about and here I was, just a kid, playing with them! And it was the first time I'd touched a tenor sax! On the way back to New York, Bix complained about pain and numbness in his legs and Carl (Kress) and I had to rub them until we got him into bed at his hotel.[3]

For the rest of the spring and into the summer of 1931, Berigan was riding on an ever faster merry-go-round of work: CBS, first and foremost; but then commercial recording sessions with Fred Rich, the Dorsey Brothers, Fred Rich *and* the Dorsey Brothers, Bob Haring, Ben Selvin, Victor Young, Sam Lanin, Hit-of-the-Week Records, and a few one-nighters with friends sprinkled in. He may have also played for a Hal Kemp record date (April 23, 1931; Brunswick).

He also found time to wed Donna McArthur on Monday, May 25, 1931, at St. Patrick's Church in Syracuse, New York, Donna's home town. Donna Berigan recalled: "My brother Darrell was best man and his wife Joyce, who was also his new dancing partner, was matron of honor. There was no time for a honeymoon. We boarded a train for New York City on our wedding night so that Bunny could report back to CBS the next day."[4] From the very first day of his marriage, the demands of Bunny's career would take precedence over his duties as a husband. This is not a negative criticism of either Bunny or Donna. It is simply a statement of fact.

During this time, Berigan also made his first records with Benny Goodman (June 20, 1931), who recalled:

> Musicians who played hot were pretty much of a clique by themselves. They hung around in the same places, made the same spots after work, drank together and worked together whenever they had the chance. In New York, they even had one place that was pretty much their own, a dive called Plunkett's on West Fifty-third Street, where the liquor was cheap and the credit pretty liberal. It was listed, in the phone book, for special reasons as *The Trombone Club*. None of us had any use for what were known as 'commercial' musicians. If a fellow happened to be a good legitimate trumpet man or a swell straight clarinet player, he might get credit for being a fine musician, who could read a part upside-down at sight, but we didn't pay much attention to him. The saddest thing, always, was a recognized hot man, who went in for that sort of work because he made good dough and got steady work around the studios. But, whenever you met him, you could tell that the work bored the pants off him and I have seen more than a few fellows crack up for this one reason.[5]

One such fellow was Artie Shaw, whose first exit from the music business came in late 1933–early 1934, after he had spent two years in the New York radio and recording studios. He fled from the never-ending grind of radio and recording work to a remote cabin in eastern Pennsylvania. Bunny Berigan, who never left the music business and rarely took vacations from it, coped somehow, probably with the ever-increasing "help" of the distilled spirits that were still quite illegal in 1931.

Around October 5, 1931, Bunny stopped his CBS studio activities abruptly. He had been persuaded by Tommy Dorsey to join the pit band for the musical show *Everybody's Welcome*. Tommy was leading this band, which included his brother Jimmy on reeds, Mickey Bloom on trumpet, and Chummy MacGregor on piano. Jack Teagarden later joined this band. The show had opened in Philadelphia on September 21, and then moved to the Majestic Theater in Brooklyn on October 5. Fred Rich was not happy to be losing Berigan's services. Sammy Prager (piano) said:

He left when the Dorsey brothers got the pit band job in the musical show *Everybody's Welcome*. Bunny, Lyall Bowen and I auditioned for that job and they were selected, so I stayed on with Rich, who was very upset as he figured he'd given Bunny a good break in his bands. After that incident, Fred said he wouldn't use either the Dorseys or Bunny again. He tried out several men to fill Bowen's lead alto chair, but didn't like any of them, so I got Artie Shaw to audition for the job. He had been playing with Red Nichols at the Park Central Hotel in New York, but Rich liked him and he joined on lead alto and jazz clarinet. The CBS job was five days a week, usually starting around 4:00 p.m. and going on until late evening, sometimes as late as midnight. We played all types of music from jazz to light classical and occasionally Bunny would get to sing the odd novelty or rhythmic type tune.[6]

There were warning signs early on that this show would not have a very long run. It is doubtful, however, that these warning signs altered Bunny's approach to his work. Away from the show, he continued to maintain as full a work schedule as possible. He undoubtedly continued making records while he was in the band for this show. There is some evidence he may have worked on a Brunswick session under Victor Young featuring Bing Crosby on October 6, but whatever trumpet solos there are on the records that were produced are straight, without any jazz. He definitely was present on a Boswell Sisters session for Brunswick, his first with them, with everyone gathering in the studio at 2:00 a.m. on November 5. Connie Boswell elaborated on how those sessions were usually handled:

Tom Rockwell of Brunswick Records, who later became our manager, took us into the studios and we made a whole batch of sides. We revolutionized trio and group singing! We didn't sing everything straight, the way other groups did. After the first chorus, we'd start singing the tune a little different, with a beat, the way jazz musicians would. We always used a lot of free-blowing guys like Jack Purvis and the Dorsey brothers on our broadcasts and we did numbers that we didn't get a chance to record. Most of our Brunswick sessions were cut between midnight and dawn. We'd finish up our show at the Paramount or the Roxy, then go over to Plunkett's and get the Dorseys, Bunny Berigan, Mannie Klein, Stan King and the rest of the boys. Then there would be a sobering-up session, while we pumped black coffee into them and we'd finally get to recording. We recorded direct on to wax and sometimes we'd spoil 20 to 30 waxes before we got an acceptable take! They were just the greatest bunch of fellows to work with. Crazy, yeah, but they were all just wonderful musicians, who understood exactly what we were trying to do.[7]

Bunny appeared on another Boswells' session on December 4. Then the Dorsey Brothers recorded on December 9, with the band they were using in the pit for *Everybody's Welcome,* including Berigan.

As 1932 dawned, *Everybody's Welcome,* starring Harriet Lake, continued to limp along, barely escaping closure each week. Harriet Lake was the older sister of Bonnie Lake, the swing era singer and composer ("Sandman," the theme song of the Dorsey Brothers Orchestra, and "The Man with the Horn"), who was for a time married to the trombonist Jack Jenney. Harriet Lake was then being pursued by Mickey Bloom, one of the trumpet players in the band, as well as Hollywood glamour boy Charles "Buddy" Rogers. (Harriet Lake would eventually decamp to Hollywood herself, change her name to Ann Sothern, appear in movies, and have a successful career that lasted well into the era of television.) Before *Everybody's Welcome* finally closed on February 14, Bunny had cut records on Columbia with Ed Kirkeby on January 15 (as Ted Wallace and His Campus Boys) and again with the Boswells on February 5 for ARC. (By this time, the American Record Company had taken over Brunswick.)

After *Everybody's Welcome* folded, Berigan was, relatively speaking, at liberty. He had to decide now whether to return to CBS, if Fred Rich would have him, or try his luck as a true freelance. He chose to be a freelance, concentrating his work in the recording studios. He seems to have secured some sort of status at ARC, because he virtually resided in their studios in late February, 1932. Here is a small sample of what his gig book looked like then: he once again recorded with the Boswell Sisters on February 19; the next day with a generic band supporting vocalists Paul Small and Elmer Feldkamp; on February 23 backing Bing Crosby and Connie Boswell; the next day, with Ed Kirkeby in the morning, backing vocalist Feldkamp; then with a house band after noon, supporting singer Chick Bullock; then at 9:45 that evening in a band led by the Dorsey Brothers, supporting the Boswell Sisters. In a span of six days, Berigan had participated in six separate recording sessions producing twenty-eight usable takes. On February 24 alone, he had worked three separate sessions backing different vocalists, making thirteen usable takes. It is not too much of a stretch to surmise that Bunny may have stopped at Plunkett's on the way home that night to unwind a bit.

Trombonist Larry Altpeter, who was working in radio in New York then, explained the difference between working "on the inside" and working "on the outside."

I didn't do many records, (I was) too damn busy with radio. Normally on a network show you'd be signed on for the run of the show, 13 weeks. Often the 'option' would be picked up, so you'd be on the same show for 26, even 39 weeks. The leader had the contract and sometimes he'd be fired, then the band would be out too. One network show would mean a rehearsal, often on the same day as the show, and a rebroadcast, later that day-evening, for the west coast. If you had 2 or 3 network shows this was a good living and you had a degree of security as well. Then too, many of us worked over and over for the same leaders or contractors. Those who were 'tied' to a radio series or a leader or worked for a set band at a hotel or club were called 'being on the inside.' Many of us were not really jazzmen but could read like crazy and made few mistakes and that was damn important in the days of live radio. Others were strictly 'free lancers,' 'tied' to no one and taking work as it came. It was plentiful for that small group that included

Tommy and Jimmy Dorsey, Mannie Klein, Dick McDonough, Artie Bernstein, Chauncey Morehouse, Larry Binyon and others. Often they were 'first call' at Brunswick records. Most of these guys had fine jazz skills plus they could read and while some also did radio work it was not their main job, as it was with me. Bunny 'did the outside' as it was called, for a period in 1932 I'm sure. Then later he turned up in the Smith Ballew band, but was still able to do records and some other 'casual work.' I still have my 1932 date book which shows Bunny then living at 4309 West Fortieth Street, with a phone number of Stillwell 4-2728.[8] (Note: 4309 West Fortieth Street would be somewhere in New Jersey, if such an address existed. The correct address was either 430 or 439.)

As winter melted into spring, Bunny Berigan was kept very busy in the ARC recording studios. In March there were sessions with a house band backing vocalists Scrappy Lambert and Smith Ballew (March 1); with Victor Young and Bing Crosby[9] (March 8); with Bennie Krueger (March 9); with the ARC house band (theater discs), (circa March 19).[10] In April, he had sessions with the ARC house band with Chick Bullock and others (April 4); Bennie Krueger/Dick Robertson, (April 6); and on and on. Yet Bunny still found time to sub into various bands at locations in and around New York during this period. He worked with Eddie Duchin in March, and may have subbed for Andy Secrest in Paul Whiteman's orchestra in May. On numerous occasions, he definitely subbed into the band behind Russ Columbo at the Woodmanston Inn, which had been brought together by Benny and Harry Goodman.[11]

By mid-May, Berigan was growing restless under the constant grind of making records. His occasional outings with bands playing for audiences did not provide enough stimulation for him, and with the warmer weather approaching, he was looking for an opportunity to get out of the stuffy pre-air-conditioning recording studios and join a band of kindred souls. He didn't have to look far. Smith Ballew, the singer he had met in the Hal Kemp band and backed on records, had formed a band that included Glenn Miller on trombone and Ray McKinley on drums. Ballew's booking agent had secured a two-week stand at the Summit Ballroom in Baltimore,[12] near Pimlico Racetrack. Bunny joined them there. McKinley remembered:

> I knew Smith Ballew from my days as a kid in Fort Worth, Texas, so when I got the call from Glenn Miller to join Ballew's new band, I jumped at the chance. He was a nice sort of guy, but he really didn't know much about leading a band. He was very handsome, but too easygoing to make a successful bandleader. Miller, however, was a bundle of energy and knew exactly where he was going. Unfortunately, Ballew's bands always seemed to break up after each location job. Then there'd be a long layoff until the next job. I don't think I had met or played with Bunny prior to the Smith Ballew band. He was with us for the 'summer' as I recall, out on Long Island. The Ballew band was more or less 'reforming' when I joined. I recall J.D. Wade, Sid Stoneburn, Bill Barford, Rex Gavitt and Eddie Bergman I'm sure.[13]

Eddie Bergman (violin) recalled:

I remember going to play a long club date in Miami, but the club folded before we got started and we were out of a job again. Later that spring, we were summoned for a date in Baltimore, and that was where Bunny joined on second trumpet, replacing Johnny McGhee. After that job, we went into the Pavilion Royal on Long Island, which was one of the better dance spots on the East Coast. We had Hap Lawson and Sid Stoneburn on saxophones, J.D. Wade and Bunny on trumpets, Glenn Miller on trombone and doing most of the arranging, Bill Barford on guitar, Rex Gavitt on bass, Fulton McGrath on piano and Ray McKinley on drums. I used to front while Ballew, like many other leaders, spent a lot of time off the bandstand, mixing with the customers. Glenn was the real backbone of the band, mixing up many of the stock arrangements with a shrewd cut here or a new intro there. He handled all the rehearsals, often coaching each section separately. It was quite a drinking band, I guess, but Glenn and I would do our best to keep the rest of the guys on the straight and narrow! I had to go into a little bar one night to fetch Bunny, who, after arriving early for work, had gone in for some liquid refreshment to pass away the time. I really gave him a bad time, castigating him for letting the band down and when he got on the stand, he started crying and couldn't stop![14]

The Baltimore job ended on May 21, and the band returned to New York, where they would open a long engagement at Pavilion Royal, Valley Stream, Long Island, New York. Here is what *Variety* reported:

John Steinberg's Pavilion Royal has been a consistent money maker and this season should be no different. Smith Ballew and his Orchestra, a well-known crew of society musicians with a mild radio reputation, is set for the summer or until August 1st at least, when there might be a change. Ballew has a pleasing style on instrumentals and with a WABC wire, which is forthcoming this week, should prove a draw. The Pavilion can accommodate 2000 persons, 1500 in the garden and 500 under the roof. There is no cover, but a minimum check of $2 per person. Marque and Marquette, a dance team, are featured on the floor. The couple are expert society dancers. Opening night, Friday (27th) saw the usual quota of uncomplaining music publishers. Tex Guinan's café, down the road a few miles at Lynbrook, staged a premiere opening night, but the Pavilion drew its share of business.[15]

Smith Ballew gave some insight as to how the business end of this engagement was handled: "Bunny was paid $200 a week and at the same time he and Glenn were doing free-lance studio dates. The job at the Pavilion Royal was split with us doing the first six weeks and Guy Lombardo doing the second six weeks. I went with MCA (Music Corporation of America, the largest and most powerful band-booking office) at that time and they needed a new radio wire at the Pavilion, so I got stuck for $1,500 for it, while Lombardo, who could afford it much more than me, paid nothing!"[16]

As Smith Ballew recalled, Bunny augmented his work with the Ballew band by accepting some choice record dates, among them June 14 and 17 with Victor

Young, the Dorseys, and the Boswell Sisters. The Ballew band itself also recorded during this time, on July 6. They closed at Pavilion Royal on July 21.

On July 23, 1932, Bunny and Donna's first child, Patricia, was born. This event, no doubt, was a joyous one for Bunny. He had been raised in the bosom of a close-knit extended family in rural Wisconsin, and had received much love, support, and musical education, among many other benefits, from his family. His desire to marry and start his own family, very likely, resulted from his wish to replicate as much as possible the family life he had always enjoyed so much. Unfortunately, for numerous reasons, this was not to be. What he could not have known then was that his pursuit of any conventional mode of family life was almost certainly doomed to failure because of the course he was on as a supremely gifted musician in New York City. In almost every conceivable way, what was required of him as such a musician in that place and at that time undermined his marriage. Also, Bunny's spouse quickly demonstrated that she was not mature enough to discharge the responsibilities of motherhood and housekeeping. The frustrations Bunny was to encounter first and foremost in his relationship with his wife, and then in his relationship with his children, were tremendous, and would have far-reaching negative consequences in his life.

Robert Dupuis, while preparing his biography *Bunny Berigan—Elusive Legend of Jazz*, conducted a series of interviews with Donna McArthur Berigan in September of 1984. Those interviews are valuable in many ways, especially in Donna's recollections of how she and Bunny met, and to some extent, what life as the wife of Bunny Berigan was like. But like all personal recollections of events that occurred many years before, Donna's memories were not always completely accurate. And more importantly, Donna could not be expected to be totally objective about herself or her relationship with Bunny. Her marriage to Bunny, like all marriages, was filled with many moments that affected her emotionally, and a lot of those moments were undoubtedly hurtful to her. But there are always two sides, and the negative aspects of Donna's behavior as Bunny's wife and the mother of his children have not previously been explored to any great degree.

I have come to the belief that being the spouse of a famous or very talented person is always much more difficult than marriage to a more average person (if there is such a person). Great talent is very often an all-consuming force. It requires the person having it to be something of a slave to it. The same can be said for great success. Bunny Berigan undoubtedly had great talent, and as his career progressed, substantial success and fame also came his way. As a result, over a period of time, he gradually ceased being the charming, carefree young man who arrived in New York in 1929 seeking a career in music, and gradually became, depending on who you were, a powerful musical force, a commercial asset, a meal ticket, a star. Also, at the very same time that Bunny gradually became an alcoholic, he became a workaholic. His obsession with working almost nonstop would eventually have grave consequences. With all of this came a lot of responsibility, a lot of irritation, and a lot of pressure. The Bunny Berigan of

1939 was a vastly different husband than the Bunny Berigan of 1931 had been. This, and the fact that Donna herself became an alcoholic during this time, explains, in very general terms, the inexorable disintegration of Bunny and Donna's marriage through the 1930s.

The Dupuis biography, probably out of courtesy to Donna, did not really provide a very complete picture of Donna as Bunny's wife. The available evidence strongly suggests that as Bunny's alcoholism took root and progressed, Donna herself also began having problems with alcohol, and was very often a codependent facilitator of Bunny's ever-increasing drinking. In addition, and this was referred to only obliquely in the Dupuis biography, Donna was far from an ideal mother. This caused not only immediate problems in the Berigan household in New York, but great tension with Bunny's family in Wisconsin. Also, what has never been reported, but what Robert Dupuis told me, is that he learned from the Berigan daughters directly (daughter Joyce was born in 1936) is that shortly after Bunny's death, they went to live with Donna's brother Darrell McArthur and his wife, Joyce. They did not stay with their mother. This situation continued until they grew up. There are many other clues present in the White materials and the Dupuis biography that strongly suggest that, irrespective of Bunny's many failures as a husband, his wife likely had many of the same shortcomings, and was also quite responsible for the failure of their marriage.

Donna Berigan was twenty years old when the first Berigan daughter, Patricia, was born. Donna's life as a vaudeville dancer who traveled from place to place in the very unreal world of show business had done nothing to prepare her to be either a nurturing mother, or a supportive wife. Within a short time after she met Bunny, she found herself married to a handsome, charismatic, highly paid performer who was prone to overwork, drink more than he should, and be away from home a lot. She was an emotionally immature girl, who soon became pregnant. She was also isolated from her family and other supporting people, living in the midst of New York City, a place that can easily overwhelm even the most secure and stable person. Within a brief period of time, she also had an infant to care for and deal with. It could not have been easy.

In the meantime, Bunny continued to work with the Smith Ballew band. After a short time off and some rehearsal, the Ballew band was featured in late July–early August in what very quickly became a Broadway flop. It was a show entitled *Chamberlain Brown's Scrapbook*. It closed on August 9 after ten performances, and Ballew did not get paid. "I was stuck for the musicians' wages and the guys refused to accept a nickel from me, except the string players!"[17] For the next couple of weeks, the Ballew band had no work. By August 27, they were ensconced at the Post Lodge in Mamaroneck, just outside New York City, for a five-week stay. It is unclear whether Berigan worked any part of this engagement.

By mid-September, Bunny had returned to his former position as a frequent participant on recording sessions at ARC/Brunswick. Before the month ended he had played for Victor Young (backing Harlan Lattimore, as "Abe Lyman & His California Orchestra") on the 17th; with the ARC house band (behind Morton Downey, Annette Hanshaw, Singin' Sam, and Will Osborne) on the 20th; the Dorsey Brothers Orchestra (backing Jean Bowes) on the 24th, (Note: It was at this session that Tommy Dorsey first recorded "I'm Getting Sentimental over You"); Young again (behind Chick Bullock), and on an instrumental, on the 26th; Young again (supporting Will Osborne) on the 27th; and the Dorseys (backing Connie Boswell and Jean Bowes) also on the 27th.

Harry Hoffman, a violinist who was also on many of these sessions with Bunny, explained how they were organized:

I did many records at ARC under Vic Young, and Bunny was on most of them. It wasn't really a 'set' house band, but rather a group of free-lancers on 'first call,' like Bunny, the Dorseys, Mannie Klein, Stan King and the others. I played second violin and did quite a bit of arranging and we used different musicians according to the type of session it was. A vocal session with the likes of Chick Bullock or Dick Robertson was more formal than the jazz-type session so loved by the Boswell Sisters. Quite often the men on first call might not be able to make a date because of prior commitments, so the second call men would be contacted. Men like the Dorseys, Bunny, Mannie and Larry Binyon were always first call men because it was known they could play anything. Bunny wouldn't be called as a lead man because he mostly played hot. The lead men were normally Charlie Margulis, Frank Guarente or Ruby Weinstein, who could really carry a section. Bunny was too individual to play lead and although he was a good reader, he didn't really care for lead work. I didn't play any jazz solos; they were left to Joe Venuti, who brought Eddie Lang along on guitar. Victor Young had some reservations about Joe, though, because he was such a 'cut-up' and you never knew what he'd do next with his practical jokes, which could easily break up a session! Vic was a very serious person and all business! If he decided he couldn't risk calling Joe, Eddie (Lang) would always insist he call me. Walter Edelstein would usually play first violin and help me with the arranging, particularly for the Ponds show (later, 1933) which featured Lee Wiley. Victor Young's studio dates were fairly informal as a rule, though he would indicate what he wanted in regard to certain harmonic patterns and choice of tempos. It was all valuable experience, which was to serve me in good stead later, when I became assistant conductor to André Kostelanetz.[18]

At this same time, Berigan started to work with Rudy Vallee,[19] on his weekly NBC radio program, a job like so many others that he got through his association with Tommy Dorsey. According to violinist Buddy Sheppard:

I was the concertmaster, associate conductor and contractor for Rudy Vallee on the *Fleischmann Yeast Hour* from 1929 to 1932. Whenever Vallee added musicians to our regular orchestra, I would engage them and they would usually include Tommy Dorsey and Bunny Berigan. Tommy and I had been close friends for a long time, and around 1931 he brought to my attention one Bunny Berigan, a most talented trumpet player. He played the Fleischman show for several months before I left Vallee to join CBS as concertmaster. Shortly afterwards (at

CBS), I was asked to recommend a jazz trumpet player and I suggested Bunny, who was given a tryout and subsequently played almost all shows on which I played or conducted. He was quite sensational, even then, and would thrill us, if not shock us, with his improvisational jaunts! As a person, Bunny was something of an enigma. He could be very nice, but sometimes, particularly after a bout of very heavy drinking, he could be very nasty, too! He would break into a ping-pong game, which we often played during intermissions between shows or re-hearsals, grab my racket and smash it, if he lost the point. He was a big, strong man and I wasn't about to test him on such an occasion! Neither were any of the other musicians. We thought it best just to leave him alone until he calmed down. He was a very handsome guy, too, but he always had to prove that he was all man and could outdrink anyone.[20] (I am somewhat skeptical of the part of this recol-lection where Sheppard says he recommended Bunny for a job at CBS. Berigan was already well known at CBS, having worked there for the better part of 1931. Nevertheless, Sheppard may well have asked for Bunny to be reemployed by CBS.)

On October 13, 1932, singer Lee Wiley appeared as a guest on Rudy Val-lee's radio program. Bunny was in Vallee's orchestra that night. This evidently was the first time they worked together. It is unlikely that anything more than a casual meeting between Berigan and Wiley, if that, occurred at this time. But soon they would meet and be drawn to each other, and an intense but spasmodic relationship would develop between them. Beginning probably in early 1936, and for the next several years, Bunny Berigan's relationship with Lee Wiley would deeply affect him personally as well as professionally.

Between mid-October and mid-November, Berigan subbed briefly into Abe Lyman's band. Two of Lyman's sidemen recalled that time, with obvious plea-sure: Jimmy Welton (saxophone) remembered:

> Abe Lyman's orchestra was playing the Capitol Theatre in New York, when our first trumpet player, Moe Ferguson, was involved in an auto accident. There we were, with a tough hour and a half stage show to do, minus the leader of the brass section! Somehow, Abe contacted Victor Young, who knew all the musicians in town, and he sent Bunny Berigan to step into the breach without even a brief re-hearsal! He looked over the book for about 20 minutes, then proceeded to play a phenomenal show and got famous—fast! Lyman heard notes that night he never knew existed! On things like 'Tiger Rag' and 'Milenberg Joys,' which had take-off choruses for trumpet, Bunny really went places far off and back! He was just unbelievable and I was privileged to hear him and marvel! Frank Papile (accor-dion): Yeah, Bunny played the show without a mistake, like he'd been playing it forever. The band was due to go back to the West Coast to play the Coconut Grove the following summer and Lyman badly wanted Bunny to go along, but Bunny had bigger ideas and we left for California without him.[21]

Notes

[1] White Materials: March 1, 1931.

[2] Cornetist Leon Bix Beiderbecke was born on March 10, 1903, in Davenport, Iowa. Beiderbecke began to absorb jazz influences as a child listening to music being played by New Orleans musicians on riverboats plying the Mississippi River, which flows next to Davenport. In response to his poor academic performance as a boy, his parents sent him to a boarding school in Chicago where he soon discovered jazz in many nightlife venues, and left school permanently. By the early 1920s, he was a professional jazz musician, making his first recordings in 1924 with a group called the Wolverines. He also slowly slipped into alcoholism during this time. He moved through various jazz-based dance bands in the mid-1920s, employing his unorthodox method of playing the cornet. Beiderbecke also played the piano, though he did so only rarely as a professional. At this time, he was not a very proficient reader of music. But his cornet sound was so beautiful and his solos were so creative that bandleaders would often hire him simply to feature his solos. Beiderbecke was one of the earliest jazz musicians to absorb the harmonic and rhythmic lessons of such composers as Claude Debussy and Maurice Ravel. These influences quickly found their way into his cornet and piano playing, and were subsequently emulated by many jazz musicians. Although he made some remarkable recordings while with Jean Goldkette's band in 1927, the acme of Beiderbecke's career was the time he spent as a featured cornet soloist in Paul Whiteman's orchestra beginning in late 1927. His overall musicianship improved greatly during the time he spent with Whiteman; however the stresses of performing at virtuoso levels before large audiences on an ongoing basis caused his alcoholism to become worse. He collapsed on more than one occasion while in Whiteman's employ, and Whiteman attempted to help him deal with his alcoholism. But by late 1929, his tenure with Whiteman was at an end. From then until his death, he worked only sporadically. Bix Beiderbecke died on August 6, 1931, in Sunnyside, Queens, New York.

[3] White Materials: May 8, 1931. There is also evidence that Bix and Bunny played a third date together, on May 16, 1931, at Yale University's Derby Day dance, again as members of a band put together by the Dorsey Brothers. See *Bix, Man and Legend,* by Richard M. Sudhalter, Philip R. Evans, and William Dean Myatt, Schirmer Books, (1974), 318.

[4] White materials: May 25, 1931.

[5] *The Kingdom of Swing,* by Benny Goodman, with Irving Kolodin, published initially by Stackpole Sons (1939), cited in the White materials: June 20, 1931, without reference to pages where this quote was found. The quote that actually appears on page 101 of *The Kingdom of Swing* has been used here, courtesy of big band historian Christopher Popa.

[6] White materials: September 10, 1931.

[7] White materials: November 5, 1931.

[8] White materials: February 20, 1932.

[9] Harry Lillis "Bing" Crosby was born on May 3, 1903, in Tacoma, Washington. Crosby was a titanic presence in the entertainment world from approximately 1930 to the mid-1950s. He achieved hugh success first and foremost as a singer whose mastery of microphone use made him one of the first and certainly one of the largest stars of radio and recordings. Crosby was also influenced early in his career by the rhythmic elasticity he heard in the cornet solos of Bix Beiderbecke, with whom he worked in the Paul White-

man orchestra, and he translated some of this to his singing. He had an enormous influence on popular singing in the 1930s and 1940s. In addition, Crosby, though hardly possessed of matinee-idol good looks, projected a hip, droll, ironic humor very effectively, and this enabled him to gain a foothold in films as well. Eventually, he became a very effective film actor and one of the most bankable stars for Paramount Pictures. Crosby died from a massive coronary attack after playing a round of golf in Madrid, Spain, on October 14, 1977.

[10] The discography at the end of the liner notes booklet that accompanies the Mosaic Berigan CD set at page 22 contains this information regarding theater-use ARC recordings: "In addition to the regular 78s released to the public, ARC also recorded background music for use in theaters only, which were almost always instrumentals ranging from organ solos to dance band material. Pressed with the same matrix on both sides of a 10" 78 rpm recording ("F" series) as well a 33 1/3 rpm recording, these rare theater-use sides were cut as a part of a regular ARC session." The one theater-use recording included in the Mosaic Berigan set is "Stop the Sun, Stop the Moon," which was recorded in March of 1932 and then on March 19, 1932, dubbed from the commercially issued ARC/Brunswick releases onto theater-use discs. Liner notes—*The Complete Brunswick, Parlophone and Vocalion Bunny Berigan Sessions;* Mosaic Records (2003) MD7-219, by Richard M. Sudhalter, hereafter "Mosaic Berigan Set."

[11] White materials: March–May 1932. Harry Goodman was Benny Goodman's older bass-playing brother. His important role in the founding, development, and early success of the Benny Goodman band has been almost completely overlooked by jazz historians.

[12] It was at this same ballroom ten years later that a mortally ill Bunny Berigan would rejoin his own band after having spent more than two weeks in a Pittsburgh hospital.

[13] White materials: May 8, 1932.

[14] *Ibid.*

[15] *Variety:* May 31, 1932, cited in White materials.

[16] White materials: May 27, 1932.

[17] White materials: August 1, 1932.

[18] White materials: September 17, 1932.

[19] Hubert Prior Vallee was born on July 28, 1901, in Island Pond, Vermont. He took up saxophone in his youth and was greatly impressed by the playing of 1920s saxophone virtuoso Rudy Wiedhoeft, so much so that he changed his name to Rudy. He recorded as early as 1921, but did not immediately gain fame. He was one of the first persons to achieve national renown by appearing on network radio, on NBC's *The Fleischmann Hour,* which debuted in 1929, and ran successfully for the next ten years. In late 1932, Vallee changed the format of the show to what is now known as "variety," thus pioneering the kind of program that was to be important on radio and later TV for the next forty years. Vallee went on to success in Hollywood in films, and late in his career, achieved resounding success on Broadway in *How to Succeed in Business without Really Trying.* Vallee died on July 3, 1986, in Hollywood, California.

[20] White materials: September 22, 1932.

[21] White materials: October 14, 1932.

Chapter 8
Whiteman Sideman

The mention of the name of Paul Whiteman[1] to jazz fans over the last eighty years has almost universally caused an immediate outpouring of vitriolic negative criticism, if not outright hostility. It seems as though a lot of people have never gotten over the fact that Paul Whiteman was known as "The King of Jazz." And many also believe that as a result of playing the dreary musical pap Whiteman purveyed so often and so successfully to the American public, young Bix Beiderbecke was driven to drink more and more, and die far too soon. The truth of these matters is far more complex. Whiteman became known as "The King of Jazz" largely as a result of the publicity that was used so masterfully to promote his band in the 1920s, and this identity was reinforced in the public's mind by the 1930 Universal film, one of the first in color, entitled *The King of Jazz*. Bix Beiderbecke had an excellent relationship with Whiteman, who fully appreciated Bix's unique musical talent. No person was a greater patron of Bix Beiderbecke, or more understanding and supportive employer of him, than Paul Whiteman. For his part, Bix greatly enjoyed playing in the Whiteman band, and grew musically as a result of his experience there. His alcoholism predated by years his entry into the Whiteman orchestra, and unfortunately was exacerbated not by the poor quality of the music he played with Whiteman, but by the constant demands placed on him, and every other musician in Whiteman's employ, to be able to perform at absolutely top levels of proficiency constantly, before large and often highly critical audiences, all over the country. It was these audiences, who came forth in droves to hear the Whiteman band perform wherever it appeared throughout the 1920s and well into the 1930s, that made it possible for Whiteman to pay the highest salaries in the music business. Bix Beiderbecke never made more money than he did in his days with Whiteman, was always grateful to Whiteman for the opportunities he had given him, and made no secret about these facts.

Among all of the bands on the scene in the late 1920s and early '30s, Paul Whiteman's was, in terms of glamour and success, simply on a higher plateau than all the rest. Whiteman was a genius at promotion, and above all, he was a superb businessman. His success as a bandleader came before the formation of Music Corporation of America (MCA), the largest and most powerful band-booking agency of the big band era, and he was not booked during those years

53

by MCA or any other agency. Consequently, Whiteman was free to negotiate his own terms and conditions of employment, the result often being that his organization grossed far more money than any other band in the business, and that his tours suited his needs and those of his orchestra, rather than those of a booking agency. For these reasons, Whiteman had a huge advantage over his competition. One other salient point must be made about Paul Whiteman's orchestra: it was primarily a concert orchestra, not a dance band. Although it could and did play for dancers, its métier was concert music. In this regard also, it stood apart from almost all of the other musical aggregations that toured the United States in the 1920s and 1930s.

Whiteman also knew a great deal about music. He was well aware of what was good and bad in music. But he never confused that with what he knew the public wanted. He understood entirely that to maintain the most expensive touring orchestra in the country, he had to always know what the public wanted, and sell it to them for as much as the market would bear. He did this with great success, starting in the early 1920s, for over two decades.

But there was another side to Whiteman also. Duke Ellington,[2] a lifelong Whiteman admirer, captured the essence of it:

> Now there have been those who have come on the scene, grabbed the money, and run off to a plush life of boredom, but nobody held onto his band like Paul Whiteman did. He was always adding interesting musicians to the payroll, without regard to their behavior. We knew him way back at the Kentucky Club, which stayed open as long as the cash register rang. Paul Whiteman came often as a genuine enthusiast, listened respectfully, said his words of encouragement, very discreetly slipped the piano player a fifty dollar bill, and very loudly proclaimed our musical merit.[3]

In short, Paul Whiteman loved to hear good musicians play. If Bunny Berigan had subbed into the Whiteman band in the fall of 1932, and it appears that he did on occasion, replacing cornetist Andy Secrest, it is likely that Whiteman was very favorably impressed by his playing and musicianship. From then on, the days that Secrest would spend with the Whiteman orchestra were numbered.

Berigan began to work as a sideman with Paul Whiteman's orchestra in mid-November of 1932. At that time, Whiteman was playing on a radio program sponsored by Buick, was playing for dancing (and broadcasting) at the Biltmore Hotel, was making records for Victor, and was taking occasional theater engagements, all in New York City. Bunny was still working with Rudy Vallee on radio, and possibly subbing or guesting on a few CBS radio shows. It is not clear if Berigan was present on all Whiteman jobs in the early months of their association. He evidently was present for a Victor recording session on November 25, and a Buick broadcast on the 28th, however, likely his first such appearances with Whiteman.

The revelation of previously unknown Berigan recordings always causes a stir among collectors of his music. Here is the notation from the White materials that may indeed lose a few such recordings:

A series of about one hundred hours of home type recording discs, dating from February 1932 to June 1933 are known to exist. Some at least were on pre-grooved discs and were from the 'Magic Carpet' radio show. Others include at least two complete Jack Pearl–Paul Whiteman radio shows (see April 27 and May 18, 1933). Somehow these discs survived into the 1980s when they came into the possession of a well-known NYC disc jockey.[4] It is known that these are recorded at 33⅓ and they are probably on 10-inch discs. Probably most or all of those featuring Bunny will sooner or later be released on compact discs. One such is said to be from a jam session at the apartment of trombonist Larry Altpeter.[5]

One cut from these recordings, an excerpt that included only trumpet and piano, was reviewed either by Bozy White or others who edited his materials; it was "Way Down Yonder in New Orleans," and it definitely contains Berigan's playing.

Jazz fans have long wondered why Bunny Berigan would ever have joined Paul Whiteman's much-maligned orchestra. Here are a few reasons: as 1932 ended, Bunny, who had only recently turned twenty-four, had completed his most productive year as a professional musician. His place in the highly competitive and demanding New York music world was now secure. Bandleaders, conductors, and record producers knew who he was and what he was capable of. And because of his unique blend of talents as a superb studio musician, as well as an exciting, inspired jazz soloist, he was constantly in demand. As always, his employment had been widely varied. He seemed to be able, even in the ever-deepening depression, to work as much as he wanted, and in his case, that was always a great deal. Now, he was employed by the nation's leading bandleader, Paul Whiteman, earning an excellent salary, and still augmenting that income with good pay from other work, whenever time would permit. Bunny understood that Whiteman was "the top." He was "class." Through Whiteman, Bunny would be introduced into the upper echelons of not only the music business, but show business as well. From a career advancement standpoint, Bunny's move into the Whiteman orchestra made a lot of sense. Bing Crosby had launched his fabulously successful career as a singer with Whiteman. And we mustn't forget that both Dorseys had previously worked for Pops Whiteman, and they undoubtedly encouraged Bunny to get from Whiteman some of the experience, musical and otherwise, that he had provided for them.

Here is the text of an advertisement that ran several days in the *New York Times* in late 1932 that gave the essential information about Paul Whiteman's New Year's Eve party at the Biltmore Hotel, as well as the ads for two of his competitors: "Paul Whiteman Orchestra, WJZ, 11:30 p.m. to 12:00 midnight. New Year's Eve. Hotel Biltmore...Paul Whiteman and entertainers...Supper Room $12.50 per person; Main Dining Room, $10.50 per person; Palm Court, $10.50 per person." "The Park Central—New Coconut Grove—Russ Columbo and his music, $7.50 per person." "Paradise Restaurant Abe Lyman and his Orch. $7.50 per person."[6] For that time, these prices were extraordinarily high. (A multiple of fifteen would give an approximation in value of today's money.) Whiteman liked it that way—then he could pay his musicians what they were worth, and still make top money himself.

In one other relevant year-end note, Lee Wiley began to be featured on Paul Whiteman's Buick radio show at that time.

Beginning in 1933, while Bunny Berigan was settling in as a member of Paul Whiteman's orchestra, various recordings began to be made at the American Record Company by ad hoc groups of musicians gathered to back the usual ARC singers that were identified as "Bunny Berigan and His Orchestra." This was a continuation of ARC's practice of putting almost any name they could think of, in willy-nilly fashion, on the records they used to sell tunes, not necessarily those of the singers or musicians who actually made the records. The irony in this practice is that very frequently, the name on the record label had nothing at all to do with the band of musicians who actually made the recording. With respect to these early "Bunny Berigan" recordings, Bunny did not play on *any* of them and had *nothing* to do with them. Nevertheless, the fact that his name was now being printed on various record labels that circulated throughout the country began the lengthy process of creating a public identity, albeit a rather unfocused one, for the name Bunny Berigan.

In addition to whatever duties Bunny had in Paul Whiteman's band, he continued to broadcast with Rudy Vallee into 1933. The Vallee archive has a cancelled check payable to him for the broadcast of January 26, bearing Bunny's endorsement. Still, it was his employment with Whiteman that provided the greatest opportunity for professional growth and satisfaction. Whiteman performed one in the series of Carnegie Hall concerts he did in the 1930s on January 25, 1933. *Billboard* advertised the occasion as follows: "Paul Whiteman's concert at Carnegie Hall on January 25th will include 'Night Club,' by John W. Green (six impressions for orchestra and six pianos); Ferde Grofe's recently composed 'Tabloid,' (suite in four movements); and 'Land of Superstition,' from 'Africa Suite,' by Bill Still, colored composer and arranger."[7] For a jazz musician to play in Carnegie Hall in the early 1930s was practically unheard of. Benny Goodman didn't get there for another five years. There is every reason to believe that Bunny Berigan very proudly participated in this concert as a member of the Whiteman orchestra. The music performed at this concert was certainly not jazz, but rather that unique Whiteman brand of quasi-concert music with jazzy trappings. In that concert, Berigan played a solo on Johnny Green's "Night Club." The whole experience undoubtedly was interesting and exciting for Bunny—the realization of a dream for him. This was the kind of venue a musician who worked with Whiteman could expect to play—yet another reason why the Whiteman orchestra was *sui generis*, and why Bunny chose to join it when he did.

On February 2, he participated in a Victor recording session with Whiteman, taking a solo on Ferde Grofe's arrangement of "Night and Day," which was released on a twelve-inch disc. The Whiteman orchestra was also then being presented on a weekly forty-five minute Sunday evening radio program over WJZ called *Rhythmic Concert*. Ward Bond, later a well-known character actor in Hollywood films, was the announcer.

The Whiteman engagement at the Biltmore Hotel ended on February 28. Whiteman then headed to Florida for a three-week vacation. He returned to New York during this vacation for the Buick broadcasts on Monday evenings. His orchestra, including Bunny, was probably put "on vacation," meaning the musicians were, with the exception of the weekly Buick broadcasts, laid off.

While Whiteman was on vacation, Bunny returned to the ARC studios once again to back singers. The session on March 7, 1933, which was conducted by Victor Young, featured Chick Bullock on two sides, and Lee Wiley on two. Here are a couple of descriptions of Ms. Wiley from the early 1930s:

Lee Wiley, a tall, striking-looking woman with olive skin, corn-colored hair and Cherokee blood, is one bitch of a singer, which for all its robustness happens to be just about the sweetest, most terrific tribute you can pay a person, meaning, as it so richly does, that she can reach your heart with her singing. Miss Wiley has a little thing going for her called 'class.' Technically, she may leave something to be desired, but artistically she's simply magnificent, projecting emotion with dignity and warmth, expressing nuances with exquisite delicacy and making you share her bliss or heartbreak. She came here from Fort Gibson, Oklahoma, and before very long, all the right people were bewitched by her incomparable magic. (George Frazier) Born in Oklahoma with a generous strain of Indian blood, Lee Wiley grew up on Ethel Waters records. When she was only fifteen, she ran away from home. At seventeen, she was a featured singer in New York clubs and before she could vote, she was a nationally famous radio and recording star. Bing Crosby once claimed her as his favorite vocalist. Fats Waller and Bunny Berigan violated recording contracts to play behind her on obscure recording dates. And George Gershwin said he'd rather hear Lee sing his songs than anybody else. Always the musicians' favorite, Lee was limited to no school of jazz, despite her close association with Dixieland. Her most distinctive qualities were her slow, pulsating vibrato, her keen sense of phrase and the husky eroticism that warmed her work.[8]

The story of Wiley's early life was perhaps a press agency "version," although it may have originated with Wiley herself. In fact she was born on October 9, 1908, and was age twenty-three when she reached New York City. She died on December 11, 1975.[9]

Although Bunny and Ms. Wiley were beginning to work together more frequently at this time, their relationship remained musical only. Lee Wiley and Victor Young were then conducting *une affaire d'amour.* Their liaison continued until Young went to Hollywood in 1935, to work more closely with Bing Crosby and at Paramount Pictures. Wiley followed Young there, but their relationship ended when she returned to New York early in 1936.[10]

On March 14, Berigan was in the band at ARC led by the Dorsey Brothers. They recorded two instrumentals, "Mood Hollywood" and "Shim Sham Shimmy," and also provided the backing for Bing Crosby on three sides. The karma at this session was especially good—every side recorded that day is wonderfully spirited. On April 4, he recorded at Victor with Paul Whiteman, and again with the Dorseys at ARC on April 8, backing that talented songstress Mildred Bailey for the first time. On April 11 he returned to ARC to back the Boswell Sisters and Dick Robertson. In March and April 1933, various claims have been made that Bunny recorded with several other groups, notably Freddy Martin's band, the ARC band behind vocalist Greta Keller, and some records featuring vocalists Smith Ballew and Chick Bullock with the labels bearing the legend: "Bunny Berigan and His Orchestra." His presence on any of these recordings is doubtful. It was also during this time that he stopped working in Rudy Vallee's radio band. Berigan's employment with Paul Whiteman was about to become full-time.

On April 14, Paul Whiteman and His Orchestra opened a one-week stand at the Earle Theater in Philadelphia. This was the first stop on an extended tour that would last until the beginning of June. While they were playing at the Earle Theater, several of Whiteman's musicians and singers went across the Delaware River to Victor's "church studio" in Camden, New Jersey, for recording sessions on April 18 and 20. Berigan was definitely present on the April 20 session, which produced three masters: "Raisin' the Rent," "Was My Face Red?" and "I've Got to Sing a Torch Song," all with vocals by Ramona.[11] They then moved on to the Orpheum Theater in Memphis where they opened on April 22. Whiteman's road manager, Charles Strickfadden, who played woodwinds in the orchestra, added some details:

> After we closed at the Biltmore Hotel, we played a week at the Earle Theatre in Philadelphia and then jumped to Memphis where we rehearsed and played our first date on that tour with the Boswell Sisters, Jack Pearl and Cliff Hall. We were

out on the road for about three months, traveling first class in three Pullman cars throughout the mid-Western states. Most of the dates were single two-shows-a-day performances, except in Cleveland where Sophie Tucker joined and we were there for a week. We finished the tour after playing two weeks in Chicago at the Oriental Theatre, where we added a chorus line of 16 girls, Burns and Allen and another dancing act.[12]

Comedian Cliff Hall had more information about that tour:

Eddie Cantor was the first radio star to make a nationwide theater tour of one night stands, which was such a success that the William Morris booking agency decided to follow up with other tours sponsored by the American Tobacco Company. Thus Jack Pearl and the Boswell Sisters and I joined the Paul Whiteman troupe as one large entertainment package. They would set up the stage with mikes, fly in announcers and a crew of technicians and use the last hour of the stage show for the broadcast. On a few occasions, Jack and I flew back to New York for the radio program and then back to rejoin the tour. Although this was during the Depression, we were making the best money I ever made! Jack had a guaranteed $5,000 per week, plus a percentage of the take, and out of that he paid me $1,000 a week. Our first week on the road, Jack made over $8,000 with that arrangement. The whole trip was a smash success with sold-out houses all along the way, including breaking many theatre attendance records. The tour began with the first performance at the Orpheum Theatre in Memphis. Jack Pearl had top billing and 'Pops' Whiteman was given second billing! The Whiteman band had played a week in Philly, where Jack and the Boswell Sisters and I picked up the band and continued on to Memphis. The company had three Pullman cars, which would be switched on to a siding at each town and then the band, the stage acts and the technical crew would use them as their headquarters. We usually held a party in my compartment after each show. That tour included the biggest collection of 'rummies' I ever encountered! I particularly recall that Bunny was a good man with a bottle, and Jack Fulton, Mischa Russell and Fud Livingston were also prominent members of the drinking fraternity. When we pulled into a town, the members of the band would generally go into the nearest hotel to get bathed and cleaned up, then Pops and Jack and I would head for the local golf course. We were all usually treated like real celebrities by the town officials, and prominent citizens would often wine and dine us; also any hotel bills would be 'on the house.' I used to send the porter from the train on a scouting expedition in each town to contact the local bootleggers. He was usually pretty successful so that when the boys got back to the Pullman car after each show, he'd have various types and quantities of booze, ice and glasses ready for the serious business at hand. Jack Fulton, the trombone player, had a high baritone voice and did all the ballads, though how he managed it after all the booze he imbibed I'll never know. Ramona also sang ballads and did some solo piano while Peggy Healy did all the hot songs. ...Sophie Tucker joined the show for its engagement in Cleveland with George Burns and Gracie Allen being added in Chicago. Pops had shed about 110 pounds during the year before that tour and Margaret Livingston, his second wife, had made him quit drinking. He'd been very fond of his first wife and her leaving him broke him up and set him off drinking on three or four day binges, so that he'd show up with a heavy growth of beard, bloodshot baggy eyes and looking really awful. Fortunately, he had put all that behind him by the 1933 tour. I was often called 'Charlie' Hall by mistake, because on my first radio program with Jack Pearl, a couple of years before, someone had written Charlie on the announcer's script instead of Cliff. So, when he called out 'Charlie Hall,' I couldn't believe it and said, 'Who, me?' and Jack ad-libbed, 'Vos you dere, Sharlie?' That got a big laugh and eventually became his trademark. I'm sure Jack Pearl retired as a millionaire.[13]

The tour continued with one night-stands in Shreveport, Louisiana, on April 23, the Metropolitan Theater in Houston on the 24th, (where a photo of the orchestra was taken), the Texas Theater in San Antonio on the 25th, the Auditorium in Ft. Worth on the 26th, and the Palace Theater in Dallas on the 27th. At this location, they broadcast their regularly scheduled *Lucky Strike Hour* radio program, which was recorded. Of the fifteen musical selections played that night, Berigan had solos on six of them. Although Bunny had to share the stage with Whiteman's many other featured singers and instrumentalists, it appears that Pops was providing him with a fair amount of solo space. The tour moved on with one-nighters in Oklahoma City, Tulsa, Kansas City, and then Des Moines, Iowa, on May 1.

Meanwhile, on May 2 (which was an off day on the Whiteman tour being billed as *The Radio Revue*), at the ARC recording studio in New York City, a group led by Freddy Martin, and looking very much like his band, being billed as Bunny Berigan and His Orchestra, (among other pseudonyms), backed singers Elmer Feldkamp, Will Osborne, and George Beuchler. On May 4, there was a similar session led by Gene Kardos, backing Dick Robertson and Chick Bullock. Berigan again had no connection with any of the records that were produced from these sessions. Other ARC "Bunny Berigan" sessions were also recorded around this time, none of which had anything to do with Bunny Berigan.

The Whiteman tour resumed on May 3, with a stop at Davenport, Iowa, then moved onto Rockford, Illinois, on the 4th. (Trade papers of the time were reporting that RCA Victor was inaugurating their new "budget" record label, Bluebird. Bluebird records then sold for twenty-five cents. Also, at CBS, Mark Warnow had been appointed a conductor, relieving Fred Rich and others of some of their assignments.)

On May 5, 1933, the Whiteman troupe pulled into Milwaukee to play at the Wisconsin Theater. It was Bunny's first return to Wisconsin since he left Madison for New York three and a half years before. "Quite a large number of Fox Lake people are planning on going to Milwaukee tomorrow, Friday, to hear Paul

Whiteman and his famous orchestra of twenty-five pieces at the Wisconsin Theatre. Local people have an added interest due to the fact that Bernard Berigan, son of Mr. and Mrs. W. P. Berigan, is a member of the famous orchestra."[14] After appearing in Milwaukee, the Whiteman orchestra continued playing one-nighters: May 6, Minneapolis, and May 7, St. Paul.

Then they returned to Wisconsin on May 8, for a one-night performance. Here are the details: "Paul Whiteman and his Orchestra played at the Capitol Theatre in Madison, Wisconsin. The performances were at 3:30 and 8:30 p.m. Prices for the matinee were Main Floor, $1.65 and $2.20; Loge, $2.20; Balcony 55 ¢, $1.10 and $1.65. Prices for the evening were Main Floor, $2.20 and $2.75; Loge, $2.75; Balcony, $1.10 and $1.65."[15] Bunny's hometown newspaper reported his return, and a large number of family, friends, and previous musical associates attended the Whiteman show at the Capitol Theater. Bunny's older brother Donald Berigan was there:

> About thirty of us showed up at the Capitol Theatre. After the show it was so crowded backstage that we couldn't get near to Bunny's dressing room. It was then that I met his wife, Donna, for the first time and their daughter, Pat, who was about two years old. (Actually, little Patricia would not be one year old until the following July 23.) Later, we all went over to my grandmother's house for a big party, and Bunny was his old self. We all went down to the railroad station to see him off on the midnight train.

Bunny's cousin Charles Casey was also there, as were Larry Becker and Lou Hanks, two of Bunny's early sidekicks. Here are their recollections:

> Charles Casey: We had a great night when Bunny appeared on the Capitol stage in Paul Whiteman's band. The show included the Boswell Sisters, 'Baron Munchausen and Charlie,' Jack Fulton and 'Goldie' on cornet. Bunny wasn't feeling too hot, but he was featured on a couple of solos. One was on 'Burning Sands' I think, and Jack Fulton sang 'Love Letters in the Sand.' Merrill Owen: Many of us who had worked with Bunny in the early days saw him with Paul Whiteman in Madison. It was a variety show and quite spectacular! Larry Becker: Bunny was not billed; I spoke with him and recall that he said he was scared and said 'in my hometown they expect too much.' Becker recalled Bunny was drinking and had lip problems. He was featured in short solo spots on 5–6 numbers and one feature, 'Night and Day,' using a kazoo type mute. Lou Hanks: After Bunny left Madison in 1929 I didn't see him again until 1933 when he came through with Paul Whiteman's band. I got a group of 6–8 guys who had worked with him in Madison previously and we met him. I'm sure Erle Smith was included in that group.[16]

After Bunny had this small reunion with his family and friends, he left Madison with the Whiteman band and continued on tour, as follows: May 9, Springfield, Illinois; May 10, Toledo, Ohio; May 11, Valley Dale Ballroom, Columbus, Ohio; and May 12, the Hippodrome Theater, Cleveland, Ohio, for three days. After the Cleveland stand, the band had a couple of days off, then headed west toward Chicago, with a single one-nighter along the way, in Fremont, Ohio, on May 17.

The Whiteman aggregation broadcast from Chicago on their next Thursday evening (May 18) *Lucky Strike Hour* program. The entire one-hour show was recorded. The next day, they opened for a two-week engagement at the Oriental Theater, 24 West Randolph Street, in Chicago's Loop. A few acts had been added to the show including, notably, Burns and Allen. The *Chicago Tribune* reviewed it:

> The Oriental Theatre was the focal point of Chicago's elite last night for some 3,400 people assembled there to celebrate its conversion from a cinema to flesh and blood entertainment and almost as many more herded around its portals to watch the first-nighters arrive and bask in the searchlights that illuminated the festive scene. There was a Hollywood atmosphere on this first occasion that Chicago saw the performance of a revue by radio celebrities. Both Jack Pearl and Paul Whiteman have an aura of fame about them. Thirty musicians sit upon thrones surrounded by strange musical instruments with a golden glitter. Pearl works on his comic skits with passionate devotion to the tradition of Weber and Fields. Funny though he is on radio, Pearl is three times funnier on stage, his action being an important part of his humor, charging about the stage and striking his straight-man's chest in his attempts to be understood, which conveys a power to amuse that radio cannot communicate. The Boswells, three graces of sad and merry singing of the Negroid type, George Burns' and Gracie Allen's amusing chatter of jokes based upon the eternal dumbness of the human race, Sonny O'Dea, a dancing girl, works in a jazz variation of Bessie McCoy in style. Cliff Hall, Mr. Pearl's genial opposite, Ramona, who sings and plays piano, Jack Fulton, an amiable crooner, Peggy Healy of 'Fit as a Fiddle' repertory, and a certain Mr. Goldie, a trumpet blower, who also has gifts as a comedian, singer and dancer.[17]

It is likely that Donna Berigan, who was again pregnant, met Bunny in Madison with their ten-month-old daughter, Patricia, for the Capitol Theater engagement, and then stayed with Bunny's parents in Fox Lake for a couple of weeks, until the Whiteman band got settled in Chicago at the Oriental Theater. The plan, undoubtedly conceived by Bunny, was for Donna to meet the Berigan family, and get to know them, while at the same time to allow Cap and Mayme some time to enjoy their first grandchild. Donna and Patricia evidently stayed with the Berigans from May 8, when the Whiteman orchestra played in Madison, until they joined Bunny in Chicago on May 20th. After the Whiteman band closed at the Oriental Theater on June 2, the performers dispersed for a few weeks of vacation. Bunny, Donna, and Patricia all returned to Fox Lake, with Bunny remaining there with them until June 21, when he left to return to New York. This was one of the few vacations Bunny would ever have. While in Fox Lake, he did do some sitting in with his former musical coworkers to keep his lip in shape. All reports were that his playing had improved since he had left in 1929, but that success had not gone to his head. Donna and Patricia remained with Cap and Mayme in Fox Lake until mid-August, when they returned to New York. This also had been Bunny's idea. He hoped that Donna and Patricia would enjoy the hot summer more in rural Wisconsin than they would in New York City. It is also likely that Bunny and Donna both hoped that this would help Donna through some of the months of her pregnancy. All told, Donna and Patricia spent over three months in Fox Lake with the Berigan family in the spring and summer of 1933.

In late June in New York, Whiteman began his association on radio with the Kraft-Phoenix Cheese Company. Here is the background:

Paul Whiteman played but one serious selection, Gershwin's 'American in Paris,' on his new radio program with Al Jolson, sponsored by the Kraft-Phoenix Cheese Company. He showed the band's versatility by following his symphonic selection with dance tunes. Jolson was good and Whiteman was not too bad at chatter, despite being mike shy. The soloists included Mike Pingitore, banjo, Roy Bargy and Ramona, pianos, the Rhythm Boys, Jack Fulton and others. Ramona was very good with her songs, and Peggy Healy was OK. Deems Taylor, making his commercial debut, showed a great sense of humor. The two hour show is scheduled for several weeks with renewal in September, but for one hour only.[18]

The greatest stroke of good fortune came in the form of Miracle Whip salad dressing. The Kraft-Phoenix cheese company introduced the new product nationally in June. To bring it to the attention of millions of households, the company signed two of the biggest entertainers in show business, Al Jolson and Paul Whiteman. The program, soon to be known as the *Kraft Music Hall*, bowed with a two hour broadcast from NBC's Times Square studios. Paul was in fast company as he stood shoulder to shoulder with Jolson reading lines from a script. Deems Taylor, the musicologist and composer, assisted in describing such Whiteman concert selections as 'Bolero,' 'American in Paris,' etc. His annotations were brief, humorous and quietly enlightening. Jolson made frequent guest appearances on the show during its first season, before heading into his own series, *Shell Chateau*. By January 1934, the one hour program ranked 7th in the comedy-variety line-up, the first three places going to Eddie Cantor and Rubinoff's orchestra, the *Maxwell House Showboat* with Lannie Ross and Don Voorhees orchestra and Rudy Vallee and his *Fleischmann Hour*, respectively.[19]

The Kraft program was broadcast on Monday nights. Whiteman had the band available in New York for the broadcasts and rehearsals on Mondays, but played out-of-town engagements on other nights. At some point in the next few months, Whiteman's Kraft show was switched to Thursday evenings.

Bunny was kept quite busy with his Whiteman duties during the summer of 1933, and did not do a lot of recording or radio work during this time. Nevertheless he did make some recordings. He appeared with the Whiteman band on Victor recordings made on July 20, took a muted solo and played behind Ramona on "Are You Making Any Money?" and possibly appeared on the session from August 16 billed as: "Paul Whiteman presents Ramona and her Grand Piano," which had Ramona playing piano, with accompaniment of trumpet, clarinet, and drums. The White materials state that the trumpet on these sides may well have been played by Harry Goldfield, Bunny's section mate in the Whiteman orchestra.

On September 5, Berigan was reunited with his ARC house band buddies, including the Dorsey Brothers, to back the wonderful Mildred Bailey.[20] Mildred came to dearly love Bunny as both a musician, and as a person, in what was almost certainly a nonsexual way. He inspired her musically and could always make her laugh. She loved to cook and he was a frequent guest at her home in Forest Hills, including on the memorable night when the Joe Venuti,[21] the superb jazz violinist who had an outrageous sense of humor, served his infamous "Italian sausage salad" at one of her dinner parties.[22] Only two sides were recorded that day, and they appear to be rather heavily arranged when compared with later Bailey-Berigan recordings.

Two days after this, Bunny, along with Nat Natoli and Harry Goldfield, his fellow trumpeters in the Whiteman band, in summer white tuxes, posed for the much reproduced photo of them holding their instruments. This photo was taken to go along with an advertisement for Vega *Triumphal* trumpets. Berigan would appear in many of these promotional ad photos in the coming years. They provided some easy money and publicity. He also formed a long-standing friendship with Nat Natoli (or "Natalie") while they worked together in the Whiteman band. (Note: It appears that trumpeter Chelsea Qualey may also have worked on occasion in the Whiteman trumpet section at this time.)

On September 11, the Whiteman band had another Victor recording session, supporting vocalists Bob Lawrence (a new addition), Peggy Healy, and the Rhythm Boys. There are open trumpet solos on "Paper Moon" and "Sittin' on a Backyard Fence" from that session that have been attributed to Berigan. On Saturday, September 16, the Whiteman band played a dance date at the Biltmore Hotel in Westchester, New York until 1:00 a.m., and then returned to Manhattan to play a one-hour breakfast dance at Harlem's Savoy Ballroom, starting at 2:30 a.m. This was Bunny Berigan's first appearance at this legendary swing era venue as a performer.

America was truly dance crazy in the 1930s.

Harlem's marvelous Savoy Ballroom ran from 140th to 141st Street on Lenox Avenue. A great marble stairway led to a vast room with space for tables and chairs and 10,000 square feet for dancing. Colored spotlights played intermittently on the dancers. A well-stocked ice cream soda fountain offered chocolate-nut sundaes, banana splits and floats. Mostly what it sold was ginger-ale setups, into which the customers poured their own portable potables while listening to Chick Webb driving hard ahead on his snare and bass drums and flicking his sticks over the cymbals. Many whites came to the Savoy to foxtrot or to listen to Chick. More came just to watch young black couples whirling through stylized, intricate and very, very fast dances. At the Savoy, the real jitterbugs danced five nights a week to music provided by two alternating bands. The music never stopped. The dancers rested on Wednesday and Friday nights, which were reserved for private social affairs. Mondays, Tuesdays and Thursday, they came early because the admission price rose at 6:00 p.m. from thirty cents to sixty cents and rose again at 8:00 p.m. to eighty-five cents. Monday was 'Ladies' Night' and Thursday was 'Kitchen Mechanics Night,' when maids and cooks had the night off. On Saturdays, the middle-aged white squares showed up to watch the dancers. On Sundays, dancers, musicians and actors from Broadway shows jammed the Savoy. The northeast corner of the ballroom was the 'Cats Corner,' where only the best dancers could sit or dance.[23]

Paul Whiteman, ever the smart businessman, was angling for a place in New York for his band to call home for a time. The Kraft radio program kept his band tied to New York, and he was now tiring of doing the one-night stands in the territory around Gotham that had helped to cover his orchestra's hefty payroll for the previous several months. It was announced in *Variety* on September 19 that he was set for ten weeks starting on October 13 at the Paradise Restaurant, at Forty-ninth and Broadway. He then moved the band into the Hippodrome Theater in Baltimore for a one-week engagement commencing on September 22. Bunny Berigan was still a member of the Whiteman band, and he played that engagement. While there, the Whiteman troupe did their regular Kraft broadcast from the stage of the Hippodrome, to the delight of Whiteman's Baltimore fans. Whiteman followed this engagement with a similar one at the RKO Theater in Boston. Berigan was not present at this engagement. Another one-week theater engagement, at the Keith Theater in Providence, Rhode Island, may or may not have included Bunny. Finally, on October 13, the touring was at an end, for a while. Berigan's absences from these engagements were probably because he was coming to the end of his one-year contract with Whiteman, was tired of touring and playing theaters, and was once again taking on as much work as he could handle in Manhattan. There is also evidence that Donna's pregnancy had been somewhat troubled, and this may have caused Bunny to remain in New York to be closer to her as her delivery date approached.

Bunny wasted no time in returning to the ARC studios on October 16, this time with a musically compatible group led by Adrian Rollini, which backed singers Herb Weil and Clay Bryson. Bunny's playing on this session is inspired. Clay Bryson (guitar) and Herb Weil (drums) remembered:

> The Rollini sessions were always a great kick. Fulton 'Fidgy' McGrath used to collect jokes and limericks, which he wrote down in a little book so he wouldn't forget them. We all used to tell him stories for his book, most of which had Bunny in stitches! Al Philburn was usually responsible for the arrangements, such as they were. Just an introduction and an interlude or two scribbled on scraps of paper. No booze was consumed during the actual recording and Bunny appeared to be stone cold sober. At one point, Adrian wanted Goodman to split a chorus with Bunny, but Benny declined, saying, 'The way he's playing today, let him take the whole chorus.' I don't think he could have paid Bunny a greater compliment.[24]

Bunny's tenure with Paul Whiteman was circumscribed by a one-year contract, which began approximately in late November of 1932. As the term of that contract was about to end, it is likely that Berigan had decidedly mixed emotions about the experience he had had in the Whiteman orchestra. While it was true that the band was the top unit of its kind in the country, and the highest paid, and it did play the top locations, its music was for the most part rather flashy, and sometimes trashy, vaudeville fare. Although Bunny did get to play solos in the Whiteman band, that group's musical policy was simply out of phase with Berigan's jazz orientation. (It is not mere happenstance that of the many Victor recordings Bunny made with the Paul Whiteman orchestra, none have appeared on the dozens of LP and CD releases of Berigan's recordings that have been produced over the last five-plus decades. Bunny's unique talents as a jazz soloist were simply not utilized on Whiteman's Victor recordings.) Also, from mid-April until mid-October, the Whiteman band had been on an almost constant tour, and as subsequent events will show, that took a heavy toll on Bunny's marriage. Yes, there had been the pleasant hiatus in June, when Bunny was able to enjoy a couple of weeks off with his wife and family in Fox Lake. But other than that, he had been on the go almost continuously. Nevertheless, from a purely professional point of view, Bunny's service with Whiteman undoubtedly provided a big boost to his reputation. At that time, and for the next thirty years, the highest strata of the popular music world were filled with musicians, singers, and arrangers who had worked with Paul Whiteman. Bunny Berigan had now joined that select group.

On November 2, 1933, Donna delivered their second child, a girl whom they named Barbara Ann Berigan. The baby died soon after birth. The death certificate listed the cause of death as "prematurity."[25] Although decades later, when interviewed by Berigan biographer Robert Dupuis, Donna stated that she had not known that she was pregnant while she was in Fox Lake, this seems unlikely. While there is little doubt that the child Donna delivered on November 2, 1933, was not full term, if one counts backward from that date, it is obvious that Donna was at least a couple of months into the pregnancy while she was in Fox Lake during the previous spring/summer. It is certainly plausible that she and Bunny had known this, and that Bunny wanted her and Patricia to be in what for him had always been a pleasant, nurturing environment, rural Wisconsin, rather than in an apartment in hot, humid New York City. Also, he knew that he would be away from home almost constantly for several months fulfilling his commitments to Whiteman, and he hoped the time Donna and Patricia spent in Fox Lake would be enjoyable and family oriented.

In the wake of this tragic event however, Bunny undoubtedly discovered that all had not been rosy while Donna had stayed with his family. In 1986, when Dupuis interviewed Donna, here is what she said: "I'd been in Fox Lake when I was pregnant with Barbara, only I didn't know it at the time. I didn't get along with them very well and I was a nervous wreck. I lost weight instead of gaining. Bunny wanted me to live in Fox Lake, but I wouldn't have it. I couldn't get along with them. Oh, with Mayme it was all right, but Cap was hard to get along with. He was bossy and money hungry. He didn't want me to go out with the rest of the kids. Being Pat's mother, I guess I wasn't supposed to have a good time."[26]

In addition to the stresses surrounding Bunny's family situation, he encountered an uncharacteristically insensitive reaction from his employer, Paul Whiteman when Donna was about to give birth. Kurt Dieterle, a violinist with the Whiteman orchestra recalled: "Bunny went to Pops and told him that his wife was about to have a baby, so could he have some time off? He must have caught Whiteman in a bad humor, because he refused Bunny's request. The other trumpet men had agreed to cover for Bunny, but Paul said no. Unfortunately, the baby died and there were hard feelings between Bunny and Paul from then on."[27] Bunny Berigan's twenty-fifth birthday was on November 2, 1933. The sad irony of this undoubtedly hit him hard.[28] From that point on, it seems he simply went through the motions to complete his remaining month with Whiteman.

There have been persistent reports that after the death of his second child, Bunny went on a protracted binge of uncontrolled drinking. The facts indicate that this was improbable. Since November 2 was a Thursday, it meant the Whiteman band had to work on the Kraft radio program (which had by then been switched from Mondays) from 10:00 to 11:00 p.m. As was noted above, Whiteman did not allow Bunny to miss that broadcast. The next day, the

Whiteman orchestra was in the Victor recording studio making records. The White editors identified Bunny's trumpet on "Something Had to Happen" from that session. Shortly thereafter, he began subbing into various radio bands, including at least one broadcast with *The Taystee Breadwinners* Orchestra, conducted by Ben Selvin. On November 24, Berigan was again making records with a band led by Adrian Rollini at ARC. On November 30, he was present and taking solos on the Whiteman/Kraft radio show. If Bunny did occasionally drink at this time to unwind and cope, he also worked to get through those tough emotional times.

While he was employed by Whiteman, Berigan made $250 a week. By the first week of December, however, it appears that Bunny had left Whiteman, and joined Abe Lyman, who had offered him a weekly salary of $275 His chair in the Whiteman band was temporarily taken by Dave Wade, and then permanently by Charlie Teagarden, who, with his brother Jack, remained with Whiteman for quite some time. In spite of the hurt Whiteman inflicted on Berigan at the time of the birth and death of his second child, Bunny appears to have left the Whiteman band on good terms. Pops called him back in early January 1934, for the limited purpose of playing a solo on "Park Avenue Fantasy" at a concert because Charlie Teagarden had not yet had time to practice it. Bunny would continue to have intermittent but friendly dealings with Paul Whiteman for the rest of his life.

Frank Papile, an accordionist with Abe Lyman's band, remembered when Bunny was there: "Bunny Berigan left Whiteman for Lyman because he wanted to take things easier. He replaced Horace Smith in the trumpet section and after all those weeks of traveling and ballyhoo with the Whiteman organization. But the Lyman band's schedule of rehearsing, broadcasting, recording, and performing at the hotel wasn't any rest cure! Anyway, after about a month, Bunny declared it was too much for him and he quit, but he'd been on his best behavior the whole time."[29] It is safe to say that whatever drinking Bunny Berigan was doing at the end of 1933 was certainly not affecting his ability to continue to fulfill the heavy demands required of him as one of the top musicians in New York.

What appears to have been a rather strange incident may have caused Bunny to leave the Abe Lyman band after only a short time. Tommy Thunen (trumpet) recalled: "Bunny was only with Lyman for a few weeks in 1934 at the New Yorker hotel. I remember one night when Connie Boswell came in and Bunny refused to play muted horn while she was singing. This enraged Lyman, even though Bunny blew marvelously as always. It wasn't long after that before I replaced him. I don't mean that Bunny was fired, exactly, I think the parting was mutual."[30] I am skeptical about this because Tommy Thunen was not a member of the Lyman band until after Bunny left. As he stated, he replaced Berigan in the Lyman band. If this is so, then he likely would not have been present to witness the event he described. It is more probable that Bunny left the Lyman band when he did because he was returning to CBS.

Notes

[1] Paul Samuel Whiteman was born on March 28, 1890, in Denver, Colorado. He received classical musical tuition early and learned to play the violin. He worked in a variety of musical jobs prior to forming his own band in 1918. His rather revolutionary idea was to present a wide variety of music including light classical fare, dance music, and popular tunes with first-rate musicianship being a paramount objective. After his first successful recordings were made in 1920, he skillfully navigated through the sometimes turbulent waters of the popular music business over the next two-plus decades, achieving great success on tour, in film, on records, and in radio. Although he employed some of the finest jazz musicians in his band, including Bix Beiderbecke, Joe Venuti, the Dorsey Brothers, Bunny Berigan, and Jack and Charlie Teagarden, and the pioneering jazz arrangers Bill Challis and Lennie Hayton, the musical policy of his orchestra was never highly jazz oriented. Nevertheless, Whiteman knew what good jazz was, and supported it indirectly by paying the jazz musicians he employed the highest salaries they ever received as sidemen, and by providing them the opportunity to enter the highest echelons of the music business. Whiteman was among the first bandleaders to employ boy and girl singers. Bing Crosby and Mildred Bailey both went onto fame after their time as members of the Whiteman orchestra. After his years of leading a standing band, Whiteman worked with success in radio. Paul Whiteman died on December 29, 1967, in Doylestown, Pennsylvania.

[2] Edward Kennedy "Duke" Ellington was born in Washington, D.C. on April 29, 1899. As a pianist, bandleader, composer, and arranger whose career spanned the time from the early 1920s until his death on May 24, 1974, in New York City, Ellington had an enormous influence on the development and evolution of jazz. In addition, his many popular compositions have earned him a place of prominence in what is now known as "American popular song."

[3] *Music Is My Mistress,* by Duke Ellington, Doubleday (1973), 103.

[4] Bozy White did not reveal the identity of the "well-known New York jockey." Christopher Popa, who is the man behind the *Big Band Library.com* website, and is very knowledgeable about the history of big bands, speculates that person may be Phil Schaap. Mr. Popa is also a librarian at the Chicago Public Library, and as such has access to that great institution's massive collection of books, periodicals, and other information.

[5] White materials: December 8, 1932.

[6] *New York Times:* December 23–31, 1932, cited in White materials.

[7] *Billboard:* January 14, 1933, cited in the White materials.

[8] Both of these descriptions of Lee Wiley come from an undated issue of *Esquire's World of Jazz* that is contained in the White materials: March 7, 1933. Christopher Popa pro-

vided me with the full, correct citation: *Esquire's World of Jazz,* Esquire, Inc./Grosset & Dunlap (1962), 142.

[9] White materials: March 7, 1933.

[10] Victor Young, born on August 8, 1900, in Chicago, Illinois, composed the music for many first-rate songs including a few much beloved by jazz musicians: "My Foolish Heart," "Stella by Starlight," and "Street of Dreams." His work in Hollywood at Paramount Pictures and elsewhere eventually earned him twenty Academy Award nominations. He won an Oscar for his music for the film *Around the World in Eighty Days.* Young died of a cerebral hemorrhage in Palm Springs, California, on November 10, 1956.

[11] Ramona was the stage name of Estrilde Raymona Myers (1909–1972), who played piano and sang with Paul Whiteman from 1932–1936. When Ramona joined Whiteman, she was married to musician Howard Davies.

[12] White materials: April 20, 1933.

[13] *Ibid.*

[14] *Fox Lake Representative:* May 4, 1933, cited in White materials.

[15] White materials: May 8, 1933. Again, to approximate the ticket costs for this engagement in the value of 2008 dollars, multiply by fifteen.

[16] *Ibid.*

[17] *Chicago Tribune:* May 20, 1933, cited in White materials. Full citation courtesy Christopher Popa: "Jam Oriental for Opening of Stage Regime," by Charles Collins, *Chicago Daily Tribune,* May 20, 1933, 15.

[18] *Billboard:* July 8, 1933, cited in White materials.

[19] This quote is credited in the White materials: June 26, 1933, to "Pops DeLong." No further identification or explanation is provided by Mr. White. Christopher Popa discovered that the quote cited is from *Pops: Paul Whiteman, King of Jazz,* by Thomas A. DeLong, New Century Publishers, Inc. (1983), 177–178. Mr. Popa further commented: "The text (as quoted in the White materials) is heavily edited from what is actually written on those two pages in the DeLong book."

[20] Vocalist Mildred Bailey was born Mildred Rinker on February 27, 1907, in Tekoa, Washington. Her brother Al Rinker was associated with Bing Crosby in a singing group called the Rhythm Boys, which worked with Paul Whiteman's orchestra in the late 1920s. It was through this connection that Bailey, who retained the surname of her second husband, was hired by Whiteman. She remained in Whiteman's employ from 1929–1933. During this time she met her third husband, the xylophonist/vibraphonist Red Norvo. After Bailey left Whiteman's orchestra, she had considerable success on radio and records throughout the 1930s, and influenced many of the female vocalists then working with dance bands. She appeared for a time in the late 1930s as featured vocalist in Norvo's band. By then they were married, and were thus billed as "Mr. and Mrs. Swing." Bailey's career stagnated in the 1940s as a result of her declining health. She died in Poughkeepsie, New York, on December 12, 1951.

[21] Giuseppi "Joe" Venuti, born on April 4, 1898, in Lecco, Italy, was the premier jazz soloist on violin. Raised in Philadelphia, he met guitarist Eddie Lang there, and they formed a musical partnership that lasted until Lang's premature death in 1933. Venuti worked with innumerable bands throughout the 1920s, most notably with Paul White-

man's at the end of that decade. He was very active as a recording artist through the early 1930s, but then began leading bands of various sizes through the 1940s, and recorded almost nothing. From then until the 1960s, Venuti worked steadily, but without much public notice. From the late 1960s, he enjoyed a renaissance of popularity during which his playing was as inspired as ever. He died on August 14, 1978, in Seattle, Washington.

[22] Bandleader Charles Daly "Charlie" Barnet (1913–1991) was there too, and told the story in his hilarious autobiography *Those Swinging Years,* with Stanley Dance, Louisiana State University Press (1984), 49. Bud Freeman, when recalling this same incident in 1986, told me that he went to Mildred Bailey's dinner party with Bunny that night. Freeman said that this event took place "around the time Bunny and I made those records for John Hammond," which would have been in December 1935.

[23] John Stanton is credited with this quote in the White materials. No explanation is given as to who Mr. Stanton is or was, or where this quote was taken from. White materials: September 18, 1933. I assume that he was one of the persons who contributed material to Bozy White for inclusion in what eventually became the White materials.

[24] White materials: October 16, 1933.

[25] *Bunny Berigan Elusive Legend of Jazz,* by Robert Dupuis, Louisiana State University Press (1993), 67, hereafter "Dupuis." Mr. Dupuis obtained this information from the death certificate of Barbara Ann Berigan.

[26] *Ibid.*

[27] White materials: November 2, 1933.

[28] Barbara Ann Berigan is buried in the Berigan family plot at St. Mary's Cemetery, Fox Lake, Wisconsin, near her father.

[29] White materials: December 1, 1933.

[30] White materials: January 24, 1934.

Chapter 9
The Birth of the Swing Era

Bunny Berigan had stopped working at CBS in early October 1931 to join the pit band for the show *Everybody's Welcome,* after being persuaded to do so by Tommy Dorsey. At the time, Fred Rich, their frequent boss at CBS, angrily stated that they would never work for him again. Rich had apparently reconsidered, at least with regard to Berigan, because after Bunny returned to CBS in early 1934, he did indeed work again, rather frequently, with Rich.

Upon his return, Bunny found that things had changed a bit at CBS. In addition to being a utility trumpet player who might be called upon to perform just about any musical task, there now appeared to be some tiny awareness of the attractiveness of jazz to at least a small part of the large and ever-growing CBS listening audience. Bunny was assigned to work with the "morning band." Drummer Johnny Williams, father of the multi-Oscar-winning film composer John Williams, was to become a frequent associate of Bunny's at CBS, and a close friend. He recalled that time:

> The period after Bunny rejoined CBS was pretty good. We had Sundays off, at first, but later we worked Sundays and had Mondays off. We played mornings and afternoons only, and several different groups of musicians were used for those early shows. Bunny and I enjoyed that routine, because it gave us plenty of drinking time plus the chance of fitting in outside night jobs. Many a time we'd be drinking all night and try to grab some sleep in the studio on a chair or a couch or, yes a pool table! At other times we'd get no sleep at all and have to drink gallons of black coffee to get sobered up enough to play the first morning show. It was Jerry Colonna[1] who was largely responsible for CBS hiring Bunny and me. My wife Esther and I became good friends of the Berigans. Colonna was really the spark-plug in getting the morning band organized. The big band had a string section and always played written arrangements, but we'd just go in and play jazz. They used to work us eight hours, officially, and we'd have to be at the studios for eight hours, even if we only worked five. Sometimes they'd put us on overtime and we'd go into the studios at 10:00 a.m. and still be there at midnight! Also, we'd double with the big band. Anytime Freddy Rich needed a trumpet player or a drummer to play jazz, he'd send for Bunny and me, which would mean more overtime. We didn't have individual contracts, but the union had to be notified how many hours we worked and how much money we got. We were supposed to give a few days advance notice (to take a day off), but I guess Bunny

didn't think that applied to him! He'd just say, 'I'm not going to be in tomorrow.' Of course, under those circumstances, if he had a recording date, he'd send in a sub like we all did if we couldn't make a date. I always used Sammy Weiss or Billy Gussak. We both did quite a lot of outside work like club dates and some society dates with Joe Moss, who was out of the Meyer Davis office. Often we'd get more money from those jobs than we got from CBS.[2]

Announcer Del Sharbutt, also a CBS employee then, explained the workings of the CBS music department further:

I was working in radio over at station WJGD in Chicago, when I got the opportunity to go to New York and audition for CBS as an announcer. There were 44 other aspirants and only one job, but I was the lucky one. I didn't make much money, but it was a great place to work. There was no bullshit organization structure there. If you had an idea, you took it to the top and if they liked it, they'd give it a try. At that time, CBS had three regular bands: the morning band, the afternoon-evening dance orchestra and the full-sized symphony orchestra. I worked mostly with the morning band, which was a very sharp group consisting of top sidemen like Bunny Berigan, Jerry Colonna, Babe Russin, Artie Shaw, Raymond Scott, Lou Shoobe and Johnny Williams. Their rehearsals were very short! After a few bars of a new number, they'd yell, 'We've got it!' and they'd move on to the next tune. They'd play six or seven shows a day between 8:00 a.m. and 12:00 noon, using such names as the *Instrumentalists*, the *Southernaires*, the *Rhythmaires*, etc. They all worked night-time dates as well, and Bunny would often arrive hung-over. He'd reach into his trumpet case, pull out a bottle and take a quick swig. That would be breakfast! They were all pretty good drinkers, but I guess Bunny drank more than most, even then. CBS used many singers, most of them unknown, but some of them like Bing Crosby, the Boswell Sisters, Kate Smith and Morton Downey were on their way to fame and fortune. The morning band accompanied most of them in 15–30 minute programs. I also started doing remote jobs at night, some for CBS plus some outside jobs like the Dorsey Brothers and I worked seven days a week, mostly, at widely varying times depending on which guy had made up the schedule. I might have a spot at 6:00 a.m., to put the station on the air and another at 1:00 a.m. the following morning, to sign off. I first met Bunny in 1934, while working with the morning band and what a wild bunch of musicians those guys were! They had about 12 men and the afternoon band had about 30 and these would amalgamate and add more strings and woodwinds to form the symphony orchestra. The staff conductors included Mark Warnow, Fred Rich, Leith Stevens and Walter Gross. The main CBS building was 485 Madison Avenue, which had one big studio on the second floor housing shows like the *Saturday Night Swing Club* and four smaller studios used for smaller musical and chat shows. They also took over one or two Broadway theatres that were dark owing to the Depression and refurbished them for shows with live audiences, like the Chevrolet show that featured Isham Jones. That was the first show of its kind, I believe, and I got the job of MC because I wasn't afraid to go out front and talk to the audience.[3]   (Note: The flagship CBS network station in New York then was WABC.)

Bunny also resumed making records, and in this also there appeared to be (at least occasionally) more emphasis on jazz. Between February 10 and 28, 1934, he participated in two sessions at World Sound Studios in New York at which twenty-four tunes were recorded. These are the famous *Bill Dodge* transcription recordings, made by a band under the direction of Benny Goodman. (Incredibly, these recordings are not mentioned in either the James Lincoln Collier or Ross Firestone biographies of Benny Goodman.) The first session, propelled by the drumming of Gene Krupa,[4] who had just quit the Mal Hallett band to join the Buddy Rogers band (which was really the latest Joe Haymes band *led* by Buddy Rogers), contains some very spirited playing by all participants, including Bunny Berigan. The second session, which I think does not include Krupa, generally is a bit less satisfying from a jazz standpoint. Still, these recordings are essential for any serious Berigan (or Goodman) collector.

In addition, there had been changes in the scene surrounding music. The new meeting place for musicians was the latest incarnation of the Onyx Club, which was now located at 72 West Fifty-second Street. Jack Egan, who later worked for Tommy Dorsey in a number of capacities, recalled:

> The first Onyx Club opened on 13th July, 1930, at 35 West Fifty-second Street, a new speakeasy with Joe Helbock at the helm, which rapidly gained favor with musicians, friends of the manager and his co-workers. During the day, tooters would rush over from 711 Fifth Avenue and 485 Madison Avenue, between rehearsals, to find relief in a tall Tom Collins or similar stimulant. After dark, when they had completed their day's work, they would drop in again, knock on the door three times and ask for Joe, say 'I'm from 802,' in order to gain admission. Jam sessions at the Onyx were commonplace, with only one paid entertainer, Joe Sullivan. His piano tickling was an attraction for the boys from the studios as was the kitchen and bar. It would be impossible to list all the boys who sat in but among the regulars were Joe Venuti, Eddie Lang, Frankie Trumbauer, Roy Bargy, Art Tatum, Bunny Berigan, Benny Goodman, Tommy and Jimmy Dorsey, Jack and Charlie Teagarden, Arthur Schutt, Mannie Klein, Carl Kress and Dick McDonough and just about every other 'cat' on radio row. Since the clientele consisted practically exclusively of musicians, they all felt at ease. Helbock's famous greeting, 'Hya Toots' had become universally popular by the time the club moved across the street to its present site, where he took over two floors and a grand opening was held.[5]

Later dubbed "The Cradle of Swing," the Onyx launched Fifty-second Street as a music thoroughfare and helped make it the foremost jazz street in the world. The first magnet to draw the general public to The Street, the Onyx remained *hot* for more years than any other club, with the possible exception of the Famous Door, which also started as a musicians' in-spot."[6] Fifty-second Street was now becoming the street of jazz, and Bunny Berigan was very much a part of that development.

At the end of February 1934, Bunny appeared as a part of the Fred Rich's Orchestra in a Warner Brothers/Vitaphone short entitled *Mirrors*. This film was made at Warner Brothers' Brooklyn studio on February 23, 27, and 28. Also in this movie are vocalist Vera Van and the Eton Boys vocal quartet. The total running time of the film is 11:23. It contains six tunes. On "China Boy" there are solos by Bunny, Jimmy Dorsey on clarinet, Hank Ross on tenor sax, and Walter Gross on piano. (Gross later composed the lovely waltz "Tenderly.") As a result of the "mirrors" gimmick, Berigan appears to be playing left-handed. This short is on laserdisc, and is available from Turner Classic Movies as a part of the laserdisc set MGM/UA Home Video (ML-103928), is entitled *Swing, Swing, Swing–Cavalcade of Vitaphone Shorts, Volume 1*.[7]

Back at CBS, Bunny appeared almost daily in various orchestras known as: the Studio Orchestra, Mark Warnow Orchestra, the Captivators, the Merry Makers, the Dictators,[8] etc. He also resumed his recording activity at ARC with the Dorseys on March 14. By this time, the Dorsey Brothers seemed to be moving in the direction of forming a regular, standing band to play dance gigs in and around New York. They had gathered a number of former members of the Smith Ballew band at Glenn Miller's request (saxist Skeets Herfurt, trombonist/singer Don Matteson, guitarist Roc Hillman, drummer Ray McKinley, and singer Kay Weber) and combined them with some of the musicians they had been using to form what eventually became the Dorsey Brothers Orchestra.

Bunny Berigan was never a full-time member of the Dorsey Brothers Orchestra, because his full-time duties at CBS kept him tied to New York and unable to make many out-of-town one-nighters. Still, Tommy Dorsey, who occasionally played cornet himself with the DBO, would often implore Berigan to come along, and on more than one occasion, Bunny's exhaustion and too many "pops" (intended to be pick-me-ups) resulted in substandard playing by him. Bunny simply loved to play so much, especially with a good band, that he could not say no when asked to be a part of what he considered to be musical fun. (Unfortunately, the combination of overwork, fatigue, and alcohol would mar quite a few Berigan performances in the coming years.) Eventually, the Dorseys reluctantly accepted the fact that Bunny was not going to be able to anchor the brass section of their new band, and then hired the reliable but unexciting George Thow, who had been working with Isham Jones, as their regular trumpeter.

Vocalist Kay Weber was present at the beginning of the Dorsey Brothers Orchestra:

When the Smith Ballew band got to New York, the Florida job (which they had been promised) having been canceled, Glenn Miller somehow managed to get us some studio dates at Brunswick (by 1934 it was ARC) that just about kept the wolf from the door. He got Skeets Herfurt, Roc Hillman, Don Matteson and me on some Dorsey Brothers dates and we were signed up for the new band the

Dorseys were taking out on the road. We broke in with a few one nighters, including dates at Virginia Military Institute, Amherst, and Philadelphia, where Bunny arrived late after his regular radio work. And by that time he was very drunk and played very badly. He didn't remain very long with the new band, because he was making lots of money in the studios, much more than the Dorseys could match on the road. We used the Rockwell-O'Keefe office a lot for rehearsals and Tommy and Glenn were constantly striving for a particular sound, which couldn't materialize unless Bunny played his part. Glenn did most of the arranging and worked the band through the new charts, but Tommy was always the boss, even though he was the younger brother. Jimmy said very little.[9]

It is safe to say that the animating spirit for creation of the Dorsey Brothers Orchestra was Tommy Dorsey, being greatly assisted by Glenn Miller. Both Dorseys and Miller were approximately the same age, and by 1934 they had been involved in their careers as professional dance band musicians for a few years more than Berigan. They now seemed to be ready to move in the direction of forming a new jazz-oriented dance band. The brothers undoubtedly were bored and stifled as a result of spending several years on the grueling merry-go-round of working in the New York radio and recording studios. Miller had developed a reputation as a competent trombonist and arranger, but equally important were his abilities as a "straw boss," who helped harried bandleaders with myriad details like hiring the appropriate musicians, either making new arrangements or reworking stocks, and rehearsing the musicians. He had done this for Smith Ballew, was now doing it for the Dorseys, and would later do it for Ray Noble. The Dorseys and Miller also sensed that there now might be some new potential for success with a band of this sort, undoubtedly being encouraged by Tommy Rockwell and Cork O'Keefe, who booked them.

The music scene in Manhattan in 1934 for those chosen few performers who had the musical and physical ability to do what was required was rather bizarre. *Variety*, "the Bible of show business," reported in its April 3, 1934, issue:

With an estimated 5,000 active musicians in New York, a select few commute between the studios of the two networks, playing in one name band after the other. In the meantime, the unchosen many go hungry. According to a leader with a one-time weekly shot of his own, there are about 300 musicians, if that many, on the air, from whose ranks most orchestras are made up. These musicians are kept working constantly from audition to rehearsal to broadcast and back again. Some individuals average up to $600 weekly. Those on the outside, hungrily looking on, and blame this partly on the agencies, partly on the leaders. There are instances where leaders have changed rehearsal times because too many of their men have been on other jobs. Louis Sayde, violinist, is offered as one example, playing with Leo Reisman, Nat Shilkret, Lennie Hayton on Terraplane and Ipana-Sal Hepatica show and others. Charlie Margulis, trumpet, is with Hayton, Leon Belasco (Armour), Shilkret, Arnold Johnson (True Story). Tommy Dorsey, trombonist, Larry Abbott and Dick Ladd, saxes, Lou Raderman, Benny Baker and Mannie Klein, trumpets, are some of those doubling constantly. Musicians kept constantly on the move are in surprisingly high money brackets. Very minimum is $6 hourly for rehearsals, $12 for performances. Multiply that by the days of the week, including Sunday and the number of jobs they do. It's so bad that there are those who claim the players are often too physically tired out by the constant grind to give the best in them. Equally as bad is the substitute system. When those in the select circle can't fill a job, they get their own subs to replace them. This prevents the outsider from getting a look-in. Likewise, it obligates the sub. Exception offered to the clique rule is that rare occasion when a member of the circle is unavailable. Another factor working against the outsider is a union ruling regarding dues. Musicians must be paid up or no workee. This means they must often turn down calls. It gets worse for these chaps daily, the back dues being augmented by the fines for not being paid up.[10]

Bunny Berigan was deeply involved in all of this at CBS; plus he was making records and doing club dates. It appears that he was now turning to alcohol more and more "to get through," and he was certainly not alone in this.

Bunny's chronic overwork was getting to be something of a joke among musicians. Here is another example. On March 23, 1934, after working all day at CBS, he raced over to the ARC studios to record with the Dorsey Brothers Orchestra and the Boswell Sisters. After that, he had accepted what most likely was yet another recording date, this one with Frank Trumbauer.[11] Trumbauer's date book indicated somewhat ambiguously: "...hired *by* Bunny Berigan, who failed to show; date cancelled."[12] I doubt that Bunny Berigan was setting up any recording dates on his own at this time. He was simply too busy playing for other people. However, Frank Trumbauer did eventually set up a recording date with Bunny as a sideman, the famous Victor session of November 20, 1934, which produced four classic sides. Bunny may have participated in yet another DBO session on March 28, featuring vocals by Connie Boswell and Kay Weber. And on and on it went.

Meanwhile, there were many dance bands working in venues of all kinds in the United States. The dancing boom of the 1920s had continued on into the 1930s, aided greatly by constantly increasing exposure of bands on radio. Radio as a mass entertainment medium grew exponentially in the Depression of the 1930s because, among other reasons, it was free after one stood the initial expense of purchasing a radio. Radio was the perfect medium for music. The explosion of popular music and other music-based entertainment in the 1930s was directly related to the huge number of radios that had been sold in the 1920s, and in the years that followed. Touring dance bands, like all other business enterprises, were negatively impacted by the Depression initially. But within a relatively short time, the use of radio to build a band's name and musical identity had allowed booking agents to gradually increase the asking prices for their clients as they toured doing one-night stands. By the spring of 1934, the Casa Loma band, booked by Rockwell-O'Keefe, was getting $1,000 per night.[13] This was possible largely because the Casa Loma band had begun broadcasting its *Camel Caravan* radio series on December 5, 1933, on approximately sixty-five stations scattered across the nation, and had consequently built its name with dancers.[14]

By June 1934 there was still more activity on the hot music front. Benny Goodman had organized a jazz-oriented dance band to play at Billy Rose's Music Hall in New York City.

> The Music Hall was located on the site of the old Manhattan Theatre at Broadway and Fifty-third Street and had been scheduled to open as early as May 1st or June 1st and according to *Variety*, 'Ushered in another new phase of show business.' Three shows were presented nightly with a three-hour 'turn-over' including five top vaudeville acts, 100 hostesses, 100 singing waiters and news reels. The club had a capacity of about 1,000, equally divided between the ground and upper floors. Supper prices ranged from $1.20 to $1.50 according to the hour and the show was conducted by Lou Froman. Jerry Arlen's band played in the afternoons and the Goodman band played for dancing in the evenings. The decor and setting of the Music Hall were patterned after the 'Wonder Bar' set in the Al Jolson movie of that name. Later the Billy Rose Music Hall site became the Ed Sullivan Theatre.[15]

Bunny Berigan subbed into the Goodman band occasionally during the summer of 1934 at the Music Hall. Sammy Shapiro, a formidable first trumpet player, later well known as a leader of studio bands at CBS as Sammy Spear, recalled working with Bunny then:

> The original lead trumpet for the Music Hall date was Eddie Wade. I had rehearsed with Goodman prior to the opening and had recorded with him several times under fictitious names like the Modernists, but I did not start the engagement. I joined in August 1934. It was a great band, but the toughest job I ever had. We worked about seven hours a night, seven days a week! I had the lead book all by myself and it wasn't until Bunny Berigan actually joined the band for the *Let's Dance* radio program that I was able to unload half the book on him. Bunny was without any doubt the best in his field and a pleasure to work with. [16]

In spite of all of this musical activity going on "on the outside," Berigan focused the vast majority of his energies on his demanding but lucrative work at CBS, sprinkling in a few record dates and other gigs. On May 21, he was at ARC in the "Smith Ballew Orchestra" (which by then was really the Dorsey Brothers Orchestra; Ballew had nothing to do with this session) to back the always pleasant sounding singer Chick Bullock. After Bunny left Paul Whiteman's band, he purchased a home in Queens and was trying to have some sort of family life. He elected to stay in New York for the summer of 1934, as opposed to joining another band and doing one-nighters. (Bunny may have taken a short two-week tour with Fred Rich's band at about this time. CBS booked it for limited engagements within about a one hundred mile radius of NYC.) His friend trombonist Larry Altpeter remembered that summer: "Bunny and his family at about this point were living in Rego Park, West Forest Hills, Long Island, in single family house they had purchased with furniture. I saw a lot of Bunny in the studios then and can still recall his phone number: HA9-1634."[17]

The Dupuis Berigan biography reported that Bunny went home to Fox Lake sometime in 1934.[18] However this is not mentioned in the White materials, which usually reported such visits via citations from the local Fox Lake newspaper, which scrupulously gave the details of these events. Whether this visit happened or not, Bunny somehow recruited a local Fox Lake girl, Eunice Sheskey, who sang and hoped to be discovered in New York, to act as his and Donna's housekeeper. This undoubtedly was done to help Donna, who evidently was still weakened from the pregnancy of the previous year, and was also probably lonely in the Rego Park house. Eunice reported to the folks back home that the Berigans had a large police dog (to help allay Donna's fears about being in the house with only little Patricia and Eunice), and a lot of parties.[19] Bunny named the dog "Cozy" after drummer William Randolph "Cozy" Cole, whom Bunny had met in 1934, while Cole was working in Benny Carter's band.[20]

In the meantime, Bunny's friends who had decided to become the leaders of their own bands began to experience the joys and sorrows of bandleading. The Dorsey Brothers Orchestra was working at the Sands Point Bath Club in Great Neck, Long Island.[21] Bing Crosby's younger brother Bob, who was also a singer, recalled how he joined the DBO:

> Anson Weeks knew that Bing Crosby had a brother who also sang, so he sent for me. I was picking cucumbers at home in Spokane, Washington, when I got the call. I did pretty well with Anson for the next couple of years, and then Tommy Rockwell, the booking agent, came to hear me. He said, 'We're organizing a new band with the Dorsey brothers and I'm going to put you with them.' Although I liked their records and enjoyed Jimmy's sax work, I was reluctant. Tommy Dorsey, in my opinion, was never a great jazz trombonist. Anyhow, I joined the band at Sands Point Bath Club in Great Neck, Long Island, NY. Those opening nights burned in my mind like a nightmare. The first two nights, nobody spoke a word to me and I didn't sing a single note, just sat at a table. The beginning of the third night, Tommy came over to me and in his very tender way said, 'Look, this is the best band in the whole world and you ain't the best Crosby singer. I didn't want you in this band, Tom Rockwell put you here. I'm not going to have any arrangements written for you, but if you find something in the book that you can sing, get up there and sing it. If you can't—tough!'[22]

For whatever reason, Bob Crosby and Tommy Dorsey never got along. With the exception of the hyperbolic reference to the DBO as "the best band in the world," nothing Tommy said to Bob Crosby was untrue. But I doubt that Tommy would have been so gratuitously brutal to young Bob. Not because he was such a nice guy, because he certainly could be vicious when provoked; but because he valued the friendship of Bob's older brother Bing too much. In any event, Bob would soon be promoted by Tommy Rockwell to the position of titular leader of the band Gil Rodin was soon to assemble, and he sailed through the swing era quite contentedly and successfully in that role.

At about the same time, Benny Goodman's struggling new band was suddenly thrown out of work.

(Headline) Billy Rose Quits Casino. Also withdraws from Music Hall and Threatens Suits. Alleging he had not been paid for his services, Billy Rose yesterday announced that he had withdrawn from the Casino de Paree, 254 West Fifty-fourth Street and the Billy Rose Music Hall, 1697 Broadway, both of them among the more popular of the city's post-repeal 'hot spots.' Lawsuits to settle the differences between the theatrical producer and Yermie G. Stern, president of the corporation operating the two enterprises, were promised by Mr. Rose and his attorney, Julian Abelees. Mr. Stern said 'We could not agree on certain policies and decided a change would be best.'[23]

Dateline, September 8th, New York... Billy Rose Out of Music Hall. He says he quit; others say he was fired. Rose claims he has not been paid since June 21st. He is also out of the Casino de Paree. He discovered when he returned from Europe that changes had been made in his shows and demanded his money. When it was not forthcoming, he walked out. Yermie Stern, who produces and finances both the Casino de Paris and the Music Hall, says Rose was fired for spending too much on the shows in both spots. Rose took a train for Chicago (September 15th) and has no definite plans but is talking of suing to get his name removed from the Music Hall and also to get monies due him and return of stage properties he says are all his. Both places were successful, so the break came as a surprise to the trade press. Acts at both places on notice.[24]

Another bandleader, Ray Noble, after having been enticed into coming from a successful career in England to the United States by Tommy Rockwell: "...was refused permission by American Federation of Musicians to do café work (in New York) with his new orchestra, and left for Hollywood to do some movie work around October 13th. Glenn Miller (in New York) continued to rehearse the Noble band."[25]

We don't know exactly what Bunny's feelings about these matters were then, but it is likely that he considered himself lucky not to have been a bandleader. Although he was working very hard at CBS, his duties there did not greatly interfere with his outside recording activities, or his ability to sub into many bands. He was making a great deal of money, was not on the road, was able to return to his home after work (when he chose to), and did not have to worry about personnel matters, booking agents, clubs folding, and the union meddling in his business. In short, he was probably pretty happy.

A major development on the pop music scene in the summer of 1934 was the establishment of the American Decca record label.

Decca Phonograph Company of England is to help finance a new Decca company in the U.S.A., to be called Decca and headed by Jack Kapp, who resigned from Brunswick on Monday (16th). He had personal contracts with all the stars at Brunswick and they will follow him in the breakaway. Decca (U.S.) is to get a strong start with Bing Crosby, Victor Young, Casa Loma, the Mills Brothers and the Street Singers, all of whom are transferring from the Brunswick roster. The new company will start around August 1. Justin Ring has officially left Brunswick to join Kapp at Decca as recording manager.[26]

John Hammond[27] amplified on this development later:

(E.R.) Lewis, with Jack Kapp of Brunswick, E.F. Stevens, a former sales manager with Columbia, and Harry Kruse, the promotion manager of Columbia, formed the American Decca Company in the summer of 1934. They moved much of the (Brunswick) equipment from Michigan to 619 West Fifty-fourth Street in New York. Decca was fortunate enough to start at the beginning of the juke box era, a tremendous market for popular records. It also went into business with Guy Lombardo and Bing Crosby, lured from Brunswick, and sold Deccas for thirty-five cents while all other important popular labels were selling for seventy-five.[28]

These moves were a big blow to ARC/Brunswick, whose losses were Decca's gains. Almost immediately, Decca Records became a force to be reckoned with. In addition, ARC brought in a new recording director, Russ Morgan. He seemed to eschew a jazz-oriented backing for singers, preferring instead a more nondescript string-oriented approach. Consequently, Bunny's work at ARC abruptly stopped in the fall of 1934.

But Berigan was busier than ever at CBS. Singer Bonnie Lake, who composed the Dorsey Brothers' theme song "Sandman" (which in my opinion received its best recorded treatment by Benny Goodman on November 22, 1935; arrangement by Fletcher Henderson), as well as the later "The Man with a Horn," had memories of Berigan that were similar to those of many others: "I am the sister of Harriet Lake (Ann Sothern) who worked with Bunny in the Broadway show in 1931. "I often saw Bunny at CBS, 485 Madison Avenue; I was doing office work there then. I recall Bunny's eyes most of all—it was the first thing you'd notice about him, *those eyes!*"[29]

By September 1934, Bunny's good friend from the Whiteman band, trumpeter Nat Natoli, who decided to settle in New York, had also been hired by CBS. According to drummer Johnny Williams, "Bunny helped to get Nat Natoli into the first trumpet chair at CBS, replacing Vincent Gentile. When he heard that Nat was leaving Whiteman, Bunny told me how Nat had helped him with some problems when they were both with Whiteman. Apparently Nat had shown him how to play for very long periods without his lip getting tired, so Bunny now wanted to do something in return. I advised him to talk to Mark Warnow, who had a great deal of influence at CBS."[30] Nat and his wife were already good friends of Bunny and Donna, and the two couples would frequently socialize.

At about the same time, Kate Smith, who had recently been signed to a long-term contract by CBS, started her various CBS network radio programs. Also at this time, Mark Warnow's brother Harry, known professionally as Raymond Scott, began to create his unique if somewhat eccentric brand of music by using musicians from the CBS morning band, including Bunny Berigan. Some recordings made on September 18, 1934, that are housed in the Scott archives include Bunny on trumpet.[31]

Generally, business was booming at CBS. The network by now needed more space for its many programs, and it began buying legitimate Broadway theaters, whose business had been hard hit by the Depression, to house some of its studios. These theaters were used to broadcast musical programs that were produced with a live audience. Some of the best music of the swing era would originate in these theaters, via CBS network shows like *The Camel Caravan* (first with Casa Loma, and later, Benny Goodman, then Bob Crosby); Old Gold's *Melody and Madness* series (with Artie Shaw); and one of the most successful of all, Chesterfield's *Moonlight Serenade,* with Glenn Miller.

CBS didn't always know how best to utilize its ever-growing corps of top-flight musicians, however. The success of the Kate Smith hour afternoon show has prompted CBS to launch four more of the same length, one going on at 9.00 a.m. The CBS Playhouse is being used for these shows with invited guests. The a.m. show is called *Morning Minstrels* with Leith Stevens' orchestra to be used. Harry Von Zell is the announcer and a total of thirty-five persons are to be involved in its production."[32]

Trumpeter Harry Gluck recalled:

> I was auditioning for CBS in the Leith Stevens orchestra, which was loaded with top class musicians and overloaded with about sixteen fiddles and cellos, not to mention a full legitimate woodwind section and a separate complement of saxes, all getting in each other's way! The tune was 'Poor Butterfly,' a semi-classical, symphonic arrangement up to a point where Bunny soloed with a pickup to a rhythm chorus. He stood up and played with such brilliance and power that he carried that enormous weight of orchestra, making it really swing or, more accurately, float on the broad tone and solid beat of Bunny Berigan.[33]

After an inordinately long hiatus for him, Bunny Berigan returned to the recording studios on November 20, 1934. On this occasion, the session, under the direction of Frank Trumbauer, took place at Victor's Twenty-fourth Street studio.[34] Bunny first had recorded in this space, rather unremarkably, with Paul Whiteman in late 1932 and several times thereafter. That had certainly not been his fault, because as other recordings he made during the time he was with Whiteman show he was at that time quite capable of delivering remarkable performances, if given the chance. Later, after the door of the swing era had opened, he would make some of the most memorable recordings of that epoch here with Benny Goodman, Tommy Dorsey, the *Metronome* All-Stars, and his own band. But this session, like so many before, had no advance planning as far as he was concerned. He simply showed up at the designated time and place, looked around the studio to see with whom he would be working, unpacked his horn, and took care of business.

This session was in most ways the same as dozens of sessions he had made previously, and yet was just a little bit different. It looked backward in many ways, but where Berigan's playing was concerned, it looked ahead into the swing era. The singer on this session was Dick Robertson, one of a number of pleasant, if fungible, performers whose job it was to sell the song. He sang two titles in conventional fashion: Rodgers and Hart's timeless "Blue Moon," and a Tin Pan Alley special, "Down t'Uncle Bill's." The assembled musicians did their jobs well. The records were made and that was that. Of slightly more interest, however, were the two instrumentals recorded: "Plantation Moods" and "Troubled." Trumbauer had a hand in composing both of these. Although there are moments of interest in "Plantation Moods," it is the last tune recorded, "Troubled," that brought forth a full measure of the Berigan magic. The perceptive and poetic Richard M. Sudhalter described it this way:

> After a quiet reed passage, Nat Natoli's cup-muted trumpet sets out a minor-key melody, a prelude to the entrance of Berigan, playing on open horn with a tone so huge that for a moment it sounds like a trombone. The effect is startling... Berigan—unfettered, rhythmically free, totally commanding—makes Trumbauer and the arrangement sound outdated. ...Then, gloriously, it is Berigan slamming out his high C sharp to begin a 16-bar solo that is like a giant searchlight beam piercing a night sky. Working against an unvarying harmonic background that is little more than an extended D minor chord, he builds his first eight bars on a series of descending cascades. He drops far down, then climbs back up for a longer, more sweeping descent highlighted by an original device: a chromatic drop that concentrates actively on the second and fourth beats of the bar. Again and again he hammers away at a high B natural, a slight rasp edging his normally heraldic tone, generating to the end a tremendous intensity and momentum.[35]

It is obvious from this recording that jazz was in a period of transition in 1934. The cross-pollination of black and white influences had begun some time earlier, but now the message of Louis Armstrong, that is *swing,* was moving to the center of the jazz stage. The soloists on "Troubled" were each at different stages of their rhythmic development. Berigan, being under the influence of Armstrong for almost as long as he had been playing the trumpet, had completely embraced Louis's rhythmic vocabulary, which was the essence of swing. Frank Trumbauer, bouncing along on the beat, and sounding rhythmically stilted as a result, clearly had not. Artie Shaw, whose playing was then in transition, was somewhere in between. His playing would not fully develop rhythmically until the later 1930s.

Notes

[1] Jerry Colonna, who was born Gerardo Luigi Colonna in Boston on September 17, 1904, was an excellent professional trombonist before he became a professional comedian. His handlebar moustache, rolling eyes, and high piercing tenor voice were trademarks. He worked as a staff trombonist at CBS from 1931 to 1936. There he became well known for his manic hijinks, which frequently entertained his fellow musicians and others between broadcasts. This led to him doing live on-air warm-ups for stars who performed on CBS radio. He worked for a time with Bing Crosby and Fred Allen, before he joined Bob Hope, with whom he was associated for decades on radio and in films. Colonna's career was effectively ended by a stroke in 1966. He died in Woodland Hills, California, on November 21, 1986.

[2] White materials: March 1, 1934.

[3] *Ibid.*

[4] Eugene Bertram Krupa was born on January 15, 1909, in Chicago, Illinois. He began playing drums professionally in the mid-1920s in Wisconsin, but by 1927 was tapped to be the drummer in bassist Thelma Terry's touring band. He made numerous records in Chicago in the 1920s with musicians such as guitarist Eddie Condon, singer Red McKenzie, and cornetist Bix Beiderbecke. In 1929, Krupa moved to New York where he began a long association with cornetist Red Nichols. He worked with other bands in the early 1930s including those led by Mal Hallett and Buddy Rogers. By late 1934, he was the drummer in the Benny Goodman band that was beginning its ascent to great popularity. Gradually, Krupa's drumming and stage demeanor became much more flamboyant, and this added greatly to the popularity of both the Goodman band and Gene Krupa himself. In 1938 Krupa formed his own big band, and led it almost continuously for the next thirteen years. Thereafter, he appeared at Jazz at the Philharmonic, and in other engagements that he chose with care, well into the 1960s. Gene Krupa died on October 16, 1973, in Yonkers, New York.

[5] *52nd Street; The Street of Jazz*, by Arnold Shaw, Da Capo Books (1977), 60, hereafter *52nd Street*.

[6] *Ibid.*

[7] Total running time for this ten-disk set is eight hours and twenty-six minutes. *Mirrors* is on side six. No date or personnel is given. There are no other films in this set that include Berigan. White materials: February 24, 1934. The six tunes performed in *Mirrors* are "China Boy" (instrumental); "I Want to Be Loved" (vocal, Vera Van); "I Want to Go Back to My Little Grass Shack" (vocal, Vera Van and the Eton Boys); "Way Down Yonder in New Orleans" (vocal, the Eton Boys); "Chloe" (vocal, Vera Van); and "Daybreak" (instrumental).

[8] The Studebaker Corporation produced an automobile model throughout the 1930s called the Dictator. Obviously this noun had a different, more positive connotation in the years before the crimes of Adolf Hitler and Joseph Stalin were committed and became known.

[9] White materials: March 14, 1934.

[10] *Variety:* April 3, 1934, cited in White materials.

[11] Frank Trumbauer, born on May 30, 1901, in Carbondale, Illinois, was one of the earliest exponents of jazz saxophone. Trumbauer played the C-melody saxophone, which is between an alto and a tenor, and has a uniquely melancholy sound, but which fell out of favor with jazz performers before 1930. Trumbauer worked with Bix Beiderbecke in the 1920s in a number of settings, the most notable of which was the recording, on Okeh Records in 1927 of "Singin' the Blues." This recording was hugely influential at the time, especially for young saxophonists. Although Trumbauer's rhythmic approach to jazz was rather stilted, his cool, delicate style and minimal vibrato caught the attention of many, including Lester Young, who incorporated these elements into his playing. In the late 1930s, Trumbauer worked in a variety of bands, often as a leader, yet he never achieved much success. After World War II, his activities as a musician were minimal. He died on June 11, 1956, in Kansas City, Missouri.

[12] *Ibid.*

[13] *Variety:* April 21, 1934, cited in White materials.

[14] "Glen Gray and the Casa Loma Orchestra" by George A. Borgman, *Mississippi Rag,* October 2006, 6.

[15] White materials: June 21, 1934.

[16] *Ibid.*

[17] White materials: July 7, 1934.

[18] Dupuis: 102.

[19] *Ibid.*

[20] Donna Berigan recounted how the Berigan dog got his name to Robert Dupuis. Dupuis archive, UW–Madison. Patricia Berigan also recalled Cozy to Mr. Dupuis.

[21] Like so many venues where big bands played during the swing era, the Sands Point Bath Club was destroyed by fire. Chris Popa informed me this particular spot burned to the ground in March of 1986.

[22] White materials: July 27, 1934.

[23] *New York Times:* September 8, 1934, cited in White materials.

[24] *Variety:* September 11, 1934, and *Billboard:* September 15, 1934, cited in White materials.

[25] *Billboard:* October 13, 1934, cited in White materials.

[26] *Variety:* July 24 and 31, 1934, cited in White materials.

[27] John Henry Hammond Jr. was born on December 15, 1910, in New York City into a family of great wealth and prominence. His mother was a Vanderbilt. Hammond's activities, beginning in the early 1930s as talent scout, record producer, and writer, had a major impact on many careers in jazz, including those of Billie Holiday, Benny Goodman, Count Basie, and Teddy Wilson. Later, he was instrumental in launching the careers of Aretha Franklin, George Benson, Bob Dylan, and Bruce Springsteen. One of Hammond's sisters, Alice, married Benny Goodman in 1942. Hammond's activities as critic were always somewhat dubious because he was a man of extreme opinions, which he had the wealth and power to indulge. His criticisms, which were delivered as sermons from on high, often were extreme: "he's maaahvelous," or "he stinks." Moreover, he was known to write criticism about artists whose music he recorded as producer for many record labels, a blatant conflict of interest. Hammond was an early and passionate crusader for racial equality, but again his arrogance often undercut what he was trying to do to bring about—racial parity. Black jazz musicians, whose work he preferred, often tolerated his meddling patiently to his face, but among themselves referred to him ironically as "the great white father." Often in spite of himself, Hammond was a bridge builder whose efforts helped the cause of jazz and jazz musicians. John Hammond died on July 10, 1987, in Manhattan.

[28] *John Hammond on the Record, an Autobiography of John Hammond,* with Irving Townsend, Ridge Press/Summit Books, (1977), 216. Hereafter *Hammond.*

[29] White materials: July 11, 1934.

[30] White materials: September 11, 1934.

[31] White materials: September 18, 1934.

[32] White materials: October 12, 1934.

[33] White materials: *ibid.*

[34] The Manhattan studios used by RCA Victor in the 1930s (and for many years after) were located at 155 East Twenty-fourth Street, just east of Lexington Avenue. Today the place where those studios stood is occupied by Baruch College, which is a part of City University of New York.

[35] Liner notes—*Giants of Jazz—Bunny Berigan,* by Richard M. Sudhalter Time-Life Records, (1982), 30–31. Hereafter *Giants of Jazz.*

Chapter 10
The Kingdom of Swing

As the series of events in the previous chapter clearly indicate, the birth of the swing era was taking place in a number of places and in a number of bands in 1934. The role of Benny Goodman in the birth of the swing era has perhaps taken on a larger significance in retrospect than it actually had when these events were taking place. There are many reasons why this is so. Probably the largest reason is that Benny Goodman, who early on was dubbed "The King of Swing," enjoyed a tremendously successful career, lasting long after the end of the swing era, well into the 1980s. The length of Goodman's career was possible in large measure because of the surprise success, in the early 1950s, of the recordings from his 1938 Carnegie Hall concert, followed shortly by the success of a set of his live radio broadcast recordings from the late 1930s. (Both sets of recordings were well produced, handsomely packaged, and heavily promoted by Columbia Records.) These successes led directly to the making by Universal Pictures of the Hollywood film version of his life, *The Benny Goodman Story*. As hokey and inaccurate as that film is, people are still watching it over fifty years after it was released, and will undoubtedly continue do so for as long as it remains available. As the renowned film composer (and former Tex Beneke band pianist/arranger) Henry Mancini was wont to say: "films are forever." And as long as people watch that film, they are going to get a distorted picture of what actually happened at the birth of the swing era. I do not intend to minimize the role of Benny Goodman in the birth of the swing era. I merely want to place his part in that process into the context of what was actually happening then.

Even though there had been much publicity surrounding the departure of Billy Rose from the Billy Rose Music Hall in September of 1934, Benny Goodman's band apparently continued to work there until October 17.[1] After that gig ended, the Goodman band had spotty work at best for several weeks. (Berigan did not play on the Adrian Rollini session of October 23, 1934, as claimed by Adrian's brother, tenor saxist Arthur Rollini, who was then in the Goodman band. The trumpet on that session was played by the ubiquitous Mannie Klein.) On November 6, 1934, Benny Goodman and His Orchestra auditioned for the *Let's Dance* radio program at NBC.[2]

The story of the NBC *Let's Dance* radio series is an essential part of any review of how swing came to be a part of the mainstream of American popular music in the 1930s. The White materials give us many insights about the start of that now legendary radio program:

This (the December 1, 1934 broadcast) was the first of the 'Let's Dance' programs, which had been in the planning stages for several weeks, and the public relations executives of the agency handling the account had been filling the trade press with many handouts. Here is what the trade papers reported:

Let's Dance is the first sponsored, three hour show, coast to coast, in radio history.' (*Variety:* October 23, 1934) 'The National Biscuit Company is throwing a shindig November 21. (*Billboard:* October 24, 1934); *Let's Dance* is to be on 57 NBC stations and supplement others. The first show is to be December 1, 10:30 p.m. to 3:30 a.m., going three hours into each time zone in the U.S.A. (*Broadcasting:* November 1, 1934) The National Biscuit Company radio show, *Let's Dance*, is being extensively ballyhooed with a party last week, reams of releases and a 'Hollywood' opening with searchlights and 'names' at the first broadcast. (*Billboard:* December 1, 1934).[3]

The basic personnel of the Benny Goodman band that broadcast on the first several *Let's Dance* shows from the NBC studios[4] New York City was set by Saturday, December 1, 1934. Here it is: Benny Goodman, clarinet, directing: Sammy Shapiro, lead, Bunny Berigan, second/jazz, Jerry Neary, Russ Case or Charlie Spivak, third, trumpets; Jack Lacey, lead/jazz, Red Ballard, trombones; Ben Kanter, lead alto/clarinet, Hymie Schertzer, third alto and bass clarinet, Arthur Rollini, second tenor/jazz/doubled clarinet, Gil Rodin, initially fourth tenor/clarinet, soon replaced by Dick Clark, who also played jazz, reeds; Frank Froeba, piano; George Van Eps, guitar; Harry Goodman, bass; Gene Krupa, drums. Joe Lippman, Fletcher and Horace Henderson, and Lyle "Spud" Murphy, were the arrangers. Helen Ward and Buddy Clark were the vocalists.

Helen Ward: "This was the first time I ever worked with Bunny Berigan. The shows emanated from NBC's Studio H. The band sat on tiered platforms with the brass section perched on the top tier at the back. One night, Bunny fell over backwards, right off the stand! They had to rush out and get Mannie Klein to sub for the remainder of the show"[5] (See comment below by saxist Ben Kanter about the December 29 New Year's Eve show.)

Fellow musicians expect the *Let's Dance* show to have trouble building. They figure that established name orchestras on other networks will not be turned off for newcomers Kel Murray and the not-so-well-known Benny Goodman and Xavier Cugat even though these outfits all have good musicians. A few of the opposition names are Hal Kemp, Wayne King, Freddy Martin, Enrique Madriguera, Joe Haymes, Glen Gray, Will Osborne, Eddie Duchin and Claude Hopkins. Another expected difficulty will be orchestrations for approximately fifty tunes, that being the number played during each three hour show.[6]

Here is a detailed review of *Let's Dance* from the January 1935 issue of *Metronome:*

Dancing Party (fair) *Let's Dance* sponsored by National Biscuit with Kel Murray's, Xavier Cugat and Bennie *(sic)* Goodman's bands, vocalists: Phil Duey,

Frank Luther, Carmen Castillia, Connie Gates, Helen Ward, Jack Parker and Luis Alvarez, three hours, Saturday night, WEAF.

Musicianship: Fifty-six stations on the red web carry these three hours of terpsichore to the four corners of the country. It means a five hour work out for the bands since they will be on the air from 10:30 p.m. in the East to 1:30 a.m.; 9:30 p.m. to 12:30 on the Pacific Coast. The three hours set up is for straight dancing, each dance running approximately three minutes in quarter hour period, for each band. Titles of numbers are announced. Cugat dishes out tangos, rumbas, waltzes and others of South American influence; Benny Goodman hands out the hot stuff and Murray comes smooth and sweet. Each band holds forth for four or five numbers, when another one is switched on *(sic)*. Still greater variety would be secured if the bands alternated each number although that would not give them much of a rest. For a dance routine the bands mesh nicely. Kel Murray who is a first class musician, comes through with a sonorous and well balanced ensemble. Benny Goodman and his clarinet capers are outstanding. The vocalists singly and in combination are adequate.

Showmanship: There is nothing new about dance music on the air. Anyone can tune in on a Sat Night especially and get all they want from the best name bands. The only difference with this program is that you can set the dial at one spot and let it ride which makes it a little easier for lazy fans and the majority are. Neither is it the longest sponsored program as announced. The Metropolitan Opera rambles on for four and sometimes five hours. But there are enough angles to this as a three hours strictly dance routine to make a spread about it, and Sat Night is a likely spot in the week.[7]

Each band played for fifteen minute alternating sets. Some trade press reports indicated that commercial skits were repeated late in the shows, but it is not certain if that also applied to band numbers. Reviews were generally unfavorable at first, asserting that the commercials were twenty years behind the times, and that there was plenty of good dance music being broadcast during those hours, without commercials. Don Carey, who hosted a long-running children's show as "Uncle Don," appeared on the first two shows, but then was dropped because, according to *Metronome*, "he was ribbed by every radio scribe in town."[8]

This program was an expensive undertaking in the middle of the Depression. In addition to all of the costs involved in paying the bands, and arrangers, copyists, and so on, for new music, and paying the large technical staff needed to stage the show, there was the cost of "renting" the lines over which the NBC radio network's programs flowed to its affiliates."The *Let's Dance* show, a Saturday night dancing party, will run for three hours, beginning December 1. The sponsor is the National Biscuit Company and the program begins at 10.30 p.m. and continues until 1.30 a.m. Sunday in the East, with earlier times for Central, West and Pacific coast. The line cost for the three hours will be $30,000, approximately, which ordinarily would run the ante up to $45,000, since after 11:00 p.m. is quoted at half rate."[9]

Ben Kanter, who for a time was the lead alto saxophone in the Goodman band on the *Let's Dance* show recalled: "Bunny wasn't a regular member of the Goodman band at this time as he was still working at CBS. He would not normally be present at rehearsals, but would just show up for the broadcasts. Connie Gates sang with the Kel Murray band, which included Mannie Klein, Arthur Schutt and Lyall Bowen."[10]

Berigan continued working full-time at CBS during the day in December 1934, appearing in all manner of combos, bands, and orchestras on the air, including as a member of the Instrumentalists, led by Harry Warnow, CBS conductor Mark Warnow's younger brother, professionally known as Raymond Scott. He also took club dates on some evenings. Drummer Johnny Williams worked with Berigan at CBS and elsewhere then: "I did a couple of Benny's *Let's Dance* shows. Bunny was definitely on the early shows, even though he was still working over at CBS, plus doing some society dates with Joe Moss, who ran Meyer Davis's New York office. He would get as much as $50 from Moss, which was big money then for a dance job."[11] Clearly, Bunny Berigan's work with Benny Goodman at this time was strictly on the side.

Nevertheless, it appears that he played on the December 8, 15, 22, and 29 *Let's Dance* shows, and made a one-nighter with BG on December 25, 1934, at the George F. Pavilion, in Binghamton, New York. Ben Kanter later had vivid recollections of the December 29 *Let's Dance* show: "That was a special New Year's *Let's Dance* program and Bunny had gotten so drunk he passed out in the middle of the opening theme! Once again Mannie Klein came over from Kel Murray to fill in for the show. Also, about that time, Dick Clark came in on 4th tenor for Gil Rodin, who was only there on a temporary basis."[12]

The destructive pattern of Berigan overworking, followed by him collapsing as a result of being drunk had started. His use of alcohol had progressed to the abuse stage during the year 1934 while he was at CBS. Undoubtedly, the long hours, and downtime between broadcasts, on top of the incredible demands of playing a wide variety of music on live network radio on a stop watch schedule, plus his outside work, all combined to increase his perceived need for alcohol to help him get through. Unfortunately, when the rare opportunity to play a little jazz came along, Bunny was often too tapped out and/or inebriated to play at the top of his ability. His use of alcohol to "help" him at such times often had precisely the opposite effect. Still, he was able to stop drinking periodically, or reduce his intake to levels where he was not incapacitated, no doubt to convince himself that he didn't have a problem. His coworkers knew differently. He now had to have alcohol to perform at all. He was in the process of learning how to be a functioning alcoholic.

Alcohol was not only affecting Bunny Berigan's ability to play the trumpet and his professional reliability, it was also beginning to affect his behavior.

Buddy Sheppard recalled how Bunny was beginning to behave at CBS:

Members of the various bands would receive a weekly schedule of the shows we'd play and the names of the conductors, Fred Rich, Howard Barlow, Leith Stevens, etc. Bunny Berigan at that time was a sensational musician who would almost shock us with his daring improvisations. It was always a thrill to hear him. As a person, however, he was an enigma. He could be very nice, very easy-going, but after a heavy drinking bout he could get nasty. He had many run-ins with the authorities, like the famous one with Kate Smith[13] on her radio show. Kate was very proper and very religious and reacted strongly to an outburst of Berigan profanity! Bunny was banished from the studio and the whole episode took an awful lot of smoothing over![14]

The incident Buddy Sheppard referred to, like so many others involving Bunny Berigan, has been greatly embellished over the years. He was certainly not fired by CBS for whatever he did. He was simply removed from the Kate Smith show, temporarily. Indeed, there is evidence that he returned later in 1935 to play on the Kate Smith show. "Bunny's famous 'run-in' with Kate Smith was indeed well known to many members of the CBS staff orchestra(s), but none interviewed could offer details of the event nor help 'date' it. All agreed Smith attempted to have Bunny fired, but he had only been 'removed' from her shows.[15] Kate Smith and her manager, Ted Collins, were held in very low esteem by most of the CBS musicians, but by 1935–36, when the event probably took place, Smith was an important source of income for CBS and she certainly had the ability to demand that something be done."[16]

There can be no justification of this lapse in professional demeanor by Berigan; however, there were undoubtedly reasons why it happened. Bunny, like all musicians, resented people like Kate Smith, whose musical background was limited, telling him how to play. Moreover, the musical level of the Kate Smith show was minuscule, so Bunny was probably already irritated by having to be a part of that. Add the exhaustion and boredom that were becoming greater the longer Bunny stayed at CBS, a bit of alcoholic fuel, and you have a blowup.

By January of 1935, Bunny Berigan had completed another full year as a CBS staff musician since returning to the network the previous year. Although he was superbly equipped to be a studio musician from the technical standpoint, he was far less well suited temperamentally to do this kind of work. He was first and foremost a jazz musician, and his duties at CBS gave him almost no opportunity to play jazz there. He chafed at the constant restrictions and confinement his employment at CBS imposed on him. His increased reliance upon alcohol and chronic overwork away from CBS were direct results of the ongoing frustration within him caused by this situation. There were indeed other run-ins with the authorities at CBS. Trumpeter Ruby Weinstein recalled:

I first met Bunny Berigan when I was working with Victor Young on the Ponds radio show and we also did the Lucky Strike program with Lennie Hayton's forty-piece orchestra, when Mr. Hill, president of the tobacco company, was alive. He gave strict orders not to deviate from the melody, so when Bunny was given a chorus, he obeyed the instruction at rehearsal. But when we went on the air, he took such liberties with the tune that Mr. Hill nearly had a fit and fired the entire orchestra! Hayton had a thirteen weeks contract and as we'd only worked for three, they had to pay him for the remaining ten weeks. Naturally, we, the musicians, didn't get paid![17]

Yet there were other aspects of Bunny's CBS employment that were extremely positive and enjoyable. CBS, in the mid-1930s, was a haven for some of the most creative people on the entertainment and broadcasting scene at that time. The musical fare at CBS then was so widely varied that it boggles the mind, especially when compared with the generally homogeneous and unimaginative offerings found on radio today. At CBS, one could within one broadcast day, run the gamut from outright concert music *(The Ford Sunday Evening Hour)*, to the light classics, with André Kostelanetz, to Kate Smith to Raymond Scott to *The Saturday Night Swing Club* (which had a great deal to do with establishing jazz as a part of the American cultural landscape). In addition, there was a wide variety of what are now called "scripted shows," from soap operas to dramas to comedies. The *Mercury Theater of the Air,* under the wildly unconventional leadership of the prodigious Orson Welles, was allowed to appear and thrive on CBS radio. The music for Welles's radio dramas was provided by CBS staffer Bernard Herrmann, who followed Welles to Hollywood, and composed the music for Welles's classic film *Citizen Kane*. Herrmann later went on to a now legendary collaboration with film director Alfred Hitchcock, composing the music for such memorable films as *Vertigo, North by Northwest, The Birds,* and *Psycho*.[18] The mid-1930s also marked the beginnings of the renowned news division at CBS, which ultimately produced the first superstar news person: Edward R. Murrow.[19] By 1938, CBS was broadcasting, via live relay from WGAR in Cleveland on Sunday afternoons, the first network radio program that was dedicated to Afro-Americans: *Wings over Jordan*. It came to be recognized as the first radio program of the American civil rights movement. CBS was not the largest radio network in America, but it could certainly claim to be the most creative and inclusive. Bunny Berigan was at CBS in the midst of this heady atmosphere, and he encountered many people there whose creative outlook must have been a healthy antidote for the very often grueling and stultifying work he had to do in the music department.

The nation was deeply mired in an economic depression in the mid-1930s. Berigan's work at CBS, tedious and exhausting as it was, paid very well, and due to his schedule there, he was free most evenings to take outside jobs. Some of these, like the ones with Joe Moss at the Meyer Davis office, were hardly satisfying in the musical sense, but they paid well. Financially speaking, Bunny was (or should have been) doing very well. There were few musicians in New York or anywhere who were making more money in 1934–1935 than he was. His wife reported that he was often earning $500 weekly,[20] and if this amount is multiplied by fifteen, we can approximate the value of those Depression era dollars today. It appears that by 1935, Bunny had his own car, and he and his family resided in the comfortable house at 83-28 Sixty-third Ave. Rego Park, in Queens that he had purchased upon his return to CBS in early 1934.[21] This residence is located near Juniper Valley Park and St. John's Cemetery, and was not far from the Forest Hills home of Mildred Bailey and Red Norvo.[22]

Nevertheless, ominous signs started to appear in Berigan's financial life at about this time. His Ford automobile was repossessed.[23] Trumpeter Dave Wade, a colleague of Bunny's at CBS recalled:

> Raymond Scott's group also recorded backing singers Red McKenzie and Midge Williams. My solo on 'Wanted' (with Red McKenzie) fooled some people into thinking it was Bunny. I did my best to sound like him, as Ray Scott told me I had to sound like Bunny to get the CBS job. While Bunny was still on staff at CBS I recall that Nat Natalie was in the 'night band' at that same time and was a good friend of Bunny's. Bunny and I were in the so-called 'morning band.' Nat and I went out to visit Bunny for some reason, it was mid-winter and cold, and when we arrived we found the house with no heat; the kids were on the floor with their coats on. Nat was so mad! He wanted to fracture Bunny! While Bunny was still on staff, but before I had joined, I used to do a lot of sub work in his place; he was always so busy.[24]

If Bunny was irresponsible with money, and he certainly was, Donna was too. Bunny provided large sums of money for Donna to run the Berigan household, and she used that money as she saw fit. He was not one to bother with things like a family budget, and he was not around enough to monitor the family's finances in any event. It appears that Donna's overall immaturity extended into the area of family finance. Consequently, there was never enough money to keep things running smoothly at the Berigan home no matter how much Bunny earned. As a result of both Bunny's and Donna's spendthrift ways, he and Donna were always short of funds. Although he was clearly the dominant partner in their marriage, he was not domineering or cruel. Donna was undoubtedly aware of the fact that her husband was capable of making a lot of money, and she seemed to defer to him in most, if not all matters. It appears that she was along for the ride, and for a long time, that ride included a lot of laughs, a lot of fun, and a lot of goodies. She seems to have come to the conclusion that whatever Bunny did, and his conduct was becoming more damaging to their marriage, that conduct was necessary for him to continue his very successful career. Donna was using denial to deal with Bunny's behavior, especially his deepening dependence on alcohol. Her way of dealing with Bunny's drinking, more and more, involved her having a few with him, whenever he was around, which was less and less. Nevertheless, Donna was by this time also developing her own problem with alcohol.

The repeal of Prohibition was certainly not a factor in Berigan's advancing alcoholism. He was well on his way in that direction long before repeal. However, the repeal was a substantial factor in the economic revival of the dance band business in the mid-1930s.

The long awaited repeal of Prohibition finally became a reality shortly after President Roosevelt took office. Light wines and beer were made legal first, with hard liquor available on a legal basis early in 1934. The former speakeasies now became respectable nightclubs. Hotels, which had previously experienced difficulty in underwriting top talent, suddenly had a profitable revenue source, which permitted them to do so. Every phase of the entertainment business was given a healthy shot in the arm and the band business was the first to benefit since it was the backbone around which every show was built.[25]

One of many remarkable things about Bunny Berigan was his ability to bounce back from the most humiliating, ego-crushing experiences, like falling off the bandstand at the *Let's Dance* radio broadcast in a drunken stupor, and then somehow pulling himself together and playing well (sometimes magnificently) within a short time thereafter. There is no doubt that after that sad incident with Benny Goodman, Bunny returned to CBS (probably the next day) to once again resume his demanding and exacting duties, which likely included playing in the band on the Kate Smith show, appearing with the Instrumentalists, a forerunner of the Raymond Scott Quintet, and working with various bands under the direction of Mark Warnow.

Far more musically significant for jazz fans however, was his appearance at the Columbia recording studio on January 25 as a member of Red Norvo's swing octet. The sides made that day were harbingers of the swing era. In addition to Berigan's splendid playing, all of the other musicians also contributed greatly to these recordings. The tunes were "Honeysuckle Rose," "With All My Heart and Soul," "Bughouse," and "Blues in E Flat." The musicians were Norvo on xylophone; Berigan; Jack Jenney, trombone; Johnny Mince, clarinet; Chu Berry, tenor saxophone; Teddy Wilson, piano; George Van Eps, guitar; Artie Bernstein, bass; Gene Krupa, drums. "Bunny and Jenney were on staff at CBS; Mince was with Ray Noble; Krupa with Goodman; and Van Eps doubling the two leaders. Chu Berry was with Teddy Hill, and Teddy Wilson with Willie Bryant."[26]

Note should be made at this juncture of the almost certainty that Bunny Berigan *did not* record with bands led by Freddy Martin and Richard Himber during the early and mid-1930s, many reports to the contrary notwithstanding. He also did not sit-in with or sub into the Casa Loma band, based on the recollections of trumpeter Sonny Dunham, who was then a member of that band, and who surely would have remembered such an event.[27] On the other hand, it is quite possible that he *did* play in the André Kostelanetz Orchestra at CBS from time to time.

On May 13, 1935, Berigan participated in another recording session with kindred spirits. The musicians who took part in this session with him were Bud Freeman, tenor saxophone; Matty Matlock, clarinet; Morey Samel, trombone; Claude Thornhill, piano; Dick McDonough, guitar; Pete Peterson, bass; Ray Bauduc, drums. The band was led by Gene Gifford, the first great arranger to work with the Casa Loma band. The trumpeter/vocalist Wingy Manone was also present, wisely confining his contributions to singing on three of the four titles recorded that day. Gifford arranged all four tunes. The first title cut was "Nothin' but the Blues," an original twelve-bar blues that was co-composed by Gifford, Manone, and Joe Bishop, an arranger/composer who was then working in the Isham Jones band with a very young Woody Herman. Bunny's passionate first blues chorus before the vocal is a perfect miniature jazz statement, stamped indelibly with Berigan's musical personality. After Manone's whiskeyfied singing he returns to play two more moving choruses, above the accompaniment of the other musicians, delivered with the utmost authority.

The next tune cut was the very rarely reissued instrumental "New Orleans Twist," which was co-composed by Gifford and Bishop. It and the equally rare "Dizzy Glide," featuring another Wingy Manone vocal, are basically off-the-shelf mid-1930s jazz-based pop music fare. Berigan's work on these sides is confined to his uniquely spirited lead trumpet playing.

I have heard "Squareface" frequently, and enjoy it every time. It is another blues that opens with a lovely, subdued ensemble passage that spots Berigan's cup-muted trumpet and Claude Thornhill's glistening piano. Matty Matlock's woody clarinet sound and cogent jazz ideas are well presented in the chorus he takes. Manone's vocal chorus is half spoken and half sung, backed by McDonough's chorded guitar and Samel's cup-muted trombone. It is followed by Berigan, once again playing movingly on his open trumpet, first way down low, then leaping dramatically into his high register with no discernable strain. Bunny's cadenza at the end, capped by a ringing high D, is extremely rewarding. Clearly, Bunny Berigan was at the peak of his powers on this recording date.

On April 23, 1935, Benny Goodman's band opened at the Roosevelt Hotel in New York. Aside from the weekly *Let's Dance* radio show, the Goodman band had worked very little in the spring of 1935. But one very big thing had happened in early 1935 that augured well for BG: his struggling band had been taken on by Music Corporation of America (MCA), the largest and most powerful band-booking agency in the nation. This was a significant development because MCA's roster of bands, up to the signing of Goodman, was comprised exclusively of either "sweet" dance bands like Guy Lombardo's or Wayne King's, or "entertaining" music-cum-burlesque bands, typified by Kay Kyser. The complete story of why this happened has never been told, and never may be, not that there is any mystery to it. The bottom line is that MCA's people were well aware of the success of the Casa Loma band, and knew of the potential for success that the Dorsey Brothers Orchestra had. (When the Dorseys went their separate ways in mid-1935, Jimmy stayed with Rockwell-O'Keefe and Tommy went with MCA.) Both Casa Loma and the Dorsey Brothers Orchestra were booked by Rockwell-O'Keefe, precursor to General Artists Corporation, which would later be a significant part of the success of the Artie Shaw, Glenn Miller, and Woody Herman [28] bands. Someone at MCA sensed that now there might be a niche market for jazz-oriented dance music, and MCA didn't want to miss an opportunity to get into the action against Rockwell-O'Keefe.

Even though MCA had managed to secure for Goodman a recording contract with Victor, it had not been able to stimulate much interest in the Goodman band among ballroom operators. The *Let's Dance* radio show was soon to end. (The last *Let's Dance* show was broadcast on May 25, 1935. A few days earlier, the Goodman band auditioned for a radio show to be sponsored by "Life Savers," but did not get the job.)[29] Goodman's MCA liaison/manager was a young man named Willard Alexander. He shared what John Hammond in his autobiography described as a "swinging apartment in the Alrae Hotel" with Guy Lombardo's MCA liaison/manager Sonny Werblin. Alexander "implored (Werblin) to put Benny into the (Roosevelt) Hotel to replace the Lombardo-like Bernie Cummins orchestra, which was going out on tour. Everyone was aware that this was hardly the ideal room for Benny's type of music, but there was really no other choice. 'We wanted to get work for the band,' Alexander explained. 'Hell, we would have booked the Holland Tunnel.'"[30]

The Roosevelt Hotel gig immediately became a disaster when the room's staid patrons, accustomed to the dulcet tones of the Guy Lombardo and Bernie Cummins bands, were jolted by the volume and syncopations of the Goodman band. BG was given notice on opening night. After the Goodman band left the Roosevelt Hotel, they played a few widely scattered one-nighters around the eastern United States. Clearly, the future for the Benny Goodman band looked very dim in the spring of 1935. But Benny, iron willed and ambitious, with substantial help from his bass-playing brother Harry, who was now also a member of the band and a large stabilizing influence on his younger brother,[31] forged ahead. He agreed to let MCA put together a cross-country summer tour, culminating with a stay at the Palomar Ballroom in Los Angeles. MCA had long before learned the power of radio in developing an audience for dance bands. The expectation was that the Goodman band's six months on NBC's *Let's Dance* program would make folks in the hinterlands hungry for the music of Benny Goodman. Eventually, that would be the case, but it did not really happen for Goodman until the following year, after he had spent another six months broadcasting from the Congress Hotel in Chicago.

Fortunately, the same obtuse stubbornness that so often was such an exasperating part of Benny Goodman's dealings with humanity in general in this situation worked to the benefit of jazz fans. Goodman's analysis of the situation was likely as follows: (1) I've put together the best band I've ever played in; (2) I've gotten a great many wonderful arrangements for this band as a result of the budget for new music on the *Let's Dance* show; (3) I am now represented by the strongest booking agency in the band business; and (4) I've got a contract to make records. Therefore, I'm going to use all of this to make the best records possible, and I'm going to work with this band for as long as I can, and continue to make it a better band. If I succeed, fine. If not, then I'll return to the radio and recording studios and earn a good living.

The Goodman band produced a total of eight sides at Victor recording sessions on April 4 and April 19, 1935. The records they made at those sessions were good. But in spite of all the talent present on those recordings, and a number of fine arrangements, the whole of the performances was somehow less than the sum of the parts. I am quite certain that Benny Goodman himself had these same opinions when he listened to these records. The spark that elevates solid, professional dance music into the realm of the inspired and exhilarating was missing. Maybe that is why Benny invited the great jazz trombonist Jack Teagarden[32] to play on the April 19 session. For whatever reason, the band with Teagarden did not sound appreciably more stimulated than it had sounded without him. I suspect that Benny knew all along what, or rather who, might solve this problem. But he was not about to call the man whose last stint with his band had ended so disgustingly, when he fell of the bandstand, drunk—at least not without some persuasion. Maybe that persuasion came when Benny listened to the records Bunny Berigan had recently made with Red Norvo. Maybe it came when Bunny subbed into the Goodman band at the Roosevelt Hotel. Whenever or however it came, the conclusion Goodman drew was clear: drinking or not, Bunny Berigan would energize the Goodman band like no one else.

A most vivid example of the effect Bunny Berigan's trumpet had on the Goodman band in the spring of 1935 is to be found by simply playing, in chronological order, the Victor recordings Benny made then. When you go from the gentle, lilting Irving Berlin tune "Always," which was arranged by Horace Henderson, and was recorded on April 19, with a rather stiff rhythmic feel, to the scintillating "Get Rhythm in Your Feet," arranged by Fletcher Henderson, and recorded on June 25, you feel as though the band had now somehow been supercharged. It swings hard from the first trumpet chair all the way down through all of the other instruments, and sitting in that first trumpet chair was Bunny Berigan. Mannie Klein, a trumpet virtuoso himself and an ardent Berigan admirer, summarized the unique effect Bunny's playing had on a band: "You didn't know sometimes whether he was gonna show up for a session. But when he did show up—well, nobody played with the balls and the beat he did."[33] Another example of the difference Berigan's huge, warm first trumpet sound, and perfect rhythmic conception, made in the overall sound of the Goodman band is to be found in the lovely "Ballad in Blue," arranged by Spud Murphy. Irving Berlin's classic "Blue Skies," in a Fletcher Henderson[34] arrangement, is also indelibly stamped with the mark of Berigan, both as a first trumpeter on most of the performance, and as a perceptive, dramatic soloist whose playing so perfectly captures and enhances the mood of Henderson's arrangement. "Dear Old Southland," arranged by Horace Henderson, is jump-started by Berigan's careening high-register intro, and then carried along by the irresistible swing of his lead trumpet playing.

Six days later on July 1, 1935, Berigan once again played first trumpet and marvelous jazz solos with the Goodman band at the Victor recording session that produced "Sometimes I'm Happy," "King Porter Stomp," "Jingle Bells," and "Between the Devil and the Deep Blue Sea." On this last title, the Berigan-led brass *bristled*. His electric presence in the Goodman band once more elevated all of these performances into the realm of instant classics.

"King Porter Stomp"[35] is a quintessential example of Berigan's artistry. It is also one of the best recordings of the swing era. As arranged by Fletcher Henderson, "King Porter Stomp" swings from beginning to end, and provides a perfect showcase for the jazz solos that are a part of this classic performance.[36] Here is what musician/historian Gunther Schuller said about Bunny's playing on this recording:

> Certainly Berigan's solos on "King Porter Stomp" must count as among his very finest creative achievements. His performance here represents the mature Berigan in full opulent flowering. It exemplifies his unerring sense of form, and a virtually infallible clarity of statement. His two solos, one muted, the other open, are miniature compositions which many a writing-down composer would be envious of having created, even after days of work. This structural logic transmits itself to the listener in the absolute authoritativeness of his playing. The ingredients in both solos are really quite simple: great melodic beauty combined with logic and structural balance. Every note, every motivic cell, every phrase leads logically to the next with a Mozartian classic inevitability. And each phrase, whether heard in two-bar or eight-bar segments, has its own balanced structuring and symmetry. ...But that is not all. As always, there is Berigan's incomparable—and irrepressible—swing. On every given Berigan recording he usually outswings everybody else. ...His sense of swing was an innate talent, a given talent, a feeling beyond study or calculation, one that he heard in the playing of both Beiderbecke and Armstrong, but which he synthesized into his own personal rhythmic idiom.[37]

Berigan plays the joyous introductory trumpet passage with a straight mute. After this, the saxes take over for a bit, ably led by Toots Mondello. BG then plays an excellent full chorus jazz solo. Richard M. Sudhalter described what happens next:

> Pow! goes Berigan, pealing out a single massive high concert D-flat to fill his first bar. Charleston beat in bar two, an octave down. Pow again, for a two-bar figure built from the top down. Then again, this time a four-bar summation, bringing the chorus to a mid-point. Then two more terse two-bar phrases, each beginning on that same top D-flat, and another four-bar comment to close things out. It's both forceful jazz, simply and logically constructed, and superior trumpet playing. For a trumpet player to begin a solo on this kind of fortissimo high note, then use it as a structural pivot, returning to it five times in sixteen bars without strain, without a hint of effect for its own sake, is notable by any standard.[38]

The Berigan-led rideout is a prime demonstration of how his first trumpet playing could ignite a band. His power and rhythmic thrust vault the band onto a higher, more exciting musical plane. This is what is meant by *hot* music.

There was also Bunny's trumpet sound or "tone." "Berigan's other great asset was the beauty of his tone. Though technically based in perfect breath support, the purity—and amplitude—of his tone was controlled at the moment of emission by his inner ear. ...He could project in his mind and ear a certain sound, and then the physical muscles (embouchure, breathing, fingers) would, in coordination, produce the desired result."[39]

Benny Goodman undoubtedly shook his head after this recording session, and likely said to himself over and over again: *somehow I've got to get Berigan into my band!*

The fact of the matter is that Bunny Berigan did *not* join Benny Goodman's band until a couple of weeks later, after it had begun its cross-country tour. He had been, as always, very busy making records and working at CBS. He'd recorded with Glenn Miller and Smith Ballew on April 25–26; with Red McKenzie and the Mound City Blue Blowers on May 9, both on Columbia; and then with an ad hoc group led by Casa Loma's ace arranger Gene Gifford, (with Wingy Manone as a vocalist), on May 13, on Victor. Prime Berigan trumpeting is to be found on the recordings made at these sessions.

Meanwhile at CBS, Bunny was beginning to be featured on the radio network with a group called Bunny's Blue Boys. Drummer Johnny Williams recalled:

> Bunny's Blue Boys grew out of the band at CBS. We were on the air before Bunny joined Benny Goodman and we had Jerry Colonna on trombone, Pete Pumiglio on clarinet, Babe Russin on tenor sax, Raymond Scott on piano, Lou Shoobe on bass and me on drums. Our theme was "Chicken and Waffles," a tune that Bunny composed in a hurry for an early show. Mark Warnow, the conductor, organized a bigger group called the Instrumentalists, which added Artie Manners on clarinet and alto sax, Mike Miolla on trumpet, Vincent Maffei on guitar and Buddy Sheppard on violin. They usually aired in the afternoon and the Blue Boys in the morning.[40]

This was a significant development for Bunny's future career, because his name was now being announced over the CBS network as the leader of Bunny's Blue Boys. This occurrence marked the gradual emergence of Berigan from being a rather anonymous (to the public) studio musician to being a readily identifiable jazz trumpet soloist. From this point on, the name Bunny Berigan would be used more and more often to tell the nationwide CBS audience that he was the trumpeter whose exciting playing they were hearing. Also, he was now being identified in the radio listings of various New York newspapers. CBS was definitely promoting Berigan:

> (Headline) Hottest Man In Town—Is kept busy at CBS. His program *Bunny and his Blue Boys,* is heard on CBS each Tuesday at 11.45 a.m. He plays regularly in studio orchestra and is a feature of Mark Warnow's popular band heard on CBS. Four years ago, Freddie Rich brought Bunny to Columbia. He left for a time to play with Abe Lyman, but in a year and a half he was back on CBS. Bunny likes a tune that wasn't written to be a hot tune, but one that has plenty of pretty harmonies in it. A good hot trumpet player breaking into a sweet harmonious number, can gain by the contrast. He dislikes the 'wah wah' style, says it's 'passé.'

He says good hot music is not a lot of noise. It's a matter of real rhythm, what we call 'swing.'[41]

Berigan also got a good write-up in the July 6 issue of *Billboard*.

A month before, on May 30, the famous blow–up between Tommy and Jimmy Dorsey occurred at Glen Island Casino, New Rochelle, New York. The next day, Ray Noble, now having resolved the problems he had with the musicians' union, opened at the Rainbow Room, on the sixty-fifth floor of the RCA Building in Rockefeller Center. Notable Noble sidemen included Glenn Miller and Will Bradley, trombones; Claude Thornhill, piano; Charlie Spivak and Pee Wee Erwin, trumpets; Bud Freeman and Johnny Mince, reeds; and George Van Eps, guitar. At around this same time, Gil Rodin (and Rockwell-O'Keefe) had installed Bing Crosby's younger brother Bob as titular leader of the band he (Rodin) had organized and had recorded with under the name the Clark Randall Orchestra. (Crosby's place as vocalist with the Dorsey Brothers Orchestra was taken by a singer with superior vocal equipment and dark good looks, Bob Eberly.) Rodin's new band, a cooperative outfit now known as Bob Crosby and His Orchestra, was ready to begin working.[42] The swing era was beginning to take a recognizable form.

Bunny Berigan joined the Benny Goodman band at Ocean Beach Pier, Clark Lake, near Jackson, Michigan, for a one-night stand there on July 16, 1935. Also joining the Goodman band there was pianist Jess Stacy. It was understood by all concerned that Bunny's stay with the Goodman band would be temporary, lasting only until its tour ended, which would be when its engagement at the Palomar Ballroom in Los Angeles was over. Previously, the Goodman band had played a one-week engagement at the Stanley Theater[43] in Pittsburgh (July 5–11), then returned to New York, where Benny and his drummer, Gene Krupa, joined with pianist Teddy Wilson to make the first Benny Goodman Trio recordings at Victor on July 13. (Note: Teddy Wilson would not actually join Benny Goodman as a member of the Goodman Trio until early 1936.)

The itinerary for the remainder of the Goodman band tour is as follows: July 17, Toledo, Ohio;[44] then Olentangy Park, Columbus, Ohio (July 18); Luna Pier, Lakeside, Michigan (July 19); the Mile-a-Way Ballroom, Grand Rapids, Michigan (July 20); and two nights (July 21–22), at the Modernistic Ballroom, 81st and Greenfield, in Milwaukee. It was at this venue that the perceptive (and lovely) Helen Oakley, later the wife of jazz writer Stanley Dance, heard the Goodman band and was bowled over by the playing of Bunny Berigan. (See below.) From there, the Goodman band, in a caravan of automobiles, made the big jump to Denver, where they opened at Elitch's Trocadero Ballroom on July 26. This engagement lasted until August 15. On August 16, they played at Grand Junction, Colorado, the next night, August 17, at the Cocoanut Grove Ballroom in Salt Lake City, Utah. August 18 was a travel day. (They needed it because the next stop on the tour was almost 600 miles away.) They then played a one-nighter at McFadden's Ballroom, Oakland, California, on August 19. On August

20, they appeared at Pismo Pavilion, Pismo Beach, California. The next day, they opened at the Palomar Ballroom, on Vermont Avenue between Second and Third, in Los Angeles, for what was originally scheduled as a three-week engagement.

The many stories about Bunny Berigan that originated on this tour have been told often, so I will not repeat them here. Instead, I am including at this point a few bits of information that will perhaps make the picture of the Palomar engagement a bit more vivid and accurate: Tenor saxophonist Dick Clark, who was a member of the Goodman band then, recalled: "Pismo Beach was a beach-type booking and a pretty poor one. After we finished the job, we drove to Los Angeles in fog, arriving there the next morning just as the sun was rising. We had a rehearsal for the Palomar opening and quite a number of local musicians showed up to listen."[45]

MCA made sure that Benny Goodman's opening at the Palomar Ballroom was well publicized. The following are a series of items that appeared in one Los Angeles newspaper:

Benny Goodman and his hot clarinet make their debut over western airlanes tonight at 11.00 p.m., KHJ, when Goodman begins an engagement at the Palomar, his first in California. Goodman's sensational rise this year in the affections of both musicians and laymen speaks well for the merits of his music. Supplying vocal chores is Helen Ward, torch singer par excellence, whose work on 'Dixieland Band' won her a place among the nation's finest jazz singers.[46]

Last night, Benny Goodman's famous band was welcomed to Los Angeles at a colorful premiere at the Palomar ballroom, Vermont and Second. Scores of notables were numbered among those who turned out to greet the world's greatest clarinet player and his all-star organization in their initial west coast appearance. A novel entertainment spectacle was presented with the new orchestra, starring several Orpheum circuit acts and the dazzling Hudson Metzger girls.[47]

Tuesday August 27, 1935: Benny Goodman Orchestra, KHJ, 8:00 to 8:30 p.m.; Benny Goodman Orchestra, KHJ, 11:00 to 11:30 p.m.; Goodman Orchestra, WABC, 12:00 midnight to 12:30 a.m. (New York time). This was the first of four broadcasts by the Goodman band heard in the east and probably coast-to-coast on CBS network. The 8:00 p.m. starting time was probably correct for Los Angeles as not all of the country was on Daylight Saving Time. Kenneth Frogley, super announcer for Benny Goodman's aggregation of musicians, broadcasting nightly on a Pacific coast network, will have the thrill of knowing that his voice will be heard throughout the nation for the first time tonight at 8.00 p.m., when his musical program goes country-wide.[48]

MCA knew well that radio was an essential tool for promotion of a band. That is why they made sure that the Goodman band was often broadcast while it was at the Palomar Ballroom, and why they placed so many blurbs in the print media announcing and reinforcing the idea that the band could be heard on radio from there: "Benny Goodman band to be on CBS from Los Angeles."[49]

There appear in the White materials and elsewhere several recollections from Goodman band members of the drinking that Bunny did while at the Palomar. Art Rollini said: "The crowds at the Palomar grew nightly, and after the two weeks the floor was jammed. Soon there was no room to dance, and people just listened. Bunny Berigan was drinking heavily. He would play great until about 11 p.m., and after that he was impossible. Bunny was such a sweet man, it was a terrible shame. He had a pleasant personality, but was a loner. He preferred to drink and eat by himself while he was with the Goodman band."[50] Benny Goodman remembered "We were supposed to be at the Palomar only a month, but the engagement was extended, and we were doing radio broadcasts at night. They came and asked me 'What time do you want to be on the radio? Do you want an eleven-thirty slot, or twelve-thirty?' I told them I thought eleven-thirty would be good. The earlier the better—largely because if it were any later, Bunny would usually be wiped out."[51]

Only one broadcast of the Goodman band from the Palomar was recorded, the one that occurred on August 22. That broadcast aired on the Don Lee Network, which evidently was a West Coast consortium of radio stations owned by Don Lee, and fed live to all of the CBS radio network via KHJ Los Angeles. I have heard this entire broadcast, and it is quite good overall. Curiously, Benny opened it with "Goodbye," his *closing* theme song. BG had Bunny playing lead trumpet most of the time; however Berigan also had a few solos. He has some inspired moments on "Star Dust" (not the classic Fletcher Henderson arrangement BG would later record for Victor, but a rather ordinary score by Spud Murphy), and a stirring chorus on "Basin Street Blues," in the same Fletcher Henderson arrangement that Goodman would record later in 1935. The closing "Goodbye" is played while Ken Frogley sends the broadcast back to the KHJ announcer, who identifies that station by employing the quintessential 1930s pronunciation of Los Angeles, using a long—*o* and hard—*g*.

MCA took note of the Goodman band's ever-increasing momentum at the Palomar, and set up a series of Saturday afternoon concerts for them to play at football rallies at nearby universities.[52] This promotion added to the excitement that was already being generated by the band's nightly appearances at the Palomar. As a result, the Goodman band's engagement there was extended until October 1.

Bunny evidently was celebrating his freedom from the various confinements of his life in New York City, including his employment at CBS, and his outside work in the recording studios and with commercial dance bands. He was also away from his wife and daughter, not that they were confining him to any appreciable degree in New York.[53] It was probably while Bunny was on this tour that Donna informed him that she was pregnant again, for the third time. At some point during the Goodman tour, Donna and little Patricia, now three years old, went to Fox Lake, to stay with Cap and Mayme Berigan again. There they would wait for Bunny until he came off the Goodman tour in early October.

The Benny Goodman band made one Victor recording session in Los Angeles while they were resident at the Palomar Ballroom, on September 27. Three tunes were recorded: "Santa Claus Came in the Spring"; "Goodbye" (printed as "Good-Bye" on the label of Victor 25215-A); and "Madhouse." "Santa Claus Came in the Spring" is a pop tune that was arranged by Spud Murphy, featuring a vocal by Joe Harris,[54] and a tasty sixteen-bar solo by Berigan, using a tightly fitted cup mute. Bunny also played first trumpet throughout most of this performance.

"Goodbye,"[55] a lovely ballad, was composed and arranged by Gordon Jenkins, then working in the Isham Jones band. (Jenkins was friendly with Goodman during the time BG was forming his band, and recommended that Benny hire the marvelous, but almost never featured trombonist Sterling "Red" Ballard, who had been working with Jenkins in the Jones band. Ballard remained with Benny until 1940.) This recording of "Goodbye" is magnificent, indeed one of the most memorable of the swing era. The performance is superb, and the fidelity excellent. The Jenkins arrangement has Goodman playing the somber melody, with Berigan behind him, playing a recurring three-note phrase on his straight-muted trumpet. Bunny's playing here is purely straight, but strangely evocative. The trumpeters in the Goodman band quickly dubbed these three notes the "go-to-hell" notes, and joked among themselves about who was going to play the "go-to-hell" notes behind the boss in the closing theme. The brief trombone solo is played by Jack Lacey, and the big-toned first trumpet part by Ralph Muzzillo.

Two takes of "Madhouse" have circulated almost from the time of the issuance of the original 78 rpm shellac Victor disc. The tune was composed by jazz pianist and legend Earl Hines's arranger Jimmy Mundy (Hines's name is also listed as a co-composer), and recorded by the Hines band for ARC/Brunswick/Vocalion on March 26, 1934, using the same arrangement that is played by the Goodman band here. Berigan takes the introductory (written) trumpet solo using a straight mute, with the band chugging along behind him at a brisk tempo. Although this arrangement spots some acrobatic work by the sax section and a few well-placed Berigan-led brass flares, it is really a showcase for Goodman's clarinet and Jess Stacy's piano. "Madhouse" so impressed Benny Goodman that he began buying more and more arrangements from Jimmy Mundy. Mundy eventually contributed more arrangements to the Goodman book than any other arranger, except Fletcher Henderson.

As the Goodman band's engagement at the Palomar came to an end on October 1, BG began inviting various trumpeters from the Los Angeles area to audition for Berigan's soon-to-be vacant chair. The musician who eventually filled that chair was Harry Geller: "I had auditioned for Goodman a day or so earlier, when I got a message to take my horn over to the Palomar Ballroom. When I arrived, I saw Bunny, standing in front of the bandstand, drunk as a skunk and carrying his trumpet in a bag under his arm. I got the idea he was going to mail it back to New York. I moved into the third chair, as Nate Kazebier took over

Bunny's chair." Johnny Williams remembered: "Bunny sent his trumpet to me C.O.D., in New York. The case was unlocked and it came by ordinary mail. Bunny came to claim it a few days later."[56] Immediately after the Goodman band closed at the Palomar, Berigan left the band. He departed Los Angeles by air, flying from the Burbank airport. Family members picked him up at the Chicago airport, and took him to Fox Lake. There he joined Donna, Patricia, and his parents, probably on October 3. He stayed in Fox Lake until leaving for Manhattan on October 16. Bunny Berigan was just shy of his twenty-seventh birthday.

While he was in Fox Lake, Bunny sat in with some of his old musical associates. Larry O'Brien (leader and saxophones) recalled: "On the first night when Bunny came in, he was very drunk and couldn't play at all, but he came back the next night and he really blew his head off! He sounded like a million dollars and thrilled everyone in the place. I played alto sax with my band only on specialty numbers and directed. I had, of course, worked with Bunny in Madison in 1929 before he left." Orch Edgerton (drums) said: "Yes I'm sure I recall Bunny sitting in with the Larry O'Brien band one time he came down with a gang of folks from around Fox Lake. At least once when he sat in it was announced that he was 'late of The BG band' and he was featured on some numbers. I remember Bunny was wearing small brass, or gold frame glasses." Norman Phelps (bass) remembered: "Bunny was around for a week or so after he left Benny Goodman. He sat in with our band at the Chanticleer a couple of times while he was resting at home in Fox Lake. We had all thought he was a great musician and we had our opinions confirmed. He was definitely the talk of the region."[57] Also in the O'Brien band then was saxophonist Erle Smith, with whom Bunny had worked in Madison.

I suspect that there were many lessons that Bunny Berigan learned while working with Benny Goodman's band in the summer of 1935. The largest lesson by far was that it was now possible to have a jazz-oriented dance band that audiences could both accept and enjoy. Of only slightly smaller significance was that the simple, straightforward, yet swinging arrangements of Fletcher and Horace Henderson and Spud Murphy allowed audiences to be exposed to jazz without being overwhelmed by it. In the wake of his experience with Goodman, which included much appreciative applause for his solos, I think it likely that Berigan began to consider leading his own band as an alternative to the endless grind of radio and recording work where he functioned as little more than a well-paid anonymous cog in the commercial music machine. In his own band, he could play the music he liked, and be recognized and appreciated for it by ever-larger audiences.

Notes

[1] *Thirty Years with the Big Bands,* by Arthur Rollini, University of Illinois Press (1987), 36–7. Cited hereafter as "Rollini."

[2] How Benny Goodman got to perform that audition is explained in *Swing, Swing, Swing, The Life and Times of Benny Goodman,* by Ross Firestone Norton (1993),106–108, hereafter "Firestone."

[3] White materials: December 1, 1934.

[4] The "NBC studios" referred to by Helen Ward and contemporary press reports was the huge studio 8H, located in the then newly completed RCA Building in Rockefeller Center. Studio 8H could comfortably seat an audience of over a thousand people. It was from studio 8H that Arturo Toscanini would broadcast with the NBC Symphony, starting on Christmas night 1937. Later, after the advent of network television, this studio became the home of NBC's *Tonight Show,* first hosted by Steve Allen, then Jack Paar, and finally Johnny Carson. With Carson, the show moved to Burbank, California, in 1972. Studio 8H has for many years been home to *Saturday Night Live.*

[5] White materials: December 1, 1934.

[6] *Variety,* December 4, 1934 ; cited in the White materials, December 1, 1934.

[7] *Ibid.*

[8] *Metronome:* December 1935; cited in the White materials: December 1, 1934.

[9] *Ibid.*

[10] *Ibid.*

[11] *Ibid.*

[12] White materials: December, 1935.

[13] Kathryn Elizabeth Smith was born on May 1, 1907, in Greenville, Virginia. As Kate Smith, she began her recording career in the late 1920s, then moved on to a popular radio program on NBC, then on to a series of ever more popular radio shows on CBS built around her singing, starting in 1931. Smith was a large woman who weighed about 230 pounds, and was the object of many jokes by musicians at CBS. Her commercial success was no joke, however. She went on to even greater popularity in the 1940s, fueled by her singing of Irving Berlin's "God Bless America" during the trying years of World War II. She made the transition from radio to television and had continued success in that medium in the 1950s. She died on June 17, 1986, in Raleigh, North Carolina.

[14] White materials: January 1, 1935.

[15] Robert Dupuis offered an explanation of what happened between Berigan and Kate Smith in his Berigan biography, at page 97. There is no indication as to where the information to support this report came from however.

[16] White materials: January 1, 1935.

[17] White materials: April 20, 1935.

[18] A vivid summary of so-called serious music at CBS in the 1930s is to be found in *A Heart at Fire's Center, The Life and Music of Bernard Herrmann,* by Steven C. Smith, University of California Press (1991).

[19] Edward R. Murrow gathered around him at CBS a great number of exceptional broadcast journalists including: Eric Sevareid, Charles Collingwood, Howard K. Smith, and Daniel Schorr. Mr. Schorr was the last survivor of that illustrious group, working as a senior news analyst on National Public Radio until his death in 2010.

[20] Dupuis: 127.

[21] White materials: April 20, 1935. One recollection has the Berigan family living in a house. Another has them living in an apartment. Currently, 83-28 Sixty-third Avenue,

Rego Park, Queens is in a residential neighborhood block that contains spacious brick homes

that are contiguous, so I guess both characterizations are correct.

[22] Kenneth Norville was born on March 31, 1908, in Beardstown, Illinois. As Red Norvo, he was a part of Paul Whiteman's orchestra in the late 1920s, where he met Mildred Bailey. In the early years of his career, Norvo played the xylophone, and also piano. His approach to jazz from the beginning was harmonically rich and rhythmically supple, making him a pioneer in many respects, albeit a largely unappreciated one. He began to record in the early 1930s, and began leading his own band in the mid-1930s. Though Norvo tried again and again to make it commercially acceptable, his big band was a failure. By the mid-1940s, he was playing the vibraphone and appearing as a featured artist with the Benny Goodman and Woody Herman bands. Late in the 1940s, he began to lead a series of small jazz groups, all of which were musically inventive. He achieved some success in these ventures, appearing with them in a number of films during the 1950s. Norvo continued to work well into his later years. He died in Santa Monica, California, on April 6, 1999.

[23] White materials: December 4, 1935.

[24] White materials: February 20, 1937. The incident referred to by Dave Wade probably took place in late 1936 or early 1937. By then, baby Joyce would have been able to crawl.

[25] *The Wonderful Era of the Great Dance Bands,* by Leo Walker, Da Capo Press, Inc. (original copyright 1964), 62.

[26] White materials: January 25, 1935.

[27] White materials: February 7, 1935.

[28] Clarinetist/singer/alto saxophonist Woodrow Charles Herman was born on May 16, 1913, in Milwaukee, Wisconsin. As a child, Woody Herman worked as a singer in vaudeville. By the time he was fifteen he was a professional dance band musician. He served his apprenticeship in the bands of Tom Gerun, Harry Sosnick, Gus Arnheim, and most notably Isham Jones. After Jones retired from bandleading in 1936, Herman and five other former Jones sidemen formed a cooperative band in the mode of the Casa Loma and Bob Crosby bands, and began touring. This group was billed as "The Band That Plays the Blues." The Herman ensemble languished in the ranks of secondary bands until approximately 1944. By then, Herman had gathered a group of exciting musicians and arrangers, and they gained considerable success with a series of excellent recordings, and a sponsored network radio show. This band was dubbed "The First Herd." Thereafter, Herman formed and broke up numerous ensembles, remaining very active as a bandleader into the 1980s. His later bands attempted to blend elements of rock and jazz, sometimes with considerable success. Due to a defalcation of funds by his longtime manager Abe Turchen, Herman spent his last years deeply in debt to the Internal Revenue Service. He died on November 2, 1987, in West Hollywood, California.

[29] White materials: May 21, 1935.

[30] Firestone: 130.

[31] There is evidence that Harry Goodman was a part owner of the Goodman band with Benny until probably mid-1939. The checks used to pay the sidemen in the late 1930s contained the legend, "The Goodman Brothers Orchestra." The public was unaware of this because Benny was undoubtedly the music director of the band, and often its most impressive soloist. Harry Goodman was simply a workmanlike bassist who blended in.

[32] One of the foremost trombonists and singers in the history of jazz, Jack Teagarden was born on August 29, 1905, as Weldon Lee Teagarden in Vernon, Texas, into a musical family. He was playing the trombone by age ten. He worked his way through myriad bands in the Texas/Southwest territory throughout the 1920s, before joining Ben Pollack in June 1928. He remained with Pollack until 1933, but during this time made many recordings with other groups. He worked with a number of bands throughout 1933, prior to joining Paul Whiteman at the end of that year. Teagarden remained with Whiteman until the end of 1938, but again took some time to make records with others, and to appear with his brother trumpeter Charlie Teagarden and Frank Trumbauer in a short-lived group called the Three Ts, in early 1937. From early 1939 until 1946, he led a succession of big bands that were either not successful, or only moderately successful. After the final demise of his big band, he led a small group for several months before joining Louis Armstrong's All Stars from 1947 to 1951. Thereafter, he led his own small bands with considerable success until his death from bronchial pneumonia on January 15, 1964, in New Orleans, Louisiana.

[33] *Lost Chords:* 496.

[34] Pianist/arranger/bandleader James Fletcher Henderson was born on December 18, 1897, in Cuthbert, Georgia. He was one of the pioneering jazz/dance band leaders in the 1920s, who helped to launch the careers of many of the greatest jazz soloists of the 1920s and 1930s, including Louis Armstrong, Coleman Hawkins, Benny Carter, Rex Stewart, Roy Eldridge, Chu Berry, and Ben Webster, among many others, who played in his bands. He also employed some of the **most** innovative arrangers, most notably Don Redman, from whom he and his younger brother, the vastly underappreciated arranger/pianist Horace Henderson (1904–1988), learned a great deal about how to make a dance band swing. Although Fletcher Henderson's band was a formidable performing unit from the late 1920s into the 1930s, it was a victim of Henderson's sometimes lax leadership, the Great Depression, and racial discrimination which barred it from many lucrative engagements. From late 1934 until 1936, he and his brother supplied Benny Goodman's band with dozens of arrangements on jazz originals and current pop tunes that codified swing band arranging to a large degree to that time. Henderson attempted again in the late 1930s to lead a successful band, but it was not to be. From 1939 on, he worked intermittently with groups of various sizes, achieving neither wide public recognition nor notable musical achievement. He died on December 29, 1952, in New York City after having been previously disabled by a stroke.

[35] "King Porter Stomp" is identified on the label of Victor 25090-A as "King Porter."

[36] The Fletcher Henderson arrangement of "King Porter Stomp" had been in the Goodman book since at least March of 1935, and the Goodman band loved to play it. Another excellent version was recorded off the air on the *Let's Dance* broadcast of March 9, 1935, with Pee Wee Erwin taking the trumpet solos. It is interesting to compare his effort, which is first-rate jazz (including his interpolation of "Rhapsody in Blue" in his second solo), with Berigan's on the Victor recording. Truly a golden age of jazz had dawned.

[37] *The Swing Era: The Development of Jazz—1930–1945,* by Gunther Schuller, Oxford University Press, (1989), 468–469. Hereafter *The Swing Era.*

[38] *Lost Chords:* 500.

[39] *The Swing Era:* 469–470.

[40] White materials: June 11, 1935.

[41] CBS press release dated June 13, 1935, cited in White materials: June 11, 1935.

[42] *Stomp Off, Let's Go—The Story of Bob Crosby's Bob Cats and Big Band,* by John Chilton, self-published, (1983), 17–25. Hereafter: "Chilton."

[43] The Stanley Theater in Pittsburgh was one of the prime venues for swing era vaudeville shows featuring name bands. This theater, located at 719 Liberty Avenue, was opened on February 27, 1928. Like all big theaters in major cities, it had its glory days in the period from the 1920s to about 1950, when the advent of television and increasing suburbanization caused entertainment-hungry people to stay at home rather than go to a downtown theater. The Stanley was restored in the 1980s by the Pittsburgh Cultural Trust, and renamed the Benedum Center for the Performing Arts, after Claude Worthington Benedum, whose trust made the largest contribution to the $43 million restoration cost. A wide variety of entertainment is presented there now.

[44] The White materials of July 14, 1935, indicate that the Goodman band played at Olentangy Park in Toledo, Ohio. I think that this is a slightly confused reference to the place the Goodman band played in *Columbus*, Ohio, on July 18, 1935.

[45] White materials: August 21, 1935.

[46] *Los Angeles Evening Herald-Express:* August 21, 1935, cited in the White materials.

[47] *Ibid.:* August 22, 1935, cited in the White materials.

[48] *Ibid.:* August 27, 1935, cited in the White materials.

[49] *Variety:* August 28, 1935, cited in the White materials.

[50] Rollini: 46.

[51] *American Heritage,* October–November, 1981, cited in the White materials: August 1935.

[52] Firestone: 150.

[53] It should be noted that while Bunny Berigan was in Los Angeles with Benny Goodman's band, Lee Wiley was also in Los Angeles. On August 25, 1935, with an orchestra led by Victor Young, she recorded Noel Coward's torchy "Mad about the Boy." It can be safely assumed that she was in the audience at the Palomar Ballroom on a number of occasions to hear the Goodman band during its stand there from August 21 to October 1, 1935.

[54] Trombonist Joe Harris (1908–1952) was a splendid instrumentalist and fine jazz player, as his solos on the Benny Goodman records of "Basin Street Blues" and "Stompin' at the Savoy" plainly show. However, he did not play trombone in the Goodman band during its 1935 cross-country tour. He was used only as a "boy vocalist." The jazz trombone solos then were handled by Jack Lacey, also an excellent trombonist. Harris moved into the trombone section only after Lacey left the Goodman band, which was immediately after they closed at the Palomar Ballroom.

[55] "Goodbye," according to D. Russell Connor, was at first entitled "Blue Serenade." See *The Record of a Legend—Benny Goodman,* by D. Russell Connor, Let's Dance Corp. (1984), 58. I suspect that Gordon Jenkins or his publisher changed the title to avoid confusion with a then very popular song entitled "A Blues Serenade."

[56] White materials: September 29, 1935.

[57] White materials: October 1935.

Chapter 11
Swing Street

Once back in Manhattan, Bunny Berigan immediately resumed his duties at CBS, including his broadcasts with Bunny's Blue Boys and as a member of "the Instrumentalists" with Raymond Scott. "Bunny's Blue Boys on Tuesdays, 12:15 a.m. over Columbia, put on a few of the old jam numbers with the genuine swing. This outfit is led by Bunny Berigan, lately of Benny Goodman's orchestra, and play right up to time.' *(sic)* "The singer on Mark Warnow's Blue Velvet orchestra, Alice Blue (really Helen Forrest),[1] has changed her name to 'Bonnie Blue.'"[2]

Bunny also returned to his work as a freelance recording musician. Even though there was a preponderance of commercial music made on most recording sessions where he participated, now there was also an increasing number of sessions that were either all jazz, or strongly jazz influenced. On December 4, 6, and 13, Bunny participated in three of the most memorable recording sessions of the middle 1930s. They are memorable not only because of his great contributions on each session, but also because these were strictly jazz sessions. There was no commercial singer or other gimmicks used to "sell the song." The sole purpose of these sessions was to record some of the finest jazz musicians then playing. On December 4, Berigan was a part of the group gathered by John Hammond to make some records for the English Parlophone label, which had some affiliation with Decca. The personnel were: Berigan; Bud Freeman, tenor sax and clarinet; Claude Thornhill, piano; Eddie Condon, guitar; Grachan Moncur, bass; and Cozy Cole, drums. Bud Freeman remembered:

> One night after finishing (with Ray Noble's band) at the Rainbow Room, I went down to the Famous Door on Fifty-second Street. The place was packed. Humphrey Bogart and Bea Lillie were there. They were jazz fans. One of the first people I saw was John Hammond, who called me right over. He apparently had a deal with the English Parlophone label to record some American jazz and wanted me to lead a group, which would include Bunny, Benny Carter's drummer, Cozy Cole, and a young bass player called Grachan Moncur, who Hammond had heard on a Newark, New Jersey, radio station. I got hold of Eddie Condon, but when I asked Claude Thornhill, who was playing piano with Ray Noble, he turned me down, saying, 'C'mon, Bud, I'm not a jazz player, I can't play with those guys.' I told him I wanted a good pianist and he was the one. So he finally agreed to do it. He played wonderfully too.[3]

The musicians assembled in a tiny, stuffy studio at 799 Seventh Avenue, near Fifty-fourth that had been abandoned by Decca. 'It was awful,' said Hammond. 'Like a broom closet. In fact, I think that's what it became. But Parlophone had a tie-up with American Decca, so we were stuck with it.' After knocking off a pop tune, the band tackled a Freeman original, 'The Buzzard,' an up-tempo exercise on the chord sequence of 'Basin Street Blues.' 'It was an utter joy,' Hammond said. 'I'd always thought Bud was sort of an unsung hero and I was delighted to hear him prove me right. But Bunny—my God, he just stood apart from everybody!'[4]

The musicians joyously recorded 'What Is There to Say?' (one take); 'The Buzzard' (three takes); 'Tillie's Downtown Now' (three takes); and 'Keep Smiling at Trouble' (one take).[5]

This session includes a rare treat in Freeman's clarinet, heard on all but the final side. Though he plays it with less facility than the tenor, he gets very personal results, with traces of Pee Wee Russell. His tenor work was in transit between gutty Chicago style and the smoother, more sophisticated playing of a few years later. Thornhill's solos are rather nondescript; while he had a distinctive style on ballads, he was not a remarkable jazz soloist. Berigan gleams on this date. On 'Keep Smiling at Trouble,' he is economical in the Armstrong tradition, and creates a nice riff on the bridge. His lead in the 'out' chorus sings and leaps. On the swingingly-paced 'The Buzzard' he begins in the lower register and works his way up. His tone has the crackle that Roy Eldridge loved in him. Unlike most white trumpeters, Bunny used lip vibrato. The ride-out gives an inkling of his drive. On 'What Is There to Say?' he improvises and Thornhill's bridge does not disrupt his thoughts. His two choruses on 'Tillie's Downtown Now' are typical and moving. In the second, he reaches for a high note, doesn't quite make it and reaches again. Soulful is the word.[6]

"Tillie's Downtown Now" is based on the chords of the then-current pop tune "Take Me Back to My Boots and Saddle." (The original Tillie's was located at 148 West 133rd Street in Harlem. By 1935, Tillie's Kitchen, as it was known, had moved downtown to 106 West Fifty-second. It featured soul food and mellow music.)

Two days after recording with Bud Freeman, Bunny returned to the Seventh Avenue "broom closet" studio for another John Hammond session with another all-star line-up.

'It was a completely happy session,' said Hammond. 'Mildred (Bailey) loved Bunny. I chose him here, I guess, because I felt he was the best trumpet player around. I'd considered Red Allen, but I thought he had too much of his own personality, whereas Bunny would fit in so perfectly. The black musicians didn't know Bunny all that well, but once they started to play, they realized how wonderful he was.' By dispensing with a drummer, Hammond hoped to recapture the supple, lyric texture of records by the great blues singer, Bessie Smith, accompanied by trumpeter Joe Smith.[7]

Backing Mildred Bailey with Berigan were Johnny Hodges, alto sax; Teddy Wilson (a particular Hammond favorite), piano; and Grachan Moncur again on bass. The tunes: 'Willow Tree,' 'Honeysuckle Rose,' 'Squeeze Me,' and 'Downhearted Blues.' 'They were among the most beautiful records I ever made. Although Mildred was paid only $37.50 per tune, and complained bitterly, these records turned her into a jazz singer. She continued to sing these songs for the rest of her career.'[8]

The final session in this Berigan/Hammond triptych took place on December 13. The musicians assembled this time were Berigan; Eddie Miller, tenor sax and clarinet; Edgar Sampson, alto sax and clarinet; Cliff Jackson, piano; Grachan Moncur, bass; and Ray Bauduc, drums. The tunes were "You Took Advantage of Me," "Chicken and Waffles," "I'm Coming Virginia," and a blues. This session was billed as "Bunny Berigan and His Blue Boys," and it is evident that Berigan was not only the leader, but the star. His now completely mature trumpet style is on display here in all of its glory. Richard M. Sudhalter, who was a jazz trumpeter himself, described some of the more salient features of that style:

> Berigan displays his masterful control of such trumpeter's devices as shakes and lip trills. (These techniques, used to inject force and drive into rhythmic passages, produce a rhythmic cracking of the tone, usually upward, and an oscillation at the same speed as regular vibrato. The shake is most often achieved by shaking the instrument with the right hand, the lip trill by oscillating the air column with the lip or the lower jaw.) ...Everything is shaped new, fashioned out of a melodic imagination inspired by Armstrong and Beiderbecke in its formative stages but by now owing nothing to anyone.[9]

When commenting on the "Blues" recorded in December 13, an astonished Sudhalter said: "So complete is his mastery that even the expert listener takes a moment to realize that Berigan has played a note that is not on his horn: a low F on the last half of the last beat in the second bar. The trumpeter's lowest note, in the traditional sense, is a G flat half a step above, but Berigan, by fingering that note and expertly manipulating the air stream, squeezes the pitch down half a step. The size and fullness of his tone do the rest."[10]

The year 1935 marked the beginning of the swing era as both a musical phenomenon and as a cultural trend. A number of jazz-influenced musicians had either started bands in 1935, or they began to find success with their bands then. These bands were first and foremost *dance bands*, as had been the many bands that existed prior to 1935. The difference was that the rhythms of jazz, as defined most prominently in the trumpet playing of Louis Armstrong, were now being intentionally incorporated into the ensemble playing of these dance bands. And the instrumental and vocal solos were also moving in the direction of having at least some of Armstrong's rhythmic elasticity. There was a marked movement away from the choppy, vertical rhythmic style that so clearly defines the "businessman's bounce" mode of dance music, to a more horizontal or flowing rhythmic approach. This approach would soon be epitomized in the playing of the Count Basie band in general, and of tenor saxophonist Lester Young [11] in particular. Bunny Berigan, an Armstrong disciple from childhood, had the rhythmic message of Louis in his bones.

Of equal importance was the beginning, in 1935, of the representation of various jazz-oriented bandleaders by Music Corporation of America. So pervasive was MCA's power in the dance band business that without its active involvement in promoting and selling swing bands, there would likely have been no swing era, or it would have been a much smaller blip on the cultural radar screen than it eventually became. MCA, and its chief rival, Rockwell-O'Keefe (later General Artists Corporation or GAC), for the next decade engaged in a brutally competitive tussle to represent the top swing bands of the day. Overall, MCA continued to reap huge profits selling sweet bands like Guy Lombardo, Eddy Duchin, Horace Heidt, Xavier Cugat, Kay Kyser, Sammy Kaye, Wayne King, and Hal Kemp. But it realized that there was also some market for hotter, jazz-based dance bands, and decided to try them out on the mammoth circuit of ballrooms and other venues it controlled (often with exclusive contracts that allowed only MCA bands to play there) across the country. MCA learned quickly that swing bands would sell, and could command good money, *on occasion.* But no ballroom presented swing bands every night. They were never more than a small fraction of the overall dance business at most ballrooms, but that small fraction tended to include very enthusiastic music and dance fans. So MCA began to represent a few swing bands. They included Benny Goodman and Tommy Dorsey, at first, then a little later, Bunny Berigan, Harry James, Count Basie (for a while), Jan Savitt, Jack Teagarden, and (sometimes) Charlie Barnet. GAC hit pay dirt initially with the Casa Loma band, then with Jimmy Dorsey, Bob Crosby, Artie Shaw, Glenn Miller, Woody Herman, and Claude Thornhill.

The world of swing was, like Depression era America, a racially segregated place. Black bands existed because of this fact of life, and as a result, swing era audiences were the beneficiaries of the often wonderfully unadulterated blues-saturated Afro-American music they made. The two major booking agencies almost never handled black bands. Duke Ellington always existed in his own world, and that world was governed in large measure by his first booking agent and manager, Irving Mills, who also controlled Cab Calloway and the Mills Blue Rhythm band. Fletcher Henderson, with the help of his wife Leora, booked his own band in the 1920s and early '30s. Fats Waller was booked first by Phil Ponce and later by Ed Kirkeby. Louis Armstrong was booked by Joe Glaser, and Jimmie Lunceford by Harold Oxley. Still, all of these agencies together were much smaller and less powerful than MCA. They formed a sort of "minor league" in the band-booking business that profited considerably from the MCA-dominated road band business model because most ballrooms would also present black bands on occasion. When they did, even as far north as Ohio, oftentimes a rope would be strung across the dance floor, with black dancers on one side, white on the other. In most ballrooms in the North, when a white band was on the bandstand, black dancers were not welcome. Of course, rigid segregation of the races was the practice everywhere south of the Mason-Dixon line.

If the year 1935 was a very momentous year for jazz and swing, it was also the beginning of very good times for the dance band business. A lot of good things happened that year. Radio was booming. The record business was enjoying a resurgence largely because of the advent of jukeboxes. Movie musicals were a favorite pastime for millions of Americans. People were dancing more than ever. There was a feeling among the businessmen of the music industry that jazz in the form of swing, might have a wide public appeal, if it was packaged and sold "properly."[12] The musicians took care of the music, as always. But now, the businessmen began to deeply involve themselves in promoting and selling this "new" type of music. Since the Depression was at its height (or depths depending on one's point of view) everything cost less, including the salaries musicians were being paid. The business plan that allowed the swing era to take place was based on low costs, the unceasing promotion of bands by MCA, and to a lesser extent the musicians' union, for dancing and live music. It had to be a wonderful time to be a jazz-influenced dance band musician if for no other reason than that NBC was presenting the fabulous Art Tatum[13] *every morning* at 10:00! [14]

The beginning of 1936 saw Bunny Berigan return to his work pattern of previous years with a vengeance: mornings and into the afternoons at CBS, and then recording sessions outside of CBS as his schedule would permit. A review of the Berigan discography for 1936 indicates that he probably made more freelance recording sessions in that year than in any other year of his career. In January alone he participated in the following nine or ten recording sessions: the 3rd: at Decca[15] with the Mound City Blue Blowers and Red McKenzie; on the 8th–9th again at Decca with the same band, but this time with Hal "Spooky" Dickinson, later a member of the Modernaires vocal group, doing the singing; on the 15th again at Decca, with an ad hoc group including Casper Reardon on harp and vocalist Wayne Gregg; on the 18th at ARC-Brunswick backing Chick Bullock; back at Decca on the 20th, with a group supporting vocalists Red McKenzie and Slim Green; possibly a session on the 22nd at ARC-Brunswick with Jack Shilkret and Chick Bullock; on the 26th at Decca, in a band with reedman Dick Stabile, then a sideman with Ben Bernie, backing vocalist Harry Richman; on the 27th at Decca backing singer Dick Robertson; on the 28th at Decca backing vocalist Bob Howard; again at Decca on the 29th, with Dick Stabile and singer Billy Wilson.[16]

This hectic pace continued. On February 4, he was a member of the band supporting his idol, Louis Armstrong, at Decca. One can imagine how Berigan felt finally getting the chance to work with Armstrong, even though the two tunes recorded that day were unabashedly commercial—"I'm Putting All My Eggs in One Basket," and "Yes! Yes! My! My! (She's Mine)"—and Bunny's work in the supporting band could have been done by any competent pro. Nevertheless, Armstrong undoubtedly was aware of Berigan's professional reputation by then, and was from that point on (if not before) an equal member in the Armstrong-Berigan mutual admiration society. The next day Bunny returned to the Decca studios to support the much more prosaic vocal stylings of Dick Robertson, along with some more worthwhile efforts by Red McKenzie. On February 10, he returned to Decca to back Bob Howard and the Top Hatters Trio.[17]

Of far greater significance was Bunny's opening, on approximately February 10, with a small band led by singer Red McKenzie[18] (with considerable help from guitarist Eddie Condon),[19] at the Famous Door, then located at 35 West Fifty-second Street. The Famous Door was one of many clubs on Fifty-second Street then featuring live music. The "concept" that led to the creation of the Famous Door was to have a small club where musicians could come and jam, in the mode of Plunkett's. The originators of this concept were musicians who worked in the nearby radio and recording studios, mainly under pianist/arranger Lennie Hayton who was then the conductor on the Ipana Troubadors and Fred Allen shows. The original investors in the project were: violinist Harry Bluestone; trombonist Jack Jenney; trumpeter Mannie Klein; bassist Artie Bernstein; trombonist Jerry Colonna; arranger Gordon Jenkins; Jimmy Dorsey; and Glenn Miller. They each put up $100. The major investors however, were Hayton and Jack Colt, who was not a musician, but who had experience in the club business. They each put up $1,000.[20]

The name of the club came from a door that trumpeter/singer Wingy Manone said he bought at a lumberyard, had the original investors sign, then shellacked. It was also signed later by the musicians who played in the club, and celebrities. Sam Weiss (not the drummer), who was a host at the Famous Door, explained how the club looked and how the door was displayed: "You went down a few steps to enter the building. Then you would go down a dark, narrow hallway that took you to the club entrance on your left. The bandstand was to your right and the bar to your left. The 'famous door' itself rested on a small platform near the bar."[21]

The Famous Door had opened on March 1, 1935, with a small group led by a then unknown trumpeter who also sang, Louis Prima (which included clarinetist Pee Wee Russell), on the bandstand. Prima's dynamic showmanship, which later made him a fixture in the lounges of Las Vegas, soon had nonmusicians lining up to come into the Famous Door, and the club became a commercial success with the general public, something its organizers had never intended. By the summer, Prima had moved on and trombonist George Brunies replaced him. At about the same time, trombonist Mike Riley and trumpeter Eddie Farley were packing them in at the nearby Onyx Club, with a show that had more to do with comedy and hokum, typified by their smash recording "The Music Goes Round and Around," than music. The management of the Famous Door then made the decision to return to their original concept. Red Norvo's Swing Sextet opened a stand there on September 29, 1935. Norvo was followed by Wingy Manone, and then the small group co-led by singer Red McKenzie and guitarist Eddie Condon, that featured Bunny Berigan.[22] Also in the McKenzie-Condon band with

Berigan were: Paul Ricci, clarinet and tenor sax; Joe Bushkin, piano, trumpet, and singing; Morty Stulmaker, bass. There was no drummer.

Here is how *Metronome* reported this engagement some weeks later, after Forrest Crawford replaced Ricci:

> This is one of the best, if not *the* best strictly jam band to be heard around town. It's purely a case of the boys getting together, sitting down (or standing up), deciding on a tune and doing what they feel with it. Fortunately for all concerned, the individuals at the Famous Door are ace jam men. There are few hot trumpeters in the country today who can touch Bunny Berigan, when he's right. He of the high squeezes, the individual and free style, the phenomenal, but not often heard, lower register and the oft misspelled name, is a grand hornman, grand to listen to, not only because of his acts of execution, but, even more so because of his refreshingly different style. The one danger, though, is catching Bunny on an 'off' night. There's no doubt that this man, doing all the house work at Decca studios, broadcasting regularly over CBS and putting in his 42 hours a week at the 'Door,' is doing too much. Either overwork or staleness can account for the occasional disappearance of the Berigan trumpet vitality. The other melodist, tenorman Forrest Crawford, a recent importation from St. Louis, displays an equal amount of vitality in attack, ideas and execution. Possessor of a really 'dirty' tone, typified by growls that are bound to send you, this man has already won himself a host of swing admirers. The three rhythm-masters stick it at you plenty. Little Joe Bushkin has become a much improved pianist, Eddie Condon still remains the greatest tenor guitarist in the business today, while left-handed Morton Stulmaker is a fine bassist with a big tone, at times much too big for the room into which it zooms. Leader McKenzie has been a favorite with this department for years. The man has an entirely distinctive low-slow vibrato that either gets you or leaves you cold. If it gets you, you're lucky and you'll get much kick from Red's few offerings, wisely done in extremely slow tempos as contrasts for the more wild jamming that precedes. All in all, the six men swing well. Swing fans should have an evening of much fun.[23]

As was noted by the writer of the above-cited *Metronome* article (probably George T. Simon), Berigan was once again overworking, this time to a preposterous degree. If one adds to the forty-two hours a week he was working weekly at the Famous Door, even a low estimate of the time he spent each week at CBS, say thirty-five hours, he was working seventy-seven hours a week. And then there were the hours he was working at Decca. What drove this man to work eighty to one hundred hours a week? Whatever it was, something eventually had to give.[24]

The meeting of nineteen-year-old Joe Bushkin with Berigan in this band was fortuitous for Bushkin, and began a professional association between the two men that would last, with interruptions, for the following four and a half years. Joe Bushkin recalled:

> I wound up at the Famous Door in 1936, playing piano. I was living at home with my parents. George Zack started the gig on piano. Sometimes Dave Tough[25]

would sit in, along with a good tenor player named Forrest Crawford. One night, George Zack passed out and they asked me to fill in. I played all the bridges wrong, which disturbed Berigan, and I guess what made me nervous was the beauty of Berigan's playing and being exposed to the clarity of the guitar bass. Condon had a marvelous chord sense. I learned from him how to keep chord patterns simple and colorful. In fact, Condon sketched out the chords for the opening and middle section of Berigan's 'I Can't Get Started.' The Famous Door was in the bottom of a narrow town-house. It had a bar and about 14 tables and the piano was near a window that looked out on Fifty-second Street. It got its name from a fake door with signatures of famous people, which was set up on a little stage near the bar. I guess the place had some trouble, because the sheriff shut it (later in) 1936. Berigan used to play behind me when I sang and he let me do duets with him on trumpet. It was beautiful.[26] (From the 1940s until his death on November 3, 2004, Joe Bushkin was a fount of stories about Bunny Berigan.)

Berigan was also working on Rudy Vallee's NBC network radio program during February 1936. Since Vallee's show aired over NBC on Thursday evenings from 8:00- 9:00 p.m., and Kate Smith's aired on CBS from 7:30-7:45 p.m., it can be assumed that the Berigan-Smith contretemps had occurred prior to this time, and Berigan was free to take other (non-CBS) employment on Thursday evenings. An incident apparently led to Berigan's final departure from the Vallee show.

A letter from the Rudy Vallee office to Berigan indicates that Bunny was paid for the Vallee radio show of February 20, check #17456 in the amount of $38.00, and advises him that he was overpaid by $10.00 and asks he pay it back. A second letter to Berigan, dated February 25, 1936 advises him that a change in the Vallee radio show format is being made and that he will no longer be used after the show of March 5, 1936. Although the wording of the letter is circumspect, there seems to be little doubt that Bunny is being 'fired.' How long Berigan played in the Vallee radio band of this period is not known; it may have been a number of weeks or even months. The Vallee shows of this period had few or no instrumental solos and the one show heard (February 27th) has not a note of 'identifiable' Berigan, although we know he was at hand.[27]

I have no idea how (or if) this little matter was resolved, but Berigan did indeed work the March 5 Vallee show, and was paid $30.00 for doing so.[28]
Despite all of his other work, Berigan found time to work a little more at the Famous Door, and he did this particular gig for free.

On Sunday, February 16, 'The United Hot Clubs of America presented a jam session at the Famous Door club in New York City. Instead of holding a meeting at the Decca studios, as was done last month, it was decided that the Famous Door should be the scene of the festivities this time. Although the invitations stated the meeting would start at 4.30 p.m., actually it was 5:45 p.m. before anything happened, with no less than 250 persons attending. Before the session ended at 7:30 p.m., the manager volunteered the information that about 300 persons had attended this jam session. The first jam band consisted of Bunny Berigan, Forrest

Crawford, Morty Stulmaker, Joe Bushkin, Dave Tough and Eddie Condon. A partial list of the names who took part in the proceedings: Bud Freeman, Eddie Miller, Crawford, tenor saxes; Berigan, trumpet; Joe Marsala, clarinet; Sid Weiss, Stulmaker, bass; Bushkin, Teddy Wilson, Putney Dandridge, piano; Condon, Hilton Lamare, Carmen Mastren, guitar; Tough, Ray Bauduc, Manny Berger, drums. The most important features of the afternoon were the appearances of Bessie Smith[29] and Mildred Bailey. Bessie sang 'St Louis Blues,' 'Buggy Ride,' and 'Empty Bed Blues' in a manner that could only be described as colossal. The musicians who accompanied her were as much entranced by her singing as was the audience. Mildred Bailey sang 'Honeysuckle Rose' and 'Someday Sweetheart' and sufficient to say that she is to white female vocalists what Bessie is to the colored folk. Because of the size of the crowd in attendance, it has become necessary for the club to charge a small admission for future jam sessions, the proceeds of which can be used to recompense the guest artists and to aid the unemployed musicians of local 802.[30]

Bessie came in upstairs one Sunday afternoon. She came in, she planted those two flat feet firmly on the floor, she did not shake her shoulders nor snap her fingers. She just opened that great kisser and let the music come out. Backed by Bunny Berigan's muted trumpet, the great blues artiste sang 'Baby, Won't You Please Come Home?,' 'Mama's Got the Blues,' 'I'm Wild About That Thing,' 'The Gin House Blues,' 'Dirty No-Gooder's Blues,' and 'Nobody Knows You When You're Down and Out.'[31]

Brick Fleagle (guitar): 'Mildred Bailey was invited to sing, but she refused, I think wisely. Bessie left as soon as she was through. No liquor was served at those upstairs sessions, so she just came, sang and left us all in a daze!' With the cream of New York swingsters swamping the Famous Door, the UHCA (United Hot Clubs of America) local ran an informal crack-up for the jitterbugs. Thereafter, admissions will be charged to fill the coffers and compensate the performers, with a share going to the relief fund. Berigan, Tough, Freeman, Chick Webb and a new trumpet player, Otis Johnson, from the Connie's Inn relief band, are furnishing the highlights.[32]/[33]

On February 24, Bunny was back at the ARC-Brunswick-Vocalion (they had merged by then) studios to record some current pop tunes with vocalist Chick Bullock. His fellow musicians that day were all from his Famous Door combo, with Dave Tough and Bud Freeman (both of whom would soon be joining Tommy Dorsey's band) as added attractions, at least for jazz fans. His work at CBS, largely commercial dross, nevertheless allowed him the continuing opportunity to appear on network radio weekly with his little jam band Bunny's Blue Boys. This undoubtedly provided him with excellent publicity and helped to establish his name among the general public, and it also was a strong reason for him to continue at CBS during this time of other very heavy work commitments.

On March 12, Berigan took part in a broadcast over New York superstation WOR. This program was one of the earliest attempts to seriously analyze "swing." There was some trade press interest in the proposed event.

The features department of station WOR, under Jerry Danzig, is readying an air session for March 8th *(sic)* at 10:30 p.m. over the Mutual System. The intention is to supply the public with a ready-made definition of 'swing.' Marshall Stearns and K. K. Hansen of Rockwell-O'Keefe were lined up to put a finger in the jam. A final compromise between shrewd businessman Hansen and swing devotee Stearns has led to a mixed group with Louis Armstrong, Bud Freeman, Teddy Wilson, George Van Eps, Joe Marsala and Bunny Berigan giving the swing angle with Stearns as MC, and introducing Hansen, who will face the tough assignment of defining swing by example. (*Variety:* March 11, 1936)

Swing Music Fest being set by WOR...scheduled by WOR and probably over Mutual with a tentative line-up and date of March 8th at 10.30 to 11:00 p.m. K. K. Hansen of Rockwell-O'Keefe is involved and the line-up so far includes Louie Armstrong, Wingy Manone (trumpets); Stuff Smith (violin); Glen Gray (clarinet); Lennie Hayton (piano); Red Norvo (xylophone); Stan Dennis (bass); George Van Eps (guitar); Ray Bauduc (drums) and Bob Crosby and Mildred Bailey (vocals). (*Billboard:* March 7, 1936)

After this broadcast (which was recorded), *Metronome* provided the details in its April issue: 'What Is Swing' (was a) demonstration with Marshall Stearns, production man, K. K. Hansen, commentator, and Gordon Jenkins, leader-arranger. There were a number of setbacks at the last minute; Louis Armstrong and Mildred Bailey couldn't make it. Nat Brusiloff, who rehearsed the orchestra, collapsed, and Gordon Jenkins took over. The personnel had Bunny Berigan, trumpet; Joe Marsala, clarinet; Bud Freeman, tenor saxophone; Teddy Wilson, piano; Stan King, drums; Lou Shoobe, bass and Harve Ellison, guitar, plus members of the house band. The session, although lacking in finesse, was interesting and enlightening.[34]

One of the more interesting club dates Berigan played during this time period was a wedding, on March 15: "Hoagy Carmichael [35] married Ruth Merrarch at Fifth Avenue Presbyterian Church in New York City. George Gershwin played piano at the ceremony and additional music was provided by the Red McKenzie–Bunny Berigan band from the Famous Door club. Bud Freeman was also present."[36] Joe Bushkin related his memories of this event to Robert Dupuis, and they are to be found in his Berigan biography.

The next day, Bunny was in the Decca studios as a member of the band supporting vocalist Dick Robertson.

At about this time, Bunny Berigan left his job as a regular member of the CBS pool of musicians. His place in a number of CBS bands was taken by Gordon "Chris" Griffin, then twenty years old, who immediately received substantial criticism for not playing as well as Berigan. (By May, Griffin was out of the CBS band and in Benny Goodman's trumpet section, where he would remain for the next three years. After that experience, where he played mostly with Ziggy Elman[37] and Harry James[38] as trumpet section mates, there was no job in commercial music he could not do.) There appears to be no reason for Berigan's departure other than that he was required to spend too much time at CBS during the day, time he could spend as profitably (or more profitably) making records on a freelance basis, without the confinement. And of course, he could still sub into jobs at CBS, if he wished to. It is also possible that his meeting of K. K. Hansen of Rockwell-O'Keefe on the March 12 WOR swing fest led to some sort of contractual relationship between Bunny and Rockwell-O'Keefe. (Berigan did in fact sign with Rockwell-O'Keefe at some point in 1936.)[39]

But it was probably under the guidance of personal manager Arthur Michaud, who apparently began to represent Berigan at about this time, that Bunny organized his first big band in May of 1936. (See below.) If he did sign with Rockwell then, it is very likely that they or Michaud would have advised him to change his relationship with CBS so that his appearances on the network would be more in the nature of "guest star" visits, and as such, be more special and of greater use to Berigan in building his name for future endeavors, specifically leading his own band. As we will see, this change in Berigan's relationship with CBS certainly did not mean the end of his association with the network. In fact, the most musically rewarding part of that relationship was about to begin. It is certainly possible that the developments taking place at CBS which ultimately led to the creation of *The Saturday Night Swing Club* were the idea of someone outside of CBS (Rockwell-O'Keefe/Michaud) who recognized the existence of a substantial audience not only for swing music in general, but for Bunny Berigan's brand of swing music in particular. Nevertheless, someone *inside* of CBS allowed this idea to be tried on the network, and for that, jazz fans should always be grateful.

Swing was very much in and *on* the air in March of 1936. NBC, apparently following up on the WOR swing program which aired on March 12, tried its own swing fling on March 29:

'Is Swing The Thing?' hit the ether March 29th on NBC with little or no publicity. Readied by Britisher Austen 'Ginger' Croom-Johnson of the BBC, who plans to repeat the program, which offered Red Norvo, Mildred Bailey, Adrian Rollini, Ray Noble, Meredith Willson, Kay Thompson and the guitar combo of Dick McDonough and Carl Kress, with Casper Reardon swinging on the harp. It lasted for an hour from 8 to 9 p.m. and stated the case for swing fully, by giving examples of both sweet and swing. Mildred Bailey's performance was tops, with the work of McDonough-Kress a close second. By some mistake, Stuff Smith was cut off just as he was getting under way on 'I's A Muggin,' and the Norvo combo was held down by (an) arrangement. Noble played a Glenn Miller arrangement of 'Truckin,' with Sterling Bose and Johnny Mince getting off some nice solos. As a round-up of swing styles, the program was the best to date.[40]

Notes

[1] Helen Forrest, born as Helen Fogel, on April 12, 1917, in Atlantic City, New Jersey, was one of the best and most popular singers of the swing era. After working on CBS

radio, she was hired by Artie Shaw in the fall of 1938, at the time his band was rising to national prominence. Consequently the many records she made with Shaw brought her wide recognition. After Shaw left his band at the end of 1939, Forrest went to work for Benny Goodman, and then Harry James. She left James in late 1943 and began a long career as a soloist. She had success on radio in the 1940s, most notably on a radio program she shared with vocalist Dick Haymes, appeared in a few films, and then settled into a career where she would sometimes record, sometimes sing with big bands, and sometimes be featured as a soloist in various venues. Helen Forrrest died on July 11, 1999, in Woodland Hills, California.

[2] *Variety:* November 20, 1935, cited in the White materials.

[3] White materials: December 4, 1935.

[4] *Giants of Jazz:* 33–35.

[5] White materials: December 4, 1935.

[6] Liner notes—*Swing Classics: Bunny Berigan, Bud Freeman, Jess Stacy, Joe Sullivan* (1969), Prestige LP 7646, by Dan Morgenstern.

[7] *Giants of Jazz:* 35.

[8] *Hammond:* 130.

[9] *Giants of Jazz:* 36

[10] *Giants of Jazz:* 36–37.

[11] Lester Willis Young, one of the most influential musicians in the history of jazz, was born on August 27, 1909, in Woodville, Mississippi. After a lengthy apprenticeship spent in numerous black territory bands in the Midwest, Young learned to read music at sight, achieved complete control of the instruments he played (which by then were tenor sax and clarinet), and developed some extraordinarily original jazz ideas. By the early 1930s, he had grown to six feet one. His height and the combination of his light skin, penetrating green eyes, and tiny feet (size seven), made him a striking individual. He also had begun to accumulate a number of personal eccentricities that only heightened his individuality. His dress, manner of speech, and humor were exceedingly different, even in the somewhat unorthodox world of dance band musicians. But it was in his music that Lester Young was most unique. His professional activity in the early 1930s was continuous, though hardly high profile. The low point came when he was hired by Fletcher Henderson in the spring of 1934, replacing Coleman Hawkins, whose stentorian tenor saxophone stylings had been a prominent feature of Henderson's band for years. Young's entire approach to the tenor saxophone was antithetical to Hawkins's, and this employment with Henderson was short lived and exasperating. (Young requested a letter from Henderson stating that he had not been fired for musical inadequacy, which Henderson gladly provided to him. Young's playing simply didn't fit into the Henderson band's style.) Incredibly, even though Young had been a professional musician since approximately 1923, he did not make his first record until the autumn of 1936. His playing on the recording of "Lady Be Good" (ARC/Vocalion on October 9, 1936), with a small group of musicians from Count Basie's earliest band, can only be described as astonishing. Young's approach to jazz, which in my view was an extension in many ways (principally rhythmic) of what Bix Beiderbecke had started, was the first full-scale alternative to the approach developed by Louis Armstrong. His tenor saxophone sound was also quite different from that used by all others then. He attributed its light "coolness" to the influence of C-melody sax pioneer Frank Trumbauer. After disastrous experiences in the military in World War II, Young was dishonorably discharged. After this, he gradually descended

into a misama of alcoholism. Paradoxically, it was during this same time that he achieved his most widespread success as a performer, dividing his time between Jazz at the Philharmonic and leading his own small groups. His influence on other tenor saxophonists was greatest in the later 1940s and 1950s. Lester Young died in Manhattan on March 15, 1959, suffering from symptoms very similar to those Bunny Berigan had at the end of his life.

[12] By *properly,* it is meant that the bands would be sold according to the business plan developed and perfected in the late 1920s and early 1930s by MCA, and to a lesser extent, Rockwell-O'Keefe.

[13] Pianist Arthur Tatum Jr. was born on October 13, 1909, in Toledo, Ohio. He suffered from cataracts in both of his eyes as a child, causing blindness in one eye and very limited vision in the other. He was a child prodigy who played the piano obsessively as a youngster, developing an enormous technique by copying the playing of piano rolls on his mother's player piano. After receiving considerable formal piano training, Tatum returned to Toledo in 1927, and was soon featured on local radio. Many leading jazz musicians sought out Tatum in Toledo and encouraged him to go to New York, where musical opportunities were greater. He did so in late 1932, and immediately established his credentials as a virtuoso jazz improviser of unequaled technique by outplaying Fats Waller, James P. Johnson, and Willie "The Lion" Smith, all formidable masters of stride-style jazz piano. Between 1932 and 1945, Tatum established a national reputation as a jazz piano virtuoso, and began to be presented as a soloist on concert tours, which continued this until his death, caused by kidney failure, which occurred on November 5, 1956, in Los Angeles, California.

[14] *Variety:* December 18, 1935, cited in White materials.

[15] It appears that Berigan had developed some sort of relationship with Decca Records during this period that was similar to the one he had with ARC, where he was more or less "on call" for recording sessions. The Decca studios were then located at 50 West Fifty-seventh Street in Manhattan.

[16] White materials: January 1936.

[17] White materials: February 1936.

[18] Vocalist William "Red" McKenzie was born in St. Louis, Missouri, on October 14, 1899. He was raised in Washington, D.C., until the deaths of his parents, after which he returned to St. Louis, working at a variety of jobs including as a professional jockey. McKenzie began singing, as well as playing the kazoo and the comb, with tissue paper placed over the tines, in the early 1920s. With two others, he formed a novelty act called the Mound City Blue Blowers, and began recording in February 1924. The group's initial release, "Arkansas Traveler," became a hit, and they toured extensively in the United States then went to London. Upon returning to the United States, McKenzie led the group over the next several years. He spent a year with Paul Whiteman, 1932–1933, then reorganized the Mound City Blue Blowers, and began to appear at clubs on Fifty-second Street as well as on record both with and without the group. He returned to St. Louis in 1937, and was seldom seen in New York thereafter. The years prior to his death were spent in ill health owing to the progression of cirrhosis of the liver. McKenzie died in New York City on February 7, 1948.

[19] Guitarist, bandleader, and impresario Albert Edwin Condon was born in Goodland, Indiana, on November 16, 1905. He moved to Chicago in 1921, and spent most of the next decade there playing with many of the young white musicians who were then em-

bracing jazz. He went to New York in 1928 and began musical associations with an ever-widening group of performers both on and off record, including Louis Armstrong, Fats Waller, and Red Nichols. He continued an earlier association with Red McKenzie while in New York in the 1930s, and also began long but intermittent associations with Joe Marsala, Bobby Hackett, and Bud Freeman. During World War II, Condon began to lead bands for various concerts in Manhattan, and for residencies at Nick's in Greenwich Village. At the end of 1945, he opened the first of his own jazz clubs, which would remain on the scene for many years, though most of the time without Condon on their bandstands. Condon was successful on TV in the 1950s, and was a master of the *bon mot*, often delivered with just the right mixture of sarcasm and irony. He toured widely throughout the 1950s and 1960s, and died in New York City on August 4, 1973.

[20] *52nd Street:* 106.

[21] *Ibid.*

[22] *Ibid.,* 106–112.

[23] *Metronome:* April 1936, cited in White materials: February 10, 1936.

[24] It is certainly possible that by this time, Berigan was in discussions with Arthur Michaud about forming his own band. Michaud may well have told Bunny that in order to form a band, a lot of money would be needed. That could explain Bunny's incredibly heavy workload in the early months of 1936.

[25] Drummer David Jarvis Tough was born in Oak Park, Illinois, on April 26, 1907, into an affluent family. He attended the Lewis Institute in Chicago for three years, then began his association with the Austin High Gang of white teenagers who were exploring jazz in the early 1920s in Chicago. He worked with a succession of bands in and around Chicago until he went to Europe in 1927, where he worked for two years mostly in Berlin and Paris. Tough returned to the United States in mid-1929, finding only sporadic work in New York. Tough was an alcoholic, and may also have been an epileptic. (Joe Bushkin recalled to Whitney Balliet in the early 1980s that when Tough returned to New York from Chicago in early 1936, his childhood friend from Chicago, Eddie Condon, invited him to sit in with the McKenzie-Condon band at the Famous Door. See *The New Yorker,* November 18, 1985. Everyone, including Bunny Berigan, was very favorably impressed by Tough's drumming. Even though Tough had spent about a year in New York in 1929–1930, there is no evidence that he worked with Berigan during that time.) By 1936, Tough had developed into a marvelously subtle yet dynamic rhythm master who had the uncanny ability to lift the playing of any band in which he worked. Soon, through the good offices of his lifelong friend, Bud Freeman, Tough was a member of Tommy Dorsey's band. From there, he went on to a long series of high-profile jobs with the leading big bands of the day, including Benny Goodman's, Bunny Berigan's, Artie Shaw's 1941 civilian band and his 1942–1943 navy band, and finally Woody Herman's First Herd in 1944–1945. After that, Tough kept busy playing in many different musical settings, but was fighting a losing battle with his alcoholism. He died after falling in a street in Newark, New Jersey, on December 6, 1948. By far, the most illuminating and scholarly writing about Dave Tough is to be found in the articles by Harold S. Kaye that appeared in *Storyville,* in 2000–2001.

[26] White materials: February 10, 1936. The White materials quote Bushkin from the recollections he shared with Whitney Balliett for an article about Bushkin that appeared in *The New Yorker.* Unfortunately, they do not give any citation to *The New Yorker* or the date of the article which was November 18, 1985. Balliett later included this article in a

compendium of articles he had written over the years about jazz musicians for *The New Yorker* entitled: *American Musicians—56 Portraits in Jazz*, Oxford University Press (1986), 216–223. A slightly more detailed account of how Joe Bushkin came to meet Bunny Berigan at the Famous Door can be found in Dupuis, at pages 121–122.

[27] White materials: February 20, 1936.

[28] White materials: March 5, 1936.

[29] Bessie Smith, billed as "The Empress of the Blues," was both a formidable singer and a formidable woman. Born on April 15, 1894, in Chattanooga, Tennessee, she began performing as a child outside of saloons in her home town. By 1913, she began performing with her own act at Atlanta's 81 Theater, and by 1920 had established a solid reputation throughout the southeast United States as a powerful blues singer. By the early 1920s, she had taken up residence in Philadelphia, and had become a headliner on the all-black Theater Owners Booking Association vaudeville circuit. Starting in 1923, she began a remarkably successful association with Columbia Records, and was among the highest paid black performers in the nation for the rest of the decade. By 1930, her career was on the wane. She made a few records for John Hammond in 1933 which show that she was adapting her singing to a more swing-oriented approach. Smith died from injuries she received in an automobile collision on September 26, 1937, in Clarksdale, Mississippi.

[30] *Tempo:* March 1936, cited in the White materials: February 16, 1936.

[31] Robert Paul Smith in *The Record Changer,* date not provided, cited in the White materials: February 16, 1936.

[32] *Variety:* February 26, 1936, cited in the White materials: February 16, 1936.

[33] Regarding the above citations from the White materials, February 16, 1936, I must point out that almost all of this information on Bessie Smith's appearance at the Famous Door was taken, without attribution, from *Bessie*, by Chris Albertson, Stein and Day (1972), 205–206. Bessie Smith was then in the midst of the last comeback of her career, mixing pop songs with the blues for which she was renowned. The one source that was not taken from the Albertson book is the quote from the publication *Tempo*. That quote came from almost contemporaneous information, and appeared in *Tempo* in March 1936. Based on it therefore, I think it is safe to say that Mildred Bailey did indeed sing after Bessie Smith that afternoon. There is a similar review of this event in *52nd Street,* 113.

[34] White materials: March 12, 1936.

[35] Hoagland Howard Carmichael was born on November 22, 1899, in Bloomington, Indiana. He was one of the foremost composers of popular songs from the 1920s well into the 1950s. Carmichael was also a performer who appeared frequently on radio and in films. Later in his life, he continued to compose, but found that fewer and fewer people in the music business were interested in his music. He died in Rancho Mirage, California, on December 27, 1981.

[36] White materials: March 15, 1936, quoting *Variety:* March 25, 1936.

[37] Trumpeter Harry Aaron Finkelman, known by his stage name Ziggy Elman, was born on May 26, 1914, in Philadelphia, Pennsylvania. Elman's father, who was of Russian-Jewish heritage, was among other things, a part-time cantor and klezmer violinist. Young Harry absorbed these influences early, and they became a part of his musical personality. A natural musician, Ziggy Elman could play, in addition to trumpet, violin, trombone, and the woodwind instruments. His family moved to Atlantic City, New Jersey, when he was a child, and by age fifteen he was playing at Jewish weddings and in nightclubs. As he grew into manhood, he began to fuse elements of Louis Armstrong's jazz style to his

strongly klezmer-influenced playing, the result of which was a highly individual musical identity. He began working for Alex Bartha, who led the house band at the ballroom on the Steel Pier in Atlantic City in 1932. It was here that Benny Goodman heard him in 1936, and quickly hired him. With fellow trumpeters Chris Griffin and Harry James, he formed Goodman's famous "biting brass" trumpet section in the years 1937–1938. From 1939 to 1940, Elman gained prominence as Goodman's principal trumpet soloist, and as the leader of a band of Goodman sidemen on Bluebird records. From August 1940 until early 1943, Elman was the featured trumpet soloist in Tommy Dorsey's band. By this time, he had developed a brash, colorful style that was immediately identifiable. Elman served in the army in World War II, and returned to Dorsey after leaving the military. He also led his own big band after World War II, but it was unsuccessful. He settled in Hollywood thereafter, working as a freelance in the early 1950s. Illness slowed down his career considerably in the late 1950s, and he died on June 26, 1968, in Van Nuys, California.

[38] Trumpeter Harry Haag James, born on March 15, 1916, in Albany, Georgia, was one of the most spectacular trumpet virtuosos of the swing era. James's father was a bandleader in a traveling circus, and he trained young Harry from childhood in the basics of trumpet technique. This, along with James's prodigious talent, enabled him to begin to impress people with his trumpeting prowess in the environs of Beaumont, Texas, where his family had settled, starting in 1931. By 1935 he was a member of Ben Pollack's band, and moved on in January of 1937 to Benny Goodman's band. While with Goodman, James gained national prominence. He started his own band (booked by MCA) in early 1939, but had only marginal success with it until mid-1941, when the public suddenly embraced his music. His popularity was greatly enhanced by the singing of Helen Forrest, who joined his band in September 1941. James went on to great success during World War II because he remained out of military service during those years due to a mastoid condition/punctured eardrum. During the recording ban of 1942-1944, James's music continued to be presented to the public via many radio broadcasts, and numerous Hollywood feature films. He continued with his big band well after the 1940s, operating on a fairly full-time basis until literally days before his death, which occurred on July 5, 1983, in Las Vegas, Nevada.

[39] *Swing Era Scrapbook—The Teenage Diaries & Radio Logs of Bob Inman, 1936–1938,* compiled by Ken Vail, Scarecrow Press, Inc. (2005), 167.

[40] *Variety*: April 8, 1936, cited in the White materials.

Chapter 12
Making it in Manhattan

As March of 1936 gave way to April, events of great significance in the life and career of Bunny Berigan began to occur more rapidly, not that he or anyone else would have necessarily realized it then. The singer Lee Wiley and Bunny probably began their romantic involvement at about this time, while Berigan was appearing at the Famous Door. Wiley had recently returned to Manhattan from Hollywood (and Arizona [?] see below) after her affair with Victor Young ended. Young remained in Hollywood working on film scores with increasing frequency, and success. Donna Berigan was then in the last weeks of her third pregnancy (Berigan daughter Joyce was born on April 22, 1936), but given the hectic nature of Bunny's work life in Manhattan, he could not possibly have been spending much time at the Berigan home in Rego Park. At this time, Ms. Wiley was very much on the scene near Bunny. Lee Wiley recalled: "I had to spend a year in Arizona *(sic)* for my health. When I got back to New York, I was so hungry for music that when I had to stay home in bed. My brother-in-law, who was running the Famous Door, would call me, leave the phone off the hook and let me listen to Berigan, Bushkin, Bud Freeman and the intermission pianist, Teddy Wilson."[1] Meanwhile, Bunny was reveling in his new-found freedom from the drudgery and long hours at CBS. The gig at the Famous Door was relaxed in the extreme: "Bunny Berigan was caught playing the piano, while little Joe Bushkin trumpeted and vocalized on 'I Never Knew.' Several spots along Fifty-second Street are staging unofficial jam sessions on Sundays to attract business."[2]

Another momentous pairing was also about to take place, this one being musical: Bunny Berigan and the Vernon Duke–Ira Gershwin song "I Can't Get Started with You." "Within the span of the next ten days Bunny would twice record a tune from a then-current Broadway show that would forever change his life and would remain a part of it until his death and far beyond. He would transform the tune from a minor selection in the show to a standard, still preformed and recorded today, a song now considered by most to be a part of the 'Great American Songbook' 'I Can't Get Started with You,' written by Vernon Duke (music) and Ira Gershwin (lyric), was introduced by Bob Hope in the *Ziegfeld*

Follies of 1936, which had opened in New York City on January 30, 1936."[3] Eddie Condon recalled Berigan had first played the tune at the Famous Door (in the early part of 1936) and within a few weeks it became a feature number for him with Bunny singing the lyric. Shortly after the first recording under his own name (April 13th) (of "I Can't Get Started") Berigan and the Famous Door band took part in the first "Swing Concert" at the Imperial Theatre on Sunday, May 24th. There the song with Bunny's vocal was featured. A few weeks after that event, CBS rehired Bunny and built a show around his talent, the famous *Saturday Night Swing Club*, which used "I Can't Get Started" as part of its opening theme.[4]

The first recording Bunny Berigan made of "I Can't Get Started" was made at Decca on April 3, 1936. The Decca record label on the 78 rpm disc that carried this performance reads "Red McKenzie and His Rhythm Kings." It was McKenzie who sang the lyric. This session was just another of the many where Berigan was a member of a backup group, there for the limited purpose of providing support for a singer. The "arrangement" used for this performance was pretty much "off the shelf," and contained little of distinction. There is no intro. Bunny, with his warm-toned open trumpet, sets out the main strain of the eight-bar melody twice in the first chorus, followed by a rather lachrymose tenor sax on the eight-bar bridge, likely played by Sid Trucker. Berigan returns for the last eight bars of the first chorus again playing the melody. Red McKenzie takes a typical vocal chorus. His singing was certainly several levels above that of many 1930s male singers, and he was always himself, showing none of the influence of the most dominant male singer of those years, Bing Crosby. Still, he is doing nothing here but turning in a professional job of "selling the song," which was the purpose of this record. Behind McKenzie's singing in the three eight-bar segments containing the main theme of the song, there is an unobtrusive clarinet obbligato probably also played by Trucker. Trombonist Al Philburn does much the same thing behind McKenzie on the bridge. After the vocal chorus, pianist Frank Signorelli takes a rather old-fashioned solo on the bridge, and then the Berigan-led ensemble takes it out. It is all very conventional and very predictable, like hundreds of other commercial records of the time. This performance clocks in at around three minutes, and sounds a little fast to me.[5]

On April 13, at what otherwise was another strictly ordinary recording session, Bunny Berigan was given the opportunity to record the version of "I Can't Get Started" he had been working on with the small band at the Famous Door. In the ten days between the April 3 Decca recording session and this session at ARC-Brunswick, Eddie Condon suffered an attack of pancreatitis, and had to be hospitalized. The little band that accompanied Berigan on this recording, billed as: "Bunny Berigan and His Boys," consisted of Artie Shaw, clarinet; Forrest Crawford, tenor sax; Joe Bushkin, piano; Tommy Felline, guitar; Morty Stulmaker, bass; and Stan King, drums. (Also on the session was vocalist Chick Bullock, an ARC mainstay, who sang the other three tunes recorded that day.)[6]

It is in this recording of "I Can't Get Started," issued initially on Vocalion 3225, later on Brunswick 7949, and backed by "Rhythm Saved the World," that we begin to see the outline of what eventually became the definitive performance of this song, recorded by Bunny some sixteen months later for Victor. The "arrangement" that we hear in this performance was largely devised by Berigan himself, except for the succession of chord changes after the vocal and tenor sax solo, over which Berigan plays, and which serve as a modulation from concert C to D flat, springing Bunny into the stunning solo trumpet passage which closes the record. That part was worked out by Eddie Condon.

This performance starts out with Bunny stating the melody on open trumpet, the clarinet and tenor sax noodling quietly behind him for eight bars. Berigan wisely slowed the tempo down, knowing that would highlight what he had in store for later in the piece. Then he sings for an entire chorus. On the main strain of the song, the quality of his voice is pleasant and unaffected, with a fast vibrato. On the bridge, he attempts to croon, in the manner of *der Bingle* (Bing Crosby) which I'm sure sounded more musical in the mid-1930s than it does today. In his last eight bars he returns to a more genuine mode of singing, which to my ear sounds much better. Morty Stulmaker uses his bow to provide an *arco* bass foundation behind the vocal that is different, but it unfortunately imparts a rather lugubrious feeling to what is otherwise a peaceful and gentle rendering of the lyric. Thankfully, Stulmaker sets down his bow after the vocal chorus so as not to weigh down in any way the musical fireworks that are about to begin. Forrest Crawford then plays a softly melodic eight bars that lead into the Condon-fashioned series of chord changes. Richard M. Sudhalter best described what happens next:

A drum tap brings (Berigan) on for the piece de resistance. He begins it with four self-contained episodes, announced by single rhythm section chords but all, in effect, part of one great cadenza. The first establishes mood and expectancy. The second changes the key and moves effortlessly through the entire range of the horn in developing the idea. The third is delivered sotto voce and intimately. The fourth takes him deep into his low register for some final thoughts. Now he is ready. Leaping nearly two octaves, Berigan chimes out a cluster of clear, ringing high Cs and takes flight, avidly supported by the band. Working in the taxing range above high C, he tosses off E flats and one titanic high F, turning Vernon Duke's enchanting melody into an anthem. Totally in charge of his instrument and material, he lowers the intensity level to a hush for a reprise of the melody, contemplative and soothing, then parades it home, as Shaw fills in the spaces, crowning his performance with a high B flat and a glorious, resounding E flat above that. It is all fresh and new, the apotheosis of Berigan's art as trumpet soloist in the bravura tradition established a decade earlier by Armstrong— romantic, rhapsodic, emotionally unrestrained.[7]

This recording began to garner critical plaudits soon after its release in May, and it began to sell in numbers higher that the run-of-the-mill pop tune vocal records that were being churned out by the dozens by ARC, Decca, and other labels.

If we may, for a moment, set aside the substantial musical merits of this recording, it seems that now there was some promotional push being applied on Bunny's behalf, probably by either Rockwell-O'Keefe and/or Arthur Michaud, the personal manager who figured prominently in the rise of Tommy Dorsey to fame. In a blurb that appeared in *Metronome* in June of 1936, one senses the fine art of press-agentry at work. It sets forth Berigan's professional resumé, an obvious clue that he was being represented by someone who was "selling him," and steering his career in a definite direction:

> You've probably heard Bunny Berigan's trumpeting much more often than you realize. For years he was the ranking hot trumpeter at the CBS studios and right now his two lips are responsible for much of the trumpeting heard on Decca records, some of the CBS house work and 42 hours of trumpet jam at the former Famous Door every week. He's one of those chaps who just can't get enough of his horn, who lives and loves trumpet and whose colossal enthusiasm is reflected in his work. First came the usual school bands, but in 1928, Hal Kemp heard him. A year later, Bunny came to New York on his own and hooked up with Frank Cornwell's crew at Janssen's Hofbrau. Kemp found out that Berigan was in town and a short time later, Berigan found out that he was in Kemp's band. Two years of that and then a shift to the CBS studio to play in the house band there under Freddy Rich. In and out of those studios at various times, with engagements in the pit band of the *Everybody's Welcome* legit show, with Paul Whiteman at the Biltmore and, most recently, with Benny Goodman tossed in here and there. Berigan is one hot trumpeter you can pick out any place, if only because of that inspirational squeeze of his that he's made famous. Listen to him on the Benny Goodman Victor records of 'King Porter Stomp,' 'Sometimes I'm Happy,' and 'Dear Old Southland.' Hear, too, his latest work on 'I Can't Get Started' on Decca. And, on top of that, Berigan is a wonderful legitimate man, not only is he death on high notes, but his lower register tone is absolutely phenomenal; note it on Red Norvo's Columbia record of 'Blues in E Flat.' A well-mannered chap, this Bunny Berigan, popular with his musicians and admired, not only because of his musicianship, but because of his personal qualifications. One of the latter is raising a family. Any minute now, his second child is expected; then listen to Berigan blow his horn![8]

I suspect that as a part of Bunny's deal with Rockwell-O'Keefe and/or Michaud to make him a bandleader, he was told that he had to bring his drinking under control. There is evidence that he tried to do that: Joe Bushkin remembered:

> The Famous Door was only supposed to hold 80 people, but more were packed in like sardines most nights. It was run by Jimmy Doane, who was Lee Wiley's brother-in-law, and it was he who hired Red McKenzie, who in turn got Bunny and the others. Some nights, as a gag, Condon would play piano, Bunny would

play Condon's guitar, (he was the only guy in the band, other than Eddie, who could play it, because it was tuned differently) and I would fool on trumpet. Although we had no drummer, Dave Tough would just sit in whenever he came over, often with Tommy Dorsey and Bud Freeman. Bunny was pretty much on the wagon for most of that period, especially when Condon got ill and had to go into the hospital.[9]

"The wagon agrees so well with Bunny that he is becoming increasingly more consistent. If there are better trumpet players in the world, I'd certainly be surprised. He deserves either to have, or to be in the greatest band in the country."[10] Forrest Crawford: "I remember the (famous Imperial Theater) concert very well. Bunny, around that time, was putting on a little weight. He'd given up smoking and cut way down on his drinking."[11]

But as fate would have it, as Bunny was trying to control one of the demons in his life, another situation began to develop that would eventually bring him substantial pain, both personally and professionally. His relationship with Lee Wiley had by April of 1936 definitely moved beyond the platonic stage. Clarinetist/saxist Artie Manners, with whom Berigan worked at CBS, later remembered a significant episode: "When Donna was having the baby, Bunny asked me if I would drive him to the hospital. I guess he didn't have a car at the time, so I said OK. On the way there, we had to pass Lee Wiley's apartment. 'Stop the car!' shouted Bunny and no amount of argument from me would make him change his mind. He came out after half an hour and we continued our journey to his wife's bedside."[12] It does not require an extraordinary amount of deductive reasoning to conclude that Bunny's inspiration for his first great recording performance of "I Can't Get Started" (and very likely his second) came from Lee Wiley.

Lee Wiley was at that time a strikingly beautiful woman who, like Bunny Berigan, was twenty-seven years old. Her birth date (October 9, 1908) was approximately one month prior to his. Unlike Donna McArthur, whom Bunny had married when she was only nineteen, Lee Wiley was a sophisticated, alluring woman of the world. She had begun singing with Leo Reisman's band in the late 1920s, and then moved through a succession of other singing engagements, the most notable of which was her association personally and professionally with the composer and conductor Victor Young in the early 1930s. With Young, she appeared on radio, made records, and composed songs, including "Got the South in My Soul" and "Anytime, Any Day, Anywhere." They also had a rather intense affair. After that association, which ended shortly after Young went to Hollywood in 1935, she was regarded within the music profession as a *femme fatale,* and her relationship with Berigan only heightened her reputation in that regard.

Donna was now the mother of a newborn and a four-year-old, somewhat isolated in the Berigan house in Queens,[13] confined to a world of child rearing and trying to provide a home for the Berigan family. Bunny's idealized vision of that world, based on his own upbringing in Fox Lake, is exactly what had impelled him into his marriage with Donna in 1931. But things had changed in the intervening five years. He was no longer just an outstanding trumpet soloist. His career was now in high gear moving forward in a definite direction where his name would be on the labels of the records he made and on the marquees of the venues where he appeared. His days of making other, lesser talents look good were just about over. Bunny Berigan was now on the road to stardom, and as a star, he would not be spending very much time at home with his wife and children.

Lee Wiley was completely comfortable in the world that Berigan now inhabited, which was not the home and family world he grew up in. Donna was not. Lee Wiley was glamorous. Donna, though quite attractive, was not. But Donna was Bunny Berigan's wife, the mother of his children, and Lee Wiley wasn't. Eventually, Bunny found himself in a never-never land between these two women. For the next few years, while Bunny continued his liaison with Wiley, the tensions between him and Donna escalated steadily until there was a rupture in their fragile marital relationship, one that never healed. Donna refused to divorce him because she understandably wanted to retain as much financial security as possible, and the workaholic Bunny had always provided well, often handsomely for her and their daughters. At the same time, even though it appears that Bunny did come to love Lee Wiley, it eventually became obvious to him that their relationship was doomed. He couldn't marry Wiley because he was still married to Donna, and even if he had been able to marry her, it is likely that such a marriage would not have been successful, especially if one considers how unsuccessful the high-maintenance Wiley's later marriage to pianist Jess Stacy was, and how bitter Stacy was about it. Bunny's unrequited love for Lee Wiley undoubtedly triggered many of his melancholy plunges into drunkenness. If "I Can't Get Started" applies to anything in the life of Bunny Berigan, it applies at least in part to his ultimately ill-starred relationship with Lee Wiley. His affair with her effectively ended his marriage, but it never offered him the opportunity for a truly fulfilling relationship with her. The frustration of this situation would eventually weigh heavily upon Bunny, and it would be painfully compounded when the ongoing demands of his work and his continuing estrangement without divorce from Donna prevented him from building much of a relationship with his daughters, whom he dearly loved, as they grew and began to develop their own personalities.

But in the spring of 1936, all of this was in the future. The present was a time of new and exhilarating experiences and opportunities for Bunny. He continued making records as a sideman at ARC/Brunswick/Columbia. Sessions he made at that time included one with pianist Frank Froeba backing vocalists Tempo King and Ted White (April 17, 1936), and with Chick Bullock (May 8, 1936). But now, sprinkled in more frequently, were sessions at ARC that were billed as "Bunny Berigan and His Boys," where Berigan's trumpet artistry was the main feature.

Meanwhile, illness sidelined another member of the Famous Door band, tenor saxophonist Forrest Crawford. He had "a shadow on his lung,"[14] which presumably meant tuberculosis. He left New York in the spring of 1936, returned to his family home in St. Louis, and never again was a part of the New York jazz scene.

The Famous Door closed abruptly in early May. Press reports then stated that four of its creditors had forced the enterprise "into bankruptcy."[15] I am not sure what that actually meant from a legal standpoint, but from the standpoint of the McKenzie band, it meant that they suddenly had no place to work—but not for long. Very shortly thereafter, they moved a bit east on Fifty-second and across the street, to the Club 18, which was on the south side of the street, directly (south) across from "21," the famous restaurant. The Famous Door would soon appear again at a different address on Fifty-second Street, and would be the site of the "birth" (at least as far as swing fans in America were concerned) of the Count Basie[16] band in the summer of 1938.

On May 15, Red Norvo and His Orchestra opened at the Palm Court of the Commodore Hotel. Berigan was in the Norvo band for the opening and perhaps a few more nights, but this association was very brief. It is likely that Bunny was doing Norvo a favor because, according to Stew Pletcher, the other trumpeter in the band, Bunny played only lead for Norvo during this short interlude.[17] When the McKenzie band opened at the Club 18, probably on May 18, Bunny left the Norvo band to rejoin McKenzie.

During this same period, press reports began to appear that Bunny was rehearsing a big band of his own, "under the sponsorship of Arthur Michaud."[18] Arthur Michaud had had a brief association with Benny Goodman, but a much longer relationship with Tommy Dorsey. It is likely that TD introduced Michaud to Berigan in the spring of 1936. After being almost inseparable in the early 1930s in New York's radio and recording studios, Tommy Dorsey and Bunny Berigan had moved apart professionally since mid-1934, largely because of Tommy's work on the road, first with the Dorsey Brothers Orchestra, and later with his own band. The life of any bandleader necessarily required that he travel a great deal, and Tommy had logged a lot of miles on the road with his bands since 1934. But by early 1936, he was finally working for a period of time in New York, at the Commodore Hotel, and he quickly renewed his friendship with Berigan by often stopping at the Famous Door after work at the Commodore. I suspect that TD was frequently involved in conversations with Bunny about the band business in general, and the possibility of Berigan having his own band in particular. This would have led naturally to Arthur Michaud, who was known in the business as someone who could help a musician do the things necessary to organize a big band. It is safe to assume that by this time, regardless of Berigan's association with Rockwell-O'Keefe, Arthur Michaud was representing Bunny as his personal manager.

In its May 1936 issue, *Metronome* reported the following about the new Berigan big band: "The news is out! Bunny Berigan, ace trumpeter, is to have his own band. It's rehearsing now. Many stars enlisted with present line-up, consisting of saxes: Noni Bernardi (1); Artie Drelinger (2); Carl Swift (3); trumpets: Ricci Trattini (1); Irving Goodman (2); Bunny (3); trombones: George Mazza (1); Bud Smith (2); piano: Joe Lippman; bass: Morton Stulmaker; drums: Bill Flanagan. If the above outfit materializes as per schedule, there is going to be much conflict. Red McKenzie's bunch would be split wide open."[19] Although some of the musicians who were a part of this Berigan band were interviewed by the White researchers, and did recall that the band played some jobs, no independent verification of any of those jobs has been found.

Regardless of what Bunny may have been doing with a big band at that time, he definitely was a participant in the now famous Imperial Theatre Swing Concert, which took place on May 23, 1936. The White materials give an extensive review of the entire event, but with respect to Berigan's part in it, the following excerpts are relevant: "Joe Helbock, owner of the Onyx Club, presented a Swing Concert at the Imperial Theatre on 45th Street, west of Broadway, in New York City. Tickets priced $1.00 to $2.50 were on sale at the Onyx Club. The Masters of Ceremonies were Ben Grauer, Paul Douglas and Budd Hulick."[20]

The group Berigan led was the small band he had been working with at the Famous Door, and more recently, at the Club 18. (Artie Shaw was summoned by Bunny on short notice to replace Forrest Crawford. Berigan also tapped his friend from CBS, trombonist Jack Lacey, to augment the group.) They were the seventh group scheduled to appear, and were listed in the program for the event as follows:

Bunny Berrigan and his Swing Gang. (sic) Bunny Berrigan (trumpet) (sic); Forrest Crawford (tenor sax); Joe Bushkin (piano); Eddie Condon (guitar); Marty (sic) Stulmaker (bass) (sic); Sam Weiss (drums) (Courtesy of '18' Club) As was frequently the case, there were some changes in the lineup of talent to be presented before the curtain rose: 'Note that neither the Joe Venuti nor Red Nichols bands appeared. The concert was given high marks for keeping to the stop-watch timing, which was necessary because various bands, e.g. Whiteman's, had Sunday night commercials, hotel engagements or re-broadcasts, etc. *Down Beat's* review of the concert indicated that Chick Webb and Artie Shaw both played with Berigan's group, which was billed as 'from the 18th Club.'

The program moved briskly with only one intermission in the three hour grind. Bands played on stage against the 'On Your Toes' sets, which was the current attraction at the Imperial Theatre. Prices were $2.75 tops, and program receipts came to $925. The gross for everything was $3,200, including $2,300 for ticket sales. All bands, including leaders, were paid union scale, which totaled $1,700! The concert was standing room only, both upstairs and down. Promoter Joe Helbock was to get a certified accounting for disseminating amounts to musicians. He intended giving the profits to the musicians' union, but it's likely that he went into the red.[21]

When the different bands started laying it in the groove, the house pounded with them. Individual honors went to many players. Tommy Dorsey's Clambake Seven was a high spot...Dorsey and Teagarden playing in the Paul Whiteman brass section. Wingy Manone solid on 'Isle of Capri.' The Crosby band, with Bauduc featured, on 'Pagan Love Song.' One of the best and most unusual offerings was Artie Shaw's string ensemble, which opened playing chamber music but clicked with some solid swing. Shaw, with his own group and later with Bunny Berigan, Joe Marsala and Wingy Manone, was tops. Berigan, his trumpet and band, jammed to one of the best hands of the evening. Berigan is generally accepted as the 'white Louis Armstrong.' Armstrong, himself, closed the show with the best trumpet in jazz, he couldn't do enough. Carl Kress and Dick McDonough were featured, as were Casper Reardon and Meade Lux Lewis, Negro pianist from Chicago sponsored by John Hammond.[22]

Bunny Berigan followed with a 7-piece band, including Artie Shaw on clarinet, Chick Webb on drums, Jack Lacey, trombone, Joe Bushkin, piano, Eddie Condon, guitar, and Morty Stulmaker, bass. Berigan also caught a big hand on his fine vocal-and-trumpet version of 'I Can't Get Started.'[23]

Next came Bunny Berigan and his group opening with 'I Can't Get Started' and first I thought this would be impressionistic music for the first three choruses were organized and only Chick Webb's encouragement on drums here gave Bunny the courage to go on, but once in the groove, he got off with some fancy tootin' and even sang a chorus. 'In a Little Spanish Town' gave him a chance to redeem himself with some high-note reachin' and on 'Tiger Rag', Chick Webb stole the bit. I think Bunny is overrated, not because he can't play trumpet, but because he's the most inconsistent performer in the field. He can play marvelously for two or three selections and then get off on a tangent that would have the N.Y. Schools of Music (25 cents per lesson) sending out, circulars.[24]

If Bunny was inconsistent in his trumpet playing, *Down Beat* was inconsistent in its opinions regarding his trumpet playing. (See the blurb below regarding Bunny's playing at the Club 18.) It appeared in the same issue of *Down Beat* as the above criticism, and was written by John Hammond: "The two surprise hits of the evening were those scored by Bunny Berigan and Mildred Bailey-Red Norvo, where musicianship was the primary factor. Bunny's playing is now so close to perfection that even a society audience at the opera would appreciate it and Chick Webb's drumming was a definite stimulus to everybody. Chick's own solo was the flashiest of them all, even though he did actually double up the tempo."[25]

Sam Weiss (not the drummer), who handled the tickets, confirms that the concert was an absolute sell-out. Weiss remembers that composer-arranger Gordon Jenkins sat in the front row with his feet on the rail over the orchestra pit. Excitement ran so high that no one left the theatre until the Casa Loma band had sounded its last big brassy chord. It was two and a half hours after the curtains had gone down in all the other Broadway theatres. The crowd pouring out on dark 45th Street was a harbinger of the college hordes that were soon jamming ballrooms around the country. Despite the attendance, the concert was apparently a financial bust, due to fees demanded by the Musicians' Union for the long-list of performers.[26]

Exciting things were happening at the Club 18 as well. Shortly after Benny Goodman's band returned to New York at the end of May from the tour it had begun in July of 1935, Benny stopped by to visit, with his clarinet in hand: "Benny showed off to best advantage two nights ago, while playing with Bunny Berigan at the Eighteen on 'That's A-Plenty,' driven to it by Eddie Condon's terrific swing and actually made the joint rock. Bunny himself is more consistent and more inspired than at any time in history."[27]

Bunny did another recording date at ARC on June 9, as the leader of "Bunny Berigan and His Boys," once again backing vocalist Chick Bullock. The other sidemen, in addition to his small band regulars from the Club 18, were Don "Slats" Long on clarinet, Jack Lacey on trombone, and Cozy Cole on drums.

Then Berigan returned again to CBS. Although the White materials are somewhat sketchy regarding this development, to me it is not likely that Bunny returned to CBS with the same duties he had had previously, working as a more or less on-call "pool musician." The big difference was that now CBS was launching the weekly *Saturday Night Swing Club* program that at least in the beginning was built around Bunny Berigan.[28] We also know that Lee Wiley was then being featured regularly on CBS. In fact, Bunny and Wiley appeared together on a half-hour CBS broadcast immediately before the inaugural *Swing Club* broadcast, and on several other occasions. The first *SNSC* show featured, in addition to Berigan, Frank Trumbauer, Lee Wiley, Red Norvo, and "swing commentator" Paul Douglas.[29] What Bunny's other duties at CBS were in addition to *SNSC* and his occasional appearances with Lee Wiley, is not clear. But a careful review of Bob Inman's *Swing Era Scrapbook* (see below) seems to indicate that although Bunny could have been a member of one or more of CBS's jazz-oriented bands (with names like: the Dictators, the Merry Makers, the Instrumentalists) that broadcast at irregular times during the week, Inman did not ever identify any such appearance by him. My opinion therefore is that Berigan did not appear with these groups regularly, and possibly not at all.

On June 13 at 8:00 p.m. over station WABC, a new and better swing program went on the air. The program is in the capable hands of Paul Douglas as announcer and commentator and Bunny Berigan with his band augmented by CBS staff musicians.

The plan is to air the best swing musicians who understand it and who have always been its prophets. Therefore, guest artists are invited to sit in. On June 13 it was Red Norvo. On June 20 the guest was Red Nichols and his Five Pennies and again the program clicked. On June 27 the time was given to the Democratic convention, but for the first Saturday in July more good swing and more good swing artists are promised.[30]

Here are the recollections of a number of people who were involved with the *Saturday Night Swing Club,* starting with Phil Cohan, the head of CBS's program department, and producer of the show:

The ingredients of the *Saturday Night Swing Club* included a good house band, couple of good staff arrangers, producers, writers and announcers who are hot fans themselves. Big name guests, two hours of rehearsing, available radio time on a Saturday night. The first shows were not so hot; they needed to have 'balance' i.e.: variety. Rehearsals were not called before 4 p.m. which didn't leave much time to do all things, and not too many hot soloists were in New York City in the summer. Assistant producer Ed Cashman had a lot of radio experience to bring to the show. Hot men were not only willing but eager to play the show for union scale. Frankie Trumbauer flew all the way from Maine to guest. Bob Smith worked on scripts. When Bunny Berigan left, Leith Stevens, a CBS staff conductor, took over.[31]

Lee Wiley, who was very much a part of the New York jazz scene then recalled: "the *Saturday Night Swing Club* show was one I dearly loved. Bunny was playing so great at that time. The orchestra consisted mostly of regular studio men at CBS, with the addition of some famous guests each week. Leith Stevens used to conduct the band and Bunny did the playing. Later on (pianist) Walter Gross took over and Ray Scott played the piano."[32]

Guitarist Frank Worrell had a more detailed recollection:

I started at CBS in late 1932 after working for about a year with Freddy Martin's first band and remained as staff guitarist for about eight years. I guess Bunny came in first around 1934 and returned a couple of years later. He really was without fear and would play anything that came into his head. As a result, he probably hit more clams than any of his contemporaries. If you were to have a meal with him, he would talk very little and usually had to go somewhere right after. We all drank quite a bit and Bunny was no exception, but no worse than the rest of us. But he let it affect his life, indeed it took his life. Sometimes he might be late for a broadcast; sometimes he might not show at all, I vaguely knew about the Lee Wiley affair, but nobody talked about it much. She seemed to be doing very well, but after Bunny she suddenly disappeared back home and out of the limelight. Bunny never prepared a solo, although many guys did, particularly for radio, even writing out little sketches. If Bunny was in any doubt as to a chord in the tune, he'd check the piano part during a 'five' (five minute recess) and when he came to that bar, he would have something ready that was damned nice. One time, Nat Natoli was talking about the days when he and Bunny were playing together with Paul Whiteman. Bunny was making $300 a week, pretty good money for those days, and hating the whole thing. He was always bitching that if he could only get $200 together all at once, he'd leave the damn band and go into business for himself in radio or recording! But he was always in hock to somebody. He owed his paycheck often before he got it! His reputation was pretty bad as far as reliability and maturity went, but from my own experience, you didn't have to be late very often to get that kind of reputation. And let's face it, when he did show up, you had a pretty fair trumpet player![33]

Drummer Johnny Williams was also there, as was bassist Lou Shoobe:

The *Saturday Night Swing Club* program was really an extension of Bunny's Blue Boys. We got a terrific amount of mail for the 'Blue Boys' shows, especially as they were daytime programs. Anyway, Cohan comes up with the idea of expanding them at a better time, with Bunny taking over as leader. We were all pretty excited. Here was a chance for the jazz guys to do something on the air. But Bunny had to screw it up after the first couple of shows. Would you believe he couldn't even walk—in the middle of the afternoon! They had to send out for Leith Stevens to come and take over the orchestra and Bunny didn't stay to finish the show! It was such a shame, because we had real freedom at first on the choice of material, guests, etc. We'd sit down with Bunny and map out our plans for the program. However, despite Bunny's unreliability, the show was more successful than many commercial programs of the period, which surprised the 'powers-that-be,' who had given us Saturday night, which was considered to be a poor night for radio, because everybody went out.

Lou Shoobe:[34] I worked with Bunny on the *Saturday Night Swing Club* program and also many other shows. The guests on that show included just about everybody with any rating in jazz or popular music. Everybody at CBS liked the show, including conductors, musicians and administrators. Freddy Rich, Leith Stevens, Ray Block and others all wanted to conduct the orchestra on that show.[35]

While the *Saturday Night Swing Club* was taking shape, the trade press reported the goings-on at the Club 18 in the wake of his departure from its cozy confines: "Bunny Berigan has left the 18 Club. CBS has asked him to come back and lead a swing unit for them. Bunny and his 14 Little Hares swing out regularly on Saturday evenings for that web. At the club Berigan left behind, Red McKenzie is carrying on with Stew Pletcher on trumpet, Herbie Haymer on tenor, Slats Long on clarinet, plus the original Famous Door rhythm section." "Bunny Berigan has left Club 18, where he played with Red McKenzie, and now has rejoined CBS. On Saturday, June 13, he appeared on WABC's first swing program at 8.00 p.m., leading his own combination and in future he will be a regular feature on this hour."[36]

I must comment about the recollections of the musicians cited above, specifically Frank Worrell and Johnny Williams, who both worked with Bunny at CBS over a period of several years. This observation applies to the recollections of others made many years after the occurrence of a given event as well. It seems to me that peoples' memories often jumble facts after a lengthy period of time separates them from the incidents they are recalling. Memories from 1933 are scrambled with those of 1936, for example, when being recalled in the 1950s, '60s, or later. Also, people very often superimpose on their incomplete remembrances after the fact information to "fill out the story." The result may be an entertaining anecdote, but as history, it is of dubious value, and often outright misleading. I will therefore attempt to balance these anecdotes, as much as possible, with facts from other sources that contain information that was recorded almost contemporaneously with the events under discussion.

I have found *The Swing Era Scrapbook—The Teenage Diaries and Radio Logs of Bob Inman, 1936–1938,* compiled by Ken Vail, Scarecrow Press (2005), to be an absolute treasure trove of information about the New York swing scene during that time. Inman was a high school student who lived near New York City then. He was also a very bright and perceptive young man who had the resources, critically and financially, to seek out and listen to hundreds of live performances by just about every major, and a good many minor bands that played in and around New York in those years. The truly remarkable thing is that he meticulously made and kept notes of these experiences. It is these notes that are now *The Swing Era Scrapbook.* Inman saw Bunny Berigan perform in person on many occasions, and heard him on radio on many more occasions. He met and talked with Berigan and a number of his sidemen, both from the *SNSC* band and, a little later, from Bunny's own band. The details of each such occurrence were recorded shortly thereafter in his diary. *The Swing Era Scrapbook* contains dozens of entries concerning Bunny Berigan. Although I have found a few minor errors in *The Swing Era Scrapbook,* I regard it as a very authoritative source of information about both the swing era and Berigan.

Inman made note of the first *Saturday Night Swing Club* broadcast, but then seemed not to have listened to or made any notes about another *Swing Club* broadcast until August 1, 1936. From that date until February 27, 1937, when Bunny appeared for the last time on *SNSC* as a "regular," Inman attended at least eleven shows within the intimate confines of CBS Studio One, 485 Madison Avenue, and he took detailed notes of these and all the other shows while listening to them over WABC–New York. The first weekly *SNSC* show, on June 13, 1936, aired at 8:30 p.m. The next show aired at 8:00 p.m., and this time continued until October 3, 1936, when it changed to 6:45 p.m. The show was a half hour in length, fast-paced, and packed with music. Frequently, at least ten different selections were played. The CBS band on *SNSC* during this period was conducted by regular CBS conductors, including Leith Stevens, Mark Warnow, Fred Rich, and Johnny Augustine, who alternated in some fashion. From June

13, 1936 to February 27, 1937, there were thirty-one *SNSC* shows, and Bunny Berigan appeared on twenty-eight of them. On one show that he missed (November 7, 1936), he was in Boston working in the musical production *The Show Is On.* (See below.) On December 26, 1936, it was announced that he was ill, and he may have been; but he also worked with Tommy Dorsey's band during Christmas week on one of the few gigs outside of Manhattan that he did with them. On the other date (February 20, 1937), he was on tour with his own new big band. Ultimately, his duties as leader of his band are what took him away from the *Swing Club.* As will be detailed below, Bunny was also extremely busy with other activities during this period. Given these facts, I do not think much credence should be given to anecdotes recalled long after the fact about Berigan's "irresponsibility" during this time.

Although there are reports that Bunny was rehearsing a big band and taking it out for occasional dates near New York City, it does not appear that whatever band he was leading that summer occupied a great deal of his time. He continued to make records at ARC as both a sideman and leader for the remainder of 1936. I suspect that now, he chose the dates he made at ARC more carefully than he had in the past. On June 23, he worked a session as a part of what was billed as "Dick McDonough and His Orchestra," which really was a small group used to back singer Buddy Clark. There is also a possibility that on occasion in the summer of 1936, he worked with Mark Warnow's "Blue Velvet" orchestra, which broadcast over CBS on Thursday evenings at 9:00.[37] My opinion is that if he worked on any CBS shows other than *SNSC,* it would have been infrequently if at all. Bunny's managers were trying to build up his name, and that is best done by carefully managing how and when the name and the talent behind it are used.

One recording session he undoubtedly accepted with alacrity was the one he made at ARC with Billie Holiday,[38] on July 10. Bernie Hanighen, an associate of John Hammond's, and a songwriter who in 1936 was just starting to become known in the profession, like Hammond was enthralled by the singing of Billie Holiday. Holiday had been involved in an extremely productive musical relationship as a featured artist on records with Teddy Wilson for some time. However, she felt, with justification, that she now deserved her own record dates. Hanighen made the necessary arrangements with ARC, and began to gather the musicians. The band supporting Billie was Bunny; Artie Shaw (then putting together his first band, the one built around a string quartet), clarinet; Joe Bushkin, piano; Dick McDonough, guitar; Pete Peterson, bass; and Cozy Cole, drums. Bushkin recalled: "I got involved because Bernie called me and had me come down to his Village pad to rehearse with Billie, and try to put together the four tunes she was gonna do. Bernie put the band together—Bunny and Artie and the other guys he dug."[39] The four tunes recorded that day are classics: "Did I Remember?" "No Regrets," "Summertime," and "Billie's Blues." These records began to sell briskly, and Billie Holiday was thus launched as a recording artist "with her name on the records." I do not think it was coincidental that Billie appeared the next evening on the *SNSC.*

It should also be noted that Cozy Cole then began to work with some frequency as a session man at ARC records. To my knowledge, even though there had on rare special occasions been recording sessions with black and white musicians, there had been little or no real integration (i.e., that a black musician was regularly on call) in the commercial recording studios of New York prior to that. New York's radio studios remained lily white until the early 1940s.

Like almost every trumpet player who worked with Bunny in those years, Manny Weinstock had detailed and colorful recollections of him at CBS:

Bunny Berigan was highly regarded and much respected by all his colleagues for his improvisational and inventive, natural ability, his intriguing stylization and phrasing. His sound, not necessarily classical or schooled, but, paradoxically, perfect for jazz, was big and fat in the low register and powerful up high and I do mean high. For he didn't pop in a very high note now and then just to impress anyone, but if his innovative ideas and advanced configuration of the moment took him up there, he would play up there, interestingly and courageously. He always played with lots of heart, and musicians, especially trumpet players, loved to hear him play, sober or otherwise. Of course, Bunny was capable of late appearances for both rehearsals or recording dates and sometimes produced complete disappearing acts to the discomfiture of producers and musicians alike. Irresponsible for sure, but he wasn't acting the 'Big Man' when he did those things, merely registering an uncontrollable disdain for having to play some of the musical garbage required of studio men in New York. It is difficult to understand Bunny's continued presence in the studios, but he must have needed the bread to get his beloved juice, for he surely ran up an enormous booze bill in the local bars, e.g. Hurley's and Plunkett's. There were many times when he was 'feeling no pain' and hardly capable of precision section playing of the complex commercial arrangements, much to the distress and frustration of the brass section! But Bunny cared little for the whole phenomenon of commercial music. He always wanted free rein, ad-lib solos without inhibitions of any kind. The fact is—we all idolized the man. As his professional peers, we could understand his fearless cavortings on the horn, full of surprises and delightful experiences. Bunny was a most colorful player, worth the risk of possible unreliable behavior to any leader or contractor, for when he laid eight bars on the line, it was there for posterity! I think the remark of Arthur Pryor best demonstrates how some unpredictable, but otherwise excellent players fit into the musical scheme, "Give me a band full of bastards, as long as they are great players. I can't do anything with nice guys if they can't play!' Bunny had a very amusing 'chronic cough,' for which he always carried a small bottle of Dr. Brown's, a euphemism for rye or scotch. Summer posed little problem for Bunny's capacity on the job. He'd pour off two thirds of a bottle of Coke and fill it up with booze, quenching his thirst at frequent intervals, perfectly understandable on a very hot day.

During the mid-1930s, the radio networks would rent old theatres and broken-down beer and urine-smelling catering or banquet halls, because of their surprisingly good acoustic qualities, to say nothing of their cheap rents! They included the Lotus Club, Liederkranz Hall, Webster Hall, Manhattan Center and the old Ritz, Hudson and Hammerstein theatres. In one of them, we were asked to try and get Bunny through the day sober, because they said his job was in jeopardy. So we told him not to leave the bandstand when the rest of us took 'five' and he sat there, right through the rehearsal breaks, reading a book. Yet at air time he was completely smashed! All alcoholics are ingeniously cunning in hiding their booze and Bunny was no exception. He'd arrived very early for rehearsal, removed his suspenders, tied a quart bottle of scotch to them and hoisted it up into a potted palm next to his seat. After we left the studio, he pulled the elastic down and took a good swig before returning the bottle to its hiding-place in the palm. By the time we were ready to go on the air, Bunny was stoned! Despite all that, he was a gentle, docile fellow most of the time - tall, good-looking, blond and friendly, but not gregarious. You would never see him drink 'party-style.' He preferred to stand alone at the end of the bar.

Raymond Scott's tricky, highly disciplined Mickey Mouse type originals with their screwy titles must have been anathema to Bunny, when he was in the morning band at CBS, but he never fussed nor argued unpleasantly about them. He merely groused quietly to the point of dejection and carried on playing and carried on drinking! Of course, the music business evaluation of a successful freelance performer was a guy capable of playing anything from symphony, salon, show, club date, Latin, jazz, Mickey Mouse style, sight reading and transposing; capable of displaying versatility above all else and naturally all this potentially did produce mediocrity in some departments. Well, Bunny lacked some of these qualities and was unhappy about being plagued by all those rigid requirements. He therefore was quite unable to remain in studio work on a long-term basis. Those of us who didn't have his extraordinary talent or inclination to jazz, were prepared for studio work, playing in dance halls, theatres, burlesque, vaudeville, circuses, grill rooms, amusement parks, resort hotels and salons, etc. so that when we finally reached our aspirations to be New York studio musicians (sessioneers) we had little difficulty in coping with the infinite variety of broadcasting and recording demands. The money was good, the hours long and the jobs most prestigious. Obviously, the work was varied and exacting, running the gamut from exhilarating to boring, challenging to depressing and Bunny was present in many of the brass sections, rolling with the punches, sometimes like a fish out of water, at other times, blowing up a storm like nobody else! [40]

On July 20, 1936, Bunny Berigan took a group of musicians into the RCA Victor studios at 155 East Twenty-fourth Street to record twenty tunes[41] for NBC's *Thesaurus* transcription service. Although Bunny would have scarcely suspected it, he would be making a good bit of musical history in these studios in the next couple of years. RCA's files do not contain any information about this session, and the personnel, aside from Berigan himself, remains a mystery. The personnel that has been reported for many years is: Ralph Muzzillo, Harry

Preble, Bunny, trumpets; George Mazza and/or Artie Foster, trombones; Carl Swift, possibly Artie Manners, altos and clarinets; Artie Drelinger, and unknown, tenors and clarinets; Joe Lippman, piano; Morty Stulmaker, bass; Bill Flanagan, drums. The vocalist who sang with the Berigan band at this time has been identified as "Peggy Lawson, a brunette from Indianapolis" by drummer Flanagan.[42] Aside from Berigan's trumpet solos, and he is in fine form here, there is little of distinction about these recordings. Still, the workmanlike arrangements are competently performed, especially when one considers that each of them, like all *Thesaurus* recordings, was made in one take. It is obvious that Bunny had taken considerable pains with the musicians in rehearsal to prepare them for this marathon recording session. He had to have done this because this band was definitely only a part-time operation.

Since all *Thesaurus* transcriptions were identified with some nondescript language like the "Rhythm Makers Orchestra," these recordings did nothing to promote Bunny Berigan as a "name" performer or bandleader in the marketplace. At best, they could have been used by him or his handlers as demos, simply to show that Bunny was capable of preparing a band for a recording session, and leading the musicians at that session to produce acceptable recordings. I find it very interesting to compare these recordings with similar transcriptions made by other bands early in their existence, like those led by Benny Goodman, Tommy Dorsey, Artie Shaw, Charlie Barnet, and others. There is really not much difference in the overall quality of the repertoire, or the performances. Over the years, many critics have disparaged these recordings by Berigan as dull performances, devoid of any spirit or individuality, except for his trumpet solos. While these criticisms are valid, the same could be said for similar recordings made by many other bands that were just beginning to find themselves. And these recordings undoubtedly provided some cash not only for the sidemen, but also for whomever (Bunny? Michaud? Bunny *and* Michaud?) was bearing the cost of keeping this group of musicians together for rehearsals.

Metronome's August 1936 issue reported: "Bunny Berigan is readying himself a permanent swing band. He's been hitting out of late fairly well on CBS with what has always sounded like a bunch composed mostly of house men. But now it is said that Bunny is going to go on NBC with a picked band, a band that he's been rehearsing for quite a while now and which is supposed to have some swell swingers in its midst."[43] (This never materialized.) *Billboard* carried a blurb in its July 25, 1936, issue stating that the Berigan band was being handled by Consolidated Radio Artists. If this is accurate, it probably meant that what few engagements this band played, if any, were booked by CRA. Given Bunny's commitment to CBS and the *SNSC*, and his ongoing work in the New York recording studios, there would have been little time for him to be playing jobs on the road with this band. Saxophonist Murray Williams, who was a member of the Berigan band in late 1938, was a part of this band in the late summer of 1936: "The band of 1936 as I recall was an attempt by Bunny to have a big band. He was still on staff at CBS and doing the *Saturday Night Swing Club*, but wanted his own band. I'm under the impression it played no dates at that time, but was strictly a rehearsal unit. Joe Lippman wrote some arrangements and played piano. I joined Charlie Barnet at the Glen Island Casino and lost contact."[44] As in his personal life, Bunny Berigan was now carrying on a dual existence in his professional life: he was not a full-time studio musician nor was he a full-time bandleader.

It is difficult to fathom what Arthur Michaud had in mind during this period. Clearly, his ultimate goal was to make Bunny Berigan the leader of a full-time, touring band. Whatever Bunny was doing with the band he was then leading part-time may have been simply on-the-job training. And then, maybe Michaud was testing Bunny's resolve, trying to determine how much he wanted to be a bandleader, or, considering his numerous peccadilloes, whether Berigan was in fact bandleader material at all. While Arthur Michaud played *Pygmalion* with Berigan's career, Bunny continued working at CBS, principally on the *Swing Club*, and making records. His "band" such as it was, remained strictly a sideline activity for him.

On July 27, Bunny returned to the RCA Victor studios to make some recordings with bandleader Richard Himber. There have been many reports of Berigan appearing on many Himber records, but this session is likely the only one where his presence is plainly discernable. On August 4, he checked in at ARC to make some records with a small band under the leadership of Dick McDonough. Two instrumentals were made ("Dardanella" [two takes] and "In a Sentimental Mood"); and then two vocals with Buddy Clark singing. This session may have continued past midnight. Berigan took a brief solo and also played a muted obbligato behind Clark's vocal on "Midnight Blue."

On Friday, August 14, Bunny was a part of the Fred Rich band that went to the Paramount Film studios located in Astoria, Queens[45] to record the sound track for a "short." They returned the following Monday to do the filming. The band consisted of musicians who were on staff at CBS. Visible in the band are Jerry Colonna, and I think Jack Lacey on trombones, Babe Russin on tenor sax, and Joe Venuti on violin. The film runs about ten to twelve minutes. Bunny is plainly shown in the band, and plays a solo and sings a tune entitled "Until Today," which is introduced by a display with his name on it misspelled, as so often it was, as *Berrigan*. The other tunes presented are "You Can't Pull the Wool over My Eyes" as an "instrumental novelty," and "Tiger Rag." There appears to have been another tune included, using a female vocal group. (Among the singers featured in this three-girl group called the Blue Flames, was Beverly Freeland, later to become Mrs. Gordon Jenkins.[46] This group also appeared on the *SNSC*.) Recorded and filmed at the same time was a novelty number called "Take My Heart," with Fred Rich playing the piano, Jerry Colonna the trombone, and Bunny his tin whistle. This sequence was used in another short,[47] but unfortunately I have not found any information about that short.

Berigan returned to the ARC studios on August 27, this time as a part of a band led by pianist Frankie Froeba to back the sweet voiced and on-pitch Midge Williams. The lineup of musicians was Bunny; Froeba; Joe Marsala, clarinet; Artie Drelinger, tenor sax; Bobby Bennett, guitar; Artie Shapiro, bass; and Cozy Cole, drums. Berigan evidently used his pull to get Drelinger on this session. Bunny undoubtedly liked him because he was a good section man and sight reader. As a soloist, he left much to be desired however, and his hoarse sound on these recordings is almost painful to listen to. He was a part of Bunny's big band then, such as it was, and would remain so on into 1937. Bunny and Marsala play well. Froeba plays a lot of runs and arpeggios. Artie Shapiro's powerful bass comes through very clearly.

As an aside, the world of swing was evolving in 1936, and as always, younger musicians were present in the wings, waiting for their chance. At about this time, Harry James, then an unknown twenty year-old trumpeter, arrived for the first time in Manhattan as a member of the Ben Pollack band. Singer Carol McKay recalled: "I was with the Ben Pollack band which included Harry James. After we got back to New York City, one night Harry took me to a Fifty-second Street club where Bunny was playing—or sitting in, and James said: 'this is the greatest living trumpet player.' He really loved Bunny's horn."[48]

There were more ARC sessions that September, one on the 17th, with Dick McDonough and Chick Bullock, and another, on the 29th, with Billie Holiday. Both of these sessions feature excellent trumpeting by Berigan. Then Bunny's apparent progression toward becoming the leader of his own big band seemingly veered off course temporarily. This item appeared in the October issue of *Tempo:* "Bunny Berigan, who rocked radio these past three months with music a la jam on the CBS Saturday Night Swing sessions, is taking time out for lessons in make-up and footlights technique. Bunny will head a swing combo in the forthcoming Vincente Minnelli[49] Broadway musical comedy, *The Show Is On,* which will have Beatrice Lillie and Bert Lahr. Gordon Jenkins may direct."[50] Trombonist Sonny Lee, who would soon be joining Bunny's big band, recalled: "We began rehearsals for *The Show Is On* at the Winter Garden Theatre in New York City a couple of months before the Boston opening. Those rehearsals, which were called practically every day, were preceded by much discussion and planning. Gordon Jenkins was the musical director and it was he who rounded up the musicians."[51]

There is speculation in the White materials as to whether Berigan left the *SNSC* during the time of the rehearsals for *The Show Is On.* He did not. There were no *Swing Club* shows broadcast on September 12 and 19, and then again on November 14. On those dates, Bunny obviously was free to do other work. As was noted above, Bunny missed only three *Swing Club* shows from June 13, 1936, to February 27, 1937, and he had valid reasons for each of those absences. One of those absences, the one occurring on November 7, 1936, was because of his appearance in Boston in the production *The Show Is On.* Nevertheless, there was an item in the October issue of *Down Beat* that had him "divorced from the *Saturday Night Swing Club*" in order to participate in *The Show Is On.*[52] Although press reports from the time in question are very valuable in providing details of what was happening then, they are sometimes incorrect.

What actually took place was that while Berigan was very much a part of the New York rehearsal process for *The Show Is On,* and traveled with the cast to Boston for its tryout run, and appeared in the show there for a few nights, the scene in which he was featured was cut from the production. Arranger/conductor Gordon Jenkins explained :

The pit orchestra included Milt Yaner on lead alto, Phil Napoleon on trumpet and Sonny Lee on trombone. We had intended to present the first jazz band in a Broadway show. Vincente Minnelli, the producer, had a giant mirror erected to project Bunny's silhouette on to a large screen while he played. Unfortunately, it failed to work satisfactorily, so it was taken out of the show. The stage band consisted of Bunny with Sonny Lee on trombone, Cozy Cole on drums, Milt Yaner on clarinet and Red McKenzie blue-blowing, but after their speciality number was axed, Bunny, Cozy and Red all went back to New York. I can't recall the tune they were to play, other than it wasn't a jazz standard.[53]

Bunny did return to New York, but not before sitting in with cornetist Bobby Hackett's band at the Theatrical Club in Boston.

Meanwhile back in New York, MCA operatives had been working for some time to get Tommy Dorsey's band on a sponsored network radio show. The break finally came in late October when it was announced that Tommy's band would be appearing on a new show built around the comedian Jack Pearl, sponsored by Raleigh and Kool cigarettes. The Dorsey band was in the middle of an engagement at the Mayfair Casino in Cleveland at the time, but MCA pulled them out of there so they could return to New York. The first Raleigh-Kool show emanated from New York over NBC on November 9, 1936.[54]

Bunny Berigan returned to the *Saturday Night Swing Club* on November 21. How important he was to the ongoing success of the *Swing Club* is reflected in this blurb from *American Music Lover,* December, 1936:

The Saturday Night Swing Sessions on WABC continue to grow and improve. During November the sessions were deprived of Bunny Berigan for two weeks while he was in Boston opening with a new show. In that time one of the sessions was canceled because of the New York auto show. His absence served to whet the appetite of the many swing enthusiasts who look forward to this Saturday night period, so that when he returned on the 21st he was greeted with special enthusiasm. Bunny was in excellent form. On that same program was Lucky Millinder with some of his band including Red Allen, and Will Hudson, who directed two of his own compositions.[55]

That Bunny was not ready to make commercial recordings with his own big band yet is clear from the fact that at his next ARC recording session on November 23, he did not use the band he had been rehearsing, or any musicians from that band, but instead relied on musicians who were proven recording professionals. This session, though billed as by Bunny Berigan and His Orchestra/ Bunny Berigan and His Boys, was actually a small group similar to dozens of other small groups he had been a part of on records for the previous five years. Three tunes were cut that day, two with vocals by Art Gentry ("That Foolish Feeling" and "Where Are You?") and one instrumental ("In a Little Spanish Town," two takes). The personnel were Bunny; Red Jessup, trombone; Toots Mondello, alto sax and clarinet; Babe Russin, tenor sax; Joe Bushkin, piano; Eddie Condon, guitar; Morty Stulmaker, bass; and George Wettling, drums. Everybody plays well on this session, with Bunny being particularly brilliant. Joe Bushkin commented:

> Bunny had roughed out a few arrangements for the date, but when he finally showed up at the studio, he explained that he'd lost the charts and couldn't find them anywhere. He thought that his daughter might have taken them to school! (This is unlikely because his older daughter was only four years old at the time.) So we just had to ad-lib and when things got a bit sticky, we'd throw in a piano solo or some such. Even those places on the records where it sounds arranged, Bunny just explained things like the Duke used to do. He'd say, 'You play this and you play that,' and the guys did the rest.[56]

> Eddie Condon: 'This bum could play the trumpet! Joey Bushkin is on piano here, one of his early efforts. This was when Joe's father had a beauty parlor on 126th Street and Park Avenue. He used to cut my hair when I needed a trim. When Joe started playing around town, his dad tried to talk like Joe to his musician friends, but he always got things backwards. One day he came downtown and I heard him remark, after a good piano chorus, that 'Joe's ass was playing off!'[57]

Starting with the recordings from this session, ARC began to issue Bunny's discs on the higher priced Brunswick label, instead of the budget-priced Vocalion label on which they had appeared previously. This is a sure sign that the name Bunny Berigan, after several months of being "built up," was starting to mean something in the marketplace.

Trumpeter Dave Wade had been called upon to substitute for Bunny on the *Swing Club* on those few occasions when he was not there due to other commitments. "Believing that Bunny's departure from CBS was imminent, I practiced for hours trying to assimilate his style. The record I most worked to copy was 'That Foolish Feeling.' I still think it was one of his greatest solos, although few people remember it now."[58]

One of the "facts" that has been handed down over the last seventy-plus years is that Bunny Berigan was a regular member of Tommy Dorsey's band in late 1936 and into 1937. A careful review of all relevant information in the White materials and elsewhere indicates that this was not really true. He undoubtedly appeared with TD's band on a number of its weekly NBC Raleigh-Kool radio programs which aired on Monday nights, and he most certainly made some records with Tommy's band in January and February of 1937. But at the same time, he continued to appear weekly on the *SNSC*, and was stepping up his commitment to his own big band.

He also sat in for an unknown time, several nights perhaps, with Frank Trumbauer's little band (The Three Ts) at the Hickory House on Fifty-second Street, probably as a favor to Trumbauer, after Jack and Charlie Teagarden, who had been the other two "Ts," had to depart with Paul Whiteman's band to tour. Frank Trumbauer recalled: "Jack and Charlie Teagarden left on January 15, 1937. I was lost without those two. A lot of the boys around town came over to help out. First, Johnny 'Scat' Davis, from Fred Waring's band played a week, and then Bunny Berigan finished the month."[59] Aircheck recordings from a night while Bunny was present with Trumbauer's band do exist and are currently available on Sterling CD 1-15-07. The discographical information with that CD indicates that in fact Johnny Davis sat in for the January 8 broadcast, and Bunny for the January 15 broadcast. On the broadcast where Bunny plays, the announcer does not identify him, but repeatedly mentions the tag "The Three Ts." I'm sure Jack and Charlie were there in spirit!

The first documented appearance by Bunny Berigan with Tommy Dorsey's band occurred on Monday, December 28, 1936, on the NBC Raleigh-Kool show. The exact personnel of the TD band on that date, or on the January 4, 1937, show, is not known. Bunny's presence is obvious from the trumpet solos on those two shows. However, when the Dorsey band recorded on January 7, 1937, for Victor, the personnel was known, and that personnel included three trumpet players, *in addition to Berigan.* Those three were Bob Cusumano (lead), Steve Lipkins, and Joe Bauer. My conclusion from this, and from listening to the recordings made that day, and indeed for the remaining TD-BB 1937 Victors, is that Bunny was present *only to record solos.* He certainly did not play first trumpet on any of the four sides recorded on January 7. His distinctive presence as a lead player in any trumpet section is easily identified, and I do not hear anything in the ensemble playing of this trumpet section that would allow the conclusion that he played lead with them. All available information indicates that Bob Cusumano, a New York studio trumpet player that TD used on occasion, played first trumpet on this recording session. Also, if Bunny was playing any other chair in the trumpet section, then why would Tommy have had *three other* trumpet players on this record date? The Dorsey band then had only three trumpets because the arrangements were written for three trumpets. If Bunny was to have played in the section, TD would certainly have told one of the three other trumpeters to stay home. They all showed up, I think, to play the regular three trumpet parts in Tommy's arrangements. Bunny showed up to play solos. Guitarist Carmen Mastren, who was with the Dorsey band for several years in the late 1930s, and who helped out with arranging, was a member of Tommy's band when these recordings were made. He told Herb Sanford, who wrote a book about the Dorsey brothers in the early 1970s: "The only thing Bunny did on that date (January 29, 1937) was play choruses on 'Marie' and 'Song of India.'" [60] (Note: Steve Lipkins left the Dorsey band immediately after the January 19 recording session and was replaced by Jimmy Welch. After the January 29 Victor session, Andy Ferretti replaced Bob Cusumano on first trumpet. Ferretti was a much respected first trumpet man who would be in and out of TD's band many times over the next three years.)

On January 11, the Dorsey band played Irving Berlin's song "Marie" on the Raleigh-Kool program for the first time. Bunny's solo on it was far less impressive than the one he would record a few weeks later on TD's Victor recording.

On January 15, Tommy's band opened an engagement at the Meadowbrook, a ballroom on the Newark-Pompton Turnpike, in Cedar Grove, New Jersey, about fifteen miles outside of New York, which would last until January 30. I doubt that Bunny would have played many/any nights of that engagement.[61] At that stage of his career, what would he have gained from playing another dance engagement with somebody else's band?[62] However, he *was* with the Dorsey band on their radio show on the 18th, playing a slightly more provocative solo on "Marie." He also appeared on the Raleigh-Kool show on January 25, taking a solo on "Limehouse Blues." And he did appear on the other Raleigh-Kool shows with the Dorsey band during this time, and at their January 19 and January 29 Victor recording sessions. These appearances made sense: he was a radio/recording musician, and a jazz soloist. Tommy used him in precisely that fashion. Others took care of the routine work in the trumpet section.

Notes

[1] White materials: March 19, 1936.
[2] *Variety:* March 18, 1936, cited in the White materials.
[3] White materials: April 3, 1936.
[4] *Ibid.*
[5] In addition to Red McKenzie, there was another singer on this date—Mae Questal. She and McKenzie each cut two sides. Mae Questal, the voice of Betty Boop, Olive Oyl, and Casper, the Friendly Ghost, was a favorite of comedian/film director Woody Allen. She appeared with him in his film *Oedipus Wrecks/New York Stories* (1989).
[6] White materials: April 13, 1936.
[7] *Giants of Jazz:* 38–39.
[8] *Metronome:* June 1936, cited in the White materials: April 13, 1936.
[9] This quote by Bushkin appears in the White materials, April 13, 1936, with no indication of where it came from.

[10] *Downbeat:* May 1936 (article by John Hammond), cited in White materials: May 23, 1936.

[11] White materials: May 24, 1936.

[12] White materials: April 22, 1936.

[13] At some point, Donna's younger sister Maddie came to live with her and Bunny, at least on occasion. She remembered babysitting both Berigan daughters, so these visits would have been after Joyce was born in April of 1936.

[14] White materials: April 23, 1936.

[15] White materials: May 8, 1936.

[16] Pianist William James Basie was born on August 21, 1904, in Red Bank, New Jersey. His early career in touring vaudeville shows brought him into contact with many jazz musicians. By the mid-1920s, he was in Harlem, where he again met many of the leading exponents of jazz, including, most notably, the pianists James P. Johnson, Willie "The Lion" Smith, and Fats Waller. Waller taught him how to play the organ, something he did, occasionally, for the remainder of his career. He joined the band led by Kansas City pianist Bennie Moten in 1929, where he would remain until 1935. The years Basie spent in the Southwest and Kansas City resulted in his being steeped in the blues, and he would retain this orientation for all the years he led his own bands. By 1936, Basie had developed a very economical piano style that provided immeasurable lift for any band he played in and any soloist he backed. He began leading a small band in Kansas City at the Reno Club, which was broadcast over radio. It was at this time that he was dubbed "Count." The producer/critic/impresario John Hammond heard one of Basie's broadcasts, and was so taken by Basie's music that he went to Kansas City to personally scout the band. He was overwhelmed by the group's swing, especially that of tenor saxophonist Lester Young. From that time on, Hammond endlessly promoted the Basie band. Basie's band of the late 1930s and early 1940s was in many ways the quintessence of swing. Basie continued leading a big band until approximately 1950, when he cut down the size of the ensemble for a couple of years. But by 1952, he had reformed a big band and continued to lead it successfully for the rest of his life. Count Basie died on April 26, 1984, in Hollywood, Florida.

[17] White materials: May 15, 1936.

[18] *Down Beat:* May 1936, article by John Hammond, cited in White materials: May 23, 1936.

[19] *Metronome:* May 1936, cited in White materials: May 23, 1936.

[20] White materials: May 24, 1936.

[21] *Variety:* May 27, 1936, cited in the White materials: May 26, 1936.

[22] *Billboard:* May 30, 1936, cited in the White materials: May 30, 1936.

[23] *Tempo:* June 1936, cited in the White materials: May 24, 1936.

[24] *Down Beat:* June 1936, cited in the White materials: May 24, 1936.

[25] *Ibid.*

[26] White materials: May 24, 1936.

[27] *Down Beat:* June 1936, cited in White materials: May 26, 1936.

[28] There is much excellent Berigan playing on the extant recordings made of the *Saturday Night Swing Club* broadcasts on which he appeared. Presumably, all of the shows were recorded. Unfortunately, only a few of those recordings have been issued to date.

[29] *Swing Era Scrapbook:* 25.

[30] *The American Music Lover:* July 1936, cited in the White materials: June 13, 1936. *The American Music Lover* was a monthly periodical published from 1935–1944 in New York City by Peter Hugh Reed. Reed was the editor, and the *AML,* which was subtitled "The Record Conoisseur's Magazine," consisted of record notes and reviews. After August 1944, it was known as *Listener's Record Guide.* Information regarding this publication comes from big band historian Christopher Popa.

[31] *Down Beat:* April 1938, cited in the White materials: June 13, 1936.

[32] White materials: June 13, 1936.

[33] *Ibid.*

[34] Lou Shoobe was a bass player who worked at CBS in the 1930s, and became known to the public as a result of his work as the bassist with the Raymond Scott Quintette. He later became a music contractor at CBS and independently, and as such was responsible for hiring musicians for literally thousands of radio and television shows and recording sessions in New York during a career that extended into the 1960s.

[35] White materials: June 13, 1936.

[36] *Metronome:* July 1936, and *Tempo:* July 1936; both cited in White materials: June 13, 1936.

[37] White materials: June 24, 1936; See also *Swing Era Scrapbook:* 37.

[38] Born Eleanora Fagan Gough, on April 7, 1915, in Philadelphia, Pennsylvania, as Billie Holiday, she was one of the most individual of jazz singers. Her early childhood was spent in poverty in Baltimore. As she grew into womanhood, she became strikingly beautiful, and was assaulted sexually probably on more than one occasion. She and her mother moved to Harlem in the late 1920s, and for a time she worked there as a prostitute to earn enough money for her mother and her to survive. After being jailed for this, she turned to singing for tips in various Harlem speakeasys. It was in one of these that she was discovered by John Hammond, who arranged for her to make her first recordings in 1933. Shortly after, in 1935, she began a lengthy and successful association on records with the pianist Teddy Wilson. These recordings reveal the fully formed Holiday style: a very relaxed, almost elastic rhythmic approach, gentle improvisation, and great intimacy. On these sessions as backup performers were some of the finest jazz musicians of the time. She worked in Count Basie's band in 1937–1938, and then spent the balance of 1938 in Artie Shaw's band. Since she had her own recording contract, she could not make records with either Basie or Shaw. After leaving Shaw, she embarked on a career as a soloist which would continue, with varying degrees of success, for the next two decades. Because of the harrowing experiences of her early life, Holiday sought refuge in drugs, starting in the 1940s, and later, alcohol. This caused her much personal and professional pain. She died on July 17, 1959, in Manhattan from cirrhosis of the liver.

[39] Mosaic Berigan Set, page 17.

[40] White materials: July 18, 1936.

[41] The titles Berigan recorded on July 20, 1936 for *Thesaurus* are: "Take My Word," "Rendezvous With a Dream," "On a Cocoanut Island," "On the Brach at Bali-Bali," "But Definitely!," "Sing, Sing, Sing," "I'm an Old Cowhand," "Empty Saddles," "On Your Toes," "Did I Remember?," "San Francisco," "I Can't Escape from You," "I Can't Pull a Rabbit Out of My Hat," "When I'm with You," "Dardanella," "When Did You Leave

Heaven?," "You're Not the Kind," "You've Got to Eat Your Spinach, Baby," "Sweet Misery of Love," and "That's a Plenty."
[42] White materials: July 20, 1936.
[43] White materials: late July 1936.
[44] White materials: September 8, 1936.
[45] The Paramount Studios at 34-12 Thirty-sixth Street, Astoria, Queens, opened in 1920. For the next twenty years, over 120 silent and sound feature films were produced there. In addition, this studio was the home of the famed Paramount Newsreels ("the eyes and ears of the world"), as well as Paramount's short-film division. This studio continues operation to this day at the Kaufman Astoria Studios New York Production Center.
[46] Arranger/composer/pianist Gordon Hill Jenkins was born on May 12, 1910, in Webster Groves, Missouri. A child prodigy who could play several instruments well, Jenkins began his professional career in Missouri by playing numerous instruments in bars and roadhouses for tips. He also was presented, playing piano, organ, accordion, ukulele, and banjo, over St. Louis radio station KMOX while still in his midteens. In 1928 he joined the Joe Gill band in St. Louis, playing residencies at the Chase Hotel there. It was during this time that he began to learn how to arrange. Jenkins joined the Isham Jones band in St. Louis in early 1932. Although Jenkins worked with the Jones band until its leader retired in 1936, he increasingly worked as a freelance arranger during this time, and also began to write songs. His hauntingly lovely "Goodbye" was recorded by Benny Goodman in 1935 (with Bunny Berigan on trumpet), and was used by Goodman for the next fifty years as his closing theme. In 1938, Jenkins moved to Hollywood, where he continued to have much success as an arranger and conductor. Like most other musicians of his age, Jenkins found less and less work as the 1960s moved into the 1970s. He died in Malibu, California, on May 1, 1984, a victim of amyotrophic lateral sclerosis (Lou Gehrig's disease).
[47] White materials: August 14, 1936.
[48] White materials: September 16, 1936.
[49] Vincente Minnelli (1903–1986) later became famous as a director of Hollywood musical films, and husband of Judy Garland. They are the parents of entertainer Liza Minnelli.
[50] White materials: October 17, 1936.
[51] *Ibid.*
[52] White materials: October 31, 1936.
[53] This quote from Gordon Jenkins appears in the White materials: November 7, 1936, with no citation of its source.
[54] White materials: November 9, 1936.
[55] White materials: November 20, 1936.
[56] White materials: November 23, 1936.
[57] *Ibid.*
[58] *Ibid.*
[59] White materials: January 14, 1937, citing the Trumbauer biography *Tram,* by Philip R. Evans and Larry F. Kinder, wth William Trumbauer, Scarecrow Press (1994).
[60] *Tommy and Jimmy: The Dorsey Years,* by Herb Sanford, Arlington House (1972), 63. Herb Sanford was the director-producer of the Raleigh-Kool radio show on NBC radio, on which Tommy Dorsey's band was featured in 1937–1939.

[61] We know for sure that he was broadcasting with Frank Trumbauer from the Hickory House on January 15. (See text.)

[62] Moreover, the next name band scheduled to appear at the Meadowbrook was Bunny Berigan's. I am quite sure that Arthur Michaud/Rockwell-O'Keefe would not have allowed Bunny to have appeared at the Meadowbrook as a sideman with Tommy Dorsey immediately before he appeared there as the leader of his own band. That would have undercut his value in that venue as the leader of his own band.

Chapter 13
Big Band Berigan

We must remember that during this interval, Bunny Berigan was completing the final preparations for the debut of his own full-time big band, and CBS was preparing for his final departure from the *Saturday Night Swing Club*, which was by this time a recognized success that would remain on the air into 1939. During the day he was finishing the selection of musicians, commissioning arrangements, rehearsing, and generally setting up the organization that is necessary to support a standing big band. The new Berigan band was scheduled to open at the Meadowbrook on February 3, following Tommy Dorsey.

On January 22, he finally took his own big band into the ARC studios for its first recording session. Four sides were made: "The Goona Goo," "Who's Afraid of Love?" and, "One in a Million," each with a vocal by Art Gentry, and a rollicking instrumental, "Blue Lou," which contains a titanic solo by Bunny. The personnel for that date were: Harry Greenwald, Harry Brown, Berigan, trumpets; Walter Burleson, trombone; Carl Swift, lead alto; Matty Matlock, alto and clarinet; Art Drelinger, tenor; Les Burness, piano; Tommy Morgan(elli), guitar; Arnold Fishkind, bass; Manny Berger, drums. A girl singer, Louise Wallace, was added to the band for the Meadowbrook gig. She possibly had sung with Frank Dailey's band at the Meadowbrook, and would return to that job after her service to Bunny.[1] Trombonist Walter Burleson provided a recollection of that first Berigan big band recording session:

> I'd only been in New York a couple of weeks, finding it hard to get a job but after much skimping, scraping and existing on ten cent hamburgers, I got a break auditioning for Bunny Berigan at the new Haven studios on Fifty-fourth Street. Apparently, I was the 12th trombonist to try out, so imagine my surprise when I got a call later from Mort Davis, Bunny's manager, to report to the Brunswick studios for a recording date! It was a bitterly cold day and I was hungry, but this was my first taste of the big time. The date lasted about five hours and I was the sole trombone in the brass section. Matty Matlock was the clarinet soloist but the rest of the band members were unknowns like me. We had a special arrangement of a tune called 'One in a Million' and after rehearsing for about a half-hour, the recording director discovered it was the wrong 'One in a Million'! So Bunny got somebody to rush out and buy a stock arrangement of the right song, which he doctored up with a new introduction and such.[2]

Trumpeter Harry Brown also recalled that time:

Bunny held auditions for his new band in New York, followed by rehearsals and a couple of one night stands in New England for the Schribman brothers.[3] We had a recording date while Bunny was still working for Tommy Dorsey off and on. They were good friends and their occasional feuds were usually patched up pretty quickly. Bunny had the greatest talent as a player, but not as a leader. When he laid off the booze, he was moody, but after a few belts, his spirits would soon rise again. It wasn't a good band, but it was a happy one and that was the way Bunny liked it. We followed Tommy Dorsey into the Meadowbrook for a couple of weeks and neither the public nor the critics seemed to like us, but I enjoyed being in the band and learned a hell of a lot from Bunny, who was a happy-go-lucky guy as a rule and a marvelous musician. He loved life, travel, women and liquor. He never cared too much about money and always seemed to be broke.[4]

At nights, before the new Berigan band opened at the Meadowbrook, Bunny was probably either working with Frank Trumbauer at the Hickory House, or sitting in elsewhere to relax a bit. On Saturdays, he was still rehearsing for and playing on the *Swing Club* program on CBS; on Mondays, he was broadcasting with Tommy Dorsey's band on the Raleigh-Kool program on NBC. He also participated as a soloist at three Victor recording sessions with TD's band in January: on the 7th, 19th, and 29th. As usual, Bunny Berigan was a very busy man in January of 1937.

Berigan's solo on Dorsey's January 7 recording of "Mr. Ghost Goes to Town," a then current pop tune composed by Will Hudson, was excellent. His solos on "Song of India" and "Marie," both recorded on January 29, were superb. "Marie" became a very substantial hit, and since it was paired with "Song of India" on the original issue Victor record, it also carried that piece along to enduring popularity. Both of these arrangements remained in the repertoire of the Dorsey band until Tommy's death in 1956, and indeed are still played by any band that reprises the music of Tommy Dorsey. Richard M. Sudhalter analyzed Bunny's solo on "Marie."

> After the vocal chorus, the band members in unison shout Mama! Then Berigan steps forward with two notes, a clarion F-to-high-F…that sends him vaulting into his top register and instantly changes key, mood, intensity level, depth and rhythm. …His solo here, pursued at a remarkably consistent level of inventiveness and execution, is more than a piece of jazz improvisation. With its daring reaches into the topmost range of the horn, its imaginative, bold figures (like the triplets in bars 13–16 that plunge more than an octave down and straight up again), its heraldic, Armstrong-inspired *bel canto* statements (such as the last eight bars, beginning on a high concert E-flat), it is a composition, a paraphrase and a development of the original.[5]

After Berigan's death, TD had Bunny's solo transcribed and harmonized for four trumpets, and whenever his band would play "Marie," which was nightly, the entire trumpet section would rise and play Bunny's famous chorus.

The Berigan band followed Tommy Dorsey into the Meadowbrook, opening there on Wednesday, February 3. It was a gala event: "Bunny's Meadowbrook opening was attended by many of his friends and many trade representatives. Congratulatory wires were received from many notables in the music business, including Martin Block, Ray Block, Joe Higgins, Glen Gray and the Casa Loma Orchestra, Tommy Dorsey and His Orchestra, Benny Goodman, Ray Noble, Jerry and Flo Colonna, Dave Harris, Johnny and Esther Williams, Edythe Wright, Cork O'Keefe and many others."[6] The appearance of the name Cork O'Keefe in this list is significant. It indicates that by this time, Bunny's band was definitely being booked by Rockwell-O'Keefe.

Lead alto saxophonist Carl Swift also recalled the early days of the Berigan big band, including the Meadowbrook opening:

> There were a lot of important people there and, of course, the ever-present song pluggers. Bunny didn't know how to deal with them, so he just had another drink and didn't! I recall seeing Artie Shaw at the opening. Although I later played pretty good clarinet and fair tenor, with Bunny I played strictly alto sax and I was very unhappy with my lead sax playing on the band's first record date, particularly on 'Blue Lou.' So I insisted that Bunny get someone else for the next recording date. Hymie Shertzer played on the date, but didn't work with the band at the Meadowbrook, where I continued to play lead alto. (Note: I have listened to this recording of "Blue Lou" very critically, and can find no fault with the playing of Carl Swift on it.) I don't remember whether we used a guitar on the recording dates. The band sounded pretty bad and the press reviews reflected that, but there were changes in the brass section almost every night and that sure didn't help! I'd first come to New York from Boston in 1932 and played with Red Nichols and Jerry Blaine prior to joining Bunny. After the job at the Meadowbrook the band more or less fell apart. There was little or no work and Bunny didn't seem to have the necessary backing to keep the band together. While we played the Meadowbrook, Bunny and I used to go to the local pool hall nearby. He was an extra-fine pool player.[7]

The band did broadcast from the Meadowbrook over WOR–New York on Friday, February 5, from 10:00 to 10:30 p.m. The next day, Bunny rehearsed for and played on the *Swing Club* broadcast from 6:45 to 7:15 p.m., then rushed from CBS's Studio One on Madison Avenue across Manhattan and the Hudson River to join his band at the Meadowbrook. They were again on the air over WOR from 11:00 to 11:30 that night. He repeated this sequence on Saturday, February 13. Throughout the Meadowbrook engagement, the Berigan band broadcast frequently. Unfortunately, no airchecks from those broadcasts are known to exist. Their two-week stand there ended on February 17.

Critical reaction to the new Berigan band was almost unanimously negative. Here is a survey of reviews of the Berigan band's engagement at the Meadowbrook:

From *Down Beat*, March 1937:

(Headline) Shaw's Ork Follows Bunny Berigan's Outfit: 'When Artie Shaw moved into the Meadowbrook the other night, he supplanted Bunny Berigan and his newly-formed organization. This proved to be a real break, not only because Artie Shaw's music is both good and unusual (too seldom do those adjectives come together) but also because listening to Berigan's band proved almost embarrassing. Bunny is probably the greatest white trumpeter in the business today, but when he gathers about him a group of musicians who are so utterly incapable of even approaching their leader's ability, something should be done about it. Matty Matlock, the fine clarinetist formerly with Bob Crosby's band, played with Bunny's band during their engagement at the New Jersey roadhouse, but the task of swinging the rest of the men was a little too gigantic for even these two stars to undertake.[8]

From *Tempo,* March 1937:

Bunny Berigan made his debut as a full-fledged batoneer this past month by playing a two weeks engagement at the Meadowbrook. His band was composed (we use the past tense because, at this writing, an almost complete change is taking place in the orchestra) of twelve unknown instrumentalists and distinguished itself only by its leader's contributions plus Matty Matlock's clarinet work. Matlock joined as a favor and since has returned to the Bob Crosby unit. The band, however, did make one recording session, which should give you an idea of how things were running. Artie Shaw followed Berigan into the Meadowbrook for a fortnight of syncopation. From *American Music Lover* 'Swing Notes,' March, 1937: In addition to his activities with the *Saturday Night Swing Club,* Bunny Berigan has found time to assemble an orchestra of his own. On February 3rd he and his new band opened at the Meadowbrook, Cedar Grove, New Jersey and the band proved to be an instant success. It followed Tommy Dorsey and it filled the spot excellently. A band of ten players with a vocalist their playing was surprisingly homogeneous for a group that had played together less than two weeks. Of course there were rough spots here and there on opening night which could have been attributed to poor acoustics, lack of rehearsals, conflicting styles of playing, etc., but these were, on the whole, minor defects. The band played with a terrific swing and the crowd which turned out to greet the band enjoyed the music.[9]

From George T. Simon in *Metronome,* March 1937:

Roasts and Toasts: Possibly he's been spoiling us by his consistently great trumpeting and so when he takes on his own band, we expect something on as high a plane. Whatever it is, it's quite obvious that the band Bunny Berigan aired recently from the Meadowbrook is not really a fine outfit. For some reason, neither the brass nor the reed sections get together at all. The subsequent pushing and pulling make everything sound mighty rough. The really saving graces, though, were Bunny's playing and Matty Matlock's clarineting. The rest can be tossed into a corner.[10] (It appears that Simon's review was based on his listening to the Berigan band on radio.)

There is some confusion about when the Berigan band closed at the Meadowbrook. I think it was on Tuesday, February 16. Other sources have it on

Wednesday, the 17th. To sort this out a bit, we must isolate the facts we are sure of: (1) The Berigan band recorded on the 17th for ARC; (2) Hymie Schertzer, then playing first alto saxophone for Benny Goodman, was on that record date with the Berigan band; (3) The Goodman band was then playing at the Hotel Pennsylvania in New York in the evening. They broadcast that evening over WABC–New York; (4) Bunny also was present at Tommy Dorsey's Victor recording session on the 17th, and that session took place from 9:00 to 12:30 (We don't know if this was in the morning or the evening.); and (5) Tommy Dorsey's band was working at the Commodore Hotel in New York in the evening. In light of what we know actually happened on Wednesday, February 17, I have concluded that the Berigan band's last night at the Meadowbrook was Tuesday, February 16. From February 3rd to the 16th encompassed exactly two weeks. I think it would have been physically impossible, (even for Bunny) to have (1) worked with Tommy Dorsey's band on a Victor recording session from 9:00 a.m. to 12:30 p.m.; then (2) led his own band through a four-tune recording session at ARC in the afternoon of that same day; and then (3) traveled with his band to the Meadowbrook in New Jersey, and played a four-hour gig that evening. Since the Dorsey band was working at the Commodore Hotel in the evening, I must conclude that they recorded in the morning of February 17. Since Bunny's band probably did not have an engagement on the evening of the 17th, it is likely that he rested a bit in the afternoon, then started recording with his own band later in the day of the 17th. Bunny likely paid Benny Goodman to release Hymie Schertzer for the evening, and get a sub in the Goodman sax section, because Benny's band was then working at the Pennsylvania Hotel. I do think that Goodman may have done this favor for Bunny under the circumstances. It is days like this that truly give one a deeper understanding of why Bunny Berigan drank.

The interesting thing about the Berigan band's recording session of February 17 is that it gives us the opportunity to judge for ourselves how good or bad they sounded at the Meadowbrook. Since no recordings of those broadcasts are known to exist, I cannot express an opinion as to how the band actually sounded at the Meadowbrook.[11] I have however listened carefully to all of the sides Bunny's band recorded on February 17, and I have concluded that the Berigan band that played at the Meadowbrook was probably pretty good. On this recording session, they played the arrangements with accuracy, unity, and spirit. Bunny's playing was excellent, indeed inspired. The recordings are certainly acceptable. The arrangements, though competently written, are not in any way distinctive, (with the exception of "Dixieland Shuffle," see below), but the band cannot be faulted for that. The band's solo strength, aside from Bunny of course, and clarinetist Matty Matlock, was not what it should have been, therefore there was not enough variety in its presentation. But, it was a brand-new band that was trying to evolve some sort of group identity. Unfortunately (and quite unrealistically) the critics expected Bunny to start with a fully mature, distinctive band, and unfairly criticized him for not presenting such a band at the Meadowbrook. Still, there are valid criticisms to be made. They are: (1) that whoever was booking the Berigan band (probably Rockwell-O'Keefe) should have taken it out of the greater New York area for at least a couple of weeks to break-in. Then the band could have had a little time to play together in front of relatively less critical audiences, accumulate at least a couple dozen good arrangements, and gain some *esprit de corps*. (2) There should have been at least a couple of other musicians in the band capable of playing jazz solos to lessen the load on Bunny in that area. (3) More effort should have been exerted to have several special arrangements in the band's book that not only provided Bunny a showcase, but that also allowed the band to shine a bit. To have dealt with each of these criticisms would have cost someone some money, and I'm sure that is why these things were not done. Plus, Bunny apparently was still tied to the *Swing Club*, and that factor alone would have made much travel impossible.

"Dixieland Shuffle" is precisely the kind of music that would have appealed to Bunny, and brought out the best in his playing. He undoubtedly had heard King Oliver's record of the tune it was based on, "Riverside Blues," featuring Louis Armstrong, as a boy. Sudhalter attributed the arrangement Berigan played to Matty Matlock,[12] and this might seem to be reasonable since Matlock, who was a very capable arranger, was then in Bunny's band. However, this tune, which is ascribed to Gil Rodin and Bob Haggart, in almost the same arrangement, had been recorded by Bob Crosby's band on April 13, 1936. Brian Rust's discography attributes the arrangement used for that recording to Bob Haggart.[13] Since Haggart excelled at reorchestrating recordings that had been made previously (often by Louis Armstrong) for the Crosby band, I am of the opinion that he did indeed write this arrangement. Regardless of who wrote it, it was a good piece of music, and the band plays it well. There were two takes made. Upon issuance of the record in May, it received a positive review in *Down Beat*.

Despite the generally poor critical reaction to the Berigan band at the Meadowbrook, Bunny's management team was still behind him, pushing hard. Right after they closed at the Meadowbrook, the Berigan band auditioned for a sponsored radio program. *Billboard* carried this item in its February 27, 1937, issue: "Admiracion Shampoo auditioned Bunny Berigan and his Orchestra, and Tim (Ryan) and Irene (Noblette) for a coast-to-coast Mutual set-up last week."[14] At about this same time, Rockwell-O'Keefe, which was definitely Bunny's booking agent by then, was angling to get his band a job making transcriptions for a series of shows to be sponsored by the Norge appliance company. Here is some of the trade paper buzz about that project:

Norge Refrigerators is readying a series of transcriptions to be used this spring and summer for an extensive spot campaign. Bands and guest stars are being used for each 15 minute recording, with each recording using a different aggregation. The deal is being set through the Cramer-Kraselt Co., Milwaukee." (*Variety:* February 19, 1937.)

The Cramer-Kraselt Company, Milwaukee, has started cutting the 39 quarter-hour discs for Norge Refrigerators. The campaign will run 39 weeks, starting April 1st. Talent is booked for the series through the Rockwell-O'Keefe agency and includes Ray Noble, Annette Hanshaw, Barry McKinney, The Mills Brothers, 'Aunt Jemima,' Louis Armstrong, Victor Young, Connie Boswell, Josephine Tumminia, Cliff Edwards and Tim and Irene." (*Billboard*: February 24, 1937.)

"Norge Sets Wax Name Campaign: ' The biggest name splash by the transcription route in a long time by an advertiser is the series just closed for the Norge refrigerator company. The ad agency is Cramer-Kraselt, with Rockwell O'Keefe setting the talent. Included among the names to do spots are Annette Hanshaw, Barry McKinney, Ray Noble and his Orchestra, Victor Young and his Orchestra, 'Aunt Jemima' (Tess Gardella), Louis Armstrong, Cliff Edwards, The Mills Brothers, Josephine Tumminia, Connie Boswell, Tim Ryan and Irene Noblette. Decca is grinding the platters which will run for 39 weeks, quarter hours weekly. (*Variety:* February 27, 1937)[15]

It would appear from the above that the Bunny Berigan band, Frances Faye and the comedy duo of Howard and Shelton were probably added to the parade of talent for the Norge transcription series after the above items went to press. Two of the very few Norge programs discovered feature the Berigan band. It is likely that others from the series may be extant in view of the number of shows recorded.

Immediately after the February 17 recording session, the Berigan band began to play a few one-night dance jobs in New England, and this kept Bunny away from New York for the *Saturday Night Swing Club* broadcast of February 20. He returned to Manhattan however for the *Swing Club* show that aired on February 27. This was his last appearance on the *Swing Club* as a regular.

Shortly thereafter, Bunny learned that his band had been chosen for both the Admiracion Shampoo radio show, and the Norge transcription series. He was scheduled to do his first and possibly second of the Norge shows almost immediately. The first session Bunny recorded for Norge (program #5) was probably done on March 7, as an entry in trombonist Larry Altpeter's diary indicates that he worked with Berigan on that date "from 12:30 to 2:30."[16] On this fifteen minute program, Bunny was introduced with a few bars of his theme song. Alice Faye, who by then had already become a film star, was also on the program. (She had started her rise to stardom by singing with Rudy Vallee's band on *The Fleischmann Hour* from 1932–1934, so she was definitely an experienced singer.) She belted out three songs, and the Berigan band played two instrumentals: "Stompin' at the Savoy" and "There's a Small Hotel." The band performs acceptably at a brisk tempo on "Stompin' at the Savoy," though the sometimes busy arrangement was far from distinguished (or swinging) and the drummer, presumably Mannie Berger, sounds rather stiff at times. In this arrangement are several bars of fairly complicated writing for the saxophone section which I'm sure took some time to rehearse. The chart also includes brief solos by a clarinetist, either Frank Langone or Don "Slats" Long, and a tenor saxophonist who sounds very much like young Georgie Auld.[17] Bunny's open trumpet solo is sweepingly authoritative. Incidentally, Berigan handles the inane patter with the announcer immediately after "Stompin' at the Savoy" very well. "There's a Small Hotel" was taken at a slower tempo. It contains a solo clarinet in the opening bars with Bunny playing an eight-bar melodic solo later on using a straight mute. The arrangement is again off-the-shelf middle-1930s dance music, except for another quite involved passage for the four saxophones.

The second appearance Berigan made in this series of transcriptions was identified as "program # 37." There were a total of thirty-nine programs in the series. It is unclear when this program was recorded. It is likely that it was recorded at the same time as the one described above. The ambient sound on both shows is identical, and the band itself sounds the same. Once again, Bunny was introduced with a few bars of his theme song, and then the announcer comments that Berigan is "modestly referred to by musicians as the greatest living trumpet player." Appearing with the Berigan band on this program were comedians Howard and Shelton who did a skit that resembled Abbott and Costello's *Who's on First?* (Since this was March of 1937, I don't know who borrowed from whom.) The band sounds a little more relaxed on "Organ Grinder's Swing." The solos are by Berigan, Georgie Auld, and probably Joe Lippman on piano. One can detect traces in this arrangement, which I would say was written by Joe Lippman, of the ensemble sound of the Berigan band that would soon develop. Vocalist Carol McKay sang "You Turned the Tables on Me," and generally did a good job of it despite the rather fast tempo. Bunny's trumpet lead is quite noticeable in this performance. He emerges from the ensemble only briefly with some high note bursts. There is no conversation on this show between Bunny and the show's announcers.[18]

The confining format of these shows allowed very little opportunity for Berigan's musicians to be presented in anything like a relaxed setting, so it is difficult to judge the merits of the band at this early phase of its development.. Nevertheless, they seemed to have done what was required of them quite acceptably. Bunny undoubtedly realized that if he was going to be a successful bandleader, he and his band would have to be versatile enough to fit into a wide variety of entertainment situations, something he himself had been doing for years.

Listening to these programs gives one an insight into what daytime radio programming in the 1930s was like. The advertising techniques used on them are certainly quaint by today's standards. These shows were obviously directed at housewives (*Miss Mary Moderne*) who were at home during the day attending to the tasks of housekeeping and child rearing. Presumably the discs that contained these transcribed shows were sold or leased to radio stations across the country to be programmed as each local station's broadcast schedule would permit. Indirectly, they were also a small part of the promotional buildup of Bunny Berigan that was now under way.

Variety reported, in its March 10, 1937, issue: "*Fun in Swingtime*, sponsored by Admiracion Shampoo, opens on WOR, April 4 (Sunday), to go over the full

Mutual network. There will be a special guest of swing music each week. Tim and Irene, who subbed for Jack Benny on the Jello show last summer, Del Sharbutt, special commentator, and Bunny Berigan and his Orchestra are set for the show. Admiracion is manufactured by the National Oil Company."[19] The immediate results of this development was Berigan's departure from the *Saturday Night Swing Club*, and the reorganization of his band. With some cashflow now assured, Bunny finally got the green light from Rockwell-O'Keefe and Michaud to seek out better musicians whom he could now afford to pay. Bunny Berigan had finally become a full-time bandleader leading a full-time band.

At this juncture, circumstances conspired to give Bunny a number of opportunities to acquire better musicians for his band. First, after following Bunny's band into the Meadowbrook and completing its two weeks there, Artie Shaw's string quartet band broke up for lack of work. This occurred on approximately March 1. Bunny's band manager, the astute and experienced Mort Davis, who had worked previously with Benny Goodman, made it his business to know about the comings and goings of dance band musicians. He knew of Shaw's plight and undoubtedly contacted several musicians who had worked with Shaw, and told them that Bunny now had some steady work on radio lined up. Two very important additions to the Berigan band resulted: the veteran drummer George Wettling,[20] and the pianist and arranger Joe Lippman.[21] From the beginning, it was understood that Lippman would be the band's primary arranger. Second, Bunny was now in a position to benefit from Tommy Dorsey's temper tantrums. Lead trumpeter Steve Lipkins, who'd had a run-in with TD recently, jumped at the opportunity to join the Berigan band. The veteran saxist Clyde Rounds, also disenchanted with TD, left at about the same time to join Berigan. Others who joined in early March were Cliff Natalie (Nat Natoli's younger brother), trumpet; Frankie D'Annolfo, trombone; Slats Long and Hank Freeman on altos/clarinets. Tenor saxophonist Georgie Auld and vocalist Carol McKay had probably joined Bunny immediately before the Norge shows were recorded.

By March 15, the revamped Berigan band began playing some dance engagements within about a 200 mile radius of New York City to break in.[22] Singer Carol McKay recalled this transitional period:

> I had a few lessons on classical piano. I was with Ben Pollack and we did a record date (September, 1936) before leaving for the West Coast. I left Pollack later and came back east with Harry James and another trumpeter around the Christmas holidays, joining Bunny in late February or early March 1937. The band was doing mostly one-nighters. Jimmy Van Heusen, the song-writer, who wasn't yet very well known, was a good friend of Bunny's. I think they'd known each other back in Wisconsin. Anyway, Jimmy told me, 'This is the band for you,' which impressed me, so I joined. Arrangers included Joe Lippman, (and a little later) Abe Osser, Fred Norman and Dick Rose. Soon after I joined we auditioned for that shampoo radio show. 'The Goona Goo' was one of Bunny's favorite numbers and the band played it a lot. I recall Joe Bushkin being on piano for a bit at the Pennsylvania Hotel while Joe Lippman was busy with arranging. I don't remember Bunny ever warming up; he'd just come out and play! Arthur

Michaud and Mort Davis were both around the band, but Michaud was roundly disliked by almost everybody! Bunny hardly ever rehearsed the trumpets, but the saxes were always being worked on and he never seemed happy with them. I remember one rehearsal when I left to go shopping as it wasn't time for my songs, and when I got back a couple of hours later, they still hadn't gotten to my numbers! Bunny was very definite about what he wanted soundwise. He and Joe Lippman worked closely together on most numbers and got along well. Bunny would make quite a few suggestions about how the brass was to be written for. He would say, 'This is real good,' or 'Keep this in here,' etc. He loved ballads and folk tunes and he'd say, 'Well, let's go get 'em!' when the band was going to play a fast tune like 'King Porter Stomp.' I remember we did a date, maybe a radio show, for a soda water commercial. Bunny really joked about that! We also attempted a movie short when everyone in the band showed up, everyone except Bunny, that is! It was canceled, of course.[23]

At about this time, it was announced that Bunny had also secured a recording contract with RCA Victor Records. Berigan, like Benny Goodman and Tommy Dorsey, would produce recordings for RCA's prestigious Victor label, which then sold for seventy-five cents a disc. The thinking at Victor in the mid-1930s was that the music of swing/jazz bands appealed basically to affluent young college students, a niche market. These were the people who made up the largest part of the audiences that showed up at venues like the Pennsylvania Hotel, where Goodman had been such a hit, and the Commodore Hotel, where TD's band had been so well received. If these students had the money to buy a phonograph and go to those upscale venues for entertainment, Victor's marketing department reasoned, then they could certainly afford seventy-five cents a record. The incredible series of jazz recordings Lionel Hampton[24] produced with various ad hoc groupings of musicians for RCA Victor, starting in February of 1937, were all issued on the Victor label. However, the ongoing strong sales of upstart Decca's thirty-five cent discs would, by mid-1938, change the thinking of Victor's decision makers on this issue. The success of Decca's entire catalog, including such swing bands as Jimmy Dorsey, Casa Loma, and Count Basie, persuaded the people at Victor, by mid-1938, to offer the records of their stable of new swing bands to a wider market at a lower price. Thus, the bands RCA signed in 1938, including Les Brown, Van Alexander, Erskine Hawkins, Artie Shaw, and Glenn Miller, would have their recordings issued on RCA's thirty-five cent Bluebird label. The first major beneficiary of this change in direction would be Artie Shaw, whose recording of "Begin the Beguine," released in the late summer of 1938, rapidly became the most successful record RCA had issued in years. Soon thereafter, Glenn Miller's record sales on Bluebird took a vertical leap with a number of hits, most notably "In the Mood," which was released in the summer of 1939. While all of these changes were taking place, RCA would continue, inexplicably, to issue the recordings of Bunny Berigan's swing band on the Victor label, where their sales were steady, but hardly spectacular.

But all of these developments lay in the future. For the present, Berigan was elated to have a recording contract with Victor, widely regarded at that time as "the Cadillac of record labels."[25] As if to celebrate, Berigan joined with friends and kindred spirits in a "Jam Session at Victor," which occurred on March 31 in the RCA Victor studios on 24th Street. With him there were: Fats Waller, piano; Tommy Dorsey, trombone; Dick McDonough, guitar; and George Wettling, drums. The two takes that resulted, an exuberant performance of Waller's "Honeysuckle Rose," and a moving "Blues," have been a part of the classic jazz landscape ever since. George Wettling provided some background:

> It was supposed to be a four-side date with little planned, just the instrumentation. Tommy and Bunny weren't on speaking terms at that time. They'd had a row over something or other, but that didn't stop them talking to each other with their horns! (Note: Tommy was undoubtedly unhappy about some of his former sidemen going to the Berigan band.) Bunny and I came along to the studio together, the others by themselves. Everybody was feeling fairly high, as I remember. Berigan had a pint in each pocket and doubtless Fats, as usual, had his. We just went in there and cut loose! We never did get more than two numbers finished. On one of the takes, we just went on and on. Nobody wanted to stop. It was too long to use though. When it was all over, we all took off on our separate ways. Just like that.[26]

March of 1937 had been a very good month for Bunny Berigan.

On April 1, 1937, the Berigan band gathered at RCA Victor's recording studio 2 at 2:30 p.m. Their first recording session there, supervised by Leonard Joy, lasted for four hours. The band consisted of Steve Lipkins, Cliff Natalie, Berigan, trumpets; Ford Leary, Frankie D'Annolfo, trombones; Hank Freeman, first alto and clarinet; Slats Long, alto and jazz clarinet; Georgie Auld, jazz tenor; Clyde Rounds, tenor and baritone, saxophones; Joe Lippman, piano; Tommy Morgan, guitar; Arnold Fishkind, bass; George Wettling, drums; and Carol McKay, vocals. Four masters were made that day and they reveal a very well-prepared band. The arrangements were on a par with most of what Tommy Dorsey's band was then playing in terms of quality. They were not stylized to any great degree, but were well written with numerous changes of instrumental color. Bunny is in fine form. His impassioned high register playing on "Carelessly" is superb. (For whatever reason, the people at Victor did not issue this recording until twenty-three years later, when it appeared in an LP collection of his Victor work entitled *Bunny*, RCA Camden CAL-550 (1960). Vocalist Carol McKay sang well on two sides: "You Can't Run Away from Love Tonight" and "Carelessly." Bunny sang the lighthearted lyric to "'Cause My Baby Says It's So," and trombonist Ford Leary, who specialized in novelties and rhythm numbers in the manner of Tony Pastor and Butch Stone, did the vocal on the novelty "All Dark People Are Light on Their Feet," the lyric to which in the Jim Crow America of the late 1930s was regarded as inoffensive. This last title showcases the seventeen-year-old Georgie Auld on tenor sax. The lad obviously had excellent command of his horn, a good sound, nimble fingers, and a lot to learn about playing jazz, especially rhythmically. He would mature greatly as a jazz soloist during his stay in the Berigan band. There is considerable variety and charm in these performances. It was an auspicious beginning.

Now well launched, the Berigan band, under the management of Arthur Michaud, hit the road for a bit more seasoning. There may well have been a problem at this time that began the process of moving Bunny's booking agent representation from Rockwell-O'Keefe to MCA. It seems that Rockwell could not place the Berigan band on Victor Records (they had a tie-in with Decca), and this clearly was an essential part of the plan devised by Bunny's personal management team of Michaud and John Gluskin, with additional input from Tommy Dorsey. After Bunny's management team secured a Victor Records contract for him without Rockwell, the move from Rockwell-O'Keefe to MCA was clearly under way. CBS Artists handled the few one-night stands the Berigan band was able to play whenever its Manhattan broadcast schedule would permit.[27]

Bunny played a series of dates in New England, including back-to-back battles of music at Boston's Roseland State Ballroom. On April 9, they battled the even-newer Artie Shaw New Music band, which was nothing more than a band with conventional swing band instrumentation, as opposed to Artie's earlier string quartet band. The consensus opinion is that Bunny and his boys overwhelmed Artie's band that night, in spite of a heroic effort by Shaw himself. The next night, they battled Andy Kirk's crew, and again did very well. The following night, they once again bested the Shaw band, this time at Reade's Casino in Asbury Park, New Jersey. Carol McKay recalled that event: "My folks came out to listen to the band that night. They lived only 50 miles away and everybody agreed that we outplayed Shaw's crew. We all went out to dinner to celebrate and though Bunny was having car trouble, he was in a very benevolent mood and said that beating Shaw was a step in the right direction for the band. Bunny would never allow me to sit on the bandstand like most vocalists, because he felt it cheapened the singer and took away the element of surprise when he would announce, 'And now, the lovely Carol McKay!' He also said he didn't want guys talking to the singer during the gig, trying to get a dance or a date."[28]

Bunny's band was featured at an RCA Victor employee dance in Camden, New Jersey, at around this same time. The purpose of this was to generate some goodwill among the folks at Victor, who, working constantly with recording bands, were probably pretty good judges of dance music.

On Sunday April 18, the band debuted on the Admiracion Shampoo radio show, which had been named *Fun in Swingtime*. The half-hour show aired at 6:30 p.m., emanating from WOR–New York over the Mutual network.

Sunday, 6:30–7 p.m. (EDST) Style—comedy and music. Sponsor—National Oil Products Co. Agency—Charles Dallas Reach Inc. Station—WOR (MBS network): Tim Ryan and Irene Noblette still haven't hit the comedy heights that have been expected of them for some time. When they first came east from the coast, the team showed definitely it had the stuff. Since then, though on sustaining and commercial programs, the expected socks have failed to materialize.

Even Miss Noblette's delivery is bound to bring Gracie Allen comparisons, though that still is no barrier to the pair being funny. The only barrier to that is the same old cry: material. Proving again that comedians, for radio, must have funny stuff to say or they ain't funny. Then too, there's another factor on this show that's important. It's that Sunday night is the big comedy night of the radio week, with all but one or two of the air's top comics on some time during the day or evening. The musical end is well held up by Bunny Berrigan *(sic)*, his top trumpet and his band. It's Berrigan's first real radio break and he doesn't let matters get by. The commercials are satisfactorily managed.[29]

Del Sharbutt, the announcer on the show, recalled other details:

> I was the announcer on the Tim and Irene radio shows that featured the Bunny Berigan band. We used to rehearse on the day of the show. The band would arrive a couple of hours before the others and run through their numbers. Then the rest of the cast would arrive for a run-through, followed by a dress rehearsal to get the timings right. Then we'd get a break until airtime. The band would usually get two or three tunes and the rest would be comedy dialogue with Tim and Irene singing one number. Bunny had an occasional speaking part, but it wasn't really his scene and he was not very good and neither were the scripts. Tim and Irene wrote most of their material and it was pretty sad. Neither they nor the sponsors had any money to splash out on writers like those on the Fred Allen or Jack Benny or Bob Hope shows. Tim had once gone to Fred Allen in desperation to get some ideas for the show, but Allen spent the entire afternoon telling him many stories about his family, but nary a gag to be heard. But as he was leaving, Allen gave Tim a packet of stuff he'd written for the show! After the broadcast, the whole cast had to return three hours later and do it all over again for transmission to the West coast, because of the different time zones. This was common practice for all coast-to-coast broadcasts as everything was done live.
>
> Bunny was a hell of a musician, like a very talented child, but he wasn't a strong bandleader, not really cut out for it. His drinking was starting to get really bad—not that he was drunk on the job—he just had to have it to function at all. The sign of a true alcoholic I guess. The regular (Berigan) band played on the show. There was no augmenting with studio musicians as they were working on a very tight budget. There were very few guest artists as far as I remember. I suppose Tim and Irene were being promoted as competition for Burns and Allen, but they were not nearly good enough.[30]

"In fact, the Tim and Irene show was heard on the West coast at 3:30 p.m. which was a direct feed of the New York 6:30 p.m. broadcast, and heard in Chicago at 5:30 p.m. (Del Sharbutt was probably thinking of another show on which he was MC.) The writer for *Fun in Swingtime* was Hal Kanter and the program was broadcast from the New Amsterdam Roof in New York City, which WOR used as a studio. Tim and Irene had been working in comedy for several years, having broadcast as early as January 1935 (fifteen minute spots over WJZ). Later they appeared in a program sponsored by Goodrich Tires with the B.A. Rolfe Orchestra. Much later, in the 1960s, Irene gained far more fame as Granny in *The Beverly Hillbillies* TV series."[31]

Meanwhile, Bunny continued to move men in and out of his band in an attempt to get the sound he wanted out of each section. Early on, he was particularly critical of the saxophones, especially the first alto players. Carl Swift was temporarily replaced for a recording session by Hymie Schertzer, but then he (Swift) stayed on while Bunny waited for the *Fun in Swingtime* show to materialize. Then Hank Freeman replaced Swift. Shortly after the Berigan band battled the Artie Shaw band, Bunny and Freeman came to a mutual parting of the ways, and Hank moved over to Artie's band, playing third alto. (Artie's protégé Les Robinson had the lead alto job sewed up in that band.) Bunny then brought Sid Perlmutter in on first alto. The other alto chair passed from Slats Long to Frank Langone to Joe Dixon, whom Bunny had wanted all along because he was also an excellent jazz clarinetist. The game of musical chairs would continue for a time, in the best tradition of Tommy Dorsey, who was notorious for tinkering with the personnel of his bands.

In April, the trade papers announced that the Berigan band would follow Benny Goodman's into the Madhattan Room of Hotel Pennsylvania,[32] opening there on April 29. Bunny appeared at the Madhattan Room on the night of the 28th, as was the custom, so that Benny could introduce him to the patrons. Trombonist Jesse Ralph was subbing in the Goodman band that night and remembered the incident vividly: "I was subbing for Red Ballard in the Benny Goodman band at the Pennsylvania Hotel, when Bunny came in on closing night (28th). Benny introduced him to the crowd, and although Bunny was drunk to the ears, Benny insisted that he come on the stand and play! Harry James lent Bunny his horn and he made a horrible showing. I think Benny got some sort of kick out of it."[33] It was yet another ignominious experience for Bunny involving Benny Goodman.

The Berigan band opened the next night to generally good reviews and good business. "Bunny Berigan is doing well at the Madhattan Room of the Pennsylvania Hotel. He and his band will be downstairs until June 1 and then will go up on the Roof, with the grill closing for summer. The Roof is really better, since the low ceiling downstairs allows occasional suggestions of blasting. There is almost a constant double audience, dancers and those who pause to watch the band as they dance by."[34]

The band also began broadcasting regularly from the Madhattan Room over WABC–New York, which was the flagship station of the CBS radio network. Some recordings from these broadcasts are known to exist, but I am unaware of any commercial issuance of them. They were professionally recorded initially on acetate discs by the Harry Smith Recording Service. Based on the information in the White materials, there are more than enough of these recordings to make up several full eighty-minute CDs.[35] There are also some recordings of the band's featured tunes from the *Fun in Swingtime* radio series, but these appear to be far less numerous.[36]

The Berigan band's second Victor recording session took place on May 13. Once again, the music they made that day compared quite favorably with recorded performances of other top bands that had been on the scene much longer. Bunny was very efficient in the studio that day. He recorded the requisite four commercial tunes, one with a vocal by Ford Leary, "The First Time I Saw You," and three by Sue Mitchell, who was subbing on short notice for the ailing Carol McKay. Mitchell, whose real name was Susan D'Amico, had to struggle with the arrangements, because they were new to her, and because they were not in keys that fit her vocal range. Bunny patiently facilitated her three vocals, which when released by Victor caused quite a stir because people thought she was black. The three tunes Sue Mitchell recorded were "Love Is a Merry-Go-Round," "The Image of You," and "I'm Happy, Darling, Dancing with You." Possibly to give Bunny some approval and reinforce his confidence, Leonard Joy, who was supervising that session, and by all accounts was well liked and much respected by musicians, allowed Bunny to also record a special arrangement he had commissioned from Larry Clinton on the old Stephen Foster tune "Swanee River." Bunny and his band gave "Swanee River" a spirited performance. It soon became a staple of the Berigan repertoire. This recording session ran from 1:00 to 6:00 p.m.

I have not heard the Madhattan Room or *Fun in Swingtime* aircheck recordings of the Berigan band, but would like to for many reasons. I cannot imagine that the performances would differ greatly from those captured at around this same time in the Victor recording studios, or a bit later, on the aircheck of the Berigan band (playing "Am I Blue?") from the Pennsylvania Roof on June 12, on the first anniversary broadcast of the *Saturday Night Swing Club*, or the next night on the *Magic Key of RCA* broadcast (playing a bit of the theme, then "You Can't Run Away from Love Tonight" and "Swanee River.") I have listened carefully to these recordings and I cannot discern anything in them that is subpar. Nevertheless, at about this same time the following write-up appeared in *Metronome*, most likely penned by George T. Simon:

Bunny Berigan is doing his damndest at the Madhattan Room of the Hotel Pennsylvania, but he who follows Goodman follows flat. Bunny gets off with consistently beautiful trumpeting, but a thoroughly ragged band and the unlyrical Carol McKay's vocals make the show a bit of a flop. The theme, 'I Can't Get Started,' is slow persuasive swing that sounds like Bunny used a lot of the Goodman solid block phrasing; 'Star Dust' shows Bunny taking a swing chorus with inspirational backing from the saxes. Carol McKay sings a whole second chorus in a near monotone, thereby ruining Hoagy Carmichael's lovely strains. The first chorus of 'It's Swell of You' is very swell of you, Bunny Berigan; the dixieland offering, 'Mr Ghost Goes to Town,' got a little sloppy, with Bunny lifting it in the third chorus. The band gives the impression of uncertainty. There are moments of some well-built rhythm, a good, relaxed piano, but drum breaks are better omitted. Leave 'em to Gene Krupa or Dave Tough right now. The Berigan band as yet lacks integral color and personality, but they provided some high spots and hit some okay danceable swing tempos.[37]

Simon had written a similarly critical review of the Berigan band that had appeared in February at the Meadowbrook. Commercial recordings made at the same time conflict with that review. Simon would go on in the next few years to write numerous generally negative reviews of the Berigan band. I do not know if there was any history between Berigan and Simon, but I think it is safe to say that George T. Simon was not terribly enamored of Bunny's various bands, and probably did not like Bunny himself, though he did tepidly acknowledge Berigan's prowess as a jazz trumpeter. Simon's tastes ran in the direction of the old Ben Poilack band, and those who had been in it were later his favored subjects. He adored the Bob Crosby band (which was the remnants of Pollack's band), was unstinting in his praise for Benny Goodman's bands, and worshipped Glenn Miller, even though Miller had some differences with him, and on more than one occasion put him in his place. His idea of a thrilling trumpet player was Charlie Spivak.[38] The point I want to make here is that I do not consider George T. Simon's criticisms of the Berigan band to be of great value because they almost always seem to be distinctly at odds with the many contemporaneous performances by that band that have been preserved either on commercial recordings or airchecks. Also, his critical appraisals were often colored by his personal relationships and/or his personal musical preferences. I will acknowledge, however, that Simon did write one fair appraisal of the Berigan band, undoubtedly derived from a visit to the Pennsylvania Roof while the band was there in June of 1937. That review appeared in the July 1937 issue of *Metronome*. Most of his other critiques, however, were almost certainly derived from what he was able to glean from listening to the band over radio.

Whether the reviews of his band had any influence on Berigan is not known. I doubt that Bunny needed any help from the trade papers to judge whether personnel changes in his band were necessary. Nevertheless, personnel changes continued. Bunny was still not satisfied with his first alto, was looking for better jazz soloists on trombone and alto/clarinet, and a singer with more "charm."

It is also noteworthy that while the band was at the Pennsylvania Hotel, probably in early June, Bunny had a series of publicity stills made at the photographic studio of "Bruno of Hollywood" in New York. He was photographed in many poses at this session (at least a dozen), wearing a beige double-breasted suit with a striped tie. The photos from this session have been used hundreds of times since they were taken, in almost every article about or recording of Bunny Berigan. I think that this photo session occurred very soon after Berigan left Rockwell-O'Keefe to go to MCA.[39] (See below.) MCA used these photos on promotional materials for Bunny until he died. Indeed, these photos have been used continuously since they were made, in most articles, recording liner notes, and books that refer to Bunny Berigan. In only two of the photos from this shoot was Berigan shown smiling. The original smiling pictures show his dead tooth. They were later retouched to reveal a perfect smile. Bunny was very self-conscious about the unsightly appearance of his teeth, and forbade MCA to use any photos of him that revealed his teeth, unless they were retouched.

At about the time the band moved from the Madhattan Room to the Pennsylvania Roof, Bunny finally snagged alto saxophonist/clarinetist Joe Dixon, who recalled: "I joined Bunny at the Pennsylvania Hotel replacing Frank Langone. I first worked with Bunny on a Chick Bullock recording session, which I subbed on. I jammed with him many times on Fifty-second Street, at the Famous Door and other spots. My first records were with Bill Staffon's band which included Joe Lippman, Max Smith and Frank Crolene, all of whom worked with Bunny later. In May 1935, I worked at the Tap Room, Adrian Rollini's spot in NYC, then Tommy Dorsey hired me. TD was not an easy man to work for, and I left him to join Gus Arnheim briefly. (Stan Kenton was on that band.) Bunny then induced me to join his new band. TD wanted me to rejoin him and when I joined Bunny instead, Tommy never spoke to me again."[40]

For what it's worth, Tommy Dorsey had secured the services of clarinetist Johnny Mince by the time Joe Dixon joined the Berigan band. In light of the fact that Mince quickly became a TD favorite, and remained Tommy's featured clarinetist for the next four years, I doubt that TD would have been seeking Joe Dixon's services after Mince was in his band. This is no criticism of Joe's playing however. He was a fine clarinetist and alto saxophonist whose playing with the Berigan band was always quite acceptable.

Very soon, Joe Dixon realized, probably after discussing this issue with Berigan, that he needed to make some adjustments in order to fit into the Berigan band: "I had to change mouthpieces on clarinet to play in this band. Bunny's idea of a clarinet player was to get out there and wail and scream while the brass went doo-wah, doo-wah. You had to pierce through all that like a piccolo in a marching band, otherwise you wouldn't be heard. I had to use a very open mouthpiece to get that kind of sound—and you can hear it on the solos I recorded with Bunny's band."[41]

Bunny replaced trombonist Ford Leary with the veteran jazz trombonist Thomas Ball "Sonny" Lee (1904–1975). Four years older than Berigan, he, along with George Wettling, was one of the few veteran musicians in the band. By 1937, he had been a professional for fifteen years. He had worked with Bix Beiderbecke, Frank Trumbauer, Pee Wee Russell, then moved into the commercial dance bands of Gene Goldkette, Red Nichols, Cass Hagen, Roger Wolf Kahn, and Isham Jones. In 1936, he became a New York freelance working, among other places, at CBS. He was an absolutely first-rate first chair trombonist in addition to being an excellent jazz improviser. Bunny's concerns over his trombone section leader and jazz soloist were now at an end. Sonny Lee later recalled how he came to join the Berigan band:

Bunny had first talked to me about playing in his band when we both worked at CBS and it was more or less agreed that I would join when he'd gotten sufficient commercial deals going, with money guaranteed, so he could pay me a decent salary. Eventually, I got a call from his manager, guaranteeing me at least $100 a week. In all the time I was with the band I never drew less than $150 a week. From the minute I came on the band, I played both lead and all the jazz solos as

Morey (Samel) had only slight ability as a 'ride' man, so the book was written accordingly. Cliff Natalie was on the band very briefly when I joined, but then Irv Goodman came in. Joe Dixon joined at almost the same time. He replaced Frank Langone, who went over to Jan Savitt. Bunny gave definite instructions as to what he wanted on ensembles, but never on solos. On 'The Lady From Fifth Avenue' he used a cup mute reversed and did a 'flutter-tongue' growl on his solo, which really impressed the other trumpeters in the band. The band worked harder than any other band I was with, and Bunny worked harder than any other leader I ever knew, even when he was ill. Sy Devore made the clothes for the Berigan band as well as Bunny's own suits. He always favored a light brown, double-breasted style. We each had three sets of uniforms tailored by Devore, who was just getting started in men's fashions then. He became very big later in Hollywood. I think he may also have made the Jimmy Dorsey band's uniforms.[42] (After leaving Berigan, Lee spent many years in Jimmy Dorsey's band.)

As Sonny Lee remembered, there were a few other changes in the personnel of the Berigan band at the time. Benny Goodman's trumpet-playing kid brother Irving replaced Cliff Natalie, who had been in the band more or less on an interim basis. The second trombone chair also changed, with journeyman Morey Samel coming in, replacing Frankie D'Annolfo.

Bunny also replaced singer Carol McKay (she would soon marry Benny and Irving Goodman's brother Freddy) with a musicianly singer named Ruth Bradley. "My background included working with several all-girl bands such as Ina Ray Hutton's in which I played sax and clarinet. I was 22 when I joined Bunny at the Pennsylvania Roof. I had been working with Ruby Newman in the Rainbow Room when I heard that Bunny was auditioning singers and went down between shows. It was my biggest break to-date. I never met Sue Mitchell, or Gail Reese who replaced me, and I stayed with the band until the end of the Pavilion Royal date. I didn't really want to leave, but the band was going on the road and I wanted no part of that."[43]

By the time the Berigan band returned to the Victor studios for their next recording date on June 18, Bunny had almost completed the process of building his band. That process had stretched over a six-month period, and had involved about two dozen musicians. Bunny had been very particular about the composition of his band. The personnel now consisted of Steve Lipkins, first trumpet, Irving Goodman, Berigan, trumpets; (Bunny would very frequently play lead to "pick up" a part of an arrangement); Sonny Lee, first and jazz trombone; Morey Samel, trombone; Sid Perlmutter, first alto saxophone; Joe Dixon, alto sax and jazz clarinet; Georgie Auld, jazz tenor saxophone; Clyde Rounds, tenor and baritone sax; Joe Lippman, piano and arranger; Tommy Morgan, guitar; Arnold Fishkind, bass; George Wettling, drums; and Ruth Bradley, vocals. The primary arranger was Joe Lippman; however arrangements were also beginning to be commissioned from Abe Osser and a few others.

The first tune recorded on June 18 was "All God's Chillun Got Rhythm."[44] The arrangement, by Joe Lippman, is his first truly distinctive work for the Berigan band. The eight-bar intro is very ingenious: the trombones and Wettling's tom-toms set up a low pedal point over which three clarinets come on wailing. Then the trumpets come in, low and growly. The reeds and brass then mass for a burst of sound out of which George Wettling's tom-toms finish this dramatic opening sequence. From there on, the band romps on into the first chorus. Lippman reprises the sonorities of the intro on the modulation leading into Ruth Bradley's vocal chorus. This girl could sing *and swing.* She sang on pitch, had a good beat and excellent voice quality. After her vocal, Steve Lipkins demonstrates that he learned a great deal from Berigan in the previous couple of months. He plays the eight-bar upward modulation on his ringing open trumpet in a way that undoubtedly had Bunny smiling. Then the maestro and Joe Dixon take brief but pungent solos as the band swings the performance to a close. This recording clearly demonstrates that as a performing unit, the Berigan band had arrived. They were now capable of doing full justice to a good jazz arrangement.

Two then current pop tunes filled out this recording session: "The Lady from Fifth Avenue" and "Let's Have Another Cigarette," both with good vocals by Ruth Bradley.

No one was more favorably impressed by Berigan's trumpet artistry than fellow trumpeter Irving Goodman.

> Steve (Lipkins) and I would sit there in the back row, night after night, set after set and watch and listen to Bunny and be totally amazed at what he could and would do. I think most jazz musicians could appreciate Bunny's improvisations and many of the things he did, but I think you have to be another trumpet player to really, totally, understand and appreciate what Bunny was able to do on the trumpet. Oh, Bunny had his off nights and on occasion he was less than inspired, but even then his playing was far above many of us. Steve was a fine lead player; I was a less than average soloist. But night after night Steve and I would look at each other often with a nod or a raised eyebrow, etc. in acknowledgment of what we'd just heard Bunny do. Playing the trumpet is damn hard work and Bunny would often make it seem so easy! But Steve and I knew how hard it was. Bunny, being able to drink as he did and still play, was even more amazing to us. Sonny Lee in our band had played with many of the greats including Bix. He told Steve and me on a number of occasions how great Bunny really was. I know Muggsy (Spanier) told Ralph Muzzillo, another very fine lead trumpet player, how much he admired Bunny's playing. We all did![45]

The Berigan band was again in the Victor studios on June 25. Joe Lippman was by now very busy writing arrangements for them, and Joe Bushkin frequently subbed for him on piano during the band's stay at the Pennsylvania Roof so that Lippman could devote more time to writing arrangements. In addition, Bunny began ordering more arrangements from Dick Rose and possibly Fred Norman, who played trombone in the Claude Hopkins band. Four sides were recorded on June 25, two evanescent pop tune vocals ("Roses in December" and "Mother Goose"), and two instrumentals: "Frankie and Johnnie"[46] (three takes) and "Mahogany Hall Stomp" (one take). Both of these were probably arranged by Dick Rose, though it is possible that Van Alexander arranged

"Mahogany Hall Stomp." These last two titles also quickly became a part of the Berigan canon, and were frequently played by the band. Bunny's recordings of them began to sell in greater numbers than most of the pop tunes the band recorded.

Although Bunny had been making personnel changes for the previous six months and had greatly strengthened his band as a result, he was still not completely satisfied. His fixation on the first alto sax chair resulted in yet another change there. Sid Perlmutter, who undoubtedly was a fine musician, but a bit too stiff in his phrasing to please Bunny, was replaced by yet another veteran dance band musician, the rotund Robert "Mike" Doty. Doty (1910–?) was one of the leading first alto players then on the big band scene. He had worked with Gene Kardos, Joe Haymes, Phil Harris, Ray Noble, and Tommy Dorsey before joining Berigan.

Bunny also replaced the young but extremely capable bassist Arnold Fishkind with another veteran, the powerful and dynamic Hank Wayland (1906–?). Like Mike Doty and Sonny Lee, Wayland had worked with many top bands (including Benny Goodman's before Benny hired his bass-playing brother Harry) and was much respected by his peers. The second trombone chair was also changed with Morey Samel giving way to Al George. At about this same time, Mort Davis was replaced as road manager by saxophonist Jack Stacy's brother George Stacy.

It appears that the band's day off at the Penn was Sunday, so on Sundays throughout the band's residency there, after they finished the *Fun in Swingtime* radio show at 7:00 p.m., they hurried to whatever one-nighters Rockwell-O'Keefe (or MCA?) could book for them within a one-hour drive from New York.

It is strange that the White materials do not contain any information about one of the most momentous changes that occurred during this time involving the Berigan band—its move from Rockwell-O'Keefe to Music Corporation of America. There is no doubt that MCA was the biggest and strongest band-booking agency in the country then, by far. Why had MCA so suddenly taken over booking the Berigan band in the middle of Bunny's "buildup"? The only information I have found on this development is in Bob Inman's *Swing Era Scrapbook*. The reference there is under the date Wednesday, June 23, 1937. After Inman and his buddies had visited the New York office of MCA to get pictures of Peg La Centra and Edythe Wright (adolescent boys!), they "...then walked down to Rockefeller Center where we met Vincent Prior at Rockwell-O'Keefe. He certainly is a swell guy. When I asked why Rockwell-O'Keefe had dropped managing Bunny Berigan's new band, he told us that the band was always 'getting drunk' so they let MCA take over the band."[47] How magnanimous of Rockwell-O'Keefe to unload this bunch of drunkards on poor, unsuspecting MCA!

I am rather dubious about the reason for this change given by Vincent Prior. While Bunny's drinking was a fact beyond dispute, and while it is likely that

Rockwell-O'Keefe probably told him from the beginning that he would have to control it to be a successful bandleader, drinking by bandleaders or indeed by entire bands in the swing era was hardly unusual. One of Rockwell-O'Keefe's most successful bands, Casa Loma, was one of the boozingest bands in the business, and one of the most profitable. (The Casa Loma band practically lived on the road.) Also, there is no evidence of Bunny's drinking (or that of his band) creating any problems for the Rockwell office during the time they were client and agency. My speculation on this development focuses instead on the relationships of Benny Goodman and Tommy Dorsey, especially Dorsey's, with MCA. I have no hard evidence of this, but I suspect that BG and TD, by then MCA's biggest swing stars, realized that if the Berigan band were also with MCA, it would benefit them in that MCA could use the Berigan band as a substitute for their bands when the need arose, and not disappoint promoters who had contracted for a hot swing band. Shortly after Bunny went to MCA, this item appeared in *Tempo:*

> Tommy Dorsey and Benny Goodman helped Bunny Berigan, heard on Mutual's *Fun in Swingtime* program. 'I'd still be putting out hot licks on an old beat-up trumpet if it weren't for them,' said Bunny, who was playing his trumpet in a hot five at a Fifty-second Street restaurant before they persuaded him to try for a sponsored radio show. 'Goodman persuaded me to take a crack at radio. I did, and I clicked.' Then he got a band together, borrowed some of Tommy Dorsey's arrangements and began to play outside engagements, principally at colleges. Soon after, he signed for the present Tim and Irene commercial. 'Benny's interest in me continued,' said Bunny, 'even though I began to be a serious competitor. When he decided to go to Hollywood, he recommended that my band follow him at the Pennsylvania Hotel.' Bunny considered following Goodman at the Hotel Pennsylvania to be one of his toughest jobs. He made good and went into the Roof for the spring season and on July 8 he moved into the Pavilion Royal.[48]

What this article (MCA press-agentry?) does not relate is anything about the ongoing relationship between Bunny Berigan and Tommy Dorsey. Yes, Bunny was taking musicians from Tommy, and yes, his band was becoming in some ways a "competitor" for TD. But I doubt that Tommy ever felt threatened by Bunny's band, or the success he would have with it. Tommy Dorsey was a man of extremes. He hated and he loved with equal passion. What is really interesting about Tommy is that he frequently hated and loved the same person with equal passion. This was the case with his brother Jimmy, and, I think, with Bunny Berigan. (He had similar feelings later for Frank Sinatra and Buddy Rich, though with those two he had more admiration for their talent than love for them. He could, on occasion, hate them quite intensely though.) He had boundless admiration for Bunny's musical talent and ability as a jazz soloist. He enjoyed Bunny's easygoing personality and genial company. Yet he detested what Bunny was doing to his musical talent as a result of his ever-increasing intake of alcohol. I think that Tommy Dorsey, who battled the bottle himself, discussed Bunny's drinking with him on many occasions, and warned him that drinking and bandleading made a bad combination. I am also reasonably certain that Bunny listened and agreed, over and over again. The tragedy is that Bunny Berigan's addiction to alcohol was by now so profound that he could not stop drinking on his own. He had tried many times, and when he did, his friends and coworkers rejoiced because they could see how much better he was able to play the trumpet without alcohol. I also think that Tommy Dorsey wanted Bunny to be able to benefit from the superior agency relationship MCA could provide for him and his band, and did whatever he could to move Bunny from Rockwell-O'Keefe to MCA. The obligatory lecture on drinking undoubtedly came from MCA as it had from Rockwell-O'Keefe, when Bunny signed with MCA. Everyone involved hoped it would help him. Nevertheless, as I have suggested, there also had to be something in this deal for Tommy. Indeed Tommy may have either loaned Bunny some money to get his band going ("Marie" by then had become something of an annuity for TD) or intervened with MCA or someone else[49] to do this. Whatever backstage maneuvering really occurred, Bunny's move to MCA was definitely a move up.

By the time the band closed at the Penn, then opened at the Pavilion Royal on Long Island on July 8, for what was to be a six-week engagement (it was extended one week), the personnel was set and, with only one exception, would remain intact for many months. Bunny had painstakingly built his band, chair by chair. He had also assembled a group of arrangers who would continue to provide the band with increasingly interesting music to play. Although the band included a mixture of older seasoned musicians and talented youngsters, everyone in the band was capable of playing at a high level on an ongoing basis. Bunny was conscientious in rehearsing his band, and their performances, both in person and on records, were disciplined yet enthusiastic. Joe Lippman recalled how Bunny rehearsed the band:

> Bunny was pretty much in charge of rehearsals. At rehearsals all arrangers take over; it doesn't matter which band you're in. Even in studio work, it's the arranger who rehearses the band, then when the conductor takes over he might make a change or two. That's par for the course; it's not a thing that's contrived. The conductor wants to get used to the arrangement. After all, the arranger has lived with the arrangement for days or weeks maybe; he knows every note of it. The leader has to listen to it, get the feel of it. Then he might make some changes, but generally they're minor. Bunny was particular about musical detail like most good musicians are. He didn't hop on any of the guys for making mistakes because he knew they'd rectify them. They wouldn't be there if they wouldn't do that. There was an awful lot of pride in those Berigan bands. Like most of the groups of that day, we wanted to be better than anybody. I don't remember anyone ever being fired in Bunny's bands. The sidemen supplied their own discipline quite well.[50]

In the 1950s, Joe Dixon found himself in a recording studio adjacent to where Duke Ellington was recording. He was admitted by Duke to observe. As he watched Ellington interact with his musicians, he had a powerful feeling of déjà vu: Berigan had worked in exactly the same way.[51]

By July of 1937, the Berigan band had reached a musical plateau, where it would remain for a substantial period of time. We have a somewhat distorted picture of the band's capabilities because of the poor quality of many of the tunes they recorded for Victor, all of which have been readily available to collectors for the past twenty-five years. A much more representative sampling of the band's repertoire is to be found in the selections they played on their frequent broadcasts from the Pennsylvania Hotel during their engagement there in the spring of 1937, and slightly later from the Pavilion Royal. Many of these selections were recorded as airchecks, but to my knowledge have never been issued in any commercial release. Among those titles are "Peckin,'" "Big John Special," "The Goona Goo" (with Bunny singing), "Royal Garden Blues," "So Rare," "If I Had You," "Dark Eyes," "Wang Wang Blues," "They All Laughed," "Louise," "Rose Room," "Trees," "The Prisoner's Song," "Swanee River," "Black Bottom," "Yes, We Have No Bananas," "A Little Bit Later On," "Thou Swell," "Easy Living," "That Old Feeling," "Russian Lullaby," "Satan Takes a Holiday," and "Gone with the Wind."[52] Only a few of these were recorded by the Berigan band for Victor. Instead, mediocre to poor current pop tunes being pushed by song-pluggers would continue to make up the bulk of Berigan's recordings with Victor.

Aficionados of Berigan's recordings have long questioned why Bunny's band so frequently recorded the dreary pop tune ephemera that makes up so large a proportion of their Victor output. One theory that has not been advanced is that if Arthur Michaud had an ownership interest in the Berigan band, and it is likely that he did, he could have accepted the financial or other inducements of the ever-present song-pluggers, since Bunny didn't want to deal with them, and also gotten "free" arrangements of these tunes as a part of the "deal." Song-pluggers would do just about anything to get their tunes recorded or broadcast. These arrangements could then have been "doctored" by one of Bunny's regular arrangers, most often Joe Lippman, and then be recorded. Sonny Lee corroborated this theory: "I recall that some of the tunes we did might have been written by people who worked for the music publishers and given out by the song-pluggers to Bunny or Arthur Michaud or even to Eli Oberstein as the recording supervisor—usually for free, if the band, any band, would record them or play them on the air. They were often pretty bad and we'd get Joe Lippman to 're-work' them a bit."[53] Bunny, who had a tendency to be penny wise and pound foolish, may have allowed this to happen because it saved him money on arrangements, and allowed him to build his band's book in the process. His analysis of the situation was undoubtedly short term. (Michaud's outlook was basically how to maximize his own short-term profits from the Berigan band, as we shall see.) For Bunny, recording sessions had always been a no-cost source of quick cash. Now that he had to incur some costs in having recording sessions, specifically the cost of paying a band of very expensive musicians, and of buying new arrangements and having them copied, he very likely would have been amenable to any scheme to reduce these costs. Unfortunately, what Bunny did not seem to appreciate is that these often desultory recordings would more and more be used as the sole basis for critics and others in the music business to judge the quality of his band, and that would negate to a large degree his hard work in assembling a good band and working with it carefully in rehearsal and on the job. This counter–productive situation started almost immediately upon release of Bunny's initial Victor recordings, when critics reviewed them harshly, and it has continued ever since. The overall critical appraisal of Berigan's work has undoubtedly suffered as a result of the continuing negative reaction of people to many of his Victor recordings.

Nevertheless, by the time the Berigan band left the Hotel Pennsylvania in early July, they were widely regarded as one of the best new bands in the country, with a bright future before them.

Notes

[1] See the text (chapter 14) for an account of the Berigan band's triumphant return to the Meadowbrook in September 1937, for a full explanation of who Frank Dailey was and what his role was as bandleader/co-owner of the Meadowbrook.

[2] White materials: January 22, 1937.

[3] The Shcribman brothers, Si and Charlie, started in the music business in the 1920s as ballroom operators in New England. They would frequently book up-and-coming bands in their string of ballrooms, and occasionally would also invest in new bands. Three bands they invested in were those led by Artie Shaw, Glenn Miller, and Woody Herman.

[4] *Ibid.*

[5] *Giants of Jazz:* 42.

[6] Tom Cullen, one of Bozy White's early collaborators, gathered this information, which is cited in the White materials: February 3, 1937.

[7] White materials: February 3, 1937.

[8] Cited in the White materials: February 17, 1937.

[9] *Ibid.*

[10] *Ibid.*

[11] Bob Inman did listen to a couple of those broadcasts, and his notes concerning the band's performances are certainly not negatively critical. (See pages 116–117, *Swing Era Scrapbook.*) Inman had no compunction about judging something he heard as being "lousy." This stinging appraisal was applied by him to the performances of many bands. It should also be noted that some great bands made many less than exciting broadcasts during the swing era.

[12] Mosaic Berigan set: 18.

[13] *Jazz and Ragtime Records (1897–1942),* by Brian Rust, Mainspring Press (2002), 401. The arrangement of "Dixieland Shuffle" that was recorded by the Bob Crosby band was also attributed to Bob Haggart by John Chilton in his excellent book *Stomp Off, Let's Go—The Story of Bob Crosby's Bob Cats and Big Band;* Jazz Book Service (1983), 31. Bassist/composer/arrganger Bob Haggart (Robert Sherwood Haggart) was born on March 13, 1914, in New York City. One of the most popular members of the Bob Crosby band (1935–1942), he arranged many numbers in that band's repertiore. He was also a com-

poser of note, writing "What's New?" "South Rampart Street Parade," "My Inspiration," and "Big Noise from Winnetka," which was an unusual duet for bass and drums. Beginning in 1942, Haggart entered the radio and recording studios of New York, remaining there for the next twenty-five years as a freelance musician. In the late 1960s he began coleading (and arranging for) a nine-piece band that was called the World's Greatest Jazzband with trumpeter Yank Lawson, with whom he had worked in the Crosby band. This band found success playing music much in the manner of the original Bob Crosby band, with a few more modern sounding arrangements sprinkled in. From approximately 1980, Haggart performed as a freelance, traveling widely. Bob Haggart died on December 2, 1998, in Venice, Florida.

[14] White materials: February 15–19, 1937.

[15] All citations regarding the Norge transcriptions are in the White materials: February 27, 1937.

[16] White materials: March 7, 1937.

[17] Saxophonist Georgie Auld was born John Altwerger on May 19, 1919, in Toronto, Ontario, Canada. He began playing alto sax as a child in Toronto. He moved with his family to Brooklyn, New York, in 1929, won a scholarship to study with the saxophone virtuoso Rudy Wiedhoeft in 1931, and acquired many characteristics of Wiedhoeft's playing style during the nine months he studied with him. By the mid-1930s, Auld had switched to the tenor sax, and began gigging as a jazz musician working on occasion at Nick's in Greenwich Village. It was there that he was discovered by Bunny Berigan. Auld played in 1937–1938 with Berigan; 1939 with Artie Shaw (also leading the remnants of Shaw's band into 1940); then most notably with Benny Goodman later in 1940 and into 1941. Auld returned as Shaw's featured tenor sax soloist in August 1941, remaining until early 1942. Thereafter he began to lead bands of various sizes for the next eight years. In 1949 he left music to work as an actor on Broadway in a play called *The Rat Race*. He returned to jazz working briefly with Count Basie's small band in 1950. Illness forced him to leave music again, but by late 1951 he was working again in Los Angeles in a variety of settings. Auld returned to New York briefly in the late 1950s, but then moved to Las Vegas. Starting in the 1960s, Auld took various sized groups to Japan and acquired a substantial following there. In 1977, he appeared as an actor in the feature film *New York, New York,* playing a bandleader. Georgie Auld died in Palm Springs, California, on January 8, 1990.

[18] For a complete listing of the aircheck recordings made by Bunny Berigan and Bunny Berigan and His Orchestra in 1937, see appendix 1.

[19] Cited in White materials: March 6, 1937.

[20] George Godfrey Wettling was born on November 28, 1907 in Topeka, Kansas. By 1921 he was residing in Chicago, and three years later he became a professional drummer. An early and continuing influence on his playing was derived from Warren "Baby" Dodds, who worked in a succession of black bands in Chicago in the 1920s. By 1935, Wettling was a member of a specially formed touring band led by English maestro Jack Hylton for a tour of the United States. He settled in New York in 1936, and played with Artie Shaw's first (string quartet) band in late 1936–early 1937. He joined Bunny Berigan in early 1937 and remained until December of that year. He then joined Red Norvo for about a year, then spent several years with Paul Whiteman, during which time he frequently made records with jazz artists on the side. He worked with Benny Goodman, Abe Lyman, and Miff Mole during World War II, and in 1943 joined the staff orchestra for ABC radio, where he remained until 1952. Thereafter, he worked and recorded with most

of the top Dixie-oriented musicians in New York and on tour for the remainder of his life. He died in Manhattan on June 6, 1968, from lung cancer. George Wettling was an accomplished abstract painter whose work was exhibited many times during the last two decades of his life. He was also a witty and trenchant writer whose articled appeared in *Down Beat* and *Playboy* magazines.

[21] Arranger/pianist Joe Lippman was born on April 23, 1915, in Boston, Massachusetts. He got his first big break in late 1934 when arranger George Bassman and saxist Ben Kanter recommended him to Benny Goodman, who was then in need of an arranger for his NBC *Let's Dance* radio program series. Lippman then joined Vincent Lopez for several months in 1936, then Artie Shaw, mid-1936 to March 1937. He was with Bunny Berigan from March 1937 to December 1938 as chief arranger, sharing piano duties on occasion with Joe Bushkin. He freelanced as an arranger for the first half of 1939, then joined Jimmy Dorsey's band as pianist (replacing Freddy Slack) and sometimes arranger until early 1942. After military service, Lippman worked as a freelance arranger, contributing work to notable recordings by Charlie Parker and Sarah Vaughn in the early 1950s. After that, he went into television in Hollywood, working often with Dean Martin in that medium. Joe Lippman died on January 21, 2007.

[22] One such break-in date was Monday, March 15, 1937, at the Commodore Ballroom, Lowell, Massachusetts.

[23] White materials: April 1, 1937.

[24] Lionel Leo Hampton was born on April 20, 1908, in Louisville, Kentucky. (Although there appears to be some confusion about the place of Hampton's birth, I have taken this information from Hampton's autobiography entitled *Hamp,* which Hampton wrote with James Haskins, and which was published by Warner Books in 1989. This book contains literally hundreds of unchecked and incorrect assertions, but I must assume that Hampton knew where he was born.) After spending his early childhood in Birmingham, Alabama, Hampton's family moved to Chicago in 1919. It was there that he absorbed many musical influences. His early musical training took place in the *Chicago Defender* band, led by the renowned music teacher Major N. Clark Smith. His earliest musical employment came as a drummer. Hampton moved to Los Angeles in the late 1920s and eventually was hired by Les Hite, the most successful black bandleader in Los Angeles. Hampton worked for several years with the Hite band, during which time he took up the vibraphone and studied music. In the summer of 1936, a couple of sidemen in Benny Goodman's band (the Goodman band was then working in Los Angeles) discovered Hampton playing in a small club with his own band. They were impressed enough to get BG himself to come and listen. He jammed with Hampton, invited him to make a record with the Benny Goodman Trio, and duly hired him, thereby expanding the trio to a quartet. Hampton remained with Goodman until 1940. From 1937 to 1940 he made a series of jazz recordings for RCA Victor where he surrounded himself with the finest jazz musicians, and often produced remarkable music. Hampton led his own usually raucous bands from 1940 well into the 1980s. He died in New York City on August 31, 2002.

[25] Duke Ellington's drummer Sonny Greer told me of Duke's joy when he returned to the Victor label in 1940, after several years of tepid success recording for other labels. It was Greer who informed me that musicians regarded Victor as "the Cadillac of record labels" during the swing era.

[26] White materials: March 31, 1937. This quote by George Wettling appears without any indication of when or where it originated.

[27] There is evidence that these few engagements were booked by CBS Artists. An ad announcing the Berigan band's appearance on Tuesday April 6 1937 in Lowell, Massachusetts, stated that Bunny was then being booked by CBS Artists. This information is from the April 3, 1937, *Lowell Sun,* provided by Carl A. Hallstrom.

[28] White materials: April 9–11, 1937.

[29] *Billboard:* May 15, 1937, cited in the White materials.

[30] Comments of Del Sharbutt and other information about the *Fun in Swingtime* show are from the White materials: April 18, 1937.

[31] *Ibid.*

[32] The Hotel Pennsylvania is located on Seventh Avenue between West Thirty-third and West Thirty-second Streets, across Seventh Avenue from the site of the original monumental Pennsylvania (Railroad) Station, which was erected in 1908 and demolished in the mid-1960s. Both structures were built and operated by the Pennsylvania Railroad Company during the heyday of railroad travel, with the hotel being erected in 1919. They were connected by subterranean passageways. Although a press statement was issued in late 2007 indicating that the Hotel Pennsylvania was going to be demolished, as this is being written (summer 2011) Hotel Pennsylvania, though now far less glamorous than in its heyday during the swing era, remains very much in business.

[33] White materials: April 28, 1937.

[34] *New York Sun:* May 8, 1937, cited in the White materials: May 8, 1937.

[35] White materials: May 1937. See also appendix 1.

[36] These recordings are also listed in appendix 1.

[37] *Metronome:* June 1937, cited in the White materials: May 12, 1937. There is evidence that the Berigan band was broadcast from the facilities of CBS/WABC–New York via shortwave to England on June 10, 1937. The shortwave signal was relayed to the BBC, and then broadcast over the British Isles and into Europe. *Charleston* (West Virginia) *Daily Mail:* June 6, 1937. Information provided by Carl A. Hallstrom.

[38] I do not wish to leave the impression that Charlie Spivak was anything less than an excellent trumpet player. Should there be any doubt, I recommend Spivak's recording of his lovely theme song "Stardreams" and of "Star Dust" (a transcription from 1943) which includes that song's beautiful verse. Although Spivak was basically a first trumpet player whose solos were melodic and rarely improvised, he nevertheless played exceptionally well within those parameters.

[39] Reference to at least one of the photos from this shoot is made in the *Swing Era Scrapbook* on June 29, 1937, pages 198–199. In fact, the entire Berigan band, including Bunny, autographed one of those photos for young Bob Inman. Bunny remarked to Inman that he had not yet seen one of the two photos Inman showed him that night.

[40] White materials: June 1, 1937.

[41] *Giants of Jazz:* 44.

[42] White materials: June 10, 1937.

[43] White materials: June 13, 1937.

[44] The music for "All God's Chillun Got Rhythm" was composed by the wonderful Bronislau Kaper (and Walter Jurmann) for the 1937 Marx Brothers film *A Day at the Races,* with lyrics by Gus Kahn. It was introduced in that movie by Ivie Anderson and Duke Ellington's band. Kaper composed at least two other themes that jazz musicians have long found attractive: "Invitation" and "On Green Dolphin Street."

[45] White materials: June 18, 1937.

[46] "Frankie and Johnnie" is how the title of this tune appears on the label of Victor 25616-A

[47] *Swing Era Scrapbook:* 192.

[48] *Tempo:* August 1937, cited in the White materials: July 11, 1937.

[49] The "someone else" who could have loaned money to Bunny Berigan at the time MCA began to represent him was attorney John Gluskin. Gluskin had played some role in Tommy Dorsey's early career as a bandleader, and was described by some of the musicians in Berigan's band at the time as "a money man." See note 4 in chapter 14 for more information on John Gluskin.

[50] Dupuis, 171.

[51] *Ibid.:* 172

[52] White materials: May–August, 1937. See also appendix 1.

[53] White materials: September 3, 1937.

Chapter 14
Balancing Act

Every human life has some degree of schizophrenia in it. In the case of Bunny Berigan however, the duality of what he wanted to do, and what he was actually doing, was often extreme. On the personal level, he had married a young, immature, unsophisticated girl so that he could have a home and family, like the one he had grown up with in rural Wisconsin. He showered Donna, his wife, and the two daughters they had, with all of the material goodies his princely income as one of the most successful musicians in New York would allow. Yet, as time passed, Bunny was with them less and less, and his increasingly wayward ways began to affect Donna's own behavior. She gradually went from being the co-dependent alcoholic's (and workaholic's) wife, to being someone who had her own drinking (and other) problems. As a result, the Berigan home was a place that was always more or less in a state of disarray. No matter how much money Bunny made, it was never enough for Donna to run the household. Bills did not get paid. His relationship with his wife had been in a steady decline since he had commenced an on-again-off-again affair with the sultry chanteuse Lee Wiley, probably in early 1936.[1] By 1937, Bunny was appearing publicly with Wiley; indeed they were photographed together on at least one occasion. Lee Wiley was with Bunny very much throughout the months of 1937 when he was building his band and his name in New York by appearing on radio and at the Hotel Pennsylvania and the Pavilion Royal. The White materials are replete with recollections of musicians and other professional associates of Bunny who saw her with him very frequently during this period. By the time Bunny's band left New York on its first road trip, many of these people were relieved that at last Wiley would not be around Bunny anymore, at least while they were away from New York. They had the distinct feeling that, moral issues aside, Lee Wiley, like booze, was not good for Bunny Berigan. Unfortunately, Bunny did not feel this way. In fact, indications are that he had fallen in love with Lee Wiley.[2]

Professionally, Bunny Berigan had grown up as a jazz musician. Unlike most jazz musicians of his time, he also possessed the skills to be a superb studio musician. As a result, Bunny had been forced to sublimate his jazz nature, and perform for the better part of six years basically as a studio musician, which allowed him to earn a handsome income in the depths of the Great Depression. But the ongoing confinement, regimentation, and frustration of doing this, and his sense that his career was going nowhere, had caused him to become an alcoholic. By the time he was very dependent on alcohol (1934), circumstances had combined to allow him, and many other very talented musicians, to start jazz-oriented dance bands that the public supported sufficiently to allow their ongoing existence and, in a few instances, commercial success. After Bunny Berigan formed his own band, he was allowed to be himself musically more than at any other time in his professional life. Indeed, most of Bunny's happiness for the remainder of his life was derived from leading and playing with his own bands. He became obsessive about maintaining his various bands, and stubbornly continued to lead them when, during tough times, a more prudent person would have laid off for a while, and regrouped when circumstances were more favorable.

However, by 1937 Berigan's alcoholism was an unremitting counterweight: the harder he tried to do what was necessary to be a successful bandleader in the musical/commercial world in which he lived, the more bedeviled he was by his alcoholism. He would periodically cut down his drinking, would play marvelously, would thrill audiences and inspire his musicians. At the same time, he became sullen and alienated from those around him. He would begin to suffer from delirium tremens (i.e., "the shakes"). Then, he would take a few drinks, his playing would suffer a bit, but the happy-go-lucky Berigan would return. This was the day-to-day physiological reality that Bunny Berigan confronted in the summer of 1937, in addition to the other myriad musical and business challenges inherent in leading a big band. If the anxiety caused by his relationship with the very high-maintenance *femme fatale* Lee Wiley is factored in, it becomes clear that Bunny Berigan was under an immense amount of stress at the very time his professional career was moving into high gear.

One of the constant conflicts a person faces when he or she makes music a professional career, is the unending tension between the *business* of music and the *making* of music. Bunny Berigan was fully engaged in the making of music, as we have seen. He devoted almost all of his attention, time, energy, and experience to making his band the best performing unit possible. He was passionate about leading his band and investing as much as he had to offer at any given time into his trumpet playing. By July of 1937, he had accomplished a great deal musically in building and directing his band, and by shaping that band in his own musical image and likeness. On the business side, he certainly understood that his band had to exist and survive in a business/economic environment that he neither understood completely nor liked. He accepted the business/economic realities that surrounded him, as most musicians did, with mild resentment. His way of dealing with business issues was to hire competent people, pay them well, and rely on them to take care of whatever business matters had to be taken care of. He wanted as little to do with the business side of his band as was possible. Bunny trusted his business associates to do what needed to be done competently and honestly. Unfortunately, this would prove to be a major mistake on his part.

There has been very little written about the business end of the swing era over the years. Almost all commentators have taken the position that whatever happened with this band or that, happened more or less in a vacuum because of the *music* of that band, or as in the case of Bunny Berigan, because of the music and behavior of the bandleader. Berigan often has been characterized as a simpleton drunkard, who did what he was told by others, and sort of bumbled his way through his career as the leader of a big band. This is a gross oversimplifi-cation—indeed a distortion. I cannot assert that Berigan was a businessman. He wasn't. He was first, last, and always a musician. Although he had little interest in business matters, he was aware of them, and he delegated them to others who were well qualified to handle them. Otherwise, despite his great talent, he could never have had a big band in the first place, or maintained the various bands he would continue to lead (except for one six-month hiatus) for the rest of his life.

A rare glimpse of the inner business workings of a big band was published in an early 1940 article in *Down Beat*, which reviewed some of the business details of the Bob Crosby band for the previous year. This data is invaluable in helping to understand the business/economic environment in which all big bands operated during the swing era. Here is the Crosby band's income from 1939, by source:

Income: theaters: $83,827 (31.1%); one-night stands: $79,385 (29.5%); location jobs–hotels, etc.: $44,459 (16.5%); commercial radio shows: $37,249 (13.8%); records and royalties: $24,661 (9.1%). Total revenue: $269,571.

Expenses: band payroll: $157,000 (68.5%); MCA commissions: $36,000 (15. 7%); union taxes and standbys (standbys were payments to local musicians who under union rules had to stand-by when a traveling band did a broadcast in their town): $17,059 (7.4%); theater talent: $9,685 (4.2%); advertising and publicity: $6,315 (2.7%); arranging payroll: $5,000 (2.2%); general expenses: $4,602 (2%); legal fees/auditing: $936; telephone and wires: $904; entertainment: $778; hospi-talization: $566; miscellaneous taxes: $518; hotel/miscellaneous: $208.[3]

The total expenses reported equal $229,033. Conspicuous by its absence from these expense numbers is an amount for transportation. That was a big expense for every band. I would estimate that transportation expenses for the Crosby band in 1939 were at least $10,000. There is also nothing here for band uniforms. Presumably the difference between revenue and reported expenses, $40,518, included undisclosed sums for these two expenses, and also included whatever was retained as earnings (dividends) by the Crosby band, which was a corporation owned by senior band members. We must also multiply these dollar amounts by fifteen to approximate the dollar values of today.

What jumps out from these income numbers is that theaters and one night stands account for 60 percent of the Crosby band's earnings. Location jobs, their radio show, and record income account for the other 40 percent. This is proof of MCA's basic business axiom, that all bands made the most money on the road by playing in theaters and ballrooms. No band could survive very long by stay-ing in one place, even if it had its own sponsored network radio show. (Only the most successful bands could add something to their incomes by making feature films. That revenue would allow them to stay put for a while, but not indefinite-ly.) To survive, every band had to tour.

The Berigan band's income during the first eight months of 1937 was de-rived from a sponsored radio show, location jobs, and recordings. This is the 40 percent explained above. They played very few one-night dance jobs during this time, and no theaters. The overall plan initially devised by Rockwell-O'Keefe (then taken over by MCA) and Arthur Michaud for Bunny Berigan was to keep him on radio early on as much as possible to build up his name, then send him out on one-nighters and theater jobs to earn the 60 percent every successful band needed to survive. Once the band got out on the road, its popularity there could be reinforced by its records and any radio broadcasts it could garner. This was the famous "Three Rs" of the band business: first (in terms of revenue) the road; and then radio (a sponsored show was the only kind that paid money; sustaining [unpaid] broadcasts served only as promotion); and then records. Without all three Rs in their proper proportion sustaining a band, its very existence was in jeopardy. Everyone connected with the Berigan band knew that it was only a matter of time before the band would have to begin to tour in order to survive.

But after the band left the Pennsylvania Hotel in early July, they did not tour. Instead, they began a lengthy engagement at the Pavilion Royal, on the Merrick Road, in Valley Stream, Long Island, New York on July 8. Although the organization of the Berigan band was now in place, on both the music and business sides, there undoubtedly was not enough money coming in to offset the expenses of running such a high-priced outfit. Nevertheless, Bunny's management evidently thought that his name had not yet been built up enough to command substantial fees on the road, so he continued at a location that had a radio wire, but only on a sustaining, that is, nonpaying basis. It is not known how the shortfall between expenses and income was handled. I suspect that it came out of loans from either MCA and/or Michaud and/or John Gluskin[4] (and/or possibly Tommy Dorsey) to Bunny. On the one hand, this scenario proved the faith MCA and Michaud had in Bunny as a bandleader; on the other, Bunny was beginning to go from a condition of not having any personal money to creating substantial personal debt. This threatening development was something that most if not all bandleaders had to deal with effectively at one time or another in order to survive and succeed. So Bunny did what MCA and Michaud told him to do, which was to stay in the greater New York area while he was still on the *Fun in Swingtime* radio show, stay in a place with a sustaining radio connection to keep the band's music (and the Berigan name) before the public, make records as time permitted, and go in debt all the while.

Whatever the financial issues, Bunny and the band greatly enjoyed the Pavilion Royal engagement, at least at the beginning. Clyde Rounds remembered:

> The Pavilion Royal engagement was a delight. All the members of the band gave their time and best efforts to rehearsals, first by section and then by the full band. Some great new arrangements were added to the book and we fully prepared for our forthcoming road tour, where the big money was to be made—we hoped! However, there were always some musicians who were unwilling to travel, regardless of financial inducements. Some had children in school, wives who would threaten to leave, while others cradled hopes or expectations of secure studio jobs. One such was Morey Samel, who stayed on until his replacement, Al

George, got familiar with the book. The same was true for Hank Wayland *(sic)*, who took over on bass. (Since the only change on bass occurring at this time was when Hank Wayland replaced Arnold Fishkind, it can be assumed that Rounds had confused the two bass players, and that Fishkind did not want to leave New York.) Sid Perlmutter was a well-trained saxophone player with a fine tone, who was capable of playing anything at sight, but his somewhat legitimate style caused him some difficulties with the bends and slurs and rather loose style of our band. His one burning ambition was to work for Tommy Dorsey, whose lead man, Mike Doty, knew what was going on and turned in his notice to TD in order to take Sid's chair with Bunny, but poor Sid never did get to play for Dorsey![5]

Here is a blurb that appeared in the *New York World Telegram* during the Berigan band's stay at the Pavilion Royal:

The Pavilion Royal out at Valley Stream, Long Island, is now giving the citizens of that district a representative of swing music. Mr. Bunny Berigan especially attracts the youngsters of both Long Island and New York and it looks as though they may have to hold him over. Among the numerous roadhouses, the Pavilion Royal is one of the oldest and is situated in a fairly cool and open spot. Then there is a sprawling ceiling overhead, tall trees poke their limbs out of the dance floor and, being nearly dead from the roots up, are garlanded with fake, but attractive willows. There is enough room in the Pavilion Royal for more than a couple of hundred and there is a show at dinner and supper supervised by Al Shayne, the Broadway MC.[6]

Another item proved that MCA's press agents were busy trying to counteract the rumors that were rife about Bunny's drinking, and, perhaps his other activities:

Headline: To Write Hot Licks for *Down Beat*—Bunny Berigan is strictly on cokes as a liquid diet these days—and that's official—as well as his sport is confined to golf. He's a 14 handicap man who yearns for fried ham and his wife and his two kiddies, both gals, of two and four and a half. The eldest eats crackers in bed, which doesn't bother her daddy half as much as a hooked drive. He thinks that Jonah Jones is strictly 'kicks,' 'Pops' as *(sic)* trumpet and enjoys Joe Marsala's wacky doings after the job. Berrigan's *(sic)* ambition is to have a top-flight band and if the wishes of all the cats around town were put end to end, Bunny can't help but get his wish but soon.[7]

While Bunny continued to prepare the band for its tour, the last personnel change took place. This one was unfortunately to result in the loss of one of the best female vocalists he ever employed. Ruth Bradley explained what happened: "I'd joined the Berigan band while it was still at the Hotel Pennsylvania and I left at the Pavilion Royal as I knew they were going on the road and I wanted no more of that. I'd been on the road with bands like Ina Ray Hutton's, but Bunny really wanted me to stay. He was a generous, relaxed person who liked his scotch."[8] Bradley's replacement was Gail Reese, who started singing with the band at the Pavilion Royal on August 3 so she could get used to her arrangements, and generally acclimate to life in the Berigan orchestra. Ms. Reese later recalled joining Bunny:

> I was born Virginia Vieser, and my name was changed by a radio announcer. I was about 20 when I joined the Berigan band, having already worked with Bert Block, Charlie Barnet and Carl Ravell (Ravazza). I was back with Barnet when I got the job with Bunny. My big influence was Mildred Bailey and I took a few lessons from Joe Smith, Frances Langford's teacher. I joined Bunny at the Pavilion Royal, having auditioned at the recording studios a week or two earlier. I was with Charlie Barnet at the Hickory Lodge in Larchmont, Westchester, when I was approached by Chuck Rinker, brother of Al Rinker and Mildred Bailey, who was a song-plugger and the contact with Bunny's manager. When I did the audition for Bunny, he had Lee Wiley at the studio with him.[9]

Even though the Berigan band had spent the six weeks since their last Victor recording session in New York, they had not recorded during that time, I think, because Bunny wanted the numerous new band members to have the chance to settle in before they made any new discs. By August 7, Berigan was finally ready to make some more records. Four titles were recorded that day: "Let 'Er Go" and "Turn On That Red Hot Heat," with vocals by Gail Reese; "I Can't Get Started," which forever after would be Berigan's signature tune; a miniature trumpet concerto, with a vocal chorus by Bunny; and an unlikely instrumental "blowing piece" "The Prisoner's Song," which provided the band's jazz players with plenty of solo space.

"Let 'Er Go" was composed by Larry Clinton and Julian Kay. Although some sources have attributed its arrangement to Clinton, I cannot say that with certainty. The vamping opening with Hank Wayland's bass and Wettling's cymbals is very different. The band swings with authority on this and the other recordings made that day. Here, Ms. Reese tries hard, but the lyric is so contrived and hackneyed that it makes it impossible for her to accomplish very much with it. After the vocal, Sonny Lee comes forth with sixteen bars of splendid jazz on his muted trombone. Lee later stated that he achieved the muting sound he got on this solo by covering the bell of his trombone with a felt hat with holes cut into its crown.[10] Bunny follows in exuberant fashion on his blazing open trumpet.

"Turn On That Red Hot Heat (Burn Your Blues Away)" is undoubtedly one of the best recordings Berigan ever made, though it has only rarely been released as a part of the many anthologies of Bunny's recordings. The arrangement, the band's performance, and especially Berigan's trumpet playing, are all superb. Once again, newcomer Gail Reese is saddled with a pedestrian lyric, but such was often the lot of girl vocalists in big bands then. Joe Lippman reprised his very successful opening from "All God's Chillun Got Rhythm" with a few new dramatic twists here: Wettling's pounding tom-toms and the growling open trombones of Sonny Lee and Al George, followed by the wailing clarinets, then the ooh-aah trumpets tell the listener that this heat is to be found in Equatorial (or is it *Ellingtonian?*) Africa. In any case, it is a masterful use of contrasting registers and timbres. Then the maestro steps out, plunger in hand, growling away on his otherwise open trumpet, to state the melody for sixteen bars, backed by those tasty clarinets. Joe Dixon then takes his turn, with sixteen bars that start in the juicy lower register of his clarinet. He is backed by the open brass. As he moves up into his high register, there is a corresponding heightening of excitement. Dixon's solo is first-rate jazz. The band then struts on into the vocal chorus, which Gail Reese does invest with some enthusiasm. Bunny returns on open trumpet for another sixteen bars with a sound so huge that it almost overloads the microphones. His exultant solo is the quintessence and culmination of everything he had been working to achieve as a jazz soloist for the previous ten or more years. There is a beginning, a middle, and an end to this solo: it is a perfect musical statement, and marvelous jazz. It is also technically dazzling, but not at the expense of the music in his playing.

This tune was written by Louis Alter (music) and Paul Francis Webster (lyric). Webster would do much better in later years with the lyrics to memorable songs like "The Shadow of Your Smile" (the title to which Johnny Mercer *hated*); "Somewhere My Love," "Love Is a Many Splendored Thing," "The Twelfth of Never," and "Black Coffee."

As great as "Turn On That Red Hot Heat" is, it was merely a warm-up for what followed. In the summer of 1937, Berigan was notified by Victor that he and his band would be featured on one-fourth of a four-record album release utilizing extended play twelve-inch 78 rpm records. He would have to come up with two pieces of music that would highlight what he and his band did best, and fill up two sides of a twelve-inch record. The two tunes he chose for this record were "I Can't Get Started" and "The Prisoner's Song."

> When Berigan formed his first big band in the spring of 1937, the logical choice for the band's theme was 'I Can't Get Started', and Bunny used it until the very end. The definitive Berigan recording of the song was made on August 7, 1937, Victor 36208, a twelve-inch disc that was included in what was almost certainly the first jazz album of 12-inch 78 rpm records to ever be released. The album and Bunny's performance of 'I Can't Get Started' have long since become jazz classics. Except for a brief period in the middle of World War II, when shellac shortages became critical, the Berigan Victor recording, in one form or another, has never been out of print. It can still be heard on radio, in Hollywood films (most notably *Chinatown*), and found on juke boxes. A number of 'tributes' have been done, almost all using the 'formula' of the Berigan Victor record. Since 1936 and with the passage of time the song and Bunny Berigan have become almost inseparable. Some people believe Bunny wrote the tune, so close is his association with it. Both Vernon Duke and Ira Gershwin credited Berigan's classic Victor performance with helping to keep the song alive through the years. While it never became a huge hit, never reached the 'Hit Parade' nor led in the sales of sheet music, Bunny's Victor recording of 'I Can't Get Started' long ago reached the million sales mark, when such things had meaning, and it continues to sell today. Vernon Duke, in private conversation with the Bozy White, gave Bunny full credit for making 'I Can't Get Started' into a standard.[11]

We know that the basic outlines for Berigan's classic performance of "I Can't Get Started" had been created by him in early 1936 when he first began to perform it at the Famous Door. The Vocalion recording he made of the song on April 13, 1936 provides an early snapshot in the evolution of his treatment of it. But over time, Bunny made subtle changes in the arrangement. By the time he was ready to record it with his own band, his conception of how it should be presented had been carefully refined, and now included an extended *rubato* opening cadenza to display his virtuosity on trumpet, *and* fill space on a twelve-inch record. Trumpeter Richard M. Sudhalter analyzed this classic recording:

> An introduction—an extended cadenza over four different sustained chords in the key of C—had been added by this time, but otherwise Berigan's routine had not changed since the Vocalion recording. But whereas the Vocalion comes across as a virtuoso performance of a great song, the Victor version presents itself as a kind of concerto, a tour de force for a trumpeter of imagination and daring having impeccable command of his instrument. A younger player, raised on the finger-snarling complexities of bebop, might listen to this recording and wonder what all the fuss was about—until he tried to play it and learned the killing difficulty of executing this kind of top-to-bottom endurance contest with polish, power, and Berigan's broad tone. It is both an athletic feat and a supreme test of musicianship and emotional strength.
>
> The introduction itself is no small feat, ranging from the lowest note on the trumpet to more than two octaves above that, with every note struck square, full, and fat. Berigan follows with eight bars of straight melody, as he did on the Vocalion record. But there is a different feeling here: something tighter, grander in scope, more aware, perhaps, of the importance of this performance. His tone is especially broad and lustrous, his phrasing generous.
>
> The saxes take eight more while Berigan moves to the microphone for his vocal. He sings the Ira Gershwin lyric again in that curiously appealing voice. His phrasing constantly recalls his trumpet playing: Note the snap he gives to 'still I can't get no place with you' and his note-for-trumpet-note rendering of '...cause I can't get started with you' at the end of the chorus.
>
> There is no tenor solo after the vocal on this one—just the full band sustaining big, fat chords and George Wettling laying down a solid beat as Berigan takes to his horn for the climax. Again, there are four little episodes of two bars each: two in the upper middle register, two lower down, then a final clarion call, a series of strong, singing high Cs, balanced on perfectly controlled lip trills, to push off his half-chorus assault on the summit. It is all done in that punishing high register, and all with no loss of power, tone size, or melodic shape. There is a magnificent lunge to a high F in bar three, the chimelike E flats at the end of bar four, the same descent with its echo of Louis Armstrong. There is no longer the thrill of discovery in this performance. Berigan is retracing familiar steps by now, but because of that this performance radiated a greater assurance. At the end, rather than going straight to the high E flat as he had a year and a half earlier, Berigan spins things out a bit for the sake of drama. He plays first his B flat, drops to a G for a moment to build tension, and then, after an artful pause, vaults to the high E flat and finds it waiting there for him as the band chimes in underneath to finish the performance.[12]

Numerous trumpeters have pointed out to me that the contrasting low-register and high-register playing for which Bunny Berigan was renowned, and which is on full display in this classic performance of "I Can't Get Started," is something that was facilitated by his uncommon control of the trumpet's lowest range. Berigan's frequent vaults into the highest register of the trumpet were very often "set-up," both technically and musically, by his playing in the lowest range of the horn immediately before. This allowed his chops to receive maximum blood circulation so that when he went upstairs, his sound would remain full and rich, not pinched or piercing.

Another interesting sidelight to both this recording and its predecessor is how much Bunny had altered the original Ira Gershwin lyric. Most of this retooling had been done by the time the Vocalion recording was made. But the process of evolution had nevertheless continued after that recording. Here is a comparison between the original lyric as written by Ira Gershwin and what Bunny sang on the Victor recording:

IG: I've flown around the world in a plane;
BB: I've flown around the world in a plane;

IG: I've settled revolutions in Spain;
BB: I've settled revolutions in Spain;

IG: The North Pole I have charted, but I can't get started with you.
BB: And the North Pole I have charted, still I can't get started with you.

IG: Around a golf course, I'm under par;
BB: On the golf course, I'm under par;

IG: And all the movies want me to star;
BB: Metro-Goldwyn have asked me to star;

IG: I've got a house, a showplace, but I get no place with you.
BB: I've got a house, a showplace, still I can't get no place with you.

IG: You're so supreme, lyrics I write of you;
BB: 'Cause you're so supreme, lyrics I write of you;

IG: Scheme, just for the sight of you;
BB: I dream, dream day and night of you:

IG: Dream, both day and night of you,
BB: And I scheme, just for the sight of you,

IG: And what good does it do?
BB: Baby, what good does it do?

> IG: In nineteen twenty-nine I sold short;
> BB: I've been consulted by Franklin D.;
>
> IG: In England I'm presented at court;
> BB: Greta Garbo has had me to tea;
>
> IG: But you've got me downhearted,
> BB: Still I'm broken hearted,
>
> IG: 'Cause I can't get started with you.
> BB: 'Cause I can't get started with you.[13]

I'll leave it to the reader to judge which lyric works best.

The classic recording of "I Can't Get Started" that all Berigan fans are so familiar with was actually the second take of it he made in the Victor studio on August 7, 1937. The first take was made minutes before the issued take. To my knowledge, the only readily available commercial release of this alternate take was on RCA *Black and White/Jazz Tribune* (France) PM 43689, a two LP set, issued in 1982. I have listened to this first (alternate) take recently and am absolutely positive that it was the first take made of "I Can't Get Started," and that it was made on August 7, 1937. The recording balance on the band and Bunny and ambient sound are identical to the issued performance. Nevertheless, there are numerous plainly noticeable differences between this take and the one that was released by Victor. They include a couple minor trumpet blips in the opening cadenza; Bunny phrasing the vocal quite differently from the issued take; a lapse in pitch when Bunny went down for a low note in the vocal chorus; and an overshot high note in the final trumpet solo. Also, to my ears, Bunny's ending trumpet solo on the first take has a slightly more precise pitch than what is on the issued recording. The alternate take also clocks in at 4:33, which is twelve seconds faster than the issued version.

With the Victor recording of "I Can't Get Started," Bunny Berigan went from being a virtuoso trumpeter and bandleader to being a star. As Sudhalter correctly observed, Bunny was well aware of the importance of this performance. He had come to realize that however excellent his band was, and no matter how great its arrangements, for it to mean anything to his audiences, *he* had to deliver. And on this recording, he *did* deliver.

He also delivered on the last recording made that day, "The Prisoner's Song." Clarinetist Joe Dixon recalled how this tune entered the Berigan repertoire:

> Dick Rose came into Nola, or one of those studios on Broadway where we rehearsed, one day with this arrangement. I don't know if he'd been invited in or just walked in. Anyway, Bunny said 'Pass it out. ' Bunny would always said 'Pass it out,' and then he'd sit there and listen. So Dick Rose kicked it off and when we got through playing the thing Georgie Auld and I went over to Bunny and said, 'This tune is a pig; we don't want this.' And Bunny said, 'Aah, it isn't that bad.' Then Bunny got the idea for the introduction, with the tom-toms and

his growling with the plunger. The funniest part of it is, it became a hit. So we were wrong![14]

The Victor recording of "The Prisoner's Song" hints at what Berigan would do with his band on theater and dance dates—he would extend arrangements to allow everybody plenty of room to blow. Once again, Bunny had the guys well prepared to record this tune—the band is tight, yet swinging. His own playing is superb, both as soloist and as leader of the brass. Then there are the jazz solos from Georgie Auld on tenor sax; Joe Dixon on clarinet; and Sonny Lee, on trombone. Joe Lippman:

> 'The Prisoner's Song' was first spotted by Dick Rose, who used to be a copyist. He thought it would be a natural for the expressive Berigan trumpet. So it started out as his arrangement, but as extra choruses were added during performances on the stand, it went on to become more of a 'head' arrangement, incorporating ideas from the guys in the band. It was fashionable for all the bands to have a few so-called 'killer dillers' in the book, which would be used to close out broadcasts or sets. They were real rabble-rousers like Benny Goodman's 'Roll 'Em' and Artie Shaw's 'The Chant' and I guess Bunny used it in the same way. Thus 'The Prisoner's Song' finished up about half Dick Rose and half the rest of the band, but it provided a really jumping finale to many a broadcast![15]

The Berigan band's recordings of "I Can't Get Started" and "The Prisoner's Song" were issued back-to-back on the twelve-inch Victor record 36208, and were a part of an album of four such records entitled *A Symposium of Swing*, Victor C-28. This was something of a coup for Bunny, as the critical comments below reveal:

> RCA Victor has given the wax cult something to really shout about. Spreading their stuff on 12 inches of wax and packeted in an album dressed up with concert notes by swing critic Warren Scholl, candid camera shots of the wand-wavers and personnel of the tooters, Victor Hall of Fame's *A Symposium of Swing* (C-28) features Tommy Dorsey, Fats Waller, Benny Goodman & Bunny Berigan. (*Billboard:* September 18, 1937)

> Victor's first swing album, *Symposium of Swing*, is a big hit. The public acceptance (and sales) was almost double the estimate by the company. The set was backed by a special advertising and display campaign. (*Billboard:* October 23, 1937)

> Biggest record news of the month is Victor's release of a *Symposium in Swing (sic)* album of four 12-inch records, which follows their recent Bix Beiderbecke memorial album. The four discs provide an opportunity to hear Goodman, Tommy Dorsey, Waller and Berigan at their best. Only serious question that might be raised is the inclusion of Berigan, whose band is just rounding into shape. Other leaders naturally should occupy Berigan's place in the *Symposium* but these leaders are not recording for Victor. Since this is strictly Victor's *Symposium* and judged on its merits the album deserves a top notch spot in any record library. Here is a compilation of what swing really is, as played by the present Victor

swing masters. For a swing banquet, don't miss this sumptuous swing meal. (*Orchestra World:* October 1937) [16]

Benny Goodman's contribution to this collection was the two-sided blockbuster "Sing, Sing, Sing." Tommy Dorsey's was "Stop, Look and Listen," backed by "Beale Street Blues." Fats Waller's disc in this set had "Honeysuckle Rose" on side A, and "Blue Turning Gray over You" on side B. Both of these performances were by Fats Waller and His Rhythm. [17]

The Pavilion Royal engagement provided the band with a home base close to New York, so they could continue their weekly Sunday evening broadcasts on the sponsored *Fun in Swingtime* show which was being broadcast over the Mutual radio network. Presumably the money involved was enough to justify keeping the Berigan band off the road, where the real money was to be made. The radio exposure also helped to build the Berigan name. The band's frequent broadcasts from the Pavilion Royal were over WABC, CBS's New York flagship station, and presumably on at least some other CBS affiliates throughout the region, if not on the national CBS network, at least on occasion. These broadcasts were sustaining, meaning the Berigan band made no money doing them. But again, they gave the band and the name Bunny Berigan valuable public exposure.

Among those who recalled the Berigan engagement at the Pavilion Royal was George Stacy, Bunny's new road manager. He was one of the new faces in the Berigan organization at the Pavilion Royal:

I replaced Mort Davis as Bunny's road manager. My brother Jack knew Bunny through having worked with him in the Dorsey Brothers band, so he put in a word for me. My main duties consisted of watching the gate at dance halls, making sure that Bob 'Little Gate' Walker, our band boy, had the stands all set up and the music ready, and preparing all the advance bookings and publicity. A year of one-nighters could be back-breaking with all the traveling, inadequate eating facilities, lack of sleep, to say nothing of keeping track of the money, checking the weekly payroll, etc. Every night, after the final high note of his closing theme, Bunny would throw his horn back over his head, high in the air, and 'Little Gate' was supposed to catch it behind the stand. Now and then, he would miss and then I had a real problem: How in hell do you find a trumpet in 'Nowheresville,' Pennsylvania, on a Sunday morning? Assisting 'Little Gate' around that time was a keen, young aspiring bassist called Grieg Stewart Jackson, better known a few years later as 'Chubby'! [18]

On August 18, the Berigan band checked in again at the Victor recording studio in New York City. The session ran from 1:30 to 6:45 p.m. after which they rushed from Manhattan to the Pavilion Royal. They recorded three tunes that day: the then current pop "Why Talk about Love?" with a Gail Reese vocal; and two good instrumentals, "Caravan" and "A Study in Brown." "Caravan" was a new tune, composed by Duke Ellington's valve trombonist Juan Tizol. The Berigan version, in a great arrangement by Joe Lippman, with Bunny featured throughout using a pixie straight mute in his trumpet, and a plunger over its bell, was well received by the more cultivated swing commentators, albeit with some rather overheated adjectives:

'Caravan' is an eerie, satanic interpretation in slow tempo of Juan Tizol's note-worthy melody. It testifies to the steady improvement of Berigan's group and is far and away the finest of its recordings. The significance of the disc lies in the fact that it is an exceptional and imaginative arrangement, which never for a moment hesitates to utilize the most colorful harmonies and techniques at the command of the modern jazz orchestra. Against a coherent and deftly articulated background of clarinet choir, strongly accented percussion led by bass saxophone *(sic)* and subtone clarinet and delicate pianissimo brass figures, Berigan introduces the theme on solo trumpet. It's sensuous and feverish and played with tremendous feeling; its phrasing and intonation complete the bizarre atmosphere conjured up by the background counter-themes. Except in the finale, which returns to the opening motif, the source is ensemble. Unity of design, however, is so well maintained that the concerted unison chorus with the crescendos, diminuendos and modulations creates a powerful climax in keeping with the original mood. Wettling's drumming considerably strengthens the driving rhythmic background. All in all, this is a fit companion piece for the Ellington and Ambrose versions.[19] (Note: There is no bass saxophone on Bunny Berigan's recording of "Caravan." There is, however, a bass clarinet, which was played expertly by Mike Doty.)

This performance of "Caravan," wherein Bunny and the band bring Joe Lippman's brilliant chart vividly to life, executing the many crescendos, diminuendos, and brass *oo-ahs* perfectly, is one of many bits of recorded evidence that refute the hoary canard that the Berigan band was little more that a ragtag group of undisciplined musicians.

The riffy "A Study in Brown" was composed by Larry Clinton, but arranged for the Berigan band by Joe Lippman. It contains an excellent solo by Bunny on open trumpet, some bouncing tenor by Georgie Auld, sixteen bars of good clarinet by Joe Dixon, and a superb muted trombone solo by Sonny Lee, which again has him covering the bell of his trombone with a perforated felt hat. This was one of Lee's finest recorded solos as a member of the Berigan band. Note the use of Dixon's clarinet to lead the reeds in the finale: this device was becoming a hallmark of Lippman's writing for the Berigan ensemble.

Then Bunny was required by Victor executive Eli Oberstein to participate in preparing a "welcoming record" for British bandleader Henry Hall. It consisted of brief cuts by the Berigan band and five other Victor bands, and a short speech by each bandleader. The resulting music and talk made up one side of a twelve-inch record. Presumably, only one copy was pressed, and regrettably it has been lost.

There have been various stories of how the Berigan band's engagement at the Pavilion Royal ended. Unfortunately, those stories do not always jibe with the known facts. Here is one such account, that of Bunny's guitarist Tommy Morgan, recalling, among other things, Lee Wiley's constant presence at Pavilion Royal:

> She was a character. She used to follow us around a lot. When we played at Valley Stream, Long Island, she was there every night—every night! Bunny'd go out in the car with her between sets and when he'd come back he'd be...spent. After he was with her he used to fold up sometimes. We lost that job on account of her.

It was a beautiful job out there. The boss finally told Bunny: 'Look, either she goes or the band goes.' Bunny said, 'Well, the band goes!' Oh my God! Everybody was real unhappy with Bunny. The job was so good, and we had to go out on one-nighters and crap like that. He wasn't thinking of the guys in the band that time. But we wouldn't fool with him. He could be thick-headed at times too. We were frustrated because there were no bookings. We had to scramble around.[20]

The facts are that the Berigan band played exactly *seven* weeks at Pavilion Royal, not just the six that were originally scheduled. They closed there on August 25. This suggests that Bunny's management was possibly doing the Pavilion Royal's management a favor by extending what had apparently been a very profitable engagement for them for another week. Anyone in the band business should have known that a location job like this never allowed a band to break even, much less make a profit. Since the Berigan band was tied to the New York area because of their ongoing commitment to the successful *Fun in Swingtime* radio show, Bunny's management had to find the most profitable employment possible for the band, but within an hour's drive of New York, for as long as his commitment to the radio program continued. It is extremely possible that there were negotiations between Bunny's management and the Pavilion Royal to extend the Berigan band's stay even longer, but that these came to nothing, and the Berigan band then left after the one-week extension. MCA was still in the process of trying to book a highly lucrative tour of one-nighters and weeklong theater engagements for the Berigan band, but again, this tour could not commence until Bunny could leave the *Fun in Swingtime* show. It is likely that MCA and/or Michaud would have tried to free Berigan from *Fun in Swingtime* at this juncture, but the radio show's management refused to let Bunny go because the band's presence on the show was helping its popularity. (The Berigan band was playing four or five selections on the show each week. See appendix 1.) So, the waiting game continued. Bunny and his band could not hit the road to make good money because of their ongoing commitment to the *Fun in Swingtime* radio show. Nevertheless, the Berigan band did not scramble around for lack of bookings, as Tommy Morgan said. Immediately after departing the Pavilion Royal, Bunny's band went to another location in or near New York (not specified in the White materials) and played there for a few days. They broadcast from this location over WABC on August 31.[21]

The real challenge Bunny's management had then was to fill in the band's schedule with good jobs in and around New York while they completed their *Fun in Swingtime* contract. As subsequent events would eventually make clear, Bunny could not leave the *Fun in Swingtime* show until mid-October, at the earliest. So, in early September, MCA announced that the Berigan band would open a two-week engagement at the Meadowbrook in Cedar Grove, New Jersey, on September 7.

Between September 1 and the Meadowbrook opening, the Berigan band remained very busy. On September 3, they made some more records at Victor. The titles were: "Sweet Varsity Sue," "Gee but It's Great to Meet a Friend,"

"Ebb Tide," "Have You Ever Been in Heaven, and "Mama, I Want to Make Rhythm." All five tunes were either current pops, or novelties, and all had vocals by Gail Reese, except "Mama, I want to Make Rhythm," which featured Bunny singing, and scatting a bit. All of theses sides contained spirited playing by Berigan and his band members.

"Sweet Varsity Sue" starts with a Dixie bit, and then after the vocal has a somewhat stilted solo by Auld, good Berigan, and a romping out-chorus. "Gee but It's Great to Meet a Friend (from Your Home Town)" at first has Gail Reese singing and then the band vocalizing. But the real excitement comes after the vocal: Wettling starts rattling away on his snare drum, and for four bars it is just him, backing Bunny's ever higher trumpet. This is a very effective transition which leads to a flowing full chorus solo by Berigan that is first-class jazz.

"Ebb Tide," from the then current film of the same name, is not to be confused with the hit tune from the 1950s, which was later recorded by the Platters, Lenny Welch, and the Righteous Brothers. This "Ebb Tide," a pleasant pop ballad that has been almost completely overlooked by Berigan aficionados, contains some skillful arranging touches, applied by Joe Lippman, and a superb Berigan solo after Gail Reese's vocal. It begins with the two trombones, playing a pedal point, contrasted with clarinets, which anchor the first statements of the melody played with a melancholy tinge by Berigan, using a tightly-fitted cup mute. Lippman was coming to be very imaginative in his use of the contrasting sonorities and registers of trombones and clarinets in his arrangements for the Berigan band.

As good as Lippman's arrangement is, it is because of Bunny's solo after the vocal that this performance will be remembered. After a brief pause, Berigan enters, playing in the low register of the trumpet, and then glisses *lower.* His sound is sumptuous and velvety: he lovingly shapes each note as a sculptor would shape the details of a fine statue. The effect is to immediately transport the listener from the realm of 1930s dance music into a warm and magical place not defined by time, space, or anything else. Then, by playing three ascending notes, he is suddenly in the upper reaches of the trumpet's range, and ends his solo by perfectly lip-trilling the climactic last note (a high E flat) as the band returns to finish the performance. After this, the members of Bunny's band no doubt looked at each other all thinking the same thought simultaneously: where did *that* come from?

"Have You Ever Been in Heaven?" is a rhythmic pop that spots some good drumming by Wettling, and good solos by Sonny Lee on trombone and Joe Dixon on clarinet. Bunny's first trumpet solo is notable for being executed completely in the lower range of his trumpet. He returns a bit later for some more characteristic playing. There are even a few bars of Joe Lippman's solo piano, surely a rarity.

"Mama, I Want to Make Rhythm" is a relaxed swinger that is highlighted by Bunny's singing and exuberant trumpeting. Georgie Auld's brief solos on this recording, and on the previous ones made at this session where he had a few bars to himself, are among his poorest efforts while he was a member of the Berigan band. Perhaps he was not feeling well on this date. Usually, he played well, indeed sometimes very well. As we will see, his jazz solos improved steadily during his tenure with Bunny.

On September 4, the Berigan band played at Roton Point, South Norwalk, Connecticut, and broadcast over WABC. One month later, *Metronome* reported on that gig, as well as the one Bunny had played at Roton Point on the prior July 4:

> With all the poor weather, this has been the worst season for business since the Point started booking name bands seven years ago. For last July 4, Bunny Berigan, then riding the crest of a wave with broadcasts on Mutual and Columbia, was booked by special planning, which caused him to hurry up to the Park after his Sunday evening commercial at the WOR studios. The job started more than an hour late, but Berigan, nevertheless drew the largest attendance for that part of the season. His audience response compared with the first showing of such as Goodman, Bob Crosby and the Dorseys in years before. If Bunny could match his on-the-air performances in the ballrooms, he would be on his way. The following Labor Day weekend brought the season's end with an encore return of Berigan, who did not equal his first date, principally because of the opening of a winter room in the territory with Ted Lewis as the attraction.[22]

On September 5, they did their weekly *Fun in Swingtime* broadcast, and then went to a dance date at Niantic, Connecticut. They may have had a much-deserved day off on Monday, September 6, before opening the next day at the Meadowbrook.

Clyde Rounds recalled the Berigan's band's triumphant return to the Meadowbrook: "The Meadowbrook was the most sought-after spot in the east. It had better broadcasting facilities than Glen Island Casino, and its manager Frank Dailey was a good friend of Bunny's. That two weeks stand gave us time to let the newer members of the band familiarize themselves with the charts, and by the time we finished the date, our band was much better known."[23] Rounds's memory may have been a bit hazy on the issue of new band members because there hadn't been any personnel changes in the Berigan band for many weeks prior to the Meadowbrook engagement. He was not mistaken however about the importance of that venue to the bands that played there:

> Meadowbrook Country Club is unique in that, it is the only major dance spot in metropolitan New York that is owned and operated by musicians. This all-year round club is operated by 'Vince' Dailey one of the youngest operators in the business. Vince buys not only the music but all the other necessities for the 'Brook.' Bandleaders find this spot convenient not only for building up their New Jersey reps but for a shot at the several CBS coast-to-coast wires emanating from there. Frank Dailey, who has one of the leading swing bands, is the president of a corporation of five members of his first band who own the Meadowbrook. His latest band is built around Joe Mooney, arranger, who plays a swinging piano and accordion and Louise Wallace (formerly of the Wallace Sisters) whose vocal

style is a cross between Ella Fitzgerald and a Billie Holiday. Casa Loma holds the house record for one-nighters for a date in 1934. At present, Dailey is back on his own bandstand. December and January will bring a flock of names to the Meadowbrook among them Red Norvo and Mildred Bailey.[24]

Frank Dailey was born in 1901 and attended Seton Hall College in South Orange, New Jersey, studying to be a priest. While in school, he organized a 5-piece group, which he led on violin, but in 1918 his father's death caused him to drop out of school, though he continued to lead a band, which he enlarged to 9 pieces in 1923. From then until 1925, he played at a spot in Cedar Grove, New Jersey called Four Towers across the road from the Pavilion Royal, later renamed the Meadowbrook. This place opened and closed many times, before being taken over by Dailey in 1930 and featuring his band until late 1936–early 1937. The band included at one time or another drummer Buddy Schutz; Ralph Muzzillo, trumpet; Bud Freeman, tenor sax; Paul Tanner, trombone; and vocalists Connie Haines, Dolly Dawn and Edythe Wright. In 1937, Dailey started to bring in name bands, using his own group as relief band, and he made it a point to attract a younger crowd. He had no cover charge: 'a young fella with $2.00 could come with his gal and have a good time there all evening.' The spot had a Mutual wire and bands got lots of airtime. It switched to a CBS wire in 1940. (Note: Late 1939 Glenn Miller and early 1940 Tommy Dorsey broadcasts from the Meadowbrook were carried over NBC. Benny Goodman's remotes from there in 1941 were over Mutual. Later, CBS broadcast remotes from there, including ones of Woody Herman's 'First Herd.') The 'Matinee at Meadowbrook' radio show started in 1938. Dailey had a mailing list of over 23,000, with about 5,000 being added and dropped each year, and he continued to poll his customers to see what they wanted. He had only a small staff, which included his two brothers, Vince and Cliff. The spot now (1941) holds 1,700 up from a capacity of about 800 when he took it over, and has a beautiful outdoor garden with tables for dining on hot summer nights.[25]

Clearly, the Berigan band was marking time while they were at the Meadowbrook. It is assumed that the band would have broadcast from that location, but there is no information about any such broadcasts in either the White materials or Bob Inman's *Swing Era Scrapbook*. The Meadowbrook engagement ended on September 22. Promoters throughout the eastern and midwestern states were now clamoring for the Berigan band, but MCA could not firmly book a long succession of one-nighters or week long theater dates because the band had to return to New York every Sunday evening for the *Fun in Swingtime* radio show. This show, which had been secured for Bunny by Arthur Michaud and Rockwell-O'Keefe, and which had initially provided Bunny with the financial stability to greatly strengthen his band, was now seriously limiting his ability to capitalize on the demand for the band that had been created by its lengthy radio buildup. MCA tried to continue to book some strategic one-night dance jobs in the territory near New York. There were such dates in Clearfield, Pennsylvania (Hecla Park), on Wednesday September 15 (an off-night at the Meadowbrook); Scranton, Pennsylvania on September 23; and at the well-known Sunnybrook Ballroom in Pottstown, Pennsylvania on Saturday night, September 25 (1584 dancers). They returned to New York on Sunday the 26th for the *Fun in Swingtime* show from 6:30 to 7:00 p.m. and then played for the first time at the legendary Savoy Ballroom in Harlem. Bunny's music proved to be very popular with the dancers at the Savoy. He would return there a number of times. On Tuesday, September 28, the Berigan band played at Worcester, Massachusetts, and on October 2 at the State Armory in Syracuse, New York.

Immediately after this, MCA booked the band into the Arcadia Ballroom in New York for a week. Press reports then had him "breaking in a vaude act" while at the Arcadia.[26] He would need these supporting performers when his band began to play theaters on tour. It was another expense that he would have to front until he could recoup his losses on the road. While the waiting game continued, the stakes and Bunny's debt were growing larger each day.

The Victor recording session of October 7 was devoted to four unremarkable pop tunes with Gail Reese vocals that someone, probably a song-plugger,[27] wanted the Berigan band to promote. The titles were: "I'd Love to Play a Love Scene (Opposite You)," "I Want a New Romance," "Miles Apart," and "A Strange Loneliness." There is nothing in these performances, aside from Bunny's unique trumpet contributions, that would even remotely suggest the kind of band he was then leading. It seemed like he was walking in place at Victor on this session, not that this was his fault. He undoubtedly was told what to record, and he was probably very happy to do what he was told, if for nor other reason than to earn some money to partially offset his unremitting overhead in operating his band. The few ballroom one-nighters he did play could not have generated enough revenue to come close to equalizing the band's costs during this lengthy waiting period.

Finally, Bunny was able to announce to the band that the long-awaited road tour would soon begin. He told his musicians that the *Fun in Swingtime* show to air on October 10, their 26th weekly appearance with Tim and Irene, would be their last. Sonny Lee remembered: "The program continued with the D'Artega orchestra. Bunny's participation was ended by him and Arthur Michaud, rather than him being dropped by the sponsor. Michaud had negotiated the original contract, which wasn't renewed because he advised Bunny that he was now a big property and should go for the colleges and large theatres in order to build up an 'in person' following in eastern and Midwestern states. Staying in New York would not permit this, so Bunny agreed to drop the radio show."[28]

On the night of October 10, Bunny guested on Martin Block's radio program with the WNEW orchestra for a swing concert which was broadcast from 11:30 p.m. to 12:30 a.m. He took solos on "Black Bottom," "The Ubangi Man," "Honeysuckle Rose," and "Russian Lullaby." Recordings of this broadcast do exist.[29]

After this, Berigan was finally free to leave the greater New York area for extended periods of time to meet the American public in person. The full power of MCA was now brought to bear on theater and ballroom operators to make sure that they had the opportunity to present Bunny Berigan, "The Miracle Man of Swing," and His Orchestra at their venues. No one was happier at this development than Bunny himself. His entire professional life had been a preparation for this golden opportunity. Berigan, just a couple of weeks shy of his 29th birthday, was in his prime, and national success at last was beckoning.

Notes

[1] Although the Berigan-Wiley affair was definitely in full bloom by early 1936, it may have started the previous summer, when Wiley was in Los Angeles at the same time Berigan, who was with Benny Goodman's band, was also there.

[2] A number of Bunny's musical associates from the mid to late 1930s expressed the opinion that Bunny did indeed love Lee Wiley.

[3] *Chilton:* 108–109.

[4] Joseph M. Herbert was Tommy Dorsey's accountant, and through TD, he was introduced to Bunny Berigan, and then retained by Bunny. Herbert reported to Mort Goode, in the liner notes for *The Complete Tommy Dorsey, Vol. III, 1936–1937,* RCA Bluebird AXM2-5560 (1978) that "John Gluskin was a well-known litigating attorney, associated in those days with the Ferdinand Pecora Law Firm. He had a ten percent management interest in the (Tommy Dorsey) band's income, and Tommy and Arthur Michaud owed him a good deal of commissions. They were in a business discussion one night when Tommy said (to Gluskin): 'I'm going to pay you more money than I even owe you to settle my debt.' Gluskin enthusiastically replied: 'Okay Tom, that's great kid.' Tommy said, 'Fine, here are all of the stock certificates for those oil wells I went into with Morton Downey and the boys. They're all yours.' That's how he paid him off. Every one of those wells came in dry." Such a gambit would never have occurred to Bunny Berigan. Indeed, Bunny would never have invested in oil wells. Despite the ongoing involvement of Gluskin in the Berigan band's finances, it appears that he never represented Berigan as an attorney.

[5] White materials: July 17, 1937.

[6] Cited in White materials: July 31, 1937.

[7] *Down Beat:* August 1, 1937, cited in the White materials.

[8] White materials: August 3, 1937.

[9] White materials: August 8, 1937.

[10] *Ibid.*

[11] White materials: April 3, 1936.

[12] *Giants of Jazz:* 43.

[13] This comparison was first made by Vince Danca in his self-published booklet entitled *Bunny* (1978), 18–19.

[14] Dupuis: 169.

[15] White materials: August 7, 1937.

[16] All cited in the White materials: August 7, 1937.

[17] The information concerning the Waller disc in the album *A Symopsium of Swing* came from big band historian Christopher Popa, who operates the *Big Band Library* website.

[18] White materials: July 8, 1937.

[19] This review was by Paul Eduard Miller, and it appeared in the November 1937 issue of *Down Beat,* cited in the White materials: August 18, 1937. Miller conducted a lengthy interview in April of 1938 with drummer Dave Tough which contains most of the information that now exists about Tough's early career. That information was the basis for the

scholarly articles about Tough that Harold S. Kaye wrote, which appeared in *Storyville,* 2000–2001.

[20] Dupuis: 159–160.

[21] White materials: August 31, 1937.

[22] *Metronome:* October 1937, cited in the White materials: September 4, 1937.

[23] White materials: September 7, 1937.

[24] *Orchestra World:* December 1937, cited in the White materials: September 7, 1937.

[25] *Billboard:* August 30, 1941, cited in the White materials: September 7, 1937.

[26] *Orchestra World:* November 1937, cited in the White materials: September 30, 1937.

[27] The great jazz pianist Teddy Wilson, a most thoughtful and articulate man, who led many of the recording sessions in the mid and late 1930s that featured Billie Holiday, once made a concise summary of how the music publishers essentially decided what tunes were to be recorded then: "In those days, the publishers made the hits. They had what they called number one, two, and three plugs, these being the songs they were pushing. The publishers would send all the sheet music to the recording companies each month, but the one, two, and three tunes were given to other people. We had our choice of the rest. That's why many of those songs we recorded you never heard anybody singing besides Billie." Liner notes for *Billie Holiday—God Bless the Child,* Columbia G30782 (1972).

[28] White materials: October 10, 1937.

[29] *Ibid.*

Chapter 15
The Business of Success

No one has ever recounted their experiences as the leader of a big band more compellingly than Bunny's fellow CBS and freelance recording comrade Artie Shaw did in his book *The Trouble with Cinderella.* The dislocations of constant travel; the discomforts, and occasional pleasures of road life; the insanity of constant ballyhoo and celebrity—it erodes the human spirit and breaks down one's health. Shaw didn't drink, but he suffered several nervous collapses and other health problems while he led various big bands during the swing era. He repeatedly formed then broke up bands to deal with the stresses of leading a big band on the road. He left the music business, then returned, several times. He finally walked away from the music business permanently to preserve his sanity and his health. He managed to survive though, to ripe old age, and tell the tale.

Bunny Berigan was another type of cat entirely. He was a big, strong man, and he was stubbornly idealistic. He firmly believed that if he presented the best band possible to audiences, and played his best, he would have ongoing success. He had dedicated the first nine-plus months of 1937 to doing precisely that. Berigan, like all successful bandleaders, completely understood the compromises that had to be made to allow him to keep his band together. These were more or less the same compromises he had been making for years at CBS and in the recording studios: you must play a certain percentage of bad music in order to play some good music. Bunny had compromised to get his band going, and he would continue to compromise to keep his band going.

Once his band got rolling however, and it moved into high gear in the autumn of 1937, he would not, indeed he could not entertain even the possibility of laying off, or heaven forbid, breaking up his band. Leading his band was far more intoxicating for Bunny Berigan than alcohol. It was through his band that Bunny Berigan *lived.* Almost everything else he did during the course of the day, no matter how important or inconsequential, was more or less irrelevant to him. What mattered most was what he and his band did onstage that night. He *had* to perform; he had to do what he did to the best of his ability—every night. And when he didn't or his band didn't, it was much more than a small disappointment. In this way, he was very much like his idol, Louis Armstrong. Both men lived through their music, and were unhappy when they were not making music. Vacations and layoffs made them feel very uncomfortable. They reveled in the love and appreciation they felt when they played for appreciative audiences. Armstrong dealt with the inevitable challenges and disappointments of life as a star performer perpetually on tour by habitually smoking marijuana. He was able to live a long, full life as a result. Bunny Berigan's musical associates repeatedly tried to get him to use marijuana instead of alcohol as a coping tool. Unfortunately, by 1937, his addiction to alcohol was so profound that nothing else was powerful enough to get him to stop or reduce his drinking for very long. Moreover, given the constant demands of his work as a star bandleader, it was now impossible for him to stop drinking completely, go through withdrawal, and obtain the constant follow-up required to deal with breaking alcohol addiction. He simply could not do that and maintain the career he had worked so hard to build. Indeed, the progressive nature of his alcoholism made it necessary for him to consume more alcohol each day merely to function. Every day he had to gauge how much liquor he needed to get through the day, yet not be impaired. It was difficult to find the right balance; he frequently missed. But he tried, every single day. So, he worked and he traveled, and he drank. This would be the pattern of his life for the next four and a half years, with his overall consumption of alcohol increasing steadily all the while. This could not go on for very long, his associates thought. Or could it?

We do not know who loaned Bunny Berigan the money to balance his band-operations budget for the long months in 1937 it had taken to organize the band, build its personnel and book of arrangements, and then forge it into a formidable performing unit. As I have said earlier, MCA was the most likely source of at least some these funds. Arthur Michaud, John Gluskin, and/or Tommy Dorsey were also possible sources for some of the money. (John Gluskin was an attorney who had an association with Arthur Michaud. He [Gluskin] was certainly involved with Michaud in the business of Tommy Dorsey's band in the 1930s, and was similarly involved in the Berigan band.) After months of incurring an operating deficit with his band, it was now time for Bunny to balance the books. And for MCA and/or Michaud/Gluskin/TD, it was payback time. The numbers cited above in chapter 14 for the Bob Crosby band reveal the stark realities of how a big band could survive: 60 percent of a band's income would have to come from theaters and one-night stands, and that was in a successful band that also had a sponsored radio show adding considerably to its revenue. MCA now put the Berigan band on the road where for a solid two-month period, all they would do was play theaters and one-night dance dates.

Much of the detail regarding the late 1937 Berigan band tour was taken from the records created by the band's road manager, George Stacy. The job of road manager for a big band was an important one. George T. Simon, in his biography of Glenn Miller, devoted a number of pages to reviewing just how important having a good road manager was to having a successful band on tour. Here are some of his observations regarding one of Miller's most effective road managers, Johnny O'Leary:

> He was a stickler for details and a master at following routines. A graduate of the Schribman office, he knew all the tricks promoters played, and he'd catch all of them at each and every one of them. He was a genius at clocking the gate, with his hidden clicker in hand, counting every paying customer and every freebee

who walked in, and then at the end of the evening coming up with the correct total paid attendance on the basis of which the band would be paid. With O'Leary on the job, Glenn never again had to worry about any promoter shortchanging him. As road manager it was also his job to check on the musicians, on what uniforms they were to wear, when the bus left, what hotel they'd be staying at, whether they'd arrived on time, whether they'd left on time, and all sorts of other routine details.[1]

In his years as a bandleader, Bunny Berigan had several road managers. Not all of them performed up to the high standards of Glenn Miller's Johnny O'Leary.

Here is the band's itinerary then: October 12, Roseland State Ballroom, Boston; drive 314 miles to Carbondale, Pennsylvania, for a dance date on October, 13; drive 134 miles back to New York; October 14, appear on Martin Block's *Make Believe Ballroom* radio show from 6:00 to 6:30 p.m., then play a dance in New York after the broadcast; October 15, drive 200 miles to Baltimore, then open a one-week stand at the Hippodrome Theater in Baltimore playing numerous shows each day. These shows featured vaudeville performers that Berigan had to pay. Here is the review of Bunny's theater debut that appeared in *Variety:*

Berigan's First Vaude Date: Baltimore, October 16. Bunny Berigan, trumpet tooting maestro, made his first theatre appearance this week, set by MCA, at the Hippodrome, with a week of one nighters following taking him to the Stanley Theatre, Pittsburgh, on October 29. Recognized in band circles as a hot trumpeter of top rank and established over the air, Bunny Berigan is now essaying a stage unit and as such has the makings of an entertaining outfit. With some interpolated specialties, the unit as caught here runs 44 minutes. Working in his own set, an attractive sunburst background nicely lit, Berigan fronts a 12-piece combo, pitching in on the brass choruses and introducing the various numbers. A good opening by the band, with Horace Nichols and Dixie Roberts, 'King and Queen of Shag,' going to town in hotcha style, starts the doings nicely and sets the spot for Gail Reese, the band's femme vocalist who gives out with 'That Old Feeling' and 'Baby.' An interpolation here by the theatre of the winner of a recently conducted accordion contest, a stage-scared youth who gives out with 'Dark Eyes' and an unnecessary encore, had a tendency to slow matters up, but Berigan took hold quickly with a version of 'Frankie and Johnny', showing off the various members of his ensemble in special choruses. Okay stuff, but some of the jamming a bit too drawn out. Limiting each soloist to a minimum contribution would help the pace considerably. An arrangement of 'Caravan' next: very good, and audibly greeted by the customers. A femme hoofer then took hold for an okay interlude, preceding Berigan's version of 'The Prison Song' *(sic),* in which he demonstrated his torrid trumpet giving out with some high ones in the upper register. Another number, 'I Want to Make Rhythm' *(sic),* announced as recently recorded, starting with a vocal by Berigan and the femme and winding up in more trumpet stuff. With some cutting down of the band stuff and bunching of Berigan's trumpet contributions into one sock spot, the unit should make an entertaining adjunct to any combo bill.[2]

After closing at the Hippodrome, the band drove 102 miles to Philadelphia for a dance date on October 22 at the Broadwood Hotel opposite the Claude Hopkins band. They then moved on to New Haven, Connecticut, and a one-nighter at the Roger Sherman Hotel on the 23rd. The band was traveling in automobiles owned by various band members. George Stacy, the band's road manager recalled: "Bunny, 'Little Gate' and I rode in Bunny's Plymouth; Hank Wayland and George Wettling each had a 1935 Olds; Mike Doty, Tommy Morgan and Al George were in Mike's DeSoto; Joe Dixon, Steve Lipkins, Georgie Auld and Irv Goodman had Chrysler Royals. We did a helluva lot of driving!"[3]

After the New Haven gig, they returned to New York. Clyde Rounds recalled that time and the first personnel crisis in the Berigan band:

We drove back to New York from Connecticut for a long and arduous day preparing for the theatre engagements ahead. New arrangements had to be rehearsed, new uniforms were delivered and dire warnings were issued regarding the behavior expected by all from our booking agents. Rehearsals continued through the weekend (24th–25th) and on Tuesday night, we played at a private party in Harrisburg, Pennsylvania, where Rollo Laylan first came on the scene. Laylan was an enigma. I'd never met him before, and after his short-lived tenure with the band, I never saw him again. It was rumored that he was either a relative or a long-time friend of Bunny's wife, Donna, but since he came from Bunny's home state, it's more likely it was Bunny he knew. Anyway, Bunny said he could sit in on drums at this party, where everyone was getting well juiced, including Wettling. Well, George blew his top when Rollo sat down at his drums and it looked as though things might get out of hand. Eventually, we managed to calm things down, but we were to realize later how much this incident had hurt Wettling.[4]

This is the first reference to the problem Bunny was having with someone else's (George Wettling's) drinking. Wettling's drinking was so bad while he was with the Berigan band that even fans were aware of it.[5] It undoubtedly affected his ability to perform, and moreover impeded the swing of the rest of the rhythm section and the band as a whole. Bunny was now in the uncomfortable position of having to deal with the problems Wettling's drinking was causing for the band. Bunny genuinely liked George Wettling, who, when sober, could be a truly inspiring drummer. I'm sure Bunny talked to Wettling and told him that he could drink, just like Bunny drank, but that he couldn't get so drunk that he couldn't perform. This is the type of conversation that seems absurd to non-alcoholics, but makes perfect sense to alcoholics. Wettling then probably said he would control his drinking, and everything seemed settled. Things were not settled however. Wettling's pride had been wounded, and Bunny was growing increasingly dissatisfied with Wettling's behavior, both behind the drums and with other members of the band. When intoxicated, Wettling could be mean and violent. Joe Dixon recalled: "George was a delightful guy, but he just drove us crazy. He and Joe Lippman were constantly fighting. Fistfights, everything. He really beat Joe up once. When George left, Joe just relaxed." Lippman's view on this: "George and I loved each other. It was just that when Wettling drank, he seemed to get on his friends."[6] Between Bunny, and MCA/Michaud, it was decided that a backup drummer should be available in case Wettling fell off the wagon (or the bandstand). Bunny no doubt realized that Lippman was becoming more of an asset to the band because of his arrangements than Wettling was with his erratic drumming and behavior. In what can be judged a truly bizarre decision, the backup drummer chosen was Rollo Laylan, who was indeed an old acquaintance of Bunny's from his Wisconsin days. Undoubtedly, Bunny alone was responsible for the choice of Laylan, who quickly demonstrated that he was completely unsuited to be the drummer in the Berigan band. (See below.) Nevertheless, he was available now on short notice.

After the Harrisburg gig on October 26, the band played one-nighters in Wheeling, West Virginia, on the 27th, and possibly one in Akron, Ohio on the 28th before opening at the Stanley Theater in Pittsburgh on Friday, October 29. Bunny had retained the services of different vaudeville performers for this engagement. They are certainly the ones referred to above by Clyde Rounds who had rehearsed with the band in New York a few days before. The *Pittsburgh Post-Gazette* reviewed the Berigan show at the Stanley:

> It is practically a parade of youthful veterans at the Stanley this week. Heading is that sizzling cornet *(sic)* player, Bunny Berigan, who's been around for some time, but only recently took over a band of his own. Swing, of course, is Mr. Berigan's meat and what came out of his horn when he pushed that valve down is almost unbelievable. He should pay a little more attention to his arrangements; they're just a bit too long and pruning the scores would heighten their effect considerably. That new dance craze called the Shag gets a frenzied demonstration by the team of Nicholas and Roberts, and Mr. Berigan presents his attractive vocalist, Gail Reese, all too briefly.[7]

Gail Reese explained why she didn't sing more at the Stanley Theater: "Unfortunately, I was taken ill during that engagement and Bunny was most considerate, cutting down my numbers before finally packing me off home to recuperate."[8] When the Berigan troupe closed at the Stanley on November 4, it was reported that they had grossed $21,000 during their stand there. This was for six days, because Pennsylvania's "Blue Laws" prevented performances on Sundays. Ticket prices were in the twenty-five to sixty-five cent range. (Again, to get an approximate value in today's dollars, multiply by fifteen.) The band likely moved the show twenty-five miles west to the Capitol Theater in Steubenville, Ohio, on Sunday October, 31, where it probably performed at least two shows.[9] That would have upped the weekly gross number.

The next stop on the tour was the Fox Theater in Detroit, where the band opened on Friday, November 5 for a week. While he was in Detroit, Bunny was joined by his parents, whom he had not seen in over two years. The last time he had seen them was right after he came off the Benny Goodman band in October of 1935. Since then the pace of his life had accelerated enormously, and his fame was now spreading across the nation. His parents were most certainly proud of their son as they saw him on the stage of the mammoth Fox Theater, leading his own band and playing to good business. They were also likely shocked and dismayed at the amount of alcohol he had to have each day to function. But they were hardly in a position to be critical because to that point, Bunny's career had been an unbroken series of ever greater successes.

The Berigan show was received very well in Detroit for the entire week it played there. In July of 1938, *Billboard* carried a blurb that revealed just how successful that show was: "The Fox Theatre, Detroit, is a 6,000 seater and now is the only house in town playing vaudeville. The highest take of the year was grossed by Ted Lewis with $40,000 and the lowest was Hal Kemp with $11,000. The biggest surprise to manager David M. Idzal was Bunny Berigan, who grossed $33,000 on his first appearance here. A Ritz Brothers picture helped. Guy Lombardo was the next lowest draw to Hal Kemp. A lot of moderately priced bands do better than the big salaried boys. For example, Berigan, drawing only a third of Lombardo's money, almost doubled his business."[10] These statistics reveal a number of things: first, Detroit was obviously a swing-oriented town, preferring the hot music of Bunny Berigan's band to the sweet offerings of two of MCA's highest-grossing bands, Guy Lombardo and Hal Kemp. It also reveals that Bunny's name in the market had not reached the point where his band could command the top money that long-established bands like Kemp's and Lombardo's were getting. MCA had to constantly make sure that their bands were getting as much money as possible, so the MCA accounting department probably examined the numbers from Bunny's Fox engagement very carefully. In the meantime, MCA continued "building the brand" by promoting Bunny Berigan to every theater and ballroom operator on the MCA circuit of venues.

On the bill with the Berigan band and acts in Detroit was the thirteen-year-old pianist and singer Bobby Short.[11] He later remembered this engagement:

> At the beginning of November, we were booked into the Fox Theatre in Detroit, which was the biggest house I'd ever played—a castle—and my salary was $250 a week. They'd assembled Bunny Berigan's orchestra, a troupe of colored 'Big Apple' dancers, a comic or two and Bobby Short. Berigan, even then deep into his drinking problem, kept very much to himself, withdrawn and removed from everyone around him. I became friendly with all of Berigan's musicians and his piano player taught me 'In a Mist,' a Bix Beiderbecke piano classic. Another Berigan classic I heard that week at the Fox was his arrangement of 'Black Bottom,' which was an old song and dance unto itself.[12]

After closing in Detroit, the Berigan band played a one-nighter in Cleveland on Friday, November 12. On the 13th, they played a dance at the Valley Dale Ballroom, in Columbus, Ohio,[13] from which location they broadcast over WABC–New York. Recordings of this half-hour remote do exist. On the 14th they performed at the Rainbow Garden Ballroom in Fremont, Ohio. Monday, November 15 was a travel day as the band drove back to New York City, approximately 600 miles, most of which was through the hills and mountains of

Pennsylvania. In Manhattan, a most important engagement awaited, at the Paramount Theater.

The Paramount Theater, at Broadway and Forty-third, was the quintessential showcase for the big bands of the swing era. The man whose idea it was to put swing bands on the vaudeville stage was the Paramount's managing director, Bob Weitman. An excellent summary of the Paramount Theater's history in the big band years was carried in both *Billboard* and *Variety* at the end of 1941–beginning of 1942:

> Robert M. 'Bob' Weitman, managing director of the Paramount Theatre, joined the Paramount organization in 1926 and has been at the New York Paramount, which has a staff of 200 people, since 1931. Weitman, a 'graduate' of the old Publix manager training school, was at the Rialto, New York, for 18 months, then manager of the Brooklyn Theatre for five years prior to joining Paramount. The Paramount was the first Broadway theatre to go to a name band policy, which rescued it from its depression-dug grave. It had a low gross of $8,000 a week, which increased to $56,000 the first week of using bands. The first band show was Christmas week 1935, using the Glen Gray Casa Loma orchestra, and the policy was started on a tight budget of $6,500. Tommy Dorsey was the top grosser with a $79,000 week in 1940. He was also the top money-getter, with a pay of $14,000, which included the acts on the bill also. The theatre itself was opened in November 1926 as a straight movie house and prior to the band policy was the biggest 'white elephant' of the Paramount chain. It now spends over $570,000 annually for talent. Cost are tightly controlled; by using a rising pit instead of the stage, $4,000 a week is saved in production costs. Part of the policy is to catch new bands on the way up—some are signed for dates as far as eight months in advance. As of the end of 1941, the average gross for the first week of a show is $48,000 to $52,000, the second week $40,000 to $44,000 and the third week around $36,000. Paramount is the most successful theatre operation in the USA. As of December 1940, the house had grossed close to $10 million in the period since 1935, averaging a million dollars a year. Only once in 260 weeks has the house dropped into the 'red,' and then only slightly. The biggest year was 1937, with 1940 only slightly behind. The scale of admissions is only 25¢ to 85¢ and better than $60,000 has been grossed on six different occasions. By January 1942, a total of 78 different bands had played the house, 28 of them returning. 72 of those bands are (or were) making phonograph records. Acts or specialty artists have also been rebooked. The record for the house is the 14 weeks Red Skelton played in a nine month period. The Andrews Sisters did 15 weeks in the past three years. Tommy Dorsey has the record with 22 weeks in eight engagements; Glen Gray second with 7 dates totaling 17 weeks. A new high was reached on the 5th anniversary show, December 1940, with $77,500 for the Tommy Dorsey orchestra and show.[14]

The Berigan band opened a two-week engagement at the Paramount Theater on Wednesday, November 17. They were truly playing in the big league now. This would be the acid test. If the Berigan band could play a successful two-week stand at the New York Paramount, they had truly arrived. If they failed, MCA would banish them to the road forever doing whatever small theater engagements and one-nighters were available. Bunny had a great deal of help in making the Paramount show something audiences would enjoy. As usual, Bob Weitman made sure that his audiences received great variety, and plenty of it, for their money.

Thursday eve, November 18: the current show, slated for two weeks, is a Technicolor picture, *Ebb Tide*, combined with Bunny Berigan's band and Frances Langford. Miss Langford, a lovely sight in a white-beaded gown, clicked from the time she came on. Without gushing Hollywood talk, she swings right into her singing, landing an appreciative hand after each number and going off to heavy applause. A sweet personality, she delivered a varied set of songs, including a medley of tunes she introduced in recent films, giving each number attention-compelling delivery. She knows how to sell her songs. Berigan, making his Broadway theatre debut as a bandleader, makes fair impression. He's got a flashy swing combo, but Berigan himself lacks real stage presence, despite valiant attempts at singing and comedy banter. When he gets down to tooting that trumpet, he is at his best, providing a brilliant tone and showing off some pretty fancy licks. His 12 men (comprising four saxes, two trumpets, two trombones, string bass, piano, guitar and drums) form a rather solid unit. The sax, clarinet, trombone and bass fiddle standouts in the catchy 'Prisoner's Song' arrangement drew individual hands, each man doing a swell job. A swing arrangement of 'Frankie and Johnny' is another standout, the band as a whole making a good impression. Specialties are offered by Edna Strong, Bob Williams and Fred Sanborn, with Miss Langford closing the show. Miss Strong, a charming brunette, won her audience quickly and completely with fancy loose-jointed taps spins, while Sanborn worked his funny eyebrows overtime to wean a steady run of laughs. His silent cavorting and expert comedy and straight xylophoning put him over solidly. Helen and Bob Williams bring on their remarkable dog, Red Dust, with Bob putting the handsome canine through comedy and acrobatic contortionistics. Bob uses more comedy now and it's a good idea too. The show is preceded by the usual organ session by Don Baker, who can certainly finger that keyboard.[15]

The show, really a vaudeville review, was a success, and during its second week was being called a "smash" in not only the trade papers, but also in the *New York Times*. Weitman extended the review for a third week. Bunny Berigan and His Orchestra had passed the test. Everyone connected with the Berigan band was ecstatic. This was a major triumph.

But in the last week of the engagement, Clyde Rounds saw something happen that seemed insignificant at the time:

We were received most enthusiastically at the Paramount and we also played for *The Hollywood Hour*, which starred Frances Langford, who shared the stage with us. All this helped to enhance the band's reputation with the public, but during our last week an incident occurred, the significance of which didn't strike us at the time. In order to get on to the Paramount stage, we had to go through the basement, past the huge organ and on to the bandstand which was lowered for that purpose. The bandstand rose from the pit like the organ and it was quite a small area, so we had to proceed more or less in single file. Suddenly, on that occasion, the stand started going up before we'd all managed to get on! Bunny was bringing up the rear, giving us a shove, but by the time it came his turn to mount the stand, it was almost level with his head and still rising. All he could do was hang on and pull himself up, but by then he was in full view of the audience and it took him a little time to regain his balance and composure. Of course, word soon spread around that he was drunk again! Despite this injustice, the rumor persisted, resulting in the band being turned down by at least three top locations, the Roosevelt, Biltmore and Commodore hotels in New York, all of which had valuable air-time. At least the Biltmore did us the courtesy of an audition, but to no avail. Gail Reese didn't work the Paramount date, probably because of Frances Langford's act in the stage show which also included Freddy Sanborn, a comic xylophonist. The film was *Ebb Tide*, starring Ray Milland, and we grossed between $30,000 and $40,000 each week.[16]

In spite of this strange mishap, there was no denying that the Berigan band had done well at the Paramount Theater. A sampling of band grosses at the Paramount appeared in *The International Musician* at various times in late 1937– early 1938 reveal where he ranked among other top bands:

New York Paramount grosses for Bunny Berigan: first week unknown; second week $43,000; third week $30,000. The top grosses in 1937 were by the sweet bands, e.g. Shep Fields with $64,000, $42,500, $34,000 in September; followed by Russ Morgan. Berigan out-grossed Tommy Dorsey for his two-week stand in November. Dorsey did $38,500 and $28,000. Fred Waring had the top gross up to early 1938, with a single week record of $70,000 plus weeks of $50,000, $35,000 and $26,000. Benny Goodman grossed $57,000 for the first of his three-week stand in February 1938, which was the third best in two years.[17]

The Berigan band was on a roll. In addition to its continuing success in theaters and ballrooms, its Victor records were beginning to sell, especially the disc that contained "I Can't Get Started" and "The Prisoner's Song." In early December, Victor edited both of these tunes to fit onto a ten-inch record that could be played in jukeboxes. But at that moment, Bunny was simply too busy to take his band into Victor's Manhattan studios to make more records. More lucrative opportunities existed outside of New York City.

After closing at the Paramount Theater on Tuesday December 7, the Berigan crew drove to a one-night dance engagement at the Ritz Ballroom in Bridgeport, Connecticut, on the 8th that had been postponed due to the band's Paramount engagement being extended. They then moved on to "The Showplace of New England," the Metropolitan Theater in Boston for a one-week stand. George Stacy provided the details: "The band shared the stage show with Freddy Sanborn, who had appeared with us in New York, Frances McCoy, another singer who kept Gail Reese at home, plus a couple of comedians, Kepple and Betty and a dance troupe. The film was *Submarine D-1*, which starred George Brent, Pat O'Brien and Wayne Morris. There were four stage shows a day. Prices 25¢ until 1 p.m.; 45¢ 1 to 5 p.m.; 65¢ after 5 p.m.[18]

Vocalist Gail Reese had been unable to work at a number of theaters with the band, because she would have been competing with the starring female singer in the various shows. She explained how this was handled: "I played the Hippodrome Theatre date, but I didn't play the Met in Boston because Frances McCoy was on the bill, or the New York Paramount, when Frances Langford was the headliner. So I wasn't allowed to sing and went home for three weeks. We had one comedy routine, we used in theatres: I was a girl reporter sent to interview Bunny and it would end with me being chased off the stage by his high notes! On one-nighters, we would occasionally split vocals and that was fun. The greatest I ever heard Bunny play was on 'Dark Eyes' at a slow tempo. When he felt like playing that, he was so great!"[19]

The Berigan band closed at the Metropolitan Theater on December 15, having grossed $24,000 while they played there.[20] They then played a couple of dance dates in New England before moving on to the Valencia Ballroom in York, Pennsylvania, for a one-night dance engagement on Saturday December 18. The next night they were back at the Ritz Ballroom in Bridgeport, Connecticut, and then played one-nighters in New England on December 20–22. They returned home to New York on December 23, 1937, an exhausted but elated bunch. Their first big-time tour of theaters and ballrooms, lasting over two months, had been a resounding success.

On December 23, Bunny led his bandsmen into Victor's Twenty-fourth Street studios in Manhattan. The last time they had been there was on October 7, before they went on tour, when they had recorded four forgettable pop tunes with vocals. This session began at 1:00 p.m., ran until 5:30, and produced five instrumentals, something that was virtually unheard of in the swing era. All of the performances are good, and a couple of them are more than that.

"In a Little Spanish Town," as arranged by Joe Lippman, shows that he had learned to simplify his writing so as not to interfere with the overall rhythmic momentum of the band and the jazz solos. After a sort of Dixie beginning, his chart on "Spanish Town" unfolds with minimal, riffy backgrounds that propel the soloists, rather than impeding them. As a result, Georgie Auld, Joe Dixon, and Sonny Lee play freely, and with considerable swing. After a reprise of the Dixie-styled theme, Bunny soars above the band with a flowing solo. The entire ensemble joins in the finale to conclude an excellent, spirited performance.

Dick Rose's swinging arrangement of "Black Bottom" had proved to be a real audience-pleaser when the band played it on the road. Bunny was thus able to persuade the Victor people that it would be successful on record as well. He was right! Once again, the uncomplicated riff-based backgrounds really help the band and soloists to build up a head of steam. I suspect Rose and Lippman had compared notes while preparing the arrangements that were to be recorded at this session. Dick Sudhalter elucidated the goings-on in this performance splendidly:

Nowhere is Berigan's affinity for Louis Armstrong so explicit as in his solo on this recording. (It) is practically a *quodlibet*, a collection of fond memories of his mentor, but delivered in the inimitable Berigan style. In his first two-bar breaks he offers a taste first of Armstrong's solo on 'Sugar Foot Strut' and then a taste of 'Cornet Chop Suey.' Four bars of his own then send him rolling into a 16-bar so-lo that combines a whiff of 'Weather Bird,' a hint of 'Put 'Em Down Blues' and an oblique nod to 'Potato Head Blues.' Georgie Auld bounces through the bridge, and Berigan returns up high with a quote from the old barn-dance favorite 'Ar-kansas Traveler,' working that into an attractive figure that is pure Berigan: a descending chromatic scale, each step of which is 'sprung' from two lower notes for strong rhythmic push.[21]

Auld then returns, for his own solo, which shows that he had grown consi-derably as a jazz player since the previous spring. Dixon also has a good solo, (hear Bunny's sizzling lead trumpet in the background) followed by a bit of Wayland's slapped bass, Wettling's drums, and yet another good solo by Sonny Lee. Bunny adds the high-note capper. Berigan's various bands would play this arrangement, which picked up steam over the years, for the remainder of his life.

It would seem that the vintage tune "Trees (written in 1922 by Oscar Ras-bach as a melody for the poem previously written by Joyce Kilmer while he was serving in France during World War I, shortly before he was killed in action) was a rather odd choice as a vehicle for the dramatic Berigan trumpet, and his hard-charging band. Nevertheless, Bunny utterly transformed it into one of the essential performances not only of his career, but of the entire swing era. The arrangement, this time by Abe Osser, is once again open and airy, and is taken at a perfect dance tempo. It provides an ideal showcase for Bunny's unique talents as both a first trumpeter and as a jazz soloist. Joe Dixon on clarinet leads the reeds, which play the background figures while Bunny leads the cup-muted brass, which carry the melody through the first twenty-four bars. Berigan's very personal sound, phrasing, and expressive vibrato utterly permeate and define the sound of the brass choir: no one else could ever play this music in precisely this way. When Dixon switches to alto saxophone, the four-man sax team steps out for sixteen bars of its own superb melodic playing under the supple lead of Mike Doty's first alto, with the still muted brass punctuating behind them. At about bar 10 of this chorus, the brass are suddenly open, and warm; they then finish the chorus with eight glistening bars of melody. The saxes modulate into Beri-gan's open trumpet solo. Sudhalter explained what happened next:

(H)e chooses the trumpet's lowest register to begin a solo that after many hear-ings seems less an improvisation than a commentary on both Kilmer's poem and (Rasbach's) melody. Especially poignant is a drop to his F sharp (concert E) in bar six, followed by a low F (concert E flat), a note not actually on the horn, but which Bunny 'lips' into being. A magnificent upward sweep to his high B flat and he sings out a legato passage in his horn's highest register, culminating a cla-rion high F—all with no diminution of power or tonal breadth. He lets Lipkins carry things for four bars, then returns to play his own strong, sure lead, bearing the performance into immortality.[22]

This performance is obviously a *tour de force* in the technical sense, but more than that, it is a magnificent, passionately made musical statement. The emotional and musical content of Berigan's playing here is so powerful that the technical wizardry is all but completely subsumed by it. All in a day's work, I guess—if you are Bunny Berigan.

Irving Berlin's "Russian Lullaby," as arranged by Dick Rose, was recorded next. An intro that suggests a Russian march leads into the first chorus where the four saxes set out the melody, with the open Berigan-led brass kicking them along. The brass then take the bridge, and the reeds finish the chorus. Georgie Auld takes a typically bouncing tenor solo; Joe Dixon follows on clarinet. Then Berigan plays a fiery solo where he in effect duels with the entire brass section in places. The smooth reeds and Bunny's excellent first trumpet playing carry this brisk performance to a satisfying close.

The final tune recorded that day was Jerome Kern's "Can't Help Lovin' Dat Man." This song and the preceding "Russian Lullaby" are two of the relatively few selections in the Berigan-Victor catalog that were composed by major figures in the realm of what is now called American popular song.[23] Bunny's agile open trumpet is featured in the first chorus. Both Auld and Lee (with a straight mute) solo at length, with a spot of Dixon's clarinet added for contrast in Sonny's chorus. Berigan returns to wrap it up. This arrangement, attributed to Lippman, is a first-class swing treatment of a fine song.

Bunny Berigan's first year as the leader of a big band had been very successful. He had worked hard, and followed the advice of his manager Arthur Michaud and his booking agent MCA, to the letter. His had built his band carefully, chair by chair. After July, there had been no personnel turnover. He had let the identity of the band evolve around his virtuoso trumpet playing and the arrangements of Joe Lippman, but he was frequently utilizing the arrangements of Dick Rose and Abe Osser, among others, as well. The Berigan band was principally a hard-swinging unit, and although Bunny was most comfortable when the band was swinging away, he was also a nonpareil ballad player, as his renditions of "I Can't Get Started" and "Trees" proved. His relationship with Victor Records through 1937 had been good. His Victor recordings were selling—not in huge numbers, but steadily, even though many of the sides he recorded for them were of substandard pop tunes. His band had proved itself to be quite capable of holding its own on a sponsored radio program, and on the stages of the largest theaters in the United States, being presented there as a part of a package of vaudeville entertainers. In ballrooms, the band was probably at its best, not being constrained by the needs of vaudeville theater or commercial radio. Also, the Berigan band had broadcast regularly on innumerable sustaining broadcasts from many different venues in the eastern United States, building its reputation as one of the more exciting new bands then on the scene.

Last, but certainly not least, the Berigan band ended the year 1937 in the black. All of the weeks when Bunny was required to keep the band in the greater New York area to finish his commitment to the *Fun in Swingtime* radio program had cost Berigan and his financial backers a lot of money. It was reported that Berigan's debt at the beginning of his band's first tour had reached $10,000 (multiply by fifteen to get the value in today's dollars).[24] The tour of theaters and ballrooms from mid-October to the Christmas holidays had been so financially successful that everybody had been paid back, with some money left over to carry the band into the new year. A handsome picture of Bunny Berigan playing his trumpet graced the cover of the December 1937 issue of *Metronome* magazine. It had been a very good year.

In spite of all of this success, Bunny's associates couldn't help but wonder when the ticking time bomb within him might explode. His drinking had continued to increase throughout 1937. He now required great amounts of alcohol simply to get through each day. In addition, his spasmodic relationship with Lee Wiley continued. Their liaison tended to be in its "on" phase when Bunny was in New York. It was at these times that items in various newspaper gossip columns referring obliquely to them began to appear.

Also, even though the Berigan band had achieved substantial success, certain limitations had been recognized as the band progressed through 1937. Bunny could not conduct a show for the various vaudeville acts that appeared in theaters with his band. I do not think this was really a major drawback, because it would have been rather poor showmanship to have a featured performer entertain an audience for an hour or so, then remain onstage to conduct his band as they backed jugglers, dancers, or comedians. No other major bandleader conducted shows for the vaudeville acts that accompanied them in theaters. Also, even though Bunny tried valiantly, he was usually not very good at onstage (or on-air) repartee. And despite his memorable singing on his Victor recording of "I Can't Get Started," Bunny's singing was rarely lauded by contemporary critics. Nevertheless, audiences enjoyed Bunny's vocalizing. He wisely chose to sing only a few numbers each night, making it something of a special treat for his fans.

After the December 23 Victor recording session, Bunny hosted a party for all of the band members—and their wives and girlfriends. Clyde Rounds, in many ways Bunny's Boswell in the 1937–1938 time period, remembered it well:

> We had a big Christmas party after that recording session and Bunny presented each member of the band with a watch, individually inscribed. Gail Reese got a traveling case, and he gave Donna a fur coat. We'd all clubbed together to buy Bunny a matching set of luggage. The day after Christmas, Bunny had called a rehearsal and Rollo Laylan put in another appearance, which really upset George Wettling, who went out during an intermission and had a few belts in a nearby bar. He stormed back into the studio full of Dutch courage, ordering Laylan to 'get-the-hell-out-of-there' and yelling at Bunny that he'd quit if Laylan wasn't out in one minute! It was all very awkward for Bunny and very embarrassing for the rest of us. In the end, I guess Bunny felt George had gone too far this time and let him leave the studio and the band [25]

Even though George Wettling was a fine drummer whom Bunny liked musically and personally, his work with the Berigan band seldom rose to thrilling heights, based on the recordings that the band made while he was a member. It seemed that he was very often trying to utilize various Dixieland devices that did not really fit with what the band was playing. Although his playing did seem to get less busy the longer he was with the band, overall, his playing did not fit in too well with the musical concept of the rest of the Berigan ensemble. This may have been at the root of the sometimes violent disagreements between Wettling and the band's chief arranger and pianist, Joe Lippman.

Bunny's flirtation with the idea that Rollo Laylan would be a suitable replacement for Wettling did not last long. The band members disliked his playing, and referred to him as "Rudimental Rollo."[26] Bunny allowed Laylan to play with the band for only a short time, perhaps only a few days, then a number of other drummers were tried out, and Laylan was replaced. Nevertheless, for the rest of his career, Laylan's resumé included the proud assertion that he had played with Bunny Berigan.

The Berigan band opened at the Earle Theater in Philadelphia for a one-week stand on Friday, December 31, 1937. It was a part of the customary vaudeville show format then being used in theaters. Unfortunately, during this engagement, Bunny became ill with the flu and simply could not perform with his band. Being unable to perform because of illness is every performer's worst nightmare. The rumor mill went into high gear, with George T. Simon, *Metronome's* editor and major writer, leading the charge:

> Philly news: Bunny Berigan stepped into a flock of tough breaks when he played the Earle Theater. Besides being ill with grippe, Bunny was in a constant state of anxiety over his little daughter, who was dangerously low with pneumonia in New York. Berigan was forced to leave the stage in the midst of solos. For the several shows in which Bunny didn't appear at all, the management put a pit-man into his clothes and stuck him out front. The cash customers were not told the circumstances and the substitution did not do Bunny any good.[27]

What actually happened was that after Bunny was forced to leave, trumpeter Irving Goodman directed the band, and a trumpet player from the Earle Theater pit band was used in the section. There is no indication that Irving Goodman was ever misrepresented as Bunny Berigan. This was explained in a letter to the editor of *Metronome*, that appeared in the March, 1938 issue. However, this bad publicity, and the resulting gossip in the music business, hurt Berigan at a critical time in his band's existence. After they closed at the Earle Theater, Bunny returned to New York with them and took a few days off to recuperate from his illness.[28]

Then the wildly swinging pendulum of luck suddenly moved into a more positive phase for Bunny. After being fired by Tommy Dorsey for drunkenness, the drummer Dave Tough was hired by Berigan, probably around January 15.

Bunny and his sidemen were elated. Clyde Rounds recalled the diminutive Mr. Tough:

> Davey, as we all called him, was a man of many parts. Of Scottish descent, he could be as dour as any true member of the kilt set or convulse us with his outrageously wild sense of humor. Also highly intelligent and imaginative, he could have been a successful writer, poet or composer. He was the best and most solid drummer I ever worked with, who despised the idea of a drummer being a flashy soloist in the Krupa tradition, and played very few solos himself. Like Bunny and his predecessor Wettling, Davey had a strong affinity for hard liquor, and also like Bunny, he couldn't stay on the wagon for long. Rollo Laylan couldn't swing the band, and the difference with Davey Tough in the driving seat was obvious to musicians and listeners alike. Bunny had auditioned several drummers, but none of them had what he was looking for. When he heard that Tough was available, he went all out to get him and dispensed with an audition.[29]

The band did some one-nighters within a 150 mile radius of the New York area for a few days before they opened for a week at the Brunswick Hotel in Boston on Tuesday, January 18. That job ended on the 24th. They then returned to New York for a Victor recording session on the 26th. Once again, the Berigan band was used to promote four current pop tunes with Gail Reese vocals, the most notable of which was "Heigh-Ho (The Dwarfs' Marching Song)," which was a part of the musical score for Walt Disney's first full-length animated feature film *Snow White and the Seven Dwarfs*. By this time Joe Lippman was remaining in New York to write arrangements for the Berigan band. His place in the band had been taken on an interim basis by pianist Fulton "Fidgey" McGrath. McGrath gets substantial solo space on the novelty "Piano Tuner Man," which also includes Bunny and Gail Reese "talking" to each other. The White materials include speculation that McGrath may also have written the arrangement. On this recording, the band is obviously energized by Dave Tough's electric presence on drums.

"Heigh-Ho" is given a romping up-tempo treatment in 2/4 time. This is a happy-sounding performance that I'm sure the band didn't take too seriously. But that doesn't mean they did not invest the music with great spirit. Again there is speculation in the White materials about the source of the arrangement; this time Deane Kincaide is mentioned as the possible writer. I cannot say who wrote this chart, but it certainly does not sound like anything Kincaide was writing then for the Bob Crosby, Woody Herman, or Tommy Dorsey bands. Nevertheless, Kincaide himself recalled "doing a Disney tune for a Berigan record date," so on that basis, it is certainly possible that this arrangement is his. Bunny states the melody using a straight mute, Ms. Reese sings well, then the maestro returns with a few bars of torrid open horn trumpeting.

Richard M. Sudhalter commented many times about why it is worthwhile to listen to these Berigan performances of evanescent pop tunes: "A Serenade to the Stars," recorded next, is the kind of performance that could be taken for granted by anyone except a trumpet player. Berigan's lead and velvety low register solo in the first chorus, the casual way he enters over the tutti after the vocal, then the majesty of his solo statement when the band modulates into B flat for the final passionate half-chorus in the high register—it's all staggeringly difficult to do so well." On "Outside of Paradise," the final tune recorded that day,"...Bunny states the melody in his lower middle register, then up an octave. After the vocal and a brief Dixon solo, Berigan leads the full ensemble to the end in dramatic corroboration of bassist Arnold Fishkind's remark that: 'no one could play lead the way Bunny could.'"[30]

Bunny was delighted to have Dave Tough in his band, and Davey, the little giant of the drums, was very happy to be there. Unfortunately, the records they made together in the winter of 1938 gave Tough very little opportunity to demonstrate why he was one of the greatest drummers of the swing era.

It seems that MCA was uncertain of what to do next with the Berigan band because the bookings it had lined up revealed no overall plan: scattered one-nighters, including one at the Ritz Ballroom in Bridgeport, Connecticut, on Sunday January 30, followed by several days at New York's Roseland Ballroom, starting on Saturday, February 5. After the Roseland gig, they returned to the road, playing at Davidson College, near Charlotte, North Carolina, on Friday and Saturday February 11-12, and then the Sunnybrook Ballroom in Pottstown, Pennsylvania, on February 13. It was at this time that road manager George Stacy left the band, being replaced temporarily by Bob Parke. On February 14, the Berigan band opened for a week at the Carmen Theater in Philadelphia. *Billboard* reported at the time that the purpose of this engagement was to build the band up for its upcoming engagement at the Arcadia International Restaurant in Philadelphia.[31]

After closing at the Carmen Theater, the Berigan band traveled to an afternoon gig on February 20 at the Fordham Club in New York City, playing opposite Count Basie. The Basie band had been the beneficiary of the ongoing enthusiastic support of John Hammond, and had been improving steadily in the year since they had arrived in New York. Their first engagement in New York was at Roseland during Christmas week 1936. *Metronome's* George T. Simon welcomed them with one of the most brutally negative reviews he ever wrote. On the issue of the early Basie band, King George and King John disagreed completely. Hammond had just recently persuaded Benny Goodman to include Basie and Basie sidemen Lester Young, Buck Clayton, Freddie Green, and Walter Page in his Carnegie Hall swing concert, which took place on January 16, 1938. After that momentous occasion, the full Basie band then invaded Harlem's Savoy Ballroom, where they battled the local favorite Chick Webb[32] to a draw. That event had to be fabulous: Basie and Billie Holiday, and Chick and Ella Fitzgerald.[33] Heaven! The swing era was nearing an early apogee.

I can imagine that Bunny gave his band a pep talk before the Fordham Club engagement, telling his boys that if they weren't careful, the Basie band would blow them off the stage. It must have worked. The always gracious Bill Basie, after hiring Georgie Auld for his early 1950s small band, remembered this encounter with the Berigan band: "The first time I met Georgie Auld was when Bunny Berigan's band battled ours one Sunday afternoon in the Bronx, and cut us. Georgie was great and has been ever since."[34] For his part, Bunny took tremendous admiration of the Basie style of swing away from this battle. In fact, he became somewhat obsessed with the light but powerful way the Basie band's rhythm section functioned, and on at least one occasion a few months after this event, had his musicians deliberately study what the Basie band did so well. (For those interested in how Count Basie's band sounded at the time it battled the Berigan band, listen to the recordings they made for Decca a few days before, on February 16, especially "Every Tub" and "Swingin' the Blues.")

Pianist Graham Forbes, who followed Fulton McGrath into the Berigan band, recalled, among other things, that Davey Tough may have been a casualty of this battle with Basie:

> My real name was Charles Graham Forbes but I went by C. Graham. After the big band period I was a vocal (male) accompanist for a number of years into the 1960s. I also did solo work including a gig at Eddie Condon's club in NYC. I'd been introduced to Bunny by George Stacy, his road manager, when he was looking for a pianist. My parents came to my first date with the band at the Fordham Club, where we shared the bill with Count Basie. I think Jo Jones, Basie's drummer, was called on by Bunny to sub for Davey Tough, at least part of the time. I guess Davey was under the weather. Soon afterwards, we traveled back to Philadelphia, where Bunny hired Harlow Atwood as permanent replacement for Stacy as road manager.[35]

The Berigan band opened at the Arcadia International Restaurant in Philadelphia on Thursday, February 24 for two weeks. They broadcast from there on opening night and regularly thereafter at various times over WABC, WOR, and WMCA. Graham Forbes recalled that engagement: "Bunny did terrific business at the Arcadia. He and Davey Tough were both on the wagon and playing great. During the second week, Benny Goodman, Tommy and Jimmy Dorsey and Larry Clinton were all playing in or around Philadelphia, and one night both Tommy Dorsey and Gene Krupa were on the stand, jamming with Bunny for about an hour! I believe the local union officials didn't take kindly to such goings-on."[36] Indeed, the local musicians' union did make a big issue about this, which was reported on in the trade papers. The Berigan band closed at the Arcadia Restaurant on March 10.

On March 3, while the Benny Goodman band was on the stage of the Earle Theater in Philadelphia, Benny and Gene Krupa had an argument, after which Krupa abruptly left the Goodman band. The ultimate significance of this event would be very great for Bunny Berigan for a number of reasons.

The next night, the Berigan band was on the air (WABC) and their entire thirty-minute broadcast was recorded. I have not heard these recordings. They have never been issued commercially. But I would bet that they are excellent if for no other reason than that they present the Berigan band with drummer Dave Tough playing at least a few jazz tunes. The selections: "Back in Your Own

Back Yard," as an instrumental; then "Serenade to the Stars," "Heigh-Ho," "Goodnight Angel," all with vocals by Gail Reese; three more instrumentals; "In a Little Spanish Town," "Thanks for the Memory," "'Tain't So Honey, 'Tain't So;" then "The One I Love," with a Reese vocal; and finally "The Prisoner's Song," which Bunny had been using for some time as his wrap-up tune. This lineup shows that Berigan was playing a mixture of jazz vehicles, tunes he had recently recorded, and some new ("Thanks for the Memory") and old ("The One I Love") goodies. It was a very well-balanced program. Musically, Bunny continued to make the right moves.

MCA then announced that the Berigan band would begin an lengthy engagement at the Paradise Restaurant in New York on March 20, with frequent sustaining broadcasts over the entire Mutual network, originating from WOR–New York. Their plan had finally emerged: build up the Berigan name again via radio broadcasts, then send the band out on tour again to play weeklong engagements in theaters, with fill-in one-night dance jobs along the way. A sponsored radio show would have provided Berigan with a financial base to continue to operate his band in the black. Unfortunately, despite a number of auditions, one was not forthcoming.

Nevertheless, before Bunny started the Paradise stand, he kept very busy playing dance dates and making records. On March 15 and 16, the band made two separate recording sessions at Victor. These were Dave Tough's last appearances with the Berigan band. Almost immediately after the departure of Gene Krupa from the Benny Goodman band, probably through machinations engineered by MCA, it was decided that Tough was needed to hold the very successful, but somewhat shaken, Goodman band together. He was now on the last days of his two-week notice with Bunny. It was obvious to everyone, including the people at MCA, that Tough was a marvelous big band drummer. His work, first with Tommy Dorsey, and then with Berigan, had been exemplary. His services would be of greater benefit to MCA if he worked for Goodman. This development greatly pleased Benny, who had for some time been growing more resentful of Gene Krupa's loud (and crowd-pleasing) drumming and histrionics. By comparison, Tough's drumming and persona were almost unnoticeable to audiences. Musicians in the Goodman band (and fans attuned to the rhythms of jazz) took note of what Tough was doing however, and they liked it.

This development did not please Bunny Berigan. After George Wettling departed, Bunny had greatly miscalculated when he thought "Rudimental Rollo" Laylan could take Wettling's place. After a few weeks of frustrating uncertainty, a stroke of good luck brought Dave Tough into the Berigan band, and Bunny could not have been happier. Tough's unobtrusive, though powerful swing had freed Berigan's musicians to play with greater abandon than they ever had previously. As anyone who knows anything about jazz knows, if the drummer is not right the band is not right. With Dave Tough, the Berigan band was *right*. Unfortunately, the ten Victor recordings made while Tough was a member of the Berigan band are all very ordinary (at best) pop tunes, each with a Gail

Reese vocal chorus, that the band performed professionally. They probably felt that with this material, the best thing they could do was get acceptable takes as quickly as possible, and move on to more stimulating endeavors outside of the recording studio. That they found it difficult to work up much enthusiasm for these run-of-the-mill songs is understandable. Bunny, however, usually invested a lot of thought and feeling in his solos, even on the most pedestrian of these songs, as the produce of the next two Victor recording sessions shows. And the arrangements, mostly by Joe Lippman, contain some excellent writing.

The critic Leonard Feather, in 1938 only recently arrived in the United States from England, was a guest at the Berigan band's March 15 recording session which ran from 1:30 to 6:00 p.m.:

> When you hear a band in person, it is customary, indeed instinctive, to pardon a slip here and there and if the ensemble work is less than perfect, a few faults may not prove offensive. But it was not until I heard Bunny and his boys down at the Victor studios that I realized the difference between a band that sounds fine and one that records well. As I entered, Bunny was growling his way into one of those very low register choruses which have become his forte. The tune was a popular number, 'Down Stream,' and the arrangement by the talented pianist, Joe Lippman. Bunny had already made several masters, but all had been spoilt, generally through some slip in his solo. As the buzzer called for silence and the next master went into action, Bunny got going nicely, then came just one sour note and he knew the master was wasted. Next time, the band didn't even get past the introduction as Irving Goodman took a bow for the fluff that held up proceedings. Rose-cheeked and petite, Gail Reese sat in her chair, waiting for them to make a master in which they'd get as far as her vocal in the second chorus. 'Now, just take it easy, this is going to be the one,' said Bunny, quite calmly, for the seventh time. Because he has been a rank-and-file musician and feels the way the men do, Bunny is unlike many bandleaders. The master-and-pupil disciplinary method is entirely absent. Possibly he has erred on the side of leniency for it was difficult for him to maintain law and order between takes and it was clear that no amount of rehearsal would pave the way for a perfect master of 'Down Stream.' It was just a matter of playing on until luck gave them three minutes of flufflessness! After the next take, Bunny called out, 'Wrap it up!' By now, he was feeling the strain and to let off steam he started on a glorious impression of a street musician. This was funny enough to take everybody's minds off 'Down Stream' and there was a fresher approach to the next waxing. The time had come for me to leave Bunny floating 'down stream,' so I slipped out as the much-too-familiar strains of the introduction were striking up yet again.[37]

"Down Stream" was the first tune recorded on March 15. To my ears, whatever strain there was in producing this recording is totally absent from the issued take. Bunny's playing is exemplary throughout. He lobs out huge sounding low notes in his first exposition of the melody. When he returns, it's in the middle register, and he's moving up, heightening drama. After the vocal, Auld plays effectively on the bridge; then Bunny returns low at first, then high and fiery. He growls over the humming reeds to finish this recording. All things considered,

Bunny's treatment of "Down Stream" was exceedingly musical, and thoughtful. It made no difference. Feather's story was later embellished, and became a typically apocryphal Bunny Berigan tale: that Bunny required approximately forty takes to make an acceptable master. There is no evidence in the RCA Victor files indicating that Berigan made an amount of takes or tries even remotely near to forty for "Down Stream."

Will Hudson wrote the simple but attractive melody to "Sophisticated Swing," and Mitchell Parrish the mundane lyric, replete with references to Depression era America. Once again, Bunny first sets out the melody in his lower register, then returns a little higher, slurring notes to add a bit of jazz interest. The band plays the rhythmic arrangement with finesse and swing, gliding along atop Tough's high-hat swishes. There is music going on here. Bunny plays the eight-bar main strain of the song once more before the vocal chorus. After the vocal, Bunny leads the brass, his unique vibrato prominent. Based on the writing for the swirling reeds under the brass here, I would say this arrangement was done by Joe Lippman. Both Dixon and Auld make the most of their eight-bar solos. Then the master returns: "...on a rip up to his high F, winding it up with three magnificent Armstrong-inspired breaks."[38] Berigan's trumpet playing, and a good performance by the band, raised the musical level much higher than one would expect, given the rather ordinary source material.

"Lovelight in the Starlight" is rescued from oblivion by Berigan's velvety low-register melody statements in the first chorus.

The recording session the next day was scarcely more productive in terms of the quality of the songs. "Rinka Tinka Man" has almost nothing to recommend it. "An Old Straw Hat" is a little better, with solid playing by Berigan, Tough, and Lee. The band sounds strangely energized on "I Dance Alone," Bunny's solo after the vocal chorus is excellent. They were probably looking forward to leaving the Victor studios where they had exerted so much effort over two days to record seven mediocre to poor tunes.

This session would be Gail Reese's last with the Berigan band. She was a beautiful girl, and undoubtedly dressed up the Berigan bandstand quite nicely. But, based on the twenty-one Victor recordings and the few airchecks she made with the band, she was at best an average singer. Although no one could have done much with most of the tunes she was assigned to sing, her voice quality and pitch frequently left something to be desired. She was also unable to project much enthusiasm, and didn't sing with a beat. I don't know if Bunny, like many other bandleaders, thought girl vocalists were supposed to be merely decorations for the bandstand. If he did, he was making a mistake. Any band that had a good-looking girl vocalist who could also sing well had a much greater chance of pleasing audiences, and of achieving success before live audiences, and on records and radio. As an experiment, I have excised the Gail Reese vocal choruses from a number of otherwise hard-to-listen-to Berigan recordings with the digital remastering equipment I have. Without the cloyingly mawkish lyrics, and Reese's rather listless singing, these sides come remarkably to life. It is obvious that a top-flight band, and a great soloist, were being vastly underutilized by Victor to produce these recordings.

I do not know of the details of Bunny Berigan's contract with Victor Records. I suspect that he was paid a certain sum per side made, and this payment was probably an advance against royalties earned from the future sale of his Victor recordings. In his first year as a Victor recording artist, he made forty-seven sides for the company. Of that forty-seven, thirty-six were vocals, and eleven were instrumentals. Of those eleven instrumentals, at least eight are still, over seventy years after they were recorded, essential items in Bunny's recorded canon. Those recordings are "Swanee River," " Frankie and Johnny," " Mahogany Hall Stomp," "The Prisoner's Song," "Caravan," "A Study in Brown," "Black Bottom," and "Trees." The other three, "In a Little Spanish Town," "Russian Lullaby," and "Can't Help Lovin' Dat Man," are in my opinion also fairly good representations of what the band's actual character was. Among the thirty-six vocals, obviously "I Can't Get Started" is one of the Berigan essentials. There were a couple of other diamonds in the rough: "Turn on That Red Hot Heat" is superb by any measure. Bunny's solo on "Ebb Tide" is magnificent, certainly enough for that performance to be included in any omnibus collections of his Victor recordings, which it has not been.

Of the remaining thirty-four vocals, although many of them contain rewarding musical moments, supplied mostly by Bunny himself, they are really not recordings many people, aside from Berigan aficionados, would get much enjoyment out of. It is a most sad irony that *every one* of the ten recordings the Berigan band made while the great Dave Tough was with them falls into this group. I think it likely that these recordings, with Gail Reese vocals weighing them down like an anchor, did not sell in significant numbers when they were first issued. It is also likely that the decision makers at Victor would have noticed this. Whatever their analysis of this situation was, it did not bring about any immediate changes in the ratio of worthwhile instrumentals versus insipid vocal tunes the Berigan band recorded for Victor. It seems that Victor used the Berigan band in a very similar manner to the way he had been used when he was a freelance recording musician—merely to sell current pop tunes. The big difference for the career of Bunny Berigan then (and this has definitely affected how his work has been judged ever since), is that almost no one knew he was involved in the making of the dozens of rather insipid pop tune vocal records he made before he became a bandleader. Now, *his name was on the records.* Consequently, he was being judged by recordings that very often did not even remotely show the real character of his band. I think it also very possible that in the first year of their association, Berigan himself may have not cared what he recorded for Victor. If they told him to record four lame pop tunes at one session, fine; if they allowed him to record one or more of his band's special arrangements, fine. He led his band either way; he played his trumpet either way; he got paid either way.

Having said all of this, Berigan probably began to get some heat from the people at Victor and/or MCA after these records were made because they clearly indicated that he needed a more effective female vocalist, and maybe even a male vocalist, to enhance his band's commercial appeal. Thus, the wheels of change were set in motion.

The next day, March 17, the Berigan band traveled to Rochester, New York, where they played a St. Patrick's Day dance in that city's armory. The luck of the Irish was with Bunny that night—4,500 persons attended. It was also the first date for the band's new drummer, Johnny Blowers (pronounced like *flowers*). Following Dave Tough into the Berigan band was a daunting challenge for Blowers, who was just shy of his 27th birthday when he joined. Blowers had been working at Nick's in Greenwich Village, with Bobby Hackett's little band. The musicians' grapevine had worked with lightning speed after Tough gave Bunny his two-week notice. Red McKenzie quickly learned that Bunny was going to need a drummer, and asked him to stop in at Nick's when he got back to New York, and listen to Blowers. Bunny showed up at Nick's soon thereafter, without his trumpet. He listened to the band, visited with old friends, met several new ones that night, then left. The next night, he called Nick's and asked to speak with Blowers. He offered Johnny the job as drummer with his band, and, according to Blowers, after brief negotiation agreed to pay $185 weekly, plus extra for recordings. Blowers had been making $45 a week with Hackett.[39] I am somewhat skeptical about the $185 a week salary figure Blowers recalled. My skepticism is based on what Bunny was paying almost everyone else in the band, which was a base salary in the $80–$100 a week range, plus extra for recordings. There is much hyperbole in Blowers's book.

Johnny was welcomed into the Berigan band with some skepticism. Bunny's sidemen had not yet gotten over the "Rudimental Rollo" episode. They quickly realized however that Blowers was a very capable drummer, somewhat in the mode of Dave Tough, but with considerably more technique and flash. Blowers could drive a band almost like Tough, but when called on, could also solo, in the showy then popular Gene Krupa fashion. Soon, the Berigan rhythm team was meshing very well again. Bunny had weathered another potentially damaging personnel changeover without much damage to his band.

On March 18, the Berigan troupe moved on to a Sigma Phi Gamma dance at the Hotel Fillmore, Delaware at Chippewa, in Buffalo, New York. Dancing started at 9:30, with the cost being $1.40 a person, which included thirteen cents for tax.[40] Presumably, they played another one-nighter on March 19, which was a Saturday. On the following night, they opened at the Paradise Restaurant in New York City.

Variety reported the basic information concerning the new Paradise "review" in its March 16 issue: "Bunny Berigan orchestra heads the show opening Sunday, March 20. Acts include Lionel Rand and his boys (rhumba band), Barbara Parks, Liberto and Owens, Alan Carney, McNally Sisters, Grand Quartet and Johnny Coy." A dinner menu dated Saturday April 16, 1938, lists three shows nightly—"7:30 p.m., midnight, and 2 a.m. 'Never a cover charge' but there was a minimum 'spending charge' per person for dinner of $1.50. Saturday and Holidays: $2.00, Ringside: $2.50." Shortly after the show opened, *Variety* published this review:

> A light and spring-like show, fittingly costumed and carrying special music, opened here Sunday (20th) night under a new policy to frequently change orchestras. Changes will be made probably every two weeks. Rudy Vallee is due in next. Management is making a pull for the dancing public. Figured that any deficits can be made up if the Paradise gets the younger generation. Bands will be booked with that in mind. The new floor show doesn't include any name acts, but the Berigan band is being depended on for box office. However it's an agreeably entertaining production with capable talent. Well rounded and moving along at a good clip, show is effectively emceed by Alan Carney. Special music is by Dave Oppenheim and Henry Tobias. Singers include Barbara Parks, Four Grand Quartet, while the McNally Sisters sing and dance. Johnny Coy also sings and tap dances.[41]

The personnel of the band remained unchanged, except that Joe Lippman returned on piano because Graham Forbes did not have a Local 802 union card. There have been reports by Berigan sidemen that during the first part of 1938, they auditioned for a number of sponsored radio shows, but did not get hired for any of them. One of these, for which the band auditioned while they were at the Paradise Restaurant, was for Griffin shoe polish. Hal Kemp got that gig. There had also been rumors in the trade papers for several months (planted by MCA no doubt) that the Berigan band would soon be heading for California to work on radio with Bob Hope.[42] This had not come to pass either. Some of the veteran sidemen, most notably Sonny Lee, sensed that these strikeouts indicated that the Berigan band had perhaps topped out in terms of its commercial appeal.

Even though Berigan was drinking no more (or less) than he had previously, and the band was in fine shape musically, the reasons given as to why they were not getting these jobs were that Berigan was unreliable because of his drinking, and that he could not engage in the jovial repartee that was so much a part of network radio then, without stumbling. (As an aside, no one was more awkward than Benny Goodman when he first began speaking on radio broadcasts featuring his band. On one notable occasion during the Christmas holidays, Benny was required to introduce the tune "Jingle Bells" to a national radio audience. He did so as follows: "*And now, in honor of the season, 'Jingle Balls.'*" His MCA handlers quickly arranged for him to take elocution lessons, after which his radio voice was a cross between the south side of Chicago and Park Avenue. Benny wanted success very badly, and would do what it took to move his band ahead.) Bunny wanted success very badly too, but there were certain things he would not/could not/did not do to move his band ahead. He never took elocution lessons; never got his dead front tooth fixed; and of course, never stopped drinking, at least not for long. In spite of all of this, as the summer of 1938 approached, he was still a spectacular musician, and his band was now one of the hottest swing bands in the country.

Notes

[1] *Glenn Miller and His Orchestra—The Story of America's Most Unforgettable Band-leader,* by George T. Simon, Thomas Y. Crowell Co. (1974), 236–237.
[2] *Variety:* October 20, 1937, cited in the White materials: October 15, 1937.
[3] White materials: October 15, 1937.
[4] White materials: October 24–26, 1937.
[5] *Swing Era Scrapbook:* 167.
[6] *Giants of Jazz:* 45.
[7] *Pittsburgh Post Gazette,* cited in the White materials: October 29, 1937.
[8] White materials: October 29, 1937.
[9] This practice was reported in *Billboard:* October 2, 1937, cited in the White materials: October 31, 1937.
[10] *Billboard:* July 30, 1938, cited in the White materials: November 5, 1937.
[11] Robert Waltrip Short was born on September 15, 1924, in Danville, Illinois. One of his schoolmates was the actor-comedian Dick Van Dyke. Short went to Chicago as an eleven-year old singer/pianist, and began what would eventually be a sixty-plus-year career as a performer. He worked in vaudeville in the 1930s and 1940s, but gradually evolved into a superb interpreter of the best of classic American popular song, frequently working in supper clubs. By the 1970s, he had begun his long association with the Café Carlyle in New York City. This venue would be the base of his operations for the rest of his life. While at the Carlyle, Short became an institution and key performer in the growing cabaret singing movement, which remains vital in New York and other major U.S. cities to this day. Bobby Short died in New York on March 21, 2005, of leukemia.
[12] This excerpt is from *Black and White Baby,* which, though not identified as such in the White materials, is the autobiography of Bobby Short. There is no citation to publisher or date of publication. White materials: November 5, 1937.
[13] Valley Dale Ballroom, 1590 Sunbury Road, Columbus, Ohio, opened originally in 1919, but burned to the ground on New Year's Eve 1923. A new and larger ballroom was built on the same site and opened in 1925. Valley Dale was one of the prime venues for big bands during the swing era. It has been meticulously restored and continues to operate to this day as a multi-purpose banquet facility.
[14] This article appeared in the December 1941 issue of *Billboard,* and in *Variety* on January 8, 1942. Cited in the White materials: November 17, 1937.
[15] *Billboard:* November 27, 1937, cited in the White materials: November 17, 1937.
[16] White materials: November 17, 1937.
[17] Cited in the White materials: December 7, 1937.
[18] White materials: December 9, 1937.
[19] White materials: October 15, 1937.
[20] *Down Beat:* December 1937, cited in the White materials: December 15, 1937.
[21] *Giants of Jazz:* 44–45.
[22] Liner notes—*The Complete Bunny Berigan, Vol. 2* (1986); RCA/BMG Bluebird 5657-1-RB, by Richard M. Sudhalter. Hereafter *The Complete Bunny Berigan, Vol. 2.*
[23] The term American popular song gained currency after the monumental *American Popular Song—The Great Innovators: 1900–1950,* by Alec Wilder, was published in 1972.

[24] A feature article in the *Milwaukee Journal,* February 27, 1938, entitled "Boosting the Rabbit" detailed the costly buildup of the Berigan band and Berigan name.

[25] White materials: December 23, 1937.

[26] White materials: January 1, 1938.

[27] *Metronome:* February 1938, cited in the White materials: January 6, 1938.

[28] White materials: January 1, 1938.

[29] White materials: January 26, 1938.

[30] Liner notes—*The Complete Bunny Berigan, Vol. 2.*

[31] White materials: February 14, 1938.

[32] Drummer William Henry "Chick" Webb was born on February 10, 1905, in Baltimore, Maryland. From childhood he suffered from tuberculosis of the spine, which left him with the appearance of a hunchbacked dwarf. Nevertheless, because of his iron willpower and great ambition, he became a spectacularly flashy drummer, and successful bandleader. He moved to New York City in the early 1920s, and by 1926 was leading his own band in Harlem. By 1931, Webb's band was in essence the house band at Harlem's Savoy Ballroom, where he built a fanatically loyal fan base. In 1935 he began to feature the singing of Ella Fitzgerald, and this and a Decca recording contract caused his band to move from the category of local favorite to one of national prominence. By the late 1930s, the Webb band was one of the most formidable swing units. Unfortunately, his health began to decline dramatically in late 1938, and he died on June 16, 1939, in Baltimore. After his death, his band was led for a time by Ella Fitzgerald.

[33] Singer Ella Jane Fitzgerald was born on April 25, 1917, in Newport News, Virginia. She had a lovely, sweet, but rather callow vocal quality as a youngster that bandleader Chick Webb successfully exploited in the mid and late 1930s. Consequently, Ms. Fitzgerald was catapulted to success very early in her career. She led the Webb band for a few years after its leader's death in 1939, then commenced a long career as a soloist, where she was even more successful. As her voice matured, she began to invest her performances with a bit more emotional depth, but she seemed to eschew an overtly emotional approach to singing, perhaps in reaction to the deeply emotional approach of one of her earliest competitors, Billie Holiday. Nevertheless, her vocal equipment and sense of pitch were so fine that she could make anything sound good. Her series of recordings of songs by America's greatest popular song composers in the 1950s–1960s are landmarks. She could swing as well, and starting in the 1950s, began to feature scat singing in her shows to the delight (and dismay) of many of her fans. Her later career, when she was known as "the First Lady of Song," was expertly guided by impresario Norman Granz. Ella Fitzgerald died on June 15, 1996, in Beverly Hills, California.

[34] *Down Beat*: June 15, 1951, cited in the White materials: February 20, 1938.

[35] White materials: February 20, 1938.

[36] *Ibid.*

[37] *Melody Maker:* June 11, 1938, cited in the White materials: March 16, 1938.

[38] Liner notes—*The Complete Bunny Berigan, Vol. 2.*

[39] *Back Beats and Rim Shots—The Johnny Blowers Story,* by Warren W. Vaché, Scarecrow Press. Inc. (1997), 34–35. Hereafter: *Blowers.*

[40] White materials: March 18, 1938.

[41] *Variety:* March 30, 1938, cited in the White materials: March 20, 1938.

[42] Leslie Townes "Bob" Hope was born in Eltham, London, England on May 29, 1903. Hope emigrated to Cleveland, Ohio, with his family in 1908, and became a U.S. citizen in 1920. He spent most of the 1920s as a touring vaudeville performer, dabbling in song and

dance, and developing a comedy routine that became increasingly successful. By the middle 1930s, Hope began to appear in comedy/musical short-subject films for Warner Brothers/Vitaphone. He was signed by Paramount Pictures in 1938, and it was there that he met Bing Crosby, then fast becoming one of Paramount's biggest stars. Their pairing in many films over the next dozen years proved to be very successful. Hope initiated his own network radio program in 1937 on NBC, first sponsored by Woodbury Soap. A year later, he began an association with Pepsodent which lasted for fifteen years. By the early 1950s, Hope had made the transition from radio to television, and achieved much success in that medium which continued into the 1970s. Hope was also very well known for entertaining U.S. military personnel around the world from the 1940s until the 1970s. Bob Hope died at age one hundred on July 27, 2003, in Toluca Lake, California.

Chapter 16
Maintenance

One of the most fortuitous (for Berigan fans) developments to have occurred while the Berigan band played at the Paradise Restaurant was the recording of many of its sustaining broadcasts emanating from that location. Most of these airchecks began to appear in the late 1970s, and have been commercially available since then. They reveal much more clearly the capabilities of the Berigan band, and the true breadth of its repertoire, balancing in large measure the grossly distorted and limited picture that one gets by simply listening to their Victor recordings from 1937 and the first few months of 1938. These airchecks also reveal that contrary to conventional wisdom, Bunny Berigan was very much taking care of commercial business by frequently playing on the air many of the tunes he had recorded for Victor, to promote those recordings, as all other successful bandleaders also did. The first such recordings from the Paradise were made on March 27, one week after Berigan had opened there. The tunes played were Berigan's theme, briefly; "Back In Your Own Back Yard" (a swinging instrumental); the much maligned "Down Stream"; "Rose Room" (instrumental); "Sweet as a Song" (vocal, Gail Reese); "Let 'Er Go" (as an instrumental); "'Round My Old Deserted Farm "(which would soon be recorded with a vocal); "How'd Ya Like To Love Me?" (vocal); a romping instrumental version of "Louisiana;" and then the closing theme. It was a great broadcast in 1938, and still is today. An excellent cross-section of the off-the-air recordings of the Berigan band from the Paradise Restaurant (seventeen tracks) is to be found on Jazz Hour-1022.[1]

The august *New York Times* took note of the proceedings at the Paradise Restaurant thusly: "The Paradise Restaurant has come back to life with music for dancing provided by Bunny Berigan, one of the better trumpeters, in a new show, which is considerably wilder than some of the institution's prior editions, but very entertaining."[2]

On April 1, Bunny guested, along with Mildred Bailey, on a Paul Whiteman concert that was broadcast over WABC from 8:30 to 9:00 p.m. It scarcely seemed possible that four and a half years had passed since Bunny had been a member of Pops's orchestra. After a brief chat between Bunny and Whiteman (with trumpeter Charlie Teagarden playing "I Can't Get Started" quietly in the background), Berigan played "Dark Eyes," then rushed back to the Paradise to rejoin his band in its show there.

As an aside, Whiteman's drummer on that broadcast was Rollo Laylan. He would shortly be replaced by George Wettling, something that undoubtedly gave

Wettling a sense of payback, since Laylan's presence in the Berigan band was the reason for his sudden departure. Also, former Berigan saxophonist Artie Drelinger was by then ensconced in the Whiteman reed section.

On April 14, Berigan appeared on the *Steinie Bottle Boys Swing Club* on NBC, playing solos on "Posin'" and "Dinah."[3]

In spite of the success of the Paradise engagement (it was extended several times and eventually lasted from March 20 to May 6, a total of seven weeks), there was some personnel turnover among the Berigan bandsmen. Guitarist Tommy Morgan was replaced by Dick Wharton, who in addition to playing guitar, sang in an "Irish tenor" fashion.

> I was born in Philadelphia in 1907. I studied violin and voice originally. I then played with Ted Lewis in 1928–29. Later, I did studio work with the Jan Savitt radio station studio band at KYW Philly (1934–35). Art Michaud was also from Philly and he got me the job with Bunny. Art seemed to be very concerned about the Berigan band then and its possibilities. He, with help from men in the band and the band boy, was trying to keep Lee Wiley & Bunny apart whenever possible—she was 'around' a lot then. I joined Bunny at the Paradise Restaurant. I was hired primarily as a singer, but Tommy Morgan had already given his notice. So, for playing in the rhythm section as well, I got $80 a week after a little argument with Bunny! Arthur Michaud got me the job when I was sweating out my union card in New York and the guys in the band nicknamed me 'Rev' because I was married and not much interested in the usual wild lifestyle associated with jazz musicians. Nat Lobovsky came in on first trombone, and Ruth Gaylor took over the gal vocal spot about the same time.[4]

Another notable change also took place during this period. Trombonist Sonny Lee, indisputably the most accomplished jazz soloist in the band after Berigan, accepted an offer from Jimmy Dorsey for more money than Bunny could pay. Once again, the musicians' grapevine went into high gear: Ray Conniff (trombone) recalled:

> I ran into Joe Dixon one day at the Forrest Hotel in New York and he told me that Al George had just had a run-in with Bunny and as a result, he was working out his notice. Bunny was auditioning trombone players at the Paradise, so I went down and was lucky enough to get the job. The trombone parts had been written for Sonny Lee, who had not only played lead, but took all the jazz solos as well. Nat Lobovsky had inherited that situation although he didn't consider himself a jazz player and was quite content to confine himself to playing lead parts after I joined. I took all the jazz solos after that. I soon got to know all the stories that were told about Bunny. For instance, not long before I joined, the band had played an important audition at which Bunny had gotten stinking drunk, with the result that his playing suffered. So, that particular job was offered to Glenn Miller. (Conniff may be referring to the radio show job that was awarded to Hal Kemp. Glenn Miller was scuffling in early 1938 and certainly had no sponsored radio show then.) Of course, Bunny was a marvelous musician, who could outplay all of us, a very warm-hearted guy, but the world's worst businessman! Although I got my salary, which was $60 a week, I didn't get paid for any of my ar-

rangements! I did a couple of originals, 'Little Gate's Special' and 'Gangbusters' Holiday' and I was told I would receive $35 per score. Well, I waited for what I thought was a reasonable time and when I heard nothing, I reminded Bunny that I hadn't been paid. 'How much was I going to pay you?' he asked. '$35 was it? We'll make it 40.' And each time I asked him for payment, he'd raise the offer, but I never did get any money for those charts! I recall Andy Phillips with the band when I joined at the Paradise in April '38 and about a week before Joe Bushkin I think; he replaced Joe Lippman; Lobovsky was still the other trombone.[5]

Years later, Ray Conniff (1916–2002), as the leader of and arranger for the Ray Conniff Singers, went on to become the most financially successful ex-Berigan sideman by far. From the mid-1950s until his retirement around the year 2000, he made over ninety albums, won a Grammy, two Golden Globe awards, had two platinum albums, and at least ten gold albums. But his big-time musical career started with his association with Bunny Berigan. Ray's daughter Tamara, who has worked in the music industry for many years, once asked him about his early years and recorded his recollections. Among them were his memories of joining the Berigan band:

I was sitting at the Forrest Bar with Joe Dixon, a friend of mine from back in New England. He told me that Bunny Berigan had just had a run-in with one of his trombone players, so there was a spot open, and asked me if I would like to give it a shot. Would I! The next night I went to the Paradise Restaurant and sat in. The band started playing 'It's Wonderful.' So Bunny came over to me and asked, 'Do you know this song, kid?' Of course I did because I was making the rehearsal band scene, so instead of giving the girl singer the chorus, I played it solo on trombone. I knew it note for note in any key, so I could watch the band as I played. Bunny looked over at Georgie Auld for approval, and Georgie gave him the code—the old index finger to the eye trick—meaning 'get a load of this!' I knew that I was in. Touring with Bunny was my first big-time gig, and it was one of the highlights of my life.[6]

Arranger Andy Phillips also came on the scene then:

I graduated from high school in Cortland, New York in 1934. Went to North Carolina State College; played guitar, violin and sang and arranged with the big school dance band there. Then I got a job with Frank Daily's band. Joe Mooney was their arranger and as he was blind I took down the stuff he picked out on the piano. He was a great talent and I learned a lot from him. I then went to NYC and studied with Joseph Schillinger. I'd done an arrangement of 'Lullaby of Rhythm' (*sic* "Lullaby *in* Rhythm") was a then current jazz tune composed by Edgar Sampson) and a publisher told me Bunny Berigan was looking for an arranger. He was at the Paradise Restaurant, and after the job one night, I went up to him and asked him to try out my arrangement. Bunny said, 'Look, stick around and we'll try it after everybody has gone home.' Anyway, he liked it and offered me a job at $85 a week to supply two arrangements a week, mainly of ballads and pop tunes. The band was on the air over the Mutual network from the Paradise which had three bands at that time. Lionel Rand had the house band that played all the floor shows and there was a rumba band that alternated with Bunny, who I found to be a nice guy to work for.

He and Donna were living with their two kids in an apartment house around Eightieth Street[7] where he use to invite me over for dinner now and again. We'd listen to records of classical music, one of his favorites being Rachmaninoff's Second piano concerto. He always maintained that the slow movement would have made a good pop song! I only traveled occasionally with the band. Normally I mailed my arrangements to them. Bunny didn't interfere much, just indicating where he wanted a vocal, etc. But there were always song-pluggers trying to persuade him to play their stuff in return for some financial handout. This 'payola,' as it was (later) called involved music publishers and disc jockeys as well as singers and leaders. Bunny would often choose a number that wasn't too well-known and get it scored just because he liked it and thought he could do something original with it. He was very selective, except with his records, when he often did not have any choice, being given some real 'dogs' to record. That really burned him up, because he knew leaders like Dorsey and Goodman were getting the best material and he was getting the dross. He wasn't very critical of any of his arrangers, but he always knew exactly what he wanted and always played the same chart in the same tempo. He was quite adamant about that. Although other leaders might vary their tempos, his metronomic mind wouldn't allow that. Joe Lippman was the principal arranger and the copyist was Jack Maisel, an old friend of Bunny's, who always made an extra copy of each chart for his own library! Once, we were doing a college dance and the students' band played an arrangement that I had done not too long before! Bunny paid Maisel good money for some of the things he brought in, but I'm sure he knew that other bands were using the same charts. Arthur Michaud was the 'man behind the scenes'—the manipulator as far as schedules and personnel were concerned, and lawyer John Gluskin was the money-man. He was a professional band backer, treating it as an investment which he hoped would bring him a profitable return, just like someone backing a Broadway show.[8]

First trumpeter Steve Lipkins now encountered a situation that would eventually take him out of the Berigan band: "My father took ill around that time and as it sounded pretty serious, I asked Bunny for a few days off so I could go home and see him and assess the situation. Bunny wasn't too keen and I guess we had a slight argument, but I went home anyway and he got Max Herman to sub for me."

Lipkins however returned to the band after a few days, in time for the next Berigan record date. The somewhat revamped Berigan band entered the RCA Victor recording studios on April 21[9] for an almost six-hour (1:00 to 6:45 p.m.) recording session. The tunes were; "Never Felt Better, Never Had Less," "I've Got a Guy," "Moonshine over Kentucky," "'Round My Old Deserted Farm," and "Azure." The new personnel were: Berigan, Lipkins, Goodman, trumpets; Nat Lobovsky, first trombone; Ray Conniff, jazz trombone; Doty, Dixon, Auld, and Rounds in the reed section; Lippman on piano; Dick Wharton, guitar; Wayland, bass; and Johnny Blowers, drums. The new girl singer was Ruth Gaylor.

Although Andy Phillips and Ray Conniff were new arrangers, none of their work was recorded on this date. Once again, most of the charts were done by Joe Lippman, with possibly a few by Abe Osser. Personnel changes or not, the band sounded fine.

I think that the arrangement on "Never Felt Better, Never Had Less" is by Abe Osser based on the reed voicings, which are similar to the ones Osser had used on the arrangement on "Trees," which the Berigan band recorded the previous December. The new vocalist, the pert Ruthie Gaylor, had a deeper, more resonant voice than her predecessor Gail Reese. Although she sometimes had pitch and enunciation issues, she sang with a beat and some enthusiasm. She transferred to Berigan from the Hudson-DeLange band with whom she had made some good recordings. The overall impression is that she sings a little better and with substantially more feeling than Ms. Reese. The rhythm guitar of Dick Wharton is also more prominent, and is excellent. Joe Lippman was a fine accompanist—unlike Graham Forbes and Fulton McGrath, who tended to be a little too fussy behind soloists, and especially behind the singers. Blowers's drumming is definitely heavier than Tough's had been, but this is something Bunny seemed to encourage.

"I've Got a Guy" is another somewhat remote pop tune, by Marion Sunshine composer of "The Peanut Vendor." There is nothing exceptional about the Berigan band's performance of it.

"Moonshine over Kentucky' is also somewhat remote. But on this song the Bunny and the band swing hard from the downbeat. Indeed, they romp all the way through this performance, with Bunny leading the charge. His exposition of the melody in the first chorus, played with a cup mute, and his open trumpet on the bridge after the vocal, sizzle. Johnny Blowers's use of his high-hat cymbals shows that he had been listening profitably to Dave Tough. Ruth Gaylor's vocal is pleasant and swinging. Following her, there is something completely new: Georgie Auld's rhythmic tenor saxophone solo backed by a rocking heavy backbeat laid down by drummer Johnny Blowers. This kind of drumming became something of a cliché in the rhythm and blues bands of the late 1940s and early 1950s (and on many Motown records in the 1960s and 1970s), but was seldom used in the late 1930s. Bunny liked it, and often exhorted his drummers to use it from this time on. The Berigan band was getting rhythmically "heavier" and its leader was not complaining. "Moonshine over Kentucky" is a highly spirited recording.

The next tune recorded was Willard Robison's "'Round My Old Deserted Farm," often incorrectly denominated as "'Round *the* Old Deserted Farm," or "'Round *an* Old Deserted Farm." Robison was a composer/lyricist who was much a part of the New York radio scene of the 1930s, hosting his own *Deep River Hour* then. The songs he wrote often had a rural, melancholy feeling to them, similar to many written by Hoagy Carmichael. (Among my favorites are "Old Folks," "Guess I'll Go Back Home This Summer" [which in a marvelous Bill Challis arrangement was recorded memorably by Glenn Miller, with Tex

Beneke singing], and the wonderful "A Cottage for Sale.") Robison also composed one of Bunny's favorite "blowing pieces" "'Tain't So Honey, 'Tain't So." It is likely that he and Berigan met sometime during Bunny's association with CBS. It is also likely that Robison brought "'Round My Old Deserted Farm" to Berigan while his band was appearing at the Paradise Restaurant, and asked Bunny to have it arranged and played there to provide some promotional push. We know Berigan did this because aircheck recordings of it were made on March 27, and April 8, and Bunny played it there again on April 24. Obviously Bunny liked this song, and persuaded the Victor people to let him record it. (It is also probable that Lee Wiley liked this song, and if this were so, then that would have been one more reason for Bunny to record it.)

The Berigan band's arrangement on "'Round My Old Deserted Farm" has been attributed to Joe Lippman, and I am of the opinion that he did indeed arrange it. Bunny sets out the melody using a straight mute in the first chorus. Ruthie Gaylor sings with feeling; then the band shines on the out-chorus, with Bunny's throaty open trumpet being prominent.

Having paid the rent and warmed up with the previous tunes, Bunny and the band finished this recording session with one of Joe Lippman's special arrangements. The Berigan band's recording of Duke Ellington's "Azure" is certainly one of the best treatments this sixteen-bar composition ever received. Lippman's masterful arrangement is somewhat reminiscent of his chart on "Caravan." In it are frequent changes of timbre and dramatic uses of register and dynamics. Bunny set a perfect dance tempo for this performance, which opens with three of the four saxists playing B-flat clarinets, with Joe Dixon on lead, and Mike Doty playing his bass clarinet. They play the eight-bar intro over Blowers's soft tom-toms, and *oo-ah* brass. Then Bunny sets out the sixteen-bar melody with an open trumpet displaying his unique low register sound; here it is velvety, indeed sumptuous. Behind him, the reeds provide color, Doty's bass clarinet again being noteworthy, with the brass adding subtle emphases. After this, the open brass play what amounts to a miniature fanfare, and Bunny's suddenly brilliant high register trumpet projects a powerful and stirring transitional figure that ushers in the four-man Berigan reed section, now playing their saxophones. Their sixteen-bar chorus is a model of unity and singing (and swinging) expressiveness. Behind them are Blowers's insistent high-hat cymbals, solid bass and guitar rhythm, and a few strategically placed brass *oo-ahs*. A brief muted brass interlude is followed by a few more bars of splendid work by the saxophones. Then Lippman's arrangement sets the reeds against the open brass, after which Georgie Auld plays a few bars of solo tenor saxophone. The climax arrives when the Berigan-led open brass, with warm reed voicings beneath them, reprise the melody again, but in the high register. (Hear them shake on their high notes!) The denouement comes via a bit of Joe Dixon's clarinet, and Bunny's warm, low register trumpet. This is a remarkable performance of a magnificently constructed arrangement. Few, if any critics have noted what superbly creative use Joe Lippman made of the rather limited instrumental resources available to him in Berigan's thirteen-piece band with this arrangement. The most salient of those thirteen instruments was one singularly expressive musical voice: Bunny Berigan's trumpet. This is another one of the "essentials" for Berigan aficionados.

The Brian Rust discography states that the arrangement for Duke Ellington's recording of "Azure," recorded by Ellington for Irving Mills's Master label on May 14, 1937, was written by *Joe Lippman.*[10] This assertion was denied by Lippman himself. It is significant however that the record that contained Duke's "Azure (Master 131), had "Caravan" on the other side. This disc probably provided Lippman with the inspiration for the splendid arrangements he wrote for Berigan on both "Caravan" and "Azure."

Bunny's April 21 Victor recording session was his most successful in many months. The band's engagement at the Paradise Restaurant was extended. The recent personnel changes had actually improved the band. Once again, it seemed that Bunny Berigan had weathered a number of challenges, and emerged unscathed.

The recollections of everyone connected with Berigan's band during its run at the Paradise Restaurant were extremely positive. The band members were very happy to be off the road and at home in Manhattan. New drummer Johnny Blowers got to know Bunny during that stand:

We spent a lot of time together. I believe he liked me as a drummer and also as a person. When we were working at the Paradise, the band would play for two hours and then break for the floor-show, after which we would go back and finish the night. But it was a long intermission, and Bunny would ask me 'are you going to join me tonight?' And I usually did. That meant a fast trip to Mama Leone's, the Italian Restaurant on Forty-ninth Street, for a spaghetti dinner or pizza, and always a large bottle of wine. I would fill my glass halfway, and Bunny would drink the rest. Bunny was an alcoholic, and eventually it killed him, but I don't think he drank for pleasure. It was a compulsion, and I know he tried to fight it. He took the cure two or three times. I really believe that if AA had come along sooner than it did, he would gladly have joined. I know, too, that he was concerned about his family and wished he could see them more often. But a musician has a hard time trying to spend much time at home.[11]

I have found that some of Blowers's recollections are less than one hundred percent accurate. I do not really know what he meant when he said that Bunny "took the cure two or three times."[12] There is certainly evidence that on many occasions, Berigan tried to greatly reduce the amount of alcohol he drank daily. But he was in no position to take time off and go somewhere to dry out and try to modify his behavior. He was far too busy. He had a lot of commitments, and most of them were sources of pressure for him. Invariably, when Bunny would try to drink less, his mood would turn from jovial and fun loving to sullen and standoffish. His trumpet playing would improve. The multitude of irritants he had in his life as a bandleader would bother him more. He would feel more and more stressed. The quick fix that always seemed to make things better was to take a few more drinks. Bunny was now completely ensnared in the vicious cycle of addiction, but he was still able to function well enough when drinking to do what was necessary to perform as a virtuoso trumpet soloist and leader of one of the best swing bands of the day.

As happy and musically successful as Bunny and the band were during the Paradise engagement, things were happening behind the scenes that would ultimately affect the business side of the Berigan band negatively. Gene Krupa, now the leader of his own band, was also being managed by Arthur Michaud. Michaud had continued representing Tommy Dorsey through the time he was involved in launching Bunny Berigan as the leader of his own band. Most of Michaud's attention during the spring of 1938 was being absorbed in activities involving the fledgling Krupa band. Michaud and attorney John Gluskin, the "money man" referred to by arranger Andy Phillips, as well as MCA, had all been involved first with TD, then Bunny, and now Gene. It was only a matter of time before a conflict of interest would occur.

This item appeared in the April 13, 1938, issue of *Variety:* "Berigan's crew holds forth for another four weeks at the Paradise Restaurant, New York City. Tommy Dorsey, Gene Krupa and Bunny Berigan are being booked under a policy which permits a dance promoter or theater operator a refund from a guaranteed figure if the date doesn't turn out a profitable one."[13] This was one of Arthur Michaud's ideas. It put the risk of the success or failure of an engagement on the bandleader instead of the promoter. Consequently, if a promoter was incompetent, or if a more famous band happened to be playing in the area, or if there was bad weather, or if there were any other circumstances that caused a gig to be unprofitable, the refund would come out of the band's guarantee for the gig, not out of the promoter's pocket. This scheme favored more established bands that were proven box office draws, and worked against newer bands that were still trying to establish themselves in the marketplace. Gene Krupa's band in particular languished in the minor leagues for the next three years as Gene followed the directions given to him by his management team to the letter. And if anyone thinks Bunny's band was the only one recording dud tunes, check out the Tommy Dorsey or Gene Krupa discographies for the period 1938–1940. Only when Gene deviated from the formula his managers had devised, and in 1941 hired singer Anita O'Day and trumpeter Roy Eldridge, both of whom his managers disliked, did his band move up the food chain. But Gene did not have Bunny's bad habits, especially drinking. He was able therefore to wait for the right time to do what he thought was best for his band without suffering major setbacks in the daily operation of his organization.

Bunny Berigan did not need to bear any additional risks as a bandleader. His alcoholism hung over his career as a virtuoso trumpeter and bandleader like the sword of Damocles. MCA was now billing him as "The Miracle Man of Swing." His sidemen, with an ironic humor so typical among jazz musicians, were now also referring to him among themselves as "The Miracle Man of Swing," not necessarily because of his feats of trumpeting, but because they were constantly amazed that he could play at all after consuming so much alcohol each day. There was a feeling among them that it was only a matter of time until Bunny would crash and burn as a result of his toping. Nevertheless, throughout the spring of 1938 positive things continued to happen for the Berigan band, and the musicians continued to enjoy the good pay and musical kicks that resulted.

The MCA/Michaud/Gluskin management troika staged a public relations lovefest on the stage of New York's Paramount Theater, while Tommy Dorsey's band was being presented there in April: "By way of exploiting Gene Krupa's new litter of cats, which made its debut last Saturday at Atlantic City, N.J., Krupa, Bunny Berigan, Jimmy and Tommy Dorsey staged an impromptu swing session during the last show at the Paramount Theater, New York City, where Tommy Dorsey's band is currently filling a two weeks stand. The session jammed the Paramount to near capacity, but didn't induce any shagging in the aisles. Playing as a unit the quartet wasn't outstanding in view of their individual talents, but the solo licks were in the groove!"[14] Photos from this gathering have been published many times in the last seven-plus decades, invariably without a correct caption.

In early May, MCA announced that the Berigan band had been booked for a week at New York's Paramount Theater, to start on May 11. They would be following MCA's top grossing band, Kay Kyser's, at that venue. Between the date the Berigan band closed at the Paradise Restaurant (May 6) and their opening at the Paramount Theater, they likely played one-nighters near New York City. One such engagement has been documented, at the Palorama Ballroom in Colonie, New York, just north of Albany. Berigan fan Al Gage, who also played trumpet, was there on the night of May 10:

> I saw Bunny and his band at a one-nighter in Colonie, New York in the spring of 1938. My recollections include Bunny having a guy passing out post cards with photos of himself before the dance. After the band warmed up and tuned up, the band boy came out and placed a gold trumpet on a chair in front of the band. The crowd was jammed around the bandstand. Bunny walked out with a sheepish, friendly grin. Big fellow-well fleshed but very pasty white complexion; teeth seemed stained. He picked up that horn, stormed off a beat with a peculiar sideways stomp of his right leg and the band was off. Bunny put his horn up and played as though he didn't care what came out...and what came out was so great! The band played every major recorded solo he ever did, from 'Started' to 'Spanish Town,' one after another, as fast as the crowd requested tunes. Before and after solos he stepped back so that he lined up with Irving Goodman and Steve Lipkins and played lead. Bunny did this for about an hour and a half before taking a break. 'On Spanish Town,' I recall, Bunny, Auld and Mike Doty *(sic)* did a combo and Bunny bent toward Auld pointing his trumpet right at him, as they played the 'dixie' stuff.[15]

When the Berigan band returned to the Paramount Theater, it was again a part of a vaudeville review. Here are the relevant details, provided by Dick Wharton: "The movie was 'Stolen Heaven.' Gene Raymond, Cass Daley, and the dance team of Nichols and Roberts were on stage with the band, but I wasn't allowed to play the date because Gene Raymond, the big star, objected to any other male singer being on the same stage as him. Bunny, as part of the stage show did a bit using a hat, with Cass Daley called 'Hot Pertater.'"[16]

Variety, as usual, had a reporter in the audience on opening night. Here is his report:

> Bunny Berigan's orch; 40 minutes; band setting, Paramount, NY. Berigan's hot trumpet originally came to attention through the swing sessions conducted by CBS. During the forepart of last year he was on the Admiracion Shampoo session over Mutual network with Tim and Irene. Aggregation which made its bow at the Paramount with him consisted of a crack brass four-some, a like number of reeds, a pianist, a drummer, a bass player and a guitarist. From this combination plus a number of fetching arrangements Berigan draws a jitter brew that's up to the minute in tang and flavor. For stage purposes his layout's in the groove. The items are so varied as to keep the interest on the upbeat. It's straight music from start to finish, with no imitation of top-blowing or any other outbreak of nut be-havior by some member of the band. Berigan blends a keen sense of musician-ship with a hard grasp of the current trends in dansapation, and the outlook for him should be a bright one. Gene Raymond—Songs-patter 10 minutes, Para-mount, NY. Date is Raymond's first on Broadway since he quit the legit for films. While he's no great shakes as a crooner, Raymond carries a tune easily enough...with the uke accompaniment filling in nicely with limitations and style. Between vocal numbers Raymond had several of the musicians out of the Bunny Berigan contingent join him and his uke in a jam session. The incident went big with the jitterbugs in the assembly.[17]

Bunny did well once again at the Paramount. Here's how his gross for the week compared with two of MCA's biggest box office draws: Kay Kyser, the week prior: $35,000; Hal Kemp, the week after: $47,000; Bunny Berigan: $32,000.[18]

People in the music business were also beginning to take note of the many fine arrangements Joe Lippman had been writing for the Berigan band. Lippman recalled how he finally left Bunny's employ as his band's pianist: "I was getting pretty tired of all the traveling and I'd gotten a few good offers to write scores for some network radio programs. Larry Clinton had asked me to do some ar-ranging for his band and Joey Bushkin needed a job anyway! So, after we fi-nished at the Paramount, I left the band and Joey took over. It was all done very amicably with no ill-feeling between Bunny and me."[19] Even though Lippman was no longer a playing member of the Berigan band, he continued writing ar-rangements for Bunny until the end of 1938.

Lippman's departure as band pianist created an opportunity for Bunny's pet, Joe Bushkin, to become a member of the Berigan orchestra. The experiences Bushkin would have over the next fifteen months with Bunny were the source of many stories Joe would tell for the next sixty-plus years. For his part, Bushkin played fine jazz piano while a member of the Berigan band, giving Bunny another very individual soloist on an instrument that had not been featured previously in the Berigan band. Bushkin was also a very good accompanist.

In the wake of Bunny's initial success as a bandleader, he had taken a lovely apartment in one of the beautiful new art deco buildings on Central Park West around west Eightieth Street.[20] He and Donna still also maintained their home in Rego Park, and it seems that Donna and the girls would move between these two places. Because he was so busy, Bunny seldom went to the house, preferring to stay in Manhattan whenever he was in New York. As the young arranger Andy Phillips reported, Bunny would sometimes take one of the band members home with him after work. One such person was Joe Bushkin, whom Bunny liked as a person as well as a pianist. Bushkin took note of conditions in Bunny's relationship with Donna at the time: "One night, Bunny and I went back to the apartment they had on Central Park West. This is after we had busted our ass and played five shows at the Paramount. I remember dinner being the lousiest fuckin' hamburger I ever ate, with some canned peas. If that's the way you treat Bunny Berigan, who just played five shows at the Paramount..."[21] Donna had by now descended into her own drinking problems, and the effect of this was to make her even less effective as a mother to her daughters and as a homemaker. Her relationship with Bunny, at this juncture, can be described as a marriage in name only.

Nevertheless, she was still Mrs. Bunny Berigan. Many of the comments she made to Robert Dupuis reveal an almost incredible lack of awareness of what was going on in Bunny's life at the time. In fact, there was almost a total disconnect between the two of them. She told Dupuis, for example, that she was informed about Bunny's affair with Lee Wiley, which had been going on rather openly for at least two years, by one of Bunny's best friends, the trumpeter Nat Natoli, while the Berigan band was playing at the Paramount Theater in the spring of 1938. She decided to confront Bunny:

> So I came down from Rego Park. I decided I would go and see what was going on. He had to make up his mind one way or the other and not embarrass me by cheating on me. My bringing up was pretty straight-laced, even though I was in show business. The doorman let me in, and I went to the dressing room; he was on the third floor. I knocked at the door. He told me 'Wait a minute.' I waited. He let me in. I said, 'I can't go on this way. You're either going to be right with me or you're not—one way or the other. Do you want her or do you want me?' He stopped...and he thought...and he said, 'I'll take *her!*' [22]

After this confrontation, Donna, no doubt in a highly emotional state, stormed out of Bunny's dressing room and went directly to the band room and told the musicians in Bunny's band what had just occurred. This is significant in that she felt it necessary to justify to Bunny's band members that she was now going to leave him. She had to secure her victimhood with them before she did anything else.

Soon thereafter, Donna returned to Syracuse where she settled into a com-modious house with the girls. Bunny sent her $100 a month, which was enough for them to live quite comfortably.[23] Bunny was now paying the bills to keep three residences operating, while at the same time paying his own living ex-penses on the road, which increasingly would become his full-time home.

Phase two of MCA's plan for the Berigan band in the summer of 1938 was to put it out on the road to play in ballrooms. After closing at the Paramount, the band played for two evenings in Reading, Pennsylvania. Then on Sunday May 22, they battled Artie Shaw's band again, this time at Danceland Ballroom, Ocean Beach Park, New London, Connecticut.

After more than a year of scuffling, Shaw had forged his group of mostly young unknown musicians into a formidable performing unit. Unlike the Beri-gan band, Artie Shaw's band had not enjoyed several months on a sponsored network radio show, and it had not played at some of the top theaters in the na-tion for a week or more at a time. Indeed, since the end of 1937, it had not had a recording contract. Instead, Shaw had played widely scattered one-nighters until March of 1938, when, with vocalists Tony Pastor and Billie Holiday, he opened at the Roseland State Ballroom in Boston, broadcasting from that location only on Tuesday and Saturday nights. On other nights, Artie took whatever gigs Si Schribman[24] could get for his band around the New England territory. If that didn't cover the weekly "nut," Schribman would cover the shortfall.[25] At the time of this meeting between the Berigan and Shaw bands, Shaw was once again cast in the role of underdog. But even though Artie and his boys played very well that night, they still weren't strong enough to overcome Bunny, and his contingent of strong jazz soloists which now included Georgie Auld, tenor sax; Joe Dixon, clarinet and alto sax; Ray Conniff, trombone; Joe Bushkin, piano; the flashy and exuberant bassist Hank Wayland, and Johnny Blowers on drums. In one department however, Artie had the much stronger performers: Tony Pastor excelled at singing/swinging lighthearted novelties, and Billie Holiday sang the songs of love and loneliness as only she could. The consensus was that the hard-swinging Berigan band edged Shaw's group that night, but not by much. Beri-gan's musicians sensed that the Shaw band was "happening." They were right. Artie's first record date for RCA Bluebird two months later would include the instrumentals "Begin the Beguine," "Indian Love Call," "Back Bay Shuffle," and Billie singing "Any Old Time."

After this contest, the Berigan band again hit the road, playing one-night dance jobs until May 25, when they returned to New York to rehearse for a Vic-tor recording session the next day.

The White materials indicate that the Berigan band was in the studio from 9:30 to 1:30 on May 26, but the Victor session sheets did not specify whether this was a.m. or p.m. I think this session started at 9:30 p.m. because the band apparently did not work elsewhere that night, and its next engagement was in New York City the following night. Jazz musicians are night people, and they prefer to work at night, whenever possible.

The first tune recorded was "Somewhere with Somebody Else," a then cur-rent pop by Edgar Leslie and Johnny Burke. Joe Lippman wrote the arrangement which spots Bunny with some type of straight or possibly an altered Harmon mute in the first chorus, playing very high. Nat Lobovsky's lead trombone is also heard briefly. Dick Wharton takes the vocal. His tenor voice is something I do not enjoy, but from a technical point of view, his quality and pitch were good. (I would have thought that the rambunctious character of the Berigan band would have required a male vocalist more in the earthy Jimmy Rushing[26] mode, and perhaps Bunny also thought this might work, as we shall see. But Dick Wharton was friends with Arthur Michaud, so that was that.) Bunny returns with an open trumpet for the soaring finale.

"It's the Little Things That Count" is another pop tune, composed by Haven Gillespie, who wrote numerous good songs during his career, most notably "You Go to My Head," which was the first big recording for Jan Savitt and His Top Hatters. (They would record that song on August 25, 1938. In the mean-time, the Savitt band was being used by the Victor people to promote on the Bluebird label many of the same tunes the Berigan band was recording on the Victor label. As Artie Shaw so often observed, there was tremendous pressure on *all* bands then to record current pop tunes.) "It's the Little Things That Count" is another recording by the recently invigorated Berigan band that shows a bit of swagger. The tune is not remarkable, but the band's performance cer-tainly is. It was a joke among the members of the Berigan band that young Georgie Auld was so hyperactive that he often attempted to lead the saxophone section from the second tenor chair. His section mates had to rein him in. Joe Lippman wrote this arrangement to give George a bit of lead tenor to play in the first chorus. He responds in typically exuberant fashion. Ruth Gaylor does just about everything one could hope for with the lyric before Bunny returns with a rather spine-tingling solo. Auld has a brief solo, and the band then wraps it up.

"Wacky Dust" is a fun tune with music by one of Bunny's friends from his early days at CBS, the manic pianist Oscar Levant,[27] and words by Stanley Adams. Levant would frequently come to the Paradise while the Berigan band was in residence there and add to the general atmosphere of hilarity. The rhyth-mic arrangement is by Joe Lippman, who ingeniously blends two clarinets, and a tenor and baritone sax in the intro and on into the first chorus. Bunny plays the eight-bar bridge in the first chorus. Poor Ruthie Gaylor had to contend with not only the rhythms in the music, but also a rather brisk tempo, in addition to the words of the lyric. (What is this wacky dust stuff anyway? I think the lyric pro-vides the answer.)[28] After the vocal, the improvement in the trombones becomes obvious: Nat Lobovsky was an exceptionally fine first trombonist, and Ray Conniff was clearly superior to his predecessor, Al George. When playing the brass *tuttis* here the five-man brass section plays as a unit with authority. Those horns are *ringing.* At last Bunny had an entire brass section to play up to his lead. He had to be pleased by this development. Bushkin switched to the celesta for an additional bit of fun before the reeds and brass closed. This recording ranks as one of the best novelties the Berigan band ever made.

The fourth tune to be recorded, the *piece de resistance,* was saved for last. It would be difficult to think of a more unlikely tune than "The Wearin' of the Green" to be the point of departure for one of the most splendid arrangements and memorable performances of the swing era. But, it is a natural thing, right? Bunny Berigan and "The Wearin' of the Green." Could there be a more perfect combination? With the benefit of much hindsight, yes, it is a perfect combination. But what swing bands were playing "The Wearin' of the Green" in 1938? It is unclear whose idea it was to pair Bunny Berigan and "The Wearin' of the Green." There was some comment in the White materials to the effect that Bunny was planning to record an album of Irish tunes. But this seems far less likely than Bunny simply commissioning a special arrangement and recording only one such tune. However the idea got started, it developed in the ordinary course, which is to say that Bunny instructed Joe Lippman to write an arrangement, and waited to see what Joe would come up with. When Lippman passed out his arrangement on "The Wearin' of the Green" for the first time, there had to be glee among the band members.

Richard M. Sudhalter listened carefully and analyzed:

> ...the opening phrases, arranged by Lippman as a kind of minuet for four clarinets, backed only by Blowers's swishing high-hats, has Dixon playing lead and Mike Doty playing bass clarinet, in a passage of balanced, controlled beauty. The brass, phrasing with clipped delicacy, join in for a moment as the clarinets supply Mozartean counterpoint. (I think I hear Hank Wayland's arco bass under the ensemble here. MZ) Then the woodwind quartet finishes the chorus. Berigan, playing (cup) muted, swings in on the melody with the trombones prominent behind him. The band delivers the middle section with Berigan-inspired punch, then the leader returns on open trumpet to play out the chorus with assurance, popping out a ringing high E in the process. In the next phase of the arrangement, there are solos by Georgie Auld, Ray Conniff, and Nat Lobovsky. Auld is backed by the strutting brass and Blowers's heavy back-beats. The idea of contrasting Conniff's rugged jazz trombone with Lobovsky's lovely straight trombone was a very good one that Lippman would use often in coming months. Nat's lulling solo is perfect preparation for Berigan's electrifying entrance. As the band, with Steve Lipkins's strong first trumpet leading the way, picks things up at the bridge, Berigan comes sailing in on an eerie, massive high concert F, a full octave above. The effect is hair-raising; not only is it high and splendidly played, but it typifies Berigan's almost supernatural sense of drama. It is improbable, unexpected, and quite beyond the capabilities of most jazz trumpeters of the era. After the reeds reprise the intro, the trombones take four bars in three part harmony! Three part harmony with only two trombones? Ah, yes. The same trumpeter who pierced the ensemble a few seconds ago with a resounding entrance at the very peak of his instrument's range is now using his spacious low-register tone to blend with the trombones and fill out the harmony.[29]

When Johnny Blowers listened to this recording some forty-five years after it was made, after not hearing it for a long time, he was amazed: "Wow! Tremendous! He just picked that whole band up and swung it by himself. What a guy!"[30]

Notes

[1] The tunes on Jazz Hour-1022: Theme and introduction; "Back in Your Own Back Yard," "Rose Room," "'Round My Old Deserted Farm," "Louisiana," "It's Wonderful," "Devil's Holiday," "Whistle While You Work," "Kiss Me Again," "Sweet Varsity Sue," "Shanghai Shuffle," "Star Dust," "A Study in Brown," "I'll Always Be in Love with You," "Moonshine over Kentucky," "Downstream," and "Black Bottom." See appendix 2 for a complete listing of the airchecks that were made during the Berigan band's residency at the Paradise Restaurant in the spring of 1938.

[2] *New York Times:* March 27, 1938, cited in the White materials: March 27, 1938.

[3] This information was provided to me by Carl A. Hallstrom, who obtained it from the NBC Archive, Library of Congress.

[4] White materials: April 14, 1938.

[5] White materials: April 30, 1938.

[6] This quote was taken from the Ray Conniff website called: "my web pages.comcast.net Ray Conniff," January 2008.

[7] Numerous people have stated that Bunny's apartment in Manhattan was on Central Park West, near Eightieth Street. The only "apartment house" located near that area then and now is the luxurious Beresford, located at 211 Central Park West, between West eighty-first and Eighty-second Streets. It became a co-op in 1962. South of Eighty-first extending to Seventy-seventh Street is the Museum of Natural History.

[8] White materials: April 17, 1938.

[9] I think it fair to assume that Arthur Michaud had secured another one-year contract between Berigan and RCA Victor shortly after the March 15, 1938, recording session that marked the end of Bunny's first one-year Victor recording contract.

[10] *Jazz and Ragtime Records (1897–1942),* by Brian Rust, Malcolm Shaw, Editor, Mainspring Press (2002), 537–538.

[11] *Blowers:* 39.

[12] The only time when Berigan may have actually sought professional help to deal with his alcoholism was in July of 1940, when he was in and out of Tommy Dorsey's band.

[13] White materials: April 20, 1938.

[14] *Variety:* April 20, 1938, cited in the White materials: April 14, 1938.

[15] White materials: May 10, 1938.

[16] White materials: May 11, 1938.

[17] *Variety:* May 18, 1938, cited in the White materials: May 11, 1938.

[18] *International Musician:* June 1938, cited in the White materials: May 17, 1938.

[19] White materials: May 11, 1938.

[20] Both Andy Phillips, and especially Joe Bushkin, a native Manhattanite, remember Berigan's Central Park West apartment being located near Eightieth Street. Donna Berigan, whose memory proved less than accurate on many details, told Robert Dupuis in the 1980s that the apartment was near Eighty-sixth. I am inclined to believe Phillips and Bushkin.

[21] Dupuis: 155. Bushkin's remarks indicate that he may have worked with the Berigan band at least a part of the time they were at the Paramount Theater.

[22] Dupuis: 160.

[23] Additional information about Bunny and Donna's initial breakup is from Dupuis.

[24] Si Schribman was a businessman who, with his brother Charlie, owned a number of ballrooms in the New England area during the swing era. In addition to employing bands in his ballrooms, he would on occasion invest in fledgling bands that he thought had a bright future. Two such bands were Artie Shaw's and Glenn Miller's.

[25] Shaw and Schribman later (after the Shaw band became a success) had a disagreement over whether Si was buying small pieces of the Shaw band, or merely loaning Artie money. This was settled amicably by Shaw paying Schribman a sum of money in exchange for Si releasing all rights he may have had in the Shaw band.

[26] Vocalist James Andrew Rushing was born on August 26, 1903, in Oklahoma City, Oklahoma. He developed his powerful blues-shouting approach to singing in the 1920s, before microphones were widely used in dance halls and cabarets. He worked with many bands in the Oklahoma City and California territories in the early 1920s, then joined the bassist Walter Page in his band entitled the Blue Devils in 1927. He joined Bennie Moten's band in 1929, and remained with Moten until 1935. He then joined Count Basie in 1935 in Kansas City, and remained a stalwart and very popular performer in the Basie band for the next fifteen years. Thereafter, he performed as a soloist for the rest of his life, never straying too far from the blues. Jimmy Rushing, who was known as "Mr. Five-by-Five" because he was short and very rotund, died in New York City on June 8, 1972.

[27] Pianist Oscar Levant was born on December 27, 1906, in Pittsburgh, Pennsylvania. He began his musical studies as a child in Pittsburgh, then continued them after he moved to New York in the early 1920s. By the late 1920s, Levant was composing musical scores for films, but began to concentrate more on his career as a concert pianist after he met and became very close friends with composer George Gershwin in the late 1920s. Nevertheless, in the mid-1930s, Levant studied with Joseph Schillinger (at Gershwin's recommendation), and with Arnold Schoenberg, and composed several classical pieces. After Gershwin's death in 1937, Levant became more of a personality (albeit an extremely neurotic and brilliant one), and began appearing regularly on network radio, in films, and by the 1950s, on television. Unfortunately, Levant became progressively addicted to various drugs, and this caused his career as a concert pianist to grind to a halt by the late 1950s. Oscar Levant died on August 14, 1972, in Beverly Hills, California.

[28] Stanley Adams, who wrote the lyric to "Wacky Dust," emphatically denied that this title or the lyric he wrote had anything to do with the drug culture. (Given the predilections of the composer of the music to "Wacky Dust," Oscar Levant, this denial is rather dubious.) The only other artist who recorded it during the late 1930s was Ella Fitzgerald. However, much later, in the 1980s, the singing group Manhattan Transfer recorded it, and it became a hit in Europe. See *Let's Dance— Popular Music in the 1930s,* by Arnold Shaw, edited by Bill Willard, Oxford University Press (1998), 129.

[29] Sudhalter, in *Giants of Jazz:* 45

[30] Blowers, in *Giants of Jazz:* 45.

Chapter 17
Golden Boy[1]

It is abundantly clear from the Berigan band's recording of "The Wearin' of the Green" that from a musical standpoint, Bunny Berigan and His Orchestra were among the top swing bands in the country in May of 1938. They had developed an assurance as an ensemble that bordered on swagger. When they chose to, they *strutted* the music. The band had very good, exciting soloists, most of their arrangements now were first rate, and Joe Lippman had shown again and again that he was capable of writing special arrangements that highlighted not only his skill and creativity, but the capabilities of the Berigan band, and their virtuoso leader. Bunny himself had worked without letup for seventeen months to build every aspect of this band. He had been totally involved in assembling its personnel and arrangements. He had constantly tried to infuse the band's performances with his fiery jazz spirit. At last, his band had arrived at a point where to a large degree, it reflected his musical personality. He had to be pleased.

He had endured the vicissitudes of the band *business* more or less with equanimity, but basically entrusted business matters to others. He paid these people well, and expected that they would guide his band's fortunes in a positive direction. To this point in the band's history, Bunny's management team had functioned reasonably well. Not perfectly by any means, but well. Bunny had every reason to be encouraged about the future of his band as the summer of 1938 began.

Immediately after the May 26 Victor recording session, the Berigan band played for one or two nights at New York's posh Essex House. One wonders how well this romping jazz band fit in there. The next night, Sunday, May 29, they were in a much more congenial jazz atmosphere, Harlem's famous Savoy Ballroom. There they were to do battle with the "King of the Savoy," Chick Webb. At this time, Webb's band was also one of the leading swing bands in the nation, having good arrangements, strong soloists (especially Chick himself on drums, trumpeters Bobby Stark and Taft Jordan, and alto saxophonist Louis Jordan), and the lilting vocalist Ella Fitzgerald. (To hear what the Webb band was up to in May of 1938, listen to their recording of "Spinnin' the Webb," with its great Bobby Stark trumpet solo, Mario Bauza's fiery lead trumpet, and Chick's superb drumming.) Once again, coach Berigan very likely told his boys to watch themselves lest they be embarrassed by the hard-swinging Webb musicians. The consensus drawn from the throng that attended this event was that Webb won by a whisker on his home turf. But the Berigan band had nothing to be ashamed of: it was said that *nobody* ever outplayed Chick Webb's band at the Savoy.

After this stimulating experience, the band played a number of dance dates within about a 150 mile radius of New York City until they returned to Manhattan for another Victor recording session on June 8. One of the gigs the Berigan band played during this period was at the Al-Dorn or Castle Rock Ballroom, Dorney Park, Allentown, Pennsylvania, on Thursday June 2, 1938. In the third volume of his monumental Benny Goodman biodiscography, D. Russell Connor included some financial data he obtained from the owners of Dorney Park that provide a very revealing insight into the realities of the band business in the spring of 1938. Dorney Park presented name bands only on Thursdays because these bands charged more on weekends and holidays.

Here is the information from left to right: band name; date of appearance; band fee; paid/comp admissions; ticket price; profit/loss.

Hal Kemp	(4/21)	$1,000	774/6	$1.10	$226.26-
Sammy Kaye	(4/28)	$ 750	1096/67	$1.10	$346.80+
Louis Armstrong	(5/5)	$ 800	282/82	$1.10	$516.80-
Benny Goodman	(5/12)	$1,250	1327/110	$1.10	$76.99+
Red Norvo	(5/19)	$ 500	271/60	$0.85	$190.48-
Kay Kyser	(5/26)	$1,000	674/70	$1.10	$328.00-

Bunny Berigan   (6/2)   (After racking up losses with four out of six name bands, Dorney's management insisted on a deal where they would pay the band a percentage of paid admissions up to $400. Consequently, Bunny grossed $142.15 for this dance date. He drew 383 paid and 63 comps. The ticket price was seventy-five cents, and the park made a profit of $12.85. This date had to have yielded less than one-seventh of the weekly Berigan band "nut," an ominous sign.)

Here is the rest of the information gathered by Connor:

Count Basie	(6/9)	$250	342/30	$.50	$79.09-
Paul Tremaine	(6/16)	$200	165/30	$.50	$117.50-
Casa Loma	(6/23)	$700	722/92	$1.10	$22.71+
Sammy Kaye	(6/30)	$500	319/78	$1.10	$191.10-[2]

Many conclusions can be drawn from these figures. The first and probably least speculative one is that more established bands commanded higher fees. Hal Kemp and Kay Kyser were by 1938 among MCA's top grossing bands. Benny Goodman, also represented by MCA, was then riding the crest of a sponsored network radio show, a Hollywood film, frequent sustaining radio broadcasts, steady if not spectacular record sales, and the recently completed Carnegie Hall jazz concert. Also, MCA was then putting a vast amount of promotional push behind the Goodman band—publications everywhere contained something about Benny Goodman. BG's career was definitely at an early peak in the spring of 1938.

By 1938, Sammy Kaye's band, also represented by MCA, had been in existence for several years. It was modeled to some extent on Kay Kyser's and played acceptable dance music, with a lot of gimmicks along the way. People loved it. Even so, it was not guaranteed top dollar, or a hugely successful date, as the numbers from June 30 show. Louis Armstrong, who was being booked by Joe Glaser, received an excellent guarantee, but the date was a bomb for Dorney Park. Rockwell-O'Keefe's top band was Casa Loma. They too got a good guarantee, but their date was also successful for the ballroom. Count Basie's band, then also booked by MCA, was similar to Bunny's in that it was a heavily jazz-influenced dance band, and it had existed (at least in the East) for a similar length of time. Dorney Park lost money on Basie, Kemp, Armstrong, Norvo, Tremaine, and Sammy Kaye's second appearance. It essentially broke even with Berigan and Casa Loma. The only really successful date was the first one with Sammy Kaye. Overall, their name band program for the above-cited period was a big loser.

Since MCA was notorious for "block booking" its talent, that is, offering promoters a package of talent, rather than booking individual bands on individual dates, their tack here could well have been "take the package and you get Benny Goodman, Kay Kyser, and Sammy Kaye. Don't take the package and you get whatever is available." And MCA would make sure that not too much was available. Bands like Berigan's, Norvo's, and Basie's were hardly in a position to negotiate: the bandleader's overhead continued nonstop regardless of where the band played, or for how much.

If a band was on the road, it was always preferable, from the bandleader's standpoint, for that band to play a "cheap date," that is one at less than market rate, as opposed to not playing at all. But if a bandleader did that then he undercut the efforts of his booking agent to get the most money possible for the band. So MCA would advise their clients to take a night off rather than play a date at below market rate. While the band rested, the bandleader's overhead continued unabated. The secret to having a financially successful band on the road however, was to secure a guarantee on each date that at least covered expenses, and balance these high-risk/cost one-night dance jobs with more lucrative theater dates, which normally lasted for a week, or a split week, where a band would play in one theater for three or four days, then hop to a nearby town and finish up the week there. This usually resulted in more cash and less financial risk on the revenue side, and less transportation costs on the expense side. Also, it was essential to pull a band off of the road for periods of time and fill its engagement book with something other than one-nighters, preferably a hotel booking with sustaining radio broadcasts. Then supply would not overwhelm demand; indeed the radio exposure would strengthen demand. It was during these longer "residencies" in New York, Chicago, or Los Angeles that most bands also made their recordings. If a week at a theater could also be secured while a band was in one spot for a period of time, all the better. It was up to the bandleader's manager to see to it that the proper balance of engagements was being maintained for his client so that revenue met or exceeded expenses.

Any band that constantly played one-night dance dates, no matter what they were paid, was on a high-risk journey that would almost always eventually lead to complete exhaustion and bankruptcy for the bandleader. Booking agencies loved one-night dance dates however because they got their full commission off the top of the guarantee, before the bandleader paid his expenses and got his share. They had no cash flow problems; indeed, their costs and risks were minimal. The bandleader had to pay all of the costs for the band, including extremely variable transportation costs, out of whatever was left over at the completion of the gig. From the bandleader's perspective, the classic MCA-devised business plan was extremely risky. If Bunny Berigan thought about this at all, and I suspect that he did, he undoubtedly hoped that Arthur Michaud would look after his best interests in these often perilous business matters. Michaud after all had guided Bunny in the months he was organizing and strengthening his band, and had directed its first very successful tour. At the end of that tour, Bunny was able to pay back all of the loans he had taken to keep his band going while MCA built his name, and have quite a bit left over. Unfortunately, during the spring and summer of 1938, Michaud's attention was being stretched between Tommy Dorsey's established band and Gene Krupa's new band, as well as Bunny's.

On June 8, the Berigan band recorded four more vocal arrangements for Victor. In spite of some good trumpeting by Bunny, and enthusiastic performances by the band, this session represents another example of Victor greatly underutilizing a band that was capable of making remarkable music. The titles recorded that day were: "The Pied Piper," "Tonight Will Live," "(A Sky of Blue and You) And So Forth," and "(How to Make Love In) Ten Easy Lessons." Bunny's use of a kazoo mute on "And So Forth" is certainly noteworthy, though not necessarily in the best of taste. "The Pied Piper" and "Ten Easy Lessons" are novelties sung by Ruth Gaylor. Dick Wharton warbles on "Tonight Will Live." This session lasted from 2:00 to 8:00 p.m.

As one would expect, critical reaction to these records was mixed, at best. *Tempo's* August 1938 issue carried this review:

> Bunny Berigan tops a small swing output from Victor this month with a tune that might have been written for him. It's 'The Pied Piper,' backed by 'Ten Easy Lessons' and well played the whole distance. Maybe I'm getting soft, but Ruth Gaylor does some fine chirping and Georgie Auld really busts me on tenor sax. The kick is Bunny, however. He takes those breaks with a variety of stuff that puts him right back on top. Just remember that a lot of the stuff and things you hear today on trumpet can be traced back to Berigan.[3]

A review also appeared in the August issue of *Metronome*. George T. Simon, as usual, had sharpened his hatchet: "Typical Bunny Berigan playing, not at all inspired either, pops up in 'Pied Piper,' while 'Ten Easy Lessons' is another one of the 'accent the four-beat' things. Georgie Auld, though, adds interest to both sides. Bunny himself ruins an otherwise pretty arrangement of 'Tonight Will Live' by some sloppy, tasteless high-blowing in the opening chorus."[4]

After this session, Bunny led his musicians to Baltimore for a one-nighter on June 9, followed by an engagement the next day at the Windberry Forrest School for Boys, in Culpeper, Virginia. They were scheduled to play an afternoon "tea dance" followed in the evening by a regular dance. On the way to this gig, the band's equipment truck containing all of its instruments and music, being driven by Robert "Little Gate" Walker, skidded off a rain-soaked country road and into a ditch. In those days long before civil rights and cell phones, Little Gate, who was black, found himself in the unenviable position of being stranded in segregated rural Virginia. He had to call upon all of his resourcefulness simply to get the truck out of the ditch and on the road again, without coming to harm himself. The Berigan band was forced to play the tea dance without its instruments. Johnny Blowers later recalled this incident to Albert McCarthy:

> The band was due to play a tea-dance and an evening dance at a military academy in Virginia, but en route became parted from its instruments, when the truck, driven by band-boy 'Little Gate,' slithered into a ditch. For the tea-dance, a variety of instruments were exhumed from the academy band stock. Berigan fronted the band on a cornet with a fiber mouthpiece. Hank Wayland played tuba, and Johnny Blowers made do with a field drum and a huge bass drum, the latter 'emitting a noise like a cannon every time I struck it!' Blowers recalled. Fortunately, the errant 'Little Gate' arrived with the regular instruments in time for the evening dance.[5]

The band forged on through a series of one-nighters in Pennsylvania and Ohio. They played at Moonlight Gardens, Meyer's Lake Park, Canton, Ohio, on Thursday, June 16. *Billboard* reported on this engagement in its June 25, 1938, issue: 'With Glen Gray the attraction less than twenty miles away at Summit Beach, Akron, Ohio, Bunny Berigan drew almost 1,000 dancers here last Thursday at Moonlight Gardens in Meyer's Lake Park. Harry Sinclair, Moonlight Gardens manager, was pleased with the $460 take."[6] The next night, Bunny's band was broadcast over WABC–New York, probably from somewhere in Pennsylvania. Johnny Blowers kept a diary of places he played with the Berigan band, but sometimes did not place a date with the location. Here are some of the venues the band played for the period June 17 to June 25: Tyrone, Pennsylvania (west of State College); Hershey, Pennsylvania, at Starlight Ballroom, Hershey Park, (15 miles east of Harrisburg); Shamokin, Pennsylvania, at Edgewood Park; on June 23, at the Crystal Ballroom, Cumberland, Maryland; Ithaca, New York, at Cornell University; Middletown State Armory, Kingston, New York, on Saturday, June 25; Greenwich, Connecticut. At some point in this eight-day span, a mix-up occurred involving a date at Old Orchard Beach, Maine.

Blowers recalled this venue in his biography *Back Beats and Rim Shots— The Johnny Blowers Story*: "Wherever we played the crowd loved the band, and there were hundreds of dancers, but we had a peculiar tendency to be in the wrong place, or in the right place at the wrong time. Even sometimes the wrong day. Once we went to Old Orchard Beach a day ahead of schedule, so we spent it enjoying rides and games. We played the following night. I really believe that band could have been very successful if more care had gone into planning and management."[7] The fact is that in the summer of 1938, the Berigan band *was* very successful. Its management (MCA and Michaud) however was by then focusing most of their attention elsewhere, primarily on the development of Gene Krupa's new band. Engagements that otherwise might have gone to Berigan now were going to Krupa. As a result, there seemed to be no real plan as to how to achieve maximum financial return for the Berigan band on the road. Also, logistical slipups started to occur. These snafus have long been attributed to Bunny's lackadaisical attitude about business matters. However, he was paying others to attend to these important issues, as all other bandleaders did, and had every reason to expect that they would be handled properly. Increasingly, they were not being handled properly, and Bunny's normally sanguine attitude sometimes turned edgy. He, not MCA or Michaud, had to pay the band while they enjoyed an unplanned off day, rode amusement rides, and played games at Old Orchard Beach.

Berigan returned to New York City on June 26 to play on the RCA *Magic Key* radio show, which was broadcast over the NBC radio network. Here are the details: "*Magic Key* broadcast, WJZ (NBC Blue), 2:00 to 3:00 p.m.; Frank Black and NBC concert orchestra. Guests: Marie and Anneda Ohia, songs; Bob Hope, comedian; Bunny Berigan Orchestra. And from Buenos Aires, Linton Wells, commentator." A bit of Bunny's theme was played, followed by 'Somewhere with Somebody Else,' and 'The Prisoner's Song.'"[8] It is apparent that Bunny often used "The Prisoner's Song" as a closing piece on broadcasts.[9] This version, which was recorded, shows that there had been some evolution in the band's performance of it since the Victor recording had been made the previous August.

The source of the recording I have of this aircheck performance is the LP entitled *Hot Trumpets*, which was issued on the Historical label in the 1970s. At the time this record (HLP-28) was issued, the information contained in the White materials was not available, and there was widespread ignorance about the details of Bunny Berigan's life and career. "The Prisoner's Song" is listed in the liner notes of HLP-28 as having been performed in June of 1937. In listening to this performance since learning when it actually took place, I have been able to arrive at some conclusions about the solos, especially the trombone solos, which for years had baffled me. This scintillating performance (which is approximately five minutes and thirty seconds long) once again shows the true nature of the Berigan band far more accurately and fully than most of its Victor recordings. In addition to Bunny's trumpet solos, and he is in fine form here, there are solos by Georgie Auld, Joe Dixon, and on trombones first Ray Conniff, then Nat Lobovsky. Conniff's solo is in his rough-and-ready style; Lobovsky's first sixteen bars are reminiscent of players who were slightly older than Conniff. (Ray was twenty-two years old when this recording was made; Nat was thirty-one.) Still, Lobovsky has complete control of his instrument: he plays sixteen improvised bars, followed by another sixteen of perfect trilling, which he does in one breath. (Lobovsky was able to do things on trombone that only Tommy Dorsey and the two Jacks, Teagarden and Jenney, could then do.) Hank Wayland slaps his bass for sixteen bars; then drummer Johnny Blowers plays an interesting solo that shows that he too was a complete master of his instrument. His provocative use of cymbals in this performance is noteworthy.

We must remember that a primary purpose of the *Magic Key* program was to promote Victor records. Too bad Victor did not take this opportunity to publicize Bunny's recordings of "Azure," or "The Wearin' of the Green." On the other hand, we should be thankful to have this great live performance of "The Prisoner's Song."[10]

Bob Hope appeared on this *Magic Key* program with Bunny, and I'm sure he was very favorably impressed by the hard-swinging Berigan band. Rumors immediately began to circulate (again) that Bunny and his band would soon be headed to Hollywood to be the featured band on Hope's soon to be debuted NBC network radio show, and/or in an upcoming Hope movie.

The next day, June 27, Bunny again visited the RCA Victor studios, but this time he and his musicians were scheduled to make recordings for NBC's *Thesaurus* transcription service. The sixteen inch 33 1/3 rpm discs on which the music was marketed were leased or sold to radio stations under the generic name "Rhythm Makers" or "The Rhythm Makers." No identification of the many bands that made *Thesaurus* transcriptions was ever done. It is extremely fortuitous that this opportunity existed for the Berigan band, because this *Thesaurus* recording session, and one which would take place in the not too distant future, like the airchecks of the band from the Paradise Restaurant and elsewhere, allow us to have a much more complete understanding of the Berigan band's capabilities. The difference between this band and the one Bunny had led on his previous *Thesaurus* session almost two years earlier is immense. The earlier band sounded very much like what it actually was—a part-time band with no identity. This Berigan band had now reached the place where it was imbued with its leader's passionate musical persona: it was powerful, exciting, and sometimes a bit unpredictable, even reckless.

They recorded twenty tunes that day, and as always was the case on transcriptions, only one take on each tune was made. There is no indication of when the session started or ended. Indeed, there is some question as to whether this session took place in New York, or at RCA's Camden, New Jersey "church studio." I think that this session was recorded in New York because I know that other *Thesaurus* recording sessions with many other bands, including Benny Goodman, Artie Shaw, Les Brown, Joe Haymes, Charlie Barnet, and Chick Webb, took place in New York. Although Joe Dixon on at least one occasion recalled recording these transcriptions in Camden, every other source I have ever checked indicates that all *Thesaurus* sessions took place in RCA's Twenty-fourth Street studios in Manhattan. (See appendix 3 for more detailed information about the Berigan/*Thesaurus* recordings made in 1938.)

The Berigan band obviously recorded for *Thesaurus* many of the same tunes they had recorded for Victor. As we can see from appendix 3, sometimes the vocal chorus was omitted, sometimes not. It is always interesting to listen to versions of the pop tunes Berigan recorded with the vocal chorus excised. Very often, removal of the vocal improves the performance. Why Bunny would not have allowed an instrumentalist to play a solo in lieu of the vocal on these *Thesaurus* recordings is not known. That would have improved these performances even more.

Of much more interest however, are the titles that Bunny recorded for *Thesaurus* that he did *not* record for Victor. Among these are some of the best and most representative recordings the Berigan band ever made. Irving Berlin's "My Walking Stick" was recorded on Victor by Tommy Dorsey (April 27, 1938) with a vocal by Edythe Wright, so Bunny was unable to record it for Victor. That is too bad, because this arrangement, with solos by Dixon, Conniff, and Auld is excellent. Bunny, using his kazoo mute very effectively, gives new meaning to the term "dirty" trumpet. Based on the use of the reeds and trombones, I would say that this is almost certainly a Lippman chart.

"Flat Foot Floogie" was a current pop tune composed by the absolutely wild pianist/guitarist Slim Gaillard, the fine bassist Slam Stewart (then performing together as "Slim and Slam"), and Bud Green. Bunny was aced out on this by Benny Goodman, who had a good recording of it on Victor (May 31, 1938). In this version, Bernard N. "Bernie" Mackey, who had subbed for an ailing Little Gate Walker as the Berigan band's equipment manager/truck driver earlier in the year, then remained as Little Gate's assistant when he returned, was tapped by Bunny to sing the jivey lyric. Although this seems rather improbable, Mackey was then studying guitar, and later joined the Ink Spots[11] playing guitar and singing, so he no doubt had some singing experience. Bunny contributes an exuberant trumpet solo; Bushkin, Conniff, Auld, and Dixon also play some jazz. Clocking in at 3:43, this performance hints at what the Berigan band would do in front of audiences, by extending arrangements to allow for more solos. There is no indication anywhere as to who wrote this chart. It was possibly one of Andy Phillips's earliest contributions to the Berigan library of arrangements.

Drummer Johnny Blowers related an incident that occurred in the wake of this *Thesaurus* recording date that is indicative of the way Arthur Michaud handled the Berigan band's business, and probably led directly to Blowers leaving the Berigan band. After not being paid extra for the *Thesaurus* recording session, Blowers went to Michaud and asked where his money was for the transcription date. "'What transcription date?' he said, trying to look innocent. 'My contract states that I'm to get paid extra for recording. That transcription date was supposed to pay over $400. (Probably for the whole band.) I want my money or I'm going to report you to the union.' The threat worked, and everybody in the band was paid for the date."[12]

After the *Thesaurus* recording session, the band returned to the road, settling on July 4 at the Raymor Ballroom in Boston. This was Johnny Blowers's last night with the band. He had gotten a very good financial offer from Ben Bernie, who after a period of retirement, was returning to the music business with a swing-oriented band. (Among the other sidemen Bernie recruited then was trombonist Lou McGarity, who would go on to star with Benny Goodman.) After the gig that night, Bunny threw a surprise going-away party for Blowers, who overindulged, missed the train back to New York, and almost blew the job with Bernie before it started. Regardless, Bunny had secured the services of another drummer: Buddy Rich.

Bernard "Buddy" Rich, perhaps the most technically astonishing drummer in the history of jazz, was born on September 30, 1917, in Brooklyn, New York. His parents were vaudeville performers, and almost from infancy Buddy was onstage performing with them. His prodigious drumming talent manifested itself when Buddy was only eighteen months old. This led to a very successful vaudeville career for Rich, which lasted through his childhood years. By 1937, he began his career as a jazz drummer, first with Joe Marsala, then in 1938 with Bunny Berigan. Rich's big break came when he joined Artie Shaw's band at the beginning of 1939. With Shaw, his stunning drumming technique was first put on display before a national radio and movie audience. From Shaw he went, in late 1939, to Tommy Dorsey, who featured him as a soloist almost as much as Gene Krupa was featured in his own band. His tenure with Dorsey lasted until 1945, although he did serve in the Marine Corps during World War II. After World War II he led his own big bands with modest success in the late 1940s. He worked for many bandleaders in the 1950s and into the 1960s, including Les Brown, Tommy Dorsey, and most notably, Harry James. He also worked extensively with Norman Granz's Jazz at the Philharmonic, and on his own with small groups. In 1966, Rich formed a big band, which he led with considerable success, until his death. Rich was helped immeasurably in this endeavor by television personality Johnny Carson, who was an amateur drummer, a personal friend, and an idolator. Rich appeared on Carson's *Tonight Show* dozens of times from the 1960s to the 1980s. In addition to his virtuoso drumming, Rich would easily trade witticisms with Carson. Rich also had an explosive temper and the sidemen in his last bands took delight in surreptitiously recording his rages to band members within the confines of the band bus. Buddy Rich died on April 2, 1987, in Los Angeles, California.

Georgie Auld related how Rich got into the Berigan band:

Y'know I met Buddy when I was 14 and he was 16, which means we knew each other for 54 years. I got him in Bunny Berigan's band and I got him in Artie Shaw's band. He and I both lived in Brooklyn. Bunny was looking for a drummer, he was upgrading the band at the time, and I said 'there's a buddy of mine that's a genius behind the drums but he can't read a note of music.' Bunny said 'well, that's no good.' In those days we played theaters and we usually had 5 acts of vaudeville. He said, 'What's gonna happen when we play a theatre and we get a dance act or something and he can't read music?' I said, 'He'll do more without reading than any 30 drummers you get that can read.' Then Bunny said, 'All right let him sit in for a tune.' The exact same thing happened with Artie Shaw.[13]

Rich joined the Berigan band at Manhattan Beach in New York City. Dick Wharton remembered the gig, and Rich's impact on the Berigan band: "Manhattan Beach was an amusement park with an open-air bandstand next to Coney Island. Johnny Blowers had just left and Georgie Auld was Bunny's contact for enticing the young Buddy Rich away from Joe Marsala and persuading him it was a great opportunity for him. Buddy was loud from the very start and Bunny would have to insist on his cutting down the volume. But Bunny apparently liked the rhythmic 'figures' Rich played and had Buddy's 'licks' worked into some of the arrangements."[14] The Berigan band, with their new drummer, played at Manhattan Beach for one week, closing there on July 11. Buddy Rich began to slowly settle in.

After the Manhattan Beach stand, they played one-nighters west to Michigan, including one at the Queen's Ball for the National Cherry Festival at Traverse City, Michigan on July 13.[15] They opened on Friday July 15, at the Fox Theater in Detroit,[16] for a one-week engagement. Here is the review of the show that the Berigan band was a part of:

> Berigan blows into the Fox with his trumpet and band to keep the jitterbugs happy and it's a lively package of talent that Berigan has with him in the stage show. Bunny's band is plenty smooth and keeping up the festivities are the Frazee Sisters, song stars of Billy Rose's Casa Manana, returning by popular demand, three sophisticated ladies whose knockabout antics get plenty of laughs. Sharpe and Armstrong do a very clever satire on ballroom dancing, and Ruth Gaylor and Dick Wharton sing several popular lyrics. It is sixty minutes of lively stage fare to accompany the movie, *We're Going to Be Rich*, starring Gracie Fields, Victor McLaglen and Brian Donlevy.[17]

While appearing at the Fox Theater, Bunny invited his mother and father to Detroit, as well as his brother Donald, who had only recently married, and Don's new wife, Loretta. He also insisted that Donna, who had been living separately from him in Syracuse, join this family gathering. Loretta Berigan recalled this family reunion to Robert Dupuis:

> At first Donna was not going to be there. Then she decided to come, apparently to put up a united front and welcome me as a new family member. This seemed very important for Bunny. At first it was very strained; Don and I both sensed it. Then things began to loosen up. Bunny and Donna had a few drinks and he started teasing and joking with her. She couldn't keep from laughing. It ended up that we all had a good time. I remember wondering at the time if there was ever any down-to-earth conversation between them. It was all fun and games.[18]

Bunny gave Don and Loretta $50 as a wedding present, which in the value of money today would be about $750. It was a generous gift, but certainly not extravagant. In the summer of 1938, Bunny was making a lot of money.

While Berigan was in Detroit, he also apparently "...visited and dined with Dr. Cliff Benson, with whom he had worked in Madison in the late 1920s. Benson was a practicing medical doctor and said 'Bunny visited my office. He very briefly discussed his problem. I never was his medical advisor.' Dr. Benson told Bunny that he should know the cause of his 'shakes' and advised him to cut down on his drinking. Dr. Benson never saw Bunny again."[19] Joe Dixon recalled what it was like traveling with Bunny: "Bunny's doctor, Dr. Goldberg, was telling him he had cirrhosis of the liver and if he didn't stop drinking he wouldn't last long. I drove his big Chrysler Imperial on the road once in a while, with him in the back seat, and sometimes he'd wake from a dead sleep all perspired and hysterical, and I'd have to head for the nearest bar or liquor store and get some brandy. He'd have to swallow at least a half a pint before he'd calm down."[20]

After the Fox Theater engagement, which ended on July 21, the band headed east, and probably played a one-nighter in Syracuse, New York, on July 22. Dick Wharton recalled a very strange rehearsal that occurred the next day: "We drove back to New York City from Syracuse, arriving about 4 a.m. Later that day we had to rehearse for our forthcoming engagement at the Casa Manana and it was a rough one, because they had a very tough, tricky floor show with lots of cues and changes and neither Buddy Rich nor Joey Bushkin could read music. And Bunny wasn't really experienced in leading for stage shows of that type, so it was all rather a mess with everybody getting sore at everybody else."[21] Immediately after the rehearsal, the Berigan bandsmen drove to Atlantic City, where that night they opened what was supposed to be a one-week engagement at the Marine Ballroom on the Steel Pier, a prime venue.

That same night, the band participated in another transatlantic radio broadcast: "Remote from Marine Ballroom of Steel Pier, Atlantic City, relayed through CBS station W2XE (19.64M), received by BBC England, on a Murphy A40C, direct on a Philo A847 *(sic)*. 10:30–11:00 p.m. Greenwich Mean Time (which would mean midafternoon in New Jersey.) 'I Can't Get Started' (theme-partial); 'Shanghai Shuffle;' 'Somewhere With Somebody Else' (vocal); 'My Melancholy Baby;' 'Flat Foot Floogie,' (BB vocal?); 'Wacky Dust;' 'Devil's Holiday;' 'I Can't Get Started' (theme-partial)."[22]

The British publication *Melody Maker* carried this review:

Headline: 'Bunny Berigan Battles Against Static.' If I awarded stars on reception as well as performance this broadcast would have earned about two. The reception was about the poorest we have had in the present series of relays from America, one of its peculiarities being that, in contrast to the Lopez reply last week, the bass resister came over not only thick and lacking in definition, but at times so heavy that it almost swamped out the rest of the ensemble. Nevertheless we were left in no doubt that Bunny Berigan has a band that can hold its own with the best in the states. And in saying this I am saying an ocean full. One of the things the better American swing bands have developed is an overwhelming force of personality...a vitality that cannot be described in the terms of style or technique which have for so long been the accepted means of assessing a dance band, because it comes from something much deeper; from, it would seem, the power, one might almost say, with an abandon that is purely spontaneous. If not, how else does one account for such performances as Berigan's 'Flat Foot Floogie'? The number had some singing that would hardly have been a credit to a music hall comedian; the arrangement, breath-taking as it was, did little more then use the melody of the number, when it used it at all, as an excuse for the licks, riffs and other orchestrator's devices which are the fashions of the moment in swing scoring. But doubtful as these points may have been if looked upon separately in cold blood, in the blaze of the performance they meant little. They were completely obscured by the inevitable rhythmic urge of the interpretation, the character of the playing, the creativeness of the solos, the terrific momentum of it all. And every number more or less had the same irresistible exhilaration. Which, my children, is the spirit if not the letter of swing.[23]

The Berigan band continued its engagement at the Steel Pier the following night, Sunday, July 24. Then, abruptly, they were removed from the Steel Pier job by MCA and replaced by Little Jack Little's band. Why this happened gives some indication as to how MCA handled its talent. The following is a comment from the White materials about what went on, as well as the recollections of a number of performers who were on the scene then. "Possibly the Berigan band opened at the Steel Pier for a week's stand, but when Vincent Lopez was transferred by MCA to a more important engagement at Piping Rock, Bunny was pulled out of the Pier job and moved into the Casa Manana, as he was already scheduled there. Then when Bunny and Billy Rose got into a big hassle, the band was given notice almost before they had opened. The Casa Manana show was due to close at the end of the month in any case."[24]

Clyde Rounds: That engagement lifted the band back to something like its earlier status among its contemporaries. The artists featured at the club included Jimmy 'Schonzzle' Durante, John Steel, a singing favorite of the time, Benay Venuta, and the relatively unknown Danny Kaye. The show girls were so beautiful and so distracting for the musicians! Often the boys had their eyes glued on the girls rather than the music. Needless to say, the crowds packed the place every night and we got good notices. We really thought we were set for a nice long season with everyone near home, but it wasn't to be.[25]

Dick Wharton: Bunny would play us on with his theme, 'I Can't Get Started,' followed by the opening number. Then four experienced show-type musicians would replace Bunny, Joey Bushkin, Buddy Rich, and me, while the band would accompany the various vaudeville acts. The floor show lasted for about an hour, after which we'd rejoin the band to play for the dancing session. Louis Prima led the interval band and I remember there was a minor hassle as to whose theme song should introduce the show. And soon after that was settled, Bunny got into a major row with Billy Rose, who owned the club, and the band was out! It was a very abrupt ending to what had promised to be a most successful date.[26]

Benay Venuta: I was in the show at the Casa Manana. Jimmy Durante and I were the headliners. Danny Kaye was on hand but had only a small part. I recall the 'changes' in the Berigan band yes, while it played the show, which was a tough one for sure. I think I worked someplace about this time with Bunny's wife's brother named 'McArthur' who had a dance act.[27]

What is curious about the recollections of Clyde Rounds and Dick Wharton is that the show that they joined in midrun at the Casa Manana was scheduled to close on July 30, and *did close* on July 30, with an entirely new cast opening with a new show the following night. The Berigan band played with the Durante show every night from July 25 to July 30, when it closed. The net result of the moves made by MCA was that it removed the Vincent Lopez band from the Casa Manana show in the middle of its run, removed Bunny's band from a plum booking at the Steel Pier to replace Lopez with little or no notice, then threw the Berigan band into the middle of the ongoing Casa Manana show with little or no rehearsal. It is possible however, that the Berigan band was supposed to have been the featured band in the *next* Casa Manana show, but lost that gig because of Bunny's disagreement with Billy Rose. This is only speculation on my part however. No direct evidence that this was the case is to be found in the White materials or elsewhere. Whatever actually happened, I can understand why Bunny was a bit edgy at the Casa Manana.[28]

Meanwhile, Gene Krupa's band was then in the middle of a successful run at New York's Paramount Theater, and Tommy Dorsey's was on the West Coast. But Tommy was not happy:

What was the motivating force in the recent split between Tommy Dorsey and his manager Arthur Michaud? No official statement has been issued as to the cause of the split, though it has been conjectured that a slip-up on the provision of a stand-by band during Dorsey's commercial in Chicago a few weeks ago, on which Tommy took over $1,000 loss, was the direct cause. Be that as it may, the cause is secondary to the fireworks that are likely to ensue in the near future. For Arthur Michaud, through with one trombone player, is now preparing to launch a rival in the person of none other than Jack Teagarden. True, Mr. T is still with Paul Whiteman, but from well-informed circles comes the story that Jackson may be released from contractual obligations very shortly. As soon as that comes to pass, Michaud will commence an intensive campaign to put Jack Teagarden on top. On top of what? Well, one thing is certain and that is he'll try to put him on top of Tommy Dorsey and, if possible, on top of the entire field of dance orchestras. Meanwhile, out on the west coast in the Palomar, Tommy Dorsey is doing extremely well for himself.[29]

It seems that the second victim of Arthur Michaud's inattention and conflict of interest was Tommy Dorsey. With a weekly sponsored network radio show as a base, and several hit records going for him, Tommy was able to sustain this loss. But TD correctly saw that Michaud's negligence had cost him dearly once, and he decided that it would not happen a second time. He quickly lowered the boom on Michaud, and terminated their relationship. Bunny Berigan took note of these developments.

There is little documentation as to the Berigan band's whereabouts after their Casa Manana engagement, but it is likely that they played a number of one-night dance engagements during this time, including one on August 5 at Budd Lake, New Jersey. On August 8, they were once again in the RCA Victor studios in New York to record another batch of transcriptions for *Thesaurus*. The titles of the tunes they recorded and other information related to this session are in appendix 3.

I must recount at this point a personal experience I had involving Buddy Rich that occurred in the late 1970s while I was in New York attending various events of what was then called the Newport–New York Jazz Festival. A friend and I had traveled from Ohio to New York to spend a week listening to as much music as possible. We both had enormous respect for Buddy Rich, who at that time had been leading his own big band with considerable success for over a decade. We had bought tickets to see Buddy and his band, who that night were on the bill with a few other jazz stars at Carnegie Hall for a concert that was to start at 8:00 p.m. I am habitually early for everything, so my friend and I found ourselves outside of Carnegie Hall at about 7:15. Since it was too early to enter, we decided to walk around near Carnegie Hall until about 7:45, then go in.

As we began to stroll south on the Seventh Avenue sidewalk next to Carnegie Hall, we encountered Buddy Rich walking toward us, smoking something. I knew that Mr. Rich could be nasty, but I couldn't pass up an opportunity to attempt to speak with the great Buddy Rich. As we met on the sidewalk I said, "Excuse me, Mr. Rich, I want to tell you that I have always enjoyed your playing." He glared at me and exhaled smoke through his nostrils like a bull in a bull ring. "*Yeaaaaah,*" he said. Sensing that I was getting nowhere fast, I decided to try an abrupt change of direction. Knowing that Rich dearly loved Count Basie, I then asked him: "When did you first hear Count Basie?" The expression on his face suddenly changed to a toothy smile. "How did you know about me and Basie?" he asked. I mumbled something stupid, and he cut me off: "I was with Bunny Berigan. We were in New York for a few days, and Bunny had a rehearsal and wasn't too happy with the way we were playing. So he stopped the rehearsal and said, 'You guys need to go see Count Basie's band. He's playing over on Fifty-second Street at the Famous Door. That will do you more good than rehearsing!' So I went with Georgie Auld, Joe Dixon, Ray Conniff, and Joey Bushkin. We were all overwhelmed by the way the Basie band played. They swung so hard; it was so light, but powerful. Everyone was blown away by Lester Young. Everyone but Georgie, that is. He dug Herschel Evans." Rich then took another puff, and said, "Hey, I gotta go in and do the show." He then turned and walked south on the Seventh Avenue sidewalk to the rear of Carnegie Hall and disappeared into the stage door. We entered Carnegie Hall, and watched Buddy play the devil out of his drums that night. (Note: Soon after the incident described by Buddy Rich, an arrangement of "One O'Clock Jump," probably written by Ray Conniff, entered the Berigan band's repertoire. Other Basie-inspired changes in the music of the Berigan band also started to take place at this time.)

From August 9 through the 14th, the Berigan band played one-nighters out to a week-long engagement at Moonlight Gardens, Coney Island, Cincinnati, Ohio. It was at this location that George "Gigi" Bohn joined them on first alto saxophone, replacing Mike Doty. Bunny's sax section had remained together as a unit for over a year, but Doty[30] had received a good offer from Larry Clinton, whose band then seemed to be on the upswing, so he made the move. Bohn was an extremely capable first alto player who came from the very underrated Hudson-DeLange band, and would go on to lead a superb sax section for Jan Savitt after his brief spell with Bunny. Following the Coney Island stand, the Berigan band moved on to what appears to have been a split-week engagement between the Palace Theater in Youngstown, Ohio, and the Palace Theater in Akron, Ohio. The week of August 21 started with the band in Youngstown.

During this period, several things happened that began the process of destabilizing the personnel of the Berigan band. Here is the recollection of Joe Dixon:

> From the transcription studio in New Jersey, *(sic)* we went west; we didn't come back to New York. Bunny started acting up very badly then. He was drinking and when it catches up to you after awhile, alcohol distorts your sense of person and perspective. When we got to Pittsburgh, he was getting very touchy and edgy. We were doing four shows a day at the Stanley Theater and he showed up drunk almost every night. One night Bunny walked out on stage and fell right into the orchestra pit. The band was on its way to do the Bob Hope show in California. (See the following chapter, September 27, 1938, for a description of the events surrounding the first Bob Hope radio show sponsored by Pepsodent. It is unlikely that the Berigan band was ever committed to work on the Bob Hope show.) When we got to Youngstown and Akron, he blew it. He called a rehearsal one day, which was very unlike Bunny to do. This was between shows and Mike Doty and I were having lunch somewhere near the theater. Someone came over and said 'Bunny called a rehearsal, where are you?' We didn't know anything about it. When we got there he started getting really nasty with us and that was the first time Bunny ever did that. So Mike followed him down to his dressing room, and gave his notice, and I followed about a day or two later. We thought, where are we going with this? This band is beautiful and he is drunk all the time.[31]

George Bohn himself recalled exactly where he joined the Berigan band: "I joined Bunny's band in Cincinnati, taking over Mike Doty's lead alto chair. I'd been playing with the Hudson-DeLange orchestra."[32] If George Bohn had joined the Berigan band on August 15 at Coney Island in Cincinnati, then Mike Doty would *not* have been in the Berigan band a week after that when they were in Youngstown and Akron. I must conclude that Joe Dixon's memory on some of the larger details of this particular incident was slightly inaccurate. I think that there was an unpleasant incident between Bunny and Dixon, and Dixon may well have given notice at that time (August 21–24). Nevertheless, he remained in the band until September 11. There is no evidence of anyone else giving notice or leaving the band within the weeks between August 21 and September 11.

I think that Bunny may have been feeling increasing stress as a result of the rather haphazard booking of his band that had taken place since it had left the Paradise Restaurant the previous May. Although there had been a few lucrative theater dates since then, the band was now playing more and more one-nighters, and the few theater dates they did have were often occurring in smaller theaters in smaller cities. The result of this undoubtedly was smaller weekly grosses. Yet there was no reduction in Bunny's band payroll, transportation, and other fixed costs. They kept accruing constantly.

Finally, MCA lined up a very good one-week theater stand for the Berigan band. On Thursday, August 25, 1938, they opened again at the Stanley Theater in Pittsburgh, the site of their successful engagement in the fall of 1937. Here are the details:

> The Stanley stage show headed by Bunny Berigan and his trumpet and his orchestra is aimed at the jitterbug. For less sturdy mortals, it has little to offer. Maestro Berigan, who seems to be on the upbeat these days, presents a slightly wild program in which he himself plays no small part. The Andrews Sisters, three gals well versed in the dizzy doings of swing, add their talented voices in quiet contrast to the Berigan brass and dancing interludes are provided by Ruth and Billy Ambrose and Frank Cowell and Sally Dale. The film being presented was *Mother Carey's Chickens* with Annie Shirley and Ruby Keeler.[33]

It is interesting that trombonist Walter Burleson, who had worked with Bunny in early 1937, recalled that Donna was with Bunny during this engagement: "That was my last meeting with Bunny and Donna. The Berigan band and the Andrews Sisters were appearing at the Stanley Theater and I had the pleasure of introducing to Bunny a young trumpet player called Jimmy Pupa, with whom I'd played a few state fairs. He was just a kid, full of pep and vigor, who was called later by Bunny, when he was in urgent need of a first trumpet player."[34]

It is safe to say that where drinking was concerned, by this time Donna was not a good influence on Bunny. In fact, the opposite was probably true, not that he needed any encouragement from Donna or anyone else to take a sip. The White materials contain this information about Bunny's infamous fall into the orchestra pit, which probably occurred during the Stanley Theater engagement:

> How long would he be able to withstand the pressures and pitfalls of the band-leading business? Also, his ability to hold his liquor was decreasing. At one time he could take a drink before a performance and not show it, but now he might disgrace himself in public. Once, in a Pittsburgh theatre, he came on stage to lead his band, playing his theme, 'I Can't Get Started,' staggered right off the stage and fell into the orchestra pit. Luckily, a canvas covering broke his fall and though shaken up, he was unhurt. 'You'd feel so sorry for him,' said a friend,

'Here was a wonderful guy, a fantastic talent and he was just killing himself. When he fell off the stage, he got all tangled up in the canvas, flailing around. The ushers had to extricate him. What a mess! The band played that set without him.'[35]

It seems that just as the Berigan band had arrived at its peak as a performing unit, Bunny's drinking began to take a heavier toll on him. Now, in addition to his being occasionally unable to deliver flawless performances on his trumpet, he was reacting to the stresses and strains of being a bandleader in negative ways.

Many writers have suggested that by 1938, Bunny Berigan was past his prime and was on an irreversible course headed down. *Subsequent events* have all too often provided the basis for this assertion. In fact, in the summer of 1938, he was still capable of playing marvelously, and his band was still one of the best in the country. With the benefit of much hindsight, we are now able to see that the summer of 1938 proved to be the tipping point as far as Berigan's success as a bandleader was concerned. But at that time, this was not at all apparent. Yes, Bunny's drinking had now approached a critical stage, and those who worked with him on a daily basis knew the toll that it was taking on him. But most audiences then saw Bunny as someone who often resembled a kind of mythic god. He was tall, well built, strikingly handsome, and always dressed immaculately when he appeared onstage. (MCA insisted on this, but Bunny had to pay the salary of the valet who prepared his clothing for each appearance.) When he was "on" the musical experience could be overwhelming. In addition, there was a mystique about him, and this has been lost to history, except in the recollections of those who actually saw and heard him at his peak.

Encomia praising the trumpet artistry of Bunny Berigan began to pour forth from those fortunate enough to have heard him play in person almost from the beginning of his professional career. In fact, the adjectives used to describe Bunny's playing are almost always the same—whether spoken by fellow musicians or awestruck fans: *tremendous; amazing, fiery, magnificent, impassioned.* One of the first reviews to mention and attempt to describe the trumpet playing of Bunny Berigan was written by a young and perceptive Helen Oakley[36] in the summer of 1935, when Bunny was featured with Benny Goodman's band. Ms. Oakley had heard the band during its two-night stand at the Modernistic Ballroom in Milwaukee, which had taken place on July 21-22, 1935. The following is excerpted from her full review of the band that appeared in the August 1935 issue of *Down Beat:*

Bunny Berigan was a revelation to me. Never having heard him in-person before, even though well acquainted with his work on recordings, I was unprepared for such a tremendous thrill. The man is a master...he plays so well and at the same time I doubt if I ever heard a more forceful trumpet...unending ideas and possessed of that quality peculiar to both Teagarden and Armstrong, that of swinging the band as a whole at the outset and carrying it solidly along with him without letup until the finish of his chorus. Bunny is, I believe, the only trumpeter today comparable to Louis. So much must be left unsaid; one feels stupid in attempting to evaluate Bunny's work on paper.[37]

George T. Simon, who began his long affiliation with *Metronome* magazine in 1935, was one of many whose first exposure to Berigan's trumpeting also came while Bunny was in Benny Goodman's band. Although during the years Bunny fronted a big band Simon was perhaps his most consistently harsh critic (often unfairly so), eventually, he too got the message: "He was for many of us the ultimate jazz trumpeter, a fiery player with a tremendous range and one of the fattest upper register sounds ever to emanate from anyone's horn."[38]

But in addition to the bravura, there was a touch of Irish melancholy in Berigan's playing, and it was expressed sensitively and subtly in many of his ballad performances.

Many years after Berigan's death, two of the stalwart sidemen from his 1937–1938 big band reflected on the Berigan mystique. Clarinetist/alto saxist Joe Dixon: "You can talk about one thing and another—beautiful, clear, big tone, range, power—and sure that's part of it—but only part of it. Bunny hit a note, and it had pulse, that certain ingredient that makes it vibrate right away, and—well, *inside* you. It just did something to you, that's all. It's hard to describe, but his sound seemed to, well, soar. He'd play lead and the whole band would soar with him, with or without the rhythm section. There was drama in what he did—he had that ability, like Louis, to make any tune his own. But in the end all that says nothing. You had to hear him, that's all."[39] Steve Lipkins played lead trumpet in that band, whenever Bunny didn't. His impressions were: "He was the first jazz player I'd heard at that time who played the trumpet well from bottom to top, very evenly and strongly throughout. Besides that, he had something special in the magic department, and you had to hear that to understand it."[40]

Berigan's relationship with Benny Goodman could be best described as "strained." Anyone familiar with BG knows that he was not one to pass out compliments, especially about other musicians. He well understood that Berigan's abuse of alcohol could make him unpredictable as a person, and inconsistent as a performer. Nevertheless, even he was not immune to Berigan's musical sorcery. He described Bunny's effect on his band this way: "It was like a bolt of electricity running through the whole band. He just lifted the whole thing. You can explain it in terms of his tone, his range, musicianship, great ideas, whatever you want. It's all of that—and none of it. It's a God-given thing."[41] Shortly before Benny Goodman's death in 1986, Loren Schoenberg,[42] a young tenor saxophonist and pianist who was then working with BG on a number of projects, showed Goodman a video of Berigan singing and playing in the film short that he made with Fred Rich's band in 1936. Schoenberg recalled: "Although not usually given to any form of nostalgia, he asked me several times to rewind the tape to where Bunny started; it was one of the few times I saw Benny so moved."[43]

Berigan's impact on other trumpet players was enormous. As has been noted in the comments of Berigan band members Steve Lipkins and Irving Goodman, both of whom had the pleasure of hearing a large amount of Bunny's playing while he was at the peak of his powers, he could and did do remarkable things very frequently. Other trumpeters who heard less of his playing were also impressed. Jimmy Maxwell began his career as a member of Gil Evans's band in southern California in the mid-1930s. He was a stalwart member of Benny Goodman's trumpet section from 1939–1942, and then commenced a long and distinguished career as a New York freelance and teacher. Maxwell was at home in any musical situation, including performing with symphony orchestras, which he often did. Here are his thoughts on Berigan as a trumpet virtuoso:

> I'd never heard anyone play so lyrically. It was a good deal like Louis, but it was looser. Armstrong at that point was inclining toward a more rigid, angular style. Bunny would play those beautiful, liquid solos. So fluid. By 1934, he had started to have an enormous influence on trumpet players, particularly white trumpet players. Here was somebody who played with a different feeling, but wasn't black. I felt Bunny was one of the first bridges, taking the race out of music and playing music. He had the most gorgeous sound, and that beautiful vibrato. And everything he played had a line. It was like a melody, even if it had a lot of notes in it.[44]

Although Berigan's influence on white trumpet players was huge, black trumpet players also heard something special. Cornetist Rex Stewart, long one of Duke Ellington's featured soloists, called Bunny Berigan "one of the indestructibles."[45] He also included Berigan among his favorite trumpeters, along with Dizzy Gillespie, Roy Eldridge, Bobby Stark, Charlie Shavers, Bix Beiderbecke, Russell Smith, Bobby Hackett, Alvin Alcorn, and Joe Smith.[46]

George "Pee Wee" Erwin was another marvelous trumpeter who stood in awe of Berigan's trumpet artistry. In early 1937, it was Erwin who followed Bunny into Tommy Dorsey's band as its featured jazz soloist. He later recalled one of his first challenges:

> Tommy and Eli Oberstein, RCA's recording supervisor, wanted another tune done to the same formula as 'Marie'. So we went and recorded 'Who' the same way, with me taking a full-chorus solo out of Jack Leonard's vocal. When we got there, I asked Freddy, the recording engineer, where Bunny had stood when he played that chorus into a standard RCA 44-ribbon mike. He showed me a point approximately thirty feet away from the microphone. *Thirty feet!* Well, when we recorded 'Who,' I stood about fifteen feet away—and I was known in those days for a big tone! You could never fully appreciate the tone he had, and the power, unless you stood in front of his horn and heard it. He hit a note and it was just like a cannon. I'm not talking about volume, but his sheer body of sound. He used a Bach #7 mouthpiece, which is relatively deep. In other words, he was one helluva strong man.[47]

There was more to the Berigan mystique however than his masterly and inspired trumpet playing. Bunny also had about him a personal charisma, a physical presence that was at once commanding and memorable. Joe Bushkin, the pianist who worked with Bunny's small group on Manhattan's Fifty-second Street in 1936, with his big band in 1938–39, and again with him in Tommy Dorsey's band in 1940, explained it this way: "Look, if you could have seen him there onstage in a white suit, with his blonde hair and penetrating gray eyes, holding that shiny gold trumpet—well, if that didn't knock you over when he started to play, ain't nothing gonna knock you down."[48]

The totality of the Berigan mystique hit my father, full force, on Sunday, August 28, 1938, at the Capitol Theater in Steubenville, Ohio. What follows is an amalgam of the stories he told me over many years about that memorable night. My father was born in 1918, so in 1938 he was twenty years old. He had grown up in a small town in eastern Ohio called Summitville, and had graduated from high school in nearby Salineville, in 1936. Upon graduation, he began to work at a local brickyard, where his father also worked. In those New Deal days, there was considerable union organizing activity occurring in family-owned businesses in that region of Ohio. Unfortunately for my father and grandfather, this activity resulted in a lockout that quickly reduced the meager fortunes of the Zirpolo family to near zero. In 1937, my grandfather moved to Canton, Ohio, about twenty-five miles northwest of Summitville, and lived there with his wife's family while he tried to find work. By 1938, he had secured employment at a brick yard in Canton, and shortly after, the rest of his family followed him there. My dad then worked with his uncle in Canton, in a family-owned produce business.

In the mid-1930s in Summitville, Ohio, there was little in the way of entertainment available to kids growing up. The source of much entertainment in the home where my father grew up was the massive floor-model radio that stood in the living room of my grandparents' home. They continued to listen to this radio well into the 1960s. I was always strictly forbidden from touching its dials. It was from this radio that my father first heard the sounds of remote broadcasts by the myriad dance bands that existed in the early and mid-1930s, as well as the many network radio programs that featured live music, but emanated from studios usually in either New York or Chicago. In due course, he discovered the Casa Loma band and later Benny Goodman on *The Camel Caravan,* Goodman's band on the NBC *Let's Dance* program and via the "Rhythm Makers" *Thesaurus* transcriptions BG made, and Bunny Berigan on various CBS network shows, the most memorable being the *Saturday Night Swing Club.* He also heard Fats Waller on radio, as well as the many bands that then recorded for the RCA labels on the NBC *Magic Key of Radio* programs that were used to promote RCA recording artists. Last but certainly not least, he heard hundreds of sustaining radio broadcasts of bands of all kinds from venues all over the United States.

The move to Canton provided a big boost to my dad's interest in music. In Canton was Moonlight Ballroom located at Meyer's Lake Park, where touring bands and territory bands appeared on a regular basis to play for dancing. There were also two theaters, the Palace and the Loew's, each having seating to accommodate over 2,000, which featured bands as a part of touring vaudeville shows. There was also an astonishing array of live music provided in various other venues in and around Canton by talented local musicians. There were the many malt shops and bars that then had the relatively new jukeboxes in them. My father would not only feed those jukeboxes the nickels they took to play one tune, but he often negotiated with the jukebox servicemen to buy (at a reduced price!) his favorites among the records they were removing when a new batch of sides arrived. Music was definitely in the air in Canton, Ohio, in the late 1930s. My dad began to attend local musical events regularly, and also subscribed to *Down Beat* to find out more about the bands criss-crossing the country then.

Soon, my father and a cadre of his friends (whenever finances would permit), were traveling all over northeastern Ohio to see the top bands of the day. Among the notable venues they visited were East Market Gardens and the Palace Theater in Akron, the Nu-Elms, Idora Park, and Yankee Lake Ballrooms near Youngstown, the mammoth Palace Theater in the Playhouse Square complex of theaters in Cleveland, and the Capitol Theater in Steubenville.[49] Without a doubt, his favorite place to see a band was at the Capitol Theater in Steubenville. He recalled that it was "small enough so that you could really hear and see the bands, and it had great acoustics. The music just exploded off that stage."

Steubenville, Ohio, is located on the Ohio River about twenty-five miles due west of Pittsburgh. One of its most notable sons, Dino Crocetti, later to achieve fame as Dean Martin, who in the late 1930s was dealing blackjack and poker in one of the city's many illegal gambling casinos, described it as: "a rough and tumble Ohio River town full of steel mills, speakeasies, and whorehouses."[50] The Capitol Theater there had an agreement with the Stanley Theater in Pittsburgh, then one of the major stops on the big band and vaudeville circuit, that allowed the Stanley's current attractions to play at the Capitol on Sundays when they could not perform in Pennsylvania because of that commonwealth's "blue laws." Almost every performer who played at the Stanley Theater, therefore, also played at the Capitol Theater. As noted above, Bunny Berigan and His Orchestra opened at the Stanley Theater on Thursday, August 25, 1938, for a one-week stand.[51]

By the time my father actually saw Bunny Berigan in person, on Sunday, August 28, 1938, he had known about him for probably three years, had purchased many of his Victor recordings, and had heard him many times on the *Saturday Night Swing Club* radio show. The band that Berigan led that night at the Capitol Theater consisted of the following: Steve Lipkins (lead), Irving Goodman, trumpets; Nat Lobovsky (lead), Ray Conniff, trombones; George Bohn (lead), Joe Dixon, Georgie Auld, and Clyde Rounds, reeds; Joe Bushkin, piano; Dick Wharton, guitar/vocals; Hank Wayland, bass; Buddy Rich, drums; and Ruth Gaylor, vocals. My father remembered the Andrews Sisters, who did appear at the Capitol with Berigan, only as "a corny vocal group," and didn't recall the dancers at all. He stated that there was no movie, but that the band played two one-hour shows, with the theater being cleared between them. His sole reason for going to the Capitol Theater that night was to see and hear Bunny Berigan. His expectations were high, and he was not disappointed.

The day had been "roasting hot, with stifling humidity." The 2,000-seat Capitol "was filled to the rafters with a very wild audience." My dad was seated somewhere in the first few rows, and was able to see Bunny and the band very clearly. Those there wanted hot music, and Berigan and his musicians made no apologies about swinging hard, and playing loud.

> As the curtain rose, Bunny was standing in front of the band; they came on playing his theme, 'I Can't Get Started,' for a few bars, then segued quickly into a loud up-tempo swinger, which lasted for about five minutes. The audience responded with a roar of approval, and the show proceeded in like fashion for the next hour, with little letup. Berigan himself was a big guy, probably six feet one, with powerfully built arms and shoulders (the result no doubt of lifting a trumpet to his lips for anywhere from three to seven hours a day for the past ten years). He had magnificent reddish-blonde hair, and arresting blue-gray eyes. He was wearing an immaculate light colored suit, with blue necktie and kerchief in his breast pocket. He was a very good-looking guy. He looked like a movie star. He said very little to the audience between numbers and seldom flashed his teeth, like many other bandleaders, because his teeth looked crooked. His trumpet seemed to be extra long, and he would hold it so it was straight out and level when he played. But when he would play a high note, he would point the trumpet up, at about 45 degrees.

My father recalled one or two vocals by the girl singer in each show, "to allow the band members to catch their breath between romping swingers. Bunny and all of the other soloists played much longer solos, completely different from those on the records, with the arrangements being extended by Bunny setting up spontaneous riffs in the various sections behind the soloists." This was rarely done in white bands then, and not done too frequently even in black bands (with the exception of Basie's). The Berigan band played both shows without any music stands or written music.

> Bunny's trumpet sound was awe inspiring: He had a huge sound. It was full and rich and ringing, but always very warm. He was not a blaster, like Ziggy Elman, or a screecher, like Cat Anderson and Maynard Ferguson, who came later. His sound was just enormous, in all registers of the horn. I have no idea how he did it, but when he played, and that trumpet was pointed at you, my God, it was like being enveloped by that gorgeous sound. It completely filled the theater; it was like the walls were bulging. And his ideas were fantastic: he could play an entire improvised chorus without even the hint of repetition or cliché. The music just flowed out of his trumpet. He was clearly inspired when he was onstage in front of his band playing, and that was very contagious, to his musicians and to his audience. He put a lot into his playing, both physically and emotionally. I had never seen mist come out of the bell of a trumpet before. That night, I saw it frequently. It seemed that when Bunny played a solo he was able to communicate with his

audience in a very immediate, powerful, magical way. His band gave him everything they had every second they were playing. That was one swinging band!

As a result, the audience was stirred to frenzy, and remained at fever pitch throughout the evening.

At the end of the first show, he let his drummer play, and he was fantastic. His arms were flying around the drum set and cymbals, and he was swinging. We had no idea who he or any of the others in the band were because Bunny didn't introduce anybody. He just let them play.

The drummer in question was Buddy Rich. Anyone who knows anything about Buddy Rich knows that he was not one to engage in exercises in nostalgia. He was, nevertheless, a very emotional man who was very proud of having played with many of the greatest musicians in the history of jazz, including Bunny Berigan. When he formed his big band in the 1960s, one of the first things he did was to commission from arranger Dave Bloomberg a lovely, evocative arrangement of "I Can't Get Started." I personally witnessed Rich and his band play this arrangement more than once. Buddy never made a big issue about dedicating it to Berigan, but he did clearly announce that this tune was "the theme song of Bunny Berigan." When Rich decided to record this arrangement, his tenor saxophonist Jay Corre had a solo. Here is what Corre remembered: "I had begun playing my solo when I happened to glance over at Buddy. He was playing brushes and leaning over the snare drum crying his eyes out; teardrops were running down his face and falling on the snare. I knew right then that he was probably thinking about Bunny Berigan and the times they had spent together. I got caught up in Buddy's emotions and it affected my playing as well. It's a moment that I will always remember."[52]

The Capitol Theater was not air-conditioned.

I had never seen a human being sweat like Bunny, and I had worked with guys in kilns in the brickyard. He perspired so heavily that by the end of the first show, he was completely soaked, with sweat coming through the lapels, arms, and back of his suit jacket, and indeed, the crotch of his trousers. During the show, he had a towel hidden inside the lid of the piano, and he would go over there while someone else was playing, and wipe his face.[53]

After the first show, the theater was cleared, and within about a half hour, the second show began. My dad and his friends, including some Steubenville "relatives," had paid little kids to stand on the ticket line for them for the second show. ("We gave them a dime when we went in for the first show, and then another dime when we came out. They knew if they took off with that first dime, we would go looking for them.") It was, if anything, more swinging and exciting than the first show. Berigan, who had changed suits (and probably everything else) during the intermission, "strode out from behind the curtain playing 'I Can't Get Started,' but this time he played it all the way through, exactly as he had recorded it. The audience was quiet for the first and only time that night. At the climax of the performance, as Bunny went into the high register, his trumpet pointed skyward, a clap of thunder shook the building, and wild cheering erupted." Once again, Berigan had immediately stirred the audience, and he then proceeded to play a completely different program of tunes, most of them up-tempo swingers, for the second show. "By the end of the second show, Bunny was again drenched. So were we. That theater smelled like a horse barn by then!" The audience departed and was able to cool off in a hurry as they walked out into a full-scale thunderstorm.

As I learned more about Bunny Berigan over the years, I began to wonder if my dad had noticed any indication that night of Bunny's drinking. I once asked him about this. "I have no way of knowing for sure. I certainly saw no signs of it. But I can't imagine anyone performing like he did that night if he had been even slightly under the influence. What he did was simply too demanding physically and mentally for him to have been impaired."

Notes

[1] *Golden Boy: The Timeless Artistry of Bunny Berigan* is the title of the liner notes essay written by Richard M. Sudhalter for the Mosaic set of CDs (2002) containing many performances by Bunny Berigan from early in his career. Sudhalter borrowed the title *Golden Boy* from the playwright Clifford Odets, who wrote a play by that name in 1937 for the New York Group Theater which was later made into a film and a Broadway musical.

[2] *Benny Goodman—Wrappin' It Up*, by D. Russell Connor, Scarecrow Press Inc. (1996), 17–18.

[3] White materials: June 8, 1938.

[4] Cited in the White materials: June 8, 1938.

[5] This story was published originally in *Big Band Jazz*, by Albert McCarthy, G.P. Putnam's Sons (1974), 208, and later appeared in *Blowers*, 38. Johnny Blowers kept a diary of dates he played while he was a member of the Berigan band. Much of the detail for the Berigan band's tour in May and June 1938 comes from *Blowers*.

[6] Cited in the White materials: June 16, 1938.

[7] *Blowers:* 40.

[8] White materials: June 25, 1938.

[9] See appendix 1 for a listing of all Berigan broadcast recordings (except for those from the Paradise Restaurant, which are in appendix 2) for the years 1937–1938.

[10] A complete set of *Magic Key* broadcasts are available for listening at the Library of Congress.

[11] The Ink Spots were a very popular black vocal group from the 1930s–1940s that found acceptance among white as well as black audiences. Their vocal stylings led to later developments like rhythm and blues, rock and roll, and doo-wop.

[12] *Blowers:* 40.

[13] Don Manning interview, cited in the White materials: July 5, 1938.

[14] White materials: July 5, 1938.

[15] *Traverse City Record Eagle:* Wednesday, June 29, 1938. Information provided by Carl A. Hallstrom.

[16] The Fox Theater, located at 2211 Woodward Avenue, Detroit, was built in 1928 by Hollywood film pioneer William Fox. Its seating capacity of 5,048 makes it the second

largest theater in the United States. (Only Radio City Music Hall in New York is larger.) Its twin is the Fox Theater in St. Louis, which has 500 fewer seats. The Fox Theater has remained a vital entertainment venue since its opening.

[17] *Detroit Free Press:* July 16, 1938, cited in the White materials: July 15, 1938.

[18] Dupuis: 161.

[19] White materials: July 15, 1938.

[20] Liner notes—*The Complete Bunny Berigan, Vol. 2;* interview of Joe Dixon by Richard M. Sudhalter. Hereafter: *The Complete Bunny Berigan, Vol. 2.*

[21] White materials: July 22, 1938.

[22] *Melody Maker:* July 30, 1938, cited in the White materials.

[23] *Ibid.*

[24] White materials: July 25, 1938.

[25] *Ibid.*

[26] *Ibid.*

[27] *Ibid.*

[28] While Bunny Berigan was in the midst of the Casa Manana imbroglio, Artie Shaw was busy cutting his first records for RCA Victor's Bluebird label. The titles he recorded on July 24, 1938, included "Begin the Beguine," "Indian Love Call ","Any Old Time" (with Billie Holiday), and "Back Bay Shuffle."

[29] *Metronome:* July 1938.

[30] Doty, like so many other veterans of the big bands, eventually became a freelance musician in New York. His career lasted into the 1960s. I have a recording made in September 1961 *(Desmond Blue)* where he plays various woodwinds as a part of an ensemble backing the great jazz alto saxophonist Paul Desmond.

[31] Liner notes—*Bunny Berigan and the Rhythm Makers, Vol. 2: 1938* (1992), Jass Records J-CD-638. These liner notes contain the comments of Joe Dixon, Johnny Blowers, and Steve Lipkins.

[32] White materials: August 14, 1938.

[33] *Pittsburgh Post Gazette:* August 27, 1938, cited in the White materials, August 25, 1938.

[34] White materials: August 25, 1938.

[35] This is a quote from Don Wilson, one of the White researchers, cited in the White materials: January 1, 1938.

[36] Helen Margaret Oakley was born into a wealthy family in Toronto, Ontario, on February 15, 1913. She became enthralled by jazz as a young woman and began working in various roles in the music business in the 1930s. Among those were as a writer and publicist. She became associated with Irving Mills's various enterprises in the later 1930s, and actually produced a number of Duke Ellington small group recordings for Mills at that time. Later, she married the English jazz writer Stanley Dance. They both remained lifelong friends of Ellington, with Dance publishing a number of articles and books about Duke. She was also a longtime crusader for racial integration and civil rights. She died in Escondido, California, on May 27, 2001.

[37] White materials: August, 1935.

[38] Liner notes—*Benny Goodman—The Birth of Swing (1935–1936)* (1991), RCA/BMG Bluebird 61038-2, page 17, by George T. Simon.

[39] Liner notes—*The Complete Bunny Berigan, Vol. 2.*

[40] *Ibid.*

[41] Liner notes—*Bunny Berigan—The Pied Piper (1934–1940)* (1995), RCA/BMG Bluebird 66615-2, interview of Benny Goodman by Richard M. Sudhalter.

[42] Loren Schoenberg, born July 23, 1958, in Fairlawn, New Jersey, is a talented tenor saxophonist and pianist who in addition to having a career as a jazz musician, has written extensively on jazz, and since 2002 has been the executive director of the National Jazz Museum in Harlem.

[43] Liner notes—*Benny Goodman—The Birth of Swing (1935–1936)*, 27–28.

[44] *The Complete Bunny Berigan, Vol. 2*, interview of Jimmy Maxwell by Richard M. Sudhalter.

[45] *Boy Meets Horn*, by Rex Stewart, University of Michigan Press (1991), 166.

[46] *Jazz Masters of the '30s*, by Rex Stewart, Macmillan Company (1972), 223.

[47] Liner notes—*The Complete Bunny Berigan, Vol. 2*, interview of Pee Wee Erwin by Richard M. Sudhalter.

[48] *The Complete Bunny Berigan Vol. 2*, interview of Joe Bushkin by Richard M. Sudhalter.

[49] The Capitol Theater in Steubenville, Ohio, was built in 1925, and was located at 208 South Fourth Street. It was demolished in the 1970s.

[50] *Dean and Me*, by Jerry Lewis and James Kaplan, Broadway Books, (2005), 16.

[51] White materials: August 25, 1938.

[52] Quote from Jay Corre is in the liner notes to Buddy Rich's Pacific Jazz CDP-7243-4-94507-2-1 (1998) entitled *The New One!*

[53] In order to deal with so much perspiration, Berigan used great quantities of talcum powder.

Chapter 18
Bad Boys and Bad Luck

After completing the Stanley Theater engagement, the Berigan band traveled to Detroit once again, and building on its previous successes at the Fox Theater there, opened a one-week stand at one of that city's top dancing spots, Eastwood Gardens, on September 2. It was a profitable engagement. After weeks of back-breaking touring and grueling work, Bunny finally had a little leisure time in one place to enjoy by playing golf and doing other things not related to leading his band. Joe Dixon remembered this brief interlude: "In addition to playing nightly, we had a so-called *Jitterbug Jamboree* for three hours on the Sunday afternoon. We stayed at the Detroiter Hotel and I remember one early morning around 3 a.m., after we'd finished the job, Bunny was to be seen casually knocking golf balls out of his hotel room window with an 8 or 9 iron!"[1]

After absorbing the rather spectacular lifestyle of the Berigan band for several months, Ray Conniff had formed some opinions:

> Yeah, it was quite an experience working with the Berigan band. It was a tight little band, just like a family of bad little boys, with Bunny the worst of all. We were all friends. In fact, Bunny wouldn't hire anybody he didn't like. All of us would take turns rooming with him. Oh, it was a mad ball. You should have seen those hotel rooms! Ribs, booze, and women all over the place. As a musician we all idolized him. Even when he was drunk, he'd blow good. And when he was sober—man! Whenever we'd play the Savoy up in Harlem, if we'd walk along the streets or go into a rib joint they would say, 'Hey Pops, them's Bunny's boys.' They loved him up there. He had that beat.[2]

After closing at Eastwood Gardens on September 9, the Berigan band headed east. They likely played a one-nighter in Pennsylvania on Saturday, September 10, and then appeared on Sunday evening, September 11 at Lake Compounce, Bristol, Connecticut. The trade press gleefully reported what ensued. From *Billboard:*

> One of the biggest mixups in memory occurred here (Bridgeport) at Pleasure Beach Ballroom, where Bunny Berigan was booked to play the closing dance of the season. Berigan, giving a 'Corrigan' twist to the directions, went up to Lake Compounce Ballroom, Bristol, CT, instead. The Berigan boys had their equipment set up after arriving early, when in walked Gene Krupa and his men, who were booked there. Hurried explanations followed, with Krupa staying and Berigan packing and quickly getting underway for Bridgeport, where they arrived several hours late. Meanwhile, Pleasure Beach had turned out the lights and those

who didn't return home went over to the Ritz Ballroom, where Ina Ray Hutton was holding forth.[3]

The front page of *Metronome* in a block under "Bungled Booking" had this account: "The best boner of the season occurred in Bristol, Connecticut, on Sunday, September 11. Bunny Berigan's band had just set up for its one-nighter, when in walked Gene Krupa and his crew ready to play the same place. Hasty consultation revealed that Bunny and the boys were supposed to be over in Bridgeport. Result: Krupa worked, while Bristol dancers had fun. Berigan couldn't make the job, while Bridgeport hoofers cried.[4] *Orchestra World* reported it this way: "Crossed Wires: Bridgeport, Connecticut—Pleasure Beach Ballroom booked Bunny Berigan for the final, expected-to-be-record-smashing closing attraction. The crowd showed up—but not Berigan. All the money was refunded, the lights turned out and Berigan appeared. Due to an error the band had gone up to Bristol, where Gene Krupa already was set up and playing. They hurried back to Bridgeport too late, and everyone had gone over to the Ritz to hear Ina Ray Hutton."[5]

Clyde Rounds offered a bit more insight as to why the mix-up had occurred:

It wasn't really Bunny's fault, but MCA's. When we got there, Gene Krupa's boys were already starting to set up and as we said our hellos, we realized that there was only one bandstand and guessed something was wrong. The ballroom manager said we certainly weren't booked in there, and since it was a Sunday, it took quite a few frantic phone calls to locate someone at MCA's office who knew anything about our itinerary. Meanwhile, we all pitched in to get the instruments re-packed and loaded back on to the truck. Eventually, we got instructions to drive to Bridgeport as fast as we could! That was a journey of about 60 miles and when we finally got there, cars were coming away and the place was closed. It really was a terrible humiliation and for ages after, Bunny was nicknamed 'Wrong Way Berigan,' after the famous flight of Doug 'Wrong Way' Corrigan, which had started from Long Island, New York. The papers had a field-day with the story![6]

Bunny had to be livid. As a result of the increasing conflict of interest at MCA and with Arthur Michaud involving his band and Gene Krupa's, he was once again the victim of a fiasco not of his making, the second such mess in three months. He was not only denied the opportunity to play what should have been a very profitable dance date, and was humiliated in the press, but he now had the very angry operators of Bridgeport's Pleasure Beach Ballroom to deal with because of the blown date. And of course throughout this debacle his band overhead continued unabated. The full consequences of the earlier Old Orchard Beach screwup had fallen squarely on Berigan, and now this.

There are only two possible scenarios that could have resulted in two blown dates in less than three months. The first and less likely, is that Bunny's latest road manager, Frank Carzonne, was completely inept and could not keep the itinerary he received from MCA straight. If this were the case, Mr. Carzonne simply would have been fired for incompetence after the Old Orchard Beach mistake. If Berigan had not done the firing, then Arthur Michaud surely would have. Far more likely, as suggested by Clyde Rounds, is that MCA made the earlier mistake, for which there apparently were no adverse consequences as to MCA, then made a similar mistake again. Bunny was not in a position to fire MCA, and neither was Michaud. Michaud very probably told him after the first situation to simply ignore it and go on. That would have been easy for Michaud, because he was not paying the band's expenses—Bunny was. Bunny likely took Michaud's advice, because he was paying Michaud to guide him through problems like this. However, Michaud's attention now seemed to be focused elsewhere. Bunny noticed. He was not a man prone to emotional blow–ups, like Tommy Dorsey. Instead, he would do a slow burn. From this point on, where Michaud was concerned, Bunny was definitely touchy.

What should have happened is that Berigan should have retained an attorney to get to the bottom of the Old Orchard Beach debacle. If the fault was with MCA, which it appeared to have been, then the attorney could have taken or threatened legal action against MCA so that the party responsible for the foul-up would bear the consequences. Or, at a minimum, he could have pleaded Bunny's case with MCA and tried to work out a resolution diplomatically that was less costly for Berigan. For whatever reason, Bunny did nothing about that first foul-up, and then same thing happened again, with even worse consequences the second time. Once again Berigan sustained the losses for someone else's mistake, and did nothing to protect himself. These two incidents reveal that no one was looking out solely for the interests of Bunny Berigan, and that he was incapable of doing so himself. They also mark the beginning of the chronic financial difficulties that would dog Berigan to his dying day.

From this fiasco, Bunny took his band to play a private party on Long Island the next night. It was at this gig that clarinetist–alto saxist Arcuiso "Gus" Bivona became a member of the Berigan band. "I joined Bunny for that date, replacing Joe Dixon. There was another band at the affair, one of those society orchestras organized by Meyer Davis. We played alternating sets and there was quite a difference in the types of music! I'd never met Bunny before that day, but he had contacted me at the Forrest Hotel in New York, where the band assembled before leaving for the date. Jayne Dover,[7] who had worked with 'Gigi' Bohn and me in the Hudson-DeLange orchestra, joined Bunny about the same time."[8] Following this date, the band returned to New York for a Victor recording session the next day, September 13.

Six acceptable masters were recorded that day between the hours of 1:30–7:00 p.m. One wonders when (or if) the band had the opportunity to rehearse the tunes they recorded that day. The two new members, Bivona and vocalist Jayne Dover, had joined the Berigan band only the day before. Ms. Dover had three new songs to sing at the recording date. (These are details that record reviewers and critics are seldom aware of, or consider.) Legend has it that Bunny used the private party the day before to prepare the band for the recording date. However the band rehearsed these tunes, the resulting recordings were remarkably good. The personnel of the Berigan band now was Berigan, Lipkins and Goodman, trumpets; Lobovsky and Conniff, trombones; George "Gigi" Bohn, lead alto, Gus Bivona, alto and clarinet; Auld, tenor, Rounds, tenor (and occasionally baritone) saxophones; Bushkin, piano; Wharton, guitar/vocals; Wayland, bass; Rich, drums; and Jayne Dover, vocals. More of the band's arrangements were now being written by Andy Phillips, especially those on current pop tunes. But Joe Lippman was still contributing many of the charts the Berigan band was recording, especially those on "special" material.

"When a Prince of a Fella Meets a Cinderella" is another lightweight pop tune, with a vocal by Jayne Dover. Bunny states the melody in the first chorus on open trumpet sounding a bit weary. (One wonders why Berigan, who possessed one of the most glorious trumpet sounds in jazz, so often during these months chose to mute his horn when stating the melody in the first chorus of the songs he performed.) Gus Bivona, who follows Bunny, plays the eight-bar bridge. His clarinet tone here is somewhat warmer than the often shrill sound produced by his predecessor, Joe Dixon. Ms. Dover had a pleasant contralto voice that could be husky and sensuous. In the few recordings she made with the Berigan band, she sang on pitch and with a beat. Bunny returns for a much more convincing solo after her vocal. The arranger of this song employed Bivona's clarinet leading the saxophones throughout. I would say this chart was written by Andy Phillips because he created more varied sonorities with the instruments at his disposal than Joe Lippman did when arranging current pop tunes for the Berigan band.

The chart on the early jazz classic "Livery Stable Blues"[9] has been attributed to Joe Lippman, and I agree with this. Bunny states the melody using either his notorious kazoo mute, or a Harmon with guttural growling sounds. Contemporary critics seemed to be offended by this. (See below.) I am not at all offended. The band alternately roars, then purrs on this. Nat Lobovsky must have had a lot of fun blasting out those pedal tones on his trombone. Bunny's lead trumpet is superb, as is the very personal piano solo played by Joe Bushkin. After Bushkin's solo, the band glides on into the conclusion, atop Buddy Rich's fluttering brushwork. This is a wonderful recording of another excellent special arrangement written by Joe Lippman. (Note: There have been two different takes of "Livery Stable Blues" available for many years. Both are first rate.)

"Let This Be a Warning to You" is another meaningless pop tune, but on this recording there are many surprises, all of them pleasant. Here we again have the Berigan band *strutting*, with Bunny leading the charge. The ensembles bristle throughout this performance. The first chorus is played joyously, with Bunny taking the bridge using what appears to be a straight mute with a felt hat over the bell of his trumpet. Berigan was a master of mutes, using far more muting devices than any other major jazz trumpeter. When he takes the mute out for a brief but brilliant few bars before the vocal, he tantalizes us. After the vocal,

Ray Conniff plays a robust trombone solo, and then Berigan reappears, soaring into the stratosphere with his glorious ringing tone remaining full and rich all the way.

"Why Doesn't Somebody Tell Me These Things?" also gets a rollicking performance by Bunny and his boys. Conniff is heard in the first chorus as is Bunny on open trumpet. (Hear Bunny punctuate the modulation into the vocal with high notes.) After Ms. Dover's vocal, Georgie Auld's tenor solo reveals how deeply he had been impressed by Herschel Evans's playing when he had visited the Famous Door a few weeks previously to hear the Count Basie band. Bunny then walks the high wire with his solo. This and the preceding tune were probably arranged by Andy Phillips.

The venerable "High Society" (composed in 1901) is recast here in the finery of swing by Joe Lippman. The clarinet-led reeds (probably three B-flat clarinets and Auld's tenor saxophone) play call and response in the first chorus with the Berigan-led brass, which play the melody. Then Georgie comes in with a big sigh (calling Mr. Evans!) on his tenor sax, followed by sixteen bars of solid jazz. Young Mr. Auld had progressed light-years in his jazz playing in the eighteen months he had been in Bunny's employ. Bushkin swings nicely on piano, and then a fanfare by the band brings Berigan on. Here he is at his best on open trumpet; his solo is a perfectly constructed, flowing musical statement delivered with his usual brio. Ray Conniff follows on trombone, and the band rocks through the exuberant out-chorus. "High Society" is a quintessential Berigan recording and a superb example of swing era jazz. It is one of the few Victor recordings made by Bunny that captures the irrepressible panache of the 1938 Berigan band.

"Father Dear Father" had to be a joke. Things are more than a little shaky in both Auld's tenor and Conniff's trombone solos, but Bernie Mackey's vocal is very swinging, (hear Bushkin's tasty comping behind him) as is the band's performance throughout. Bunny tried hard to sound like he cared in his solo, but after over five hours in the recording studio, he probably would have preferred to be doing something other than recording this dismal tune.

As usual, critical reaction to these records was all over the place: "When the band doesn't blare and stretch the wax, it can and does turn in some good stuff as, for example, Georgie Auld's tenor and Buddy Rich's drums combining for a short spell on 'Father Dear Father;' Buddy's brush work in 'Livery Stable Blues' and Auld and Bunny on 'High Society.' Bunny and vocalist Bernie Mackey, the band's valet, shine up 'Father Dear Father' too."[10] "Bunny's first solo on 'Livery Stable Blues' is awful. He plays it with a loose mute and if he did so intentionally, he's committing a breach of good taste; if unintentionally, the record ought never to have been released. The balance of the disc is acceptably performed."[11]

Trumpeter Bob Ballard commented on the effect Bunny had achieved in the first chorus of "Livery Stable Blues:" "I'm sure Bunny was deliberately trying for that effect on 'Livery Stable Blues,'" Art Beecher, drummer and Wisconsin friend of Bunny's, suggested that: "Bunny sometimes used a water glass for that effect and at other times used a small kazoo for a mute. I don't believe that either Bunny or Louis Armstrong ever used the so-called 'throat growl,' used by some jazzmen to produce a rough tone."[12] (I would respectfully disagree, at least with respect to Berigan.) Gigi Bohn recalled how the vocal in "Father Dear Father" came to be sung by Bernie Mackey: "We were all supposed to sing 'Father Dear Father' in unison, but after a half-dozen attempts, it just wasn't working. In desperation, Bunny called in Bernie, the bandboy, and asked him to sing it. He made a darned good job of it too, compared with our terrible efforts!"[13]

After this recording session, the immediate future prospects for the Berigan band looked good. They played a one-night dance date on September 14 at the Commodore Ballroom, Lowell, Massachusetts, on the way to a prime two-week engagement at Boston's Ritz Carlton Hotel,[14] from which point they would broadcast frequently. Engagements like this were a key part of the success of any big band—they allowed the band to relax a bit in one place, with the radio exposure regenerating demand for the band in ballrooms and theaters. After a few one-night dance dates in New England, Bunny Berigan and His Orchestra opened at the Roof Garden of Boston's Ritz-Carlton Hotel on Monday September 19, 1938. Their first broadcast from there was on September 20, over WEEI–Boston from 11:30 p.m.–12:00 midnight.

When the band left New York, it was without another of its stalwart members—first trumpeter Steve Lipkins. "My dad's illness had been getting worse and the doctor had given him up. When he finally died, I had no option but to give my notice as I had all of his affairs to sort out. So I left the band just before it took off for Boston and Bunny got Bernie Privin to sub until he could fix up a permanent replacement."[15]

As it turned out, Privin, then only eighteen-years-old but at the beginning of what would be a long and highly successful career, played in the Berigan band for only a couple of nights. Bunny had secured the services of Johnny Napton, a brilliant-toned trumpeter, to "permanently" lead the brass section while he was otherwise occupied on the bandstand. But Napton could not join the band until Wednesday, September 21. Mother Nature made sure that Napton's trip to Boston from New York was memorable. As Napton rode on the train called "The Bostonian" on September 21, a massive hurricane struck New England. The train "…was nearly washed away by wind and waves on a narrow causeway at Stonington, Connecticut. Engineer Harry Easton and his crew saved many lives by herding what passengers they could into the front cars and inching to high ground."[16]

Napton was not so lucky. He recalled the entire trip this way: 'I got a call from Bunny's manager to join the band in Boston, so I took the train from Pennsylvania Station in New York, normally a five-hour journey, and ran into the worst hurricane to hit the northeast in years! The rain was torrential, the wind was over 100 miles an hour and the water rose up the sides of the coaches, causing the train to stop and tip over on to its side. I grabbed my horn and waded out, waist deep, into the water, clinging on to the side of the train in the teeth of the gale, Finally, after what seemed like forever, I managed to find shelter for the night. The next morning, I hitched a lift into Boston, arriving at the hotel about thirty-five hours late. Joey Bushkin opened the door of the hotel suite with a flourish and said, 'What kept you?'[17]

While Johnny Napton was traveling to Boston to join the Berigan band, they were having their own encounter with the hurricane.

The day started out sunny and seasonably cool, but the sky had started to cloud over, and the air became thick, muggy. By the time the musicians took their places under the big striped awning of the roof garden for a 3:00 p.m. rehearsal, something was definitely amiss. 'It was the wind' Bernie Privin recalled. 'The wind had come up and was making a kind of howling noise, blowing up in gusts. And the sky had gone a funny yellowish color. The air was heavy. It was scary. I just thought: Oh my God, what next? All at once there was this tremendous sound, like ripping and slamming together, and a new mighty blast of air tore the striped awning off its poles and whirled it away toward the Charles River. The roof garden was suddenly a chaos of flying music, music stands, and chairs as 14 terrified musicians scrambled for cover.'[18]

Ray Conniff also recalled this incident:

We got back to our room and looked out on Boston Common just in time to see this huge tree blow down, then another. We couldn't believe it: these were big trees—you couldn't put your arms around one. But they were blowing down all over the place. By this time it had sunk in that this was something big.[19]

It was something big indeed: "The great hurricane that hit the northeast corner of the United States on Wednesday, September 21, 1938, was one of the worst natural disasters in American history. It is estimated to have cost 680 lives and $400 million in property damage, compared with the parallel figures of $350 and $450 million for the San Francisco earthquake and fire of 1906 and $200 and $250 million for the Chicago fire of 1871. Also, some 26,000 automobiles were smashed, 275 million trees were blown down and more than 6,000 boats were lost or damaged."[20]

Once again, Bunny Berigan's name was splashed across the trade papers for something other than the quality of his music. *Billboard* reported:

The hurricane blew Bunny Berigan right out of a job at the Ritz-Carlton Hotel Roof in Boston. The band was appearing for a couple of weeks on the canopied terrace, but after the gale finished its work, there was no canopy, not much roof and therefore not much need for a bunch of musicians. The hotel effected a settlement of Berigan's contract with his manager, despite the clause which, in most theatrical contracts, abrogates responsibility for any 'Act of God.'"[21]

Metronome also carried coverage of the catastrophe:

.

"WIND DEFEATS BERIGAN (Headline) That hurricane a couple of weeks ago blew the roof off the staid Ritz Carlton Hotel before Bunny Berigan and band even had a chance to pull the same stunt. As a result, Bunny's booking was postponed until a later date. The hurricane was given two weeks notice, but quit before that time. The management is reporting it to the AFM."[22]

The great hurricane of 1938 was not only a mammoth natural disaster, it was a disaster for the Bunny Berigan band as well. The fact that Arthur Michaud was able to effect some settlement with the Ritz-Carlton was of small significance to the overall future prospects for the band. The net result of this event for Bunny was that he had gone from having a good two-week gig with many radio broadcasts, to having no gig, no broadcasts, and no immediate work for his band.

This disaster also negatively affected the dance band business throughout much of New England. *Variety* carried this story at the time: "New England, cream territory, goes on Fritz for Touring Orchestras. Dance bands in, or scheduled for dates in the one night territory in New England found most of their dates gone with the big wind, following last week's storm. Concentrating most of its force in Connecticut, Rhode Island and Massachusetts, which, with the rest of the New England states, is considered one of the most lucrative areas for touring outfits, the blow washed out even location dates."[23] Danceland, Ocean Beach, New London, Connecticut, for example, didn't reopen until October 30, with the Mal Hallett band.[24]

The Berigan bandsmen, deeply shaken by this catastrophe, returned to New York in their cars as soon as the highways were cleared. Bernie Privin remembered that trip: "When we were able to drive home, I was sitting in the back seat of Bunny's car and Joey Bushkin was next to Bunny. It didn't take very long before Bunny tried to crawl up a tree—it's not very difficult when you're stoned! This awakened Joey, who insisted on taking over the wheel and I'll be damned if he didn't do the same thing! I was scared stiff and didn't know how to drive, but after a few more adventures we did, thankfully, get back home."[25]

When the musicians arrived back in New York, the lack of work for the foreseeable future and sideman burnout had a number of Berigan's musicians seeking other employment. Clyde Rounds recalled:

We had been expecting to stay in Boston for about a month, but after the disaster we found ourselves with no immediate dates. So one or two of the boys were looking around for new jobs. Gigi Bohn and Nat Lobovsky (both excellent lead men) left the band and were replaced by Milton Schatz and Wes Hein, respectively. The changes in the band had a definite long-term effect. I'm not implying that the replacements weren't capable musicians, but they altered the sound and phrasing of the sections. Also, beneath the surface there were signs of discontent rumbling within the band. We hadn't worked the New York area since our stint at the Paramount and there didn't appear to be anything in the offing. Many of the wives were unhappy about being left while the band was constantly on the road, and all these pressures were mounting.[26]

In the face of this, Bunny did what he undoubtedly hated to do—he laid the band off.

Berigan was loathe to layoff his musicians because whenever something like this happened in the band business, the musicians' grapevine went into high gear, and other leaders who were looking for sidemen would come in like vultures and offer the laid-off musicians jobs, and in a short time, a bandleader could lose a band. Bunny was extremely proud of his band, and had worked very hard for over eighteen months to organize, build, and refine it. He would have endured almost anything not to have this layoff, but he really had no choice. What may have made this a bit more palatable for him is that many other bands were in the same predicament, as the *Variety* article explained. Also, the layoff provided Bunny with a reprieve from the unremitting costs of keeping his band together. Nevertheless, he soon had lost two key musicians, and others were growing restive. Both Bunny and MCA wanted to get the Berigan band back to work as soon as possible to squelch any rumors that the band might be breaking up.

Bunny appeared on the *Saturday Night Swing Club* for the first time since the spring of 1937 on September 24, and played his standard solo feature, "Dark Eyes." Announcer Paul Douglas stated that Bunny "was laying-off this week." The White materials report his playing on that broadcast to be "spotty."[27] Also at about this time, Bunny entered a recording studio in New York to record, with Joe Bushkin, two unknown tunes for a ten-inch acetate disc, which was intended to be used as a memento for someone. Also on hand was tenor saxophonist Bud Freeman, doing his "British" double-talk routine, but not playing.[28]

In Hollywood on Tuesday, September 27, 1938, Bob Hope launched his new NBC network radio show, sponsored by Pepsodent toothpaste. Hope's comedy foil was Bunny's trombone-playing associate from the CBS morning band, Jerry Colonna. The band on the Hope show was led by former Hal Kemp singer and drummer Skinnay Ennis. Ennis's booking agency was MCA. In light of how Ennis and his band were used on this program,[29] one wonders whether all of the talk about Bunny and his band being featured on this show was not just another one of MCA's canards. MCA frequently manipulated the rumor mill to hoodwink its bandleader clients into thinking that future prospects were brighter than they actually were. Then the bandleaders relayed these rumors (fantasies?) to the members of their bands, who likewise were fooled at least temporarily into thinking/hoping/wishing that the rumors were true. When the truth finally came to light, there were always many disappointed people. The fact that Bunny was not chosen to work on Bob Hope's radio program only added to the general mood of discontent that was now infecting the Berigan band.

Between September 24 and October 1, when the Berigan band resumed activity by playing a one-night dance date in Westchester, New York, Bunny broke his leg (or ankle). Clyde Rounds recalled the surrounding circumstances:

We were all surprised to see Bunny climb on the stand with his leg in plaster. He explained that he'd been at home, spending a rare night with his family and playing ball, when he slipped on a rug and fell. He heard and felt a sickening crack as a bone broke. Donna drove him to the hospital, where they X-rayed him and put the leg in a plaster cast. Then she drove him back to their apartment, where he rested until the Westchester date. 'This crack is going to be heard all over the country,' Bunny declared. 'Anytime when I've drunk a few too many, only a very few people knew or cared, as long as the band sounded okay. And now, although I was sober, no one will ever believe it!' I don't know if it was because of that, but he went on the wagon for some time after his accident.[30]

Notwithstanding the many other tales that have circulated over the years, this seems to be the way Bunny Berigan broke his leg or ankle. (Another version had Bunny playing ping-pong while drinking as the cause of the broken ankle.)

In the meantime, MCA had beaten the bushes and lined up some work for the Berigan band. *Variety* carried this blurb in its October 5 issue:

Headline: Hazards Of Touring—Bunny Berigan back on his feet. The Bunny Berigan orchestra picks up where it left off after being blown out of a two weeks date at the Ritz-Carlton Hotel, Boston, by the recent hurricane. It starts four successive Wednesday eve one-nighters at the Roseland Ballroom, New York tonight (5th). In between, the band plays some one-nighters in New England, a society job and cuts records. The crew will have a CBS wire at the Roseland. Berigan capped a string of hard-luck deals, which included the loss of the Boston date, smacking up his own car in an auto crack-up, a ditto fate with his instrument truck plus a sprained ankle, Sunday (2nd), making it necessary for him to stay off his feet until the last minute prior to going into the Roseland.[31]

The band finally got back on radio from the Roseland on October 5, broadcasting from 11:30 p.m. to midnight over WABC/CBS. The tunes they played on the air that night were: "Gangbusters' Holiday," "There's Something about an Old Love," "Royal Garden Blues," "Small Fry," "The Wearin' of the Green," "Now It Can Be Told," "Wacky Dust," and "The Prisoner's Song."[32] (This is the first evidence that Ray Conniff now was submitting arrangements to Bunny: the Basie-influenced "Gangbusters' Holiday" was his original composition and arrangement.) This little snapshot proves that the band on this broadcast was *Bunny Berigan's;* it could have been no one else's.

In spite of the damage done by the hurricane to many venues in New England, there were some that had escaped the devastation wrought by the storm. MCA made sure to keep the ones that had not been damaged operating with MCA bands providing the music. Bunny and his boys returned to New England on Friday, October 7, to play a dance at the State Armory in North Adams, Massachusetts. They followed this up with other one-nighters in New England and New York until they returned to Roseland the following Wednesday, October 12. They again broadcast from Roseland, and here is the lineup of tunes they played: "Black Bottom," "Change Partners," "Sugar Foot Stomp," "Livery Stable Blues," "One O'Clock Jump," "So Help Me," "Wacky Dust," "Anything

Goes," and their closing theme. It was at about this time that veteran trombonist Andy Russo subbed for Wes Hein, who was ill.

Bunny's broken ankle was slowing him down considerably. Gus Bivona had vivid memories of this situation:

> Bunny had his leg in a plaster cast for five or six weeks. He used a cane to get around and a chair or a stool to rest his foot while he was playing. He claimed he'd broken his ankle at home while playing with his daughters, but I don't know how many of the guys believed that. Sometime later, while riding in the band bus, he had his foot propped up on the heater and when the bus went over a big bump in the road, it knocked his foot down on to the floor, cracked the plaster and broke the bone again![33]

Dick Wharton reported that: Bunny had to have the broken leg *(sic)* re-broken and reset. It became very painful and he went back to NYC to have it taken care of.[34]

Berigan's streak of bad luck continued.

The episode where Bunny had fallen off the stage while his band was playing at the Stanley Theater in Pittsburgh had engendered much insidious gossip in the band business. The result of this was that MCA was now finding it very hard to sell the Berigan band to the operators of major theaters. It seems that Bunny's drinking had now reached the point where he was always under the influence, to some degree. The only variable was how he was able to handle it from day to day. Trumpeter Johnny Napton remembered: "He could talk to you at the end of the evening, and you'd have no idea that he'd knocked off a whole bottle of scotch. He could drive, he could play, and you'd never be able to tell a thing."[35] Gus Bivona had a slightly different take on this situation: "Don't get me wrong. Bunny was playing good— he always played good, even when he drank. He was the best trumpet player ever! But there were times when he was sloppy, when it just wasn't up to what he could do."[36] Ray Conniff agreed: "There was definitely some deterioration. He was drinking too much, and he missed an awful lot. But when he wasn't drinking—well, he was the best. Really great! Inimitable! And don't forget, things may have been getting worse, but we were having one continuous good time, like a non-stop party. And that counted for a lot."[37]

In the 1930s, people who drank a lot were often regarded as being colorful and entertaining "characters." When pianist/arranger Claude Thornhill (later the leader of one of the most exquisite bands of the swing era), who was an alcoholic, went to Hollywood to work as an arranger with the Skinnay Ennis band on the Bob Hope radio show, he quickly established a reputation for eccentric behavior. Carmine Calhoun Ennis, Skinnay's wife, recalled how Thornhill would, on occasion, enter the posh Victor Hugo restaurant, where the Ennis band often worked: "He used to come into the Hugo, laugh hysterically, and crawl around on the floor, barking at people. Being drunk in those days was looked on differently—drinking wasn't looked on as the disease of alcoholism. If a celebrity like Claude did crazy things, it was passed off as a joke."[38] Although Bunny had numerous embarrassing experiences while drunk, he never did anything quite like this.

Donna's separation from Bunny, which had started while the band was at the Paramount Theater in New York in May, had been intermittent. Since that time, she had traveled with him on a number of occasions, especially when the band had been able to stay in one place for a week or so. Even though Berigan's almost continuous touring since that time had caused him to be away from Lee Wiley, their relationship was still not over. Bunny also had had a good many casual sexual encounters since he had begun leading his band, but the cumulative effects of alcohol were now sometimes beginning to reduce his ability to perform sexually. Voyeurism was something he experimented with, at least on occasion: "We'd check into a hotel, Gus Bivona recalled, and the first thing we'd do was to ask the porter to send up a hooker. We were just growing up then, you know. And Bunny—well, he liked to watch. I never saw him with a hooker, but he seemed to get a kick out of watching guys who were brave enough to perform in front of him."[39]

Between Bunny's ever-escalating drinking, the wildness of his band members, the endless touring, the series of misfortunes that had befallen him in the past several months, and the deepening debt he was experiencing, one wonders how the quality of the band's performances could have remained high. In spite of all of these distractions however, their performances were still at a remarkably high musical level, as the recordings they made on October 14 show.

Once again, Victor used the Berigan band only to sell current commercial pop tunes. In spite of this, there are some pleasant surprises. "Simple and Sweet" spots Georgie Auld, by now very deeply into his Herschel Evans phase, stating the melody in the first chorus. Bunny follows him with a Harmon mute. Dick Wharton sings the lyric in his tenor voice, which reminds me very much of Joe Feeney, who was the Irish tenor with Lawrence Welk's band on TV for many years. Berigan returns in the last half-chorus on open trumpet for some final thoughts. This arrangement was written by Joe Lippman.

"Button, Button (Who's Got the Button?)" is given a robust, if at times shaky, performance by the band. Jayne Dover sings the inane lyric, after which Auld and Berigan solo. Bunny's eight bars can be aptly characterized as manic. This swinging arrangement—note the incisive brass backgrounds behind Auld's solo, and the use of the baritone saxophone in the out-chorus—was likely written by Andy Phillips.

"I Won't Tell a Soul" spots Bunny with a straight mute in the first chorus, where trombonist Ray Conniff takes the bridge. Dick Wharton's excellent rhythm guitar is featured behind these solos. Wharton had two big strikes on him in the Berigan band: first, he was a friend of Arthur Michaud's; and second he sang in a style that almost everyone in the band did not like. Still, from what I have been able to discern, he was a fine musician whose guitar playing was never less than first rate, and whose singing was certainly acceptable, given the nature of much of what he was required to sing. I must agree however with the

Berigan sidemen who thought that his singing didn't fit the band's style. Auld is heard only briefly after the vocal. The arrangement on this tune was done by Andy Phillips, who used a more complicated style of writing for the Berigan ensemble than Joe Lippman did at this time.

"Rockin' Rollers' Jubilee" is a happy, straight-ahead swing arrangement by Joe Lippman that features spirited playing by everyone, and an effective vocal by Ms. Dover. Bunny solos on open trumpet before, and Auld and Bushkin solo after the vocal chorus, while Mr. B. leads the brass going out. The reeds throughout are a little more sonorous due once again to the use of the baritone sax in the ensemble, ably played by Clyde Rounds. Bunny obviously liked the deeper sonority derived from this deployment of the four saxes, and would return to it often in the future.

This recording session lasted only from 10:30 a.m. to 2:00 p.m., and the haste is evident in the somewhat rough performances the band gave to each of these then-current pop tunes. Still, there are some worthwhile moments in these recordings.

Immediately after this recording session, the Berigan band got on the bus and headed for Johnson City, New York, near Binghamton, a jump of 200 miles, where they played a one-night dance job at the George F. Pavilion. They then headed south to the Valencia Ballroom in York, Pennsylvania, then on to Keith's Ballroom in Baltimore, where they drew a crowd of over 2,000 people. Bunny and the band were now being booked haphazardly by MCA, and were teetering on the brink of exhaustion, yet they were still drawing good crowds. They continued to play one-nighters in Pennsylvania during this time, including ones at the Orlando Ballroom in Wilkes-Barre on October 22, and the senior ball at Lehigh University in Bethlehem, on the 28th. October 29 found them in New Haven, Connecticut, at Wilcox's Dance Pavilion, Savin Rock Amusement Park. Here is how Berigan compared with other bands at that location: "The Bunny Berigan orchestra with paid admissions of 890 dancers at 65 cents per person was the best draw in three weeks of name attractions at Wilcox's Dance Pavilion. Dave Hudgins, ballroom manager, realized a $578 gate and nobody was hurt. The season started with Mal Hallett at $396 for 610 dancers; and Glenn Miller on October 16, with $386 for 596 dancers."[40] The following week MCA had the Berigan band hopping all over New England and New York.

The life of a group of young men on the road in the late 1930s as members of a big band, with one woman thrown in amongst them, is difficult for us to understand now for many reasons, not the least of which is that over seven decades have passed, and so many things have changed so much since then. But some things never change, as this little vignette recalled by Georgie Auld demonstrates:

Bunny Berigan—now that was about the wildest band that was ever organized – or unorganized. I was in Bunny's sax section when I was eighteen. Things were so rough that the chick with the band reached the point where she just couldn't take it any more. Jayne Dover, that was her name. One night there was only one seat left on the bus, and that was next to her. Johnny Napton, the trumpet player, wanted to take it, but she wouldn't let him, so he started cursing her out. She ran out of the bus and told Bunny, 'I can't take this any more! All this rotten language, this foul-mouthed talk, I'm through!' Bunny, who has had one more for the road, and then some, gets back on the bus with her, and all the guys are seated in their chairs. (He'd broken his ankle and was using a cane.) He grabs the post beside the driver, starts banging on it with his cane and just about breaks the cane in half. He's furious. 'I've had it! All this language, and the girl singer wants to quit the band, and you're hanging me up in the middle of a stack of one-nighters without a girl singer. Now I want you to get one thing straight!' (The girl is sitting there while he's saying all this.) The first m----- f----- that curses on this bus is automatically through!' Everybody on the bus starts to laugh, so he catches himself and says, 'Well, I didn't mean to put it that way, but I'm serious! I don't want to hear another foul word out of you as long as Jayne is sitting in this bus!' Well, we go about 250 miles, and not a sound out of anyone. The cats were even lighting their cigarettes real quiet because we knew that Bunny was flipping. Along about daybreak, Joey Bushkin, our pianist, is in the back of the bus, and just as everybody's starting to open their squinty eyes, he runs up the aisle of the bus and he stops by the driver and turns around facing everybody, Bunny included, and yells: 'I can't stand this any longer! f---!f---!f---!f---!', and every other word he can think of. That was about the most frantic bunch of kids that were ever together.[41]

It must have been a deeply tired Berigan band that returned to Manhattan on Sunday, November 4. But tired or not, they were in for another major challenge: they were to battle Erskine Hawkins "The Twentieth Century Gabriel," and His Orchestra at the Savoy Ballroom that night. Hawkins was a very good trumpet player who had an extraordinary high register. He was more of a first trumpet player than a jazz soloist, but jazz or not, he could handle his trumpet very well. Hawkins's secret weapon however, was another trumpet player in his band, the vastly underrated jazz soloist Wilbur "Dud" Bascomb. In addition, Hawkins had a good tenor sax soloist, Julian Dash, and the crowd-pleasing blues-drenched pianist Avery Parrish. The Hawkins band was an excellent dance band, and had made a lot of friends in its many engagements at the Savoy Ballroom. Once again, Bunny and his band would have their hands full as they invaded the Savoy.

They proved to be equal to the task. As Haywood Henry, who played saxophone and clarinet for Hawkins, recalled:

There were only three bands that stole the show from us at the Savoy: Duke's, Lionel Hampton's and Bunny Berigan's. Bunny took us by surprise. Usually we'd prepare in advance by rehearsing or working over one of their specialities, just to make it more exciting. We didn't prepare for Bunny, because we thought we had him. But Buddy Rich and Georgie Auld were with him and the house came down! We had a number with a 'Rhapsody in Blue' ending, but when our drummer's foot pedal broke, we sounded so horrible after Buddy Rich had got through. As for Bunny, I've no doubt he was the best white trumpet player. And something else— he sounded like himself![42]

At least one other trumpet player was there to watch the action that night. Dick Wharton remembered: "I recall Harry James, apparently on an off night, coming to the Savoy and standing only a few feet in front of the bandstand to hear Bunny and the band. He stood there set after set."[43]

Personnel changes continued to occur. Lead altoist Murray "Jumbo" Williams replaced Milton Schatz, who wanted to get into studio work in New York; and Bob "Brad" Jenney, younger brother of trombone virtuoso Jack Jenney, replaced Andy Russo, who returned to studio work in New York. Joe Bushkin, who like everyone else in the band was exhausted from the endless one-night stands, took a job in New York with Pee Wee Russell. Unlike many of the other musicians in the Berigan band, he was a native New Yorker, and had a Local 802 card that allowed him to work where he pleased in New York City. It is unclear who replaced Bushkin on piano in the Berigan band. The White materials suggest that Joe Lippman returned, but I doubt this. He was by this time a very successful arranger, and was contributing scores to a number of bandleaders in addition to Berigan. That kept him very busy, and it allowed him to remain in New York. In fact, at that very moment he was busy on a special arranging project for Berigan that undoubtedly occupied much of his time.

At about the same time, the best girl vocalist Bunny ever employed joined the band. This was Kathleen "Kitty" Lane, a statuesque redhead whose every attribute, definitely including her voice, exuded sex appeal. She sang both ballads and up-tempo tunes with a beat, had excellent voice quality, and very good pitch control and range. Beyond that, she was a very easygoing girl who had no attitude issues. Almost immediately, she became one of the most popular members of the Berigan band.

After the excitement of battling Erskine Hawkins at the Savoy Ballroom, the Berigan band had to be a little letdown to return to the road to play more widely scattered dance dates. Some of the places they played then included: Laurenceville Preparatory School, Laurenceville, New Jersey, on November 11; Cornell University, Ithaca, New York, on the 12th; Princeton University, Princeton, New Jersey, on the 18th. On Saturday November 19th, Bunny appeared again on the *Saturday Night Swing Club.* Also on the program was Lee Wiley. He played "I Can't Get Started" with the CBS band, and then led a contingent of nine musicians from his band through Joe Lippman's new arrangement of Bix Beiderbecke's composition "In a Mist." Lippman explained Bunny's thinking behind this experiment: "We were always looking for something different to record and Bunny had the devil of a time selling the idea of doing a batch of tunes associated with Bix Beiderbecke to the powers-that-be at Victor. So we introduced 'In a Mist' on the *Saturday Night Swing Club* program to show what could be done. I guess the main idea was to have a little band within the big band, which was quite popular then, and we felt it was successful." (This appears to be the last time Bunny guested on the *Saturday Night Swing Club.* This show, which he had a major part in starting in June 1936, was taken off the air in mid-1939).[44]

After appearing on the *Swing Club,* Bunny gathered the rest of his musicians and played a dance date that same night at Hotel St. George in Brooklyn.

On the following day, Sunday, November 20, 1938, Artie Shaw, Bunny's colleague from CBS and the recordings studios, began appearing on a sponsored CBS network radio program with his band. It was called *Melody and Madness,* and it was sponsored by Old Gold cigarettes. Shaw provided the melody; comedian Robert Benchley provided the madness. In addition, Shaw's first record for RCA's thirty-five cent Bluebird label, "Begin the Beguine," was quickly proving to be the largest selling disc produced by RCA Victor in many years. Shaw's band was also about to make a Warner Brothers/Vitaphone movie short and open an engagement with almost nightly NBC radio broadcasts at the Blue Room of Hotel Lincoln in New York City. In short, Artie Shaw and His Orchestra were now on a big roll, after over two years of struggle and relative failure. Shaw was now in a position to be able to afford to really strengthen his band. He began replacing a number of his sidemen at this time. Unfortunately for Berigan, Shaw's gains in the personnel department would be Bunny's losses.

Meanwhile, the Berigan band returned to the road again, playing a couple of one-night dance jobs near New York City. In spite of the recent turnover of some of its musicians, the Berigan band that entered the RCA Victor recording studio on November 22 sounded very good. In addition, they finally had four excellent arrangements on four tunes that seemed to fit the style of the band, to record. Bunny's old friend Leonard Joy was back in the control room that day to supervise the session, and as a result, there was very good karma in the studio. It seems that Bunny's luck, if only temporarily, was back in a positive phase. The recordings he made on this date are among his finest.

"Sobbin' Blues" was hardly a current pop tune in 1938. Bunny undoubtedly was familiar with the recording of this Art Kassel–Vic Berton tune made by the New Orleans Rhythm Kings in the early 1920s. He very likely told Joe Lippman to do a straight-ahead swing arrangement on it, and the result is what is heard in this splendid recording. The band is *tight* in this performance. Bunny's solo in the first chorus on Harmon-muted trumpet sounds very good. That was not always the case. When he returns with an open horn, we hear the glorious burnished sound for which he is renowned. Ray Conniff follows with a very good trombone solo. Then Gus Bivona takes his turn on clarinet. It is clear from his sound here that Bunny had had the same talk with him that he had had with Joe Dixon about adjusting his clarinet mouthpiece to get a brighter sound. Bivona definitely did not sound this way in his many recordings with the Hudson-De Lange band. Georgie Auld is up next with a flowing, cogent jazz solo that would have been unimaginable for him a year before. The influences of Herschel Evans *and Bunny Berigan* had finally sunk in. Some antiphonal riffs follow, played perfectly by the brass and reeds (hear Clyde Rounds on baritone adding just the right touch of testosterone) with Buddy Rich's drums kicking the ensemble along. It is evident that first trumpeter Johnny Napton had become completely comfortable in the Berigan band by the time this recording was made.

L–R: Donald Berigan, Bernard Berigan, and their cousin Charles Casey, Jr. (Fox Lake, Wisconsin, 1912). *Photograph courtesy of the Harriet O'Connell Historical Room at Fox Lake Public Library, Fox Lake, Wisconsin.*

Mary Catherine, William Patrick, Donald and Bernard Berigan (Fox Lake, 1915). *Photograph courtesy of the Harriet O'Connell Historical Room at Fox Lake Public Library, Fox Lake, Wisconsin.*

Bernard "Bun" Berigan (Lyndon Dale Island, Fox Lake, June 1921). This photo was taken at a class picnic. Bunny had taken the ribbon in his hair from one of his female classmates. *Photograph courtesy of the Harriet O'Connell Historical Room at Fox Lake Public Library, Fox Lake, WI.*

The pit orchestra for the Capitol Theater in Madison, Wisconsin, early February 1928. The conductor is violinist Vernon Bestor. Berigan is in the front row at the far right. *From the University of Wisconsin Berigan Archive, Mills Music Library, Madison, Wisconsin.*

The Lacy "Speed" Young band (Philadelphia, June 1928). L–R front: Billy Southern, Speed Young; back: Julie Towers (Julio Torres), Berigan, Walt Dorfuss, Ardon Cornwell, Keith "Curly" Roberts. Not pictured: Paul La Valle (Joe Usifer) and Russ Norhoff. *From the University of Wisconsin Berigan Archive, Mills Music Library, Madison, Wisconsin.*

The Joe Shoer band at the Joyland Casino (Lexington, Kentucky, July 1929). Berigan is seated, at far left. Next to him is Benny Woodworth. In the water second from the left is Harry Haberkorn; next to him, shading his eyes, is Oro "Tut" Soper; Shoer is standing. *From the University of Wisconsin Berigan Archive, Mills Music Library, Madison, Wisconsin.*

Donna McArthur, early 1930. *From the University of Wisconsin Berigan Archive, Mills Music Library, Madison, Wisconsin.*

Members of the Hal Kemp band (London, May 1930). L–R: Berigan, Ben Williams, Skinnay Ennis, and Milton "Mickey" Bloom. *From the collection of Al Apfelberg.*

Bunny and Donna pose for a gag photo at an amusement park, late 1931–early 1932. The people behind them may be Donna's brother and former dance partner Darrell McArthur and his wife Joyce. *From the Harriet O'Connell Historical Room Berigan Archive, Fox Lake Wisconsin Public Library.*

Berigan relaxes with members of the Paul Whiteman band on tour (Texas, April 1933). *From the collection of Al Apfelberg.*

The Berigan family (Fox Lake, June 2–20, 1933). L–R: Mayme, Donald, Donna, Bunny (holding 11-month-old Patricia), Margaret McMahon Berigan, and Cap. The children in front are probably members of the Casey clan. It is possible this was the day Patricia was baptized. *From the University of Wisconsin Berigan Archive, Mills Music Library, Madison, Wisconsin.*

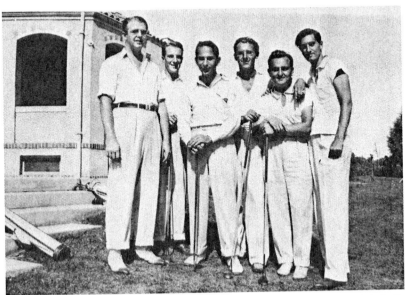

Benny Goodman bandsmen on the golf course (Los Angeles, September 1935). L–R: Berigan, Sterling "Red" Ballard, road manager Mort Davis, BG, Hymie Schertzer, and Jack Lacey. *From the University of Wisconsin Berigan Archive, Mills Music Library, Madison, Wisconsin.*

Berigan sings at the Famous Door, 35 West 52nd St., New York City, February 10–early May 1936. *From the collection of Michael P. Zirpolo.*

Lee Wiley, 1936. *From the collection of Michael P. Zirpolo*

Berigan listens while his manager/Svengali Arthur Michaud, talks, 1937. *From the University of Wisconsin Berigan Archive, Mills Music Library, Madison, Wisconsin.*

Berigan and drummer George Wettling stroll along the sidewalks of New York in summer 1937. Wettling was the first of several great drummers to power the Berigan band. *From the collection of Michael P. Zirpolo.*

On the road with vocalist Gail Reese (fall 1937). *From the collection of Al Apfelberg.*

The Berigan band onstage at New York's Paramount Theater (November 17–December 7, 1937). L–R: Clyde Rounds, Robert "Mike" Doty, Tommy Morgan(elli), Joe Dixon, Georgie Auld, George Wettling, Berigan, Irving Goodman, Hank Wayland, Steve Lipkins, Al George, and Thomas "Sonny" Lee. Not visible, pianist/arranger Joe Lippman. *From the University of Wisconsin Berigan Archive, Mills Music Library, Madison, Wisconsin.*

Berigan engages in onstage patter with vaudeville performer Freddy Sanborn during the Berigan band's first appearance at the New York Paramount Theater (November–December 1937), while Joe Dixon and Georgie Auld listen. *From the collection of Al Apfelberg.*

The Berigan band onstage at another theater (early 1938). L–R: Clyde Rounds, Mike Doty, Joe Dixon, Tommy Morgan, Georgie Auld, and Joe Lippman. More than anyone but Bunny himself, arranger Joe Lippman shaped the sound of the early Berigan band. *From the University of Wisconsin Berigan Archive, Mills Music Library, Madison, Wisconsin.*

Drummer Dave Tough with Berigan at RCA Victor Studios in New York City (January 26, 1938). *From the collection of Al Apfelberg.*

Berigan sings, 1938. *From the University of Wisconsin Berigan Archive, Mills Music Library, Madison, Wisconsin.*

Berigan sidemen take a breather between shows at the Stanley Theater in Pittsburgh (August 25–31, 1938). L–R: Hank Wayland, Clyde Rounds, Ray Conniff, Nat Lobovsky, Joe Dixon, and Buddy Rich. *From the University of Wisconsin Berigan Archive, Mills Music Library, Madison, Wisconsin.*

Kathleen Lane, 1938. *From the collection of Michael P. Zirpolo.*

At the *Metronome* All-Star recording session at RCA Victor Studios in New York City (January 12, 1939). L-R: Tommy Dorsey and his manager, Bobby Burns; Berigan; *Metronome* editor and chief writer, George T. Simon; and Benny Goodman. *From the collection of Michael P. Zirpolo.*

Berigan solos on "Blue Lou," *Metronome* All-Star recording session. The head below the clock is Jack Teagarden's. *From the University of Wisconsin Berigan Archive, Mills Music Library, Madison, Wisconsin.*

RCA Victor Studios in New York City (March 15, 1939). L–R: Kathleen Lane, Don Lodice, Johnny Napton, Gus Bivona, Jake Koven, Berigan, George Johnston, Hank Saltman, Eddie Jenkins, Larry Walsh, and Allan Reuss. *From the University of Wisconsin Berigan Archive, Mills Music Library, Madison, Wisconsin.*

Cap and Bunny Berigan at Kennywood Park outside of Pittsburgh (May 17–30, 1939). *From the University of Wisconsin Berigan Archive, Mills Music Library, Madison, Wisconsin.*

Berigan's best male vocalist was Danny Richards (pictured here in 1939 at Eastwood Gardens, Detroit, Michigan). Unfortunately, circumstances conspired against Richards making records with Bunny—he made only two commercial recordings in more than two years as the Berigan band's featured vocalist. *From the University of Wisconsin Berigan Archive, Mills Music Library, Madison, Wisconsin.*

Patricia, Joyce, and Bunny Berigan at the Schlitzberg-Berigan home (Fox Lake, July 1939). *From the University of Wisconsin Berigan Archive, Mills Music Library, Madison, Wisconsin.*

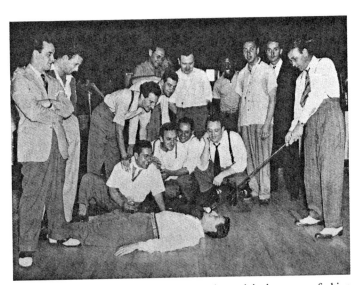

The Berigan band "takes five" from a rehearsal in humorous fashion at the Panther Room of Hotel Sherman in Chicago (July 1–August 11, 1939). L–R standing: Andy Phillips, Danny Richards, Johnny Napton, Morty Stulmaker, Charlie DiMaggio, Larry Walsh, Robert "Little Gate" Walker, Don Lodice, unknown "publicity man," Paul Collins; sitting: Jake Koven; squatting: Gus Bivona, Tommy Moore, Joe Bauer; and laying: Joe Bushkin. *From the University of Wisconsin Berigan Archive, Mills Music Library, Madison, Wisconsin.*

Berigan clowns at Jacobs Beach, Connecticut, in summer 1939. *From the University of Wisconsin Berigan Archive, Mills Music Library, Madison, Wisconsin.*

Onstage at the Loew's State Theater in New York City (August 24–30, 1939). *From the University of Wisconsin Berigan Archive, Mills Music Library, Madison, Wisconsin.*

'Swing Family' on Vacation

Meet the other three-quarters of the Berigan family. Father "Bunny" Berigan is the trumpet playing orchestra leader who won the title "King of Swing." In this picture, Mrs. Berigan, who was Donna MacArthur, professional dancer in New York, poses with their children, Patsy, 7, and Jo-Jo, 3, while on a Wisconsin vacation.

Patricia, Joyce, and Donna Berigan in Fox Lake (September 1939). *From the Harriet O'Connell Historical Room Berigan Archive, Fox Lake Wisconsin Public Library.*

Berigan solos with Tommy Dorsey's band at Paramount Theater in New York City (March 13–April 9, 1940). L–R: unknown trumpeter and trombonist; Berigan, Buddy Rich; back row: Pied Pipers Chuck Lowery, Jo Stafford, and Clark Yocum; front: saxophonist/arranger Deane Kincaide. *Photograph courtesy of the Harriet O'Connell Historical Room at Fox Lake Public Library, Fox Lake, Wisconsin.*

Backstage at the Paramount, same TD engagement. Among those pictured are second from left, Red Skelton; third Frank Sinatra; seventh, a clowning Bunny Berigan; and eighth, trombonist Les Jenkins (are they imitating Skelton?). Tommy Dorsey is at the right. *From the collection of Al Apfelberg.*

The "unknown" Berigan band of 1940–1941 at the Patio Room of the Roosevelt Hotel in Jacksonville, Florida (November 29–December 31, 1940). L–R: Berigan; back row: Max Smith, Ernie Stricker, probably Frank Perry, Jack Thompson, and Ray Krantz. The tenor saxophonist in front is probably Johnny Castaldi. *From the University of Wisconsin Berigan Archive, Mills Music Library, Madison, Wisconsin.*

A rare photo of Bunny Berigan smiling and resplendent in evening clothes, taken with his 1940–1941 band, probably at a college dance date in early 1941. The bassist is Morty Stulmaker. Possible identification of others: L–R, Tommy Moore, guitar; Frank Crolene and Joe DiMaggio, saxes. *From the collection of Michael P. Zirpolo.*

Berigan reads Louis Armstrong's kind words about him in *Down Beat* in a restaurant in Pulaski, Virginia (September 1941). *From the University of Wisconsin Berigan Archive, Mills Music Library, Madison, Wisconsin.*

Berigan with his last great drummer, Jack Sperling, in fall 1941. *From the University of Wisconsin Berigan Archive, Mills Music Library, Madison, Wisconsin.*

On the bandstand with Jack Sperling, Ed Lange, and Berigan in spring 1942. *From the University of Wisconsin Berigan Archive, Mills Music Library, Madison, Wisconsin.*

Berigan with his saxophone section in spring 1942. L–R: Berigan, Ed Lange, Walt Mellor, George Quinty, and Neal Smith. *From the University of Wisconsin Berigan Archive, Mills Music Library, Madison, Wisconsin.*

The brass section of Berigan's last band in spring 1942. L–R probable identification: trumpets—Bob Mansell, Kenny Davis, and Fred Norton; trombones—Frank Webb and Max Smith. *From the University of Wisconsin Berigan Archive, Mills Music Library, Madison, Wisconsin.*

Bunny Berigan and his road family somewhere in the midwest, early spring, 1942. *From the University of Wisconsin Berigan Archive, Mills Music Library, Madison, Wisconsin.*

Berigan solos in front of his band at a dance at Bowling Green College, Ohio, on March 21, 1942. To his left are saxists George Quinty and Walt Mellor. *From the University of Wisconsin Berigan Archive, Mills Music Library, Madison, Wisconsin.*

Mr. Trumpet casts a spell, somewhere on the road in spring 1942. *From the University of Wisconsin Berigan Archive, Mills Music Library, Madison, Wisconsin.*

A McArthur family celebration, circa 1948. L–R: Joyce and Darrell McArthur; a lovely sixteen-year-old Patricia Berigan; John J. McArthur, Darrell's father; Maddie McArthur, the youngest McArthur sister; and twelve-year-old Joyce Berigan. Donna McArthur Berigan was at this time married to pianist George Zack. *Photograph courtesy of the Harriet O'Connell Historical Room at Fox Lake Public Library, Fox Lake, Wisconsin.*

His brilliant sound and deep swing are exactly what Bunny wanted and needed for this band. This is a prime Berigan record and a quintessential example of swing at its best.

"I Cried for You" was another oldie, but goodie, dating from 1923. This recording set off a bit of a revival of the tune. Lippman provided the arrangement, and we hear Kathleen Lane's first recording with the Berigan band. I suspect that she was not yet completely acclimated, because the RCA manifest shows that three separate masters of "I Cried for You" were cut. Two of them are extant. The issued recording is lovely except for one point in Ms. Lane's vocal were she is a bit flat. (I had been annoyed by that little imperfection for over forty years. Since I have had the digital equipment to remaster vintage recordings—and spent several years learning how to use it, I tried many times to correct that flaw. Finally I did it. The resulting performance has Ms. Lane singing perfectly on pitch throughout the entire recording. I smile every time I listen to it.) After her vocal chorus, Berigan enters with that warm, velvety sound of his, and creates some truly splendid jazz. Auld plays next, and his solo is also excellent. He is clearly inspired by what Berigan had just played. The band's ensembles are again first rate. This is another great swing recording.

The tune "Jelly Roll Blues," like many things about its composer Ferdinand "Jelly Roll" Morton,[45] is somewhat mysterious. He claimed to have written it in 1905, which would have been three years after he said that he invented jazz. I suspect that Bunny was familiar with Morton's recording of it, which was made for Victor in 1926. He commissioned this arrangement from Abe Osser, who had done such a good job on the chart he had written for Bunny's band on "Trees." Here, Osser outdoes himself —the arrangement is superb, and Bunny and the band do it full justice.

Berigan starts the performance once again using a Harmon mute, adding a slight rasp for effect this time. The opening reeds are led by Bivona's clarinet; then the melody is stated by both Auld's tenor sax and Bivona's clarinet playing the lead in unison an octave apart, with the open brass humming along behind them providing a soft harmonic cushion.

An eight-bar reed section unison opens out onto the next part of the piece, heralded by three trilled clarinet notes from Bivona. The sensitive scoring uses the substance of Morton's composition, only slightly rearranging its parts in order to harvest their melodic richness. Bivona's clarinet and Auld's tenor, (again) playing in unison octaves, are an especially attractive feature here, with Dick Wharton's guitar providing good underpinning. Berigan can be heard leading the brass, and the band achieves a clean, handsome sorority. The musicians use dynamics and different orchestral textures in a way that belies all of the undoubtedly accurate stories of haphazard rehearsals and wayward leadership.[46]

I must at this point interject that there are many references both in the White materials and elsewhere that make it very clear that whatever other peccadilloes Bunny Berigan had, and we know that he had many, he was *not* haphazard in rehearsal with his band. Whenever the Berigan band sounded good, and that was quite often, Bunny's leadership in rehearsal can and should be credited with facilitating those good performances.

Joe Bushkin offers four thoughtful, delicate bars of piano to bring Berigan on for one of his most eloquent solos on record. His phrases seem to grieve with an intense and vivid humanity. The chords of this blues, differing from the norm in their construction, allow Berigan to tap two sources of emotional strength—the basic force of the blues and the lyric intensity of song—and he makes the most of both. His solo abounds in points of exquisite musical detail: His use of eighth-note triplets in bars five and six is typical of the way that he accents some and leaves others out altogether to shape a coiled spring of a phrase. His playing is right across the warmest range of his rich middle register, going for no spectacular climaxes or effects, devoting everything to melody and feeling. Even his break at the conclusion of his first chorus, with its half-valve rip up to high C and four annunciatory quarter notes, is in keeping with the moment. With the band playing quiet three-beat stop-time behind him (marking the first three beats of each bar and leaving the fourth open), Berigan follows his melodic trajectory up, then plunges to the depths of his horn, soaring back up to a glorious high D before gather in this thrilling solo an a bouncing, half-valve figure that seems to cajole before quietly taking its leave. The full ensemble, with the reeds on clarinets and Rich riding his backbeats hard, delivers an equally moving chorus, one of the most intense and beautifully played Berigan orchestral passages on record. It had the power of a Berigan solo and a single-minded unanimity of interpretation. It ends on an engaging little unison clarinet figure that brings Berigan back, muted again, for a parting comment in the spirit of his introduction but this time played more deliberately, a fitting recognition of the compelling statement that has just been made. The band takes it out with a reiteration of Morton's famous triplet phrase and a concluding thump.[47]

This is a recording for the ages. It goes far beyond its initial purpose as a commercial recording by a swing era dance band. What Bunny achieved that day on his recording of "Jelly Roll Blues" was a completely integrated, deeply profound musical statement. There is an ineffable perfection and completeness to this performance. It is not technically perfect, but it is *musically* perfect. One cannot imagine it being rendered any differently. Yet listening to it is much more than a musical experience; it is an emotional experience, rooted in the inexhaustible wellspring of jazz, the blues. For anyone who wonders what the artistry of Bunny Berigan was all about, this recording offers a complete explanation. "Jelly Roll Blues" is absolutely one of the Berigan essentials and one of the greatest recordings of the swing era.

If one is astonished that the Berigan band could have ever rendered something as intensely musical and emotional as "Jelly Roll Blues" given the totality of the circumstances in which that recording was made,[48] one must be equally amazed that they could have shifted gears so effortlessly, and then knocked off Joe Lippman's breezy arrangement of the vintage, yet worthwhile pop tune "'Deed I Do" (composed in 1926) only a few minutes later. Ms. Lane sounds a bit more relaxed on this recording than on "I Cried for You." Everyone else is very mellow. Johnny Napton's brilliant first trumpet is noteworthy throughout this performance. "'Deed I Do" is an excellent dance band record.

This session lasted from 1:30 to 6:00 p.m. It appears that the band remained in New York after completing their work in the recording studio, and enjoyed a very rare night off in Manhattan.

The next night, they were probably on the road again. We know that they played a one-nighter on Thursday November 24 (Thanksgiving night) at the Valencia Ballroom, York, Pennsylvania, where they had been received so warmly only a few weeks before. Other single-evening dance dates no doubt followed, probably through the weekend. I suspect that Bunny spent the better part of Monday, November 28 and Tuesday, November 29 in New York carefully rehearsing the music he would record for RCA Victor on November 30 and December 1. These back-to-back recording sessions would document one of the most musically worthwhile experiments in the Berigan band's history.

Notes

[1] White materials: September 2, 1938.

[2] *Hear Me Talkin' to Ya—The Story of Jazz as Told by the Men Who Made It*, by Nat Shapiro and Nat Hentoff, Dover Publications, Inc. (1955), 324.

[3] *Billboard:* September 24, 1938, cited in the White materials: September 11, 1938.

[4] *Metronome:* October 1938, cited in the White materials: September 11, 1938.

[5] *Orchestra World:* October 1938, cited in the White materials: September 11, 1938.

[6] White materials: September 11, 1938.

[7] Jayne Dover later sang with Claude Thornhill's band as Jane Essex.

[8] White materials: September 12, 1938.

[9] "Livery Stable Blues," composed by Ray Lopez and Alcide Nunez, as recorded by the Original Dixieland Jass Band on February 16, 1917, is said to have been the first jazz record. This recording, made for Victor (18255), sold over a million copies. The musicians in the ODJB were white, and in their rendition, they made comic barnyard noises on their instruments at various times throughout the performance. In reality, the ODJB had made two previous "jass" recordings on January 31, 1917, for Columbia: "Darktown Strutter's Ball" and "Back Home in Indiana."

[10] *Metronome:* November 1938, cited in the White materials.

[11] *Down Beat:* November 1938, cited in the White materials.

[12] White materials: September 13, 1938.

[13] *Ibid.*

[14] The Old Ritz-Carlton Hotel, which is located adjacent to the Public Garden and Boston Commons, is now used for luxury condominiums, ranging in price from $1,000,000 – $2,600,000.

[15] White materials: September 20, 1938.

[16] Liner notes—*The Complete Bunny Berigan, Vol. III*, RCA-BMG-Bluebird LP 9953-1-RB (1990), by Richard M. Sudhalter. Sudhalter interviewed a number of ex-Berigan sidemen and quoted them in these liner notes. Hereafter cited as *Bluebird, Vol. III.*

[17] White materials: September 21, 1938.

[18] *Bluebird, Vol. III.*

[19] *Ibid.*
[20] Christopher Lehman-Haupt is quoted in the White materials: September 21, 1938.
[21] *Billboard:* October 1, 1938, cited in the White materials.
[22] *Metronome:* October 1938, cited in the White materials.
[23] *Variety:* September 28, 1938, cited in the White materials.
[24] White materials: September 21, 1938.
[25] White materials: September 23, 1938.
[26] White materials: September 13–23, 1938.
[27] White materials: September 24, 1938.
[28] *Ibid.*
[29] Skinnay Ennis sang on the Bob Hope radio show and was often the brunt of Hope's jokes. His band functioned as a studio band, playing cues, backgrounds, and backing up musical guests and variety acts. They also backed up the show's featured vocal group, Six Hits and a Miss. Ennis had earlier been placed in front of arranger/pianist Gil Evans's band by MCA "to make it more commercial." Evans stayed with the band as its chief arranger and music director, however. When the arranging duties for the Hope show got too heavy for Evans, he was asked who he wanted to help him out. He recommended Claude Thornhill, who soon joined him arranging for the Hope show. Although neither of them knew it at the time, their association would in the 1940s and 1950s alter the course of jazz. See *Castles Made of Sound—The Story of Gil Evans,* by Larry Hicock, Da Capo Press, (2002) 16.
[30] White materials: October 1, 1938.
[31] Cited in the White materials: October 1, 1938.
[32] White materials: October 5, 1938.
[33] White materials: October 12, 1938.
[34] *Ibid.*
[35] *Bluebird, Vol. III*
[36] *Ibid.*
[37] *Ibid.*
[38] *Gil Evans—Out of the Cool; His Life and Music,* by Stephanie Stein Crease, A Cappella Books, (2002) 66.
[39] *Lost Chords:* 513.
[40] *Billboard:* November 5, 1938, cited in the White materials.
[41] *Laughter from the Hip—The Lighter Side of Jazz,* by Leonard Feather and Jack Tracy, Horizon Press, (1963) 72–73.
[42] *The World of Swing,* by Stanley Dance, Da Capo Press, (1979) 210
[43] White materials: November 4, 1938.
[44] White materials: November 19, 1938.
[45] Ferdinand Joseph Lamothe was born on October 20, 1890, in New Orleans, Louisiana. (There is some confusion about the date of Morton's birth.) He took the surname Morton by Anglicizing the last name of his stepfather, which was Mouton. Morton began working as a pianist in the brothels of New Orleans's Storyville section as a boy. In 1926, he recorded a series of classic sessions for the Victor label in Chicago with a band billed as Jelly Roll Morton and His Red Hot Peppers. These recordings show that Morton was a good bandleader and arranger. He died on July 10, 1941, in Los Angeles. In addition to "Jelly Roll Blues," Morton also composed "King Porter Stomp," and many other tunes.
[46] *Giants of Jazz:* 46. (Notes by Richard M. Sudhalter.)
[47] *Ibid.*

---

[48] It may have been at about this time that Bunny began to discover serious problems relating to the care of his daughters. See chapter 19.

.

Chapter 19
Enigma Variations:[1] Part One

It is very paradoxical that the RCA Victor Recording Company, which for the previous nineteen months had dictated to Bunny Berigan which tunes he should record for them, including such titles as "Mother Goose," "Rinka Tinka Man," and "Button, Button," should suddenly allow him to record a six-side series of compositions either composed by Bix Beiderbecke, or associated with him. I must assume that Bunny and Joe Lippman pleaded with Leonard Joy, who was now supervising Berigan's Victor recording sessions, to allow this project to go forward, and somehow persuaded him that it was worth a try. Eli Oberstein, Victor's self-styled hit maker, would undoubtedly have vetoed this concept immediately. It had nothing to do with current pop tunes, banal lyrics, girl or boy singers, song-pluggers, and the other usual commercial considerations that guided his choice of what tunes a band should record. Indeed, this set of recordings was unique in that no other swing band up to that time had ever actually recorded, as a group, a number of compositions that shared a common theme. People often attribute the origination of the "concept album" idea to Frank Sinatra, who certainly did some great things along those lines in the 1950s while recording for Capitol. But this was happening in 1938, and it was being done by an artist who certainly did not have a lot of clout with the recording company.[2] This extremely strange development is but the first of many difficult to explain (but in this case fortuitous) incidents that would occur between Berigan and Victor over the next twelve months. What is equally odd is that between the recording sessions of November 22, November 30, and December 1, 1938, a period of only nine days, Bunny Berigan recorded a total of ten sides for Victor, not a one of which was a current pop tune. This represented a complete turnabout from the many sessions he had previously made for Victor that had consisted exclusively of current Tin Pan Alley ephemera, often with mawkish lyrics. In light of Bunny's overall experience with Victor Records, we must be very thankful that the series of recordings he made on November 30 and December 1, 1938, was ever allowed to be produced.

At 1:30 p.m. on November 30, Bunny gathered eight of his sidemen at RCA Victor's Twenty-fourth Street recording studio. This small band, billed as Bunny Berigan and His Men, consisted of Berigan and Irving Goodman, trumpets; Ray Conniff, trombone; Murray Williams, Gus Bivona, and Georgie Auld, saxophones and clarinets; Joe Lippman, piano; Hank Wayland, bass; and Buddy

Rich, drums. Over the next three and three-quarter hours, they very efficiently recorded four tunes that had been composed by Bix Beiderbecke: "In a Mist," "Flashes," "Davenport Blues," and "Candlelights." "It was Bunny's idea to do these things, Joe Lippman said. He got that book—the suite of piano pieces—and we tried out 'In a Mist' on the *Saturday Night Swing Club* radio show.[3] His idea was to create a little band within the big band, and what better way to do it than with the music of Bix?"[4] The "book" Lippman referred to was the published transcriptions of Beiderbecke's piano compositions that had been done for Bix by arranger Bill Challis.[5]

"In a Mist" was the first of these compositions the Berigan men tackled. It is the most well known of Bix's four piano pieces, and the only one he recorded—for Okeh, on September 9, 1927. Lippman's arrangement is rather different from Bix's recording both rhythmically and in mood. This is definitely a *swing* interpretation of "In a Mist." Lippman plays a brief intro on piano which establishes the basic motive that recurs throughout the piece. Next is an ensemble that features brass led by Berigan and reeds led by Auld on tenor. The way that Lippman integrates the piano into his arrangement is ingenious and effective. Buddy Rich, using his sticks, ticks away on his closed high hats, adding to the rather jaunty feeling, as Bunny and then Bivona burst out of the ensembles. The next section of the arrangement is rather riffy, and played with splendid precision by the band. Ray Conniff then plays a trombone solo against a highly rhythmic background supplied by the brass and reeds. The ensemble returns to wrap things up, gently.

"Flashes"[6] begins with an absolutely lovely four-bar piano intro played by Joe Lippman that contains harmonies that would soon become a more prominent part of the swing-band–jazz-band lexicon, via arrangements by Billy Strayhorn, Paul Jordan, Eddie Sauter, Gil Evans, and Bill Finegan.[7] Auld leads the reeds on tenor saxophone in his typically robust fashion, playing much of the time in unison with Bivona's B-flat clarinet. Williams handles the bass clarinet part, which is often voiced with the brass, beautifully. The combinations of instrumental sonorities make an attractive musical blend. Bunny plays brief solo passages as he emerges, from time to time, from the ensembles, where his burnished broad trumpet tone provides both warmth and strength. Given the sound of his trumpet, it appears that Berigan slightly muted its sound, probably using a felt beret. Later, Conniff's trombone and Bivona's clarinet pop out of the delightful swirls of orchestrated sound in similar fashion. In this performance, Rich uses his brushes with delicacy and taste. Joe Lippman plays the piano parts splendidly. This arrangement is attributed to Abe Osser. It demonstrates his complete command of the art of arranging, using the nine musicians very deftly—the instruments disappear into a charming orchestral kaleidoscope. Bunny must receive the credit for having his sidemen totally prepared to deliver a marvelously cohesive and sensitive musical performance. This recording is a jewel, and has been vastly underappreciated.

"Davenport Blues," as arranged by Joe Lippman, is a bit of a swinger. This chart returns us to the conventions of the swing era: a taut rhythm section sup-

porting harmonized ensemble backgrounds supporting improvised solos. Georgie Auld is heard here in the intro on alto saxophone, an instrument he rarely
played while he was with Berigan. Then Ray Conniff steps forward with a robust trombone solo. Bunny's melodic open trumpet brings Auld back for a tasty
eight bars of solo alto sax, followed by eight bars of Bunny's open trumpet, with
Auld then returning for eight more bars. This eight-eight-eight scheme is then
repeated, with Gus Bivona's clarinet bookending Ray Conniff's trombone. Berigan's passionate trumpet moves this performance to a very satisfactory conclusion. "Davenport Blues" is another excellent recording. Auld's use of his alto
saxophone on it created a situation in which he and Bunny had a slight disagreement. (See below.)

The impressionistic "Candlelights" is much more restrained than "Davenport
Blues," and is cast in the orchestral mode of "In a Mist" and "Flashes." Lippman
again plays the band on with some rich harmonies. The reeds are voiced with
Auld's tenor sax playing lead, much of the time in unison with Bivona's clarinet. Murray Williams is once again impressive on bass clarinet. The piano and
Berigan's trumpet fill in brief openings in the music. Then Bunny plays a solo
on the second strain which, according to Dan Morgenstern, has him using a
bucket mute.[8] (To me it sounds like a straight mute, but I could be wrong.) He
returns a bit later on open trumpet to lead the ensemble to the conclusion, which
contains a perfectly executed *ritardando*. The White materials attribute this arrangement to either Lippman or Osser. It is my judgment that it was written by
Joe Lippman.

This recording session demonstrated that in spite of the chaos surrounding
him much of the time, Bunny Berigan was still functioning on a very creative
level as a bandleader. He had originated an extremely unusual but musically
valid idea for a series of recordings, had commissioned fitting arrangements for
them from writers who were very familiar with his musical orientation, had rehearsed the musicians to a state of total preparedness, and then led them through
brilliant performances that were beautifully recorded by Victor's sound engineers. He had also successfully advocated with the people at Victor to get this
series of recordings produced.[9] This recording session was an unqualified musical triumph, and these recordings will be listened to as long as people have any
interest in the music of the swing era of jazz history.

After wrapping-up "Candlelights" at 5:15 p.m., Bunny dismissed his sidemen, who then had the night off. He then probably got a bite to eat and something to drink, and headed to the Manhattan studios of WNEW, where he appeared on a jam session broadcast organized by radio personality Martin Block.
An aircheck of this broadcast is among the numerous Berigan performances that
are a part of the "Savory Recordings" now owned by the National Jazz Museum
in Harlem. It is in excellent fidelity and presents Bunny in an informal setting
with the following musicians: guitarist Slim Gaillard and bassist Slam Stewart,
then performing together as *Slim and Slam;* tenor saxophonist Joe Thomas and
trombonist Trummy Young, then with Jimmie Lunceford; clarinetist Buster Bailey and pianist Billy Kyle, then with John Kirby; and drummer Slick Jones, then

with Fats Waller. Among the tunes recorded: an ad-lib "Blues," "I Got Rhythm," and a marvelous rendering of "I Can't Get Started," which is notable for Berigan's very relaxed vocal chorus.[10]

Bunny and the same musicians who began their tribute to Bix Beiderbecke in the RCA Victor studios on November 30, returned the next afternoon at 4:00 to finish the final two of the six recordings that have come to be known as the "Beiderbecke Suite."

It is interesting to review how Georgie Auld recalled the events surrounding these two recording sessions:

> Bunny wanted me to play alto and tenor on this album. I hadn't touched the alto in a long time. I squeaked a couple of times. Bunny took his trumpet and threw it up against the wall, cursed me out and said, 'Blackie (Bunny's nickname for Auld), you sonofabitch, you're doin' the squeakin' so we can go overtime.' It broke my heart. Those were the first out-of-the-way words we ever had. I go back to the Forrest Hotel, and run into Billie Holiday and Tony Pastor. They say 'Artie has been looking for you all day. Where have you been?' They were working at the Lincoln Hotel. So I said, 'I'll come by tonight.' I went by that evening and Artie hired me. The next evening I went back to RCA to finish Bunny's album. I walked into the men's room to take a leak, and Bunny's in there taking one. He looked at me and said: 'Jeez, Georgie, I was overtrained last night. I never should have done what I did. I hope you'll forgive me.' 'I forgive you Bunny. I hope you'll forgive me.' 'Why? What did you do?' 'I joined Artie Shaw last night. I'm going with his band in two weeks.' He says: 'You make a move and I'll knock every one of your fuckin' teeth out.' One minute later, he's hugging me and saying: 'No matter who's in your chair with my band, if you're not happy with Shaw, that chair always belongs to you.'[11]

Like many jazz musicians, Georgie Auld was a good storyteller; indeed he was a good actor. He appeared on Broadway in *The Rat Race* in the 1950s, and later appeared in the film *New York, New York,* as a jaded bandleader. (In that film he stole more than one scene from stars Robert De Niro and Liza Minnelli. It was also the sound of his tenor saxophone that was heard on the film's soundtrack when De Niro was "playing" the saxophone onscreen.) I have ascertained that Auld's first night with Artie Shaw's band was December 16, 1938. That means that he probably gave his notice to Berigan two weeks earlier, on December 2. How much of the above-cited story is true is open to discussion. But I think the general outlines probably are true. Bunny undoubtedly was not happy about losing Auld. Nevertheless, their ultimate parting was on good terms, with Bunny being very gracious about it.

The Victor manifest indicates that Berigan and his small band were in the studio on December 1 only from 4:00 to 6:30 p.m. They recorded Joe Lippman's arrangement of Beiderbecke's tune "In the Dark" first. Like all of the other arrangements in Bunny's "Beiderbecke Suite," except "Davenport Blues" and "Walkin' the Dog," the mood of this performance is decidedly gentle, even a bit introspective. Most of it is played by the ensemble, with solo voices emerging only briefly. Auld is heard on tenor sax, and Bunny plays with a straight mute.

Once again Lippman's piano is an integral part of the performance, and he plays as beautifully on this as he had on all of these titles. We must remember that Lippman was an extremely competent reader of music, in addition to being a marvelous arranger. These performances required an excellent reader to play the many piano parts accurately and with appropriate feeling. Lippman did this very well. His playing on these sides is several notches above "arranger's piano." He was not, however, an especially good jazz soloist. Joe Bushkin was an excellent jazz soloist who was not a strong reader. For these reasons, Bunny's choice of Lippman over Bushkin as pianist for this project was absolutely correct.

"Walkin' the Dog" was composed by Dudley Brooks, not Beiderbecke, and was not directly associated with Bix. The arrangement, at times, has a definite retro feel to it, especially the Dixieland part right after Lippman's solo in the first chorus. After this, Bunny steps forward with his open trumpet, as the band settles into riffing background behind him. Auld follows on tenor, Murray Williams on alto, and Ray Conniff on trombone, each with a good solo. Then the band riffs for the remainder of the performance.

There is some confusion as to who wrote the arrangement on "Walkin' the Dog." Ray Conniff explained as follows: "We realized at the second session that we were one number short. I had a chart in my case that I'd done on 'I Would Do Anything for You', so I swiped the intro off that and we faked the rest. They put me down as arranger on that one because I wrote the intro. I never complained."[12] I assume that Conniff had to "downsize" what he had written previously (probably for the Berigan big band) to fit the reduced instrumentation used in this performance. Given the generally loose "head arrangement" feel that the musicians achieved, I am persuaded that Conniff's explanation is accurate.

As was usually the case, the reviews of these recordings that appeared in the trade papers were perfunctory, and not at all well considered. The fact that we are listening to these recordings more than seventy years after they were made speaks for the quality of the music that was made by Bunny and this group of musicians in late 1938. Albert McCarthy was much more thoughtful when he wrote about these recordings in his book *Big Band Jazz*:

> Beiderbecke's introspective and impressionist piano compositions aren't all that easy to transcribe into orchestral arrangements, but Lippman's scores are intelligently conceived and he makes use of a number of individual voicings. The performances are very much governed by the arrangements, with solos generally of short duration and forming an integral part of the whole. 'Candlelights' and 'In the Dark' are probably the most successful titles as they capture the emotional climate of the numbers well. Berigan subordinates something of his own musical personality while remaining tonally quite distinctive. He manages to convey an impression of the unique lyricism that suffused Beiderbecke's own playing without ever attempting to directly copy him. The wistfulness of Berigan's playing during 'Candlelights,' for example, is not recreated on any other of his records.[13]

This recording session was probably Joe Lippman's last with Berigan.[14] From this time forward, he concentrated his energies on arranging. Although

Jimmy Dorsey persuaded him to join his band on piano for a time (September 1939 to January 1942), Lippman contributed far more to the JD canon as an arranger and sometime composer of swing originals such as "Major and Minor Stomp," "Turn Left," "Turn Right," "The Spirit's Got Me," "Murderistic," and "Hoboken Rock," among many others, than he did as a pianist. Lippman went on to a very successful career as a freelance arranger, making notable contributions to recordings by, among others, Charlie Parker and Sarah Vaughn in the early 1950s, and then going into television in Hollywood after that.

After the Beiderbecke suite recordings were finished, it was back to the grind of one-nighters for Bunny and his band. On December 3 they played at the Riverside Plaza Ballroom in New York City, and then hit the road once again. Bunny had a bit of good luck when Joe Bushkin rejoined his band at this time. Clyde Rounds recalled:

> Joey Bushkin was thrown out of a job when the Little Club folded, so he returned, but Georgie Auld and Irving Goodman both turned in their notices about the same time, which made about a dozen changes in a few months. While we were playing the closing number of a set, I noticed Bunny holding up two fingers and waving vigorously. Hank Wayland was waving back and cursing, thinking that Bunny was indicating his two weeks notice. It turned out, however, that Bunny was signaling for the alternative, shorter ending to the number in order to get off the stand quickly! That was one of the few laughs we were getting then.[15]

Bunny had been extremely reluctant to lay-off his band back in September after the hurricane disaster because he feared that he might lose a number of his musicians. As it turned out, within a couple of months, he essentially lost most of the musicians who had been with him in the summer anyway. In retrospect, he would have been better off to simply have disbanded immediately after the hurricane, perhaps retaining a few key players, and then reorganize when conditions were more favorable. His stubborn insistence on keeping the band together during the fallow period after the hurricane had cost him dearly. By the end of 1938, he was having trouble meeting his band's weekly payroll. Berigan's mulish persistence in doing things *his way* was about to create some more major problems on the business side of his band.

Nevertheless, as December began, he slogged on, taking whatever one-night stands MCA had lined up for him. On December 7, he and the band played at the State Armory in Watertown, New York; on the 9th at the sophomore hop at Penn State University, College Park, Pennsylvania. On December 14, they were at the University of Maryland, in Baltimore. Clyde Rounds recalled his section mate Georgie Auld's departure from the Berigan band this way: "I remember Bunny making the announcement to the crowd that Georgie Auld would be leaving the band the next night. It was obvious that he had been offered a lot more money by Artie Shaw, and he, quite rightly as it turned out, saw it as a golden opportunity to further his musical career. I think Bunny was pretty upset at losing his number one saxophone soloist, but he gave Auld his blessing."[16] Now Bunny was casting about for a tenor sax soloist who could replace Auld.

In late 1938, trumpeter Harry James was approached by MCA to form his own band. He left Benny Goodman's band in the first few days of 1939. Benny and Harry Goodman had been using subs to fill out BG's trumpet section, where after James's departure, Ziggy Elman would be the featured soloist. Irving Goodman was now being implored by his brothers to join the Goodman band, where he would be paid more than he was making with Berigan because of Benny's ongoing network radio show, *The Camel Caravan*. Irving reluctantly decided to leave Bunny, and recalled how he worked out his notice with him: "I'd been on notice for several weeks, but Bunny didn't seem to be making any attempt to get a replacement, so I figured that if I was ever to get away, I'd have to do the job myself. So I took Jake Koven along with us on the New England dates. I knew he was a good player, because we'd worked together with Charlie Barnet and I was sure Bunny would approve. Well, he did and he duly hired Jake. For a bit we had three trumpets (in the section), myself, Napton and Koven. After Jake learned the book I left the band after a date in Scranton, Pennsylvania."[17] Irving Goodman joined his brothers in early January, after taking a couple of weeks of rest.

Irving Goodman later reflected on his time as a member of Bunny Berigan's band:

Like everyone else, I was crazy about Bunny. He was with Benny for only a short period, but whenever he was present it was another story. There haven't been many guys who could electrify Benny, but Bunny was certainly one of them. As a leader, he was great to work for. The whole band would do anything he wanted. It was like a real happy family. His attitude was so great too. Like when we played the boondocks, where it didn't really count. Bunny never let up—he gave it everything he had. Another thing, he never acted like he was anything special. Maybe he didn't think he was. Music occupied his mind a lot, and he seemed to be able to inspire everybody to play a bit better than they ordinarily could. The way he beat off a tempo, and the sound he produced, got under our skins. It was so much fun some of us were pretty near willing to work for nothing, and sometimes it nearly came to that![18]

The Scranton engagement to which Irving Goodman made reference took place on December 20. How different the Christmas holidays of 1938 were from those a year earlier. This Christmas season, there were no gifts, no parties, indeed, no gigs. The musicians were not at all sure if there would even be a Bunny Berigan band for very much longer.

The Berigan band was evolving right before its leader's eyes as 1938 ended, and Bunny had no idea exactly where this evolutionary process would end. He was extremely unhappy that so many of his stalwart sidemen had left him over the past few months, but he was not, under any circumstances, about to give up his band. He pulled the band off the road for the Christmas holidays, and set about replacing the musicians he had lost, and a few others who were associated with his band in nonmusical capacities.

Bunny Berigan cleaned house Christmas week, ending with a 10-piece combo which he will front himself. Arthur Michaud, the trumpeter's manager, no longer is affiliated with Berigan. Georgie Auld, tenor man, made a swift shift from Berigan's to Artie Shaw's ranks. Understanding here is that Auld and Tony Pastor will share hot choruses in Shaw's unit. The Berigan personnel now includes Irving Goodman, trumpet; Hank Wayland, bass; Murray Williams and Gus Bivona, saxes; Joe Lippman, piano and arranger; Buddy Rich, traps and Ray Conniff, trombone. Another sax is to be added and the new style will be slanted along 'chamber jazz' lines.[19]

As usual, this contemporary press report was a bit inaccurate. The fact of the matter was that Bunny's band was undergoing an almost complete turnover in personnel, and this turnover was not of his making. His sidemen were choosing to move on. Despite press speculation, Bunny had no intention of fronting a ten-piece band.

Almost immediately after Georgie Auld had joined Artie Shaw, he (Auld) called Buddy Rich and told him that Shaw was looking for a drummer. Buddy duly appeared at the Hotel Lincoln, sat in for a few tunes, and was offered a job by Shaw. He then gave Bunny his two-week notice, and joined the Shaw band as 1939 began. In the meantime, the Berigan band was laid off in New York, and Bunny was auditioning new musicians. He was very favorably impressed by a young tenor saxophonist from Trenton, New Jersey, by the name of Domenico Francesco Lo Giudice. As Don Lodice, he was hired by Berigan, and immediately began to light up Bunny's band with his often wild big-toned tenor sax solos. Lodice recalled the circumstances: "I joined Bunny around Christmas 1938. Gus Bivona and Irv Goodman heard me playing at a New York jazz club called Rudy's Rail and recommended me to Bunny as replacement for Georgie Auld, who, together with Buddy Rich, had accepted an offer from Artie Shaw. Phil Sillman was the new drummer, and Jerry Johnson the new band manager in place of Arthur Michaud."[20]

The rupture between Berigan and Michaud was acrimonious. Bunny had for some time thought that Michaud was favoring Gene Krupa's band over his. During the previous summer, Michaud had repeatedly told Bunny that he would be going to Hollywood to work either in films or on radio with Bob Hope. Skinnay Ennis got the job on radio with Hope. When the news broke in the trade press in late 1938 that Gene Krupa's band would be featured in a Paramount film with Bob Hope,[21] Bunny was livid. He regarded this as the last straw in the business relationship between himself and Michaud. After Berigan and Michaud parted company, which probably happened in early January 1939, Bunny made the decision to operate without a personal manager, probably to save money. This was a big mistake, for as we shall see, without the guidance of a powerful personal manager, key aspects of Berigan's career went from being managed somewhat poorly to not being managed at all. For the next two and a half years, Bunny's career went adrift. It seems that all he wanted was to keep his band intact, playing on the road. Consequently, he simply did what he was told to do by MCA, and was used by MCA for the sole benefit of MCA. *Metronome* reported the parting with Michaud this way: "Bunny Berigan has left personal manager, Arthur Michaud, with whom he has been associated for years. Each side claims the other is at fault, with the old cash problems acute. Michaud had Bunny before the local 802 Trial Board, but nothing came of it. Berigan, meanwhile, takes advice from Joe Herbert, his accountant, and books directly through MCA. Kitty Lane has joined as vocalist."[22] Once again, this press report is not entirely accurate. The White materials state that a check of the records of Local 802 revealed no such action against Berigan. Once again George T. Simon reported something negative about Bunny that simply was not true.

Despite the ongoing problems on the business side of the band, Berigan was resolute about continuing to be the leader of a big band. Filling the vacant chairs with good musicians was a challenge, but one Bunny took on enthusiastically. His reputation as a great musician made this task somewhat easier. Young musicians were thrilled to have the opportunity to play with a musician of Bunny's renown and ability. Nevertheless, the numerous problems that had contributed to the large personnel turnover in his band continued. First and foremost, Bunny's ever-increasing drinking was now beginning to have an effect not only on his playing, but on his health as well.

In spite of the fact that Bunny Berigan was blessed with a powerful constitution and great stamina, what was going on inside of his body by the end of 1938 was contributing to a gradual weakening of the magnificent performance mechanism he relied on to play the trumpet at virtuoso levels. Berigan now had two diseases simultaneously: alcoholism and cirrhosis of the liver. The former, though devastating to a human being, is not necessarily fatal. Alcoholism had been affecting Bunny's playing and personality in negative ways for some time. Cirrhosis of the liver, however, is irreversible and fatal if the alcoholic continues to drink. It is likely that as early as 1938, Bunny Berigan's liver had begun to show the signs of cirrhosis.[23]

> The liver breaks down food products reaching it in blood from the bowel, returning the nutrients to the general (systemic) circulation. This closed-circuit system of blood vessels through the liver is called the portal circulation. If the liver is partly blocked by scars caused by cirrhosis, portal hypertension (high blood pressure in that area) occurs. Attempts to establish better, collateral flow of blood between the portal and systemic circulation results in enlarged veins at the points of connection, mainly the esophagus—the tube that connects the mouth with the stomach.[24]

Thus, the mechanism of Bunny Berigan's death had already begun its inexorable process in 1938. Joe Dixon stated that Bunny was aware of this, and had convinced himself that whatever steps he was taking to reduce his drinking would halt the cumulative damage that was being done to his liver by cirrhosis. Unfortunately, Bunny's spasmodic attempts to go on the wagon were not effective to combat either his advancing alcoholism or his advancing cirrhosis. Like most alcoholics, he lived in a world of delusion and denial, and he continued to live his life more or less as he always had, and this usually included drinking more and more alcohol every day.[25]

Historically, New Year's Eve has been the best day of the year for professional musicians. Musicians kid among themselves that even *bad* musicians have a gig on New Year's Eve. Bunny had spent the Christmas holidays trying out new musicians while his band was on a layoff in New York. Although he had not yet reorganized his band completely to his satisfaction, he was able to present an acceptable group for an engagement in Philadelphia on New Year's Eve at the 103rd Regiment Armory. Here is what happened at that Saturday night New Year's Eve party:

(Headline) Berigan Fizzles in Philly With A G New Year's Draw. Bunny Berigan plus a gala 15-act show drew poorly at a New Year's Eve jitterbug frolic at the 103rd Regiment Armory here. Despite plenty of advance publicity and advertising, less than 700 customers paid the $1.50 tariff to hear Berigan's hot tootling, putting a little more than $1,000 in the till. Promoters of the affair blamed the scant attendance on the mayor's statement that all festivities would cease at the stroke of midnight due to the Sunday blue laws. Despite the fact that the town ignored the hizzoner's statement many people were afraid to plunk down any money with the prospect of being streeted at midnight. Dance was sponsored by the Garrirt Post, American Legion, and Jolly Joyce local booking agency. Promoters went into the hole for about $1,500 for the affair.[26]

Bunny hurriedly transported his band from Philadelphia to Worcester, Massachusetts the next day, to play another New Year's party. Clyde Rounds reported what happened:

Worcester is more than 350 miles away from Philadelphia, but we took that double date on account of the state of Massachusetts' 'blue laws' affecting Sunday entertainment. So the party couldn't begin until exactly one minute after midnight on Sunday! We were all pretty exhausted by then and I guess that was what finally made me decide to get off the road once and for all! I'd told Bunny that I was thinking of quitting, but he asked me to stay on to help break in the new men, including George Johnston, who took over the second trumpet chair so that Jake Koven could play third. Larry Walsh came in as my replacement and Vic Hauprich, an old friend of Bunny's from Wisconsin, joined on lead alto sax. Phil Sillman had the unenviable job of taking Buddy Rich's drum chair and Andy Phillips came in mainly to do some arranging, but also to fill in on guitar occasionally. Although Bunny was still capable of playing great horn, he didn't seem to generate the inspiration I remembered from earlier days, perhaps because of his high alcohol intake, plus having to settle for less experienced and maybe inferior musicians. Also, he was having problems meeting the weekly payroll and getting himself deeper and deeper in debt.[27]

The Berigan band then played some other one-nighters, including one at the Flatbush Theater in Brooklyn. Ray Conniff recalled that engagement: "I remember that date particularly because Bunny had some pains in his chest and thought he'd had a heart attack! He swore to us that his heart had stopped, but I guess he was just about completely exhausted from all his troubles. He was drinking more than ever and we seemed to be permanently traveling, short of sleep and proper meals, and he had plenty of money worries. Anyway, it scared him into going on the wagon for the next six weeks!"[28] I am skeptical that Bunny could have stopped drinking for six weeks. That would have involved him going through withdrawal, and he simply would not have been able to do that and continue to lead his band day-to-day on the road.

Tenor saxophonist Larry Walsh, who replaced Clyde Rounds, later provided some details of what he found upon joining the Berigan band:

> When I first joined the band, we were mostly traveling by bus, which was rented from Greyhound, but later we used our own cars. Jake Koven and I were the usual passengers in Joe Bushkin's Pontiac 2-door sedan, while Bunny drove a 1938 Buick Roadmaster with Kitty Lane, Jerry Johnson and a couple of the boys as passengers. Bob Jenney drove a Ford and 'Big Gate' drove the instrument truck, which was a 3/4-ton Dodge panel truck. Most of the single fellows tended to hang out together, but there weren't really any exclusive cliques. When Bunny got back on the booze again, he was knocking back at least a fifth of cheap whisky a day, but you would almost never see him stagger! He was generally very easy-going and slow to anger, but you always knew if he was getting mad, because his voice would pitch higher and higher! The morale of the band was pretty low on one-nighters, but would pick up quite a bit on our few longer engagements. My first official date was at New York's Roseland Ballroom, although I'd been rehearsing with the band for a couple of weeks before, learning the book with the help of Clyde Rounds. The Forrest Hotel was the band's headquarters, but Bunny and Donna had an apartment in the Central Park West area.[29]

George T. Simon, who very frequently was critical and negative in his opinions regarding Bunny's playing and his band, included this bit of insight in the January 1939 issue of *Metronome:* "Bunny Berigan, while always threatening to go someplace, reached no heights at all and towards the end of the year (1938) was still reorganizing in the hope of getting someplace near where he deserves to be."[30] In spite of Simon's frequent critical blasts against Berigan in *Metronome,* its readers voted Bunny into the 1939 *Metronome* "All Star Band," which was scheduled to make a record. On January 12, Berigan would record with this elite (but all white) group of jazz musicians. But before that could happen, Bunny had to take care of some old business.

As a result of the mistake MCA had made in the Berigan band's itinerary the previous September, Bunny and his boys showed up at the Lake Compounce Ballroom in Bristol, Connecticut, on the same night as Gene Krupa's band. Both bands were booked by MCA and both were managed by Arthur Michaud. Berigan should have been sent by MCA to the Pleasure Beach Ballroom in *Bridgeport,* Connecticut. The foul-up was not Bunny's fault. The net result of this mistake, however, was that Bunny received a lot of bad publicity, lost the income from the Bridgeport gig, and incurred the wrath of the operators of the Pleasure Beach Ballroom in Bridgeport for the blown gig. They evidently initiated legal action against Berigan to recoup the losses they sustained as a result of this incident. When he and his band were booked into the Ritz Ballroom, which was also in Bridgeport, Connecticut, on Sunday January 8, 1939, the local sheriff was there waiting for him. As usual, the trade press had a field day: *Down Beat* reported that:

> Bunny Berigan and his new band, on a one-nighter at the Ritz Ballroom here, set a record for this town. But it wasn't in attendance, because the Monday daily papers carried the story of the date. And the reason? Bunny was greeted by the sheriff and presented with a bill for over $100 which he still owed the city. It all started when Berigan failed to show up until 10:30 p.m. for the Labor Day dance at city owned Pleasure Beach Ballroom. A mix-up in bookings sent Berigan to Bristol, where Gene Krupa was playing and so the city wanted the money that had been spent for advertising the affair. Bunny agreed to pay, but up to Sunday had not done so. Knowing he was due at the Ritz, the sheriff was sent out to get the money and did. Now everyone is satisfied and the incident can be marked closed, but I'll bet it is the first time that any bandleader was greeted by the sheriff instead of the jitterbugs.[31]

Billboard gave the incident similar play:

> On this date, Bunny Berigan is forced to pay $117 to the city of Bridgeport, Connecticut. The amount owed to the city was for advance and miscellaneous preparations for the dance Bunny was scheduled to play last September at Pleasure Beach Ballroom. On that date, due to a misunderstanding, the band arrived in Bridgeport only after patrons' money had been refunded and the ballroom closed. The city claimed damages, which Berigan agreed to pay but had not done so. When Bunny was scheduled to play Bridgeport again, city comptroller Perry Rodman had a writ drawn up and the sheriff on hand to make sure the city got its money.[32]

For the second time, Berigan was publicly embarrassed by a fiasco that he did not cause. Nevertheless, he took the bad publicity, paid for someone else's mistake, which he could ill afford to do, and soldiered on.

On January 12, 1939, at 1:18 a.m., Bunny Berigan walked into RCA Victor's Twenty-fourth Street recording studio in Manhattan. In the studio already were Arthur Rollini, Jack Teagarden, Charlie Spivak, Carmen Mastren, Mr. and Mrs. Hymie Schertzer, Benny Goodman, and Harry James. Shortly after, Tommy Dorsey, his manager Bobby Burns, lawyer John Gluskin (who was also a business partner of Arthur Michaud's), and recording supervisor Eli Oberstein arrived. Also in the studio was George T. Simon, the editor of *Metronome* magazine (which sponsored the date), who in the previous two years had never missed an opportunity to report anything negative about Berigan and/or his orchestra. One can reasonably conclude that Bunny would have had some ill will toward Simon. But despite the almost nonstop lambastings Simon had given Berigan in the pages of *Metronome,* enough of that publication's readers thought enough of Bunny Berigan's playing to vote him into the 1939 *Metronome* All Star band. Even though Bunny probably would have liked to have told Simon that he thought he was an unfair little weasel, he did no such thing. He simply came in and performed as the quintessential professional he was. The rest of the musicians selected for the date, including trumpeter Sonny Dunham and four men from the Bob Crosby band (Simon's favorite in the 1930s), arrived late. The four Crosby musicians were nevertheless fine players: bassist Bob Haggart, tenor saxophonist Eddie Miller, pianist Bob Zurke (who had problems with alcoholism not unlike Berigan's), and drummer Ray Bauduc. The Crosby musicians, *sans* Zurke, entered the studio at 2:08 a.m. Zurke finally appeared at 2:21. At that point, Bunny Berigan had been in the studio for over an hour.[33]

Bunny had every reason to be apprehensive about this date. He undoubtedly had no idea what Simon had in mind, and had to feel a bit of a twinge knowing that the other three trumpeters on the session, Charlie Spivak, Sonny Dunham, and especially Harry James, were each masters of their instrument, who undoubtedly would play well. Spivak was a lead trumpeter, so it was assumed that he would play lead. Dunham was a soloist specializing in forays into the high register of the trumpet that were not necessarily done with the utmost of musical taste. He was not an especially convincing jazz player. Harry James at that time was a superb lead trumpeter, and also a spectacular and often compelling jazz soloist. In terms of sheer technique, there was no trumpet player in 1939 who could surpass Harry James. Although Simon did not reveal how it was decided who would solo at which point on each of the two tunes recorded that night, I will speculate that since the arrangement on "Blue Lou," used by both Tommy Dorsey's and Benny Goodman's bands (the first tune recorded), was used as the basic road map for the performance of that tune, and Tommy led the band through the recording of it,[34] TD had some input as to who would solo and where.

The musicians started to rehearse "Blue Lou" at approximately 2:22 a.m. Choruses were assigned at 2:40, and a test was made at 2:45. After the band listened to the playback, it was decided to make another test. This was done at 2:55, but it was still not acceptable. Dorsey was leading the musicians through all of this, and making minor revisions to the arrangement as they went on. A third test was made at 3:08, and it was much better. The first master was attempted at 3:18; a second at 3:25; and a third at 3:29, which was marred by clinkers. The final master was made at 3:30, and this is the recording of "Blue Lou" that has been released and rereleased dozens of times since 1939.[35]

This recording of Edgar Sampson's tune is certainly among the best. The solos, in order, are by Berigan, Teagarden, Miller, Dunham, Goodman (who also played third alto in the sax section on a borrowed horn), Zurke, Bauduc, and then some parting thoughts by Berigan. These solos reveal that all of the featured musicians were excellent soloists, and when compared with the solos on the alternate takes, show that they were very comfortable improvising. On the issued take, the most fascinating comparison to be made however is in the jazz solos of the trumpeters Berigan and Dunham. Berigan's sixteen swaggering bars are quintessential: he covers much of the range of his instrument, his sound is fat and round, even in the highest register, his jazz ideas are cogent, and his solo is suffused, bar by bar, with the feeling that anything might happen. There is nevertheless a very keen musical intelligence informing this solo.

Berigan charges in with a typically long-lined, shapely four-bar phrase. An aggressive edge adds intensity to his tone, and when he shouts out his high D to open the second extended phrase, the sheer size of the sound seems about to overload the microphone. He rounds out his half-chorus solo with another pair of phrases. The first one dwells for a while on some almost growled blue minor thirds, accentuating the rather tough-minded mood of the solo. Then, in another leap to his high register, he concludes with a descending phrase of considerable eloquence. Dunham, taking it from the bridge, tries to equal Berigan, opening with a long middle-register exposition before leaping to his high register for a climax. His spectacular high-note playing on trumpet and trombone with the Casa Loma orchestra had made him something of a celebrity, but here he cannot compete: he lacks the full, compelling Berigan tone and overriding sense of purpose and form.[36]

The progress of the development of the solos shown by the alternate takes reveals that Bunny was listening carefully to the way Dunham was organizing his solo, and then, when it came time to make the master, used all of that information to completely upstage Dunham. He in no way copied what Dunham had played. He simply *distilled* Dunham's approach, which was to challenge Berigan, and turned it around and used it to cut Sonny. As Sudhalter correctly observed, Bunny was definitely in the mood for combat that night: "It's an affirmation, like a prizefighter who's been on the ropes a time or two bringing his gloves together over his head to proclaim, 'See, I'm still the champ.'"[37]

I have often wondered what Sonny Dunham was thinking immediately after he heard Berigan play the solo that is on the issued record. Most likely, it was, what am I going to play after *that?*

Forty-two years later, George T. Simon made this comment about Bunny Berigan's participation at the recording date that produced this version of "Blue Lou": "All the musicians worshipped this guy. And that night he was in fine shape. No problems at all. He just pitched in—and played great."[38] It is too bad that Simon could not have said this while Bunny was struggling to keep his band together in early 1939, or indeed while Bunny was still living. He certainly could have used some good press.

Berigan returned to his band hoping that some good publicity would come out of his participation in the *Metronome* All Star record date. The Berigan band played at Princeton University on January 13, Temple University on the 14th, and La Fayette College in Easton, Pennsylvania on the 17th.

Sometime in the fall of 1938, a series of disturbing incidents relating to the Berigan daughters occurred. They set in motion a number of reactions by Bunny which were directed to improving the ongoing care of his daughters, Pat, now seven, and Joyce, three. In the wake of the initial separation of Donna from Bunny, which started in the spring of 1938 after Donna confronted him about his liaison with Lee Wiley, Donna took the girls to live with her in Syracuse, New

York, her hometown. This arrangement evidently lasted for only a few months because Donna was bored living in Syracuse with the girls. By late in the summer, she was spending a considerable amount of time with Bunny and the band on the road. During these times, she put the girls in places described by Patricia Berigan as "foster homes," probably in the Queens section of New York City. Donna asked her (and Bunny's) friend Kay Altpeter, the wife of trombonist Larry Altpeter, who lived nearby, to look in on the girls periodically and let her know how they were doing. On one such visit, Kay discovered what Patricia described as "child abuse" of little Jo. Kay notified Bunny and Donna of this, and an irate Bunny immediately returned to New York from wherever he was with his band, removed the girls from this home, and began searching, with Donna, for another place for them to stay while he and Donna were together on tour with the band. He was not satisfied with any of the places he visited, and told Donna that she would have to remain at home with the girls until he had time to find a place for them to stay whenever Donna chose to join Bunny on the road. He then returned to his band.

This development caused Donna to become very resentful. By the time Bunny came home for the holidays at the end of 1938, she was drinking too much, and was strung out emotionally. The atmosphere in the Berigan home, which had never been nurturing for the girls, or well organized, was now nearing crisis. Pat later stated that Donna was not a loving mother, and did not in any way enjoy staying at home to care for her and Jo. Indeed, when Donna drank too much, which she was now doing more often, she would berate the girls to such an extent that they hid from her to get away from her rages. When the girls told Bunny about this, he confronted Donna and there was a major blowup between them. With the girls cowering in a hiding place watching and crying, a hysterical Donna grabbed a butcher knife and came at Bunny with it. He was somehow able to deflect the assault, but she refused to put down the knife. He then told her to go ahead and stab him. As she came at him a second time, little Patty appeared and said, "Don't hurt Daddy!" A dim light-bulb of reason then switched on in Donna's addled mind. Instead of stabbing Bunny, she hurled the knife to the floor, and began screaming imprecations at him.

In the wake of this emotional upheaval, Bunny recognized that the 1938 holiday season was not filled with joy at the Berigan home. So in his own modest way, he tried to bring a little Christmas cheer to his daughters. He obtained Christmas cards, and with Pat and Joyce, signed each one himself, and then helped the girls to also "sign" them. Almost fifty years later, Patricia Berigan fondly recalled this. Bunny's girls were his "princesses" and he was never without a photo of them in his wallet, which he would proudly display to whoever asked him about his daughters. They both knew that he loved them.[39]

Seeing firsthand what was going on between Donna and their daughters, Bunny discussed this disturbing situation on the phone with his parents. Having observed Donna at close range and for extended periods of time, they weren't surprised about her inability to be an effective mother, but they were, of course, shocked by the incident of child abuse. Bunny and his parents then devised the plan whereby Cap and Mayme would come to New York from Fox Lake to live in the Berigan house with Donna and the girls. Then, whenever Donna chose to join Bunny on tour, at least Pat and Jo would be well cared for by their grandparents.

This *modus vivendi* could not have been very pleasing for Donna, but then she always had had some difficulty functioning as a mother for her daughters, and now was expressing her resentment openly and creating an emotionally harmful situation for the girls. I strongly suspect that this living arrangement is what hardened Donna's dislike for Cap Berigan who, unlike Mayme, was very blunt in his criticisms of Donna. It is unclear *where* the Berigan family was then living. It is quite possible that Bunny's strained finances had by this time (early 1939) caused him to give up the apartment he had maintained for the past couple of years on Central Park West. Presumably, the Berigans still occupied the home in Rego Park, and that is probably where the family lived in the winter and spring of 1939. This uneasy arrangement continued until early May, when Cap joined Bunny and the band on tour, acting as road manager or assistant road manager, and the distaff side of the family went to Fox Lake.

In the midst of this family turmoil, Bunny was still attempting to reconstruct his band. He finally found a drummer who satisfied him, twenty-one year old Eddie Jenkins. Jenkins joined the Berigan band in time for its January 19 engagement in Scranton, Pennsylvania. It is through Jenkins's journal, which was published originally in *The Mississippi Rag*[40] in February 1983, that we know much of the detail of what the Berigan band was doing over the next three months. Jenkins's journal entries were cross-checked by the White researchers with contemporary press reports and found to be very accurate. Jenkins recalled how he came to join Bunny's band:

> A friend of mine called George Stacy was Bunny Berigan's former road manager and he must have mentioned my name at some time, because I got a call asking me if I'd be interested in trying out for the band. Apparently, they were going on the road and the drummer, Phil Sillman, wanted to stay in New York. When I auditioned, it was only with the saxes as the others had been given a break to work over some new charts. We started and stopped several times, seldom playing anything from beginning to end. Vic Hauprich, an old friend of Bunny's, had just joined on lead alto and there were one or two other drummers there. I didn't really feel as though I'd been given much opportunity to do my stuff. However, a few days later, I got another call telling me to pack my bag and be at the Forrest Hotel on West Forty-ninth Street the next morning. I was there with bells on![41]

The band once again hit the road, playing a dance job at Carbondale Casino, Scranton, Pennsylvania on January 19. It was here that Bunny first encountered the young man who would become his most impressive male vocalist, Danny Richards:

> I was born Donato Ricciardi in 1919 in Scranton, Pennsylvania. I began singing at age 14 around in Scranton night spots with a 'rippling rhythm' type band,

Freddy Cariati's orchestra. Later, circa 1937–38, I took over the band. I'd been singing with my own band in Scranton and I went down to the Casino, where Bunny's band was playing. I got acquainted with Bunny and learned that Dick Wharton, his guitarist and vocalist, was on notice.[42]

Richards would join the Berigan band a short time later.

By this time, MCA's one-nighter "dartboard" was being used to book the Berigan band. From Scranton, their caravan of automobiles headed north to Kingston, Ontario for a gig at Queens College on the 20th, then on to the Graystone Ballroom in Detroit for a dance on the 22nd. They were off on the 23rd, which was a Monday, then played a one-nighter at the Coliseum Ballroom in Lorain, Ohio on the 24th. From there, they returned to Pennsylvania, where this wild goose chase had begun only the week before. Eddie Jenkins recalled the trip from Lorain to Bradford, Pennsylvania:

That was a bitterly cold night and after we'd finished the job, we set off for Bradford, Pennsylvania. During that long journey, we ran into a blizzard and one of the cars ran into another vehicle that had been abandoned in the snow. Bob Jenney and another of the boys were injured and required medical attention. Our car, which carried manager Jerry Johnson, singer Kitty Lane, Don Lodice and me, had skidded and spun round in a circle at one point. The band had no drum 'book,' to speak of. I took my cues from Hank Wayland's hand until I became familiar with the arrangements.[43]

The collision referred to by Eddie Jenkins, which occurred in Corry, Pennsylvania, was newsworthy enough to be reported in the Uniontown, Pennsylvania, *Morning Herald* on January 27: "Suffering bruises and cuts were Ray Conniff, driver and trombone; Frederick Wayland, bass; Larry Walsh, sax; Joe Bushkin, piano; and Bob Jenney, trombone."[44]

Bunny's band at last had another theater engagement, at Shea's Theater in Bradford, Pennsylvania, on the 25th, playing four shows. It was there that Danny Richards replaced Dick Wharton. Wharton remembered:

I left the band on good terms at Bradford, Pennsylvania and joined Vincent Lopez. Betty Hutton was with him then and it seemed like a good move. Bunny was not much of a 'stage personality,' like Tommy Dorsey. He never 'led' much—he would start a tune and the rest of it was on the music. His teeth were very dark; he smoked cigarettes right down to the very end, yet he didn't seem to worry about his teeth, as far as I could see.[45]

Danny Richards added a few more details:

I joined the band on this date, and my first experience was having to sit in Bob Jenney's chair in the trombone section, and pretend to play! Bob had been hurt in an auto accident on the way to the job and wasn't able to play, so I just moved the slide up and down as though I were playing the instrument. However, I didn't have to pretend when Bunny called me out front to sing. The first number I sang with Bunny was 'Change Partners.' I'll never forget the thrill.[46]

After doing the four shows at Bradford, it was on the road again and back to Ontario, this time to Toronto and the Royal York Hotel for a single-night dance date. Eddie Jenkins had warm memories of that date: "'We played some memorable dates in Canada, where the people were all really marvelous and just couldn't do enough for us. The Royal York Hotel was the venue for Toronto's medical college ball. There was a Canadian customs officer who accompanied us to the job and then back to the U.S. border, to make sure we hadn't sold any of our horns in Canada!"[47]

The newly constituted Berigan band now included the following personnel: Johnny Napton (lead), George Johnston, and Jake Koven, trumpets; Ray Conniff (lead and jazz) and Bob Jenney, trombones; Vic Hauprich, lead alto, Gus Bivona, jazz alto and clarinet; Don Lodice (jazz) and Larry Walsh, tenors; Joe Bushkin, piano; Hank Wayland, bass; Eddie Jenkins, drums; Kathleen Lane and Danny Richards, vocals. The bulk of the band's arrangements now came from Andy Phillips, with Ray Conniff contributing more and more jazz originals. Jerry Johnson (Ms. Lane's husband), was the road manager. Bernie Mackey was no longer assisting Robert "Little Gate" Walker, the band's equipment manager, but Little Gate had acquired another assistant.

This new lineup was different in a number of ways, the most important of which was that Bunny now had a three-man trumpet section, *without* his trumpet. One cannot imagine how taxing it must have been for Berigan to have played all of the solo trumpet in the band over the previous two years, and then to have played an enormous amount of lead trumpet in the brass section as well. Now he had the luxury to play the solos, which in this band was extremely demanding, and then play in the section only when he thought a little extra zing was needed there, but not always. The additional trumpet was initially financed by the temporary elimination of the guitar. Even though arranger Andy Phillips would occasionally appear with the band playing guitar, he was not in the band often. He usually remained in New York to supply the band with arrangements on current pop tunes.

Bunny's band now had two excellent vocalists. Kathleen Lane had had experience before her stint with Berigan, mainly with Glenn Miller. In addition to being a fine singer, she was an extremely attractive young woman with a great figure. She was equally adept presenting ballads and rhythm tunes. Danny Richards had no name band experience, but he was a very musicianly singer who sang on pitch, and had splendid vocal equipment, and good range. He sang the romantic ballads. Both of these singers were big assets to Bunny's band in the early months of 1939. By February 1, the Berigan band had been completely reorganized, and upon returning to New York, could easily have recorded successfully for Victor. Nevertheless, no recording dates were forthcoming. Instead, one-nighters piled up: January 27, at the National Guard Armory in Oneida, New York; on the 28th, at the Valencia Ballroom, York, Pennsylvania; on the 29th, at Manhattan Center, New York City; the 30th, at Westchester County Center, White Plains, New York.

On Tuesday, January 31, 1939, the Berigan band opened at the Southland Club in Boston for a week's engagement. They were billeted at Boston's number one musicians' hotel, the Avery. Eddie Jenkins, the new kid in the band, discreetly recalled the Avery: "After another dreadful drive through blizzard conditions, we all checked in at the Avery Hotel in Boston. It was a well-known hangout for visiting musicians who were working in the area. Needless to say, there were plenty of stories about crazy goings-on there, and it became known among musicians as the 'Ovary' Hotel."[48] It was at this time, according to Andy Phillips, that Joe Bushkin created quite a sensation by launching fireworks sky-rockets from a bathtub in the Avery Hotel through an open window into the still of the Boston night at 4:00 a.m. Berigan himself was in Bushkin's room with several other band members urging Joe to "shoot off one more," when a visit from the house detective, and a threat of immediate eviction from the hotel, brought the pyrotechnic display to an end.

As we have seen, Massachusetts, like several other states then, had "blue laws" which prevented live entertainment on Sundays. So when Sunday, February 5 arrived, MCA made sure that the Berigan band had not forgotten the back-breaking rigors of the road: they booked Bunny and his boys for a one-nighter at the Mosque Ballroom in Newark, New Jersey, after which they had to return to Boston to finish their week at the Southland. Once again, Eddie Jenkins provided the background:

> We drove to Newark on Sunday, because the Southland in Boston was shut in accordance with Massachusetts' so-called 'blue laws,' which prohibited such activities on Sundays. So, despite the distance and the inconvenience, which apparently meant nothing to the booking office, we had to make a quick round-trip to Newark. There was a consolation for me, however, when Mr. Avedis Zildjian, maker of the famous Zildjian cymbals, invited me to visit his factory, where I selected several new cymbals on the understanding that payment would be made through my New York retailer. But Mr. and Mrs. Zildjian came down to the Southland a couple of nights later and Bunny called me over to their table to be told that the cymbals were a gift![49]

The Berigan band's stay at the Southland was extremely successful. In fact, they had broken all attendance records at that venue.[50] But no matter how hard Bunny tried, no matter how well he and his band played, indeed, no matter how good business was where they played, it never seemed to be good enough. He simply could not keep ahead of his band's overhead.

In spite of the fact that Bunny's reorganized band was now playing very well (he had every reason to be quite happy with his new personnel), rumors, possibly started by MCA, began to circulate that he would soon rejoin Benny Goodman, replacing Harry James, who had just left Goodman to start his own band, that would operate under the management of Music Corporation of America. I wonder what Bunny thought when he started seeing or being informed about items like this in the trade press: "Rumored that Bunny Berigan may give up band and take Harry James's place with Benny Goodman."[51] Berigan had recently parted company with Arthur Michaud because of Michaud's numerous conflicts of interest, which had on more than one occasion placed him and his band in bad (and costly) positions. He undoubtedly realized that the same was true with MCA, which seemed more and more to be relegating him to a minor league status. That was bad enough when Bunny's in-house MCA competition was Gene Krupa. But Gene's band was built around his drumming, so to some extent at least, the two bands were selling a slightly different swing product. Now, MCA was also using Harry James, whose hot trumpet calling card was the same as Bunny's, to compete for the same gigs that the Berigan band had been getting in 1937 and 1938. There were only a finite number of good engagements for top grade big bands, and by 1939, those gigs were increasingly not going to Bunny Berigan.

Indeed, it seems that by early 1939, MCA had come to the conclusion that Berigan was now incapable of handling a lucrative one-week engagement at a major theater, playing four or five shows a day. They reasoned that if he was drunk on a one-nighter, and either could not play well or at all, then the damage would be relatively small. At a theater, the financial risks to MCA would be much greater. Since Bunny no longer had a personal manager to advocate on his behalf with MCA, the agency simply booked his band as it saw fit. Consequently, Berigan and his band, no matter how good or bad, would henceforth be booked by MCA almost exclusively for one-nighters. In that way, MCA would continue to make money off of the band with relatively little risk for the agency. The inevitable adverse consequences that would flow from this business arrangement would fall squarely upon Berigan, and he probably understood this to some degree. Nevertheless, Bunny had repeatedly made it clear to his handlers at MCA that he was *not* going to give up his band. Bunny Berigan was a very stubborn/willful/tenacious person. So, MCA allowed him to play out the string with indifferent (at best) support from the agency. It is possible that by early 1939 MCA's operatives were making book on how long it would take before Bunny and/or his band would implode.

After a successful run at the Southland, the Berigan band was once again scheduled to play a string of one-night engagements throughout the eastern United States. Probably because of the cold and snowy weather, a date in Charlottesville, Virginia (February 9) was cancelled. On the 10th and 11th, Bunny played at Virginia Polytech Institute in Blacksburg, VA. Vic Hauprich, who had been playing lead alto, became ill, and subs were used until a permanent replacement could be found. I am of the opinion that at this time, Gus Bivona, who had been a member of the Berigan band for six months, took over the first alto chair, in addition to continuing to play jazz on both alto saxophone and clarinet. Shortly after this, Henry Saltman joined the band playing alto. He may have played first alto at times, but Bivona undoubtedly played first alto at least some (and probably most) of the time.[52]

The one-nighters continued: "February 12, Keith's Ballroom, Baltimore; the 13th, Webster Hall, New York City; off on the 14th; the date at Berwick, Pennsylvania on the 15th, cancelled due to bad roads; 16th, Mealey's Auditorium,

Allentown, Pennsylvania."[53]. It was at this last gig that two men who would figure prominently in Bunny's later bands would encounter him. George Quinty
(lead alto sax with Berigan's 1941-1942 band): "Don Palmer (who would become Bunny's personal manager in July, 1941) and I drove up from Trenton to
see Bunny on this date. Don was related to Don Lodice. I may have met Bunny
very briefly at this time; I'm not sure."[54]

The next night, the Berigan band played at the prep school in Andover, Massachusetts. And so it went.

Eddie Jenkins later recalled life on the road with the Berigan band during
those weeks:

> On a night when the band was in rare form, Bunny would give most of the guys a
> chance to play a chorus and I think he often got more out of his men than maybe
> a strict disciplinarian like Glenn Miller might have. But it was in the realm of
> business organization that he took a beating. The agents exploited him to the full,
> as I'm sure did many of the ballroom operators. Since most of our dates were
> one-nighters, we barely had time to get checked into a hotel before we were leav-
> ing for the next job. So the only socializing would take place at a diner en route
> to the next engagement, usually in the small hours of the morning! Don Lodice
> and I often rode in the same car with road manager Jerry Johnson and his wife,
> singer Kitty Lane. We'd try to plug the cracks in the rear doors with old newspa-
> pers to keep out the cold drafts. We carried a portable phonograph balanced on
> our knees to lessen the vibration and listened to Count Basie records, especially
> 'Blue and Sentimental' with Herschel Evans's fabulous tenor solo.[55]

More one-nighters in New England followed until the band was informed
that MCA had lined up a series of dates in the south, to commence on February
24, at Virginia Military Academy in Blacksburg, Virginia. This news was no
doubt greeted by cheers of joy from the bedraggled and exhausted Berigan
sidemen because it meant they would soon be leaving the frigid northern states
and their ice-and-snow-covered roads, and heading into much warmer temperatures. From Virginia, the Berigan troupe headed further south, playing at the
University of Alabama at Tuscaloosa, on February 27–28; then to the Capitol
Theater in Macon, Georgia on March 1 (from which they made one of their now
rare radio broadcasts); the County Armory in Jacksonville, Florida on the 2nd;
and at the University of Florida at Gainesville on the 3rd and 4th. On Sunday
March 5, they arrived at Daytona Beach, and enjoyed a day off. According to
Jenkins's diary, some of the guys played golf and swam during the day, then
went to nightclubs that evening.

On Monday, March 6, they played at the Pier Casino in Daytona Beach. Despite the backbreaking traveling and work the Berigan band was doing, there
was still a good deal of hilarity in the band, with Bunny contributing more than
his share, often convulsing the sidemen with his humorous remarks delivered
with an imitation of W. C. Fields. Gus Bivona was another clown, and he later
recalled doing some "press agent" work for the band involving a lovely young
lady reporter covering the Daytona Beach gig:

That date was for the 5th Annual Junior Service League's Ball and we were being pestered by a local gal reporter called Florence Pepper. Eventually, we got so fed up that we concocted a phony story that was 100% bullshit! We did it to get rid of her. Here is the story: 'Bunny Berigan thinks jitterbugs are too noisy. The famed trumpet-leader likes sweet music and does some of his own arranging. Also arranging are Ray Conniff and Gus Bivona, members of the orchestra, and Joe Lippman, Andy Phillips and Jake Zarombie, New York arrangers. Berigan also composes numbers. His newest, yet to be published, is 'Easy to Find and Hard to Lose.' In collaboration with Bivona, he has written 'Gus Bivona Blues.' Bivona, a sax player in the orchestra, is a replica of William Powell[56] and plans to go to Hollywood to play a stand-in for the actor. An expert surfboard rider, he will be filmed in surfing sequences. Berigan's wife and two infant daughters did not accompany him on this trip. They are vacationing in Canada.' As Bivona was recounting this tale, he added: I'd never been on a surfboard in my life! I guess we really took that lady reporter for a ride! By the way, 'Jake Zarombie' was a name invented by Bunny, which he used as a gag or a brush-off, when somebody recognized him and he didn't want to be disturbed.[57]

At about this same time, Bunny's real public relations department, probably an office boy at MCA's New York office, produced a story that was designed to counteract the rumors that he would soon be disbanding. Here it is:

Berigan's going to join Goodman. That's what the crowd was saying two months ago when Bunny let several of his men go. Others claimed Bunny was planning to organize a 'chamber group' and try something new in the way of swing trumpeting. But Bunny fooled us all. He went out and got new men and a new girl singer in the person of Kathleen Lane and now he's back on the stand with a new band, which, in a few more weeks, Bunny and his men are convinced will be the best Berigan has ever assembled. The new combo includes 15 pieces: Gus Bivona, Vic Hauprich, Don Lodice and Larry Walsh, saxes; Bob Jenney and Ray Conniff, trombones; Johnny Napton, Jake Koven and George Johnston, trumpets; Hank Wayland, bass; Eddie Jenkins, drums; Andy Phillips, guitar; Joe Bushkin, piano; Miss Lane and Danny Richards, vocals and Joe Lippman and Andy Phillips, arrangers. Bunny, of course, makes it a 4-way trumpet section. Several factors point to the security of the band's future. One is that it's the most loyal gang Bunny's had. Another is the presence of Wayland, Bushkin and Jenkins in the rhythm section. Wayland and Bushkin are proven men, but Jenkins, a youngster, is the man to watch. He's young, but he is constantly improving and he plays good, solid drums. Don Lodice on tenor is about as good as Georgie Auld, but doesn't have Georgie's bite. Bivona's clarineting is exciting and his alto work is excellent. 'I'm tired of just making a living,' Bunny said recently, 'and I want the best band in the country.' It looks as if he's on his way.[58]

The story was accompanied by a photo of Bunny and Bob Jenney, and is captioned "Berigan Fools All: New Band Despite Talk Is The Best Yet." This was not just press-agent puffery: this edition of the Berigan band was quickly coming into its own as one of the more powerful and swinging bands on the scene in early 1939.

The gig in Daytona Beach received some press coverage: "Bunny Berigan's torrid tunes proved conclusively his right to the title, 'Hottest Man in Town.' Sparkling gaily-colored lights and a high revolving rainbow-hued ball trembled as the blasts from Bunny's trumpet reached the ceiling and bounced back to tickle the toes of the dancers attired in the smartest and loveliest of evening gowns. True to his word that he had the loudest band extant, Bunny was aided by the pier's peculiarly amplifying acoustics."[59]

The Berigan bandsmen were booked to play the following day in Columbus, Georgia, but before they drove there from Daytona Beach, MCA notified them that the gig had been cancelled. Larry Walsh recalled this incident: "Bunny never seemed to worry about anything. We had that date at Daytona Beach and we were supposed to go from there to the Royal Theater in Columbus, Georgia, but for some reason or other that job was canceled. Bunny didn't seem to care, so we took a vote and decided to have another day at the beach and get some sun."[60] This small holiday, like all off days, reduced Bunny's income, while the expense side of the ledger, principally his sidemen's salaries, kept accruing. Off days were slowly putting Bunny in a deep hole financially. The band then moved to their next engagement at the City Auditorium in Birmingham, Alabama, on March 8, followed by a gig at the Shrine Mosque in Atlanta, Georgia, on the 9th. Hank Wayland remembered that night well: "The place was packed to the doors when we arrived. Soon, nobody was dancing at all! They pulled their chairs across the dance floor and around the bandstand and we proceeded to play them a five-hour concert! The crowd acclaimed Bunny all the way for his outstanding playing that night."[61]

The Berigan band's southern tour was now about to end. They played on Friday–Saturday, March 10–11 at Duke University, Durham, North Carolina, and then traveled back to New York. Hank Wayland recalled what was going on with the band's personnel and schedule at that time: "Bunny phoned an old friend from Madison, Wisconsin, Doc DeHaven, to be prepared to join the band in New York, because Hank Saltman had tendered his two weeks notice. The band returned to New York that weekend and reassembled at the Jane Grey studios at 1:00 p.m. on the following Tuesday, March 14, to rehearse for a Victor recording date the next day."[62]

In retrospect, we know that 1938 was the turning point in Bunny Berigan's career and life. It was in 1938 that the business side of his career reached a plateau, and then began its decline. The waning of Berigan's career was not precipitous, but it occurred somewhat ahead of the decline in his band, which happened as 1939 ended and 1940 began. In fact, Bunny Berigan and His Orchestra were a potent musical force throughout much of 1939. When Bunny and his musicians entered RCA Victor's New York recording studio on the Ides of March 1939, they were prepared to demonstrate just how well they were then playing. This session commenced at 1:30 p.m. and ran for five and a half hours, to 7:00 p.m. Six masters were made during that time.

"Patty Cake, Patty Cake (Baker Man)" is a rhythmic confection whipped up by Fats Waller, Andy Razaf, and J. C. Johnson. Fats himself had recorded a typical Waller version of this tune on December 7, 1938, which was released on RCA's Bluebird label. RCA Victor had an in-house rule that generally prevented different artists from recording the same tune to be released on the same label. Consequently, Bunny was allowed to make this recording, which was issued on the Victor label. (Another mystery surrounding Bunny's relationship with RCA Victor is why the company never switched his records at some point from the seventy-five cent Victor label to the thirty-five cent Bluebird label. The vast majority of Berigan's fans were swing-oriented young people who found it difficult to scrape together the seventy-five cents necessary to purchase one of his Victor discs during the economic Depression of the late 1930s. These were the same kids who in 1939 were making Artie Shaw and Glenn Miller so successful on Bluebird. I suspect that such a move by Victor would have enhanced Bunny's record sales and helped his band's popularity.)[63]

The Berigan version of "Patty Cake" was arranged by Andy Phillips and sung by Kathleen Lane. Ms. Lane's performance here gives us some idea of just how good a singer she was—this lady could sing *and* swing. Her vocal chorus on this novelty tune is a delight. The band plays with unity, power, and spirit. The soloists are Don Lodice on tenor; Joe Bushkin on piano; Gus Bivona on alto; and Bunny, painting his musical picture here with broad strokes. The expanded brass section, with Johnny Napton on first trumpet, is noticeably more potent that it had been previously.

"Jazz Me Blues" is another chestnut (composed in 1921 by Tom Delaney and played by the Original Dixieland Jass Band) that Berigan asked Joe Lippman (who was by this time working as a freelance arranger) to write an arrangement on. The intro builds behind Bunny's growling, plunger-muted trumpet; then the band romps on into the first chorus. Young drummer Eddie Jenkins plays a modified backbeat behind solos by Lodice and Bivona, providing cymbal splashes along the way. The two man trombone section, led by Ray Conniff, is more aggressive here, with three trumpets to play against. Bunny's muscular solo is well supported by Jenkins's backbeats.

"Y'Had It Coming to You" is a bit of pop ephemera composed by Ben Oakland with lyrics by (would you believe?) Alan Jay Lerner. This was certainly one of Mr. Lerner's earliest and most modest efforts. Andy Phillips arranged it. The band marches into this song; then Mr. B. plays the melody in the first chorus with a mute that sounds like a Harmon mute that Bunny had altered in some way. Ms. Lane sings the lyric, investing it with a lot more vigor and sensuality than it deserved. After the vocal, the band shows just how well integrated a performing unit they were. Bunny on open trumpet, Lodice on tenor, and Conniff on trombone also have solo bits.

"There'll Be Some Changes Made" was a warhorse, even in 1939. It was also composed in 1921, by W. Benton Overstreet. This powerful exposition was charted by Andy Phillips, and opens with a lovely four-bar piano introduction by Joe Bushkin. Berigan, who rarely altered the arrangements written for his band, suggested this most effective touch. The reeds, led by Gus Bivona's alto saxophone, set forth the melody in the first chorus. Notice how much push Allan

Reuss's guitar provides here. Bunny hired him for this session only, having fore-gone a guitar in his band, at least temporarily in favor of another trumpet. Ray Conniff plays a trombone solo, followed by Bunny, who once again punches out his solo like a heavyweight boxer working out on the big punching bag. The Bivona-led (now on clarinet) reeds follow; then Don Lodice adds some punches of his own on his tenor saxophone. Bivona, on clarinet, plays a rather straight and quiet solo; then Bunny returns careening into his upper register. This is another very good Berigan record.

"Little Gate's Special," dedicated to the Berigan band's equipment manager, Robert "Little Gate" Walker, is a riffing original design on the blues composed and arranged by Ray Conniff. The band digs in here with some strutting swing, and exciting solos by Bushkin on piano (one chorus); Conniff on trombone (one chorus); Bivona on alto sax (two choruses); Larry Walsh on baritone sax (one chorus); Bunny on open trumpet, building excitement and telling a story (two choruses); and a wild foray on tenor sax by Don Lodice (two choruses). Then the band riffs, reeds against brass, riding Jenkins's heavy backbeats, and quiets down a bit as Bushkin's piano runs set up Bunny's vault into his high register for the exhilarating climax, answering the blazing brass with his open trumpet, only an octave higher. This chart, one of Ray Conniff's first successes, is a showcase for a string of jazz solos against shifting, bright, rhythmic back-grounds. It quickly became an audience favorite and a staple of the Berigan re-pertoire. "Little Gate's Special" is prime swing material, and it shows how deep-ly Conniff had been influenced by the Count Basie band.[64] It was now the tune Berigan wrapped up broadcasts with, supplanting "The Prisoner's Song."

"Gangbusters' Holiday" is another rhythmic Conniff original. Bushkin plays the band on, and then the brass and reeds riff against each other. Gus Bivona's lead alto is plainly discernable in the first chorus. Lodice is back for another frantic solo here, Jenkins's backbeats and cymbals behind him. Bivona (on cla-rinet) and Conniff then take good solos before Bunny makes a fiery statement on open trumpet. After this Berigan pops off high notes over the ensemble, before the band settles down for a bit of Bushkin's piano, and then the finish.

It should be noted at this juncture that even though Bunny Berigan never paid Ray Conniff for the arrangements he did on "Little Gate's Special"[65] and "Gangbuster's Holiday" (a story Conniff told for sixty-plus years), *he did record them.* This, coupled with the fact that Bunny did *not* put his name on these Con-niff originals as a cocomposer, allowed Conniff to receive *all* of the composer royalties on the sale of these recordings for many, many years. Most bandleaders in the 1930s and 1940s routinely insisted that before they would record an origi-nal composition by members of their bands or arrangers they did business with, they be given co-composer credit. The result for the actual composer was that his composer royalty was suddenly and forever reduced from 100 percent to 50 percent. The reasoning was that this was payment to the bandleader for the great promotional push any original composition received as a result of it being rec-orded, especially by a popular band. In terms of abstract justice therefore, I think by Ray Conniff receiving 100 percent of the composer royalty instead of 50 percent, he was very well paid by Bunny for these two arrangements. Indeed, this could be regarded as yet another example of Berigan's deficiencies as a businessman. He certainly could have used the 50 percent composer royalty revenue.

Another excellent recording session by Bunny Berigan and His Orchestra had been completed. I cannot imagine that anyone connected with this session was anything but delighted with the six sides that that were recorded that day. The band was well rehearsed and it attacked the music with verve and enthusiasm. There was excellent singing from Kathleen Lane, and good, often exciting solos from the jazzmen in the band. Bunny's trumpet solos were exemplary. The arrangements were first-rate. In fact the band had more music to record that day, but they simply ran out of time.

Boy singer Danny Richards was very disappointed that he didn't get a chance to record something at this session:

> We were supposed to have recorded two more numbers on that date and I had the vocal on one, a tune called 'Blue Evening.' However, the number was canceled out, something to do with the fact that Bob Eberly had just recorded it with Jimmy Dorsey, I think. I was quite angry and talked about quitting. Bunny defused the situation, kidding me about being a 'hot headed wop' and told me I'd have another chance. We had a good laugh and true to his word, later (in 1942) I did make records with Bunny. Allen Reuss, the guitarist, was added just for the recording date, which was one of the first to be supervised by Leonard Joy, who was a friend of Bunny's. He had just taken over at Victor from Eli Oberstein, who had left to start his own record label.[66]

Unfortunately, circumstances would conspire against Danny Richards. Although he would spend over two years, off and on, as Bunny's vocalist, in that time he would record only two sides. This was truly regrettable because Richards, who approached ballads in much the same way as the tremendously successful Bob Eberly, was an exceptionally talented singer who was very popular with audiences. His voice on Berigan records would have had considerable commercial appeal. What no one could have known or imagined on March 15, 1939 was that Bunny Berigan and His Orchestra would make only three more commercial recording sessions, yielding only twelve more sides. Only the year before, they had completed eleven recording sessions for Victor, yielding forty-three issued sides.

This recording session came almost exactly two years after Bunny was initially signed by Victor Records. It has long been assumed that his Victor recording contract continued beyond March 15, 1939, because of the Victor recoding session he had at the end of November 1939. This assumption may be false. It is my belief that Berigan's contract with Victor could well have ended with the March 15 recording session, or shortly thereafter,[67] and because Bunny no longer had a personal manager with the clout of Arthur Michaud (indeed, he had *no* personal manager at the time), he could not get it renewed, nor could he hook-up with another label. At this critical time in the Berigan band's existence, no one was pushing hard, or perhaps at all, to get the band a new recording contract. The Victor recording session of November 28, 1939 (see chapter 20) appears for a number of reasons to have been a onetime deal, indeed, an afterthought. So for the next eight-plus months, the Berigan band made no commercial recordings. The ramifications of this for Bunny, both short term and long term, would prove to be disastrous.

The next day, March 16, the band was off, but Berigan may well have participated in a somewhat unusual recording project. Bunny apparently recorded a series of short solos accompanied by piano and drums, which were transcribed and published as part of a series of booklets under the title *All Star Series—Modern Rhythm Choruses*. They were published by the Leo Feist Company of New York and the originals sold for fifty cents. Each booklet contained the featured musician's version of ten tunes. The Berigan booklet contained "'Sleepy Time Gal," "Linger Awhile," "My Blue Heaven," "At Sundown," "Swingin' Down the Lane," "China Boy," "In a Little Spanish Town," "Sunday," "Darktown Strutters' Ball," and "Ja-Da." The first series was advertised for sale in May 1939 and included interpretations by Jack Teagarden, Chu Berry, Bobby Hackett, Harry James, Toots Mondello, Glenn Miller, Bud Freeman, and others. The Berigan booklet was part of a second series, first advertised for sale in August of 1939, which included versions by Pee Wee Russell, Woody Herman, Red Norvo, Charlie Barnet, Charlie Shavers and others. Later, other booklets were added; most all were still available as late as the 1970s. The recording date of the Berigan titles is unknown, but is assumed to have been in the early months of 1939. The recordings Berigan made seem to be the only examples, by any of the musicians who may have made similar recordings, to have been preserved.

Some sources have claimed that these recordings were made in the fall of 1940, and that the accompanists are Buddy Koss (piano) and Jack Maisel (drums), but these are erroneous. Although Koss thought he recalled the titles, he did not join the band until much later in 1939. Both the pianist and drummer on these recordings were probably provided by the series producer and had no direct connection with Berigan. Eddie Jenkins, who was Bunny's drummer in March of 1939, made no mention of this session in his diary, and Paul Collins, who replaced him, could recall nothing about this session.

The Berigan family had a collection of these recordings which included a number of ten-inch acetate recording discs, and they contained what appears to be a duplicate set of the four *Modern Rhythm Choruses*, plus versions of the other six titles in the series booklet. All ten of these titles have Bunny playing open trumpet with piano and drums. Three of the titles have a second or even a third shorter attempt. Possibly, the two sets of titles are connected and it may be that those issued in the 1970s on a Shoestring LP are remakes of an earlier attempt, but this is speculation, and the reverse may be true. The discs with these titles in the Berigan family collection have been well played and are very noisy. The first parts of some are very worn, and it may well be that an announcer is present, but cannot be heard as on those same recordings on LP. Nevertheless, some of the Berigan family set do in fact have an announcer.

From oral and written information on this series of discs it would seem that the *Rhythm* titles and at least one other were done at the same session, and that both Joe Lippman and Joe Bushkin were on hand, as well as Lee Wiley, who sings on one title. It would seem also to have been a rather informal session and on one title ("My Blue Heaven") there is talking including a female voice. Some of the piano is almost certainly played by Joe Bushkin, as for example on "At Sundown" and "Sunday." Yet other titles have full chorus piano solos which are almost certainly not Bushkin, and may be Joe Lippman. In fact one title in this set is noted as "Lippman plus B."

The discs in the Berigan family collection include two untitled Bushkin originals (one has an introduction much like that on the Muggsy Spanier recording of "Relaxing at the Touro," a tune that Bushkin helped Spanier to write), and a Lee Wiley vocal with Bushkin, but no Berigan on "You Leave Me Breathless."

If the above set of the *Rhythm Choruses* titles was recorded first, then a date of late 1938–early 1939 seems likely, as Joe Lippman was still connected to the Berigan band as an arranger, though Bushkin was playing with the band on gigs.[68]

While all of this activity was going on for Bunny Berigan, Artie Shaw was causing major waves in the accepted order of big band business. This item was in the March 11 issue of *Billboard*: "Since its release some 27 weeks ago, Artie Shaw's 'Begin the Beguine' has outsold every RCA popular record in the last 9 years! At some point, it may be the best seller since electrical recordings came in."[69] "When Eli Oberstein, who had guided Shaw's recording career, announced that he was leaving RCA Victor to start his own firm, Victor, to ensure against Artie following Eli, immediately offered Shaw an almost unheard-of guarantee of $100,000.00 minimum over a two year period. Artie accepted at once."[70] (We must remember that this figure must be multiplied by fifteen to approximate the value in today's dollars.) Shaw and his band, including former Berigan sidemen Buddy Rich, Georgie Auld, and Bernie Privin, were on fire. In addition to having "Begin the Beguine" going for them as a major hit record, and a sponsored network radio show, Shaw and his band had recently completed their residency at New York's Hotel Lincoln, from where they were broadcast over the NBC radio network very frequently, and had made a couple of movie shorts. They were now on tour, playing major theaters, and soon would head to Hollywood, to make a feature film for Metro-Goldwyn-Mayer.

Artie Shaw was being booked by General Artists Corporation (GAC), successor to Rockwell-O'Keefe. The advent of Artie Shaw as a major big band star had caught MCA by surprise. While MCA had no threat to their supremacy in the sweet band market, Shaw's rise immediately undercut Benny Goodman's primacy as the "King of Swing." Shaw's success at RCA Victor so disgusted Benny that he angrily terminated his contractual relationship with Victor in the spring of 1939. MCA then toured BG relentlessly throughout the spring and summer of 1939, to keep him in touch with his fans in the hinterlands. Benny went without a recording contract until August 1939, when as a result of the intervention of John Hammond, who was by then working for Columbia, he signed with that label.[71]

Shaw also had a personal attorney and a personal manager whose services he used to protect his interests from what he saw as the inherent conflict of interest that existed between himself and GAC. Shaw resented the practices of GAC, which were patterned after those developed and perfected by MCA, specifically using his band to sell other bands as a part of a package, and being booked on the road indiscriminately to maximize GAC's commissions, while at the same time maximizing his and his musicians' exhaustion, and his transportation costs. Shaw's attorney also extricated him from his business relationship with Si Schribman, which could have cost Artie dearly, because after success came to Shaw, Si, who had covered Artie's weekly cash shortfalls before his band achieved success with loans, took the position that he was a partner with Shaw in ownership of the band.[72] In short, Artie Shaw, like every other successful bandleader, had to have someone looking out solely for *his* interests. To his dying day, Shaw understood and could explain what is meant by the term *fiduciary relationship*. That is a major reason why despite several wrong turns in his career, he died a millionaire.

Bunny Berigan never had anyone whose sole responsibility it was to look out for *his* interests. It seems that all of his business associates were in a position to take personal advantage of the conflicts of interest that invariably existed in the business milieu of the big band world of the late 1930s. Bunny couldn't have been unaware of this ongoing problem—his dealings with Arthur Michaud had been too painful and costly to him for that to have been the case. Nevertheless, he had simply allowed such situations to continue, because he had almost no interest in business matters in general, and in policing his business associates in particular. The cumulative effects of his alcoholism, specifically the denial that is such a pernicious component of the alcoholic's psychological makeup, only added to this problem.

When Berigan finally parted company with Michaud in early 1939, he petulantly chose to go it alone without a personal manager. The inevitable result was that as 1939 progressed, and he (and MCA) continued to operate his band more or less on a permanently touring basis, he ignored or attempted to avoid his constantly compounding financial difficulties. Bunny focused instead almost exclusively on the quality of music he was presenting to audiences with his band. Consequently, the Berigan band was in very good shape musically; it could and did romp. It had a varied repertoire, good soloists, and excellent singers. It was a hit wherever it went, and played to generally good crowds. Bunny himself was playing marvelously. Nevertheless, he now began to find himself in an increasingly alarming financial miasma, unable to pay some bills, including on occasion, part of his sidemen's weekly salaries. His solution was to paint a rosy picture of the band's future prospects for his musicians, while sometimes asking them to wait for a part of their pay. Since they liked Bunny, admired his musicianship, and generally enjoyed being in his band, they accepted this. With no overall plan for the band, he was able in the first half of 1939 to deliver just enough on his optimistic promises to avoid a mutiny by his band members.

After leaving New York in mid-March, the Berigan band bounced around the northeastern United States for a few days, then landed back in New York on March 19, to play on the CBS "Band of the Week" broadcast from the Hotel New Yorker. This broadcast was recorded, and it shows that the band was maintaining its repertoire with a good balance of older selections, a few new pop tunes, and some swinging originals. Here is the lineup from that broadcast: "Trees," "I Have Eyes," vocal Kathleen Lane; "I Get Along without You Very Well," vocal Danny Richards; "Gangbusters' Holiday;" "I Cried for You," vocal Lane; "A Room with a View," vocal Richards; "Little Gate's Special;" and partial theme. After this broadcast, the band was off on March 20, stayed in New York for three more days, and rehearsed.

It was at this time that saxophonist Doc DeHaven joined the band. He recalled the circumstances: "I got a call from Bunny to go to New York and meet the band at the Forrest Hotel. They had just returned from a tour of the Southern states. We rehearsed for a couple of days in a room on Forty-fourth Street, and a few days later we battled Erskine Hawkins's band at the Savoy Ballroom, and won! I was hired to play alto and utility sax if I had the equipment. After a week or so, it was decided that I didn't."[73] On March 24, Bunny and the band opened at the Riviera Theater in Brooklyn for four days. Presumably they were a part of a vaudeville review which included acts. That would explain the three-day rehearsal regimen immediately before this engagement.

On Sunday, March 26, after completing their work at the Riviera Theater, the Berigan band went to the Savoy Ballroom to once again battle Erskine Hawkins's band. These events were huge compensations for Bunny's musicians, compensations that they could never have gotten playing with just about any other band. Young Eddie Jenkins remembered the thrilling experience years later: "The crowd at the Savoy really loved Bunny and the band was always given a tremendous reception. I remember that the band swung so hard that night that I played a hole right through my bass drum! That was the only time *that* ever happened!"[74]

The Berigan band finished their stand at the Riviera Theater the next day. It was at this time that the powerful bassist Hank Wayland, who had been with Bunny for almost two years, and had been a key component in the band's swinging rhythm section, left. "The band was off the next week before Easter and I'd had a bit of an argument with Bunny, who was more than a little drunk at the time. Anyway, I quit and went home, but I soon got an offer from Larry Clinton, while Bunny got an old friend, Morty Stulmaker, to take my place."[75]

Before the week off (without pay) began, Bunny announced to the band members that they would reform at the Trianon Ballroom in Cleveland on April 5. They would use that location as their base of operations throughout the month of April. Alto saxophonist Chuck DiMaggio replaced Doc DeHaven during this interval. He recalled the situation when he joined Berigan: "The band was off for a few days and reassembled in Cleveland, Ohio, where I joined them on 3rd alto for a season at the Trianon Ballroom on Euclid Avenue. We were to play there on Tuesdays, Thursdays and Saturdays, doing one-night stands on the other nights. I was born in New York City and grew up in Madison, Wisconsin. Joe was my brother and died very young; he later worked with Bunny also."[76]

When the Berigan band resumed operations in Cleveland on April 5, it was for rehearsals only for the first three days. On Saturday, April 8, they played at the Cleveland Hotel,[77] the site a decade earlier of Bix Beiderbecke's crack-up while he was on tour with Paul Whiteman. They opened at the Trianon Ballroom (formerly the Bamboo Garden), East 100th Street and Euclid Avenue, on April 9. (The Trianon Ballroom was razed many years ago. Where it was located is now adjacent to the vast campus of the Cleveland Clinic.) The band broadcast over local Cleveland radio station WCLE on opening night, from 11:00 to 11:30 p.m., and this broadcast was recorded. Here are the tunes they played: "'Familiar Moe," (composition/arrangement Conniff);[78] "Trees"; "I Want My Share of Love" (vocal, Kathleen Lane); "This Night" (vocal, Danny Richards); "Black Bottom"; "I Cried for You" (Lane); and "Little Gate's Special." The tune "I Can't Forget You" was also recorded at some time during the Trianon stand, possibly earlier in the above-listed sequence. These recordings reveal that the band was in fine form, and that Bunny was playing very well.

The MCA plan for the Berigan band also had them doing one-nighters into the surrounding territory. The first of these occurred on Wednesday April 10, when the band drove on 1930s highways in 1930s vintage vehicles from Cleveland to Charleston, West Virginia, a distance of 240 miles, played a gig at that city's high school auditorium,[79] and then returned to Cleveland, all within the span of twenty-four hours. Bunny had learned over the previous two years that personnel changes in his band were inevitable. The only thing that was different was the reason for each man leaving. Drummer Eddie Jenkins, who was doing an excellent job with the band, decided he had to leave right after the Charleston gig: "I was violently sick on the way back to Cleveland. I guess I must have eaten some bad food in Charleston, although I'd been getting quite a lot of stomach cramps, which I thought were due to all the traveling, irregular meal-times and being strung-up all the time, playing with a name band. Perhaps my inexperience was taking over. Anyway, reluctantly, I decide to call it quits and gave Bunny my two weeks notice."[80] Consequently, Bunny had to put out the word that he was again going to need a drummer.[81]

The band did very well at the Cleveland Trianon, and over the course of its stay there established records for attendance at the ballroom. At the same time, the one-nighters into the surrounding territory continued on Mondays, Wednesdays, Fridays, and Sundays. On April 12, they played a dance date at Moonlight Ballroom, Meyer's Lake Park, Canton, Ohio; on the 14th, at the Masonic Auditorium in Detroit; on the 16th· at the Crystal Beach Ballroom, Vermillion, Ohio; and on the 17th, at the Palais Royal Ballroom in Toronto, Ontario.[82]

Eddie Jenkins left the band after a one-night dance date at Valley Dale Ballroom in Columbus, Ohio on April 23. His replacement was the veteran Paul Collins, a solid if unspectacular drummer.

No sooner had Bunny solved his drummer problem when another serious problem emerged. As Danny Richards remembered: "I recall Bunny and Jerry Johnson getting into very hot words more than once over the 'pay off' of the band and himself."[83] This dispute boiled over and Johnson left the band. That in itself would not have been a major problem. Road managers came and went, and it seems that most of Bunny's had done their jobs reasonably well. But in this case, the road manager's wife was the best girl singer Bunny ever had, and when Johnson went, Kathleen Lane went with him. That was a loss that would not easily be mitigated. It appears that Mr. and Mrs. Johnson left the band either upon completing the Trianon engagement on Thursday, May 4, 1939, or after the Cincinnati Coney Island gig, on May 7. In between these dates, Bunny and the band played at a dance in Franklin, Pennsylvania, on May 3. Berigan had to quickly find a new girl vocalist.

The Berigan troupe played a one-nighter at Lakeside Park, Dayton, Ohio, on the 5th, where Bunny was photographed playing his trumpet beneath a satin drape over the bandstand, looking very much like a star bandleader. He and the band then went to Moonlight Gardens, Coney Island, Cincinnati, where they played on May 6 and 7. It was there that Bunny's father and vocalist Wendy Bishop joined the band. Cap Berigan was summoned by Bunny to replace Jerry Johnson as road manager on an interim basis. Undoubtedly, Berigan's dispute with Johnson had been over money. Over the years there have been suggestions that Johnson was not paying bills and/or was skimming money from Bunny's part of the gate, etc. Despite the fact that a number of Bunny's bills from the latter part of 1938 had not been paid by Johnson, there has been no evidence of theft by him. In retrospect, a more likely scenario was that Bunny was wondering how his band could be playing before large audiences night after night, while he was continuing to go deeper into debt. The answer to that conundrum has also not emerged clearly in the decades since these events took place, but probably could have been found by reviewing the Berigan band's business records at Music Corporation of America from late 1938–early 1939. By all outward indicators, Bunny Berigan and His Orchestra, in the spring of 1939, should have been doing very well financially, yet they were not. Bunny was hoping that Cap would somehow help him solve his money problems. Unfortunately, Cap was in no position to fill the holes that were now constantly appearing in the Berigan band's schedule. Nor did he have the acumen to suggest to his son more profitable ways of doing business as the leader of a popular dance band. Nevertheless, Bunny seems to have appointed his father to be his band's road manager, and possibly his personal manager as well at this juncture.

Bunny's decision to appoint Cap as road manager is understandable, to a point. Certainly if Bunny couldn't trust his own father, then he couldn't trust anyone. But Cap Berigan had absolutely no qualifications to handle the myriad duties that fell upon the road manager of a touring big band. His own employment history was encompassed by only a few jobs, mostly involving selling candy on a route in rural Wisconsin. He had never made much money, never had much dealing with finances, and certainly had no experience dealing with the kinds of people he was soon to encounter in the music business. He quickly learned that the business side of the music business was populated largely by con men and thieves, while the music side had its share of kinks and deviates. Selling candy in Wisconsin had not prepared him for this. Still, rightly or wrongly, Bunny was then of the opinion that Jerry Johnson had robbed him, just like Arthur Michaud had, and whatever Cap would do as road manager, at least there would be an end to the robbing.

After a short time however, Bunny persuaded Andy Phillips to join the band on tour as its road manager. It is likely that Cap Berigan was quickly overwhelmed by the job of managing his son's band on the road, and at the same time trying in some fashion to manage his son. Cap remained however, assisted Andy in his duties as road manager, probably also gave Bunny some advice on other business matters, and attempted to help Bunny control his drinking, which had again increased alarmingly after an apparent visit of Bunny on the road by Lee Wiley. Perhaps Cap also attempted at this time to get Bunny to end his relationship with Ms. Wiley. Clearly, by early 1939, Bunny's parents were very concerned about the deteriorating situation in the Berigan home, where Donna's drinking was now interfering with her ability to care for Patricia and Joyce, and the deteriorating situation with Bunny and his band on the road. Their move a few months earlier from Wisconsin to New York to directly assist their son and daughter-in-law was a clear expression of this concern, as was Mayme's taking Donna and the girls to Wisconsin with her (see below) and Cap's joining Bunny and the band on the road at about this time.

Despite all of this tumult, Bunny and his band were still somehow able to please the paying customers at Coney Island, and there were a lot of paying customers. A review of the band's two nights at that venue appeared in a local Cincinnati newspaper: "'The Miracle Man of Swing,' Bunny Berigan and his orchestra opened the season last night at Coney Island's Moonlight Gardens. His hot swing style went over big with a large audience. His vocalists, Kathleen Lane and Danny Richards, gave a good account of themselves and won many salvos of applause."[84] (Note: It appears that vocalist Wendy Bishop probably appeared with the Berigan band at this engagement. But since MCA had publicized the event using Kathleen Lane's name, Ms. Bishop was simply introduced to the audience, per MCA's instructions, as Kathleen Lane. The occasionally abrupt comings and goings of performers with big bands sometimes resulted in this dishonest expedient.)

The newspaper account continued with some more details:

Bunny Berigan was first introduced to Cincinnati last season at Coney Island and made a big hit. He and his trumpet had previously been a feature with Hal Kemp, Rudy Vallee, Benny Goodman and Tommy Dorsey and when he decided to form his own swing band, he had the backing of his experience with them as well as his own rather advanced ideas. The Berigan swing has plenty of rhythm as well as volume and there were few who could resist its call. He leads his band by dangling his arm and snapping his fingers. But much of the time, the genial maestro is trumpeting as lustily as he did in the days before he had his own orchestra.

Edmond L. Schulitt, Coney Island president and general manager, said Bunny Berigan was the top money getter of the season at Moonlight Gardens. Bunny played to 4,849 paid admissions in a two-night stand.[85]

For the sake of comparison, consider the following: Artie Shaw was then leading the nation's top swing band. Their first week at the Palomar Ballroom in Los Angeles began on April 19, 1939. At the end of *that week*, Shaw had set a new Palomar record with 8,753 admissions.[86]

After the Coney Island gig, the Berigan band played one-night stands east into Pennsylvania. MCA had set up another location job for the band, this one at Kennywood Park outside of Pittsburgh, for two weeks commencing on May 17. It was just prior to that engagement that Bunny had summoned Andy Phillips to join the band as its road manager:

I got a call from Bunny, saying Jerry Johnson and his wife, Kitty Lane, were leaving the band. He wanted me to join them in Pottstown, Pennsylvania, and take over as road manager. I said I would, but it would mean my arrangements coming in less often. Bunny had been on the wagon for a little while, but apparently he fell off with a vengeance after a stormy interlude with Lee Wiley. Funny, no matter how hard he tried, Lee's appearance on the scene was always bad news. The guys in the band had been trying hard to protect Bunny from himself and they were all brought down when he jumped right back into the bottle.[87]

How or where this latest destructive episode with Lee Wiley took place is not revealed in the White materials. It appears however, that Ms. Wiley joined Bunny on the road for a time, as he was not in New York while these events were taking place (April–May 1939). Here is the rather cryptic note regarding this matter that is in the White materials: "This was perhaps the last major incident with Lee Wiley. A number of men in the 1939 band recall how 'let down' they were when she showed up and by Bunny's resuming heavy drinking."[88] Although this may have marked the end of the turbulent romantic liaison between Bunny and Lee Wiley, it did not end their relationship, as we shall see.

The Kennywood Park engagement was presumably successful in terms of the band's music and the paid admissions. But from several other aspects, it was decidedly unpleasant. Larry Walsh remembered some of the goings-on:

That was a bad date. The park manager wanted us to play continuous music, seven days a week, including waltzes! Jimmy Pupa joined as replacement for George Johnston and Ray Conniff quit after an argument over his (Ray's) drinking, would you believe? Ray wasn't a drinker at all.[89] He couldn't hold his liquor, but after a couple of uncharacteristic swigs and in a somewhat bemused state, he put in a wrong mute or something. Anyway, Bunny really chewed him out and that was that.[90]

Ray Conniff himself also remembered his departure from the Berigan band: "Actually, I wasn't really unprepared. Gil Rodin, who was the straw boss-manager of the Bob Crosby band, had heard my solo on Bunny's re-

322

Chapter 19

cording of 'In a Mist' and had been suitably impressed as to offer me a job at a lot more money than Bunny was paying."[91]

As 1939 progressed, the music played by the Berigan band changed slightly to include a number of original riff-based jazz compositions and arrangements by Ray Conniff. Bunny undoubtedly recognized Conniff's talent, and encouraged him to write originals so that his band would have some stimulating new music that would provide a swinging framework for jazz, and help to further differentiate his band from others. "Little Gate's Special" is by far the best known Conniff original in the Berigan repertoire. It and "Gangbusters' Holiday" were both recorded for Victor, and have been available for many years. But there were numerous other Conniff originals in the Berigan band book, including "Savoy Jump," later recorded by Artie Shaw as "Just Kiddin' Around," and the marvelous "Familiar Moe," Conniff's streamlined retooling of the then much-played Eddie Durham/Edgar Battle/Count Basie original "Time Out," with a few bits of Joe Lippman's arrangement on "A Study in Brown" also included. Both of these Conniff originals were excellent vehicles for jazz, were played often by Berigan, and should have been recorded in 1939 by the excellent band and exciting soloists Bunny had then, but were not. Fortunately, airchecks of these Conniff originals—in less than high-fidelity sound—do exist, so we can have some idea of how good they were. Conniff's departure from the Berigan band in May of 1939 stopped the flow of these bracing originals into the band's book.

Trombonist Tasso Harris replaced Conniff for the Kennywood engagement only. Just prior to the Kennywood gig, Bunny hired Tommy Moore on guitar to fill the chair that had remained vacant after Dick Wharton left the band some months earlier. The band settled in at Kennywood, trying to do their work as best they could under the rather adverse conditions. Andy Phillips took home movies of the Berigan band there that include footage of Bunny, Cap, Danny Richards, Wendy Bishop, and the following personnel: Johnny Napton, Jimmy Pupa, Jake Koven, trumpets; Bob Jenney, Tasso Harris, trombones; Gus Bivona, Charlie DiMaggio, Don Lodice, Larry Walsh, saxophones; Joe Bushkin, piano; Tommy Moore, guitar; Morty Stulmaker, bass; Paul Collins, drums. The band broadcast frequently over WCAE–Pittsburgh from Kennywood. Bunny had once again patched up the holes in his band and everything was going along very well, at least from the musical standpoint.

Then another of those tragicomic incidents that seemed to befall Berigan periodically occurred. Andy Phillips provided the details:

> Bunny's dad was traveling with the band. I guess he was supposed to look out for Bunny and try to keep him straight. The guys in the band all liked Cap and I'm sure he did have a good influence on Bunny. I remember we got involved in a brawl with some college kids at Kennywood Park. They were members of a basketball team, I think, and their coach wanted to buy Tommy Moore's wife a drink. Tom was pretty handy with his dukes and soon everybody was punching and kicking. We got police protection after that.[92]

Joe Bushkin filled in other information:

> We had to play seven nights a week, plus six afternoon concerts and Sunday afternoon dances. The bandstand was right next to the bar and some drunk upset Tommy Moore. The next thing I knew, the basketball coach from Duquesne was picking a fight with Tommy, who knocked him through a packing case, and then it became a free-for-all with Bunny and the band against the basketball team! Cap Berigan was jumping up and down, shouting, 'Give it to 'em, Bunny!' Eventually, the cops showed up and Bunny had to pay a fine for disturbing the peace! For a few nights the park and Homestead (a nearby town) police were escorting Bunny and the band to and from work. The police chief's son played trumpet and sat in with the band, Saturday to the closing Tuesday night. This was MCA's idea, not Bunny's, for sure! [93]

It appears that some of the band's instruments were damaged in this melee.

Bunny Berigan and His Brawling Orchestra left Kennywood at the end of their engagement on May 30, and headed west to Detroit. There, they opened at Eastwood Gardens, Eight Mile Road at Gratiot, a prime venue on the big band circuit, on Saturday, June 3 for a five-day stand, which included broadcasts over WWJ–Detroit. Probable personnel changes had Joe Bauer coming in on trumpet replacing Pupa, and trombonist Jimmy Emmert replacing Harris.

At this same time, Mayme, Patricia, and Joyce were traveling from New York to Fox Lake. They would stay there for several weeks, until Bunny started his next substantial location job, which was scheduled to be at the Sherman Hotel in Chicago. Donna had apparently joined Bunny on the road shortly before the Eastwood Gardens gig, possibly at Kennywood, but then had gone on to Fox Lake, so she could be with her daughters while they stayed at their grandparents' home. In light of the events that would soon unfold, I think that it was at this time that the Berigan family gave up their house in Rego Park.

The Eastwood Gardens stand ended on June 8, after which Bunny and his increasingly bedraggled bandsmen played one-night dance jobs at Grand Rapids, Michigan on June 9, and Clintonville, Wisconsin on the 11th. The Berigan band bus (they were once again using a bus, albeit temporarily) pulled into Fox Lake on Saturday the 10th, where Bunny hoped to spend a little time with his family and old friends. The local newspaper contained this item: "Bunny Berigan and his father, W. P. Berigan, visited friends and relatives here over the weekend. They made the stop here from Grand Rapids, Michigan, and returned to Detroit on Tuesday (13th). Bunny plans on being in Chicago for a month or so in the near future."[94]

Bunny's relatives added more details, some of which were rather ominous. Charles Casey recalled:

> Bunny pulled in by bus about the same time as I was begging from everyone I knew to buy out my mother's and sister's interests in the family business. He was broke and apparently in trouble with the union. They had to buy some new instruments after some kind of battle at a recent date. The guys in the band were hungry and were booked to play a one night stand at Clintonville, to the north of

Fox Lake. I had one hell of a time trying to raise some cash and finally had to take $10 out of my cash register to buy some coffee and doughnuts for the boys! What a time to be short of cash! Our one last chance for a touch was a retired cop, a cousin of Bunny's dad, but he wouldn't give us the time of day![95]

Bob Berigan remembered:

I talked with Cap about Bunny while they were visiting here but he said he (Cap) couldn't do anything with him. Bunny wouldn't listen to him, wouldn't take his advice and was paying his gal singer around $150 a week when she wasn't worth half that. Donna had been with the band, but she came to Fox Lake while he was playing Detroit and then went out to Chicago for the Sherman Hotel.[96]

On June 15, the Berigan band opened at Westwood Symphony Gardens, another good location, on Michigan Avenue, just west of Detroit, in Dearborn. This engagement ran until June 22, during which time the band made several broadcasts over WWJ–Detroit, parts of which were recorded.[97] The White materials provide some information about these recordings:

During the band's stint at Westwood Gardens, a number of 10 and 12-inch acetates were recorded from station WWJ remotes. One title plus the opening theme is on LP and others may be released. There are no dates on the acetates, nor any indication as to the number of broadcasts from which the material was taken. The band personnel definitely included Bauer and Emmert by then and vocals were by Wendy Bishop and Danny Richards with Bunny singing the opening theme. The tune 'Savoy Jump' was on a disc in the possession of arranger Andy Phillips, which, when he provided a tape copy, he labeled 'Perisphere Hop,' named in honor of the 1939 NYC Worlds Fair landmark. (Bunny also had a tune in the book called 'Trylon Trot,' which was the other fair landmark). 'Savoy Jump' and that 'Perisphere Hop' are one and the same. Possibly the tune was renamed before the Chicago engagement.[98] (See appendix 4 for a complete listing of titles recorded on these airchecks.)

Wendy Bishop's tenure with the Berigan band was very short. Perhaps Bunny took his father's advice to heart after all, and tried to economize. Trumpeter Jake Koven recalled the details surrounding the hiring of her successor: "Wendy Bishop left the band before we closed at Westwood Gardens, so Joey Bushkin, Don Lodice and I persuaded Bunny to give an audition to a girl called Ellen Kaye, whom we'd heard at the Shamrock Club in Detroit. We took her down to meet Bunny at the Hotel Detroiter, where she sang a couple of blues tunes, accompanied by Bushkin. I was rooming with Joey and he had to wire home for cash, because we were all broke and hoping for a payday when we got to Chicago."[99] Although Bunny had solved his band's latest personnel problems, the mystery of the vanishing gate receipts continued, despite the presence of Cap Berigan and Andy Phillips each night when the gate was clocked.

After the Westwood Gardens stand ended on June 22, there were a few days before the Berigan band opened at Chicago's Hotel Sherman. MCA's booking dartboard was once again used to partially fill in this opening in the band's schedule. June 23–24, Friday and Saturday, were possibly off days that Bunny spent in Fox Lake.[100] But then again, the band could have played a couple of widely scattered one-nighters on those dates. Knowing MCA's *modus operandi,* I'd say the Berigan band played on those dates.

The next certain engagement MCA had booked for the Berigan band was on the 25th, at Valley Dale Ballroom in Columbus, Ohio. They broadcast over WABC-CBS from Valley Dale from 11:00–11:30 p.m. Here is the lineup of tunes included on that broadcast: theme, (partial); "St. Louis Blues"; "That Sentimental Sandwich," vocal Danny Richards; "If You Ever Change Your Mind" vocal, Ellen Kaye; "Little Gate's Special;" "Deep Purple," vocal Richards; "Patty Cake, Patty Cake," vocal Kaye; "Savoy Jump;" and theme.

It is not known whether the band worked on June 26 and 27, (a Monday and Tuesday) but it is likely that they did not, and went to Madison, Wisconsin, to rehearse with the acts that would be appearing with them at their upcoming appearance there on June 28 and 29, at the Orpheum Theater. Here is the local press coverage of that engagement:

> Bunny Berigan, trumpet playing orchestra leader and his band will be on the Orpheum stage on Wednesday and Thursday. 'Local boy makes good' is a fitting phrase for Bernard Berigan, who signs his name musically and to the world at large as 'Bunny' and whose torrid trumpet is rapidly becoming synonymous with this name. Since Bunny left the home town, he has played with such famous orchestras as Benny Goodman, Hal Kemp, Paul Whiteman and Rudy Vallee. He has several uncles and aunts and other relatives living in Madison and his parents, who now live with him in New York, will accompany him to Madison, Bunny will give four complete shows on Wednesday and Thursday at 2:40, 5:00, 7:20 and 9:40 p.m.[101]

"Refreshingly Cool!—Orpheum—'Where The Big Pictures Play' Today and Tomorrow on stage *The Miracle Man Of Swing,* Bunny Berigan with His famous radio and recording orchestra and swing revue featuring Peggy Clarie Trio, Wendy Bishop, Russell Swan, Helen Honan."[102] Once again, the female vocalist who then was actually with Bunny's band, Ellen Kaye, was not the one who had been advertised in the advance publicity provided by MCA to the Madison newspaper. So for the Orpheum Theater engagement, Ellen Kaye was Wendy Bishop.

> Bernard 'Bunny' Berigan, orchestra leader idol of the jitterbugs who less than a score of years ago played with Madison dance and theatre pit orchestras, returned to his hometown yesterday with his orchestra and swing revue for a homecoming celebration at the Orpheum Theatre. On hand to greet the former Wisconsin High School and University of Wisconsin student were Bunny's relatives of Madison and Fox Lake, and many of his former classmates. The brand of music offered by Bunny and his music men is distinctly on the loud, brassy side. A left-handed bass player and a pianist who is also orchestra arranger *(sic)* are among Bunny's chief assets, although his organization boasts two talented singers, Wendy Bishop

and Danny Richards. Mr. Richards won instant approval when he appeared to sing a number of current popular songs. Richards has the good looks and stage personality requisite for success and should go far. Miss Bishop was a little too 'hot' in her song presentations as she 'swung' such numbers as: "Did Your Mother Come from Ireland.' Bunny himself doubled as singer on 'I Can't Get Started With You.'[103]

Merrill Owen, the first bandleader Bunny had worked for in 1925–1925, was present at the start of this engagement: "By 1939 I was tuning pianos. The last time I saw Bunny was when he had his band at the Orpheum. By then he had become a nationally famous leader. After I 'did' the piano I went back stage to talk with Bunny. He was in his dressing room preparing for a show, with two colored boys, I guess 'Big Gate' and 'Little Gate,' poised at each elbow inserting a cuff link. We chatted for a while and Bunny spoke of his financial difficulties and he complained that the booking agents 'were taking him to the cleaners.'"[104]

While Berigan was appearing at the Orpheum Theater, he was interviewed by Glenn Frank Jr., a reporter from the *Wisconsin State Journal*. His comments proved to be prophetic. Here are excerpts from that interview: "I believe the next trend in popular music is going to be away from loud and hot toward a subtle and restrained style that will concentrate on beauty, not on noise. But a band has to give the audience what it wants. That's why I play loud and hot most of the time. If I had my way, I'd play more subtly and with more restraint." When asked about criticisms of various bands being "commercial," he said: "We all have to be commercial to a degree to make a living. And anyhow, music is like love—you can't define tastes or terms; it's silly to call one man right and another wrong."[105]

Notes

[1] The title, "Enigma Variations," comes from composer Edward Elgar. He composed *Variations on an Original Theme for Orchestra, Op. 36*, in 1898–1899. This composition is a theme and a set of fourteen variations which Elgar initially worked out at the piano. He dedicated it to "my friends pictured within," but left it up to the listener to determine which theme matched which friend, thus the title.

[2] I do not think that it was a coincidence that within the year, Lee Wiley began her series of recordings grouped by composer, beginning with George Gershwin. She would do an all Cole Porter session with Bunny in 1940. Obviously one of the things Bunny Berigan and Lee Wiley had in common was their passionate love of the best of American popular song.

[3] The Berigan group played "In a Mist" on the *Saturday Night Swing Club* broadcast of November 19, 1938. Joe Lippman's arrangement, a highly integrated piece of music, contained composed solos. A comparison of the recording of "In a Mist" made that night with the one made for Victor on November 30 reveals that Bunny had the musicians well prepared to perform this piece on the *SNSC*, that he strained not to burst out of the brief

solos Lippman had written for him, and that he set the tempo slightly slower on the radio performance. Otherwise, the performances are almost identical.
[4] *Bluebird, Vol. III.*
[5] Arranger William H. Challis was born on July 8, 1904, in Wilkes-Barre, Pennsylvania. He was an early associate of the Dorsey Brothers, Russ Morgan, and other musicians who in the early 1920s were members of the fine territory band called the Scranton Sirens. Through his connection with the Sirens, he later joined the Jean Goldkette band as an arranger. It was in the Goldkette band that he became a close associate of Bix Beiderbecke's. Shortly after this, they moved on to Paul Whiteman's orchestra. Challis's arrangements for both Goldkette and Whiteman were among the most innovative of the 1920s. Whiteman made the deal with music publisher Jack Robbins to publish Beiderbecke's compositions for piano, and then Challis worked with Bix to write out the music for them. Challis went through the swing era and later years working regularly but almost anonymously as an arranger. Nevertheless, his charts were played by many of the top bands of those years, including Glenn Miller's, Artie Shaw's, and Glen Gray's. Challis returned to his home for a long retirement and died in Wilkes-Barre on October 4, 1994.
[6] Some Victor labels identified this recording as "Flashers" rather than "Flashes." This misspelling is indicative of how little concern Victor had with the records of Bunny Berigan by early 1939.
[7] We must remember that Bix Beiderbecke was enthralled by the music of Claude Debussy and Maurice Ravel, and actually met Ravel in March of 1928, when Ravel heard the Paul Whiteman orchestra, including Beiderbecke, play. Ravel was unimpressed by the music the orchestra performed, but was much impressed by the musicianship of the players, and especially by the solos of Bix Beiderbecke. As the swing era progressed, arrangers began to utilize the harmonies that had been employed by Debussy, Ravel, and Beiderbecke.
[8] Liner notes—*Bunny Berigan, His Trumpet and Orchestra, Vol. 1,* by Dan Morgenstern, RCA Victor, LPV-581 (1972). Dan Morgenstern has been the director of jazz studies at Rutgers University since 1976. He has been a historian, author, editor, and archivist in the jazz field since 1958.
[9] Although the sound engineers at RCA Victor in the late 1930s did a remarkably fine job of recording Bunny Berigan's music, reissues of these original recordings over the decades have been produced with far less than scrupulous care. If the opportunity ever arises for a reissue project to be done with integrity, the metal parts from which Berigan's records were initially made still exist, in a deep limestone mine near Slippery Rock, in western Pennsylvania. They would provide pristine sources for any such reissues.
[10] I must thank the Director of the National Jazz Museum in Harlem, Loren Schoenberg, for playing various excerpts of the Savory/Berigan recordings now owned by the Museum for me when I visited him there on April 22, 2011.
[11] *Traps, the Drum Wonder—The Life and Times of Buddy Rich,* by Mel Tormé, Oxford University Press (1991), 39–40, hereafter cited as *Traps, the Drum Wonder.*
[12] *Bluebird, Vol. III.*
[13] *Big Band Jazz:* by Albert McCarthy, G.P. Putnam's Sons (1974), 209.
[14] Although there has been speculation that Lippman played piano with Berigan on a series of jazz demonstration recordings *(Modern Rhythm Choruses,* see the text at March 16, 1939), I am doubtful that if these recordings were made on March 16, 1939, which is not certain, Lippman would have participated in such a project. He was by then far too busy writing arrangements for numerous bandleaders on a freelance basis.

[15] White materials: December 3, 1938.

[16] White materials: December 14, 1938.

[17] White materials: December 17, 1938.

[18] *The World of Earl Hines,* by Stanley Dance, Charles Scribner's Sons (1977), 196.

[19] *Down Beat:* January 1939, cited in the White materials.

[20] White materials: December 20, 1938.

[21] Gene Krupa and His Orchestra appeared in the Paramount film *Rhythm Romance* with Bob Hope. It was released in 1939. One of the tunes featured in this film was "The Lady's in Love with You," with music by Frank Loesser and lyrics by Burton Lane.

[22] *Metronome:* January, 1939, cited in the White materials.

[23] *Bluebird, Vol. II.* Joe Dixon recalled that a Dr. Goldberg told Bunny in 1938 that he had cirrhosis of the liver.

[24] *Jazz and Death—Medical Profiles of Jazz Greats,* by Frederick J. Spencer, M.D., University Press of Mississippi (2002), 106–107. Hereafter referred to as *Jazz and Death.*

[25] There is a good bit of information in the Dupuis Berigan biography in its chapter entitled "Squareface" about alcoholism in general, and Bunny Berigan's alcoholism in particular.

[26] *Billboard:* January 14, 1939, cited in the White materials.

[27] White materials: January 2, 1939.

[28] White materials: January 5, 1939.

[29] White materials: January 7, 1939.

[30] *Ibid.*

[31] *Down Beat:* February 1939, cited in the White materials.

[32] *Billboard:* January 29, 1929, cited in the White materials.

[33] *Simon Says—The Sights and Sounds of the Swing Era, 1935–1955,* by George T. Simon, Galahad Books (1971), 453–454, hereafter *Simon Says.* The liner notes for RCA Bluebird LP 7636-1-RB (1988), entitled *The Metronome All-Star Bands,* indicates that Leonard Joy supervised this session. Perhaps Eli Oberstein was "just visiting."

[34] *Ibid.:* 455.

[35] *Ibid.:* 454. The White materials state that the arrangement on "Blue Lou" was the one Benny Goodman used, which had been written by Horace Henderson, and modified by his brother Fletcher. That does not mean, of course, that Tommy Dorsey's band was not playing the same arrangement.

[36] *Giants of Jazz:* 48.

[37] *Lost Chords:* 514.

[38] *Ibid.:* 513. The second tune recorded that night was a blues on which Berigan did not solo.

[39] The information about the events leading up to Cap and Mayme Berigan coming to New York to care for their granddaughters was provided by Patricia Berigan to Robert Dupuis. It is contained in the Dupuis/Berigan Archive at the Mills Music Library at the University of Wisconsin at Madison, hereafter referred to as "Dupuis archive, UW–Madison."

[40] *The Mississippi Rag* was a monthly tabloid newspaper that specialized in news about classic jazz and ragtime. It's founder, editor, publisher and guiding light was Leslie Carole Johnson, who kept the publication afloat for thirty-five years (1973–2008), until cancer made it impossible for her to work. Leslie Johnson died on January 17, 2009, at age sixty-six.

[41] White materials: January 17, 1939.

[42] White materials: January 19, 1939.

[43] White materials: January 24, 1939.

[44] Information provided by Carl A. Hallstrom.

[45] White materials: January 25, 1939.

[46] *Ibid.*

[47] White materials: January 26, 1939.

[48] White materials: January 31, 1939.

[49] White materials: February 5, 1939.

[50] *Variety:* February 8, 1939, cited in the White materials.

[51] *Melody Maker:* February 4, 1939, cited in the White materials.

[52] To my ears, it is Gus Bivona, who had a distinctive sound on alto saxophone, who plays most if not all of the first alto on Berigan's March 15, 1939, Victor recording session.

[53] White materials: February 16, 1939.

[54] *Ibid.*

[55] White materials: February 17, 1939.

[56] Gus Bivona also (later) very much resembled film actor David Niven.

[57] White materials: March 6, 1939.

[58] *Down Beat:* April 1939, cited in the White materials.

[59] *Daytona News:* March 7, 1939, cited in the White materials.

[60] White materials: March 7, 1939.

[61] White materials: March 9, 1939.

[62] White materials: March 11, 1939.

[63] By 1940, RCA Victor had reduced the price of their Victor records from seventy-five cents to fifty cents.

[64] Indeed, the riffs in "Little Gate's Special" were "borrowed" from Count Basie's "Boogie Woogie (I May Be Wrong)," as recorded by Basie for Decca on May 26, 1937.

[65] Ray Conniff recycled many of the original composition/arrangements he wrote for Bunny Berigan's band. "Little Gate's Special," with some small modifications, was later sold to Teddy Powell, whose band recorded it on May 20, 1940, as "Feather Merchant's Ball." The same basic arrangement of "Little Gate's Special" played by Berigan was later played by Artie Shaw's band, when Conniff played trombone and arranged for Shaw. Conniff's original compositions/arrangements of "Savoy Jump" and "Familiar Moe" were later retooled by Conniff and recorded by Shaw as "Just Kiddin' Around" and "Prelude in C Sharp Major."

[66] White materials: March 15, 1939.

[67] It was Victor's custom then to enter into one-year contracts with its recording artists. Berigan's first Victor contract was signed in late March 1937, and renewed a year later. In March of 1939, there appears no evidence that Victor renewed Berigan's recording contract for another year.

[68] All commentary regarding the *Modern Rhythm Choruses* recordings come from the White materials: March 16, 1939. The whereabouts of the copies of these recordings that were owned by the Berigan family is not known to a certainty, but they may be in the Berigan archive at the University of Wisconsin's Mills Music Library.

[69] Cited in the White materials: March 11, 1939.

[70] *The Big Bands,* by George T. Simon, Macmillan Co. (1967), 418.

[71] John Hammond told the story of the resurrection of the Columbia label in 1938–1939 out of the ashes of the former Columbia label, and the moribund collection of labels operated in the 1930s by the American Record Company. See *John Hammond on Record,* an autobiography with Irving Townsend, The Ridge Press (1977), 210–221. See also *The*

Label—The Story of Columbia Records, by Gary Marmorstein, Thunder's Mouth Press (Avalon Publishing Group, Inc.) (2007), 81–94. How the art of recording music and handling recording artists has changed over the last fifty years is recounted well in *Making Records,* by Phil Ramone and Charles L. Granata, Hyperion (2007).

[72] Artie Shaw explained this in the documentary radio series entitled *The Mystery of Artie Shaw,* produced by Ted Hallock in 1998.

[73] White materials: March 19, 1939.

[74] White materials: March 26, 1939.

[75] White materials: March 27, 1939.

[76] White materials: March 28, 1939. Alto saxophonist Chuck DiMaggio's recollection that he played third alto in the Berigan band is further evidence that Gus Bivona was now the band's first alto player.

[77] This lovely hotel, located in the historic Terminal Tower complex in the center of Cleveland, continues to operate today as the Renaissance Cleveland Hotel.

[78] "Familiar Moe" is an excellent jazz original composed and arranged by Ray Conniff. He started with parts of "Time Out" from the Count Basie band, then mixed in the chord changes behind the trombone solo in Joe Lippman's arrangement of "A Study in Brown," to create this swinging framework for riffs by the band and numerous jazz solos.

[79] The engagement at Charleston, West Virginia, was heavily promoted by the local impresario. Large newspaper ads in the *Charleston Daily Mail* appeared daily for several days before the event, which turned out to be very successful. Information provided by Carl A. Hallstrom.

[80] White materials: April 10, 1939.

[81] I had the opportunity to speak with ninety-three year old Eddie Jenkins in January of 2011. In our conversation, he surprised me by asserting that Jerry Johnson gave him a two-week notice when he rejoined all the other Berigan sidemen at the Trianon Ballroom in Cleveland. When I told him I thought that his playing on the March 15 Victor session and on the airchecks from the Trianon was excellent, he agreed. "That wasn't the problem. I just couldn't handle all of the travel. Bunny saw that I was having problems, and contacted Paul Collins while we were on the short layoff before the Trianon engagement. I worked out the two-week notice and took a bus back to New York."

[82] White materials: April 1939.

[83] White materials: April 23, 1939.

[84] *Cincinnati Enquirer:* May 8, 1939, cited in the White materials.

[85] *Ibid.*

[86] *Billboard:* April 29, 1939, cited in the White materials.

[87] White materials: May 7, 1939.

[88] *Ibid.*

[89] Ray Conniff may not have been a drinker in 1939, but later, in the 1940s, he developed a problem with alcohol that he was able, fortunately, to successfully overcome.

[90] White materials: May 17, 1939.

[91] *Ibid.*

[92] White materials: May 30, 1939.

[93] *Ibid.*

[94] *Fox Lake Representative:* June 15, 1939, cited in the White materials.

[95] White materials: June 11, 1939.

[96] *Ibid.*

[97] Robert Dupuis informed me that when he was writing his Berigan biography in the late 1980s, he contacted a family friend at WWJ–Detroit and asked if the recordings of the

Berigan band at Westwood Gardens were anywhere in the station's archives. He was informed that only recently, they had been discarded as useless. Nevertheless, some recordings from that stand (loaded with surface noise, unfortunately) have survived.

[98] White materials: June 22, 1939. The identification of "Savoy Jump" as being the same tune as was recorded in 1941 by Artie Shaw as "Just Kiddin' Around" was first made by Michael P. Zirpolo in an article on Shaw that appeared in 1998 in the *IAJRC Journal.*

[99] *Ibid.*

[99] A MCA publicity poster announcing the appearance of Bunny Berigan and His Orchestra at Bemus Point, New York, on Saturday June 24, 1939, has been widely reproduced over the years. A blurb in the *Fox Lake Representative* on June 29, 1939, stated that Bunny, Cap, and four sidemen had spent June 23–24 in Fox Lake resting. For Bunny and his band to have played at Bemus Point, which is on Lake Chautauqua in western New York, they would have had to either drive there directly from Detroit (a distance of approximately 375 miles) where they had closed at Westwood Gardens at 1:00 a.m. June 23, a Friday, and then appear there on Saturday the 24th, or play a one-nighter somewhere between Detroit and Bemus Point on the night of Friday the 23rd, then travel the rest of the way to Bemus Point on the 24th. It is certain the Berigan band played a one-nighter at Valley Dale Ballroom, Columbus, Ohio (approximately 330 miles from Bemus Point) on Sunday, June 25. Given the propensities of the MCA one-nighter department, the possibility that the Berigan band played two one-nighters on June 23–24, 1939, including the one scheduled at Bemus Point on the 24th, is very real.

[101] *Madison Capital Times:* June 27–29, 1939, cited in the White materials: June 27–29, 1939.

[102] *Ibid.* June 27, 1939, cited in the White materials.

[103] *Ibid.* June 27, 28, and 29, 1939, cited in the White materials.

[104] White materials: June 29, 1939.

[105] "They Want It Hot, but Bunny Doesn't," (Madison) *Wisconsin State Journal,* June 29, 1939, 12. Information provided by Carl A. Hallstrom.

Chapter 20
Enigma Variations: Part Two

If one were to have entered the Panther Room of Hotel Sherman in Chicago on the evening of Saturday, July 1, 1939, the impression received would have been that of a gala opening night for Bunny Berigan and His Orchestra.[1] The room where they were appearing was packed with people anxious to hear Berigan's music. The band members, clad in their matching dark suits, looked good. They were happy. This was the first "prestige" residency the Berigan band played in over a year, the last having been at the Paradise Restaurant in New York in the spring of 1938. The band, in spite of several major shake-ups in personnel and months of grueling one-night stands, was still in fine shape musically.

The stubbornly idealistic Berigan had decided to run his band without a personal manager after his parting with Arthur Michaud the prior January. He simply took whatever work MCA threw his way. His idea continued to be that a musical profit would eventually put him ahead of his financial losses. Bunny himself was looking great on the outside, but on the inside, both physically and emotionally, was exhausted. It seemed that no matter how hard he tried to do a good job wherever he and the band appeared, and no matter how well he or they played, and no matter how huge or enthusiastic the audiences, it made no difference. He could not get ahead of the constantly accruing costs of keeping his band on the road. Indeed, he could not even keep up. He was now mired in debt, and his musicians had been only partially paid for several weeks. After only a short time at the Sherman, they may not have been paid at all. He was also still paying Arthur Michaud but now was completely at odds with him. He owed a long list of creditors including the Greyhound Bus Line, a hotel in Detroit, and Wanamaker's department store in New York. How he was able to keep his band together under these circumstances can only be explained in terms of the admiration his musicians had for him as a musician, and as a person.

Here is the personnel of the Berigan band that opened at Hotel Sherman that night: Johnny Napton (lead), Joe Bauer, Jake Koven, trumpets; Jimmy Emmert (lead), Bob Jenney, trombones; Gus Bivona (lead alto and jazz alto and clarinet), Charlie DiMaggio (alto), Don Lodice (jazz tenor), Larry Walsh (tenor and baritone), saxophones; Joe Bushkin, piano; Tommy Moore, guitar; Morty Stulmaker, bass; Paul Collins, drums; Danny Richards and Ellen Kaye, vocalists. For a while, all seemed well. The band, by this time a well-integrated performing unit seasoned by six months of nonstop touring and playing, performed with enthusiasm and verve. The Panther Room was full and everybody was happy. The band was off on Mondays, so right after the gig on Sunday night, Bunny would drive north to Fox Lake, about 120 miles, to be with his family and play golf on Monday. He would then return to Chicago to play on Tuesday evenings, and remain there for the balance of the week. On at least one occasion, Bunny brought Donna and the girls down from Fox Lake to Chicago with him for a week. It was during this visit that Bunny took the girls to the Sherman's swimming pool and began to teach them how to swim.[2]

The Berigan band broadcast nightly radio remotes from the Sherman during their entire run there. On many evenings there were two separate broadcasts. Their broadcasts were presented over the following radio outlets: WENR–Chicago (Chicago region) or WMAQ–Chicago and the NBC Blue Network (nationwide). MCA was finally putting a major radio push behind the Berigan band. The titles they were playing reveal that Bunny continued to feature a well-balanced mix of Berigan standbys ("Azure," "Shanghai Shuffle," "'Tain't So, Honey," "'Deed I Do," "Jelly Roll Blues," and "Sobbin' Blues") with current pop tunes ("Our Love," "And the Angels Sing," "Blue Evening," and "Don't Worry 'Bout Me.") The complete listing of tunes recorded from Berigan's Hotel Sherman broadcasts is in appendix 3.

A typical review of the Berigan band at the Panther Room appeared in *Billboard:*

> Headline: Panther Room, Sherman Hotel, Chicago: This Fox Lake, Wisconsin, lad, who has been trumpeting with some of the biggest names in the field, has been doing mighty well since he decided to swing out for himself some two and a half years ago. He fronts 13 good and true musicians (5 brass, 4 rhythm and 4 saxes), who compose a lively and balanced swing outfit. The best highlight here, however, is Bunny himself. The boys emphasize swing and make no bones about it. The arrangements by Andy Phillips are 'way above stock' caliber, although occasionally he trips up in a minor way, playing up the rhythm section too heavily. Single honors go to Joe Bushkin, a young pianist, who works fast and furiously on the keyboard. Whether or not he follows the music sheet to the minutest degree is of little concern in this case. Vocals are handled ably by Danny Richards, personable tenor *(sic)* and Ellen Kaye, a new Berigan member, who swings out juicily with both voice and personality.[3]

But as rosy as things appeared on the surface, Bunny was well aware that he was way behind in paying his musicians, and that what he was earning at the Sherman was not going to be enough for him to catch up. He also knew better than to expect that things would always go smoothly with regard to the personnel of his band. He undoubtedly realized that his inability to fully pay his band members would eventually lead to the dissolution of his band, but in the meantime, he used all of his considerable charm to hold onto his musicians. His band was strong musically, and he wanted to keep it that way. Still, there were periodic departures from the ranks. Shortly after the Sherman gig began, trombonist Bob Jenney left. Finding good replacements was difficult outside of major cities, but in Chicago, it was rather easy. Both Paul Collins and Larry Walsh recalled

Jenney's replacement: Collins said: "A few days after we opened at the Sherman Hotel, a local musician, Ralph Copsy, took over Bob Jenney's trombone chair. He played pretty good in a Teagardenish manner and was given a few solos by Bunny." Walsh recalled: "Yes I remember Copsy on the band at the Sherman. He was a terrific trombonist in the Teagarden style and had played with Ben Pollack and the Chicago NBC staff. I think he played all of the solo trombone at the Sherman. I don't think he stayed with the band after Milwaukee, which was right after the Sherman. We had only one 'bone on the trip back East."[4]

In addition to Berigan's debt to his musicians, there were other sums due and owing. (It is not clear from the available evidence whether Bunny was aware of these problems. Based on the statements of Andy Phillips [see below] he [Phillips] was clearly surprised when these matters came to light.)

As a result of the constant pressure he was under, Bunny's imperturbable cool was now subject to sudden bursts of heat. Ray Groose, one of a number of old friends from Wisconsin to visit him while he was at the Sherman, reflected: "I went to Chicago to see and hear Bunny and I was surprised at how short-tempered he seemed. He snapped at the manager that he wanted some money right away. Then later, he said, 'I wish I could be like you, Ray. Run a bar or a restaurant and get off the road for good.' He seemed very disillusioned somehow."[5]

He was also visited by Wisconsin trumpeter Clif Gomon:

The last time I saw Bunny was in Chicago. I was working there at the Atlantic Club with Hal Monroe, and I'd heard a couple of Bunny's broadcasts. His playing didn't sound too good and on my first night off I went down to the Sherman and worked my way to the front of the room while Bunny was on the stand. It was the first set of the evening and Bunny's playing was very ordinary. At the intermission, Bunny saw me and came over greeting me like a long-lost brother. He sat down and joked and reminisced about the old days. On the next set, he stood up and blew his ass off! I'd never heard such fantastic playing. His smears, his highs, his lows, everything was executed with spectacular imagination. The next day, the guys from Monroe's band told me they'd heard Bunny on the air the night before, playing stuff that was unbelievable. 'You should have heard him, Cliff,' they said. 'Yeah, I know' I replied. 'He was just great and I was there!' There was an MCA executive called Will Roland in the audience who was equally impressed. Whenever Bunny would punch out an especially stunning high note, he'd grab me and asked 'What note was that?'[6] After the show, I went to Bunny's room for more jokes and chat, but although it was a really memorable visit, I got the impression that he was generally down in the dumps. He never complained though, nor said anything was bothering him.[7]

Despite the generally dismal financial situation surrounding the Berigan band then, there were lighter moments. Trumpeter Johnny Napton recalled a couple of visits by a legendary actor who had many of the same problems Bunny had: "John Barrymore would come into the Panther Room after he'd finished work at a nearby theater. Bunny looked a bit like him and of course they hit it off, alcoholically speaking! Barrymore would sit at a ringside table and between numbers he'd say, just loud enough to be heard by the band, 'What the shit goes on here?' That used to break us up!"[8]

Bunny would occasionally be asked by Barrymore to join the group gathered around him for a taste, and for some of Barrymore's stories. One such, which was recalled later by both Joe Bushkin and Gus Bivona, two of the more manic members of the band, had Barrymore recounting some of his onstage triumphs. Barrymore, in his inimitable fashion, was discussing how he interpreted the role of Hamlet. One of the young people listening to this earnestly inquired of the great thespian as to whether Hamlet had had an affair with Ophelia. Barrymore paused, struck a pose, and then said with an absolutely straight face, "...only in the Philadelphia company." (Bud Freeman, the great tenor saxist, who idolized Barrymore, would have been in *heaven!*)

Napton also recalled that singer Ellen Kay didn't last long with the Berigan band: "Ellen Kaye left after about a week and Bunny didn't bother getting anyone to replace her at first. I guess he couldn't afford to!"[9] (Note: Ellen Kaye does not appear on any Berigan band broadcasts from the Panther Room after July 11.)

At some point during the band's run at Hotel Sherman, the storm clouds that had been gathering for a long time suddenly let loose. Andy Phillips recalled:

We got hit by a large bill from the Greyhound bus line, which I understood had been paid by Jerry Johnson. However, they insisted that Bunny owed them $875, so he agreed to pay $475 cash down and $100 a month. He (Bunny) was also served notice of an action of garnishment on behalf of a Detroit hotel corporation to appropriate the week's paycheck to cover another debt. We appealed to the Chicago local of AFM, who intervened with a ruling that the Sherman must turn the money over to the union, who would ensure that we all got paid. This was supposed to leave Bunny about $150 each week to pay off his creditors![10]

Other band members also had vivid memories of what happened. Piecing them together gives us a clearer picture of what was going on.

Morty Stulmaker: We were all flat broke by the time we got to Chicago and Bunny owed each of us at least $200. We did not mind this too much while we were playing poor dates, but we expected a better deal from the Sherman engagement.

Paul Collins: A couple of times, Bunny collected the band's wages after we finished on the Sunday night and then went up to Fox Lake. When we came back to Chicago on the Tuesday, there was no cash left! So we drew straws to see who would get to call the union and Johnny Napton drew the short straw. A guy came down from the union and got things under control so they (the union) would always get the cash and, hopefully, we would get paid!

Andy Phillips: Jimmy Petrillo, the Chicago union president, summoned Bunny to union headquarters. The offices were in an old building like a warehouse with bodyguards on the front door, real tough-looking hombres. Petrillo's command of the English language left a lot to be desired, but the gist of it was that Bunny was fined $1,000 for conduct unbecoming a member of the American Federation of Musicians![11]

Joe Bushkin: Business matters were beyond Bunny. MCA booked the band and they were supposed to take 15% of what he made, but they seemed to be taking everything, because he owed them so much money. We didn't get paid for five weeks. I was sending home for money and a lot of the guys were borrowing from a saloonkeeper across the street. We finally met in Bunny's room one night. You never saw him without a cigarette burning in the right side of his mouth and you never saw him without his whisky and his cool. He was lying on his bed smoking, his glass of whisky on the bedside table. He said, 'Go see Petrillo at the union and tell him you haven't been paid in five weeks. It's the only way you're going to get any money.' Nobody wanted to go, so we all marched over next morning like an army. We were taken into a big room with a long table and there was Petrillo—James C. himself, seated like Napoleon at the head of it. 'All right, what's the problem, fellas?' he said. Then he said, 'Boy, Bunny Berigan, he's some trumpet player, that guy.' Petrillo played a little trumpet himself. Each of us had to tell what we were paid, which was embarrassing because the salaries were so mixed up. The third trombone *(sic)* was getting maybe 85 bucks a week, while the first was only getting 60. Petrillo called MCA and told them he'd shut down (all of the) music in Chicago if our money wasn't there by two o'clock that afternoon. It was, and when we went back to the hotel, we each gave Bunny some money, because he was broke too, and we loved him.[12]

The net result of this latest tragicomedy was that Bunny's musicians were now being paid, but he was left utterly without money himself, deeply in debt. Nevertheless, despite the chaotic circumstances surrounding the Berigan band, they continued to play well and please their audiences. The Sherman gig was extended by two weeks, with continuing good business, until Friday, August 11. Bunny continued to follow the weekly routine he had established, going home to Fox Lake on Sunday after work at the Panther Room. He seemed to greatly enjoy the company of his old Wisconsin friends and family members during this trying time: Bunny's cousin Charles Casey recalled:

The band had Mondays off, so Bunny and a few of the guys would come up to Fox Lake on Sunday night and stay until Tuesday afternoon. Bunny's hair was faded by that time and he was beginning to show his age, I thought.[13] The engagement was extended so we had a fine summer. I remember the banner on the side of the hotel, which faced Lake Michigan and the Outer Drive. It said, *Bunny Berigan—The Miracle Man of Swing* and was quite the longest banner I'd ever seen! On one Monday, Bunny said he was expecting a reporter from *Down Beat* and would I mind if they held a little jam session in the tavern. (i.e., Casey's Tavern). Of course, the union mustn't know anything about it! It was about 7 p.m. then, much too late to advertise, so we figured we'd just have to see how many locals were around on a Monday. Anyway, this *Down Beat* fellow called Madison and Milwaukee and someone else called Fond du Lac and Oshkosh. Somehow, people in Beaver Dam also got wind of it, and by 11 p.m. that bar was bouncing! All we had were Bunny, Gus Bivona on clarinet, Tom Moore on guitar, and Bunny's brother Don on drums, no piano. We decided that anytime someone bought either of us a drink, we'd take out for it, but not drink it. Bunny trusted me to keep tabs. Scotch was 25 cents up there then! Besides the cash we split, we had a fifth of scotch and a fifth of bourbon to take home when we had to close at 1 a.m., because of state laws. I remember I caught hell for a year after from many people, who all thought they ought to have been invited to that session![14] Hub Keefer: I had played with Bunny in the Merrill Owen band in 1924–25. I knew Bunny's cousin well—Charlie Casey. When Bunny was 'home' for a brief period—either prior to going into the Panther Room or after he closed there, we had a whole day to talk and have fun and had a jam session at nights at Casey's Tavern. We put about 4 card tables together and Bunny got his trumpet, a man from Madison played guitar and was very good, Bunny's brother Don on drums and they found a clarinet for me and we just played and had a good time and the place was, of course, packed. That afternoon prior, Bunny and I played pool at the local hall and he beat me as he always had before.[15]

Although the ongoing lack of money was a definite problem, it did not completely dampen the spirits of either Bunny or his band members. Various sidemen would invariably accompany Bunny to Fox Lake each week to enjoy a round of golf, and the fun at Casey's Tavern. There were always many laughs along the way. Still, according to both Gus Bivona and Jake Koven, whenever they went to Fox Lake with Bunny, they had to sleep in his car.[16]

The band was in Chicago for six full weeks to play at Hotel Sherman. As the aircheck recordings from the Sherman clearly show, they were in fine form. Indeed, this band was as good as any Bunny had ever led, and he was playing splendidly. RCA Victor had recording studios in Chicago. This snippet of information appeared in one of the trade papers while Bunny was in Chicago: "Bob Chester added Kitty Lane, ex-Bunny Berigan singer; Bunny, incidentally, is set for a comeback at the wax works—this time cutting 'em for the Bluebird label."[17] One wonders what is meant by the word *comeback*. Although someone at Victor had apparently finally realized that Bunny might sell more records on the thirty-five cent Bluebird label than on the seventy-five cent Victor label, they evidently did not realize that he was ready, willing, and able to make some new records for them while he was in Chicago. (Or was his failure to record then because he no longer had a contract to record with either Victor or its Bluebird subsidiary, and for whatever reason, a new one had not been signed then?) Consequently, a golden opportunity to capture this band on commercial records was lost, and an opportunity for Bunny to earn some much needed cash was not extended to him. Yet again, whoever was managing the business side of the Berigan band[18] was asleep at the switch, and Bunny absorbed the economic consequences. The relationship between Bunny Berigan and Victor Records was now effectively over. He would make only one more session with Victor, on November 28, 1939, seemingly an afterthought. The recordings that were produced at that session marked the definitive ending to what should and could have been a much more fruitful partnership.

Before Berigan left Chicago, he did the only thing he could have done to try to extricate himself from the tangled web of debt, garnishments, and other legal actions that had ensnared him so completely while he was playing at Hotel Sherman—he filed some sort of action in U.S. District Bankruptcy Court. Here is what was reported in *Down Beat*:

> Headline: Says He's Broke: Unable to pay the $40 fee required to file a bank-ruptcy petition, Bernard R. (Bunny) Berigan, through his attorney, Paul R. Goldman, was allowed to file a special affidavit through Hoyt King, clerk of the district court here (Chicago) on August 11. The affidavit, which allowed him several days to pay the $40, did not contain a list of Berigan's creditors, but it was learned from Goldman that Berigan's heaviest obligations were to MCA, Berigan's personal manager, Arthur Michaud, John Wanamaker's of New York, and the Greyhound bus line. The affidavit was filed on the last day of Berigan's six week stand at the Panther Room of the Hotel Sherman.[19]

I am not an expert on bankruptcy law, and I am certainly not aware of how the bankruptcy laws of the United States read in 1939. But I know that the essence of bankruptcy law for the last several decades (back to 1973, at least) is that when a debtor files for bankruptcy relief, the primary objective of that legal action is to obtain *a discharge of the debtor from his debts*. There are basically two types of personal bankruptcy actions. The first is an action where the debtor has substantially more debt than he can pay, but also has assets that he wishes to retain. The second is where the debtor has more debt than he can pay, but has no assets. That appears to be the type of bankruptcy Bunny Berigan initiated. In a "no asset" bankruptcy, the conclusion of the legal proceeding comes with the issuance by the bankruptcy court of a *discharge* which has the legal effect of eliminating all of the debtor's debts. In light of the fact that Bunny was a resident of New York City, I do not know how he could have initiated any bankruptcy action in Chicago. Therefore, whatever Bunny's attorney filed in Chicago seems to have been some sort of a preliminary or interlocutory action. We know that when he returned to New York, he did in fact file a petition for bankruptcy there, which seems more in keeping with normal legal procedures.

While all of the legal wrangling was going on, Bunny remained busy leading his band. They played at the Savoy Ballroom in Chicago on August 12. Bunny's music was well regarded in the various black communities of America's large cities. While he was at the Chicago Savoy, he helped the ballroom owner out by assisting with a contest or promotion of some sort. Here is what was reported in the *Chicago Defender*: "Bunny had his photo taken shaking hands with an older colored female with four other, younger ones, looking on. This photo appeared in the black weekly, the *Chicago Defender*, and the caption makes reference to some type of contest which had taken place previously. Probably the photo was on the occasion of the winner being announced, at the Savoy Ballroom.[20] Subsequently, *Down Beat* felt it appropriate to print this item: "Letter to the Editor: 'We Fluff Berigan Off,' Louisville, Mississippi. Find enclosed a newspaper clipping and picture of Bunny Berigan and his colored friends. We just thought we would drop you all Yankee Cats a line telling you all that we thereby fluff Berigan off for having such a picture taken. Carl Johnstone and his University of Miss Ork."[21] I am sure that Bunny worried little about what Mr. Johnstone thought about his interaction with other human beings who happened to be black. This little episode however is a reminder of how virulent racism was accepted as the norm in 1939 in the United States.

Bunny and the band appeared at the Modernistic Ballroom in Milwaukee the following night. It was in this ballroom four years before that Bunny, as a member of Benny Goodman's band, had electrified the crowd with his playing. That performance garnered him one of his first mentions in *Down Beat*. Now, as the leader of his own band, he was still pleasing audiences and pulling in crowds, but he was also insolvent, exhausted, and disillusioned. Nevertheless, he was still capable of playing inspired trumpet, and was still something of a joker. Larry Walsh and Paul Collins recalled:

Walsh: Bunny was now being billed as *The Miracle Man of Swing* on all our dates. At the Savoy Ballroom on Chicago's south side, we played opposite a colored band, and at the State Fair Park in Milwaukee, we played opposite Steve Swedish and his band. Bunny was in good form on both dates and I remember thinking how he never touched the tuning slide on his horn, but would always tune up to the piano. Occasionally, he would let Joey Bushkin play a little trumpet. Bunny got a kick out of that. He would also let Jake Koven solo, particularly on Dixieland type numbers. The Milwaukee date was an outside one in an amusement park and lots of folks from around Bunny's home came down to hear him, which only spurred him on to play even better![22]

Collins: Many of Bunny's relatives, friends and people who knew of him came from around the Madison and Fox Lake areas and this did seem to inspire him, because he played really magnificently that night. Gus Bivona and I used to do a pretty bad imitation of the Ink Spots, just as a gag, while we were riding on the bus between dates. Bunny really enjoyed that and said that one day he would use it on stage. Gus used to do the gravelly, deep bass voice and I provided the high falsetto. Well, when he called on us to go into our act that night, we yelled back, 'Not now, Bunny, we're not drunk enough yet!' The crowd cheered! After we finished that job, Ralph Copsy returned home to Chicago. He hadn't really wanted to go out on the road anyway. Bunny and Donna spent a few days in Fox Lake and Bunny's dad traveled back with them.[23]

Bunny then spent a couple of days in Fox Lake, with his band. They played a dance date at the Rustic Resort, in nearby Clintonville, Wisconsin, on August 16, and then moved on to the Colonial Hotel, Rochester, Indiana, for a dance date on the 18th. He and the band then played some scattered one-nighters on the way back to New York City. There they would play what was undoubtedly their biggest job (in terms of pay) in over a year, at the Loew's State Theater, 1530 Broadway, in Times Square.

Theaters were where the big money was, and the bigger the theater, the bigger the money. The Loew's State Theater was a big theater. *Billboard* had a reporter there for opening night. Here is his report:

> Thursday evening, August 24: The vaude bill this week is not so hot, and combined with the weak film, *The Man in the Iron Mask*, will probably do only so-so business. Bunny Berigan's band is on the stage throughout, with Berigan emceeing and then highlighting the band music with some of his brilliant trumpeting. He and his 13 men snap out sharp swing-style rhythms. Their music is in the better swing class, but has a tendency to get monotonous before the show has finished. Tenor *(sic)* Danny Richards steps out for vocals, drawing generous applause. Wendy Bishop, singer, is also billed, but the theater explained there was a billing mix-up and that she's not in the show. The band dishes out 'Jumpin'Joe,' 'Jim Jam Jumpin' Jive' *(sic)* and a couple of fast rhythm numbers in the finale, with the band's drummer and the pianist-singer taking the spotlight for specialties. Eunice Healy, a lovely dancer, is featured, and Maxine Sullivan regaled the swing fans with her singing of 'The Lamp is Low,' the old ballad 'Jackie Boy,' 'The Lady's in Love with You,' and for an encore, 'Loch Lomond.' Al Trahan is back with his familiar piano and concert satire, with a new foil, Rose Perfect. Lighting for the show was above average.[24]

Business was good at the State. But while Bunny was there, word of his recent financial woes seeped out:

> Petrillo Fines Berigan 1G: (Headline) Chicago, Aug. 19—A second chaotic chapter was added to the financial woes of maestro Bunny Berigan before his pulling up stakes at the Sherman Hotel's College Inn last Friday, with the climax coming in the form of a $1,000 fine from Jimmy Petrillo, head man of the local musicians' union. Pay-off of the grand was held in abeyance by Petrillo. Berigan's moneys were already tied up by the union and the horn-tooter was forced to file a petition in bankruptcy to stave off other creditors. For 'conduct unbecoming to a union member' was the verdict of the Chicago local in meting out Berigan's fine. Petrillo started appropriating the ork's weekly paycheck to insure the members getting their salary after a garnishment had been slapped on the leader by a Detroit hotel corporation. Right after that move, Petrillo discovered that the ork leader owed his men back salaries to the tune of $3,100 before hitting Chicago and a couple of weeks after that, the boys were holding the bag for another $125 apiece since the College Inn opening. Although the Berigan tootlers did not seem too distraught over the situation, Petrillo decided it was time for Berigan to do a little straightening up. The music chief wired AFM prexy Joe Weber, for permission to stop all of Berigan's checks until such time as all indebtedness to the members was squared up. Weber gave his okay and Petrillo became Berigan's financial manager, collecting for the band on the Savoy Ballroom solo last Saturday, the Modernistic Ballroom at State Fair Park, Milwaukee and making arrangements to get the $2,100 coming to Berigan for his week at Loew's State in New York starting this Thursday. These three dates will probably put Berigan in the clear with his men, but will still leave him in the hole to the Chicago local union. The 8-ball started casting its shadow on the trumpet-tooter shortly after he organized his band, as the bookings weren't coming in fast enough to cover the

salary contracts he had with his men, whether the band worked or not. The bunch was loyal to the leader though and no doubt would have stuck it out anyway. What will happen now depends on Berigan as a financial manager and how often he can get the band booked. Otherwise, one more misstep will probably spell curtains and expulsion from the AFM. The maestro also expects to get his managerial mix-up settled in New York too, but may run into trouble on that score, since both Arthur Michaud and John Gluskin claim he has contracts with them.[25]

Trombonists Mark Pasco and Al Jennings joined Bunny for the Loew's State engagement. As the *Billboard* review quoted above indicates, Berigan played this engagement without a girl vocalist. But we must remember that even if Bunny had had a girl singer in his band at that time, she would not have been able to perform at the Loew's State because vocalist Maxine Sullivan was being cofeatured on the bill with the Berigan band. For once, a personnel problem worked in favor of Berigan—he saved the cost of having a regular girl singer whom he could not use.

In addition, for reasons that are not known, a number of photos were taken of Bunny and the band while they were onstage at the State: "Many photos of Bunny and the band emanated from this date. At least twelve different 'poses' are known to exist, many of which were still obtainable from a New York photo studio as recently as 1985. Bunny is shown in his beige, double-breasted suit and the satin draped music stands in the background have a very 'wrinkled' look! These photos have been used on many album covers."[26] One of these photos that has always struck me as particularly revealing is one of Bunny with his arms extended from his sides, his trumpet dangling from the fingers of his left hand, the index finger of his right hand pointing up. It is evident that he has just removed the trumpet from his lips, as the indentation from the horn's mouthpiece is still visible on his upper lip. His mouth is open, probably indicating that he was singing. He is dressed in his trademark khaki colored double-breasted suit, with a striped tie.[27] He looks like a big-time bandleader, but a *very tired* big-time bandleader. In light of the myriad problems he was then confronting on a daily basis, this is certainly understandable.

On Wednesday, August 30, Bunny closed at the Loew's State Theater, racking up a respectable weekly gross of $25,000. The next day, his attorney filed a petition for bankruptcy in U.S. District Bankruptcy Court in New York. The address for Bunny Berigan used on the petition, 538 Fifth Avenue, was the address of MCA's New York office. Here are some of the details: "Bunny Berigan filed a petition of bankruptcy in the New York Federal Court last Thursday. He gave his assets as $100 and his liabilities as $11,353. Among the creditors were fifteen musicians to whom he owed a total of $4,680; MCA, who were owed $1,500; and a New York finance company, $568. John Wanamaker, a New York department store, on the same day filed a judgment against Berigan for $1,054."[28] Prior to the bankruptcy filing, Bunny's share of the Loew's State money was sequestered by Local 802. The headline read: "Berigan's Coin Seized For Petrillo." Acting on a telegraphic request[29] from James C. Petrillo, head of Chicago local, the New York AFM, last week, seized the earnings of Bunny Berigan for his week's stand at the State Theater, New York City. After paying off the band musicians and giving a couple of hundred dollars to Berigan, Bill Feinberg, local 802 vice-president sent the balance to Chicago to cover Petrillo's claim against the leader for money advanced to Berigan's men in that city recently, plus taxes due that local.[30]

Clearly, the action of Petrillo in seizing Berigan's earnings from the Loew's-State engagement precipitated the bankruptcy filing. Nevertheless, Bunny's debt to the musicians' union somehow survived his bankruptcy action. Whether Petrillo's "fine" of Berigan was also a part of this continuing debt is unknown. What is known however is that for the next twelve months at least, most of whatever money Bunny Berigan earned seemed to go to the union. From this point until the end of his life, Bunny bridled at the mention of the name James Petrillo.

After finally being paid, and facing a very uncertain future with Berigan, many sidemen quit immediately following the ending of the Loew's State engagement. The band that appeared with Bunny at the Loew's State Theater had consisted of: Johnny Napton (1st), Joe Bauer, Jake Koven (trumpets); Mark Pascoe (1st), Al Jennings (2nd) (trombones); Gus Bivona (first alto and jazz alto/clarinet), Charlie DiMaggio (alto); Don Lodice (jazz) and Larry Walsh (tenors) (saxes); rhythm section of Bushkin, Moore, Stulmaker, and Collins. Those who departed were Bivona, Lodice, Napton, Bauer, and Bushkin. Napton joined Gene Krupa. Bivona and Lodice joined Teddy Powell, with whom ex-Beriganites Irving Goodman and Ruthie Gaylor were already working. (The Powell band had become a haven for musicians who had worked with and learned a lot from Bunny Berigan. In addition to the ones mentioned above, soon trumpeter Joe Bauer, and guitarist Tommy Morgan would join Powell.) Joe Bushkin joined Muggsy Spanier, who had been very favorably impressed by Joe's playing while they both were working at Hotel Sherman. Once again, there was a large hole in the Berigan band.

When one considers the many body blows Bunny Berigan had recently sustained, and these were on top of numerous other large difficulties he had encountered in the preceding fourteen months, one must ask: why didn't he simply disband after the Loew's State engagement? Clues exist that may at least partially answer this question. In spite of all of the maneuvering that had occurred in Chicago with the local musicians' union and later, according to Berigan's petition for bankruptcy, he still owed his musicians $4,680 on August 30 at the conclusion of the Loew's State stand. It appears that all of Berigan's band members were paid in full at the conclusion of the Loew's State job from the money Petrillo had seized pursuant to the court order he obtained, with any shortfall ($2,580) being covered by other Berigan receipts the union had taken, and probably by the $1,500 MCA claimed Bunny owed them. MCA then made another deal with Berigan that whatever money they advanced to pay off his band members, he would repay to them after the bankruptcy action concluded, if it concluded with a discharge of his debts. (This would be quite illegal today.) I do not think that it is a coincidence that Bunny's bankruptcy petition listed MCA as a creditor to the tune of $1,500 I do not think that Bunny owed MCA anything approaching $1,500 until the union intervened in Chicago, and essentially seized all of Bunny's earnings for the Savoy and Milwaukee dates, and indeed from the Loew's State job. Prior to that, Bunny either paid MCA its commissions, or his band didn't work. Usually, MCA secured their commissions on bookings at the time the booking was made, with the promoter paying a deposit to MCA then. And any money MCA may have advanced to Bunny in the months before his bankruptcy was likely being repaid, with interest, during that time. That, and his ongoing dispute with Arthur Michaud, are probable reasons why Bunny never had any money during the first half of 1939, even though his band was doing very good business wherever it played.

The $1,500 debt to MCA almost certainly was a loan that was made to Berigan to pay off the balance that was owed to his musicians once and for all at the conclusion of the Loew's State gig. An additional consideration flowing to Berigan from MCA was probably the Loew's State booking itself. There is no indication that this engagement had been set for very long prior to it actually taking place. When Bunny's financial situation finally imploded in Chicago, MCA could have hurriedly booked the Berigan band into the Loew's State in order to minimize the debt Bunny had incurred with his band members, and to try to preserve the Berigan band. The other side of this is that they booked Berigan into this lucrative engagement because if he didn't raise some money in a hurry, the musicians' union may have paid off the Berigan band members, then gone after MCA in some fashion to secure repayment. Whatever actually happened, Bunny Berigan emerged from this situation indebted to the union for what turned out to be a year, and as a virtual indentured servant of MCA for what turned out to be the rest of his life.

In the wake of this maneuvering, three facts became apparent: (1) Bunny Berigan continued to front a big band; (2) MCA continued to book the Berigan band; and (3) despite the bankruptcy action, Bunny remained deeply in debt. What we can assume from these facts is that the debts listed in Berigan's petition for bankruptcy eventually went away in some fashion, and that his musicians were finally paid in full. The payment of the musicians was an essential piece of the plan because if the musicians had not been paid, Berigan could never have led a band of union musicians again. And as we know, Bunny very much wanted to continue to lead his own band. So, Bunny, without the assistance of a personal manager to protect his interests, allowed MCA to devise whatever plan was necessary to enable him to continue with his band. The plan they contrived undoubtedly secured to MCA full repayment of all money advanced by MCA for Berigan's benefit, plus interest. As subsequent events seem to indicate, Berigan, at this time, jumped from the financial frying pan into the fire in order to continue to lead a big band.

The thinking processes of alcoholics are often muddled, and it is therefore sometimes difficult for nonalcoholics to understand their motivations. But in this case it seems very clear that Bunny Berigan would have done almost anything to continue to lead his band. It is likely that he looked at whatever deal he made with MCA in this way: Yes, I owe them money. But they have to continue to book my band in order to be paid back. Therefore, I will continue to get bookings from MCA if for no other reason than so they can be repaid what I owe them. This is almost too absurd to believe, and I would not believe it myself if it weren't for one fact: that Bunny Berigan worked for MCA continuously in some fashion from the time of his bankruptcy until his death on June 2, 1942. In fact, he continued working for them *after* his death by proxy, because his band continued on for a time as what was probably (after Chick Webb's) one of the first ghost bands. From MCA's standpoint, it is clear that whatever financial troubles Bunny had gotten himself into, MCA had invested in building and promoting the name Bunny Berigan, and that name would bring MCA commissions in the future as it had in the past, so long as Bunny Berigan was able to stand up in front of any group of musicians and play one-night stands. So, Bunny went about reorganizing his band so that he could do precisely that, and MCA continued to book the Berigan band and receive commissions for each gig the band played. MCA also began to repay itself the money it had advanced Berigan, plus interest.

The magical spell that Bunny was able to cast, especially on young musicians who were eager to gain some experience in his band, was still very much intact. The veteran tenor saxophonist Stuart Anderson was three years *older* than Bunny. Nevertheless, he did what was necessary to position himself to join the Berigan band: "I'd been at the State Theater nearly every night to catch the show and at the end of the week, I got a call to join the band on 4th tenor, so that Larry Walsh could move up to 2nd. Charlie DiMaggio moved into the lead alto chair and brought his brother, Joe DiMaggio, to play 3rd alto and jazz clarinet. Carl 'Bama' Warwick took Joe Bauer's 3rd trumpet chair. He was a very light-skinned Negro and most of us didn't realize he was colored."[31] Others already in the band were looking for opportunities to continue to improve their résumés. Tenor saxist Larry Walsh had not had many jazz solos while Don Lodice was in the band. Now that Lodice had left, he was given the opportunity to move up to the jazz chair.

I don't know how true it was that Bunny was maybe thinking of packing it in as a bandleader, but the Loew's State job was a very successful one with Maxine Sullivan, who'd had a hit with 'Loch Lomond,' also on the bill, but after we finished that job, Bunny was forced to reorganize, because of the personnel changes and we had to have quite a few rehearsal sessions. Truman 'Quig' Quigley came in on second trumpet, because Jake Koven had taken over Johnny Napton's first chair. Johnny left to join Gene Krupa in Chicago. I took over the 2nd (jazz) tenor chair vacated by Don Lodice. Some of the ballad arrangements had used Clyde Rounds on baritone sax, but with many of them now being replaced by jump numbers, I asked Bunny if I could drop it and he agreed. Besides the few days of rehearsals after band reorganized, we played the Palisades Park job soon after and some other one-nighters in the New York area.[32]

Buddy Koss had replaced Joe Bushkin on piano, and Bunny hired girl singer Kay Doyle. Once more, within a very short time, Bunny Berigan had effectively reorganized his band. The new personnel were as follows: Jake Koven (lead), Truman Quigley, Carl Warwick, trumpets; Mark Pasco (lead), Al Jennings, trombones; Charlie DiMaggio (lead alto), Joe DiMaggio (3rd alto and jazz clarinet), Larry Walsh (jazz/2nd) Stuart Anderson (4th) (tenors), saxophones; Edwin 'Buddy' Koss, piano; Tommy Moore, guitar; Morty Stulmaker, bass; Paul Collins, drums. Danny Richards remained on vocals and was joined by Kay Doyle. Al Jennings, in addition to playing good trombone, sang novelties and jazz numbers. The Berigan band, shaken and diminished, with its ever-optimistic leader, carried on.

A number of Berigan sidemen stated that soon after Kay Doyle joined the band, she and Bunny were in the midst of a romance. Whatever was going on seemed to be good for Bunny's playing because as aircheck recordings from this period demonstrate, he was playing brilliantly. Ms. Doyle remained with the band probably until the end of 1939.

Berigan rehearsed his new band for several days, and then took them to a break-in job at Palisades Park in Fort Lee, New Jersey, on September 13. They then traveled northeast to start a one-week engagement at the Totem Pole, Norumbega Park, Route 30, just outside Boston in Auburndale, Massachusetts, on September 15. It was from this point that the band broadcast over WOR from 8:00–8:30 p.m. on September 20. While the band was in Boston, aircheck recordings were made. Although the band plays well, it is clear that soloists Bivona, Bushkin, and Lodice are missed. Berigan however, plays as well as ever.

While Bunny was breaking his new band in at the Totem Pole, some of his old colleagues were doing very well in New York: "Glenn Miller ork and the Ink Spots open at New York's Paramount Theater on Wednesday, September 20, 1939, the first time there for Miller."[33] "Artie Shaw will get $36,000 for three weeks at the Strand Theater, New York City. He will open there on September 21."[34]

After the Totem Pole gig, the Berigan band probably played one-nighters in New England until they returned to Manhattan for an engagement, with a broadcast, that held a pleasant surprise for Bunny. Paul Collins recalled: "That broadcast was Martin Block's *Swing Session* program and Glen Gray's Casa Loma orchestra played opposite us. They played 'I Can't Get Started' as a tribute to Bunny, using his famous arrangement and featuring Murray McEachern on trombone. He played it extremely well, except for very last high note on the coda, when he stopped playing, turned and bowed towards Bunny."[35] Berigan was not a man who was given to demonstrations of emotion. But on this occasion he was moved to tears.

Despite all of Bunny's problems, the band on this broadcast is loose and swinging, and his own playing is magnificent throughout, especially on "I Poured My Heart into a Song" (hear his capacious, velvety low register before the vocal; then later the perfectly lip-trilled high C followed by the titanic high F at the end),[36] and the obscure but rewarding original "Night Song."[37] He undoubtedly had received another lecture recently from the people at MCA that he needed to reduce his drinking if he wanted to remain a bandleader. His father and the members of his band were trying to help him cut down too. It is truly amazing how quickly and dramatically his playing improved when he limited his intake of alcohol. Unfortunately, by this time, each ounce of alcohol he imbibed was adding to the severe damage that already had been done to his liver, and no regeneration or healing of that cirrhosis-ravaged organ was possible.

John Fallstich joined the band at this time on lead trumpet, replacing Jake Koven. Saxophonist Joe DiMaggio was also replaced, by Jack Goldie.

In the October issue of *Metronome,* George T. Simon inserted this squib: "I made the rounds of the booking offices and met lanky Dick Mansfield at MCA. On the way out I ran into Bunny Berigan. That recent bankruptcy trouble hasn't worried him noticeably."[38]

Maybe Bunny was being informed of MCA's latest plan for his band on that visit. It was another southern tour. Here's how it was scheduled to proceed: Saturday, September 30, Casino Ballroom, Scranton, Pennsylvania; October 2, the Hall of Swing (Lakewood Park Casino) at the Southeastern Fair, Atlanta, Georgia, for four nights. Buddy Koss remembered that engagement:

> The Southeastern Fair was Atlanta's big national livestock and poultry show, which was held at Lakewood Park in Georgia. The spacious 'Hall Of Swing' was formerly the Lakewood Park Casino, which had been refurbished. State Governor Riere and Atlanta's Mayor Hartfield opened the fair at 8 a.m. and the band went on at 9 p.m. I remember that opening night was bitterly cold, but despite that, the fair drew over 10,000 customers on the first day and the dance went on until 1 a.m. the next morning. We had broadcasts on Tuesday, Wednesday and Thursday nights, and were followed at the weekend by Gene Krupa's band.[39]

While this tour was in progress, Bunny's creditors were meeting in the bankruptcy court at the U.S. Courthouse in Manhattan on October 5. After this date, the White materials are devoid of any further information regarding Bunny Berigan's bankruptcy proceedings. Over the years, the assumption has been that Berigan concluded the bankruptcy process by obtaining a discharge from his debts. If that actually happened, then Bunny would have been free of the debts he listed on the bankruptcy petition his attorney filed with the court at the start of the bankruptcy proceedings. Since we know that after the apparent termination of the bankruptcy action, Bunny still had one or more of the debts he had listed on his bankruptcy petition, it is possible that his attorney worked out some sort of payback agreement with Berigan's creditors, and dismissed the bankruptcy action *without the bankruptcy court ever discharging Bunny's debts.* Whatever actually happened, the bankruptcy process and how Berigan's creditors were to be handled was likely viewed by Bunny in very abstract terms. He left it to others to shepherd him through the process of obtaining some relief from his debts, and continued to hope that they would protect his financial interests. He himself apparently had little or no direct involvement in this process.

The Berigan band's southern tour continued with stops in Tampa, Florida, (October 7), Mississippi State College in Starksville, Mississippi, on the 9th, and The University of Florida at Gainesville on the 11th. On October 12, they drove all the way back to New York. They opened at the Mardi Gras Casino at the New York World's Fair on the 13th, where they would remain until the 18th. While they were at the Mardi Gras Casino, they broadcast on a couple of occasions. The broadcast on October 16 was recorded. Here is what they played on that broadcast: "Ay-Ay-Ay"; "My Heart Has Wings," vocal Danny Richards; "Caravan"; "Russian Lullaby"; "Begin the Beguine"; "I Poured My Heard into a Song," vocal Richards; "Royal Garden Blues"; and "I Can't Get Started" (closing theme).

During this engagement, another personnel change took place: Trumpeter Harry Preble subbed into the band temporarily: "I played with Bunny Berigan's band for part of the engagement at the New York World's Fair, subbing for Quig Quigley, who must have been on notice. After the date, Joe Aguanno joined as permanent replacement."[40] Also, while the Berigan band played at the World's Fair, they played a night at Harlem's Savoy Ballroom, October 15. There is no indication that any other band was there with them that night.[41] After the World's Fair gig ended, the Berigan band played at the Star Theater on Lexington Avenue and 107th Street in New York. This was a theater that catered to black patrons. The Berigan band was one of a very few white bands to appear in predominantly black venues with African American talent in those years. Then the band went to Syracuse to play a one-nighter at the Syracuse Armory on Saturday October 21. It is not known if he saw Donna on this occasion.

It appears that Donna had returned to Syracuse with her daughters after their visit to Wisconsin ended in early September. Mayme Berigan had remained at the Berigan homestead in Fox Lake. Cap Berigan continued to travel with Bunny, now apparently acting as the band's sole road manager, as Andy Phillips remained in New York after the Loew's State engagement. It is unclear where Bunny and Cap lived during this period while the band worked in New York, but it was probably at a transient hotel. By this time, it is almost certain that Bunny had lost his house in Rego Park. It is probable that the Berigan family finally vacated the Rego Park house when Donna, Mayme, and the girls went to Fox Lake the previous May. By then, Bunny had already given up his apartment on Central Park West. Berigan band members had always used the Forrest Hotel as their headquarters while they were in New York, but there is no clear indication that Bunny ever lived there himself, though he may have during his stay with Tommy Dorsey's band in 1940. All we have to give some sense of what Bunny's life in Manhattan was like when he was neither travelling to a gig, or playing one, is the recollection of the trumpeter Carl "Bama" Warwick, who was then a member of his band: "He had three vices: booze, women and pool! He would frequent the pool halls and bars in the small hours, but he always needed company, so I'd often go along with him. I remember him introducing me to Willie Hoppe, the famous pool player."[42]

Now, Bunny's permanent home was on the road. Increasingly, his family was whatever group of musicians he was leading at any given time. On October 23, the Berigan band opened a two-week engagement at the Southland Club, 76 Warrenton Street, Boston. The *Boston Post* carried this item about Bunny and his band on October 22:

> That 'Superman of the Trumpet,' Bunny Berigan, direct from the New York World's Fair, where he and his grand group of musicians closed their engagement last night as the 'Band of the Week,' will open an indefinite engagement at Boston's popular Southland tomorrow eve. A remarkable orchestra with a wonderful leader, the Bunny Berigan outfit should draw to capacity while at the Southland. One swell guy with a swell voice is what they say about Danny Richards, the clever vocalist with the band, who thrilled 'em at the World's Fair. The new floor show is a rapid-fire production of all-star, all-colored performers with lots of good singing and dancing.[43]

Perhaps the gig at the Star Theater was a break-in for the acts that appeared with the Berigan band at the Southland.

There was a broadcast from 10:00–10:30 p.m. over WJZ on the band's opening night from the Southland. They played the following tunes: "Ay-Ay-Ay"; "Over the Rainbow," vocal Kay Doyle; "What's New?" vocal Danny Richards; "Swingin' and Jumpin'"; "St. Louis Blues," vocal Al Jennings; "The Jumpin' Jive," vocal Doyle; "I Poured My Heart into a Song," vocal Richards; theme; and closing. Pianist Buddy Koss recalled some of the details from that engagement: "We were at the Southland for a couple of weeks and Bunny's dad, Cap Berigan, was still around. We all tried as tactfully as possible to help him keep Bunny away from the booze. I used to lead the band during the floor shows, so that Bunny could take time off the stand and socialize with the customers."[44]

Saxophonist Stuart Anderson, after having been with Bunny for a couple of months, carefully observed what was going on:

> Bunny was not much of a leader who said 'do this or don't do that;' he just played and you played like him. When he was 'on' he couldn't help but inspire us. I don't recall his playing getting worse as time went on. His drinking would 'build up' from period of fairly dry days to where it was quite heavy. You couldn't notice his drinking in his walk, he almost never staggered, but it showed up in his playing. He was difficult to get close to, and the more he drank the more withdrawn he became. Even Danny Richards couldn't get close to him when he was drinking heavily. A couple of the musicians at different times would try to buddy-buddy with Bunny and he would tolerate that just so long, and then he would embarrass them in public in such a way that they'd be glad to keep their

distance after that. Even so, Bunny was the only leader in my experience who would tell the band that they were playing well at a given time, and mean it.[45]

Berigan's solid performances while at the Southland apparently won him at least one friend, the person who was writing the review of the band that appeared in the *Boston Post:* "At Southland, broadcasting four nights a week, two of them over the Mutual network, Bunny Berigan and his band will continue for another week, playing all special arrangements in his suave, sweet and effective swing style. As a trumpet player, Bunny Berigan is second to nobody. After watching him toot his trumpet for four hours, Dick Todd asked, 'Doesn't your lip ever give out?' 'No,' replied Bunny, 'It's standing on my feet that gets me down!'"[46] The band closed at the Southland on November 2, Bunny's thirty-first birthday. They then played two nights at the Raymor Ballroom in Boston on a trial basis. Business was good enough to merit a longer engagement.

Here is how George T. Simon described the Raymor Ballroom in his biography of Glenn Miller: "The Raymor, on Huntington Avenue, close to Symphony Hall, was once probably considered elegant, but it had aged into a typical mid-city ballroom. Heavily draped and dimly lit, it offered about as much glamour as a men's locker room. But it had a loyal clientele and a very gentle and understanding manager in Hughie Galvin."[47]

Fortunately, the Berigan band was immediately engaged to play at the Raymor-Playmor twin ballrooms for an additional two weeks, sparing them at least temporarily from the rigors of the road. They played at the Raymor, opening on November 6 and closing on the 18th, while trombonist Jack Jenney's band held forth at the Playmor. Once again, Bunny got some good publicity: "One of the greatest musicians in the world is gracing the stage of Boston, Raymor Ballroom this week. It's the personable Bunny Berigan, who blows a trumpet 'a la Gabriel.' Bunny's band is one of the nation's top swing outfits and he sure sends 'em when he gives out on the short horn."[48] While at the Raymor, the Berigan band broadcast regularly over WAAB. Unfortunately, no recordings from those broadcasts are known to exist.

After completing the Raymor engagement, the Berigan band was presented as a part of an experiment at the Westchester County Center in White Plains, New York. The general idea seems to have been to replicate the vaudeville-type variety shows then being presented in the large theaters in urban centers in a suburban setting. Here is how this venture was described in the trade press:

Westchester Country Club, White Plains, New York, opens November 19 with a policy of name bands, starting with Paul Whiteman and Bunny Berigan. The club is to be run by Les Reis and Artie Dunn, the old vaudeville team, with no dancing. The hall can accommodate approximately 500 persons with chairs on the dance floor at a price scale of 40 cents (single) and 75 cents (double) for matinees and 85 cents and $1.10, respectively, for evening shows. This is the first in a series of shows at this location. The set-up is for two bands and 7 acts of vaudeville.[49]

Show of the Week Booking...Run by ex-vaude man Les Reis. The first show with Paul Whiteman and Bunny Berigan and vaude acts. The first will be only an evening show; afterwards all will have a 3 p.m. and 8:30 p.m. show; The Berigan band, with vocalists Danny Richards and Kay Doyle, are billed second to Whiteman.[50]

After this, Bunny hit the road for several one-nighters, including a dance at Kingston, New York on the 22nd sponsored by Ahvath Israel, and another at the Arcadia Ballroom, Providence, Rhode Island on the 23rd. The band then wandered a bit or had some off days, and returned to New York and the Victor recording studios on Twenty-fourth Street for what turned out to be the last time on November 28. On this occasion, Bunny did not take a day before the recording session to prepare his musicians. This was a departure from his normal routine. There are many other rather peculiar aspects to this recording session.

There is a good bit of information in the White materials about this session that provides some insight into what occurred that day in the studio. Here are the details: RCA Victor studios, New York City (2:30–5:30 p.m.), John Fallstich (1st), Carl Warwick (2nd), Joe Aguanno (3rd), trumpets; Mark Pascoe (1st), Al Jennings, trombones; Charlie DiMaggio (lead alto), Jack Goldie (3rd alto/clarinet), Larry Walsh (2nd), Stu Anderson (4th) (tenors), saxophones; Buddy Koss, piano; Tommy Moore, guitar; Morty Stulmaker, bass; Paul Collins, drums; Bunny Berigan trumpet/leader; Joe Haymes, Jimmy Mundy, and *Johnny Sanders(?)* (see below), arrangers. Inexplicably, neither of Berigan's vocalists appeared on this recording date. This undoubtedly would have been upsetting to Danny Richards, who was a fine singer, had proved to be very popular with audiences, and had stuck with Bunny through some very difficult times. Equally perplexing were some of the choices of material Berigan recorded that day. One wonders who was calling the shots.

"Peg O' My Heart" had been in the Berigan book since the fall of 1937. In fact, Bunny had made a good recording of it for *Thesaurus* on August 8, 1938. This performance, though not particularly inspired, is certainly acceptable. Bunny's sixteen bar open trumpet solo is average Berigan, which means it is much better that what many other trumpet players could have done. The tenor solo that follows is by Larry Walsh, and it is likewise quite satisfactory. The band is tight and plays well. This arrangement, which is a straightforward swing chart, has been attributed (incorrectly in my opinion—see below) to bandleader-arranger Joe Haymes. There appears to have been only one take made on this tune. Although this is certainly nothing more than a standard dance band recording, it is in many respects much superior to many of the recordings Bunny made for Victor when others were telling him what to record in 1937 and 1938.

"Night Song" was recorded next. This tune was composed by Juan Tizol and Jimmy Mundy and recorded (at a faster tempo) by Cootie Williams and His Rug-Cutters, an Ellington small group, for Vocalion on June 21, 1939. The arrangement Berigan employed is attributed in the White materials "possibly" to Johnny Sanders,[51] about whom I have found no information. I am skeptical of this attribution. This arrangement is almost identical to the one Charlie Barnet used when he recorded "Night Song" for RCA Bluebird on March 17, 1939. In the liner notes for *The Complete Charlie Barnet—1939* (RCA Bluebird AMX2-5577, 1981), this arrangement is attributed to Jimmy Mundy, and it sounds like a number of other arrangements Mundy was then writing. Based on this evidence, I attribute the Berigan arrangement on "Night Song" to Jimmy Mundy.[52] Bunny takes this at a perfect dance tempo and plays throughout using a tightly fitted cup mute. His high notes and shakes (the *intentional* kind) are pure Berigan. Mark Pasco was the first trombone player on this recording, and I find his wavy vibrato on the brief two trombone passage to be a bit overdone. Although I prefer Bunny's aircheck performance of "Night Song" from September 26, 1939, this is nevertheless a good recording. Two takes were made, but I have never heard the alternate.

"Ain't She Sweet" is another conventional swing arrangement that was definitely written by Joe Haymes. Here it is performed very cleanly at a brisk tempo by the Berigan band. It appears that Bunny resurrected his buzzing kazoo mute for his solo on this side, and plays a creative jazz solo, finding the chord changes much to his liking. The tenor bit is by Larry Walsh. Buddy Koss has a brief solo on piano. "Ain't She Sweet" is yet another good recording spotting tight, well-played ensembles, on which Mr. B. made only one master.

"Ay-Ay-Ay" is another tune that Bunny had been playing for several months prior to this recording session, which had been recorded superbly off the air on September 26. The arrangement for this piece has also been attributed (in the White materials) to the elusive Johnny Sanders, but I am again skeptical of this. (Unfortunately I have found no information regarding who might have arranged this tune for the Berigan band. I think it possible that it was arranged by Andy Phillips.) The band attacks this chart with precision. Bunny is definitely using a Harmon mute on his solo in the first chorus. Stuart Anderson on tenor and Koss on piano have solos. When Berigan returns later to solo, it is with an open trumpet and for a full chorus. He gets off some fine jazz, but in the final bars stumbles a bit, but certainly not more than he had on many previous Victor recordings. The band riffs a bit and then he comes back and essays a very technical eight-bar passage involving about six bars of rapidly executed sixteenth notes, which he manages fairly successfully, but then he misses a few notes in the last two bars.

Despite these flaws, there were no retakes, or recordings of additional tunes. The Berigan bandsmen left the studio barely three hours after they had arrived.

Here are some of the comments contained in the White materials that relate to these recordings:

The arranger of 'Peg O'My Heart' is uncertain. Joe Haymes thought he had done it, but the chart had been in the Berigan book for at least 15 months. Haymes was sure he had arranged 'Ain't She Sweet,' recalling (quite correctly) using the same 'intro' as on 'The Lady In Red,' which he had written for his own band and recorded for Victor in April 1935. (See Bluebird LP set AXM2-5552 by Haymes.)

He was certain he did not arrange the other two titles, for which Buddy Koss suggested the name 'Johnny Sanders,' but this has not been confirmed. It is interesting to note that this last session on Victor by Bunny's band took the least time of any of his sessions (four tunes in three hours). One reason was certainly that three of the tunes, at least, were not new to the band. 'Night Song' and 'Ay-Ay-Ay' had been played since September (at least) and 'Peg O' My Heart' had been in the 'book' since 1937."[53] (It is my opinion that the arrangement of 'Peg O'My Heart' Berigan recorded on November 28, 1939, was written by Joe Lippman. The clarinet-led reed spot after the tenor sax solo is a big clue.)

Joe Haymes further recalled: "I arranged 'Ain't She Sweet' for the Berigan band and I was present during rehearsals and at the recording date. Bunny's father, William 'Cap' Berigan, was in the studio, presumably to keep an eye on his son and keep him sober!"[54] It appears therefore that Haymes's arrangement on "Ain't She Sweet" was the only new arrangement recorded that day. It also appears that by this time, Andy Phillips had gone on to other employment.

Stuart Anderson also remembered what happened on that recording date:

I played the tenor solo on 'Ay-Ay-Ay'. Larry Walsh gave me that solo on the recording date, but all the other tenor sax solos are his. During that session, Bunny was having some lip trouble, which caused him to fluff a few notes. He was quite sober, but got so upset that after an exceptionally bad clinker he was about to throw his horn against the studio wall! His father took the trumpet away from him and gave him a chair, saying, 'If you must throw something, throw this!' Whereupon Bunny proceeded to smash the chair against the wall.[55]

As always, the critics had their say, but at a remove of over one year, because Victor did not release these sides until very late in 1940 or early in 1941. The opinions cited below, are different from mine, and to my ears are at odds with the recorded evidence.

'Ay-Ay-Ay' and 'Ain't She Sweet': Made over a year ago by Bunny's big band, these were never pressed until a few weeks ago. The reason for the delay must be obvious to all who study these two performances closely. The band is unclean, Berigan's horn is inconsistent and shaky, and the material he chooses is below mediocrity. Joe Bushkin's *(sic)* piano and Don Lodice's *(sic)* tenor aren't enough to overcome the many other faults. Only the rhythm section merits a listening.[56] 'Peg O' My Heart' and 'Night Song': Peg O'My Heart' isn't too bad, but far below Tea's recent Columbia disc. Bunny plays fairly well. But 'Night Song' is a shame. It never should have been issued, for the leader's pitiful trumpet is shaky and he fluffs notes more than a few times. A few bars of Don Lodice *(sic)* on tenor sax aren't enough to overcome Berigan's inexcusable faux-pas, and these were made 'way back in early 1940 *(sic)*.[57]

These recordings are professionally done. The band was obviously well prepared for this recording session. Their performances on all the sides recorded that day were precise, and that is a characteristic one does not usually associate with Berigan's bands. Indeed, the rhythm section praised by the *Down Beat* critic, especially drummer Paul Collins, is rather stiff. Bunny's own playing was very good. He was not playing safe. His trumpet shakes are a part of the jazz lexicon, and are not indicative of illness, weakness, or poor taste. The solos by the other musicians are certainly acceptable. Relative to the choices of material, my conclusion, based on Bunny's use of three of the four tunes recorded that his band had been playing for many months before the session, was that the people at Victor by this time did not really care what he recorded, and that this session was more or less a throwaway. Berigan may have simply owed Victor four sides pursuant to their one-year contract that ran from March of 1938 to March of 1939. He chose the path of least resistance (and cost) to fulfill his obligation, and had his band perform music they were familiar with, and (except for "Ain't She Sweet") for which he would not have had to pay for new arrangements, copying, etc. (Joe Haymes's presence in the studio during the rehearsal/recording of "Ain't She Sweet" makes it likely that his arrangement was new to the band, and that Haymes helped them get it under their fingers before it was recorded.)

Bunny was undoubtedly disillusioned with Victor by this time, as he had every right to be. Victor's executives had for the most part mishandled many aspects of the relationship between the company and the artist. Their failure to record the Berigan band throughout almost all of 1939 (for whatever reason) when Bunny was playing splendidly, and leading an excellent band that included several strong soloists, had high-quality arrangements on many of the better current pop tunes and some exciting originals, and one and sometimes two very good vocalists, was inexcusable. Victor undoubtedly could have made records with the Berigan band during this time which would have competed very favorably with those being produced by the top bands in the country. This blunder only compounded the damage to Bunny's professional reputation that had resulted so often from the recordings he *had* previously made for Victor, which all too frequently were of inferior, sometimes terrible Tin Pan Alley pop tunes. Add to this Victor's failure to intelligently promote the Berigan band to the youth market, who were buying millions of the thirty-five cent Bluebird discs of other swing bands, (as opposed to the seventy-five cent Victors) and you have the outlines of a largely unsuccessful association. Also, by late November 1939, Bunny was clearly playing out the string with Victor: there would be no extension or renewal of his contract with the company, and the performer's royalties that were accruing from the sales of his previous Victor records (and probably these also) were being paid to someone else, very likely Arthur Michaud. Since Berigan's bankruptcy petition indicated that he had no assets as of August 1939, it appears that he had assigned his performer royalties to one or more of his creditors prior to that. With no personal manager or attorney to guide him through these turbulent waters, Berigan was left with only ten sides recorded in all of 1939, and no prospects to record in the immediate future. The ongoing absence of one of the magic "Three Rs" of bandleading success was undermining the popularity of the already reeling Berigan band. But, in typical fashion,

Bunny remained optimistic, assuming that a contract with another record company would be forthcoming in the near future, simply because he was playing well and leading a good band.

Nevertheless, on the musical side of the band, Bunny continued to make most of the right moves. Trombonist/vocalist Al Jennings formed some very definite opinions about Berigan during his stay with Bunny's band. Here are a few of them: "Bunny was a great leader really, but he didn't behave like a boss. True, he drank a little too much and smoked the weed occasionally, but it never seemed to hurt his playing to any great extent. He never missed any jobs that I can remember. When we cut those records, we'd start the session with Bunny holding a full glass of liquor and we wouldn't make a master until it was empty. Even if he appeared on the stand under the influence, we'd put his horn into his hand and he'd play!"[58]

On November 30, the Berigan band opened a two-night gig at the Fiesta Danceteria on Forty-second Street in New York City, following Teddy Powell's band into that spot. This appears to have been another tryout engagement because the band was then booked at the Fiesta for a week, beginning on December 7. Between the 1st and the 7th, they played one-nighters in and around New York, including one at the Arcadia Ballroom in Brooklyn, opposite Benny Carter's band on the 2nd. While the Berigan brigade was at the Fiesta, Joe Marsala's group was the other band being presented there.

All of this was a warm-up for what the Berigan band members hoped would be an exciting week at Harlem's Apollo Theater, commencing on December 15. Berigan followed Charlie Barnet into the Apollo. *Variety* included a review of the Apollo show in its December 22 issue:

> Apollo Bill: Bunny Berigan Orchestra, George Wiltshire (comedy), Lillian Fitzgerald, Apus and Estrelita, Al Hylton, Sandy Burns, Viola Underwood and the house line of eighteen. The movie is *The Escape* (Twentieth Century Fox). The show leans heavily on filth, is indifferently presented and not really staged in the accepted sense of the word, but merely tossed together with little thought of compactness, pace or development. Dance numbers are poorly conceived and insufficiently rehearsed. What laughs there are depend on the anatomical or bathroom variety. The Berigan orchestra plays the first half of the show behind a curtain, a usual procedure with guest bands. Lillian Fitzgerald, hot singer, shouts two numbers; Apus and Estrelita, a mixed pair, do songs, dance and comedy (loaded with smut). Al Hylton does a magic routine; Danny Richards sings 'My Prayer;' Miss Viola, a hefty Negro contralto, also appears with the band, doing several blues tunes to a sizeable response. Berigan vocalizes on 'I Can't Get Started,' but he's a trifle stiff as an MC.[59]

The White materials contain this note regarding the appearance of Viola Underhill with the Berigan band: "'Miss Rhapsody,' Viola Underhill, signed a contract to appear at the Apollo Theater during the week beginning December 15th at a weekly salary of $60. She appeared with the Berigan band and according to a newspaper report, 'practically stole the show from the noted bandleader and his aggregation.' And a pencilled note in her scrapbook reads, "Rhap got a raise to $75 after the first show."[60] The viewpoint of a Berigan sideman about this engagement was provided later by Paul Collins: "The Apollo was a great date, with very appreciative audiences. They had an all-colored show with a very fast, very beautiful chorus line. The drummer had a lot to do! Business was very good and the band played really great, but we had to eat smelly doughnuts and spicy spaghetti between shows!"[61]

While the Berigan band was at the Apollo Theater, a photo was taken of them onstage and in performance. A smiling and dapper Bunny in a gray double-breasted suit leads his tuxedo-clad sidemen as they play. The Berigan band's week at the Apollo was successful, as this blurb from the trade press indicates: "Charlie Barnet shattered all percentages and opening day records as he brought the first white band into the Apollo Theater. Bunny Berigan followed and also did well."[62]

After closing at the Apollo, Berigan played a dance date at the chic Carlisle Hotel in New York on December 22. The next night, he and drummer Paul Collins spent the evening together: "Bunny and I attended an ice hockey game at Madison Square Garden although he had complained of feeling rather poorly for a couple of days. He reckoned he got a further chill at the game and was taken to a nearby hospital. He was out of his head with a high fever the first night and then his hands, knees and feet all swelled up, so he had to stay in the hospital for about ten days."[63]

On December 24, the Berigan band was scheduled to begin a week's engagement at the Mosque Ballroom in Newark, New Jersey, with the 26th and 27th off for Christmas. Press reports also said the he would appear for a time on the 24th with Georgie Auld's band, which consisted of the remnants of Artie Shaw's sidemen, who had elected Auld their leader after Artie left the band and went to Mexico a few weeks earlier. Auld was then playing at Roseland in New York City. Berigan certainly did not sit in with Auld's band, and may not have played any of the Mosque engagement.[64] He entered Polyclinic Hospital in Manhattan on either December 24 or 25, and would remain there for at least ten days. The available evidence indicates that he did not rejoin his band until January 7. This illness, which caused Bunny to be away from his band for two weeks, would be very costly for him in a number of ways.

Although there has been some discussion of the symptoms of the acute illness that put Berigan in the hospital at the end of 1939, and had him walking with a cane when he got out, there appears to be very little comment about the underlying chronic illness that was causing these symptoms. That illness was cirrhosis of the liver. The symptoms described above are symptoms of cirrhosis. Edema, or swelling, is a classic symptom of cirrhosis. "As cirrhosis of the liver becomes severe, signals are sent to the kidneys to retain salt and water in the body. The excess salt and water first accumulate in the tissue beneath the skin of the ankles and legs because of the effects of gravity when standing or sitting."[65] These symptoms are in addition to those that were mentioned in chapter 18, caused by the scarring of the liver that is also typical of cirrhosis. Irrespective of the effect Bunny's drinking was having on his ability to function day-to-day, and play the trumpet, the disease within his body was now beginning to cause other serious health problems for him.

While Berigan struggled to overcome the assault on his organs that had now begun as a result of cirrhosis, his band forged on, no doubt at the behest of MCA, to honor the commitment to the Mosque Ballroom, which was then owned by former bandleader Jean Goldkette. MCA summoned various musicians to lead the Berigan band in Bunny's absence, first Jack Teagarden, on December 28 and 29, then Wingy Manone on December 31 and January 1. On December 30, the Berigan band may have played in Port Washington, New York, with Big Tea leading them. (Teagarden was having his own problems leading a big band on the road for MCA then. On February 14, 1940, would file his own bankruptcy petition, listing a staggering $45,863 in debts, including $10,000 owed to MCA.[66] When compared with Teagarden's debts, Bunny's were small.[67]) In many ways, Jack Teagarden was like Bunny Berigan. They both were, first and foremost, magnificent musicians. They both were not vigilant in matters of business, and trusted others to look out for their interests. And they both were alcoholics. Fortunately, Jack Teagarden's liver was able to tolerate his alcohol abuse for a long time. Indeed, when Teagarden died on January 15, 1964, at age fifty-eight, it was from bronchial pneumonia, not the effects of cirrhosis of the liver.

Jack Teagarden was also a gentle soul who in no way would have ever wanted to hurt Bunny Berigan, a man he liked personally and revered as a musician. Nevertheless, when Teagarden stood in front of the Berigan band for those few nights at the end of 1939, he was very favorably impressed by the quality of their performances. While he was subbing for Bunny, no one knew when Berigan would be coming back to front his band or indeed *if* he was coming back. Here is Stuart Anderson's recollection of what happened at that time: "Wingy Manone led the band for a couple of nights. He took one look at our music and said, 'Let's play the blues.' Jack Teagarden also fronted for a couple of nights, but he transposed and played Bunny's parts from the arrangements without much trouble. He also brought his singer, Kitty Kallen, with him as we didn't have a girl vocalist at that time. 'Tea' also offered all the boys jobs with him 'if the worst should happen.'"[68]

Like all bandleaders, Bunny was well aware of the dangers of layoffs, be it a layoff of the band or the layoff of the bandleader. His earlier layoffs of his band had invariably cost him at least a few musicians. This hiatus would too. Chuck DiMaggio remembered what happened while Bunny was convalescing:

> Bunny could stay away from the band for weeks at a time, like when he was in the hospital, and then come into a rehearsal cold, and just thrill everyone. He loved children and would often pick up my little boy, who was only two, and take him out for the day. The kids all loved him too. Unfortunately, he had that terrible drink problem, which caused him to go off the deep end frequently. He also

had a weakness for the ladies, which caused Donna much grief. We didn't see her or the kids very often, because she was rarely at any of the places we played. It's true that Bunny and Lee Wiley had quite a thing going and I'm certain he felt more for her than any of the other women he had. He was a handsome guy and the women used to flock around him, but I'm sure that if he and Donna had ever divorced, he'd have married Lee. He approved of most of his fellow musicians and would never put anyone down, and with that philosophy, he got the most out of his sidemen. We often starved, but how we loved and respected him! He was quite a golfer too, and would go out on the course after having driven all night from some date in the sticks. Of course, his little bottle of stimulant always accompanied him in the side pocket of his golf bag! Those were difficult times for Bunny, and besides his financial worries he was laid up from time to time with ill health, pneumonia and arthritis in particular. Then he would lose good musicians, simply because they had to keep working to earn a living and couldn't wait around while the band and its leader were laid off. So there was quite a turnover in personnel, which didn't always make for good performances. While Bunny was in the hospital, Johnny Fallstich, Larry Walsh, and Jack Goldie all accepted offers from Jack Teagarden, and I got my brother Joe into the 3rd alto chair. Stu Anderson took over the jazz tenor and Frank Rash joined on 4th tenor. A young trumpet player called Les Elgart came in on first trumpet.[69]

When Bunny rejoined the band, even though he was using a cane and had not completely recovered from the swelling that had sent him to the hospital, he was evidently playing well, and was strong enough to work with his band, then go out afterwards to sit in with friends. Paul Collins recalled: "When Bunny got out of the hospital, he was using a cane, because his fingers, knees and feet were still swollen, but it didn't seem to affect his playing, and he was drinking less."[70] Buddy Koss remembered: "Yeah, he started going down to Nick's after work. He would sit in and jam with the guys and word soon got around that Bunny was back and was in fine form."[71]

The Berigan band had a five-day engagement at Century Theater in New York City which began on January 7 and ended on the 11th. On January 12, they played a one-nighter at the George F. Pavilion near Binghamton, New York. The band probably played a couple of other one-night dates between then and their opening in Boston in the Marionette Room of Hotel Brunswick, Boyleston and Clarendon Streets, Boston, on January 15. Here is the probable personnel Bunny then was using: "Les Elgart (first), Carl Warwick, Joe Aguanno, trumpets; Mark Pasco (first), unknown, trombones; Chuck DiMaggio (first), Joe DiMaggio (jazz), (altos); Stu Anderson, Frank Rash (tenors), saxophones; Buddy Koss, piano; Tommy Moore, guitar, if present; Morty Stulmaker, bass; Paul Collins, drums; Danny Richards, vocals."[72] Bunny had no girl singer at this time, Kay Doyle having departed while Berigan was hospitalized. Regardless of Danny Richards's very good performances, I suspect that the lack of a female vocalist was something of a commercial handicap because girl singers were an important feature in all bands. Nevertheless, the band forged on, and presumably played quite acceptably at the Brunswick.

While they were there, they broadcast over WEEI–Boston, and two of those broadcasts have been preserved. (See appendix 4 for details.)

Billboard's correspondent filed this review of the Berigan band at the Brunswick Hotel:

> Bunny Berigan, one of the leading exponents of hot trumpeting art, is surrounded by 12 versatile boys, who dish out the jive in the approved manner that pleases both adults and juniors alike. The maestro handles his trumpet in a superb manner, playing almost flawless tone, he fronts and vocalizes occasionally. Joe Di-Maggio is the standout of the group, alternating between alto saxophone and clarinet. The only detriment to the band is vocalist Danny Richards. He has a pleasing personality, but is handicapped by a whispering tone which is out of place with the orchestra's brassy arrangements. Other standouts, besides DiMaggio, are Stu Anderson on tenor saxophone, Morty Stulmaker on bass and the old hide-pounder, Paul Collins.[73]

Paul Collins and Stuart Anderson added some details: "During the Brunswick Hotel engagement, we were off on Sunday and I (Collins) did a 'sub' job for Jack Teagarden, who was playing at the Southland and he made me an offer that was much more money than I was getting with Bunny. So I turned in my notice, which I worked out until we finished at the hotel. Bunny had been booked in for a two week option and he got Jack Maisel to replace me for the second stint."[74] Stuart Anderson recalled: "Jack Maisel joined the band in Boston and brought quite a few new arrangements with him. Soon afterwards, he took over the road management from 'Cap' Berigan, Bunny's father. We were out of the hotel for about a week, playing a return engagement at the Raymor-Playmor twin Ballrooms opposite Teddy Powell. Boston was really jumping at that time with Jack Teagarden and Lennie Hayton also in the city."[75]

The Berigan band closed at the Brunswick on January 27. The next day, Bunny returned to Manhattan alone to play on CBS's *Hobby Lobby* show, from 5:00–5:30 p.m. He rejoined his band in Boston the following day for a one-week gig at the Raymor-Playmor Ballrooms. From this location, they also broadcast over WEEI from 12:00 midnight to 12:30 a.m. on the 29th. No recordings of this broadcast are known to exist.[76]

While Bunny was in Boston, his friend Tommy Dorsey was in Indianapolis at the Lyric Theater with his band, and despite surface appearances, was having some problems. Here are a couple of press reports from that time:

> Rumors from the touring Tommy Dorsey ork imply a bit of more or less serious trouble within the tooter's ranks. The whispers are that three key men have already given their notices, with four more likely to follow suit, rather than take a salary pruning.[77]

> Tommy Dorsey, making a radical change in his band, put three men on notice last week. Tommy will drop one trombone, making the brass set-up six, including himself. Ward Silloway takes the first sliphorn chair. The cleaning-out is one of

the most radical the band has had in five years. Deane Kincaide, alto saxman and arranger, Elmer Smithers, trombonist, and Howard Smith, pianist, all drew notices. Babe Russin was replaced temporarily by Tony Zimmers on tenor sax. Babe is ill and will rejoin later. Meanwhile, Tommy was looking for replacements and denying that Johnny Mince, solo clarinetist, also was leaving.[78]

More details about these developments were provided by Tommy's first trumpeter, Zeke Zarchy:

All the guys in the band were called into Tommy's dressing room at the theater, one by one. We hadn't been paid for three weeks, because Tommy had suffered a series of severe business setbacks, which were going to take him some time to sort out and get back on his feet. I knew he had oil-well investments and I guess they weren't doing too well! Anyway, he was asking everyone to accept a salary cut and play ball with him until things got straightened out. He had promised me a raise after we finished the job at Chicago's Palmer House in the New Year, but asked me if I would stay on at my present salary instead of taking a cut. He added that he would give me the promised increase as soon as he was able. Now I was very fond of Tommy, who was peerless musically in my opinion, so I agreed to his proposal. Some of the guys, though, were insisting on rejecting any salary reduction and tendered their notices instead. However, departure times were always flexible, because guys would normally wait until suitable replacements could be hired and it was really just coincidental that the big exodus occurred shortly before we were due to open at Frank Dailey's famous Meadowbrook in New Jersey.[79]

Bunny closed the Raymor-Playmor engagement on February 3, and returned rather unexpectedly to the Brunswick Hotel. "Bunny Berigan and his famous orchestra return to the Marionette Room of the Hotel Brunswick on Monday, February 5. Bunny is a crowd-pleaser and a perennial favorite and we strongly suggest that you plan to visit the Marionette Room this week as his band will be there for a limited engagement."[80] In spite of this good break, Berigan himself was still not well. Former Berigan vocalist Gail Reese decided to visit Bunny while the band was in Boston: "I went down to the Brunswick Hotel to catch the band and was most upset to see Bunny in such poor physical shape. His hands were so swollen that he could hardly hold his horn. I think he must have been in a lot of pain, because he played very little that night."[81] As it turned out, Berigan's second run at the Brunswick lasted until February 14, and was very successful. "Boston was somewhat clogged by snow on its streets, but all the night spots and hotels did the largest business in some time. Bunny Berigan played to packed houses, while Teddy Powell was also playing to capacity. Berigan was at the Hotel Brunswick, where he was held over for three weeks."[82]

Sickness, snow, or a successful gig made no difference to the MCA accountants: the Berigan band had to cover its weekly commissions "nut," and that meant working whenever and wherever MCA booked the band. So, when Sunday February 11 rolled around, and MCA knew the band could not work in Boston that day because of the Massachusetts "blue laws," they booked it to play a one-nighter at the Arcadia Hall in Brooklyn, New York. The band then returned to Boston to play the Brunswick gig the next day.

Boston was buried in snow on February 15. Luckily, the MCA bookers had lined up a one-nighter for the Berigan band just across the Charles River from Boston at Harvard University for February 16. Yet again, Bunny and his boys pleased the paying customers. Stuart Anderson remembered: "We played that date in a terrific blizzard, but the campus crowd seemed to like the band. The show also included a comedian, who parodied the Roosevelts and got a big hand from the kids."[83] "The campus approved of the Bunny Berigan orchestra. Reasons were: the name, theme and the fact that he and the band's playing were much better than expected."[84]

From that gig, what the band did over the next few days is rather uncertain. There definitely was a one-night dance date at the Metropolitan Ballroom in Philadelphia on February 21, and another at Blair Academy, Blairstown, New Jersey, on the 23rd. Then on Sunday February 25, 1940, the Berigan band played a one-nighter at the St. George Hotel in Brooklyn. After the gig, Bunny unceremoniously announced that he was breaking up his band and would be joining Tommy Dorsey's band, which had recently opened at the Meadowbrook in Cedar Grove, New Jersey. Here are two remembrances of that night. Stuart Anderson recalled: "That was the band's last date. We weren't given any real notice by Bunny or the office. I guess they just ran out of bookings and that caused the band to break up." Buddy Koss added: "Bunny left the band very quickly without much warning. 'I am going back to Tommy Dorsey,' was about all he said to the band, but he added that he would definitely have his own band again at some time in the future."[85]

Ironically, what appears to be a publicity piece about Berigan appeared in *Metronome's* February, 1940 issue:

> Bunny Berigan has pointed out that the two important things that enable you to swing out are musical imagination and technique. Musical imagination gives you the various licks to play, while technique gives you the ability to execute those licks. Some of Bunny's salient points are to develop your musical imagination; the greatest help is in listening to swing soloists whose playing appeals to you. On phonograph records, study the licks you particularly like and notice the harmony that is used; you are not confined to the notes that are in the true harmony. When you develop a large stock of ideas and have the ear to know what harmonies they go with, you are ready to take off, providing you have the technique to play what's in your mind. This doesn't mean that you should always play a lot of notes. A very few well-chosen notes often create the best effect. You can always do the best job swinging a chorus on a tune you are thoroughly familiar with. Bunny often plays with his eyes closed so that nothing distracts him. Most good swing soloists, having become familiar with various chord progressions, are capable of swing in a chorus on an entirely new number. A use of various effects characteristic of swing is essential in creating a satisfactory chorus.[86]

MCA had finally pulled the plug on the Berigan band. In the previous eighteen months, Bunny had experienced a slow but inexorable withdrawal of support from MCA. Their attention was now divided between many more swing bands than had existed when they first took him on as a client in the spring of 1937. Gene Krupa, Harry James, and Jack Teagarden, to name but a few, were now also being booked by MCA. MCA had even started a "colored" department in early 1940 under the direction of Harry Moss, who oversaw the booking of dance band one-nighters by MCA.[87] In addition, there were now many other former sidemen stepping out with their own big bands. Bobby Hackett, Jack Jenney, and Sonny Dunham, had already done so; Teddy Wilson and Lionel Hampton soon would. The big band era had reached its apogee, but the supply of bands now exceeded the demand. As a result, many of these sidemen-turned-bandleaders would be driven either to bankruptcy or insolvency. Given these harsh realities, MCA undoubtedly masterminded the move of Bunny Berigan from the helm of his own struggling band into Tommy Dorsey's band. But exactly what did MCA have in mind?

Notes

[1] Also on the bill were Muggsy Spanier and His Ragtime Band.

[2] This information was provided by Patricia Berigan to Robert Dupuis, UW–Madison Dupuis archive.

[3] *Billboard:* July 22, 1939, cited in the White materials.

[4] White materials: July 6, 1939.

[5] *Ibid.*

[6] I have heard a number of the airchecks from the Berigan band's Panther Room engagement, and there is much good music on them. Bunny's playing on "Savoy Jump," "Beale Street Blues," "Panama," and especially "Livery Stable Blues" reveals that he was at the very peak of his powers as an inspired jazz trumpet virtuoso during his band's Sherman Hotel residency.

[7] White materials: July 6, 1939.

[8] *Ibid.*

[9] White materials: July 14, 1939.

[10] White materials: July 30, 1939.

[11] *Ibid.*

[12] *The New Yorker:* February 21, 1983, cited in the White materials: July 30, 1939.

[13] It was at this time that Berigan began having his hair dyed. He took meticulous care of his hair, seeking out the best hair stylists in the major cities where he appeared. As time passed, his hair color became darker, and he began dying his moustache as well. At the end of his life, his hair was a rather dark brown. By then he also was wearing a trumpeter's notch below his lower lip. At one point in the early 1940s, he appeared in a print ad promoting the hair care services of a salon in Boston.

[14] White materials: August 4, 1939.

[15] Hub Kiefer's quote is taken from a letter he wrote to Opie Austin, a White collaborator, dated 1974, and is cited in the White materials: *Ibid.*

[16] Dupuis interview with Gus Bivona; UW–Madison Dupuis archive.

[17] *Billboard:* July 29, 1939, cited in the White materials.

[18] The evidence indicates that after Berigan and his personal manager Arthur Michaud parted company in early 1939, Berigan operated without a personal manager. The absence of an aggressive personal manager could well be a reason why Berigan made no commercial records from March 15 to November 29, 1939.

[19] *Down Beat:* September 1939, cited in the White materials.

[20] *Chicago Defender:* August 19, 1939, cited in the White materials.

[21] *Down Beat:* October 1, 1939, cited in the White materials.

[22] White materials: August 13, 1939.

[23] *Ibid.* In 1942, Glenn Miller and his singing group the Modernaires hit pay dirt with their million-selling record "Juke Box Saturday Night" by imitating the Ink Spots.

[24] *Billboard:* September 2, 1939, cited in the White materials.

[25] *Billboard:* August 26, 1939, cited in the White materials.

[26] White materials: August 24, 1939. The photos of the Berigan band at the Loew's State Theater were taken on August 24, 1939 by Arsene Studio Photographers.

[27] The only copy of the photo to which I make reference that I have ever seen is in *Tommy and Jimmy— The Dorsey Years,* by Herb Sanford, Arlington House (1972), 194.

[28] *Variety:* September 6, 1939, cited in the White materials. The same information was reported in the September 13, 1939, *Madison Capital Times;* however that article stated that the $568 debt was owed to "a New York music publishing firm."

[29] Petrillo made no such request. He employed attorneys in New York to obtain a court order to sequester Berigan's earnings from the Loew's State engagement. *Madison Capital Times:* September 13, 1939. Information provided by Carl A. Hallstrom.

[30] *Ibid.*

[31] White materials: August 31, 1939.

[32] *Ibid.*

[33] *New York Times:* September 18, 1939, cited in the White materials.

[34] *Down Beat:* September 1939, cited in the White materials.

[35] White materials: September 26, 1939.

[36] Andy Phillips continued to grow as an arranger during the chaotic months of 1939 with the Berigan band just as his predecessor Joe Lippman had throughout 1937–1938. He began coaxing Bunny not to mute his trumpet on the first chorus melody exposition, and wrote modulations into vocals that were also played by Berigan on open trumpet. The result of this, which is typified by "I Poured My Heart into a Song," is thrilling music. Danny Richards also continued to grow as a performer during this time. He not only pleased audiences, but his boss as well. Hear Bunny, toward the end of Richards's vocal chorus on "I Poured My Heart into a Song," register his appreciation as he says: "Yyyyess, Danny!"

[37] "Night Song" was actually composed by Duke Ellington's valve trombonist Juan Tizol, and freelance arranger Jimmy Mundy. It was recorded for Vocalion by Cootie Williams and His Rug Cutters, a small group drawn from the Duke Ellington big band, on June 21, 1939. Previously, it had been recorded by Charlie Barnet for Bluebird on March 17, 1939, in an arrangement which most available evidence indicates was written by Jimmy Mundy, and which is almost identical to the one Berigan used. In exchange for getting this tune recorded by an Ellington small group, Ellington's then manager Irving Mills got his name added as a cocomposer.

[38] *Metronome:* October 1939, cited in the White materials.

[39] White materials: October 2, 1939.

[40] White materials: October 16, 1939. Bunny's zany sense of humor sometimes manifest itself in peculiar ways. He always referred to trumpeter Joe Aguanno as "Aguackamo." See the biographical sketch of Bunny Berigan on Christopher Popa's *Big Band Library* website.

[41] There was however a house band at the Savoy, a hard-swinging nine-piece group called the Savoy Sultans. Any band visiting the Savoy had to be on its mettle to avoid being cut by the Sultans.

[42] White materials: August 31, 1939.

[43] *Boston Post:* October 22, 1939, cited in the White materials.

[44] White materials: October 22, 1939.

[45] White materials: October 23, to November 4, 1939.

[46] *Boston Post:* October 29, 1939, cited in the White materials.

[47] *Glenn Miller and His Orchestra,* by George T. Simon, Thomas V. Crowell Co. (1974), 88–90.

[48] *Boston Post:* November 5, 1939, cited in the White materials.

[49] *Variety:* November 8, 1939, cited in the White materials.

[50] *Billboard:* November 11, 1939, cited in the White materials.

[51] This person, if he did in fact exist, was not the trombonist John Sanders who played with Duke Ellington in the 1960s, then went on to become a Roman Catholic priest.

[52] As is often the case, there is some uncertainty about the attribution of the arrangement Berigan used on "Night Song" to Jimmy Mundy. In Charlie Barnet's autobiography, *Those Swinging Years,* there is a very complete listing of tunes recorded by the Barnet band over the years, with arrangers also listed. In that list, "Night Song" is attributed to the wonderfully talented arranger Billy May. Since the Barnet recording of "Night Song" was made several months before Billy May joined the Charlie Barnet band, since one of its composers, Jimmy Mundy, was an excellent arranger who sold his charts to many bandleaders, since it sounds very unlike May's writing at that time, and since Barnet later often utilized May (as well as many other arrangers) to "revise and update" arrangements that had been in the Barnet book for some time, I still believe the arrangement that both Barnet and Berigan recorded in 1939 was written by Jimmy Mundy. May could have later revised and updated the original Mundy chart for the Barnet band.

[53] White materials: November 28, 1939.

[54] *Ibid.*

[55] *Ibid.*

[56] *Down Beat:* November 1, 1940, cited in the White materials.

[57] *Down Beat:* January 15, 1941, cited in the White materials.

[58] *Ibid.*

[59] *Variety:* December 22, 1939, cited in the White materials.

[60] White materials: December 15, 1939.

[61] *Ibid.*

[62] *Metronome:* January 1940, cited in the White materials.

[63] White materials: December 23, 1939. In 1939, Madison Square Garden was located on Eighth Avenue at West Fiftieth Street. Polyclinic Hospital was located across West Fiftieth Street from Madison Square Garden. It was here that Berigan was hospitalized.

[64] Trumpeter Joe Aguanno had a very specific remembrance of Bunny at the Mosque Ballroom. See biographical sketch of Bunny Berigan at the *Big Band Library* website. So he may have begun the engagement before being hospitalized.

[65] *MedicineNet.com, Cirrhosis of the liver* (2008).

[66] White materials: February 14, 1940.

[67] The story of Jack Teagarden's bankruptcy is remarkably similar to the story of Bunny Berigan's bankruptcy in that most of the same characters were involved: Arthur Michaud, John Gluskin, MCA, and the AFM musicians' union. The ultimate outcome was much more favorable for Teagarden however, because he employed the services of veteran show-biz lawyer Andrew Weinberger, who made a career out of extricating musicians from their improvident business dealings. See: Jack Teagarden—The Story of a Jazz Maverick, by Jay D. Smith and Len Guttridge, Da Capo Press, Inc. (1988), 132–133, for a brief explanation of the Teagarden bankruptcy.

[68] White materials: January 1, 1940.

[69] *Ibid.* Later, in the 1950s, trumpeter Les Elgart became a successful bandleader, first alone, and then in conjunction with his brother, alto saxophonist Larry Elgart.

[70] White materials: January 7, 1940.

[71] *Ibid.*

[72] White materials: January 15, 1940.

[73] *Billboard:* February 3, 1940, cited in the White materials.

[74] White materials: January 22, 1940.

[75] *Ibid.*

[76] White materials: January 28–29, 1940.

[77] *Billboard:* February 3, 1940, cited in the White materials.

[78] *Down Beat:* February 15, 1940, cited in the White materials.

[79] White materials: February 2, 1940.

[80] *Boston Post:* February 3, 1940, cited in the White materials.

[81] White Materials: February 16, 1940.

[82] *Metronome:* March 1940, cited in the White materials.

[83] White materials: February 16, 1940.

[84] *Billboard:* May 25, 1940, cited in the White materials.

[85] White materials: February 25, 1940.

[86] *Metronome:* February 1940, cited in the White materials.

[87] *Billboard:* January 27, 1940, cited in the White materials.

Chapter 21
Interlude

The move of Bunny Berigan from leadership of his own band into Tommy Dorsey's band was reported in *Variety* on February 28, 1940: "Bunny Berigan has given up his band to take his place in the trumpet section of the Tommy Dorsey orchestra. He will step into the first trumpet position vacated by Zeke Zarchy on Sunday (March 3). Dorsey is currently at the Meadowbrook, Cedar Grove, New Jersey, and goes into the Paramount Theater, New York City, on March 12."[1] It is likely that the maneuvering by MCA to effectuate this change had been going on for at least a period of weeks. Indeed, it may have started as early as late December, when Bunny was hospitalized. The fact that Cap Berigan left his duties as road manager when his son's band went to Boston in mid to late January is a possible clue that Bunny told his father then what was in the offing. From that point on, Bunny may well have been playing out the string, fulfilling the commitments MCA had made for him, while waiting for an opportune time to join TD.

Tommy Dorsey had just hired the young trumpeter Ray Linn to play jazz in his band. Linn was one of the first of his band members who was told about Bunny Berigan joining the Dorsey band:

> Tommy Dorsey was the best friend and truest fan that Bunny Berigan was ever to have. I well remember the night he took this punk teenager (me!) aside to inform him that Bunny—not Berigan, just Bunny—was coming back with the band. I remember the joy with which he said it, the excitement lighting up his face. 'Ray, Bunny's coming back with the band! He's joining us next Sunday, but don't worry, you'll still get plenty of jazz to play.' I remember my dumb-struck reply, 'Oh, Tommy, I don't want to play any solos while he's in the band. I'll just be happy to sit there and listen to him.' Tommy smiled, patted me on the arm and walked away, as happy as a clam![2]

The trade press, taking full opportunity to comment on this development, and no doubt well primed by the MCA public relations department, was full of stories about Bunny Berigan becoming a member of Tommy Dorsey's band.

> Still juggling sidemen in the most sensational shake-up his band has yet undergone, Tommy Dorsey astounded the entire music field when he persuaded Bunny Berigan to join his band. Bunny's band, rumored on repeated occasions to be breaking up or about to disband, finally did, when the leader went over to the Dorsey clan at the Meadowbrook. Bunny had been a leader since 1937 and in all

that time, despite a series of good recordings and much airtime, never seemed to get set. Rather than continue struggling along unsteadily, Bunny decided to side-step leader's headaches and return to Tommy, with whom he'd played in 1937, shortly before he organized his own crew. Carmen Mastren, guitarist, left Tommy; he'll do some writing and arranging. Paul Mason took over Deane Kincaide's sax chair. Bob Kitsis will end up as regular pianist, George Arus is in for Elmer Smithers on trombone. Don Lodice, tenorman, formerly with Bunny Berigan and Teddy Powell, succeeds Babe Russin. The band will change again after the Paramount Theater booking. Several of the veterans still remaining are tired of traveling. Hymie Schertzer, lead alto, declares he'll leave so he can remain in New York. The changes were caused by salary troubles, it was said, and also because Tommy has in mind leaning more towards a swing style in the future. Sy Oliver and Axel Stordahl remain on Dorsey's staff of arrangers.[3]

We like Tommy Dorsey's move in taking Bunny Berigan into his band. We like it musically and logically too. The Dorsey-Berigan move is healthy for Dorsey and it's healthy for Berigan. Tommy's music will obviously benefit and Bunny won't have to be tossed around with a little-more-than fair bunch, hoping that someday he'll be able to make ends meet. With moves like that, swing bands in general will benefit. There's more of a drawing card in a Dorsey band featuring Berigan than there is in a Dorsey band not featuring Berigan and certainly more than in a Berigan band featuring only Berigan.[4]

On March 4, the Dorsey band was in the RCA Victor recording studios on New York. The personnel for that session was as follows: Tommy Dorsey, trombone, leading; Zeke Zarchy, Jimmy Blake, Ray Linn, Bunny Berigan, trumpets; George Arus, Dave Jacobs, Lowell Martin, trombones; Hymie Shertzer, Freddie Stulce, Johnny Mince (altos), Babe Russin, Paul Mason (tenors), saxophones; Bob Kitsis, piano; Al Avola, guitar; Ray Leatherwood, bass; Buddy Rich, drums. The session produced two recordings with vocals by TD's new boy singer, Frank Sinatra, and one with singing by the four-person vocal group, the Pied Pipers.

In addition to the many personnel changes Tommy was then making in his band, he was greatly changing its musical policy. The prime moving force in this direction was his new arranger, Sy Oliver. Tommy had induced Sy to leave Jimmie Lunceford's band, where he had been playing trumpet, singing, and writing arrangements by offering him "$5,000 more than Jimmie is paying you."[5] In the value of today's dollar, that would be a raise of roughly $75,000.

This was quintessential Dorsey. Tommy thrived on the grandiose. While his band was playing at the Palmer House in Chicago late in 1939, Tommy noticed that the food served in the various restaurants in that hotel was especially well prepared. He made inquiries about the chef, and in due course was on a first-name basis with him. When the Dorsey band left the Palmer House to begin a tour that would eventually lead them back east for a long spell, the chef in question, William, was offered a job at Tommy's Bernardsville, New Jersey, estate. William accepted TD's offer, and soon was preparing meals at all hours of the day and night for the dozens of guests Tommy would invite on the spur of the moment to his home.[6] Frequently, one of those guests would be Bunny Berigan.

Tommy Dorsey's band had been in a process of evolution in the previous twelve months. Prior to 1939, the TD band was basically a good middle-of-the-road dance band that featured three performers: Tommy on his velvety trombone, first and foremost; then the tall, good-looking Jack Leonard its boy singer; then Edythe Wright, a stunningly beautiful and dynamic lady, as its girl singer. Its main arranger was Paul Weston, who orchestrated the vast majority of the band's recorded performances of current pop tunes. Weston was an extremely capable musician whose work was not in any way constrained by Tommy. The fact that the Dorsey band of those years was not stylized in the manner of say Guy Lombardo's, or Glenn Miller's, allowed Weston great latitude in his approach. Nevertheless, the sheer volume of music Weston had to turn out drove him into patterns. Audiences may not have noticed, but the musicians in Tommy's band certainly did, and by 1938, the TD band was sounding rather routinized.

Axel Stordahl was the other main arranger in the Dorsey band, but his work consisted almost exclusively of ballad charts, usually sung by either Jack Leonard or Edythe Wright. A small fraction of the band's library consisted of jazz arrangements by outside writers like Fletcher Henderson, and Benny Carter. These arrangements were used to give TD's very mainstream audiences a taste of swing and jazz. Slowly, Tommy also began to use arrangements by Deane Kincaide, whose approach to jazz arranging had much in common with the Dixieland oriented styles employed by arrangers Bob Haggart and Matty Matlock in the Bob Crosby band. Tommy's use of the Clambake Seven as an adjunct to his band was limited to some Dixieland, some ballads, and a good many novelty tunes. Tommy had utilized this approach to achieve substantial success in the years 1937 and 1938, when his band was featured on a weekly network radio program sponsored by Raleigh and Kool cigarettes.

But in 1939, things began to change. Overall, the dance band business had become much more competitive with the advent of many new bands led by musicians who had built their names and reputations as sidemen with established bands. This phenomenon was not limited to the swing band side of the business; the same thing was happening with sweet bands. The result of this was that rather suddenly there were more bands than places for them to play. The major booking agencies, MCA and General Artists Corporation (GAC), the successor to Rockwell-O'Keefe, had to rethink how they were going to operate going forward in this changing market. MCA's basic strategy, dating back to the late 1920s, when Jules Stein signed Guy Lombardo, was not to build bands from the ground up, but to pick bands that had already arrived in some fashion, and then promote them heavily, hoping to move them into the preeminent category. This tactic had worked again and again, mostly with sweet bands, but also with Benny Goodman's swing band. But in 1938, GAC suddenly had a major big band star on its hands in Artie Shaw, who only became bigger in 1939. They also had a fast-rising star in Glenn Miller, who after two years of struggle, began to move up the ladder of success rapidly in 1939, and then vault into the preeminent class of bandleaders in 1940. Also moving up in popularity in 1939 was Tommy Dorsey's brother Jimmy. He too was represented by GAC. At the same time, MCA's two major swing bands, Goodman's and Tommy Dorsey's, were losing market share to these GAC bands. MCA bands like Bunny Berigan's were also being edged out of the better bookings by GAC's top bands, as well as their second-tier bands, like those led by Woody Herman and Bob Crosby.[7] In addition, other newer bands like those led by Gene Krupa, Harry James, Jan Savitt, Larry Clinton, Teddy Powell, Charlie Barnet, Les Brown, and Van Alexander were now out in the marketplace competing for work. So were the black bands led by Cab Calloway, Duke Ellington, Count Basie, Jimmie Lunceford, Andy Kirk, and Erskine Hawkins, among many others. Although the bands themselves were almost totally segregated racially, the market where they competed was not.

Tommy Dorsey was completely aware of all of these developments. He decided that he would do whatever it took to move his band from the successful level it had occupied in 1937 and 1938, into the preeminent class. The hiring of arranger Sy Oliver in mid-1939 was only his first step. The gradual change in personnel from the 1939 TD band to the 1940 band took about eight months to complete, not that it was ever over, because Tommy continued to tinker with his band's personnel for some time beyond that. The major personnel acquisitions he made during this time included the pyrotechnic drummer Buddy Rich, the very musical vocal group consisting of three men and one woman (the superb Jo Stafford)[8] known as the Pied Pipers, the ultimate big band boy singer, Frank Sinatra,[9] and the man who had been the supreme swing trumpeter of the 1930s, Bunny Berigan. Although I think that Tommy Dorsey loved Bunny in a way that was very similar to the love he had for his brother Jimmy (that is to say his feelings at times were ambivalent), I do not think his hiring of Berigan in March, 1940 was an act of altruism. At the time of the hiring, Tommy knew that Bunny could still play splendidly. He also knew of the major threats to that playing, the largest then being Bunny's alcoholism. He chose to bear the risks inherent in having Bunny Berigan as a featured member of his band because he thought Berigan's playing would help to reinvigorate his band. Also, he hoped that he could help Bunny get his drinking under control, as he had done with his own drinking when he and Jimmy started the Dorsey Brothers' Orchestra.

But what was in all of this for Berigan? I am reasonably certain that the people at MCA told Bunny that if he participated in this plan to help Tommy Dorsey reorganize his band within more of a swing-oriented format, he would receive feature billing, would play in those prized venues like the Paramount Theater and Astor Hotel in New York, where only the top bands in the country played, broadcast over network radio frequently, and stay off of the road for extended periods of time. He would also make a very good salary with TD, undoubtedly more than he had been making leading his own band, probably a base of $250 a week, with extra for recordings and work on any sponsored radio show.

There is no doubt that the musicians' union was taking a substantial part of Berigan's earnings while he worked with Tommy Dorsey, pursuant to the agreement that MCA had facilitated with the union at the time Bunny's bankruptcy action was resolved. Evidently, whatever deal Bunny had made or was forced to make the previous fall with MCA and/or the musicians' union still had to be honored. Here is what *Variety* reported: "Tommy Dorsey has made arrangements with Local 802 of the Musicians' Union (AFM) to surrender a percentage of Bunny Berigan's salary each week, which will go towards liquidating salary debts Berigan owed to various members of his band."[10] Numerous sources cited in both the White materials and the Dupuis biography stated that Berigan was left with $45 a week after all deductions had been made. Less certain is whether MCA was getting any money from Bunny's earnings. It is certainly possible that they were. But from a financial standpoint, at least Bunny was not accruing more debt during the Dorsey interlude, and was probably paying off substantial amounts of whatever of his debts remained after the conclusion of his bankruptcy. I think that Berigan went along with this plan very reluctantly because he still believed that he should be the leader of his own band. But MCA probably made it clear to him that before he could lead another band, he had to eliminate as much debt as possible. In the meantime, he would be a prominently featured member of Tommy Dorsey's band, and as such, his name would be used frequently in connection with the activities of TD's band.

Ray Linn recalled how Berigan fit into the Dorsey band at the Meadowbrook:

> Bunny was added to the trumpet section, making it a foursome. He sat between Zarchy and Jimmy Blake and, not having a book of his own, played along with Zeke, only an octave lower, according to Tommy's instructions, and then played most of the jazz solos when they came up. This annoyed Zarchy to no end and I think he was only too glad to be leaving at the close of the engagement, although the main reason was a pay-out—along with most of the band—plus having had enough of one nighters for a while. My starting salary guarantee was $70 weekly and Zeke was probably asked to take a cut to around $115 a week and refused. I'm pretty sure Castaldo had left for the same reason, but there's always some punk kid available, who's ready, willing and able to work cheap, just for his big break, and that's where I came in![11]

While the Dorsey band was at the Meadowbrook, it was broadcast over WOR and WEAF–New York, and the NBC Red Network. One such broadcast, made on Saturday, March 9, was recorded. There are a few tunes which contain solos by Berigan. They are "(What Can I Say Dear) After I Say I'm Sorry," which is a feature for the Pied Pipers; "Dark Eyes," long a Berigan feature; "The Fable of a Rose," which features a Frank Sinatra vocal; and the inevitable "Marie."

When it came time for "Marie" to be played, here is how the setup went:

NBC announcer Bill Abernathy: Well, Mr. Dorsey, the time has come for you to make a speech of welcome. TD: Yes Bill, and here is the perfect tune to do it with. It's our number one record, 'Marie,' which brings back to the fold the man whose trumpet playing helped to make that number famous. Sitting right up there in the top row—Mr. Bunny Berigan! (cheers) It was over three years ago that Bunny's trumpet made its indelible mark on our 'Marie' record. Since then, Bunny has been leading his own band, and doing a swell job. But now he's back with us, and in the groove for sure on—'Marie'!

The band's heavy broadcast schedule while at the Meadowbrook saturated the greater New York area with the music and name of Tommy Dorsey. This was the big buildup for the TD band's upcoming stand at New York's Paramount Theater.

Stalwart TD sideman saxist Freddie Stulce also remembered the early weeks of Bunny's association with the Dorsey band:

Bunny played some lead horn and, of course; most of the hot. Zeke Zarchy had been the lead man and when Bunny came in, he (Bunny) would play lead on some numbers, but there was no set pattern. Tommy had gone to a 5-man saxophone section by then, which called for 5 clarinets, one of which would be a bass clarinet played by Paul Mason. The arrangements were handled by Sy Oliver, who did mostly up-tempo stuff, Axel Stordahl and Paul Weston, who shared the ballads with Weston doing some novelty numbers, plus some odds and ends by Red Bone, Deane Kincaide and myself. The vocal arrangements were mostly done by Stordahl and Weston in collaboration with the Pied Pipers, who did many of their own scores, with Stordahl or Weston doing the band parts. The relationship between Tommy and Bunny was a very friendly one at first, Tommy and the boys in the band feeling that he had gotten a very fine deal in persuading Bunny to join. But when two stars get together in the same organization, there is bound to be friction, sooner or later, both musically and personally. Not that the hassles between them were always Bunny's fault, though his drinking, which affected his performance, began to get Tommy feeling more and more fed up with his temperamental star. I remember Bunny complaining that he'd had some trouble with his fingers and his feet swelling up, but how much that affected his playing I don't know. We were paid weekly by check and I guess Local 802 got a piece out of Bunny's wages to pay off some of his debts.[12]

While at the Meadowbrook, Bunny attempted to "reduce" his drinking. Guitarist Al Avola, then temporarily in the Dorsey band, and long-time TD bassist Gene Traxler observed the result:

Avola: The Tommy Dorsey band was playing to packed houses at the Meadowbrook and Bunny was making strenuous efforts to perform up to his reputation, but he still found it necessary to obtain some Dutch courage! We drove to a record date together, a journey of only a few miles, but we had to stop several times along the way so that he could partake of some liquid refreshment. His playing was way below par, in my opinion, as it lacked both range and power.[13]

Traxler: My last contact with Bunny was at that Meadowbrook date. I remember driving him home after the job and having a hard time passing the neon-lit 'BAR' signs without stopping to allow him a taste! The Meadowbrook was situated on the brow of a rather steep hill on the Pompton Turnpike and Bunny would invariably fall down the hill! I would just wait patiently, then gather him up, pour him into the car and drive him home.[14]

Trombonist Ward Silloway also had the opportunity to observe Bunny: "I stayed with Tommy until after the band left the Meadowbrook, where Bunny Berigan joined after giving up his own band. We had regular Saturday afternoon broadcasts, but on a couple of occasions Bunny had the shakes so bad he wasn't able to play a note! I left the band at the Paramount Theater, where Tommy had to play with three trumpets and three trombones, including himself, while Ray Linn and Lowell Martin sweated out their New York union cards."[15]

It appears that Cap Berigan, after leaving his duties as road manager of Bunny's band the previous January, had remained in New York for a time. Here is an item from the *Fox Lake Representative* dated March 14, 1940: "Will Berigan, father of Bernard Berigan, arrived here (Fox Lake, Wisconsin) Tuesday (12th) from New York City." What Cap told Bunny's relatives was not encouraging: Cap's younger brother "Big Bob" Berigan recalled: "Bunny's dad had been out on the road with Bunny's band, when Bunny went back to TD (*sic*), 'Cap' came back to Wisconsin. He told me 'No use, it's no use trying to help Bunny.'" Berigan researcher Tom Cullen found others to have had the same disturbing memories: "Other family members said that when Cap came back 'home' he was broken-hearted over Bunny's condition."[16]

In light of this consensus, it seems clear that Tommy Dorsey, in order to make sure that Berigan could perform with his band, definitely tried to help him get his drinking under control in 1940. Bunny himself also tried. But in order to do this, he had to try to drink enough not to go into withdrawal, yet not drink too much, and become impaired. It would be a difficult balance to achieve, much less maintain. We now know that what Bunny actually needed was to stop drinking completely, go through detoxification with medical assistance, and then, with constant help, try to continue to remain sober. That was impossible while Bunny Berigan was a featured member of Tommy Dorsey's band.

The engagement at the Paramount Theater, which began on March 13, was far more lucrative for the Dorsey band than the Meadowbrook gig had been. Tommy was optimistic that whatever financial challenges he had been experiencing would be resolved with his earnings from the Paramount engagement. He followed Glenn Miller's now very hot band into that venue: "Miller (but not his band) was on hand to 'Welcome TD' at the first show. The movie was *Road to Singapore* with Bing Crosby, Bob Hope and Dorothy Lamour. Red Skelton was part of the stage show. Bunny is given first billing in the Paramount ads, followed by (in order) Buddy Rich, Frank Sinatra and the Pied Pipers Quartette."[17] Tommy, along with a few other leaders, had fronted the Miller band for a few days at the Paramount while Glenn had been ill. Miller's welcoming TD to the Paramount was no doubt his way of saying thanks to Tommy.

One review of the TD stage presentation at the Paramount was not glowing:

> Lackluster performance, mostly swing, and not of the relaxed type. Bunny Berigan's return to the trumpet section after leading his own crew is marked by a couple of tired solos, quite unlike the Berigan of old. There are too many lengthy tenor sax solos, which are drowned out by the bass and drums. Buddy Rich is featured way out of proportion to his worth. Credit side is TD's 'bone' and Frank Sinatra's warbling. He's new with the band and is developing into a first-rate singer. TD and the band do 50 minutes; Bunny Berigan does 'Song of India,' and the Pied Pipers do 'What Can I Say Dear After I Say I'm Sorry,' and 'Oh, Johnny.' Frank Sinatra does 'Careless,' 'My Prayer,' and 'South of the Border.' Winfield and Ford also part of the show, a sepia tap dance team.[18]

But in another review, George T. Simon at *Metronome*, never one of Bunny's big supporters, weighed in with his opinion of the TD band at the Paramount: "Tommy Dorsey's band kicks more than it ever has. All the changes he has made recently have been motivated, partially anyway, by a desire to show jazz lovers, who haven't voted him so high in recent contests, that his bunch can out-swing them all. Bunny Berigan has made a whale of a difference, musically and psychologically. The kicking Don Lodice, whose tone has improved immeasurably, also adds swing guts, and Buddy Rich, the cocky kid drummer who too often drums for himself, still gives the ensemble a mighty rock!"[19]

Tommy continued his obsessive personnel shuffling while the band was at the Paramount Theater. Ray Linn offered some insights: "Lowell Martin and I were the only members of the band who didn't belong to New York Local 802, and Tommy, wishing to avoid paying the traveling band penalty tax, found it cheaper to pay both of us for laying off. So I went home to Chicago on a four weeks paid vacation, and Lowell went home to Miami, Florida. Tommy tried to buy us a couple of 802 cards, even offering to pay $100 each for them, but they turned him down."[20]

After Tommy's version of musical chairs had slowed down a bit, *Down Beat* attempted to recap:

> Les Jenkins is back with Tommy Dorsey's orchestra. He replaced Ward Silloway during Tommy's Paramount engagement in the final round of the band's shake-up. Tommy plans to dispense with guitar work in future, except for records. He used Al Avola for a couple of Victor dates, but says there will be no permanent replacement for Carmen Mastren. Dave Tough has been recovering his health out at the Dorsey farm in Bernardsville, New Jersey, but it's just a friendly gesture and there's no intention of replacing Buddy Rich. Sid Weiss, former Artie Shaw bassist, lately of the Joe Marsala outfit, went over to Tommy's band during its Paramount stretch. Gene Traxler, vet bull-fiddle plucker with Dorsey, went to Marsala. Tommy is still making changes and declares his personnel will not be set until he opens the Astor for an eight weeks engagement on May 25. After

playing theaters and one-nighters all through April, the band will go on vacation May 4 and return for the Astor date.[21]

Accounts of how Bunny Berigan was playing during the early months of 1940 are widely divergent. One such account, that of Joe Bushkin who had grown to love Bunny over the previous four years despite his many peccadilloes and his self-destructive alcoholism, is particularly interesting:

He was playing great, beautifully. On the records that he made at that time, you can hear that he was the one guy you could count on to come up with the solos. On the jobs he was sensational, and he had so much pressure on him then. He owed everybody money; his salary was attached. There might have been a collector in the audience, but damn it, he acted like they were collecting the music, not the money he didn't have. At the Astor Roof, Tommy would come late and leave early, like Benny Goodman—a little power play going on there between those two guys. Bunny would lead the first and last sets. The band was very happy to see Dorsey leave and we were relieved he didn't show up for the first set, 'cause that's when we had fun. We were delighted to have Bunny on the band. Bunny got me the job with Tommy. I auditioned at The Meadowbrook and joined at the Paramount Theater.[22]

While the band continued its Paramount engagement, vocalist Frank Sinatra became too ill to perform for a couple of days. Bunny, who at that time was still offering Tommy suggestions about replacements, recommended his former boy singer, Danny Richards. Tommy was ready to give Richards a try: "I got a wire from Bunny, saying that Frank Sinatra was ill and would I be interested in joining the Dorsey band for a few dates until Sinatra returned? I thought about it, but I didn't believe I could cut it at that time, so I declined."[23] Richards had returned home to Scranton, Pennsylvania, after the Berigan band broke up, and reorganized his own territory band there. Tommy then summoned Allan De Witt, an excellent but now almost forgotten big band vocalist who had sung with his band briefly right after Jack Leonard left, to sub for the ailing Sinatra.

The Paramount gig was extended to April 9, for a total of four weeks. It is difficult to imagine how grueling that engagement had been with the band playing four or five shows a day on each of six or seven days every week. TD's grosses were as follows: for the week ending March 19 —$56,000; March 26 — $47,000; April 2—$39,000; and April 9—$27,000.[24] Presumably, this engagement balanced Tommy's finances, or quite possibly put them healthily into the black.

Bunny managed to keep going during that spring most probably by limiting his drinking. Otherwise he would have had difficulty keeping up with TD's breakneck pace. In Bunny's current relationship with Tommy Dorsey, one thing would remain constant and certain: that Dorsey would keep him very busy, and demand the best from him. Whenever it seemed that Bunny was either unable or unwilling to perform up to his best, Bunny, like all other TD sidemen, would have a problem with his boss. At this juncture, it seems that the initial plan was still working; Tommy kept Bunny very busy, and paid him well. Most of the money Bunny was earning was going to pay off the old debts that still somehow remained or new debts that had accrued since his bankruptcy maneuvers the prior fall. (Berigan may again have fallen behind in paying his sidemens' salaries *after* the bankruptcy filing, and borrowed money from MCA with which to catch up.) Even though he was able to keep only a small portion of his weekly salary, he had to be making large strides toward reducing his debt during this period.

The morning after the band closed at the Paramount Theater (April 10), Tommy had them in the RCA Victor studios to make some records. Six sides were cut at that session, including a Sy Oliver arrangement on "I'm Nobody's Baby," with a vocal by Connie Haines, and some fine trumpet playing from Bunny. The available information indicates that this session began at 9:30 a.m. and concluded at 6:30 p.m. Somewhere along the line, the musicians took a lunch break. We can assume therefore that Tommy Dorsey had his band in the studio on that date for the better part of eight hours.[25] Then, three of TD's sidemen, Joe Bushkin, Sid Weiss, and Bunny Berigan, went to another studio to make more recordings! Bushkin recalled that day many years later:

> We were at the RCA studios on Twenty-fourth Street between Third and Lexington. It was a long day. Tommy Dorsey was a workaholic. We all got a guarantee, including Frank Sinatra, of $125 a week. After a late closing at the Paramount, we started at 9:00 or 10:00 in the morning and had a break for lunch then worked through 6:00 or so. Then we had just enough time to get uptown and grab a sandwich or something—and in Bunny's case a number of drinks. So we showed up at the second studio at about 8:00 in the evening and played until 1:00 or 2:00 in the morning. That means that Bunny Berigan's lip held up from 10:00 in the morning until about 2:00 the next morning, with a lot of pressure on him, because there's no screwing around at RCA Victor with Tommy Dorsey.[26]

The second studio to which Bushkin referred contained Lee Wiley and Bunny's former drummer George Wettling. They were there waiting when Bunny, Bushkin, and Weiss arrived. What transpired during the six hours these musicians were in the studio has been documented to a large degree on BluDisc T-1013. Ultimately, four takes were made that were issued: "Let's Fly Away," "Let's Do It," "Hot House Rose," and "Find Me a Primitive Man," all composed by Cole Porter. There were in addition several other completed takes of these tunes, as well as numerous breakdowns, with talk among the performers about what was wrong and how to fix it.[27] (See appendix 5 for a transcript of some of this studio talk.)

After this marathon of work, the Dorsey band had a day off on April 11, which was used to travel to the next gig, a week long stand at Shea's Theater in Buffalo, New York. Young Ray Linn was once again surprised by Bunny Berigan: "I knew nothing about Bunny's relationship with Lee Wiley, but I saw her standing around a couple of times outside the band bus and kissing him good-bye, when we were leaving town to play some one nighters. I would have to assume that they weren't just toasting marshmallows together!"[28]

Bassist Sid Weiss, after playing with the Dorsey band on the April 10 recording session, joined the band full-time at Shea's in Buffalo:

I rejoined the band in Buffalo, NY, at Shea's Theater. Bunny was drinking heavily and playing mostly fourth parts in the trumpet section, plus a few jazz solos. He also had some speaking parts on the radio programs, which he missed several times. This made Tommy mad and he rode Bunny unmercifully, once holding up a Calvert's whisky sign when Bunny came down front to solo. Occasionally, Tommy and Bunny would switch instruments as a gag, but Bunny didn't play the trombone as well as Ziggy Elman did later. Bunny's theme tune, 'I Can't Get Started,' was in our book and Tommy would play it in some floor shows and occasionally on the air. I felt good playing with that band. Joey Bushkin was the pianist and I have fond memories of his great talent and swinging ability. He was a great team section player, song writer and jester. There were rumors afloat that Buddy (Rich) was disenchanted with both Joe and me being in the rhythm section, but everything came together very well. Of course, Buddy was the fastest thing afoot! Tommy was an idol, not only to most trombone players, but also to all musicians. Any bandleader with great professional aspirations must also be a teacher and Tommy had this quality. He also had a marvelous sense of humor, despite his erratic temper, and sound business acumen. He once said that the band —leader who could get $100 worth of credit from the bank would make it, because the bank couldn't allow his band to fail! Bunny's drinking, although heavy and pretty constant, hardly affected his playing, unless it had gotten so bad that he was completely gone and couldn't blow at all. Lee Wiley was always around him. She was really tenacious in her attachment to Bunny, always at his elbow, always watching every move he made. She was making quite a name for herself, recording some Cole Porter songs, arranged by Paul Weston, who shared many of Dorsey's ballad arrangements with Axel Stordahl. Sy Oliver did all the jazz standards as well as many originals like, 'Losers Weepers,' 'Swing High,' and 'Another One of Them Things.' The small group's titles, like 'East of the Sun,' were done in the recording studios, but played on stage by the full band.[29]

During its engagement at Shea's Theater in Buffalo (starting on Saturday, April 13), the TD band was broadcast, probably over a local radio station that was not linked to any network. A recording from that broadcast is known to exist. Here are the tunes they played: "I'm Getting Sentimental" (partial); "I'm Nobody's Baby," vocal Connie Haines; "Say It," vocal Frank Sinatra; "Easy Does It"; 'What Can I Say Dear After I Say I'm Sorry," vocal Pied Pipers; "Blues No More"; "'Too Romantic," vocal Sinatra; "Sweet Potato Piper," vocal Frank Sinatra and the Pied Pipers; "East of the Sun," vocal Sinatra and band; "Losers Weepers"; "I'm Getting Sentimental" (partial); and closing. This list of tunes reveals that Tommy was playing a good mix of current pops with vocals, and original instrumentals. In the process he was using the talents of all of his singers and all of his jazz soloists. Of course, his silky trombone was featured in one way or another on almost every tune. The TD band, as always, was the epitome of versatility. Their stay in Buffalo ended on April 18.

The Dorsey band then headed south to play a one-night dance date at Lehigh University in Bethlehem, Pennsylvania, on April 19. From there they went to the Sunnybrook Ballroom in Pottstown, Pennsylvania, for a one-nighter on April 20. They then returned to Manhattan where they played at the Golden Gate Ballroom for one night, Sunday, April 21. They likely[30] had the following day off, then returned to the RCA Victor studios on April 23.

Metronome reviewed the band's performance at the Golden Gate Ballroom:

Tommy Dorsey's answer to kibitzers queries whether he's going to shelve sweet for hot was given in no uncertain musical terms April 21 in Harlem's Golden Gate, when TD and his boys panicked Harlem's elite with a tremendous swing broadside. Handicapped by the temporary incapacitation of vocalist Frank Sinatra, the trombone tooter's tribe was unable to trot out many of their sweet arrangements, so they let the colored kids really have it! Biggest breaker-upper of the evening was Buddy Rich's drumming, the cats stamping and whistling as the percussionist gave out with the sticks. Bunny Berigan's trumpet also got a warm reception. Tommy's revamped line-up had Johnny Dillard on first trumpet, Ray Linn on second, Lowell Martin on trombone, Joe Bushkin on piano and Sid Weiss back on bass. Connie Haines was the girl singer. Bobby Burns, veteran Dorsey band manager, rumored to have severed connections, was present in full authoritative force. The band opens New York's Hotel Astor Roof at the end of this month, where it is scheduled for a lengthy run. TD soft pedals sweet at Harlem's Golden Gate Ballroom. One of the big features was 'Swing High,' featuring Bunny Berigan and Buddy Rich.[31]

Meanwhile, Tommy brought forth on record a new small group, called the Sentimentalists. He and RCA Victor had other marketing ideas too: "Tommy Dorsey is slated to wax on both Victor and Bluebird labels shortly. His recording for the Victor 75 cents discs will be augmented by two sides a month on Bluebird 35 centers. The full band, however, will not be waxing for the cheaper label, the idea being to use a small combo similar to Tommy's original Clambake Seven. The latter tag will probably not be used, since the exact size of the combo has not been determined."[32] Tommy Dorsey and His Sentimentalists originally consisted of the following: Tommy Dorsey, trombone; Bunny Berigan, trumpet; Johnny Mince, clarinet; Joe Bushkin, piano; Clark Yocum, guitar; Sid Weiss, bass; and Buddy Rich, drums. These musicians plus Frank Sinatra entered the studio at 4:00 p.m. on April 23, and recorded two sides, "East of the Sun," arranged by Sy Oliver, and "Head on My Pillow," arranged by Axel Stordahl, by 5:30. There was a break until 7:30; then the rest of the musicians and singers in Tommy's band arrived. They spent until 10:15 recording two songs, "You're Lonely and I'm Lonely" (arrangement Stordahl, three takes) and "It's a Lovely Day Tomorrow," both with Sinatra vocals, and then grappling with one tune, "I'll Never Smile Again." Although at least three takes were made,[33] TD was dissatisfied, and told everyone to go home. They would try to record "I'll Never Smile Again" some other time.

While all of this was going on, Tommy Dorsey, as usual, was multitasking. The following blurb shows why he was such a successful bandleader for so long a time:

> A survey reveals that nearly 100% of the bands making records have either made or are attempting to make direct tie-ups with operators of music machines (juke boxes) to increase their box office grosses on one-nighters, theater tours and night club and hotel engagements. Band booking offices indicate such promotions are given top consideration for they increase both the popularity and drawing value of the band, juke box operators say when such ties are made. They have shown a willingness to co-operate with the maestros and are interested in stunts which mean more nickels in their machines. In addition to office help, 'name' and unknown leaders alike are constantly at work furnishing such ideas. Tommy Dorsey, who spends a nice bit of change annually staging informal parties for the operators in the various sections of the country covered by the band, creates much goodwill among the trade. Dorsey is also a willing publicity subject, visiting locations with the operators, spending time in their offices and giving them all the angles he has at hand.[34]

It would be difficult to imagine Bunny Berigan doing such things; but to be fair, it would also be difficult to imagine Benny Goodman or Artie Shaw doing them. Glenn Miller and Kay Kyser, other the other hand, probably engaged in similar promotional activities enthusiastically.

The Dorsey band had April 24 and 25 off, using a part of this time to travel from Manhattan to Chapel Hill, North Carolina, where they played two nights at the University of North Carolina. There were likely other dates on this southern tour, but the White materials report only engagements at Chattanooga, Tennessee (May 1 or 2), and two nights at the University of Georgia at Athens, May 3 and 4. This report gives some indication how the band was being received on this tour: "Stormy weather and advance prices did not keep Chattanoogians from flocking to the Memorial Auditorium to hear Tommy Dorsey last week. (Dateline May 18) Tickets were on sale at advance price of $1.10, jumping to $1.50 after 6 p.m., which is rather steep for Auditorium dances here. Despite a steady downpour of rain, more than 4,000 dancers turned out and gave the band a thunderous ovation."[35]

After this tour, Tommy and the band returned to New York for a well-deserved vacation that probably ran from May 5 to May 20, after which they assembled again to prepare for their big opening at New York's Astor Hotel on the 21st. Freddie Stulce recalled how TD handled vacations: "The band was put on vacation after the southern tour. I think we must have been laid off without pay, because during all my years with Tommy Dorsey, I can't remember a layoff with pay."[36] There were many differences between the Tommy Dorsey band being "put on vacation," and Bunny Berigan's band being put on "layoff." The first difference is that each Dorsey sideman was receiving a guaranteed salary which, according to Joe Bushkin, was $125 weekly. (Young unknown members of the band, like Ray Linn, may have been paid less, as he asserted.) This base salary was augmented with money from recording sessions, which in the case of Tommy's band came rather frequently. In addition, Tommy had announced that the band would return to network radio, being named as the summer replacement for Bob Hope on NBC's *Pepsodent Show*. The news of this was broken to the public in *Billboard*: "Pepsodent Company, through Lord and Thomas advertising agency, signed Tommy Dorsey, Thursday afternoon (16th) to replace Bob Hope for the summer. The nod went to Dorsey after it was decided that an audience participation program, 'The Song I'll Never Forget,' built by Harry Salter, would cost more than the budget could stand, upwards of $3,000. Dorsey starts June 25 for 13 weeks. The program will be a straight band show."[37] This would result in still more earnings for TD's musicians and singers. Johnny Mince, long TD's featured clarinetist, once told me: "When I joined Tommy's band in 1937, almost no one knew who I was and I was broke. When I left Tommy's band in 1941, I had saved about $15,000.00, and people knew who I was."[38] On top of these financial incentives, the Dorsey band's engagement at the Astor Hotel was scheduled to be for at least eight weeks, and that meant eight weeks less of riding busses to one-nighters in the hinterlands.

TD lost no musicians during this layoff, unless he chose to fire someone, which of course he did. Ray Linn remembered Tommy's inability to get someone in the first trumpet chair who could please him.

> Bob Cusumano was one of the top studio players in New York and he came into the band shortly before we closed at the Meadowbrook, because he was going to play first trumpet at the four-week Paramount Theater engagement immediately afterwards. Tommy didn't want him coming in 'cold' on such an important booking. He only agreed to work the Paramount, plus those few break-in nights at the Meadowbrook, because he never left New York for anybody! He was top dog in the studios and could read anything at sight, the first time. He was the lead trumpet player on Tommy's first big hits, 'Marie' and 'Song of India' three years earlier. He was a great gentleman and a fine trumpet player and was certainly very nice to me, a raw young kid of 19! [39]

After the Paramount Theater engagement, Tommy got Johnny Dillard to play the first trumpet book, followed by Leon Debrow. Neither of them satisfied TD. Linn picks up the story:

> Johnny Dillard and, shortly afterwards, Leon Debrow (real name: Debrolowski) didn't really fit the band at all. After about a month in Dillard's case and maybe a week or two more in Leon's case, both got the hook. By the time we got to the Astor Hotel, Jimmy Blake and I had been designated as the lead trumpet players

by Tommy. Jimmy was allotted the sweet stuff, most of Axel Stordahl's things plus a few by Paul Weston, while I got Sy Oliver's jumpers.[40]

The fact that the Dorsey trumpet section now consisted of four men suggests to me that Tommy was not wearing Berigan out playing lead parts, but was rather using him as a specially featured soloist. Still, there were occasions when Bunny did in fact play lead trumpet for TD during this time. Overall however, Bunny was not working very hard, and this began to bother him. It was in his nature to work extremely hard; indeed, he had almost always overworked throughout his career. He felt that the only way he could keep his playing at a high level was by working as hard as possible, almost constantly.

As we have seen, the mere thought of a layoff was anathema to Berigan. Vacations made him extremely nervous. Nevertheless, for one of the few times in his professional life, he now found himself with two entire weeks off, with no work scheduled. He and Donna, perhaps as an attempt to patch-up their marriage, planned to spend at least some of this time in far upstate New York. Since Patricia was in elementary school, she would not have been able to join them for the entire two weeks. Joyce, now four years old, could. They worked out a compromise that would allow all four members of the family to be together for at least a few days. As Donna recalled it: "I remember five days at Saranac Lake, New York. It was the only vacation for Bunny in eleven years of marriage."[41] Evidently, she did not consider the summers in Fox Lake in 1933, 1935 and 1939 as vacations, because Bunny wasn't there for much of the time. But in all of these cases he was there with her and the girls more than five days. Harry Struble, a former member of the Paul Whiteman band with Bunny, recalled "Bunny, Donna and the kids up in Syracuse, New York in 1940."[42] Bunny probably paid for this vacation with the money he had received for the Lee Wiley recording date, which unlike his wages from Tommy Dorsey, was not subject to garnishment. After this brief hiatus, Bunny undoubtedly rushed back to Manhattan, and probably showed up at various clubs to sit in.

On Tuesday, May 21, 1940, Tommy Dorsey and His Orchestra opened at the Roof Garden of the Astor Hotel in New York City. Here is the information in the advertisement for this opening that was in the *New York Times:*

Tommy Dorsey and His Orchestra: Astor Roof, Astor Hotel—OPENING TONIGHT—with Sande Williams and His Orchestra—The Callahan Sisters—Hibbert, Bird & Laurie—The Top Hatters. Dinner and dancing nightly, except Sunday. Comfort is assured on the Astor Roof. Cooled by nature on suitable evenings; on other nights air conditioned. Dinner and supper dancing nightly, except Sunday. Deluxe dinners from $2.00; supper *couvert* (after 10 p.m.) 75 cents, except Saturdays and holidays, then $1.00.[43]

More information was contained in *Variety:*

The Astor show has the Tommy Dorsey band, Connie Haines, Frank Sinatra, the Pied Pipers, the Top Hatters, the Callahan Sisters, and the Hibbert-Bird-Larue trio. The band has five reeds, three trombones, not counting Dorsey, four trumpets, piano, bass and drums, no guitar. The Pied Pipers are three men and a girl, Jo Stafford; the Top Hatters are a whirlwind roller skating duo and the Callahan Sisters are a tap dance team. Buddy Rich is featured on a portable drum set down front on 'Quiet Please.' Tommy has asked ringsiders to bear with him if the blasting gets too loud during the broadcasts. Sande Williams has the house band.[44]

It seems that vaudeville was still very much alive in 1940. It also seems that although TD's singers and drummer Buddy Rich were mentioned in the blurb in *Variety*, Bunny Berigan was not.

The broadcasts referred to occurred almost nightly, alternating between NBC's Blue Network (over WJZ–New York), and Red Network (over WEAF–New York). Many recordings were taken off of the air during Tommy Dorsey's 1940 engagement at the Astor Roof. They show the development of the powerhouse band Tommy was to lead from then well into the years of World War II, and document the emergence of Frank Sinatra as a singing star. They also show how important an asset drummer Buddy Rich had become, both as a very colorful ensemble player, and as a nonpareil soloist. Other valuable commercial assets were the Pied Pipers singing group, and increasingly, their lead singer Jo Stafford, and Tommy's smooth trombone. Arranger Sy Oliver had by this time become a constant source of swinging originals for the band's jazz contingent, which included, in addition to Rich, clarinetist Johnny Mince, tenor saxist Don Lodice, pianist Joe Bushkin, and Bunny Berigan. Oliver also wrote arrangements on pop tunes for TD's band. Axel Stordahl continued to perfect his skills as arranger of ballads, most of which were sung by Sinatra. To top all of this off, Tommy used petite Connie Haines to sing mostly novelties and rhythm tunes. Paul Weston had left TD by this time, to embark on what would soon become a highly successful career as a freelance arranger/conductor.

Two days after they opened at the Astor Roof, Tommy had his band back in the RCA Victor recording studios at 1:30 p.m. They knocked off three current pop tunes in short order, then returned to "I'll Never Smile Again." Since the Pied Pipers and Sinatra are accompanied on this recording by only TD's trombone, reeds, and rhythm section (with Bushkin playing the celeste), it is likely that Tommy sent everyone else home after the first three sides were made. It appears that two takes of "I'll Never Smile Again" were completed that afternoon, including the one that has been one of Tommy's greatest hits ever since its release. TD and his sidemen left the studio at 5:30 p.m. so they could get to the Astor Roof in time for work that night. The RCA session documents contain this note: "Please RUSH process on above selection. Send Test Pressing to Mr. L. Joy as quickly as possible."[45]

The big sales for "I'll Never Smile Again" ensured that Tommy Dorsey's boy singer, Frank Sinatra, and the Pied Pipers vocal quartet would be an important part of the TD entertainment package for some time to come. In spite of TD's often-stated intentions to make his band more jazz oriented, the market was pulling him in another direction. Tommy, like all successful bandleaders, fully understood that he had to keep the paying customers satisfied first, and then indulge his liking for jazz on a limited basis, in order to survive in a marketplace dominated by Guy Lombardo, Kay Kyser, Sammy Kaye, Hal Kemp, and more recently, Glenn Miller. (Miller understood all of this as well. In the wake of TD's huge success with "I'll Never Smile Again," he too employed a vocal quartet, the Modernaires.) As a result, the Dorsey repertoire began to include ever more ballad charts featuring Sinatra, and to a lesser extent, the Pipers. At least one member of the jazz contingent of the Dorsey band was very displeased with this turn of events, and his jealous anger would soon boil over.

While at the Astor Roof, the Dorsey band continued to make hour-long broadcasts over NBC on Saturday afternoons, advertised by NBC as *The Dorsey Hour.* The first of these took place on May 25, from 5:00 to 6:00 p.m. Here are the titles of the tunes that were played and some relevant information about the recordings of them:

'East of the Sun;' 'Marie;' 'Dear Old Southland;' 'Another One of Those Things;' and 'Hold Tight.' (1)The above titles may or may not be from the same broadcast and the date(s) may be May 23, 25 or 28, 1940. (2) These airchecks came to light in July, 2001 and are on home-type recording blanks, size end speed unknown. (3) The vocal on 'Marie' does not sound like Sinatra (titles were heard via the telephone) but rather like an unknown male. Perhaps a sub for FS on this night? There is a remote possibility that this track may be from 1937 and the singer Jack Leonard. (4) Berigan's solo work on these is much better than most of his work with Dorsey; a couple of them are for two choruses.[46]

From this May 25 broadcast, I have heard "Marie," which was definitely sung by Frank Sinatra. Berigan's solo is typical, meaning he is taking risks, and playing with inspiration. "(Lights Out) Hold Me Tight," has Berigan playing an obbligato behind Connie Haines's vocal. "East of the Sun" has a bit more Bunny than the well-known commercial recording, all of it good. "All This and Heaven Too," which also was broadcast on May 25, is another feature for Sinatra, but has no Berigan solo on it.

Three days later, Tommy's band participated in the *America Dances* radio show that may have been relayed to England via shortwave signals. This broadcast emanated from the NBC studios in Radio City. John Allen Wood was the announcer. Here is the lineup from that broadcast: "Getting Sentimental," partial, announcements; "Loosers Weepers"; "Polka Dots and Moonbeams," vocal Frank Sinatra; "Easy Does It"; "I'll Never Smile Again"; "Blues No More"; "Boog It," vocal Connie Haines and band; "East of the Sun," vocal Sinatra and band; "Old Man Harlem"; theme and close. That same night, the band broadcast over NBC from the Astor Roof from 11:30 p.m. to midnight.

Many of the Dorsey band's broadcasts from the Astor Roof have been preserved by aircheck recordings. These recordings not only document the evolution of the band's style from the 1930s TD band to the 1940s TD band; they also capture the rapidly maturing singing style of Frank Sinatra, and give us a very clear picture of how Bunny Berigan was playing in June of 1940. The many recollections of the musicians who worked with Bunny during this time are contradictory I think because when these people were asked about Bunny many years later, they recalled incidents in a way that is very typical, that is by merging events that may have actually happened days, weeks, or even months apart. The resulting picture is almost always distorted to some degree. The recordings that were made then are a literal documentation of what was happening at a given time, and they greatly assist in presenting a truer, fuller representation of the reality that existed at that juncture. Fortunately, sixteen performances from June of 1940 by the Tommy Dorsey band have been gathered and presented on a CD with excellent sound, entitled *Tommy Dorsey and His Orchestra—Featuring Bunny Berigan—March/June Broadcasts to South America*, Soundcraft SC-5012 (2001). The liner notes do not contain any precise information about the dates the recordings on that CD were made. With the assistance of the White materials, I have been able to match the recordings with their proper dates, and in the process come to some conclusions about how well Bunny was playing then.

The first correction I must make is to the title of the above-said CD: *None* of the recordings on it come from March 1940; they *all* come from June of 1940. The following tunes were definitely taken from the June 1, 1940, broadcast which originated over WEAF–New York, from 5:00 to 6:00 p.m. (NBC staff announcer Lyle Van): "I'm Nobody's Baby," vocal Connie Haines, arrangement Sy Oliver; medley of "It's a Wonderful World," vocal CH; "Believing," solo TD; and "Shake Down the Stars," vocal Frank Sinatra; "Hawaiian War Chant"; "East of the Sun," vocal FS and band; and "Hallelujah!" arrangement Oliver. From the broadcast of June 5, WJZ–New York, 11:30 p.m.–12:00 midnight (Spanish-speaking announcer) are "Sweet Lorraine," vocal Pied Pipers; "Whispering," vocal FS and PP; "East of the Sun," vocal FS and band; and "Devil's Holiday." From the broadcast of June 12, probably WJZ, and probably 11:30 p.m.–12:00 midnight (Spanish-speaking announcer): "Song of India," "Marie," vocal FS and band; and "Symphony in Riffs" (announced as "Symphony in Swing"). From the broadcast of June 19, WJZ, 11:30 p.m.–midnight (Spanish-speaking announcer): theme, opening announcements; "Dark Eyes"; "March of the Toys"; and "Deep Night," vocal, FS and band.[47]

While Berigan was a featured member of Tommy Dorsey's band, he would usually lead the band during at least part of the first set on dance dates, and did so at the Astor Roof, with Tommy making a grand entrance before the first intermission. Fans constantly requested that Bunny play his theme song, "I Can't Get Started with You." Consequently Dorsey was faced with a bit of a dilemma: he wanted Bunny to be spotlighted, yet he didn't want there to be any confusion about the fact that this was Tommy Dorsey's band, not Bunny Berigan's. The solution worked out by TD had him graciously bringing Bunny down front at some time during the evening, and allowing him to play "I Can't Get Started." This did not happen nightly, but it happened frequently. There is only one time however that TD presented Berigan playing "I Can't Get Started" on a radio broadcast, and that was on a *Dorsey Hour* airshot from the Astor Roof on June 8. It is not known whether this performance was recorded, or if it was, whether it still exists.[48]

Well then, how was Bunny playing? On "I'm Nobody's Baby," he is featured in the first chorus with a straight mute, and sounds fine. He returns after the vocal with a few bars of high note playing on both sides of Don Lodice's tenor solo. On "Hawaiian War Chant," his solo is fluent and inventive with an exciting climax. "East of the Sun" was being promoted heavily by RCA Victor, and Tommy cooperated fully, broadcasting it as often as possible. After Sinatra's vocal Bunny has a few muted bars where he tried to create excitement. Perhaps he tried a bit too hard in such a short solo. In Sy Oliver's arrangement of "Hallelujah!" I think he plays at least some lead trumpet, then takes the climactic solo to conclude the performance. Johnny Mince has a splendid solo on clarinet; Don Lodice keeps the excitement going with his tenor sax. Buddy Rich's drumming is superb. Berigan's arresting entrance on a held note (a high D) shows that his sense of drama was still very much intact, as was his high register. (He ends the performance with a massive, ringing high F.) "Hallelujah!" clearly demonstrates what a great band Tommy had then, and Bunny's solo on it is top notch. "Hallelujah!" was the closing number of the June 1 broadcast.

The next group of recordings on Soundcraft-SC-5012 comes from the broadcast of June 5. This broadcast was not heard in the United States. It was relayed to Latin America via shortwave transmission, and used a Spanish-speaking announcer. The tunes that probably were taken from this broadcast were "Symphony in Riffs," in the Benny Carter arrangement used by Tommy and many other bands, and "Sweet Lorraine."[49] Berigan's solo on "Symphony in Riffs" (forty-eight bars) is again excellent and disproves the recollections of those who said he could no longer play extended solos. His playing here is fluent, his sound is full and rich, his range from the bottom of the horn to the top is unimpaired, and his ideas are interesting and exciting. Yes, he does stumble a bit along the way, but he was pursuing interesting jazz ideas and trying to create provocative music, not play safe. On "Sweet Lorraine," he has a brief solo on open trumpet before the Pied Piper's vocal where he once again is going for broke in the space of a few bars. He plays the careening trumpet lead in the finale. Based on this evidence, Bunny Berigan was playing very well indeed on June 1 and 5, 1940. "Whispering" is a feature for Sinatra and the Pipers. Bunny's jazz solo here is played simultaneously with Tommy's playing of the melody. Berigan seems to be using a straight mute, TD his famous solotone mute. Bunny as always, is searching for interesting ideas, and finding them, though not without a few minor flubs along the way. As indicated above, Tommy was pushing "East of the Sun" very hard at this time, so it was played again on this broadcast. The vocal part of this arrangement was extended, and Berigan takes his solo after the second vocal chorus. He is using a cup mute, and plays in a very clean, professional manner, indicating that he was probably becoming bored by playing this tune so often. "Devil's Holiday" is performed using the same Benny Carter arrangement that Bunny had used in his own band and recorded for *Thesaurus* in 1938. Here was some music that Berigan could get interested in. Don Lodice has the first solo on tenor sax, followed by Bunny, starting out in his low register. He returns with a downwardly cascading series of notes, and then takes the high note ending. This is another very worthwhile Berigan performance.

From the June 12 broadcast, also shortwaved to Latin America, come two of the biggest hits TD had in the 1930s: "Song of India" and "Marie." Both of these tunes were recorded by Tommy in January of 1937, with Berigan playing inspired trumpet solos. Once again, based on these aircheck performances, Bunny was at or near the peak of his powers. The comparison between the classic Berigan solos on the 1937 Victor records and these is very interesting. On "Song of India," Bunny enters in his middle register, then leaps into the high register, and goes on from there to complete an excellent solo that is totally different from the one he had recorded earlier. I am struck by how Bunny was playing in long, flowing phrases at this time. On "Marie" he enters as he had on the Victor record, then fashions some new ideas into another exciting solo. This version also spots some very good TD trombone and an extended booting tenor sax solo from Don Lodice. As anyone who knows anything about jazz will tell you, it is not easy to come up with interesting ideas on a tune that you have played for the one-hundredth time. Yet Bunny did it here on both "Song of India" and "Marie."

The last group of tunes on the Soundcraft CD was broadcast on June 19. This is also a Spanish-language program. TD started it off with "Dark Eyes." Bunny's playing on this tune is rather spectacular, but betrays the fact that he had played this song so many times that he was becoming tired of it. There are some "clams" in this spicy stew. Nevertheless, Berigan still delivers a good solo. "March of the Toys" is Deane Kincaide's arrangement. Bunny's solo on it is again quite spectacular, but this time with some good jazz ideas that are being passionately expressed. This is a performance that Berigan fans can truly savor—Bunny the gambler is at work here, and he wins! On "Deep Night," the tempo is slower, and Berigan plays a heartfelt solo that once again is excellent.

These recordings make it clear that whatever might have been going on in Bunny Berigan's life at that time, he was still capable of playing very well, and in fact played very well on these radio broadcasts.

On June 14, Berigan, along with many other top musicians, appeared at Harlem's Apollo Theater. Here is the information about that event:

> The Apollo Theater jumped so violently June 14 it almost landed across the river. A bash organized to welcome Coleman Hawkins on his opening day at the house found these high-priced, higher-talented men taking part: Bunny Berigan, Roy Eldridge, Harry James (trumpets); Tommy Dorsey, Jack Jenney (trombones); Benny Carter, Pete Brown (alto saxes); Coleman Hawkins, Lester Young, Charlie Barnet (tenor saxes); Joe Marsala (clarinet); Count Basie (piano); Carmen Mastren (guitar); John Kirby (bass); Gene Krupa (drums). They took 20 choruses on 'Lady Be Good.'[50]

Harlem after Dark (column) It was a knock-down, drag-out affair Friday morning at the Apollo Theatre when nearly 1500 swing-music mad fans were turned away when they sought to squeeze into the jampacked playhouse to attend the all-star 'dream band' jam session. The jam session was arranged by Jim McCarthy and Kay and Sue Werner, the ofay songwriters, and featured their idea of 1940's 'dream' orchestra. Held for the first show at the Apollo only, the jam session was an added attraction to the all ready top-heavy bill that featured Coleman Hawkins and his orchestra, Ralph Cooper, Pigmeat Markham and others. Willie Bryant was the wise-cracking emcee. Official lineup of the musicians who played many long choruses of the Andy Razaf–Fats Waller classic 'Honeysuckle Rose' was: Tommy Dorsey, Bunny Berigan, Harry James trumpet; he came late and had to play a solo alone; Gene Krupa John Kirby, Carmen Mastren, Count Basie, Joe Marsala, Jack Jenney and Coleman Hawkins.[51]

They all came: Jenney, Dorsey, Berigan, Eldridge, James, Krupa, Basie, Marsala, Mastren and Kirby. And people, in droves that really shook the rafters of the Apollo Theater and set jumping and howling one of the greatest crowds ever. With the collaboration of Coleman Hawkins, these stars played just as you'd imagine an all-star dream band would play. The solos flew fast and furious as, one after another, these giants stepped forward to blow great horn. The super-solid rhythm section kept things going superbly. These fine men were getting great kicks out of working together. So, late that afternoon, most of them congregated again in the small WNEW studios, whence originates Martin Block's famed *Make Believe Ballroom* and proceeded once again to fashion all-American dream music.[52]

I have heard the "Ad-Lib Blues" that was recorded at WNEW. It clocks in at twelve minutes and forty-eight seconds, and has all the assembled musicians playing spontaneous riffs behind the soloists. Berigan plays four choruses with absolutely no sign of strain. These are not the best blues choruses Bunny Berigan ever played, but they show that he was still taking chances and was certainly able to play comfortably with some of the best players in jazz at that time.

Life off of the bandstand was fairly pleasant for Bunny during this period. Since the band had Sundays and much of every other weekday off, they began playing softball games in Central Park. Ray Linn recalled that Bunny participated enthusiastically:

We all began to feel human again, playing that summer at the Astor Roof, a lovely job. Our first softball game with brother Jimmy's team was a memorable one. I was third baseman and went 3 for 5 and I think that everybody in the band, and especially those of us on the team, would have been too scared of Tommy to show up for work that night if we'd lost. Actually, we won 12 to 10 and we won the return match a week or so later which had been arranged as a publicity stunt for *Pic* magazine, by 7 to 5. Bunny really loved to play softball. He always played catcher and would keep up a stream of patter, none too complimentary, with all the opposing hitters. I guess you could say he had an 'Irish mouth,' but he was a better-than-average player, always good for a couple of hits. Of course he could be a little slow-footed, but surprisingly capable, generally, for a guy in his advanced state of alcoholism. It was really amazing that he was able to walk rapidly, let alone run. He had a good strong arm for throwing out base runners. He really loved the game, though. He'd have me call his room at the Piccadilly Hotel on Forty-fifth Street[53] every Wednesday morning when we had a game. Most of the guys in the band, the single ones anyway, stayed at the Piccadilly, and I seem to recall that Bunny was either living apart from his wife, or he and Donna were fighting a lot at that time. Anyway, whenever I would pick up the house phone to wake him for the ball game, he would reply, sleepily, 'Ray, Pootie, what time is it?' 'It's ten o'clock, Bunny,' and we're leaving for the park in ten minutes,' I'd reply. 'Aw, Pootie, I don't feel like it, I gotta get some more sleep.' And so it would go on, with me pleading with him to get up, and him demurring and yawning, 'Naw, Pootie, gimme a bit longer.' Bunny called everybody 'Pootie,' except Tommy, who was always 'Tom,' and who never called Bunny anything but 'Shanty' to his face, a name of true endearment that only one Irishman can call another. Otherwise, it's a fighting name! Bunny even called Connie Haines and Jo Stafford, 'Pootie'! In fact, even the bus-driver on our one nighters was 'Pootie' to Bunny. Anyway, to get back to my story, I would finally succeed in cajoling him into getting dressed, pour a couple of stiff jolts down his throat and join us in piling into two or three taxicabs and heading for Central Park.[54]

A couple of other musicians from Tommy's band also recalled these games: Chuck Lowry, of the Pied Pipers recalled: "Jimmy Dorsey was at the Pennsylvania Hotel and he issued a challenge to Tommy, not knowing that we had been playing regularly in Central Park every Wednesday while we were at the Astor. I was the pitcher and Bunny was the catcher, but sometimes he would fold up after a few innings, because he was out of condition. Of course, we all knew he was broke, but he was always making bets on whether he'd get a hit and which team would win."[55]

Trumpeter Clyde Hurley, whom TD hired in mid-June after he fired Leon Debrow, also played on the TD softball team: "Actually, Bunny was really a pretty good softball player. He could hit quite well and was a catcher of no mean ability. But, unfortunately, frequent refreshment would usually catch up with him before the 9th inning! [56]

Sundays were often spent at Tommy's Bernardsville, New Jersey, estate. Many people would be there, including of course Tommy's wife, Mildred, who was known to all as "Toots," and their two children, daughter, Pat, and son, Thomas Francis Dorsey, III, whose nickname was "Skipper." One of Skipper's boyhood friends recalled a humorous episode involving Bunny the prankster and the very attractive singing King Sisters, who were then being featured with Horace Heidt's band: "The girls were lying on chaise lounges at the edge of the pool. They had their straps off their shoulders. Bunny came up behind one of them and lifted up the chair and she slid into the water. Every time she treaded water, her boobs would float to the top of the water. Bunny and a group of people stood there roaring. He was a very regular guy. Mr. Dorsey was more aloof."[57]

Not everything that happened that summer was pleasant however. Lead alto saxist Hymie Schertzer remembered an incident that finally brought out into the open the lingering animosity between Frank Sinatra and Buddy Rich: "One night, backstage at the Astor during an intermission, Frank accused Buddy of messing up one of his vocals with a misplaced paradiddle. He picked up a glass pitcher full of iced-water, threw it straight at Buddy, who ducked, and almost felled me! Fortunately, it missed and struck the wall, shattering into a thousand pieces. Buddy really hated playing ballads and sometimes he'd just stop playing altogether or give a sly, most inappropriate thud on his bass drum, just when Frank reached the most sentimental part of the song!"[58] Sinatra followed up on this by having some thugs accost Rich on a Manhattan street and beat him up. *Down Beat's* September 1, 1940, issue contained this headline: "Buddy Rich Gets Face Bashed In," followed by a story detailing the assault. While Rich recuperated, Nick Pelico, the drummer with Sande Williams's house band at the Astor, filled in for him.

The hiring of Clyde Hurley in mid-June as the fourth trumpet pleased Tommy on many levels. First, Clyde was an excellent trumpeter who could play jazz in the intense Texas style epitomized in those years by Harry James. Second, Hurley had recently been with Glenn Miller's band, which was now one of the most popular in the country. Clyde and Glenn had a disagreement, after which Hurley left Miller rather hurriedly. TD immediately hired him to fill out the section for the upcoming *Pepsodent Show*, and began giving him jazz solos. (His most remembered solo with Dorsey is his manic outing on the Victor/Bluebird recording of "Quiet Please!" the Buddy Rich showpiece.) Bunny likely was not as sanguine about this development as Tommy. As was always the case in dealing with Bunny Berigan, if one could achieve the delicate balance that allowed him to work with some confidence and security, he was able to play well. Once that delicate balance was altered however, disaster usually followed. The advent of Clyde Hurley in TD's band as a jazz trumpet soloist undoubtedly upset Bunny. Nevertheless, he was ever courteous and kind to Hurley, who recalled: "Bunny was not 'close' with anyone in the TD band that I knew about. He was not that different as it were, but just not the type of guy who talked or said much off the bandstand or on the job. I recall Bunny did tell me more than once of his early influence by Louis (Armstrong) and of his admiration for 'The King,' which of course was the same as I."[59] Bunny now began to nurse a grudge against Tommy Dorsey, and his somewhat regulated intake of alcohol swiftly went out of control.

During this time, Bunny was probably living at the Forrest Hotel on West forty-ninth Street,[60] the headquarters for many big band sidemen. It had been the unofficial home of the unmarried members of Bunny's own bands from 1937 to 1940. At the Forrest, he encountered many musicians he knew, and more than a few he himself had previously employed.

Bunny's alcoholism was now reaching truly devastating levels. The drummer Ralph Collier, who later went on to some renown with Benny Goodman and Stan Kenton, recalled this tragicomic scenario that occurred at the Forrest:

> I got a call from Gus Bivona, who was organizing a band in New York and needed a drummer. I arrived there, not knowing a soul except Gus, who invited me up to his room at the Forrest Hotel. There I was astonished to see a guy lying on the floor, stoned out of his head! He was a good-looking guy, wearing a light brown double-breasted suit, which looked like it had been slept in. He was rambling, 'I'm back working with Tommy Dorsey, you know, and I'm gonna stop drinking and get my lip back in shape.' Gus told me it was Bunny Berigan. He kept on repeating over and over again about how he was the world's greatest trumpet player and how he would soon be back in shape. It was really weird![61]

Longtime TD saxist Freddie Stulce also recalled how Bunny's relationship with Tommy and his role in the Dorsey band evolved during the spring of 1940:

> Bunny got $45.00 a week for living expense and the rest of his salary was attached by the union. He managed to resist the bottle for awhile, playing with something like his old spirit and invention and his relationship with Tommy and the rest of us was very cordial. But Tom had succeeded in getting his own drink problem pretty well under control by that time and despised Bunny for being unable to get himself straightened out. As the weeks went by, their friendship began to cool, especially during the engagement at the Astor Hotel. New York was crowded at that time with visitors to the World's Fair and the hotel business was very good. Bunny's own performances, however, began to deteriorate in direct proportion to his daily alcoholic consumption and this became increasingly obvious to musicians and patrons alike. His allotted solo time was gradually, but deliberately, being reduced by Tommy, with Don Lodice having to carry the major overloading that produced. We all realized that Bunny's tenure with the band hadn't long to last.[62]

On June 25, the Dorsey band began their thirteen week stint as Bob Hope's replacement on the NBC Pepsodent radio show, entitled *Summer Pastime* during the thirteen weeks of its run. *Variety* reviewed the first broadcast:

> Tommy Dorsey presides at a thoroughly enjoyable variety session, which should make listeners Pepsodent conscious. The spot is nicely paced with other talent, including vocalists Frank Sinatra and Connie Haines, who get a single each in which to show off their nice pipes. Tommy makes an amiable emcee and is allowed a good script. Guest is Jerry Lester, a fine comedian on a night club floor, who is handicapped by poor material and bad timing from the stooges. The show is over 62 NBC stations. If proof were needed, this half-hour reveals Dorsey as a showman capable of spreading his canvas over a full-sized radio lot.[63]

One of those "stooges" may have been Bunny Berigan. Bunny never excelled at public speaking, and apparently muffed some scripted lines on the first Pepsodent show, causing TD to become enraged. Soon thereafter, probably on the very next Pepsodent show, another untoward incident involving Berigan occurred.

Sometime during the run of the Pepsodent show, for which the Dorsey band was required to leave the Astor Roof on Times Square and go by taxi to the NBC studios in Rockefeller Center for the 10:00–10:30 p.m. broadcast, the following tableau unfolded. There are numerous variations to this story, but the basic outline is as follows:

> One night, Bunny told Bobby Burns (TD's manager) that his wife was coming in for dinner, and he asked if it would be alright to sign the check. Bobby said that it was OK. Bunny sat at the table with Mrs. Berigan between sets. At the end of the dinner session, Bobby okayed Bunny's dinner check which came to about $21.00. The band went to NBC to do the Pepsodent radio show. 'Marie' was on the program. When Bunny stood for his solo, he fell off the stand. 'When we got back to the Astor Roof' said Burns, 'Tommy asked me to dig out Bunny's dinner check and see what he had for dinner. On close scrutiny it showed a tab for twelve scotch and sodas and one ham sandwich.'[64]

Ray Linn, who sat next to Berigan in TD's trumpet section that night, picks up the narrative:

> Bunny got quite a few lines of dialogue on the Pepsodent show, which also starred comedian Jerry Lester who did a lot of clowning around, including blowing a trombone. The pairing of the world's greatest trombonist along with the planet's very worst must have seemed like a natural to the masterminds at the agency that put the show together! That night, Bunny completely fell apart on, of all things 'Marie,' the opening number on the broadcast! He was the drunkest I'd ever seen him. How he was able to stand, let alone try to play, was a testimony to his rugged constitution. Attempting his F to high F glissando entrance to his 32 bar solo, nothing but a series of funny noises came out and it got worse! We were on the air, coast to coast on the NBC network, some 200 *(sic)* or more stations. Bunny stayed on his feet for about 8 bars, trying to fight it through, as he had done so many times before, but this time the booze was the winner. He literally could no longer play and putting down his horn, he fell heavily toward his chair, which he missed and dropped about four feet from the section-riser to the floor! Had he been sober, he would have undoubtedly broken several bones, but in his benumbed state he was unhurt and clambered back up on the bandstand with Blake's assistance. He didn't attempt to play another note during the remaining 25 minutes or so of the program. He just sat it out and luckily there was nothing more for him to do on the show. This created a lot of disturbance during the broadcast, because all the mikes were wide open. Tenorman Don Lodice was the one who alertly jumped up when Bunny collapsed and blew the remaining 24 bars of Bunny's chorus. Don really saved the day, because Hurley and Blake and I were dumbstruck by all this! After the show, Tommy came back of the bandstand and said to Bobby Burns, 'Get rid of him now, Burns, pay him off. I don't want to see him back at the Astor!' I was standing about six feet away, putting my horn in its case and overheard the whole thing. So Bunny was given a check for two week's salary, fired on the spot and told never to come back![65]

The date of this incident has usually been given as August 20, 1940, which appears to be the date Berigan and Dorsey finally parted company. I think it happened earlier than that, probably on July 2, because the NBC radio logs housed at the Library of Congress indicate that "Marie" was the first tune played on that broadcast,[66] and after that date, Berigan's presence with the Dorsey band was sporadic. The Dorsey band began its appearance on the Pepsodent show on June 25. Clyde Hurley had left Glenn Miller's band on May 31,[67] and joined TD's band shortly thereafter.

> I joined Tommy Dorsey in mid-June at the Astor Roof and I was given some solos right away. I figured Tommy wanted everybody to know that he'd hired me away from Glenn Miller! Bunny was still around, of course, but he was being featured less and less. Ray and Jimmy were both playing some lead parts and Bunny was still playing pretty good jazz horn, but he could only get up and blow for one chorus, after that he hadn't much left. He no longer had the stamina to play long solos, his wind and his lip were both going. He was drinking heavily and was deep in debt, always trying to borrow from anybody. Tommy was holding back part of his wages each week, but Bunny didn't gripe about it. Playing in the Dorsey band was a ball compared with the rigid inflexibility of the Glenn Miller band.[68]

After the June 19 broadcast from the Astor Roof, there was another broadcast, on June 22, which featured Berigan playing a solo on "Dark Eyes." Another such broadcast, from June 26, had him playing on "East of the Sun" and "Symphony in Riffs." The White materials indicate that his solo on "East of the Sun" is not up to par.[69] On June 27, the Dorsey band recorded five tunes for Victor, all featuring vocals.[70] There is no aural evidence that would indicate the presence of Berigan at this session. A photo of the Dorsey band from this period does not include Berigan.[71] The Dorsey band checked into the Victor recording studios again on July 17, when they recorded seven titles, including the romping Buddy Rich drum feature "Quiet Please!" with Clyde Hurley taking the trumpet solo. Berigan was not at that recording session. There is a paucity of aircheck recordings of the TD band from June 26 to July 20, so we do not know if Bunny was in the Dorsey band during that time. One source indicates that during this period "Dorsey sent Berigan away for rehabilitation."[72] This is far from an established fact, however, as I have seen only one other reference to Bunny going away for rehabilitation.[73] Nevertheless, it is possible that at this juncture (through almost all of July) Berigan sought treatment for his alcoholism.

The July 20 broadcast from the Astor Roof includes numerous tunes with trumpet solos on them. The White materials indicate that Bunny may have been present, but did not play all of these trumpet solos. The titles on which he appears to solo are "Whispering," "The Lonesome Road," and "East of the Sun." I have not heard these airchecks so I cannot comment on them. Likewise, I have not heard any of the recordings from the July 24 broadcast, but the White materials indicate that Bunny played a solo on "Swing High" on that date. I have heard "Old Gray Bonnet" from the July 27 broadcast, and can say with certainty that the trumpet solo on that tune was played by Clyde Hurley. But then, there is the aircheck of "I Found a New Baby," which appears to have been recorded from the August 3 broadcast, which definitely contains an excellent trumpet solo by Bunny Berigan. No diminution of his powers is noticeable in this performance.

We also know that Bunny was photographed on August 7 together with arranger Fred Norman, Tommy Dorsey, Lionel Hampton, Frank Sinatra, and *Eleanor Roosevelt!* This photo was supposed to promote a worthy cause, which turned out to be not so worthy:

> It wasn't only Tommy Dorsey, Bunny Berigan and Lionel Hampton who were the unwitting pawns of a conniving promoter here. Mrs. Franklin D. Roosevelt herself made a special but futile trip to New York. She was going to buy the first tickets to what was intended to be a gigantic benefit concert for the Bethune-Cookman Music School. The date was to have been August 22, the place the Polo Grounds. Mrs. Roosevelt, Dorsey, Berigan and Mrs. Fred Norman, one of the organizers, were photographed together purchasing tickets. Everything looked fine, until someone discovered that a promoter was privately turning the affair into a benefit strictly for himself! The last-minute confusion resulted in the cancellation of the concert.[74]

Bunny does not look very healthy in this photo.

Meanwhile, MCA had flexed its muscle, and the Dorsey band's stay at the Astor Roof was extended to facilitate the band remaining in New York for all of the thirteen weeks it would be playing on the Pepsodent show. They would remain at the Astor until August 28.

Tommy Dorsey had been around the music business for over fifteen years by 1940. He had slowly learned where there was money to be made, other than on the road doing one-nighters. Sometime prior to 1940, TD went into the music publishing business, founding Sun Publishing Company. At first, Tommy had no composers who wanted to place their music with him. He then decided to search out unknown composers, publish their songs, and try to get them recorded and broadcast. Not much happened until he stumbled across the song "I'll Never Smile Again." There are many divergent stories about how Tommy came to record "I'll Never Smile Again," but I find the one related by Tommy's guitarist Carmen Mastren to be the most plausible:

> I'd known Ruth Lowe (the song's composer) before I worked with Tommy Dorsey. She had once played piano with Ina Ray Hutton and I hadn't seen her for several years until Tommy's band played the Toronto Exposition in the fall of 1939. She called me, saying she had a nice song she'd written called 'I'll Never Smile Again' on an aircheck by Percy Faith, who was the music director for the Canadian Broadcasting Company. It was a beautiful arrangement, using harp and string section and I brought it back to New York, but it took me a few months before I could get Tommy to listen to that demo disc. Finally, one day at the Victor studios I told him that if he didn't sit down and listen, I'd take the song else-

where. He flipped when he heard it and I told him it was free and clear for him to record and publish. However, he first tried to hire Percy Faith to arrange it, but he was under contract to CBC. In fact, Glenn Miller recorded it first at a brighter tempo, but his version didn't take off. Tommy's record became Number One in no time, but I was no longer with the band by then.[75]

Tommy immediately signed Ruth Lowe to a contract with Sun Music, and rushed to record "I'll Never Smile Again" on April 23, 1940. As we know, he did not get a satisfactory take on that date, and planned to try to record the tune at his next recording session, whenever that might be.

Some time after TD's first attempt to record "I'll Never Smile Again," he learned that Glenn Miller had already recorded the tune, on February 19, 1940, and was playing it on remote radio broadcasts. He heard the Miller record soon after its release in April, and realized that Miller's arrangement of the tune, written by the very talented Jerry Gray, was all wrong—the tempo was too fast for the dreamy melody and sentimental lyric. Tommy worked with Freddie Stulce from his sax section (who was also a fine if underappreciated arranger), to slow the tempo way down, simplify the instrumental background, and have Joe Bushkin play the celeste instead of the piano. Against this simple, quiet background, Frank Sinatra and the Pied Pipers sang very sensitively. He finally returned to the studio to get a satisfactory take on May 23. The record was rushed into production and issued in June. By late August, *Variety* was reporting the following: "'I'll Never Smile Again' (Sun Publishing Company, aka T. Dorsey) has already sold 160,000 copies of sheet music. Weekly sales of around 20,000. Record sales of the tune figure to have gone over 500,000, with TD's Victor version 200,000 of that."[76] Tommy Dorsey's recording of "I'll Never Smile Again" continued to sell, eventually far exceeding 1,000,000 records, and probably several hundred thousand copies of sheet music. TD collected the publisher's share of the royalties, as well as the performer's share. This is another example of why Tommy Dorsey was as successful as he was as a bandleader. It also presents a stark contrast between the approaches to bandleading of Tommy Dorsey and Bunny Berigan. The word *entrepreneurism* was not used widely in the United States in 1940. Nevertheless, Tommy Dorsey and most other very successful bandleaders then were entrepreneurs, in addition to being musicians. Bunny Berigan, to say the least, was not an entrepreneur.

Clyde Hurley, and his successor in the Dorsey band, Ziggy Elman, provided some insights as to the circumstances surrounding Bunny Berigan's final departure from the ranks of TD sidemen. Hurley related:

It was a funny thing, Bunny just didn't come around for a period and then he was back and then he was out again. Finally, after a lot of talk for what seemed like weeks before it really happened, Ziggy had joined the band and Bunny was seen no more.[77]

Ziggy Elman, who replaced Berigan in the Dorsey band, recalled:

The Benny Goodman band had broken up, with Benny going into the hospital, but I and a few others, the 'key' men, had contracts with Goodman. Tommy Dorsey had actually offered me a job before Benny broke up, but I wasn't too keen and went back to New York to gig and keep my lip in shape. I'd been friends with Joe Venuti for a long period, so I started playing with him at the Meadowbrook. I was added to the band and did mostly jump-type things, the idea being to help Joe pull bigger crowds. All the time, either Tommy or his band manager, Bobby Burns, would call me up every day, trying to persuade me to join the band. Bunny was really sick by then and I actually took his place on a couple of dates before officially joining the band. They were due to go out on the road, following the Astor stand, but Tommy doubted that Bunny would be able to make it. So, I finally agreed to join Dorsey but to be fair to Joe, I said I'd wait 'til he finished at the Meadowbrook. I drove to the Meadowbrook one night, only to be told that Bunny was going to work with Venuti and I should go back to play with Tommy Dorsey. Tommy and Venuti had it all worked out.[78]

At least one other TD sideman recalled Bunny visiting the TD band on numerous occasions after he had been fired, sitting in, and on occasion playing well.[79]

After Berigan finally left the Tommy Dorsey band, which certainly was in late August, 1940, the trade papers played up the separation quite big:

Bunny Berigan again out of Dorsey crew. Bunny Berigan and the Tommy Dorsey band have parted again. After being on notice once or twice before, Berigan was let go last Tuesday (20th), following the Dorsey unit's broadcast for Pepsodent. The understanding is that Berigan will again attempt a band of his own. He disbanded his last one when he joined Tommy Dorsey several months ago. Shortly after he came back, Dorsey began paying a certain percentage of his salary each week to the AFM, to go towards paying off debts Berigan had accumulated when operating a band of his own[80]

'I fired Berigan!,' 'I quit Dorsey!' are the conflicting testimonies of the two principals in the recent withdrawal of Bunny Berigan from the Tommy Dorsey band, said action having taken place after a radio program a NBC on August 20. Said Tommy to *Metronome*: 'I just couldn't bring him around, so I had to let him go. I hated to do it.' Said Bunny to *Metronome:* 'I wasn't happy in Tommy's band, because I didn't get enough chance to play. Most of the time I was just sitting there, waiting for choruses, or else I was just a stooge, leading the band while Tommy sat at somebody's table. You can't keep in trim that way, playing just a little each night, so I thought I'd better leave and start my own band and begin to play again.' To fill his place in the band, Tommy called in Chuck Peterson, former Artie Shaw trumpeter, assigning high notes to him and giving most of Bunny's jazz parts to Clyde Hurley. Ray Linn and Jimmy Blake will also get a chance to blow some hot.[81]

Tommy Dorsey let Bunny Berigan, his ace trumpet man, go ten days ago, Chuck Peterson temporarily replacing him. Tommy had been giving Bunny terrific dialogue spots with plenty of time for the script on the band's Pepsodent show, to say nothing of the billing that Bunny got on the show every time he took a few bars solo. A spokesman in the band said that Tommy and Bunny just didn't see eye-to-eye on certain things.[82]

Berigan's statement that he was not getting enough to play is certainly borne out by the aircheck and commercial recordings made by the Dorsey band after late June. But was this a result of his increased drinking and consequent unreliability; his allegedly declining trumpeting skills; or after having been "fired" by TD, his pursuit of rehabilitation? Whatever the case, his appearances with the Dorsey band through July and August were only sporadic. The available evidence seems to indicate that Berigan was mostly being used by Dorsey as a jazz soloist, with very little other playing being required of him. When Clyde Hurley came upon the scene and began to play some jazz trumpet solos, Berigan went into a tailspin, and his drinking went out of control. This, and Bunny's apparent difficulty with scripted lines on the Pepsodent show led to the disaster on that show, and Bunny's being "fired."[83] What Berigan was doing after this incident, which probably occurred in early July, and the date of his actual final departure from the Dorsey band, which was August 20, is not clear. He did not work anywhere else during this period, but did continue some kind of intermittent relationship with the Dorsey band. Indeed, he may have sought some sort of treatment for his alcoholism during this time period.

If one assesses the six months' association Bunny Berigan had with Tommy Dorsey in 1940, the result on balance, contrary to the accepted wisdom, is overwhelmingly positive. On the plus side, Berigan spent almost all of that six-month period off of the road. He had been able to have a vacation with his wife and daughters. He had been used by TD more or less as a featured soloist, thus being spared the hard work of playing constantly in Tommy's trumpet section. Consequently, his health, which was precarious at best when he joined Dorsey, was likely restored as much as that was possible, given the ongoing harm he was doing to his damaged liver by continuing to drink. He had undoubtedly reduced his debt either to zero, or close to it. He had been on display with one of the highest-profile big bands of the swing era, and had received a lot of publicity, much of it good, indeed, encouraging.

It also appears that he was able to effectuate some sort of reconciliation with his wife during this time, and finally end his destructive relationship with Lee Wiley. That meant that he was able to enjoy at least a little time with his daughters during the Dorsey interlude. Patricia was eight years old then, and Joyce was four.

Bunny's children were blissfully unaware of the complications and problems their father was then dealing with on a daily basis. He was painfully aware of them, however, and undoubtedly realized that the source of many of these problems was his alcoholism. But with the powerful sense of denial that is a part of the psychological makeup of all alcoholics, Bunny continued to defer taking any truly decisive action then to stop his drinking, and do whatever was necessary to stay sober permanently. I think that if Bunny had decided to try to stop drinking permanently during his time with Tommy Dorsey in 1940, TD would have supported his efforts to the full. If that had in fact happened, it would not necessarily have meant that Berigan could or would have stayed sober. But he might have. And if he had, he certainly would have lived a lot longer than he did. Instead, Tommy Dorsey, like Bunny's own father had, gave up trying to help him stop drinking. But Bunny's prime objective, as August of 1940 ended, was to reorganize his own band as soon as possible, and resume touring with it. Consequently, his close personal support system would once again become the members of his band, who could not stand watching him destroy himself with alcohol, and his wife, Donna, who had her own drinking problems, would sometimes accompany Bunny on the road, and would then drink with him.

Berigan's rapidly deteriorating liver now placed his health, indeed his survival, at risk. It was no longer a matter of him trying to stay sober enough to function: each drink he took now would do more damage to his already ravaged liver. In spite of his understanding of these risks, which I think was rather complete, he would continue to deal with these dire new health challenges as he had in the past—by trying to *regulate* his drinking. But as we now know, alcoholics can deal with their drinking problem in only one way—by *stopping all intake of alcohol.* Only that plan would have effectively dealt with Berigan's alcoholism and cirrhosis. Bunny's plan was doomed to failure, and as a result, he too was doomed.

It is easy for us, with the help of seven decades of advances in the treatment of alcoholism, to judge Bunny Berigan a failure in his fight against his alcoholism. But it was infinitely more complicated than that for him in his day-to-day life in 1940. He had always been severely insecure about "laying off" playing his trumpet, and "losing his lip." He felt he had to work consistently, and fairly hard, to maintain his embouchure and playing skills. This phobia, and myriad other negative factors, militated against Bunny doing what he had to do to stop drinking. All of this, coupled with the relatively primitive understanding that the medical community had in 1940 about alcoholism as a disease, and the methods that had to be employed for a successful "intervention," made it almost impossible for Bunny Berigan to conquer his alcoholism. Nevertheless, he continued trying, in his own way.

After Berigan's departure from the Dorsey band, he began to sit in regularly with Joe Venuti's band, which was then appearing at the Meadowbrook, assuming the role of "featured guest" that Ziggy Elman had been filling just before. I suspect that Venuti's band was then being booked by MCA, and consequently would have been a welcome haven for Elman, who had been waiting for Benny Goodman to return to action after back surgery, and then for Berigan, who was pondering what to do post TD. This arrangement would have given Venuti a marquee sideman to pull customers, and would have given Berigan the opportunity to keep his lip in shape and earn a few dollars while he plotted his next move.

Soon, items began to appear in the trade papers about Berigan's plans:

Bunny Berigan lost no time after his exodus from the Tommy Dorsey band in going back to the maestro role. He is currently rehearsing, and MCA is trying to decide whether to take his crew under their wing. Although his appearance in Joe Venuti's band at the Meadowbrook, Cedar Grove, New Jersey, led to rumors that, after all, Bunny had given up ideas of forming his own band again, he nevertheless is going through with his plans to front another combo. The Venuti sojourn was merely temporary.[84]

Bunny had contacted the drummer and copyist Jack Maisel, who had been the copyist for his previous band, and who had retained copies of most of that band's arrangements. The originals that Bunny had bought and paid for when he had led his own band had apparently been turned over to his creditors after he disbanded in early 1940. Maisel and Berigan joined forces, with Jack providing arrangements, and acting as contractor to gather the musicians, as well as playing drums for Bunny's new band. Until he could get a big band organized, Berigan fronted a seven-piece group at the Brick Club on West Forty-seventh Street, between Broadway and Sixth Avenue.[85] This gig probably lasted for the first two or three weeks of September, and did very good business.

Notes

[1] *Variety:* February 28, 1940, cited in the White materials.
[2] White materials: March 2, 1940.
[3] *Down Beat:* March 15, 1940, cited in the White materials.
[4] *Metronome:* April 1940, cited in the White materials.
[5] *The Big Bands:* by George T. Simon, Macmillan Co. (1967), 167.
[6] *Tommy Dorsey—Livin' in a Great Big Way,* by Peter J. Levinson, Da Capo Press (2005), 126–127. Hereafter *Livin' in a Great Big Way.*
[7] The Bob Crosby band at some point switched from Rockwell-O'Keefe to MCA, probably in 1939, in order to be the featured band on *The Camel Caravan* radio show, following Benny Goodman's departure from that program. MCA controlled the talent on that show.
[8] Jo Elizabeth Stafford was born on November 12, 1917, in Coalinga, California. In the mid-1930s, she sang as a member of a vocal group with her sisters. They performed on radio in Los Angeles, and on the soundtrack of the Fred Astair film *A Damsel in Distress* in 1937. In 1938, she joined a vocal group consisting of eight members, called the Pied Pipers. This group was heard by Tommy Dorsey's arrangers Paul Weston and Axel Stordahl, and they persuaded TD to use the group on his radio show. Unfortunately, the show's sponsor did not like them and they were fired. Some months later, TD hired four of the Pipers, including Ms. Stafford, as regular members of his band. From 1940 through 1942, the Pipers were prominently featured by Dorsey, and gradually Jo Stafford received more opportunities to be presented as a soloist. In 1943, the Pipers left Dorsey and were signed by the then new Capitol Records, where Paul Weston was working as a house arranger/conductor. Shortly thereafter, Ms. Stafford began her career as a soloist, after having been signed by Capitol. She was featured on radio, where she had moderate success, and on records, where she had great success for the rest of the 1940s on Capitol, and throughout the 1950s on Columbia. By the mid-1960s, Ms. Stafford recognized that the

popular music landscape had changed in ways that were no longer conducive to her continuing success as a performer, so she essentially retired. Her performances thereafter were few and far between by choice. Jo Stafford died on July 16, 2008, in Century City, California.

[9] Francis Albert Sinatra was born on December 12, 1915, in Hoboken, New Jersey. Like most young male singers in the 1930s, he was influenced by Bing Crosby. Early on however, he developed a less stentorian, more intimate approach to popular music than Crosby. This, and his inexplicably powerful sex appeal, ensured that he would be a successful band vocalist. But Sinatra also had a mammoth desire to succeed in the entertainment business in the same ways that Crosby had, and this drove him to expand his career into films and radio, as well as building on his popularity as a singer. Nevertheless, Sinatra never had as much success in these media as Crosby had had. When his career was at a nadir in the early 1950s, Sinatra began one of the most remarkable comebacks in entertainment history, scoring a number of film successes, and most notably, by recording a series of superb albums for Capitol Records, most of which were done in close collaboration with the arranger Nelson Riddle. By the early 1960s, Sinatra occupied a position of great success as an entertainer in films, on television, and on record. He had also gained great acclaim as an entertainment phenomenon in the various showrooms in Las Vegas. Still, with the advent of the rock-oriented music and greatly changing approaches to filmmaking of the later 1960s, Sinatra's career was once again on the wane. He wisely retired in 1971, but missed the adulation of his audiences too much to remain away from performing, and returned to work in 1973. Although the Sinatra of the 1970s and later had much diminished vocal ability, his fans became less and less critical of his limitations, and accepted him as a pop music icon. He continued performing and recording into the 1990s. Frank Sinatra died in Los Angeles, California on May 14, 1998.

[10] *Variety:* April 3, 1940, cited in the White materials.

[11] White materials: March 4, 1940.

[12] White materials: March 10, 1940.

[13] White materials: March 12, 1940.

[14] White materials: March 10, 1940.

[15] White materials: March 12, 1940.

[16] *Ibid.*

[17] Summary of information in *New York Times,* March 13, 1940, cited in the White materials.

[18] This review, probably done by *Billboard's* correspondent, appeared in the *New York Herald Tribune,* and the *New York World-Telegram* on March 14, 1940, and then in *Billboard* on March 23, 1940. Cited in the White materials: March 13, 1940.

[19] *Metronome:* April 1940, cited in the White materials.

[20] White materials: March 13, 1940.

[21] *Down Beat:* April 1, 1940, cited in the White materials.

[22] Dupuis: 223.

[23] White materials: March 21, 1940.

[24] *International Musician:* May 1940, cited in the White materials, May 1940.

[25] Dupuis: 224.

[26] *Ibid.*

[27] A transcript of the conversation between the performers that occurred after a rejected take of "Find Me a Primitive Man" appears in appendix 5. It provides a fascinating insight into the often tedious business of recording music.

[28] White materials: April 10, 1940.

[29] White materials: April 12, 1940.

[30] It is also possible that they played a one-nighter in Bristol, Connecticut, at the Lake Compounce Ballroom.

[31] *Metronome:* May 1940, cited in the White materials.

[32] *Billboard:* April 13, 1940, cited in the White materials.

[33] The three takes of "I'll Never Smile Again" that were cut on April 10, 1940, have not been located in RCA Victor's "vaults." Liner notes/discography from *Tommy Dorsey/ Frank Sinatra—The Song Is You,* RCA-07863-66353-2 (5 CD set) (1994), 3 "sessionography."

[34] *Billboard:* April 27, 1940, cited in the White materials.

[35] *Billboard:* May 25, 1940, cited in the White materials.

[36] White materials: May 4, 1940, cited in the White materials.

[37] *Billboard:* May 25, 1940, cited in the White materials.

[38] Author's conversation with Johnny Mince, 1986.

[39] White materials: March 9, 1940.

[40] White materials: April 26, 1940.

[41] White materials: May 4, 1940.

[42] *Ibid.*

[43] *New York Times:* May 21, 1940, cited in the White materials.

[44] *Variety:* May 29, 1940, cited in the White materials.

[45] White materials: May 23, 1940.

[46] White materials: May 25, 1940.

[47] In attempting to match these tunes with the dates on which they were broadcast, I matched the actual aircheck performance timings from the tunes on SC-5012 with the same tunes and timings listed in the White materials.

[48] The information about the June 8, 1940, *Dorsey Hour* broadcast was provided by Carl A. Hallstrom from information he obtained from the NBC Archive at the Library of Congress.

[49] Both "Symphony in Riffs" (introduced by a Spanish-speaking announcer as "Symphony in Swing") and "Sweet Lorraine" (introduced by the same announcer) were a part of the June 5, 1940, broadcast beamed by NBC to South America, contrary to the suggestion in the White materials that they may have been from the June 1 broadcast. That broadcast was announced in English by NBC staff announcer Lyle Van.

[50] *Down Beat:* July 1, 1940, cited in the White materials.

[51] *New Amsterdam News:* June 22, 1940, cited in the White materials.

[52] *Swing:* September 1940, cited in the White materials.

[53] See note 60, below Berigan probably actually lived at the Forrest Hotel during the Dorsey interlude.

[54] White materials: July 10, 1940.

[55] *Ibid.*

[56] *Ibid.*

[57] Recollection of Paul Canada, contained in *Livin' in a Great Big Way,* 129.

[58] White materials: June 1, 1940.

[59] White materials: July 15, 1940.

[60] The hotel in question, located on West Forty-ninth Street, was definitely called the Forrest Hotel in 1940. It may well have changed names in later years. I do recall that there still was a Picadilly Hotel in New York in the late 1960s. The Forrest and Picadilly

hotels could not have been the same place because the Picadilly was located at 227 West Forty-fifth Street, near Broadway.

[61] White materials: March 21, 1940.

[62] *Ibid.*

[63] *Variety:* July 3, 1940, cited in the White materials.

[64] *Tommy and Jimmy—The Dorsey Years,* by Herb Sanford, Arlington House (1972), 193. Hereafter *The Dorsey Years.*

[65] White materials: August 20, 1940.

[66] The NBC radio logs housed at the NBC Archive, Library of Congress, indicate that "Marie" was the first tune played on the Pepsodent *Summer Pastime* show that aired from 10:00–10:30 p.m. on Tuesday, July 2, 1940. Information provided by Carl A. Hallstrom.

[67] *Moonlight Serenade—A Bio-discography of the Glenn Miller Civilian Band,* by John Flower, Arlington House (1972), 178.

[68] White materials: June 14, 1940.

[69] White materials: June 26, 1940.

[70] One of the tunes recorded that day was "Only Forever." After Frank Sinatra recorded "The One I Love (Belongs to Somebody Else)," he angrily walked out of the ongoing recording session because of a disagreement with TD over Tommy having Frank record cover versions of Bing Crosby tunes, one of which was "Trade Winds." One more Sinatra vocal remained to be recorded on that date, "Only Forever." TD tapped Clark Yocum from the Pied Pipers to sing the tune for the recording. When the Victor record came out, it identified the vocalist on "Only Forever" as "Allan Storr." To compound this, MCA then began circulating promotional photos of TD and his singers, with Clark Yocum being identified as "Allan Storr."

[71] White materials: June 22, 1940.

[72] *Livin' in a Great Big Way:* 131. This biography of Tommy Dorsey is worthwhile, but is not particularly scrupulous in terms of scholarship, and contains numerous factual errors.

[73] Berigan vocalist Danny Richards told one of the White researchers that Bunny attempted some sort of assisted rehabilitation on one or two occasions. If this ever occurred, it seems that the period from early July, 1940 into August, 1940, when Berigan appeared with Tommy Dorsey's band only sporadically, was when it could have happened.

[74] *Down Beat:* September 1, 1940, cited in the White materials.

[75] White materials: May 23, 1940.

[76] *Variety:* August 28, 1940, cited in the White materials.

[77] White materials: August 20, 1940.

[78] *Ibid.*

[79] Recollection of saxophonist/clarinetist Henry "Heinie" Beau, who joined the TD band in August of 1940, contained in the White materials: August 20, 1940.

[80] *Variety:* August 28, 1940, cited in the White materials.

[81] *Metronome:* September 1940, cited in the White materials.

[82] *Down Beat:* September 1, 1940, cited in the White materials.

[83] Despite my best efforts, I have not been able to pin down the date of the Berigan "incident" on the TD-Pepsodent show with certainty. As is stated in the text, there are valid reasons to assume that it happened in early July. Proof positive could be obtained if airchecks were made of the TD-Pepsodent shows, and those airchecks were positively

dated. Unfortunately, no such airchecks have emerged in the seven decades since the incident occurred.

[84] *Billboard:* September 7 and 14, 1940, cited in the White materials.

[85] White materials: early September 1940.

Chapter 22
On the Road for MCA

The story of the founding of Music Corporation of America (MCA) and its subsequent role in the development and operation of the basic business plan that the swing era was based on, is a fascinating one. MCA was founded in 1924 by Dr. Jules C. Stein, an ophthalmologist from Chicago, who had worked his way through college and medical school by playing in dance bands, and by booking engagements for them.[1] As the dance band craze went into high gear in the mid-1920s, Stein began promoting bands through the then new medium of radio. He instructed his clients to use an identifying "theme song" so that radio listeners would know whose band they were hearing from the first strains of that melody. In addition, he urged his clients' bands to adopt stylistic musical devices, and use them as frequently as possible, again to reinforce musically the listening audience's identification with the band. In this way, MCA's clients established a musical identity on radio that created a strong demand for the bands in person. MCA also engaged in all sorts of publicity activities on behalf of their bandleader clients, making them stars in their own right irrespective of their musical talents or the musical merits of their bands. Beyond the services MCA provided directly to its clients, who were the supply side of their market strategy, it also strove to control the demand side of the market. MCA used myriad methods to lock the operators of ballrooms and other venues where live dance music was presented into exclusive agreements whereby only MCA bands would play at these locations. As a result, for many years MCA controlled to a very significant degree, both the supply of dance bands in the market, and the demand for them.

MCA's costs and risks were minimal. They booked the bands, deciding when and where they would play, and for how much. Unless a bandleader was preeminent in the field, and the number of preeminent bandleaders was always very small, he had almost no input into these decisions. He either went along with MCA, or very soon would have a band with no gigs. MCA sometimes split the cost of promoting a band's appearance with the operator of the venue where the band was to appear. Far more often, they simply provided the operator with publicity materials like placards or posters, and MCA's famous publicity manual, which contained often out-of-date information, mostly fictional, about MCA's stable of bandleaders. Bandleaders absorbed the largest costs in running their bands—personnel and travel expenses, and of course, agency commissions. In addition, bandleaders had to pay for arrangements, copyists, music stands, uniforms, traveling band union taxes, and the like. MCA's business plan definitely favored the agency. Unless a bandleader had his own independent legal and/or accounting advice, he would find himself in a position where he had to rely on MCA to keep him in business. It appears that Bunny Berigan seldom if ever had such independent business advisors. Indeed, for much of his career as a bandleader he did not even have a personal manager. Basically, he relied on MCA to keep him in business.

MCA's early clients were sweet bands, like those led by Guy Lombardo, Wayne King, and Hal Kemp, or sweet "entertaining" bands, the acme of which was Kay Kyser's mixture of burlesque, hokum, and dance music. There was absolutely no interest in jazz-based bands at MCA[2] until the experiment they conducted in 1935, first with Benny Goodman's new band, and a little later, with Tommy Dorsey's. As usual, someone in the MCA brain trust had sensed, before anyone else, that for whatever reason the niche market for hotter jazz-based dance music was about to expand. They were right about that, but they also took no chances on their new "swing" clients, achieving success merely on their musical merits. All of MCA's swing band clients followed the MCA play-book: the music they presented must first and foremost be *dance music*. The bands had to have girl singers who were good looking with good figures. If they could sing well, all the better. A male vocalist, inevitably called a "boy singer" even if he was past thirty, was also a definite asset, especially if he was good looking. The bands had to feature at least some novelty tunes, so dancing audiences would be "entertained" while they danced. Whatever jazz these bands would play, and there could not be too much, would have to be danceable, with a pronounced beat. If any MCA bandleader deviated too far from this *modus operandi*, MCA would warn them that they were "not doing a good job," which carried with it the implicit threat that further such transgressions would result in fewer good jobs.

By 1935, MCA had developed into a sometimes ruthless force in the enter-tainment business. When necessary to help their clients, MCA's battalion of operatives would pretty much do whatever was necessary to obtain work for their bands. MCA was notorious for "block-booking" bands. This tactic in-volved using one of its top bands, say Guy Lombardo, as the bait; if a promoter wanted Guy Lombardo, who was almost guaranteed to make money, then he would also have to take four or five second-or third-tier bands as a part of the deal. Although MCA's clients almost universally deplored these strong-arm tactics, they nevertheless went along with them in order to work regularly in what was becoming a brutally competitive market. Musicians understood MCA's power, and they rarely fought against it. They knew that with MCA, at least they would work, at least some of the time.[3] The culture inside MCA could aptly be described as cannibalistic: agents were pitted against each other to see who could generate the most commissions for the agency. MCA was not a social service agency. It was dedicated solely, passionately, and unapologetically to making money. MCA continued its relationship with Bunny Berigan in 1940 not because he was a nice guy or because he had a problem and needed help. They continued with Bunny because he could still generate commissions for MCA.

What most musicians did not understand, and Bunny Berigan was certainly in this group, was that the MCA business model placed almost all of the business risks and costs on the bandleaders, and to a lesser degree, on the owners/operators of the venues where the bands performed. But MCA could put bands and their star leaders in front of audiences, and that was far more intoxicating for Bunny than any booze. As a result, while many bands worked almost constantly, frequently before large and enthusiastic audiences, broadcast on radio (usually on a sustaining, that is, nonpaying, basis), made commercial recordings, received good notices, pleased the dancers and the ballroom owners, and generated a constant stream of commissions for MCA, within a short period of time, their leaders were either insolvent or forced into bankruptcy. A partial list of bandleaders, in addition to Berigan, who either had to seek bankruptcy protection, or were thrown into severe financial circumstances while leading big bands contains the names of some of the greatest musicians of the swing era: Fletcher Henderson, Jack Teagarden, Coleman Hawkins, Bobby Hackett, Jack Jenney, Teddy Wilson, Billy Butterfield, Jan Savitt, Jimmy Dorsey, Buddy Rich, Ziggy Elman, and Woody Herman. Glenn Miller, one of the most spectacularly successful bandleaders, went broke once, and then with borrowed money tried again, and succeeded.

MCA rode the crest of the dance band craze from the 1920s through the 1930s. In the late 1930s, MCA's number one agent, Lew Wasserman, who earlier had developed the hugely successful "College of Musical Knowledge" on radio for Kay Kyser, began to represent Hollywood film queen Bette Davis. Although MCA continued to be a major player in the band-booking business for many years after 1940, after that year, the major focus of their business was slowly but surely moving from music to the film industry. This gradual change in MCA's business plan undoubtedly had a negative effect on the band business, even though its competitors rushed in to grab whatever business MCA left behind as it slowly exited the dance band field. But the dance band field itself was changing in major ways by 1940. The various forces then at work ultimately led to the end of the big band era. *Billboard* carried a very informative article about these market conditions in late 1940:

> Leading orchestras are getting lower prices in night clubs, hotels, theaters and one-nighters, particularly as compared to the sturdy 30s, when bands could get 50/50 on the first dollars in theaters, walk away with $1,500 on one-nighters and draw figures commensurate with their popularity in hotels and night clubs. The down-turn is blamed on three important factors: the creation of new bands faster than the demand warranted; public saturation with the same thing over and over again, even with different faces; and cut-throat competition among booking offices, personal managers and road managers. Many ballroom operators are using cheaper bands in the theory that if a name band lays an egg, the loss runs $500 to $700, while a band in the non-name class drawing only $200 to $300 for the date can only hand the ballroom owner a loss of around $50. 'A' class bands used to walk into theaters for $7,500 a week or, if that strong, a 50/50 split of the box office. 'B' bands were good for $4,500 weekly or a percentage arrangement, while

'C' bands could get $2,500 per week, every week of the year. Now, with the public at saturation point, 'A' bands have dropped into the 'B' category, 'B' bands into the 'C' and 'C' bands are now tough properties to book, even for scale. The one-nighter field, which provided the bulk of the bands revenues, is also fading by comparison. The accepted price of $1,250 to $1,500 for top bands is dimming to $650 to $1,000.[4]

What the *Billboard* article did not mention was that there was another category of big band, the "preeminent" category. In this category were the biggest names in the field: Tommy Dorsey, Benny Goodman, Artie Shaw, Glenn Miller, on the swing side, and Guy Lombardo, Kay Kyser, Sammy Kaye, and Hal Kemp, on the sweet side. These bands could be booked anywhere for top money because their leaders had developed such powerful box office names that they stood above the competition provided by very good, but less bankable bands. Black bands, because of racial segregation, were unable to enter the realm of "preeminent" bands. No matter how good they were, or well-known, they almost always were paid less than the top white bands.[5] The one black band that came closest to parity with the preeminent white bands in the marketplace was Cab Calloway's. Fats Waller was also a top earner during the swing era, but still not in the same league as the preeminent white bands.[6]

Bunny Berigan's 1940 band started out somewhere between a "B" and "C" band but it improved steadily during the ten months it existed. To MCA, the only value of a Bunny Berigan band then was if Berigan could stand in front of it and play his trumpet in a passable manner. It appears that Bunny was playing quite well during most of the time he led his 1940-1941 band. In spite of this, MCA had long before given up on the idea that he could ever lead an "A" band. The myriad problems caused by his alcoholism had, in their judgment, made that impossible as early as the fall of 1938.[7] The fact that Berigan was one of the most thrilling trumpeters in the history of American popular music and jazz meant nothing to MCA, because the audiences that came out to hear his band or any other dance band were not too concerned about those things; they just wanted good *dance music* played by a "name" band. So, under the aegis of MCA and without a personal manager, Berigan put together what initially was a workmanlike band in September of 1940. It would be a good dance band that played straightforward arrangements of current pop tunes, with jazz and musical thrills in a definitely subsidiary role. Bunny was given a budget by Harry Moss, the head of the one-nighter division at MCA, on which to run his band. He had to staff the band with suitable musicians, and pay all other expenses, including transportation, within that budget. MCA would make sure the band worked, at least part of the time. What MCA would not guarantee however, was either how often the band worked, or how much the band would be paid when it did work. Thus, even though Bunny ostensibly had control of the costs for his band, he had no control over his income. He also did not have control over the commissions MCA assessed on his earnings. He found that he had to occasionally pay a higher percentage to MCA than normal simply to secure certain jobs. This was not unusual in the band business in 1940. Charlie Barnet reported in his autobiography that at one point, he was paying as commissions to his booking agent twenty-five percent off the top on one-nighters, and fifteen percent on locations and theaters in order to work[8] These were the same risks and costs that Berigan had to assume if he wanted to be on the road for MCA. He evidently wanted this very badly because in spite of these risks and costs, which would soon submerged him in debt again, he once more took a band out on the road.

On Saturday, September 21, 1940, Bunny Berigan and His Orchestra opened a two-night stand at the Golden Gate Ballroom in New York City, playing opposite Benny Carter[9] and His Orchestra. Between the musicians he had gathered, and those Jack Maisel had secured, he somehow had put together a very passable band in an extremely short period of time. Berigan's knack for quickly fashioning a good-sounding band out of disparate sidemen is another of his talents that has seldom been acknowledged or commented on. *Down Beat* carried this information soon after the band debuted:

> Maybe it was just a coincidence, or maybe it was smart booking, but Harlem was really popping the other Sunday night, September 22, when Tommy Dorsey jammed them in at the Savoy Ballroom, while his ex-sideman, Bunny Berigan, only two blocks away in the Golden Gate Ballroom, played the second of two days in which his new band made its public debut. Berigan, who's all set with MCA backing, has Frank Tiffany, Frank Perry and Ray Crafton (Kranz), trumpets; Sam Kublin, Max Smith, trombones; Eddie Alcock, alto, Andy Fitzgerald, alto and arranger, Frank Crolene, tenor and arranger, Jack Henderson, tenor; Bill Clifton, piano; Jack Maisel, drums; and Morty Stulmaker, bass. Danny Richards, who sang with the last Berigan band, is back with Bunny, who won't use a girl singer.[10]

Here the recollections of a few of the sidemen who joined Berigan's band then: Danny Richards remembered: "Bunny called me at home in Scranton, Pennsylvania, and asked me to come back. I said OK and introduced him to Johnny 'The Face' DeSantos, and got him a job, first as band-boy and later as road manager."[11] Frank Perry (trumpet) recalled: "I was working with Jerry Arlen's band with Jack Maisel, who left to rejoin Bunny Berigan, promising to get me on Bunny's new band if there was a spot in the trumpet section. The Golden Gate stand was the band's first public engagement and shortly after we finished that job, Jack Thompson came in on first trumpet."[12] Ray Kranz (trumpet): "I was working in a hotel in the Catskills that summer in a band that also included Buddy Koss on piano and it was he who recommended me to Bunny and got me on the band. I had always held Bunny's playing in high esteem and while I was with the band, I learned a hell of a lot from him. It was my first 'name' band and I got a tremendous thrill listening to and playing alongside him every night."[13] Buddy Koss (piano): "I'd jobbed around the New York area after Bunny joined the Tommy Dorsey band and when I got his call, I joined the new band at the Golden Gate Ballroom, replacing Bill Clifton, who only rehearsed with the band. Jack Maisel was the drummer and the contractor, who called all the guys together. Bunny's library had been attached to secure a debt, but Maisel had copies of most of his old scores."[14]

Information about the band's daily activities immediately after they left the Golden Gate Ballroom is lacking. We know that on September 29, they played a one-nighter at Mike Todd's "Dancing Campus" at the New York World's Fair, alternating with Gene Krupa's band. The next night, they played at the Brooklyn Roseland Ballroom. They also may have played a few nights at Nick's in Greenwich Village in early October.[15]

On the way to a one-nighter at the Sunnybrook Ballroom in Pottstown, Pennsylvania on October 5, Bunny visited a physician in New Jersey. Buddy Koss was with him: "About this time I went with Bunny to see his favorite doctor over in New Jersey. He warned Bunny that if he didn't stop drinking, it would kill him. This seemed to worry Bunny and for a couple of weeks he actually went on the wagon!"[16]

Later, Koss elaborated on this event:

A lot of people say they saw Bunny fall off the stand. I never saw this. In all the time I was with him, I never saw him so bad. I took Bunny to a doctor in New Jersey. He put Bunny up on a table. After examining him the doctor says, 'Bunny, you've got an enlarged heart, you've got the beginning of cirrhosis, you've got arthritis. If you don't quit drinking, you'll be dead.' I always kept a pint of booze in my car for Bunny, and Bunny says, 'I'm going to go out there and smash that bottle against a wall!' We get outside and he takes it and looks at it, and says, 'Gee, it's a shame to waste it.' Bunny went to priests, fortune tellers, hypnotists. Maybe if AA had been around, it could have saved him.[17]

The Berigan band was back in New York for two nights at the Prospect Theater in the Bronx (October 12–13), and a similar gig at the Star Theater (Lexington and 107th) at around this same time. Quite possibly, vocalist Kathleen Lane appeared with the band on these engagements. Evidently, the acrimonious parting in the spring of 1939 between Bunny and Ms. Lane's husband, Jerry Johnson, did not terminate his professional relationship with her. (In the interim, Johnson had become, according to the White materials, a music contractor at ABC.)[18]

On October 14, the Berigan band returned to the "Dancing Campus." Here is the personnel lineup from that date: Remote broadcast, NBC (WEAF or WJZ) twenty-five minutes, airtime unknown. From *Jitterbug Heaven* of Dancing Campus, World's Fair, New York City: Jack Thompson (lead), Frank Perry, Ray Kranz, trumpets; Ernie Stricker (lead), Max Smith, trombones; Eddie Alcock (lead alto), Andy Fitzgerald (third alto), Johnny Castaldi (second tenor), Frank Crolene (fourth tenor), saxophones; Buddy Koss, piano; probably Tommy Moore, guitar; Morty Stulmaker, bass; and Jack Maisel, drums. Danny Richards, Kathleen Lane were the vocalists.. Fitzgerald and Crolene were writing arrangements for the band. At the beginning, the solos, other than those by Berigan, were by Koss on piano; Fitzgerald on clarinet, and Castaldi on tenor sax.[19]

Although most of the musicians who made up Bunny Berigan's band at this time were unknown, they were not inexperienced. Here are some of the ages of Bunny's new band members in the fall of 1940: Max Smith, thirty-seven; Johnny Castaldi, twenty-seven; Andy Fitzgerald, twenty-two; Ray Krantz, twenty-three; Jack Maisel, thirty; Jack Thompson, twenty-two; Ernie Stricker, thirty.[20] Berigan himself was just shy of his thirty-second birthday.

After this gig, the Berigan band headed for a two-week residency at the Chatterbox, Mountainside, New Jersey, beginning on October 18. While he was there, possibly acting on the advice of his doctor, he evidently tried, by himself, to stop drinking. Paul Whiteman somehow became aware of this, and offered Bunny some help: "Bunny had been ill and stayed at my farm for three *(sic)* weeks while the band was at the Chatterbox, which was nearby, and this was near 'the end.' He had awful nightmares, and after a couple of weeks of his shouting out in the early morning hours, I went off the wagon myself!"[21] As had happened previously when Bunny had tried to stop drinking, he suffered terribly with delirium tremens (the "DTs"). At the same time, he had to be stable enough each evening to play the gig at the Chatterbox. His solution was to have a "little" drink, enough to smooth his frayed nerves. His detoxification was thus retarded, and he remained locked in a vicious, endless cycle of reducing his intake of alcohol enough to trigger the DTs, then drinking afterwards to "straighten out." Precisely how he was able to play each evening on the job is unknown, but it can be assumed that Bunny's days were every bit as difficult as his nights at the Whiteman house.

He nevertheless did play, and he impressed people:

We went up to the Chatterbox on Route 29 at Mountainside, last Friday night and heard Bunny Berigan's new band. Bunny really has something this time and we think he is going to click. He has deserted the blasting, hot type of swing and is featuring the ballads and slow jump tunes. The band features Danny Richards on the vocals, and his top notcher is a superb arrangement of 'Maybe.' Both he and the band give out with equally good versions of 'The Nearness of You' and 'Only Forever,' the latter featuring some beautifully muted trumpet by Bunny. The standout of the band, however, is Buddy Koss, the pianist. Buddy takes the first chorus on all the jump tunes and does a terrific job of it. Bunny is still at the Chatterbox this weekend and we can think of no better place to celebrate our victory over Princeton.[22]

Andy Fitzgerald disclosed a trick Bunny used at the Chatterbox in order to make it through sometimes difficult evenings without embarrassment:

While we were at the Chatterbox, the ASCAP dispute was on and we had to pull out a tune from a broadcast at the last minute and substitute 'Dark Eyes', for which I'd scribbled a new arrangement. Bunny played lead on some tunes, but others were written for Jack Thompson, with Bunny playing solo. We still got lots of requests for things from the old Berigan book, but most of the new stuff came from Frank Crolene and me. On stage, Bunny would often do 'I Can't Get

Started,' working up to that high note ending and while he pretended to continue playing, I'd carry on up higher and higher on clarinet. Bunny would finally lower his horn and I would finish it off. On some numbers, we used a small Dixie unit, which included Bunny, Johnny Castaldi on tenor, the rhythm section and me on clarinet.[23]

Trumpeter Frank Perry later bemoaned the lack of a recording contract for this band: "I was with Bunny for about a year, I guess and there weren't too many changes, except in the second trumpet chair, but Jack (Thompson) and I stuck it out. He was an excellent player, a few years older than me and a very experienced lead man. We were fairly well rehearsed and had some good musicians, but nobody really very well known and, unfortunately, we made no records. That was a shame, but Bunny did not have a recording contract, because his old Victor contract had lapsed when he rejoined Tommy Dorsey and wasn't renewed.[24] Not only was the Victor contract not renewed, but Bunny had also been forced, during the course of his financial troubles in 1939, to assign his right to collect royalties off of the records he had made for Victor to one of his creditors. One cannot help but wonder who collected those performer's royalties for the years (decades) after Bunny's bankruptcy and death. One also wonders if Bunny had had a personal manager during this time whether he might have been able to secure a new recording deal.

After closing at the Chatterbox on October 31, the Berigan band probably played some one-nighters in the greater New York area before appearing for two nights at the RKO Coliseum Theater in New York City on November 5 and 6. While the band was there, Bunny began to experience difficulties with his horn. Johnny Castaldi reported what the Berigan sidemen did to investigate:

We did a couple of shows there, and during the first show Bunny was having some trouble with the sound from his horn. In his dressing room after the show, we examined his horn and found that the mouthpiece was almost completely blocked up! Bunny would put his mouthpiece away after each show, pick it up the next day and play the show. This would be repeated after each show, so it would gradually become almost (completely) blocked with saliva deposits. So, we'd have to get to work with a pipe cleaner, and what a difference that made![25]

After this gig, Berigan and the band headed south for one of MCA's Dixie tours. Bunny had played these before, usually to great throngs of enthusiastic fans, and usually winding up in the hole financially. This tour would be an exception in that he apparently completed it without going deeply into debt. On the way to the Deep South, the band played at the Frank Thompson Gym at North Carolina State University in Raleigh. Then they opened a week at the Roxy Theater in Atlanta, sharing the bill with the Andrews Sisters. Since Bunny had worked with the Andrews Sisters in the late summer of 1938 as the headliner, his fortunes had ebbed ever lower, while theirs had soared. The Berigan band now functioned as the warm-up act for the Andrews Sisters. Trumpeter Ray Kranz remembered: "The Andrews Sisters topped the bill, with the band playing the first half of the show and accompanying the girls for the second half. They sang 'Beer Barrel Polka,' 'Apple Blossom Time,' and all their other hits. After the last show at the end of the week, Bunny gave a big Thanksgiving party for all the acts."[26]

Nevertheless, Bunny and his band also upheld their own in their part of the show:

> The Andrews Sisters, Laverne, Patti and Maxine, who won international fame as a swing song trio, opened a week's engagement with Bunny Berigan and his orchestra at the Roxy Theater yesterday. The trio was so well received that they had to resort to a novelty, a medley of songs they have made famous in order to leave the stage. They stepped into the wings before the spellbound audience realized they were gone. Patti is featured as soloist at times, taking the melody while the other two back away from the mike and her mannerisms are a special attraction. Among the songs they performed that made them famous were 'Beer Barrel Polka' and 'Mean to Me.' The Berigan organization, decidedly on the swingy side, provided the accompaniment for the singing stars as well as holding up the first part of the stage bill. Bunny is quite a hit as a soloist.[27]

Usually, these theater engagements were very lucrative. Of course to earn the money he would have received, Berigan would probably have played four or five shows a day for the week he was at the Roxy. His generosity on closing night was typical, and unfortunately something that he could not afford. Nevertheless, Bunny's mood was probably very positive after this, his first successful big-time theater engagement as a leader in fifteen months. At this same time, the MCA publicity department had secured some positive promotion for Bunny. The November 1940 issue of a small publication called *Music and Rhythm* included a multipage article about him, with a selected discography, photos, and notated samples of his playing.[28]

After closing at the Atlanta Roxy on November 23, the Berigan band played some one-nighters in the southeastern states, including Burlington, North Carolina, on the 27th, before opening what turned out to be a month-long engagement at the Patio Grill of the Roosevelt Hotel, Jacksonville, Florida, on Friday, November 29.

Here is how his appearance was heralded in the local newspaper: "Harvey Bell presents—See It First and Best—Roosevelt, Patio Grill—New Band–New Faces–New Show—Look! He's Here—Bunny Berigan and his Orchestra. Floor shows 8:00–10:30–12:20. The Beulettes—6 dancers—Sanora Lee–Dancer De-Lux—The 3 Marvels—Arabatic Sensations—Virginia Atter–Lovely Songstress-Jimmy Bigelow–Banjo King—This Evening 7 p.m. until 2:30 a.m."[29] While they were at the Roosevelt, the Berigan band was broadcast frequently over either WJHP–Jacksonville (NBC-Blue), or WMBR–Jacksonville (CBS).

Danny Richards recalled some of the details of that residency: "We played every night in the Patio Grill Room, starting at 7 p.m. and broadcasting over station WJHP. Joe DiMaggio replaced Eddie Alcock on lead alto for that date. Bunny's wife, Donna, was also along for the engagement."[30]

By this time, Donna and the girls had returned from Syracuse to live in New York City. It is not clear where they were living in New York, but Bunny did not live with Donna during the Dorsey interlude. Nevertheless, once he got his new band rolling again, she resumed joining him on the road periodically, usually at locations where the band was in one place for a week or more. She and Bunny had carefully selected a woman Patricia Berigan referred to as "Aunt Iona" to care for the girls when Donna was away. Aunt Iona was remembered by Pat as a kindly woman whom she and Jo liked very much.[31] Bunny now had some assurance that his daughters would not be in jeopardy when Donna chose to join him on the road.

The band's two-week engagement at the Patio Grill was successful, and was extended twice, for an additional week each time. Trumpeter Frank Perry recalled the Patio Grill job very clearly: "There was an evening floor show in the Patio and we had nightly broadcasts and very big attendances during the Christmas holidays. Donna Berigan was with us in Florida and, in fact, paid us on one occasion, handing out the pay envelopes containing cash. She and Bunny were given a clock as a present by the hotel manager and I believe it was stolen later."[32] Buddy Koss also recalled Donna's presence at the Roosevelt: "While we were playing at the Roosevelt Hotel, I bought my fiancée her engagement ring and I can remember that Donna Berigan spent that Christmas in Florida with us. Bunny gave each member of the band an inscribed watch or traveling clock as a Christmas present, even though we all knew he couldn't really afford them."[33]

Bunny and the band were photographed while they were at the Patio Grill. In one of the pictures taken then, although Bunny looks rather splendid standing before his band with his erect posture, this is the first photograph of him that reveals that he was beginning to lose weight. This was an ominous sign that something insidious was going on inside of his body.

After a gala New Year's Eve party on December 31, the band closed at the Roosevelt Hotel, and headed north into the winter weather and an itinerary of sporadic one-night stands. They played a college date in Philadelphia on January 3, and then moved on. Bassist Morty Stulmaker recalled an incident that happened when they arrived at their next date, at the Sunnybrook Ballroom, Pottstown, Pennsylvania: "We drove directly from Florida to Pennsylvania and we didn't get time to get into New York City to renew our union cards for 1941 or whatever the procedure was. Anyway, when we got to Pottstown, a union representative was on hand to check our cards and we were each fined five dollars for not having the new cards!"[34] They continued to play scattered, somewhat intermittent dates: January 5, the Casino Ballroom, Scranton, Pennsylvania; January 7-8, the Academy of Music, New York City; the 10th, Carnegie Tech, Pittsburgh; the 11th, the University of Rochester, Rochester, New York. The dates in between were open.

On January 12, 1941, Berigan and his band arrived at the Trianon Ballroom in Cleveland, where he had been so warmly received in the spring of 1939, this time to play for only one night. Bunny had supposedly forgotten to do something, and King George (T. Simon), who had done so very little over the previous three years to help Bunny's career in the pages of *Metronome,* was upset. Bunny would pay: "I met Art Tatum for the first time and was greatly impressed, though a prospective phone call from Bunny Berigan in Cleveland made it impossible to stay to hear him play. Bunny, because of his high vote in the section: Trumpet Division (second to Ziggy Elman) had been tentatively scheduled to appear at the Metronome All Star Band recording session, but he just didn't bother to tell anybody whether or not he would show up. He didn't."[35] George T. could have easily called MCA's New York office, where he knew most of the personnel, and learned exactly where Bunny Berigan was going to be on the date in question. Instead he chose once again to embarrass Berigan in *Metronome.* Class guy!

The midwinter tour continued. There is no available information as to the whereabouts of the Berigan band from January 13 to the 16th. On January 17, they played at the University of Pennsylvania in Philadelphia, and on the next night at the Auditorium, Erie, Pennsylvania. Moving between these two venues required a grueling drive of almost 400 miles on icy, mountainous 1940 roads in 1940 cars. Their next gig was on the 19th, at Valley Dale Ballroom, north of Columbus, Ohio. Some homemade recordings from this gig have emerged. Here are the tunes so preserved: "Lover Come Back to Me"; an unidentified ballad; "Night Song"; "Swanee River"; and "The Nearness of You," vocal Danny Richards. The tour resumed: the Earle Theater in Washington, Pennsylvania, on the 22nd; the Nu-Elms Ballroom in Youngstown, Ohio on the 23rd. Danny Richards recalled:

> I think that was the date when Tommy Dorsey and Frank Sinatra came over to hear Bunny. I guess the Dorsey band was playing nearby. I'd met Frank previously, and he told me what a great job I was doing on his tune 'This Love of Mine,' which he had helped write and for which Andy Fitzgerald had made a great arrangement. Actually, we were playing it long before he recorded it with Dorsey.[36]

Despite the backbreaking travel, it seems that this edition of Bunny Berigan and His Orchestra was by now making fine music. Unfortunately, no recording company was interested, not that MCA (Bunny still had no personal manager at this time) was trying to get anyone to listen. In fact, Victor had inexplicably held back Bunny's final recordings for that label, which had been made in November of 1939, finally releasing them in early January 1941.[37]

But there were still more widely scattered one-nighters to play: January 24, the (Masonic) Auditorium, Detroit; the 25th, the Auditorium, Flint, Michigan; the 26th, Memorial Auditorium, Columbus, Ohio; January 31-February 1, the Auditorium, Worcester, Massachusetts; February 2, Wagenbach's Hofbrau, Lawrence, Massachusetts, at which location Bunny drew a crowd of 2,000 in two shows with acts.[38] On February 8, Berigan played the junior prom for St. Mary's College at the Cariton Hotel, Washington, D.C., as well as dance dates in February at the Universities of Pittsburgh, Delaware, and Pennsylvania. But there were many holes in the itinerary of the Berigan band as well. "Johnny Castaldi's diary indicated that he received $10.71 cents for each date and his total earnings for January 1941 amounted to $182.07 for 17 dates. February 1941 showed $107.10 for 10 dates plus $5 for Nick's (February 10)."[39]

By this time, Bunny was probably having a very powerful sense of déjà-vu. This exact scenario had played out in the early months of 1939. He had learned then that a bandleader can get into financial trouble very quickly on the road if his band is not working enough to cover ongoing expenses. In the early months of 1941, the Berigan band was playing a lot of rather random one-nighters, with many off nights in between. Whenever they had a good location to play, the crowd was large, the reception positive. Still, income was not matching expenses. All the while, Bunny's overhead continued, and his debt began to grow, again.

As March began, the schedule for the Berigan band once more had a lot of open dates in it. Here is the available information on the band's activities: Saturday March 1, a one-night dance date at the Arcadia Ballroom, Providence, Rhode Island; March 5–6, rehearsals at Haven Studios, New York City 4:00 to 6:00 p.m. each day; March 7, a dance date at Yale University, New Haven, Connecticut; March 8–9, at Manhattan Beach, New York City; the 12th and 13th, rehearsals at the Haven Studio in Manhattan for a theater job (March 15–16) in Torenton, Connecticut. From this engagement, the band headed to the always friendly confines of the Brunswick Hotel in Boston. There they opened a week's stand on March 17 at that hotel's Bermuda Terrace.

Through the arduous winter of 1941, the Berigan band's personnel had remained remarkably stable. Here is the lineup that appeared at the Brunswick Hotel with Bunny: Jack Thompson, Truman Quigley, Frank Perry (trumpets); Ernie Stricker, Max Smith (trombones); Charlie Arlington, Andy Fitzgerald, Frank Crolene, Johnny Castaldi (saxes); Buddy Koss (piano); Morty Stulmaker (bass); Jack Maisel (drums); Danny Richards (vocals). A contemporary press report and the remembrances of a few sidemen illuminate: "Bunny Berigan has made two changes: Charlie Arlington, lead alto sax from the Seger Ellis band, for Joe DiMaggio, who went to Teddy Powell; and Truman Quigley, who was with Bunny two years ago on second trumpet, from the Clyde Lucas band, for Ray Kranz, who shifted to Al Donahue".[40] Truman 'Quig' Quigley remembered: "I only stayed about a couple of weeks at the Brunswick Hotel, because John Fallstich called me there to say that Jack Teagarden was heading for the west coast and there was an opening in his trumpet section. I told Bunny, who said he hadn't too many dates booked ahead, and he let me go without the usual two weeks notice. Charlie Mitchell took my place."[41] Charlie Arlington recalled: "I had already left Seger Ellis when I got a call to go to Bunny's apartment in New York. There were a couple of other saxmen there and we played a few passages and that was it. Andy Fitzgerald was my contact who got me the audition. The band played no USO shows, did no recordings, transcriptions nor movies while I was with it."[42]

Bunny undoubtedly realized that these one-week or longer engagements at hotels were a mixed blessing. On the one hand, they allowed the band to be in one place and avoid the rigors of constant travel, especially in the north in the winter. This usually caused everyone in the band to get a little rest, eat meals at regular times, feel better, and play better. On the other hand, no hotel engagement could pay the cost of maintaining a big band. It was an axiom in the band business that if a band stayed at any location for any period of time, it had to be because of a radio hookup that enabled them to broadcast repeatedly from that location. This would "prime" the radio listening area for the band's personal appearances, and then one-nighters or theater dates could be scheduled to capitalize on the radio "buildup." But while a band was at the hotel location, the bandleader was losing money. So it is almost a certainty that the Berigan band was losing money while it played at the Brunswick Hotel. In addition, there is no indication that the Berigan band broadcast while they were at the Brunswick. But they were working and off the road!

When the Brunswick gig ended on March 22, the band headed for a one-nighter in Rutherford, New Jersey, the following day. Then they were apparently off until March 28, when they returned to the Boston area for a two night stint at the Totem Pole Ballroom at Norembega Park, Auburndale (Newton), Massachusetts. Once again, the Berigan magic was operating, as this press report indicates: "It seems that records are made to be broken here. Bunny Berigan topped Al Donahue's Friday mark of 2,600 customers by pulling 2,800 (28th), then went on to full capacity (3,000) the next night at the same prices. The two days grossed $3,915."[43] After this engagement, the band was off, except for a rehearsal session (Bunny held them frequently), for the rest of the month.

Johnny Castaldi meticulously recorded his income as a member of the Berigan band for the month of March: sixteen days worked, $164.37 earned.[44] Based on the numbers in Castaldi's diary, it seems that by early 1941, Bunny, in an attempt to further control his costs, had begun to pay his sidemen only for the dates they worked, instead of a fixed weekly salary. This shifted some of the risk of being on the road for MCA away from him and onto his sidemen. He still had to pay for their transportation from one gig to another, however, as well as all of the many other expenses related to running a touring big band. Since these expenses continued to exceed Bunny's weekly income, he then began to pay his musicians only partially each week, promising them that good-paying gigs were just around the corner, and that they would allow him to catch up. This tactic worked only because Bunny's sidemen respected him as a musician, and liked him as a person. But, as he had done before, Bunny Berigan was robbing Peter to pay Paul to keep his band going, and that can go on only for so long before something has to give.

In April, it appears that MCA once again got out the one-nighter dartboard, and used it to book the Berigan band. Here is their itinerary: April 1, Swing Club, Philadelphia; April 2, Empire Ballroom, Allentown, Pennsylvania; April 3, off; April 4, Town Hall, Philadelphia; the 5th, Rutgers University, New

Brunswick, New Jersey; the 6th, St George Hotel, New York City. Trumpeter Don Lane was with Bunny for a spell during this time period, and had this recollection: "I played in the Bunny Berigan band for a few weeks the spring of 1941. We played mostly college dates, one-nighters, including the St. George Hotel in New York. Bunny's wife was around the bandstand at the time, and she and Bunny each had their own bottles of booze. Bunny played great, but the band was always late for jobs and that was why I left."[45]

Evidently, the band was off in New York until they played a dance date (senior prom) at the Salesianum High School in Wilmington, Delaware on the 11th. They then drove to Washington D.C. for a battle of bands with Dick Stabile's orchestra. Financially, this gig was something of a bomb, as *Down Beat* reported: "A Bunny Berigan–Dick Stabile battle of jazz at the Uline Arena last month was a bad flop with less than 500 attending."[46] The Berigan band then moved on to a one-nighter in Connecticut on the 13th. From there they went to Seton Hall in South Orange, New Jersey, on the 14th. On the 15th, they were in Wilmington, Delaware, playing at Hotel DuPont. The 16th found them at Cappy's Ballroom, North Easton, Massachusetts. They were off on the 17th. On the 18th, they played at the Lincoln Park Ballroom, Worcester, Massachusetts; on the 19th, at Delmonico's Restaurant at Fifty-ninth and Park, in New York City for the Queens College junior prom. They then had a few more days off. [47]

On April 23, Berigan took part in an event that foreshadowed how jazz stars would be presented in coming years. The trade papers, as usual, did an excellent job in covering the event:

A 'Café Society Concert' entitled *Jazz and Classics* was held at Carnegie Hall on Fifty-seventh Street, New York City, commencing 8:30 p.m., in aid of the musicians' union medical fund. Included on the bill were Hazel Scott, the Golden Gate Quartet, Kenneth Spencer and Calvin Jackson (pianos), Albert Ammons and Pete Johnson, Lena Horne plus the Eddie South, John Kirby and Red Allen bands, all of whom worked at Café Society Uptown or Café Society Downtown. Guest artists included: Max Kaminsky, Henry Levine and Bunny Berigan on trumpets; Will Bradley, trombone; Tab Smith and Paul Laval, saxophones; pianists Art Tatum, Stan Facey and Buck Washington; Doles Dickens, bass and Ray McKinley and Specs Powell on drums. Also taking part were Count Basie, Buck Clayton, Don Byas, Freddie Green, Walter Page and Jo Jones from the Basie band. This group played 'One O'Clock Jump' and 'Ad-Lib Blues.'[48]

Café Society's concert at Carnegie Hall, New York City, was an artistic failure. Not until Count Basie began beating out 'One O'Clock Jump' with Bunny Berigan, Will Bradley, Buck Clayton, Ray McKinley, Henry Levine and others helping was there anything which deserved unqualified praise. The Café Society artists paraded across the huge platform for two hours, playing exactly the same music they play nightly at the two Café Society niteries. There was no new material. Then came Basie. Fresh off the road, he, Don Byas, Clayton, Jo Jones and other Basieites joined forces in an impromptu session with Berigan, Bradley, McKinley, Levine, Tab Smith and at least 30 other musicians taking part; his own 'One O'Clock Jump' and a fast blues winding up the concert, On the credit side was the financial outcome. Approximately $1,550 were turned over to AFM Local 802 for its medical fund. The gross was about $3,000 with most of the 3,000 Carnegie Hall seats filled. Prices $1.10 and $2.50.[49]

It was the first concert of its type, involving colored nitery talent from both Uptown and Downtown Café Society and drew about three-quarters capacity into the 3,000 seat hall. The audience was almost exclusively ofay. The lifeless initial three hours was forgotten in the blow-off jam session where Maxie Kaminsky cut everyone.[50]

"One O'Clock Jump" and "Ad-Lib Blues" from this concert were recorded.[51]

The day following this event, April 24, was another off day for the Berigan band, but it is very likely that Bunny spent a good part of that day in MCA's posh offices at 538 Fifth Avenue, between Forty-fourth and Forty-fifth, in New York City. Here is what leaked out shortly thereafter:

Headline: Harry Moss Handling Bunny Berigan Band: Harry Moss, MCA executive, has temporarily taken over the Bunny Berigan orchestra, putting the trumpet tooting maestro on a weekly allowance and using the rest of the money earned to pay off Bunny's creditors, mostly AFM and U.S. government taxes due. Bunny signed the agreement this week after some of his sidemen threatened to quit because of a lapse of a salary payoff. This is the second time in the past few years that Bunny has found himself in financial hot water. The first time was in Chicago, when Petrillo, then head of Local 10, took Bunny's purse to pay off the boys in the band and other creditors. Petrillo even appropriated the entire purse given to Bunny's band at a New York theatre job at that time. Since then, Bunny has been able to whittle down most of that debt, but now finds himself with a few more. Moss says the Berigan band has been doing well for MCA clients and feels that with this new arrangement between himself and Bunny, the latter will be out of the hole in another year or so.[52]

So after more than two years without a personal manager, it was decided that Bunny Berigan needed one, and MCA thought that Harry Moss could fill the bill. But Moss worked for MCA, was paid by MCA, and always placed the interests of MCA first.

Harry Moss, of all people, should not have been surprised that Bunny was once again in debt to his musicians. He was the head of MCA's one-nighter division, and knew that MCA was booking the Berigan band on only about half of the available dates each month, and often these dates were filled with money losing weeks at hotels. Bunny needed someone to look after his business interests, and those interests were different from the business interests of MCA. Nevertheless, he now accepted the plan where MCA's Harry Moss would attempt to function as his *ex officio* personal manager. This scheme seemed to be directed only at managing the costs of the Berigan band however. Subsequent events will show that nothing on the income side would really change: the band worked only 50–60 percent of the time, had no recording contract, and had precious few radio appearances. Berigan desperately needed a personal manager to look after his interests.

Yet whenever MCA did manage to secure a lucrative theater or ballroom booking for Bunny, he and his band almost always "did well." Immediately after his sit-down with Harry Moss, Bunny led his band into the always friendly precincts of Boston for a two-night stay at the Raymor-Playmor twin ballrooms. A band led by Jacques Renard was being presented in one ballroom, Berigan in the other. Here is the financial report: "Bunny Berigan, April 25–26 in Boston, booked by Ray Galvin's Eastern Orchestra Service, Boston.[53] Renard's first date and a return for Bunny Berigan brought in 2,000 Friday and 2,200 Saturday for an excellent $2,640, the best weekend in two months."[54] Yes, Bunny Berigan and His Orchestra were "doing well for MCA clients"—when given the opportunity to do so. The problem was that they simply were not being given the opportunity to do so often enough to balance the band's finances. But as always, Bunny did not have anyone looking out for his financial interests alone, and he had proved time and again that he was unable to do that for himself. So his financial interests were placed last. Harry Moss and MCA continued to call the shots, MCA continued to reap commissions off the Berigan band, and Bunny continued to be sucked more deeply into a quagmire of debt.

In a move that may sound preposterous now, right after entering into the "agreement" with Harry Moss to catch up whatever delinquencies he had accrued by not paying his sidemen fully, Berigan met with his band members and explained to them that the allowance Harry Moss set for him would not leave him enough money to keep the band going. Buddy Koss recalled: "Yeah, MCA had Bunny on salary. They allowed him $100 a week as he was way behind with his taxes, but that wasn't enough for Bunny and he was holding back about $10 from each guy every payday!"[55] So while MCA was retaining money to pay Bunny's musicians for the part of their salaries he had not paid them previously, he was incurring more debt with them by holding back a part of their current salaries. Not all of Berigan's sidemen took this well. Johnny Castaldi's diary for May 5, 1941 contains this entry: "End of Berigan: $24.71 plus $10.71; total: $35.42."[56] This would appear to be the total amount owed to Castaldi, including Bunny's new $10.00 hold-back. Castaldi angrily left the Berigan band, played a few gigs with other bands, and auditioned for bandleader Gray Gordon, an experience he described in his diary with one word: "egg." He then succumbed to Bunny's blandishments, and returned to the Berigan band on May 15. His diary entry for that date reads: "made peace with Berigan."[57] Bunny demonstrated repeatedly that he would use every bit of guile he could muster to keep his band together and as strong as possible.

While all of this was going on, Berigan had to lead his band on whatever gigs MCA tossed his way, and occasionally perform without them. On April 28, he appeared as a guest on NBC's *Chamber Music Society of Lower Basin Street* program, without his band. On May 2, he and the band appeared at Elmira College, Elmira, New York; on the 3rd, when they subbed for Harry James's band, which now, after two years of struggle, was starting to achieve large-scale success at the Lincoln Hotel in New York City. On the 5th, they again subbed for James's band, at the Armory in Natick, Massachusetts. Harry James was now MCA's number-one trumpet-playing bandleader, and he was getting all of the best work. Bunny shared what was left over with a lot of MCA's second-tier bandleaders.

The Berigan band bounced around the northeastern United States playing a gig then being off a day or two until they landed at Palisades Park, New Jersey, on May 17–18. It was from this location that Bunny received the most glowing write-up he ever received in *Metronome*. It was written by a young woman called Amy Lee, not by George T. Simon. Here is what Ms. Lee reported:

Headline: Bunny Berigan Definitely On Way Back! The trumpeter thrills in person and on the air, proving that he's by no means through. To the jibes and accusations that Bunny Berigan couldn't get with his horn anymore, Bunny himself has the best answer, and that answer he gave conclusively, without any maybes, at Palisades Park recently. It was a date replete with all the elements of nonsuccess; a dismal night, a cold stiff wind keeping the open-air casino well blown out, the guys playing with their hats and coats on, and shivering spectators. But Bunny played, and played ravishingly, his low notes pouring out full and rich, his top notes soaring clear and round. And not a clinker all night! 'That was just one night,' object the skeptics. Bunny's air shot came through with an answer to that too. It lasted only 15 minutes, an unfair slice of time in which to prove anything, even for an outfit older and more experienced than Bunny's. Nevertheless, that 15 minutes was enough to tell the listener that Bunny is playing more magnificently than ever; that he has a band with a beat, and it's a beat which fairly lifts dancers and listeners right off their seats or feet. The three-man rhythm section of piano, bass and drums held steadily together, pushing brass and saxes gently but firmly. Drummers like Bunny's don't come with every pair of sticks these days. His drumming harbored no hint of ego; it was for the band, not against it. The arrangements included wide use of cut time and simple figurations. A pretty tenor (almost an extinct species of late) graced several measures of 'Out of Nowhere' with genuine tone, technique and fluent ideas. The entire sax section and vocalist Danny Richards attracted favorable attention on 'One Look at You,' wherein the Berigan trumpet flew aloft to a top note that sounded almost like a clarinet, still without sacrificing the round trumpet tone. In the next number, 'Devil's Holiday,' Bunny was swooping down to resounding full-throated pedal tones. The thrill of his amazing talent is not to be caught by mere words. For after all's said about Bunny and about the band, its beat and blend, its push and persuasion, the only thing that really says it is Bunny's horn. His range, his conception, his lip and his soul are without compare and to hear him again is the kick of all listening kicks. Bunny plays for the love of it. So, apparently, does the band. The relaxed results hit home the awful absence of this at-ease feeling in most outfits today. 'I Can't Get Started' has been too long off the air and out of hearing. It is a great thrill hearing it once more, not only because of the song itself, but because now it announces the return of one of the greats of all jazz, the return of Bunny Berigan in full glory.[58]

Despite the rigors of the road and continuing financial difficulties, the Berigan magic was obviously still intact, at least on occasion. Cornetist Bobby Hackett,[59] who in the summer of 1941 was about to join Glenn Miller's band, had the opportunity to express some thoughts about Berigan as a jazz trumpeter: "Harry James has wonderful technique, but that certain something isn't there when he plays. Armstrong and Berigan, they thrill you, which is what real jazz should do."[60] By this time, first alto saxophonist Charlie Arlington had been with the Berigan band long enough to form some opinions about his boss: "Bunny loved to play pool, but drinking seemed to be his main interest. He was a very good leader, however, compared with others."[61]

Regardless how Berigan was perceived by fans, critics, and other musicians, he had to continue playing one-nighters to survive as a bandleader. On May 23, he and his band were in Rochester, New York; on the 24th at the Empire Ballroom in Allentown, Pennsylvania; on the 27th, they were booked onto the SS *Potomac,* departing Washington. D.C. Here is the advance publicity for that gig, and some comments on how Bunny did: "The Potomac River Boat Line reopens May 27th with Bunny Berigan ork and operates with name bands all summer. Bunny Berigan opened the boat season on the Potomac with a six days stand which impressed the large crowds. Bunny's was one of the few name bands to play Washington recently."[62] Buddy Koss remembered that occasion: "My wife and I were still on our honeymoon and we had a whale of a time on that Potomac River cruise. The boat had a small bandstand on the balcony and the band was really swinging!"[63]

After this engagement, vocalist Danny Richards left the band for a few days to marry Kay Little, who was then the vocalist with Dick Stabile's band. Their wedding took place on June 5. After a short honeymoon, Richards rejoined Berigan, and Ms. Little rejoined Stabile.

After the pleasant Potomac River stand, it was back to the old grind of one-nighters: June 5, Suburban Park, Manlius, New York; the 6th, Pawling, New York; the 7th, somewhere in Philadelphia; the 8th, Dallas, Pennsylvania; the 9th, Rochester, New York; possibly three nights at the Raymor Ballroom in Boston, June 11–13. On the 13th, Bunny definitely played at the Raymor, while his old friend Red Norvo, who was then also suffering from the big band blues, played at the neighboring Playmor. "Bunny Berigan and Red Norvo were teamed at the Raymor-Playmor twin ballrooms in Boston on Friday, June 13. Admission was 65 cents double and 55 cents single. 1,600 hoofers attended for a nice $960. The night was hot and muggy."[64]

Berigan and company jumped to Bayonne, New Jersey, for a one-nighter on June 14, then opened another location engagement, this one lasting a week, at Enna Jettick Park in Auburn, New York (near Syracuse, on Lake Owasco) on the 16th. Here is the advance publicity with a short follow-up:

Red Norvo tees off at Enna Jettick Park, Auburn, New York, summer gigs for nine days on May 24. Johnny Messner to follow on June 2– 8; George Hall on 9th to 15th, and Bunny Berigan in on 16th to 22nd.[65]

Bunny Berigan's outfit was the next to hit Enna Jettick Park. What a beat this band has! The arrangements are good, with the majority being turned out by Andy Fitzgerald and Frank Crolene. Vocalist Danny Richards is very popular. Bunny himself seems on the upbeat and with this bunch of men behind him, he can't go wrong.[66]

Andy Fitzgerald remembered that location and his time with the Berigan band generally: "Enna Jettick Park was a nice gig with good crowds. The band played a lot of out of the way places, including lots of one-nighters and college dates. Although the band worked most of the time, there were quite a few lay-offs."[67]

From the Enna Jettick Park engagement, the Berigan band moved on as follows: June 23, at the Pavilion Ballroom, Budd Lake, New Jersey; on the 24th, they opened at the Luna Pier Ballroom in New York City where they would remain until June 29. While he was there, Bunny ran into singer Joey Nash's[68] brother Julie Nassberg: "I saw Bunny on that gig and he told me MCA had him all screwed up, booking him sometimes for only three or four days and then two, three or four more days off."[69] Then it was back to New England: Whalom Park, Fitchburg, Massacuhsetts, on the 30th, and then a return to the Raymor Ballroom in Boston on July 1. From there, they went to the Old Orchard Pier Ballroom, Old Orchard Beach, Maine, a very good venue. They played there on July 3 and 4. (This is where Berigan's band had showed up a day early in the summer of 1938, and rode amusement rides on their surprise day off.) They did well there over the July 4 holiday, as many other MCA bands did across the nation: "Harry Moss of MCA, says the past 4th July weekend was the biggest in history of MCA."[70]

Was the Berigan band gathering any momentum playing successful dance dates on the road? One would think that they were, or at least should have been. Whether they were or not, they continued touring. July 5, the Chateau Ballroom, Paragon Park, Nantasket Beach, Massachusetts; July 6, a dance date in Lawrence, Massachusetts.. Bunny then led his bandsmen into another location job, this one at the Nottingham Carnival, Route 33, Hamilton Square, Trenton, New Jersey. This was to be a two-week stand, with Sundays off. No doubt the musicians heaved a sigh of relief to be off of the road for this period of time. But while the Berigan band was at the Nottingham Carnival, the discontent among the sidemen engendered by Bunny's "wage withholding" plan began to mount. Johnny Castaldi kept exact record of how this plan was affecting him: At the end of the first week in Trenton, his diary read: "Received $36.00; Coming $14.00 on scale, $6.20 on fare. $20.20 still coming." At the end of the second week: "Received $39.27. Balance due: $10.75."[71]

After closing at the Nottingham Carnival, the Berigan band had Sunday, July 20 off, and then moved to the Marine Ballroom on the Steel Pier, Atlantic City, New Jersey, another prime big band venue, where they were to play until July 25. Undoubtedly Bunny had promised his musicians that his earnings from the

Steel Pier gig would enable him to catch-up with their pay. Charlie Arlington reported what happened on the night the band opened at the Steel Pier: "Bunny had skipped out on his hotel bill in Trenton, New Jersey. They called the police, who came to Atlantic City, arrested him backstage and threatened to jail him then and there. However, they finally allowed him to do a broadcast—and then they hauled him off to jail. The band finished the rest of the evening without him."[72]

Buddy Koss completed the story:

> Bunny owed a big hotel bill and a couple of detectives from Trenton came down to the Steel Pier in Atlantic City to arrest him. They let him finish the set before taking him back to Trenton, where he may have spent the night in jail. The next day, MCA paid the bill and Bunny got released, but the guys in the band had had enough and returned to New York, where Mort Davis later got Pee Wee Erwin as the new leader. Bunny was in poor physical shape and desperately short of money. He had reached the state where he was unable to play without booze and was down to drinking a very cheap brand of rye whisky called Calvert's Special. That was about the time Don Palmer came on the scene as Bunny's new manager.[73]

In reality, the band, *with Berigan,* finished the Steel Pier gig. How Mort Davis fit into this series of events, if at all, is not known since Johnny "The Face" De Santos had been serving as Bunny's road manager since shortly after the formation of this band the previous September. He may have quit after the Trenton stand. I suspect that Bunny was using all of his persuasive (or maybe *deceptive*) powers to keep his musicians from staging a full-scale mutiny on the Steel Pier gig. Nevertheless, they moved on to a one-nighter at Old Grove Casino, Old Grove Beach, near New London, Connecticut, on July 26, and then to another dance date at Roton Point Park, South Norwalk, Connnecticut, on the 27th. Here is what Castaldi recorded in his diary: "July 28 was paid $10.71 for both the 26th and 27th. Received only $25.00 of the $60.00 which was scale for Atlantic City. Owed $6.25 on carfare from Boston, $3.71 of the balance of Clinton *(sic),* plus $10.75 due from 2nd week of Trenton, and $14.00 for the 1st week of Trenton."[74] Thus Castaldi was due a total of $69.71. If this figure is multiplied by thirteen, the number of men in the band, we see that Bunny Berigan owed his musicians approximately $906.23. The Steel Pier gig had not resulted in the members of the Berigan band being paid their back wages, as Bunny no doubt had promised. Instead, his sidemen were now owed more money. The situation had reached the point of crisis.

Johnny Castaldi's diary has this entry for July 29, 1941: "The finish with Berigan" which suggests that this was the day of the members of the Bunny Berigan band "walked out" on him *en masse.* The personnel then included Jack Thompson, Frank Perry and one other, probably Charlie Mitchell, trumpets; Max Smith and possibly Walter Burleson, trombones; Charlie Arlington, Andy Fitzgerald, Frank Crolene, Johnny Castaldi, saxes; Buddy Koss, piano; Morty Stulmaker, bass; Jack Maisel, drums; and Danny Richards, vocalist.[75]

Several veterans of that band vividly recalled this scene:

Johnny Castaldi: I think that the unrest in the band really came to a head during a date at the fair in Trenton which was about the time when Don Palmer appeared. I'm not sure how that came about, but I guess Johnny 'The Face' De Santos, our road manager, must have given Bunny his notice, and Palmer lived in Trenton. All the boys decided, very reluctantly, that they couldn't go along with Bunny's constant empty promises that we would get our money. Those who were married had certain commitments they couldn't meet and were getting plenty of hassle from their wives! However, I believe they all got their money through the union later.

Andy Fitzgerald: Most of us didn't want to leave Bunny, but the married guys had little choice. We just had to have a weekly pay check! Pee Wee Erwin liked some of the arrangements that I'd done for Bunny and though I didn't go with him, he continued to use them after he took over the band.

Danny Richards: When the band walked out on Bunny, it was a total desertion. We all knew it was coming, even Bunny himself, I think. Anyway, I talked it over with him, because I hated like hell to leave him, but he suggested that I would probably do better going with Pee Wee Erwin. Bunny owed each of us around $100, and we couldn't afford to continue on promises. We eventually got paid through the union, but it was a very harrowing experience.[76]

As fate would have it, King George T. Simon happened to be present at one of this band's last gigs on Saturday, July 26 or Sunday, the 27th. What he reported in *Metronome* soon thereafter was limned in acid:

The band was nothing. And compared with Berigan standards, Bunny's blowing was just pitiful. He sounded like a man trying to imitate himself, a man with none of the inspiration and none of the technique of the real Berigan. He looked awful too. He must have lost at least thirty pounds. His clothes were loose-fitting; even his collar looked like it was a couple of sizes too large for him. Apparently, though, he was in good spirits. He joked with friends and talked about the great future he thought his band had. But you had a feeling it would never be. And when, after intermission, Bunny left the bandstand, not to return for a long time, and some trumpet player you'd never heard before came down to front the band, play Bunny's parts, and spark the outfit more than its leader had, you realized that this was enough, and you left the place at once, feeling simply awful.[77]

This quote from *Metronome* was much later included in Simon's book entitled *The Big Bands*, which was published in 1967. In this book, and to a much larger degree in a subsequent volume entitled *Simon Says: The Sights and Sounds of the Swing Era,* published in 1971, Simon devoted many pages to quoting himself, and very often to justifying his subjective likes and dislikes. While these books are useful in providing much information about the big band era, they suffer greatly from a lack of critical scholarship and objectivity. They also point up Simon's woeful inadequacy as a journalist. (See the reports from

Down Beat and *Variety,* cited at the beginning of the next chapter for the actual details of the breakup of this edition of Bunny Berigan and His Orchestra.)

More than twenty-five years after this incident, Simon set up the above-cited quote in *The Big Bands* like this: "The last time I heard the band was in a Connecticut ballroom during the summer of 1941, and for one who admired Bunny's playing so tremendously and liked him so much personally, it was quite a shattering experience."[78] One would think that someone who admired Bunny's playing so tremendously and liked him so much personally might have gone backstage when he left the bandstand after intermission, and talked with him to find out why he and the band were not in top form that night. It seems to me that Simon would not only have gotten an answer to that question, but he would have gotten some very interesting inside information as to why this band was literally on the verge of disintegration. But it was easier and more gratifying, apparently, for King George to have a subjectively shattering experience, report that in the pages of *Metronome,* and then recycle this very incomplete story many years later for publication in a book that many people regarded as the Bible of big band information.

After the Roton Point gig, the dates MCA had secured for the Berigan band from July 28 through July 30 were covered hurriedly by other MCA bands. Bunny and most of the Berigan band members returned to New York on July 28, laid this latest financial mess at the feet of Local 802, and then went their separate ways. Bunny did what little he could to ameliorate the problem then and there, but quickly moved on to Trenton, New Jersey, to gather a new group of musicians and return immediately to the road.

Notes

[1] *The Last Mogul,* by Dennis McDougal, Da Capo Press (1998), 11. This is a very worthwhile biography of Jules Stein's "heir" at MCA, Lew Wasserman. Another excellent biography of Lew Wasserman that contains much information about the founding of MCA and how it operated is *When Hollywood Had a King,* by Connie Bruck, Random House (2003). The Bruck biography also explores the dubious but immensely profitable relationship between Jules Stein of MCA and James Caesar Petrillo, president of the Chicago musicians' union, and later president of the national musicians' union.
[2] MCA did book a few jazz performers in the late 1920s and early 1930s, but these were only on a spot engagement basis.
[3] For a highly evocative performance that points up the sometimes brutal life touring musicians had to endure while on the road, listen to Jack Teagarden's vocal on "Jack Hits the Road," by Bud Freeman and His Famous Orchestra, Columbia 25854, recorded on July 23, 1940.
[4] *Billboard:* November 30, 1940, cited in the White materials.
[5] Some of the financial records from Duke Ellington's orchestra have been preserved. Here is what they reveal: in 1939, Ellington grossed $160,000, but just broke even. In 1940, he took in $185,000, and had a small profit. In 1941, he earned $135,000, but had a loss of $1,500. In 1942, Ellington was paid anywhere from $700 to $1,200 for a one-nighter, and grossed $210,000, but netted a mere $4,000. In 1942, Johnny Hodges (El-

lington's highest paid sideman), started the year making $125 a week, which was raised to $140 by midyear. All Ellington sidemen were paid $30 each for Victor recording sessions in 1942, except Hodges, who got $50. I have personally seen these records. They were also cited in *Beyond Category—The Life and Genius of Duke Ellington,* by John Edward Hasse, Simon and Schuster (1993), 272–273. These numbers do not include Ellington's earnings from royalties on his compositions.

[6] Fats Waller, like Duke Ellington, was earning more and more money as the swing era progressed from royalties on his compositions. His objective was to get off of the road, and he was just about to do that when he died, on the road, in 1943.

[7] Berigan's failure to take elocution lessons, as Benny Goodman had when he was headed for stardom, and his failure to have his teeth capped to correct the unsightly appearance caused by his dead and crooked teeth, were also factors that militated against his being a star bandleader who could engage in breezy patter with radio announcers, and flash his perfect smile to admiring fans. These things have nothing to do with music, but nevertheless were important matters for anyone wishing to be successful in the entertainment business. Bunny, ever concerned with his precious embouchure, was afraid that if anything was done with his teeth, it could negatively affect his ability to play the trumpet.

[8] *Those Swinging Years,* by Charlie Barnet, with Stanley Dance, Louisiana State University Press (1984), 92.

[9] Bennett Lester Carter, born on August 8, 1907, in New York City, was for many years one of the most versatile musicians in jazz. Although his primary instrument was always the alto saxophone, he also played a number of other instruments very well, especially the trumpet. But possibly his greatest talent lay in arranging. Carter first recorded in 1928, and then began an apprenticeship as a sideman in the Fletcher Henderson and McKinney's Cotton Pickers bands, which lasted until 1932. Thereafter, he led his own bands intermittently until the early 1940s, when he moved to Hollywood and became increasingly involved in studio work as an arranger. (He spent the years 1935–1938 in Europe.) Throughout the 1930s, many big bands had featured arrangements written by Carter. Although he never gave up performing as a jazz soloist, most of Carter's time in the decades from the mid-1940s until the mid-1960s was spent writing scores for recording artists, television shows, and movies. He gradually resumed his career as a performer in the 1960s, continuing to perform regularly until his ninetieth birthday, in 1997. He also frequently lectured on music at leading universities including Princeton and Harvard in his later years. Benny Carter lived a long and successful life and was widely recognized and honored for his musical achievements. He died on July 12, 2003, in Los Angeles, California.

[10] *Down Beat:* October 1, 1940, cited in the White materials.

[11] White materials: September 22, 1940.

[12] *Ibid.*

[13] *Ibid.*

[14] *Ibid.*

[15] White materials: September 29, 1940.

[16] White materials: September 30, 1940.

[17] This quote is from an interview of Buddy Koss done by Debbie Mikolas, cited in Dupuis: 248. It should be remembered that Alcoholics Anonymous was founded in 1935. Nevertheless, it was not a widely known resource for alcoholics until after World War II.

[18] *Variety:* November 6, 1940, cited in the White materials. I must point out that ABC (the American Broadcasting Company) did not exist in 1940. In essence, the American

Broadcasting Company was formed out of the former NBC Blue network on October 12, 1943. (See Wikipedia entry for American Broadcasting Company for the full history.)

[19] White materials: October 14, 1940.

[20] *Ibid.*

[21] White materials: October 18, 1940.

[22] *Targum:* (Rutgers University student magazine) October 26, 1940.

[23] White materials: October 18, 1940.

[24] *Ibid.*

[25] White materials: November 6, 1940.

[26] White materials: November 17, 1940.

[27] *Atlanta Constitution:* November 18, 1940, cited in the White materials.

[28] Dupuis: 229.

[29] *Jacksonville Journal:* November 29, 1940, cited in the White materials.

[30] White materials: November 29, 1940.

[31] Information about "Aunt Iona" was provided by Patricia Berigan to Robert Dupuis, Dupuis archive, UW–Madison.

[32] White materials: December 22, 1940.

[33] *Ibid.*

[34] White materials: January 4, 1941.

[35] *Metronome:* February 1941, cited in the White materials.

[36] This quote comes from remarks Danny Richards made to Tom Cullen in September 1960, cited in the White materials: January 23, 1941. Frank Sinatra recorded "This Love of Mine" with Tommy Dorsey and His Orchestra on May 28, 1941.

[37] *Down Beat:* January 15, 1941, cited in the White materials.

[38] *Billboard:* February 8, 1941, cited in the White materials.

[39] White materials: February 28, 1941. Much of the information concerning the activities of the Berigan band from January 1, 1941, to July 28, 1941, is from saxophonist Johnny Castaldi's diary. Those who contributed to the White materials cross-checked this information with trade press and/or other contemporary sources, and found it to be accurate.

[40] *Variety:* April 2, 1941, cited in the White materials.

[41] White materials: March 17, 1941.

[42] *Ibid.*

[43] *Boston Post:* March 27, 1941, reprinted in *Variety,* April 2, 1941, cited in the White materials.

[44] Citations to the Castaldi diary are from the White materials.

[45] White materials: April 6, 1941.

[46] *Down Beat:* May 1, 1941, cited in the White materials.

[47] White materials: April 1941.

[48] *Metronome:* May 1941, cited in the White materials.

[49] *Down Beat:* May 15, 1941, cited in the White materials.

[50] *Variety:* April 30, 1941, cited in the White materials.

[51] White materials: April 23, 1941.

[52] *Billboard:* May 3, 1941, cited in the White materials.

[53] Ray Galvin's Eastern Orchestra Service was one of many regional band booking offices that would on occasion act as subcontractor for MCA and other booking agencies to secure work for touring bands.

[54] *Variety:* April 30, 1941, cited in the White materials.

[55] White materials: April 26, 1941.

[56] Cited in the White materials: May 5, 1941.

[57] White materials: May 15, 1941.

[58] *Variety:* April 23, 1941, and *Metronome:* July 1941, cited in the White materials.

[59] Cornetist Robert Leo "Bobby" Hackett, born on January 31, 1915, in Providence, Rhode Island, was influenced by both Bix Beiderbecke, to me always his greatest influence, and Louis Armstrong, his greatest inspiration. His playing was always warm and gentle, like Hackett himself, but interesting from a jazz standpoint. After going broke leading a big band in the late 1930s, he worked as a featured soloist in a number of big bands, most notably Glenn Miller's, where he was well presented on a number of classic recordings, including "A String of Pearls," and "Rhapsody in Blue." Hackett's post-big-band career was successful because he was frequently employed on recordings, and also often led bands of various sizes playing his unique brand of relaxed jazz. Bobby Hackett died June 7, 1976, in Chatham, Massachusetts.

[60] *Music and Rhythm:* May 1941, cited in the White materials.

[61] White materials: May 18, 1941.

[62] *Metronome:* July 1941, cited in the White materials.

[63] White materials: May 27, 1941.

[64] *Billboard:* June 28, 1941, cited in the White materials.

[65] *Variety:* April 23, 1941, cited in the White materials.

[66] *Down Beat:* August 1, 1941, cited in the White materials.

[67] White materials: June 16, 1941.

[68] Joey Nash was best known as the singer with Richard Himber's Orchestra 1933–35.

[69] White materials: June 24, 1941.

[70] *Billboard:* July 12, 1941, cited in the White materials: July 6, 1941.

[71] White materials: July 1941.

[72] White materials: July 21, 1941.

[73] *Ibid.*

[74] White materials: July 28, 1941.

[75] White materials: July 29, 1941.

[76] *Ibid.*

[77] *The Big Bands:* 91.

[78] *Ibid.*

Chapter 23
The Last Roundup

By early August, the trade press had reported Bunny Berigan's latest financial problems in detail:

> Front Page Headline: BERIGAN'S MEN WALK OUT—Bunny Fronts a New Crew: Almost simultaneously with the break-up of the Gray Gordon band, Bunny Berigan's band fell apart. The blow-off came after three weeks of strife. Berigan was jailed in Jersey after running up a hotel bill that MCA, which books Bunny, finally straightened out. In Atlantic City, according to Bunny's men, there was a 'slight shortage' in payment of their salaries. The musicians allegedly claimed they were paid off 'in the dark' and demanded full pay. When Berigan referred them to Harry Moss, MCA executive, the sidemen declared they were fed up and quit. In New York they filed claims with the union. Meanwhile, Berigan had dates to fill in the middlewest. For his job at Buckeye Lake, Ohio, he took a band from Trenton, New Jersey, which he rehearsed for a couple of days before heading west. Among the men in the band which folded were Jack Maisel, drummer, and Morty Stulmaker, bassist. Berigan was detained from taking the Trenton band west until his debts were cleared, supposedly by MCA, which is still booking Bunny[1]

> Headline: BERIGAN CHANGES ORK AFTER OLD MEMBERS TAKE BACK PAY BEEF TO 802. Bunny Berigan's band gave him quitting notice en masse last week in New York and filed an appeal with local 802 for approximately $900 in back salaries. Berigan immediately gave the union $300 and made arrangements to pay off the rest of the money in weekly installments, thereby avoiding suspension. The band listened to pleas to work with Bunny only two nights beyond its notice, then left him. The leader has since taken over an organized band out of Trenton, New Jersey, formerly led by Al Zahler, and has begun a four weeks stay at Buckeye Lake, Ohio. MCA has taken over the handling of Berigan's financial affairs at his request. Johnny De Santos, his road manager, left him along with the band.[2]

In attempting to review and assess the ten and a half months from the inception of this Bunny Berigan band in September 1940, to its dissolution at the end of July 1941, several facts emerge. First, it seems to have been a very good band. Unfortunately, recordings of it are extremely rare. It had no commercial recording contract, and due in part to the ASCAP-BMI dispute, its radio broadcasts were also rare and almost never recorded. The recordings from the October

14, 1940 broadcast, from the New York World's Fair appear to be the only ones that it ever made. They give some idea of how good this band was. But it must be remembered that these recordings were made after the band had been together for only a short time, less than a month. It had not yet really jelled as a performing unit. Nevertheless, there were numerous reports in the trade press throughout its existence that the band started out good, and got better as time passed. It played a mix of older arrangements from the Berigan book of the late 1930s, and some fine new ones by Andy Fitzgerald and Frank Crolene, both members of the 1940–1941 band. It also featured vocalist Danny Richards, whose singing received almost universal praise. Second, despite a chronic shortage of steady work and operating funds, the band's personnel remained amazingly stable. This always allowed a band to become a better, more unified performing ensemble with the passing weeks. Third, Bunny's playing seems to have been quite good, no doubt because he was constantly struggling to control his intake of alcohol. Bunny had always been able to play well when he limited his consumption of alcohol. The record is clear that up to the summer of 1941, whenever he was able to achieve that delicate balance between having enough alcohol in his system to function, yet not too much to render him incapable of functioning, Bunny was able to perform at a fairly high level as a trumpet soloist. Finally, there seems to have been very competent assistance provided by Johnny "The Face" De Santos, the band's road manager. The band always got to the correct destination on time (with possibly a few exceptions), and there were no allegations of theft, or incompetence in paying the band's expenses.

Although this Berigan band worked very often, it appears that its off days mounted up to approximately one-third of the total dates during the time the band was together. This steadily undermined the financial viability of the band. The mix of engagements provided by MCA did include a few lucrative theater jobs, and presumably some one-nighters that produced enough revenue to at least equalize the continuous overhead required to keep this big band on the road. But overall, there were many more dates that were at best break even. And though this band did enjoy a number of location jobs that allowed them to remain in one place for a period of time, and have a respite from the vicissitudes of constant travel, there was a downside to those "residencies." No band could survive financially by staying in one place too long. Hotels especially could not afford to pay bands enough to offset the cost of the musicians, buying new arrangements, etc., even without the cost of transportation. Bunny began to experience financial difficulties with this band early in 1941. His way of dealing with his shortage of cash was to tell his musicians that this good job or that one lay just ahead, and that if he could owe them just a little bit for a short time, he could keep the band going long enough to pay them. As a result, he began going into substantial debt to his musicians, and despite his good intentions, he could never catch up on their salaries. He had to bear the many risks of operating a big band, and these risks seemed to constantly prevent him from making full payment to his sidemen. Berigan's musicians, being young and idealistic, went along with him for as long as they could. Then the realities of their lives began to close in on them. They had expenses too, especially those of them who were married with children to support.

MCA's April 24, 1941, plan to help Bunny get out of debt had been spectacularly unsuccessful. Within three months of making whatever arrangement he had made with Harry Moss, Bunny found himself unable to pay his Trenton, New Jersey hotel bill. One wonders why Bunny didn't call Moss *before* he skipped out on that bill? Maybe he did, and Moss told him to get out of trouble the way he had gotten in. If this conversation did occur, Bunny should have told Moss that he had gotten into this predicament because of the business plan of MCA that caused constant streams of revenue to flow from touring bands into the overflowing coffers of MCA, while bankrupting touring bandleaders. But Bunny would never have considered having such a conversation with Moss. He just wanted to keep his band going. Whatever happened between Bunny and MCA before this fiasco, he chose to just bounce the Trenton hotel bill, and let the chips fall. When this incident became an embarrassment, Moss bailed him out (with a loan, plus interest) so that this MCA road band could continue to be fronted by its name leader, and keep the commissions rolling in without interruption.

The mutiny of the Berigan's musicians at the end of July was not unexpected by Bunny. In fact, it appears that he had been preparing for it, and indeed may have again (as he had in 1939) told his sidemen to go to the union to get what was due them. Don Palmer, who seems to have materialized rather serendipitously at the Nottingham Carnival in Trenton in mid-July as Bunny's personal and road manager, later gave some information about the developments then taking place:

> Don Lodice and I went to New York in late 1938, and someone told Bunny about him and he duly replaced Georgie Auld in the Berigan band. I had known Bunny on a casual basis since that time and went to see the band at the Firemen's Carnival in Trenton in July, 1941. During that couple of weeks I took Bunny to hear Al Zahler's band, which I was managing, and he was quite impressed. After dates in Atlantic City and Clinton, Conn., Bunny sent for me to take over the management of his new band, which was actually the Zahler band, because the whole of his current group, including the manager, had quit. I became Bunny's combined personal and road manager with his power of attorney to sign all contracts on his behalf.[3]

In typically Beriganesque fashion, Bunny now quickly entrusted all of his business affairs to a virtual stranger as an expedient to allow him to continue touring as the leader of his own band. As subsequent developments would show, this impulsive business decision was one of the best Bunny ever made. Berigan, like all major talents, needed a shrewd, aggressive personal manager to handle not only his daily business matters, but to guide his career. One wonders what his career would have been like if he had had a relationship with a personal manager like the canny Joe Glaser, who managed Louis Armstrong so successfully over so many years. The two and a half years Berigan went without a personal manager had been filled with financial crises and personnel problems. His career as a bandleader had had no direction. The result was that the bands Bunny Berigan led from early 1939 until mid-1941 had been "panic bands." No one knew if they would continue to exist from day to day.

The known facts about Don Palmer seem to indicate that, although he was not devoid of self-interest, he did work very hard and effectively on behalf of Bunny Berigan during the time they were associated. In addition to being an apparently honest road manager, he seemed, in his role as Berigan's personal manager, to be the nearest thing Bunny ever had to a fiduciary, who put Bunny's financial interests ahead of his own. Consequently, Berigan's financial condition improved substantially while he was being managed by Don Palmer. Of equal importance, Palmer seemed to understand what was necessary for Bunny's career to be steered in a positive direction over the long term, and took steps to move it out of the doldrums. As events over the next nine months would show, Palmer had considerable success redirecting and revitalizing Berigan's career.

Here is the information contained about Palmer in the White materials:

Don Palmer (real name: Domenico Ciro Plumeri), was born circa 1915, in Trenton, New Jersey; died January 12, 1984, Trenton, New Jersey. His father was Joseph Plumeri, part owner of the Trenton Giants (baseball) team, and his brother was Samuel Plumeri who became Trenton City Commissioner. His son Terry, a musician, was at one time with singer Roberta Flack. Palmer in his early years played with many Trenton area baseball teams including the locally famous Trenton Schroths. He started singing in local clubs at $3.00 a nite, with indifferent success. Later he became 'manager' of his cousin tenor saxophonist Don Lodice, and first met Bunny when he and Don went to see Berigan band in late 1938. In the late 1930s, he took over the management of Al Zahler's band in Trenton, and came up with the slogan 'Al Zahler and his orchestra, Music from A to Z.' After Berigan, Palmer managed Vido Musso, Johnny 'Scat' Davis, Charlie Ventura, and later the Ventura night spot in Camden, New Jersey. For 20 years he was the business manager of singer Arthur Prysock. In service in WW II with Army Air Corps as director of entertainment where he met both Mickey Rooney and Donald O'Connor, both of whom remained life-long friends. From the late 1940s into 1950s Palmer worked in Las Vegas representing the interests of Joe Glaser's Associated Booking Co. He was entertainment director with Bill Miller of the New Frontier Hotel in Las Vegas. He had two heart attacks in 1960s, but continued working with Prysock.[4]

This additional note was included in the White materials: "Palmer granted one brief interview to Tom Cullen in the late 1950s and another briefer one to Bozy White in 1960s, and then for the rest of his life refused to discuss the 'Berigan story' in spite of attempts by a number of persons. Two or three others in the 'kids band' likewise refused to be interviewed or reply to letters, etc., thus this last period of Bunny's life and career is lacking in some details in spite of the best research efforts."[5]

There are a number of accounts of Bunny listening to the Zahler band in Trenton. It appears from most of the available information that he had done this while he was playing the Trenton Carnival engagement, sometime between July 7 and July 19. That means Bunny was auditioning his "replacement" band while he was still working with his regular band. MCA may or may not have been aware of this. By that time, MCA didn't care who the sidemen were in Bunny Berigan's band. As long as he could play his trumpet in front of any competent band of musicians, preferably inexpensive ones, they were satisfied. They left the details of gathering the musicians, negotiating their salaries, putting together a book of arrangements to play, and rehearsing the men into a cohesive unit, to Bunny. He had proved again and again that he was very good at taking care of musical matters. What he wasn't good at was handling money and administering the business side of his band, or guiding his own career.

MCA probably became aware of the mutiny of the Berigan band shortly before the day it occurred, which seems to have been on Tuesday, July 29, presumably the date on which the band members took their grievances against Berigan to New York Local 802. By Thursday, July 31, Bunny Berigan was leading an entirely new band at the Luna Pier Ballroom, just south of Detroit on Lake Erie. Presumably, he spent the 30th assembling his new sidemen in Trenton, and setting out for Michigan. There was no time for the Trenton musicians to rehearse. Bunny would have to wing it with them at Luna Pier.

In the meantime, MCA did not want to waste the band Bunny had put together and trained over the previous ten plus months. MCA could make commissions by booking this band on one-nighters, with a new leader, preferably someone with a recognizable name. Unfortunately for MCA, Cork O'Keefe, previously a partner in Rockwell-O'Keefe, (now called General Artists Corporation), and now a major player at GAC, MCA's chief rival, was representing trumpeter Pee Wee Erwin. Erwin had been looking for an existing band to take over as a unit, and when the opportunity to take over Bunny's band presented itself, Pee Wee jumped at it. Thus the new Erwin band, which was the old Berigan band, would be booked by GAC, not MCA. This deal was facilitated by drummer/copyist Jack Maisel, who remained with the group of musicians who were to be led by Erwin. The idea was simply to put another leader, Erwin, who was an excellent trumpet player and jazz soloist, with fair name recognition with swing fans, in front of the previous Berigan band, and put it back out on the road without delay.

Erwin recalled how his part of this plan unfolded in his autobiography, *This Horn for Hire*: "...an old friend, Jack Maisel, the drummer, offered me Bunny Berigan's band intact, complete with Bunny's library. I immediately accepted the offer. The personnel, as I recall, included Jack Thompson, Charles Mitchell, and Charles Tessar, trumpets; Johnny Castaldi, Andy Fitzgerald, and another sax player on reeds; Morty Stulmaker on bass; and Buddy Koss on piano. Danny Richards and Kay Little were the vocalists."[6] (Ms. Little had not been with Berigan, as Bunny had not had a regular girl singer with his band since late 1939.

The following snippet of gossip reveals why she may have joined the Erwin band, and how the business of rumormongering in print was just as sordid in 1941 as it is today: "Kay Little and Danny Richards are giggly *(sic)*; she's the Stabile thrush, he's with Berigan. Does Danny know of her child in Phillie?"[7] Of course, one would expect newlyweds to be giggly!

Berigan's new band was at some point dubbed the "Kids' Band" because there were a number of musicians in it who were quite young. There were also some relatively older musicians in it. One of the members of the "Kids' Band" was lead alto saxophonist George Quinty. Born in 1916, Quinty, at age twenty-five, was one of the older members of that band. Over the years, he spoke with the White researchers, and with Robert Dupuis about his time as a member of the last Bunny Berigan band. Here is what he remembered about being hired by Berigan:

I was working in Al Zahler's 'Music from A to Z' band when Bunny played the Trenton carnival. I guess the draft board had taken a lot of his musicians and he needed subs *(sic)*. Don Palmer, our manager, persuaded Bunny to come and hear our band and suggested that we all might be willing to leave home under Bunny's leadership. He and Bunny stood outside the theatre where we were rehearsing and heard us play several arrangements that Kutchie, our pianist, Gene Kutch had copied off records by guys like Goodman, Shaw and Miller. Al called a break and when I went outside for a smoke, Bunny came up and said, 'Don Palmer has hinted that I could hire most of the guys in this band, would you be interested?' I told him I would, but that I was only a semi-pro with a regular daytime job with the Water Department. 'How much do they pay you?' he asked. '$48.40 cents every two weeks,' I replied. 'How would you like to start with me at $100 a week?' I almost fainted, but of course I accepted, and got Kutchie and Jackie Sperling, our drummer, to go along, but our bassist didn't want to leave Trenton. I also got Freddy Norton, Bob Mansell, Artie Mellor (trumpets) and Ed Cook (trombone) to join us. We had a brass section, but nobody else in the sax section wanted to leave, so I called a couple of local free-lance musicians, Walt Mellor, no relation to Artie, and Wilbur 'Weebee' Joustra, a fine tenor saxist, who both agreed to come with us. The fourth sax proved to be quite a problem, but Bunny said not to worry, we'd pick someone up on the road. Naturally, Al Zahler wasn't too happy about losing most of his band, even though I had pointed out how it was our chance to break into the big-time and prove ourselves. 'It's a dirty trick,' he complained bitterly, 'I baked a loaf of bread and Bunny Berigan is going to eat it and enjoy it!' By the end of the week, everything was set and Bunny said we'd be leaving on the Thursday morning to play the Luna Pier Pavilion in Detroit and we'd have to travel in motor cars, because he didn't have a band bus. I rode with Walt Mellor in Artie Mellor's brand-new Hudson; Ed Cook had a Hudson Commodore 8 coupe and both Mansell and Norton had new Buicks. We didn't have time to rehearse and as we'd never seen Bunny's book, but we realized that we had a lot of tough arrangements to learn.[8]

Trumpeter Arthur Mellor, who was also not a kid when he joined Berigan, provided some other details:

I was just short of my 23rd birthday when I joined Bunny. I had been with the Al Zahler band about two years prior. I played mostly jazz (2nd trumpet) with Al and some first. I recall Zahler had a drum 'act' with Jackie Sperling where they both played on two drums sets. Al played a bit then and also played vibes. I can't recall the details of how we Zahler men joined Bunny, but I think I recall Bunny hearing the Zahler band as a unit and offering the entire band a job. Don Palmer was 'involved' here, but I'm not sure just how. We did not rehearse before we left Trenton. Our first job was Luna Pier in Michigan, then a one-nighter in Dayton. I think there was only one trombone in Buckeye Lake for part of the job, then Smitty (Max Smith) joined.[9]

The Luna Pier engagement was something of a disaster. George Quinty remembered that night vividly:

There were signs and photographs all over which read: *Bunny Berigan, The Miracle Man Of The Trumpet.* I felt like I was a big star! When we got on the bandstand, Bunny and Don passed out the charts. 'They're very simple,' said Bunny, just follow the 'footballs.' He used to always call the whole notes 'footballs'! 'If I go like this,' he explained, 'It means we're going out. And if I go like that, it means cut. There are lots of little tricks you'll have to learn as we go along.' So we opened with 'I Can't Get Started' and he was pleased because it sounded good, but we screwed up the next two numbers so badly that he tried a ballad. It was terrible! We sounded like a bunch of beginners or kids taking lessons. During the first intermission, Bunny cried real, honest-to-goodness tears in his dressing room. 'How am I gonna go out and face those people again?' he wailed. But Don Palmer reminded him that we'd never really had a rehearsal and were attempting to play those scores for the first time. 'But the guys from New York could play my charts like they owned them,' Bunny retorted, 'I've never heard anything so bad in my life!' Kutchie suggested that we should play some of the arrangements that we knew well, pointing out that it would be easy for a superb musician like Bunny to work himself in (to them), much easier than it was for us to play his arrangements without plenty of time for rehearsals. Eventually, he agreed, providing that we took his music back to the hotel to study and practice. The book comprised about 300 charts, and Kutchie and Ed Lange wrote as many as time would allow while on the road. Bunny was a stickler on phrasing, standing in front of the band and demonstrating by humming how he wanted each section to sound. He especially liked the saxophone voicing of first alto and two tenors with the third alto playing mostly baritone, trying to emulate the sound of five saxes, which many other bands were using then. He didn't like a clarinet lead a la Glenn Miller. He wanted a heavier sound in the reed section. We used very few stock arrangements.[10]

The Ed Lange to whom Quinty referred was one of the surprisingly good musicians Bunny picked up at Luna Pier on that one-night stand. Edmar "Red" Langendorfer was born in 1915 in Toledo, Ohio. He later recalled that night:

I had been playing around the Toledo area for many years with many groups. My only prior contact with Bunny was in 1935 when the Benny Goodman band came into a spot near Jackson, Michigan, and I was in the house band. I saw and heard Bunny then, but did not meet him; but I sure was impressed. Tony Espen and I were playing in the house band at Luna Pier, when Bunny arrived minus a saxophone player, a trombonist and a bass player. The union asked us if we'd work with him that night and brought in Pops Faust on trombone. After the job Bunny asked us to stay with the band. Tony and I agreed, but Pops didn't want to go on the road.[11]

Red Lange proved to be a very valuable member of this Berigan band. In addition to playing saxophone and clarinet, he could arrange. Quinty, who also arranged, provided a bit more information: "Tony Espen and 'Red' Lange joined at Luna Pier, out of the Toledo local. They were good friends. 'Red' became the 4th sax, although he was a much better jazzman than 'Weebee,' but since Joustra was there first, he continued to play most of the jazz until he got canned."[12]

Thus the band Berigan had pieced together within a period of a couple of days consisted of the following: Artie Mellor (first), Bob Mansell, Freddie Norton, trumpets; Ed Cook, trombone; George Quinty, lead alto, Walt Mellor, alto/baritone, Wilbur "Weebee" Joustra, Red Lange, tenor saxophones, with Lange playing jazz clarinet; Gene Kutch, piano; Tony Espen, bass; Jack Sperling, drums. Mickey Irons, who handled the vocals, joined a few days later. Kutch and Lange also arranged. The second trombone chair was filled with subs until Bunny was able to persuade Max Smith, who had been a member of the band that had just mutinied, to return.

Much of the information about this edition of the Berigan band was derived from the diary of pianist/arranger Gene Kutch.[13] Those who contributed to the White materials cross-checked the Kutch diary with contemporary press accounts, and found it to be extremely accurate.

The very next night, August 1, at Lakeside Park Ballroom in Dayton, Ohio, there was a personnel issue: George Quinty explained: "The next job at Dayton, Ohio, was where trombonist Ed Cook got an 'or else' letter from his girlfriend back home and said he would have to return to Trenton right away. Bunny said OK and we tried a 'legit' man from the Dayton local, but he was so straight that Bunny had to pay him off and send him home after a couple of sets!"[14]

The band then moved on to a four-week gig at the Buckeye Lake Danceteria, at Buckeye Lake Park, about fifteen miles east of Columbus, Ohio. Cook continued to work with the band for a short time, and then was replaced by Max Smith. Smith's recollection of those weeks is interesting, particularly how he described the "mutiny" of the previous group of Berigan sidemen:

I really cannot recall what happened when the Berigan band broke up. I'm still not sure what took place. Some of the guys didn't get paid I guess, or got paid 'late.' We had a week at the Steel Pier, Atlantic City, then (Bunny) got a whole new band in Trenton, New Jersey. He wired me 'come join, we need another trombone' so I did, to Buckeye Lake for the summer 6–8 *(sic)* weeks, then to Jacksonville, Florida, the Roosevelt Hotel, and then a lot of one-nighters.[15]

Evidently when the prior Berigan band returned to New York at the end of July, not all of its members had been involved in reporting Bunny to Local 802.

Since Don Palmer was both the Berigan band's road manager and Bunny's personal manager, he was with the band and with Bunny constantly. He undoubtedly had some time while Bunny was trying to forge this group of musicians into a good, professional performing unit at Buckeye Lake, to figure out how to direct the fortunes of his client on something more than a daily crisis management basis. He no doubt learned during this time how MCA operated, and began to create a plan for Bunny's future. Nothing like this had happened with Bunny Berigan's career since the early days of his association with Arthur Michaud. Now someone who had Berigan's best interests as his main objective began to advise Bunny to make career choices that would benefit him over time.

At the conclusion of the Buckeye Lake engagement on September 2 or 3, *Down Beat* ran a story, probably generated through the MCA publicity department, which was both amusing and informative:

> Now shaping up at Buckeye Lake's Danceteria[16] is Bunny Berigan's new young band. Although a little rough in spots yet, the band, average age about 19, is getting a lot of fine support from the large crowds at the lake. With the inimitable Berigan on trumpet, the outfit sports one of the finest young drummers in the business in 17 year-old Jack Sperling. (Sperling was actually 19 at the time.) This tub artist has a wrist as fast as any. Another fine member of the new aggregation is hot tenorman Wilbur Joustra. The band is attracting a lot of attention with the beards they are required to wear as part of a publicity stunt at the park. The 'Bearded Snake Hunters of 1941' include all the male employees of the resort. On Labor Day, the stunt is to climax with all the men taking part in a huge patriotic panorama. Each male, including band members, is to represent some character in American history. No announcement has been released yet as to whom hornman Berigan was to depict. In addition to Joustra there are George Quinty, Walt Mellor and Ed Lange on reeds; Charles Stewart and Max Smith on trombones; Artie Mellor, Bob Munsell *(sic)* and Fred Norton, trumpets; Eugene Kutch, piano; Tony Espen, bass and Sperling on drums. 18 year-old Mickey Irons handles the vocals. Most of the boys were rounded up in Trenton, New Jersey, and Toledo, Ohio, by Bunny and his manager, Don Palmer.[17]

There is no information extant that would reveal which personage from American history Bunny represented in the Buckeye Lake "patriotic panorama."

Drummer Jack Sperling, born August 17, 1922, went on to have long and very successful career. After working with Berigan, he studied with the renowned drum teacher Henry Adler in New York, then while in military service played with Tex Beneke's[18] navy orchestra. He worked with Tex again after World War II. He moved to Los Angeles with the Beneke band, and there joined Les Brown for several years. He eventually got into freelance studio work in Hollywood in the 1950s, playing in all kinds of musical settings, the most rewarding of which were with Dave Pell, with whom he had worked in the Brown band, and Henry Mancini, with whom he had worked in the Beneke band. He was a member of Charlie Barnet's last great band in the late 1960s. Sperling died on February 26, 2004.

Jack Sperling provided much information about Bunny Berigan's last band over the years:

> The Buckeye Lake job lasted about a month and we rehearsed a lot. Charlie Stewart joined on trombone and some of the brass men had lip problems. It was a pretty tough grind. Bunny was drinking heavily and the band was ragged. We used upturned boats as music stands and we rehearsed from 1 to 4.30 p.m. every day, but by the time we'd finished that job, we had Bunny's entire library under our belts, along with Kutchie's charts. The place was called the Crystal Danceteria, and Bunny had a trombonist friend come out from New York and bring most of the old Berigan book with him. His name was Max Smith, but everyone called him 'Smitty' and I guess he replaced Ed Cook.[19]

One wonders if Jack Maisel had been holding Bunny's library for ransom, and then, after MCA/Local 802 intervened, (that is, paid Maisel what Bunny owed him) released it. Whatever the case, Bunny now had his old book of arrangements back again (for the third time), and members of his prior band were soon receiving small checks periodically from Local 802 in payment for whatever money he owed them.

Vocalist Mickey Irons recalled how he became a part of the Berigan band:

> When Bunny and Don Palmer went to hear Al Zahler's band, there was no vocal mike set up, so I didn't get a chance to sing, but Don told me if they needed a vocalist, they'd send for me. Sometime later I got a call to report to Buckeye Lake and audition for the band. I traveled there by bus and when I arrived I had to sing 'Please Be Kind' without a microphone! Anyway, after I finished, Bunny told me to report back at 9 p.m. for a broadcast. I had to borrow some clothes from the guys in the band. Guy Lombardo was also playing there and both bands stayed at the same lodge. It was a big ballroom, built on two levels with a bandstand at either end. About all we did was play and rehearse, with lots of the rehearsals held outside.[20]

MCA's Harry Moss had given Bunny a break by allowing him to keep the Buckeye Lake engagement. In addition to providing this new Berigan band some time to get themselves together as a performing unit, they were for at least a part of the time they were at Buckeye Lake, riding on the very lush commercial coattails of Guy Lombardo, one of MCA's most reliable moneymakers.

Yet more good publicity for Bunny appeared in the trade press during this time. This article also ran in the September 1, 1941 issue of *Down Beat:*

> Headline: 'Berigan Can't Do No Wrong' says Armstrong: Urged for several years by a *Down Beat* reporter to 'come on and tell us which trumpet players you yourself like best,' Louis Armstrong last week patiently and carefully typed out an answer between jumps on the road. From Huntington, West Virginia came this answer directly from Louie, who typed his words out on yellow stationary bear-

ing the single word, 'Satchmo,' in the upper left-hand corner. Said Armstrong: 'Now the question about my opinion about the trumpet players that I admire, that is actually asking an awful lot of me, because there's so many trumpet players that I admire until there would not be room to mention them on this paper. And to only name six, well, that is leaving me on the spot. But as you wished, my friend, I'll do my damndest, so here goes. First I'll name my boy, Bunny Berigan. Now there's a boy whom I've always admired for his tone, soul, technique; his sense of phrasing and all. To me Bunny can't do no wrong in music!'[21]

Bunny's reply was also included in the article:

Inspiration Was Satchmo—Berigan' (by Julian B. Bach, Columbus, Ohio) Informed that Louis Armstrong had named him first among a group of his favorite trumpet men, Bunny Berigan commented to *Down Beat*, 'You can't imagine what a kick that is, especially when it comes from Satchmo, the King. All I can say is that Louis alone has been my inspiration, and whatever style I play, you can give Armstrong the credit. Why, when I was a kid in Chicago at night I used to sneak down to the Savoy, where Louis was playing, and listen to him night after night. Later, I got one of those crank-up phonograph jobs and would play Armstrong records by the hour.[22]

After completing the Buckeye Lake engagement, the Berigan band traveled to Pulaski, Virginia, to play a one-night dance date at the Monticello Ballroom on September 4.[23] Coincidentally, Louis Armstrong was in the same town as Bunny and his band when the *Down Beat* article appeared on the newsstands. Jack Sperling recalled: "Bunny and Louis Armstrong got together in Pulaski, Virginia. I guess Satchmo was passing through town, caught the band and stopped to chat with Bunny backstage. Don Palmer bought everyone a copy of *Down Beat*, which had the story about Louis naming Bunny as his favorite trumpet man."[24]   From this gig, Bunny and his boys headed south, to Florida.

The Berigan band opened a four-week engagement at the Patio Room of the Hotel Roosevelt in Jacksonville, Florida on Saturday, September 6. This is the venue where Bunny and his previous band had done so well over the 1940 Christmas holidays. Once again, the band broadcast quite regularly over local Jacksonville radio stations while at the Patio Grill. In spite of Bunny's many troubles, he retained his sense of humor. Saxist Red Lange recalled: "We played in the Patio Grill of the Roosevelt Hotel with Joe Frisco, and Roscoe Ates, the famous stuttering movie comedian, also on the bill. One night, one of them was pretending to play the trumpet while Bunny did the real playing out in the wings. It was a very old gag. Bunny was playing 'Dinah' and on the last high note the comic dropped his horn to indicate the end of his solo, but Bunny continued playing. During that engagement, we all stayed at the Aragon Hotel, but Bunny and Donna stayed at the Roosevelt."[25]

As she had done previously, Donna joined Bunny at the Roosevelt Hotel. Her presence was not salutary for him, for by this time, she had become an alcoholic herself, and was only too happy to urge her husband to drink with her.

Their life together on these reunions was not harmonious. It seems that their marriage at this juncture was too irreparably damaged to survive; nevertheless they continued the pretense of a marital relationship. The most likely explanation as to why Bunny did not divorce Donna is that he was by this time so paralyzed emotionally by alcoholism that his life consisted only of reactions to events. He was now almost incapable of taking the initiative regarding anything other than his music. Donna was likewise paralyzed, and in addition, in an age before women's equality, saw herself as totally dependent on Bunny. They would continue to have a troubled relationship until his death.

Their two young daughters had to bear heavy burdens, having alcoholic parents. Donna took the most blame for this because she was with the girls more than Bunny, who was now living permanently on the road. But her behavior as the mother of Pat and Jo was hardly exemplary. As Patricia Berigan told Robert Dupuis many years after Bunny's death: "I never saw my father drunk. I know he got drunk, but I never saw him drunk. I saw my mother drunk many times."[26]

Unfortunately, by this time, Bunny's cirrhosis had advanced to the stage where literally every drink he took was moving him closer to death. His marked weight loss was regarded by all of his associates as merely a result of years of heavy drinking. There was seemingly a complete ignorance of what was going on inside of Bunny Berigan's body then. In spite of all of the warning signs, no one seemed to be particularly concerned that Bunny was still drinking. The general feeling was that if he would just cut down, his health and playing would respond positively, as they always had in the past. At this time, although Bunny was still drinking a great deal by all objective standards, he felt that he was drinking just enough to allow his alcohol-addicted body to function, without being completely inebriated and unable to work. He was still seeking that magic or cursed balance when it came to his drinking. He may have been achieving the alcoholic balance that allowed him to manage his life day-to-day, but what neither he (perhaps) nor anyone else was considering was the effect that alcohol was now having on his already ravaged liver.

The White materials indicate that the important job of band boy/equipment manager for the Berigan troupe had been taken over by Hazen "Doc" Pugh by this time.

At some point after the 'kids band' was formed, the bandboy spot was taken over by Hazen 'Doc' Pugh. He remained with the band until after Bunny's death, when it was taken over by Vido Musso. Later he spent a long period (1950s–1963) with Louis Armstrong. When Pugh died, Louis Armstrong was asked what was wrong with him. Louis came back with the classic: 'Man when you die everything is wrong with you.' The Dupuis Berigan biography has a photo of one Bob 'Holly' Caffey, (*sic*, see below) and says he was a bandboy on the 1941–1942 band. While he may have traveled at times with the Berigan band, and even at some point taken over when 'Doc' Pugh was ill or needed help, Caffey was not the regular band boy. Pugh was recalled by almost everyone in the 'kids band,' Caffey by none.[27]

In reviewing drummer Jack Sperling's comments to Robert Dupuis about this issue, I must disagree with Mr. White's assertion. Sperling was well acquainted with Horace "Holly" Coffey, having gone through school with him in New Jersey. Based on Sperling's very specific statements that Coffey was the band boy at some point during the existence of Berigan's last band,[28] and the fact that the trees in the photo referred to above have no leaves, I would say that photo of Berigan and Coffey, and other snapshots taken at the same time, were taken somewhere on the road in the late winter–early spring of 1942.

By the time of the September, 1941 Roosevelt Hotel engagement, Don Palmer had taken firm grasp of the Berigan band's finances. Here is Jack Sperling's take on that: "None of us knew what wages we would be getting from one week to the next. I'd been told that I would never receive less than $50.00 a week, but I always got less! Don Palmer handled all the money, even to giving Donna any spare cash when she needed it. We were all flat broke when we arrived in Florida, but I guess Bunny was too far gone in booze to either know or care much about business matters!"[29]

Meanwhile, the band was doing fine at the Patio Room, enjoying good business, good weather, and frequent sustaining radio broadcasts. The local newspaper reported what was going on: "Headline—Berigan Back at Roosevelt: The Miracle Man Of Swing, Bunny Berigan, his trumpet and his Orchestra, featuring Danny Richards, song stylist, and Connie Klaff, are now appearing in the Patio Grill of the Hotel Roosevelt. This is a return to the Patio by Berigan, who was there last season for a lengthy engagement."[30] Mickey Irons recalled that he was billed as "Danny Richards" for that engagement, which may have been a genuine mistake or an attempt (by MCA) to cash in on Richards's undoubted popularity with the Berigan band. Band members did not think the idea came from either Bunny or Irons. It is presumed that Ms. Klaff was a singer in the hotel show, as Bunny had no female vocalist until a couple of months later. George Quinty reflected: "We had no gal singer in Florida. Mickey Irons had joined and once in a while a gal would be added for specialty numbers. Gene Kutch remembered: "I think while in Florida, Mickey Irons was using the professional name of 'Dick Ames.'"[31]

If popular big band vocalist Dick Haymes was aware of this, he likely would have been amused.

During this engagement, Bunny's sidemen and Don Palmer were beginning to become infected with Bunny's optimism about the future of the band, and as a result, they conspired to try to reduce his drinking. George Quinty remembered:

> Palmer tried to take care of Bunny. He would do all he could to keep Bunny away from the booze, which wasn't possible totally. We'd try to get Bunny to eat soup and things that were good for him. Sometimes Bunny would spike the soup, but we tried. Of course, he was Palmer's meal ticket—in fact all of ours—so we wanted him to stay healthy. But it was more than that: he was such a great guy, very gentle and fun loving. By the end of the Jacksonville engagement, Bunny's spirits and physical appearance had improved noticeably. Gene Kutch recalled:

Bunny looked tremendous! He had a great tan, and he used to wear a white suit every night. He had his hair shampooed (presumably this is a reference to the hair dying treatments that Berigan got at this time) and we got his horn cleaned up. We used to go to the beach and have a great time playing around. We'd play baseball with a beach ball.[32]

A home movie taken at the time by one of the bandsmen affords a peek at this happy group doing just that, with their leader sporting a potbelly but joining fully in the fun.[33]

Quinty also recalled the repertoire of this band: "The Berigan band book contained about 300 arrangements, many of which were by Gene Kutch and Ed Lange, and including some stocks which had been re-worked. 'Song of India' and 'Marie' were both in the book, but seldom used. We got many requests for 'Trees.' The band would open each night with 'One Look at You,' an instrumental with a very good swing, arranged by Kutch, and each set would usually include a couple of ballads and one swing tune."[34] This Berigan band, like all of its predecessors, was beginning to become an integrated performing unit and take on its own musical identity.

The Berigan band closed at the Roosevelt Hotel on October 2. After two months and two lengthy location jobs, the harshness of road life immediately struck them. Quinty reflected: "We were supposed to travel to Virginia to play the Flotella Gardens, but Bunny got a wire from Harry Moss instructing us to leave immediately for a prom in Bradford, Pennsylvania, with a stop in South Carolina en route. Those of us who had their wives along had to wake them about 1 a.m. after the job! My wife, Helen, and some of the others were dropped off in Trenton, New Jersey."[35] The Berigan band then played as directed at County Hall in Charleston, South Carolina, on October 3, and in Bradford, Pennsylvania, on October 5. They then played at Berwick Park in Wilkes-Barre, Pennsylvania, on October 6 or 7. It was at this location, only a few miles from Danny Richards's home town of Scranton, Pennsylvania, that the audience realized that the "Danny Richards" advertised by MCA as Bunny's singer was not Danny Richards at all. *Down Beat* reported about this gig: "Not a few of the 1,500 crowd out to hear Bunny Berigan's Berwick Park date were disappointed to see that Danny Richards from nearby Scranton was not among the Bunny bunch. The band sounded solid."[36] The band played another one-nighter in Pennsylvania, and then headed south again to play at the University of Richmond, Richmond, Virginia, on October 10–11.

It was at around this time that Bunny once again took on a girl singer, this time Lynne Richards, who had been singing with Harry James's band. She had to leave James after Harry hired Helen Forrest, one of the best girl singers in the business. Helen had been working rather unhappily with Benny Goodman, whose band she left several weeks earlier because of differences with BG. Ms. Forrest arrived in the James band in approximately mid-September, so it is likely that Ms. Richards would have joined the Berigan band a bit after that. James and Goodman both were being booked by MCA then, and this frequently facilitated the movement of musicians and singers from one MCA band to another. Berigan's band, by now far down the MCA pecking order, nevertheless received some benefit from the MCA band talent network.

After the Richmond date, it appears that there were some holes in the Berigan band's itinerary. During these hiatuses, the sidemen would retreat to their homes, and for most of them, that was Trenton, New Jersey, and environs. Here is a blurb from the *Hopewell* (New Jersey) *Herald,* dated October 15, 1941 that explains that this particular layoff was not because MCA could not find enough bookings for the Berigan band: "A few of Bunny Berigan's band have been spending part of the week with their fellow band member, Jack Sperling, of Hart Ave., due to cancellation of southern engagements because of the illness of their leader's father."[37] Cap Berigan was now in the final stages of battling cancer. It is not clear whether Bunny took a quick trip to Wisconsin at this time to visit his father.

The next certain play date for them was October 17, at Lehigh University, Bethlehem, Pennsylvania, followed by a one-nighter at the Raymor-Playmor twin ballrooms in Boston on October 18, where the other band appearing was Dean Hudson's. The next day, they worked three shows at the Lyric Theater in Fitchburg, Massachusetts, then were apparently off again until October 22, when they played a one-nighter at the Aragon Ballroom in Philadelphia. They were back at the Raymor/Playmor on October 24–25, this time opposite Van Alexander. They played a one-nighter at Keith's Roof Ballroom in Baltimore on Halloween, October 31, and at Manhattan Center, New York City the following night. And so it went. Although there were open dates in the band's itinerary, it seemed that for whatever reason, Bunny was now working an average of five days per week, and continued to please his audiences.

The difference now on the cost side for Bunny was that in addition to not paying his musicians a guaranteed weekly salary, he would pay each man only what he could afford each week, based on what he had taken in. The result of this strategy was that Berigan was not accruing any new debt with his musicians, and that all risk for the cost of musicians' salaries was now being borne by them, not him. This was a win-win situation, because the unknown musicians now in Bunny's band were thrilled to be playing with him, and getting good experience playing before many large and enthusiastic audiences. They were also making more money than they had been making with Al Zahler. This maneuver had undoubtedly been engineered by Don Palmer. It allowed Bunny to retain enough money each week to pay off his former sidemen, and once again begin to reduce his other debts, in addition to keeping his current band on the road. *Variety,* which along with other trade papers, had previously reported the details of Bunny's financial difficulties, now had something positive to report: "Bunny Berigan is now clear of the $844 debt he owed New York Local 802 of the American Federation of Musicians. The money represented salaries he owed his musicians when the latter quit on him a few months ago. (He since has acquired another band). Settling that puts Berigan almost in the clear of debts for once. The only money he's now under obligation for is a small amount in government taxes."[38]

On November 3, the day after Bunny's thirty-third birthday, this Berigan band, after being together under Bunny's leadership for only three months, made its first recordings. The recordings they made that day were not regular commercial records, but rather were special promotional discs sponsored by the Pepsi-Cola Company to be used in promotion of the Pepsi-Cola product. For most of the musicians in the Berigan band, this would be their first experience making recordings. Great excitement and enthusiasm pervaded the band as they approached this rather modest project. "Pepsi-Cola Hits the Spot" is a two minute and forty-three second jingle that has vocalist Georgia Gibbs, then known as Fredda Gibson, singing with the Berigan band. After listening carefully to a recording of this jingle,[39] I think that the arrangement was done by Gene Kutch because of the characteristic way he voiced the brass. (See the comments below regarding Kutch's arrangements as played by the Berigan band on its Elite recordings.) The band, which is well rehearsed, swings on this, and Bunny plays a rather swaggering, though melodic, solo. A second jingle, "Get Hep with Pepsi Cola," which was definitely arranged by Gene Kutch, was also recorded, but without a vocal. The first title has been issued by IAJRC; the second has not been issued commercially. Kutch's diary reports that he was paid $30 for the recording session,[40] plus extra no doubt for the arrangements he wrote. This small bonus helped to offset those weeks on the road where the musicians had worked only a few nights. In the wake of this positive and profitable experience, Bunny continued to tell his sidemen that better days were just ahead. He probably announced at this time that he had secured another commercial recording contract, and that the band would soon be making records. It seems that Don Palmer's efforts on behalf of Bunny and the band were beginning to show some positive results.

After this recording date, the band again took to the road, heading south once more, to North Carolina State University at Raleigh to play dances there on Friday and Saturday evenings, November 7 and 8, with an afternoon tea dance, also on Saturday. During this engagement, Bunny was notified that his gravely ill father was not expected to live much longer. It is not clear if he left the Raleigh job on November 8 to go to the bedside of his dying father in Madison, or completed the gig then rushed to Wisconsin. Knowing Bunny's work habits, and his desire not to disappoint his fans (and MCA), I suspect it was the latter.

Bunny's sister-in-law, Loretta, reported what transpired after Bunny arrived on an airplane just before Cap's passing: Cap had

...cancer all through his body. We were all hard hit by it, and when Bunny came home all that activity is somewhat of a blur. I've heard that his manager, Don Palmer, came home with him, but I remember Bunny being alone. He looked just terrible: he was tired and drawn; his face was full of grief; his hair was dyed; his teeth were stained; and he was drinking a lot. But none of us suspected that Bunny was really sick. His father died in the hospital in Madison and was laid out in the home of Bunny's uncle, Dave Schlitzberg. Bunny hardly seemed to pay any attention to any member of his family; he seemed to be in a daze. His father died early in the morning on November 11, and the funeral was on the thirteenth. I just can't remember how Bunny came to town and how he left, but I'm sure he wasn't able to stay for the funeral service. And one thing I'll always remember: I was standing next to Bunny as he went up to view his father in the casket. He put his hand on him and said, 'Dad, I'll be there with you in six months.'[41]

The local Fox Lake newspaper carried the following information several days after the funeral of William Patrick Berigan: "Among those who attended the funeral services for W.P. Berigan last Thursday (November 13) were Bunny Berigan and Don Palmer, of New York City."[42]

Distraught over the death of his father, and exhausted by the return trip on a primitive airliner to rejoin his band the next night (November 14) at Convention Hall in Camden, New Jersey, Bunny sequestered himself in his hotel room that evening. *Billboard* reported how this was handled by MCA:

Headline: Shaw's Ex-leaders Pinch One-Nighter For Berigan: When Bunny Berigan was stricken with illness on his return last Friday (14th) from his father's funeral, ex-wand wavers currently with Artie Shaw took over the band chores to save the date. Bunny was scheduled to play a Police Benevolent Association dance. The Shaw band opened the same day at the Earle Theatre in Philadelphia. Jack Lear, MCA publicity chief, found Berigan sick at the hotel and got union permission for Jack Jenney, Georgie Auld, Dave Tough and others to come here following the theatre shows to fill out the night for Berigan.[43]

It may have been at this time that Bunny's old friend, Lou Hanks, from Wisconsin, visited him: "The last time I saw Bunny was in late 1941 in New Jersey. He was staying at the Stacy-Trent Hotel, I think, and I went up to visit him in his hotel room. Bunny was asleep when I entered the room and looked like death. He was unshaven and unkempt and began drinking as soon as he awoke. We talked over old times long into the night, although the phone kept ringing and he'd pick it up and say, 'I'm here with an old friend, I'll be down soon.' He looked so bad, not like old Bun at all."[44]

Bunny and the band then headed from Camden to a one-nighter at Williams College, Williamstown, Massachusetts, the next night, November 15. From there, the only dates on which we are certain the band played were November 19, near Hyde Park, New York, and November 21–22, at the El Rancho Club, near Chester, Pennsylvania. It is likely that from that date, Bunny brought the band back to New York for a day of rehearsal (November 23) before its all-important recording date on November 24, for Eli Oberstein's Elite label. Bunny was very familiar with Oberstein from their prior association when Oberstein was a Victor recording executive and Berigan was recording for that label. Oberstein had an extremely commercial orientation, and while at Victor was largely responsible for Berigan recording dozens of ordinary and sometimes poor pop tunes. That approach had certainly carried over to his own recording enterprise, as the recordings Bunny would make for the Elite label show. Once again, Bunny Berigan would have to prove himself on records before he would be allowed to have any input into what his band was allowed to record. The band Bunny took into the recording studios (possibly those of World Recording, the old NBC studios, 711 Fifth Avenue, near Fifty-fifth) that day consisted of the following musicians: Bob Mansell, Fred Norton, Addison W. Parris, trumpets; Max Smith, Charlie Stewart, trombones; George Quinty, Walter Mellor, Wilbur Joustra, Edmar Lange, saxophones; Gene Kutch, piano; Tony Espen, bass; Jack Sperling, drums; Lynne Richards, vocals.[45] Vocalist Mickey Irons was deemed too inexperienced to participate in this recording session.

This would mark the first commercial recording date for Bunny Berigan leading his own band since November 28, 1939, his final recording date for RCA Victor. In the interim, he had toured with the late 1940-early 1941 band, which had good arrangements by Andy Fitzgerald and Frank Crolene, and the talented vocalist Danny Richards. That band, which by all accounts was very good, did not make any commercial records. Prior to his last Victor session, Bunny, who at that time (1939) was playing magnificently on many occasions, had an excellent band (at least until conclusion of the Loew's State Theater engagement in August), good arrangements, and Danny Richards on vocals. But again, it made no commercial recordings. It is difficult to explain this. A perfect time to have recorded the 1939 Berigan band would have been during their long engagement at the Sherman Hotel in Chicago in the summer of 1939. The revenue from one or two recording sessions then might have averted the financial debacle that occurred in August of that year. But at the time, Bunny had no personal manager and quite possibly no recording contract. By the time those last Victor records were made in late November 1939, Bunny was exhausted and on the brink of an illness that would put him in the hospital for several days. Those recordings, though professionally done, are not among his best.

Throughout the period from early 1939 until the mutiny of the musicians who were with Berigan into the early summer of 1941, with the exception of the time Bunny was with Tommy Dorsey, his vocalist was the excellent Danny Richards. Richards sang in a robust, virile baritone that had a lot in common with Jimmy Dorsey's star vocalist Bob Eberly. In addition to his fine voice quality, Danny appeared to have been a musicianly singer with good range, relaxed phrasing, a perfectly controlled vibrato, and an exceptional sense of pitch. The information that is available indicates that in the 1939–1941 period, Bunny was steadily providing Richards with good arrangements of current pop tunes (some of which later became standards) to sing with his band, and that Danny's efforts were received very warmly by audiences. Nevertheless, Danny Richards never made a commercial recording with Bunny Berigan's band during all of the time he had previously been one of its members. He would not do so on the November 24, 1941, Berigan recording session because he was then still touring with Pee Wee Erwin's band. Insofar as making commercial recordings with Bunny Berigan, Danny Richards had some very bad luck. This is unfortunate because many vocalists who were inferior to Richards frequently recorded with a multitude of bands during the big band era. Richards could have and should have been used by Berigan's handlers to help Bunny make and sell more records during his 1939–1941 tenure as Bunny's boy singer. His time to record with Berigan would eventually come, but it would be on what turned out to be Bunny's last recording date.

Bunny used vocalist Lynne Richards on all four tunes he recorded on November 24. The first one "I Got It Bad (And That Ain't Good)" composed by Duke Ellington, soon became a standard, but then it was new. Paul Francis Webster wrote the lyric. The arrangement Berigan used is attributed to Edgar Sampson,[46] who had established a good reputation as the composer/arranger of swing originals like "Blue Lou," "Stompin' at the Savoy," and "Don't Be That Way," and the marvelous "Lullaby in Rhythm," but it has no discernable Sampson trademarks. From the workmanlike sound of this arrangement, it could have been written by any competent arranger. The band, which had been a somewhat ragtag bunch of semiprofessionals only three months before, now sounds well rehearsed and integrated. Bunny states the melody on his open trumpet against the reeds, and is followed by Wilbur "Weebee" Joustra on tenor sax, backed by brass shadings. Joustra plays the bridge. The vocal chorus has Ms. Richards singing with a rather sparse background of only the rhythm section, Kutch's piano being most audible. Bunny plays a cup-muted obbligato during most of the vocal chorus. This segment, though done well enough, would have benefited from some subtle background sounds (harmonic "pads") provided by the reeds and brass. As it is, Ms. Richards and Bunny sound kind of forlorn. (Maybe that was what the arranger intended.) After the vocal, Bunny returns with an open trumpet solo to finish the performance. Except during the vocal chorus, drummer Jack Sperling plays a heavy back-beat, which I'm sure Bunny instructed him to do. It is effective in the last chorus, when the ensembles are playing, less so in the early part of the arrangement.

"The White Cliffs of Dover" is a tearjerker composed (words by Nat Burton, music by Walter Kent) in the early days of World War II, when the British were sustaining daily devastating *Luftwaffe* bombing raids. This arrangement, by band member Red Lange, though rather straightforward, is very effectively constructed to present the singing of Lynne Richards in an optimal fashion. Alto saxophonist George Quinty is heard to advantage in the first chorus leading his section mates. The brass section is equally skillful in their interpretation of this arrangement. Ms. Richards sounds as relaxed as possible singing what is sometimes a rather maudlin lyric. After the vocal, Bunny plays intermittently with a cup mute and an open trumpet. In the final chorus, the saxophones are voiced with an alto (Quinty, playing lead), two tenors, and the third alto, Walt Mellor, playing baritone. It is an effective voicing which gives the four reeds a much more robust sound.[47]

"'Tis Autumn" was composed (words and music) by "The Neem," Henry Nemo, a denizen of Fifty-second Street, and Berigan acquaintance since Bunny's glory days on that street of jazz. This tune was very much in the air as a new pop hit in late 1941. Bunny states the melody in the first chorus with an open trumpet. His playing here is uniquely Berigan—his sound and phrasing are quintessential. Ms. Richards does a fine job delivering the lyric. The band sounds very good throughout this performance. The arrangement by Gene Kutch is certainly on a par with what the top bands of the day were playing, and recording.

"Two in Love" is the only tune recorded that day that hints at the band's ability to swing. It was another current pop tune that had been recorded quite well by Tommy Dorsey with Frank Sinatra on August 19, 1941. It was composed (words and music) by music man Meredith Willson. The arrangement is again ascribed to Edgar Sampson, and sounds much more like his work than the previously recorded "I Got It Bad," especially the pointillistic rhythmic backgrounds that keep the music bright and swinging. Bunny plays only a brief solo in the first chorus, and Joustra a short modulation leading into the vocal. The performance would have benefited from a swinging Berigan solo after the vocal, but instead ends then, rather abruptly, clocking in at a mere two minutes and thirty-two seconds.

Bunny's return to commercial records after a two-year hiatus was only moderately successful from the musical standpoint, which was always his paramount concern. It is clear from the recordings he made on November 24, 1941, that his playing was still quite good, though certainly not on a par with his greatest work. On the other hand, not much was really required of him on these recordings. Was that because he was now unable to deliver, or because Oberstein wanted him to make rather bland, middle-of-the road dance records? To my ears, his unique trumpet sound was still intact, lovely and warm, and his phrasing was relaxed. However his playing had evolved rhythmically to the point where it was almost *rubato.* If one listens to these recordings and then goes back to "The Buzzard" (December 1935), or "Let's Do It" (February 1937), when Bunny was really hopping, one finds a definite rhythmic evolution. Again, was this because Berigan's physical trumpet playing mechanism had deteriorated as a result of too much liquor and too many one-nighters, or because he was taking his playing into a looser, freer rhythmic realm? (We must also factor in that Bunny was undoubtedly still grieving for his recently deceased father.)

The band Berigan presented on these recordings was good. He had once again taken a group of musicians (some of whom were only semipros) and molded them into a cohesive professional-sounding band. Much has been said over the years about Bunny's supposed lax leadership, but very little has been said about his ability to gather disparate musicians, some having limited ability, and make them sound good when playing together within a relatively short time. These recordings clearly document his ability in that regard, and listening to them makes it is easy to understand why Bunny, Don Palmer, and the members of his band were optimistic about the future of this organization.

But these are *musical* considerations. No band could thrive, indeed a band could not even exist, without someone dealing skillfully with the *business* challenges that were constantly presenting themselves. With Don Palmer seemingly making the right managerial moves, it seems that Berigan had finally employed someone who tried to look after *his* business interests. Palmer obviously understood that Bunny's financial interests were not the same as MCA's financial interests. Under Palmer's guidance, Bunny had at last controlled the payroll of his band. He now paid his musicians only for the dates they played, rather than paying them a fixed weekly salary, and in addition, he adjusted the weekly payout commensurate with the week's receipts. This business arrangement was possible only because the musicians Bunny was now using to staff his band were unknowns, who, irrespective of their skills, had not developed professional reputations. His leadership abilities and renown as a musician enabled him to weld them into a good, if not excellent band, and to retain their services during the frequent gaps in the work schedule set by MCA. Presumably, Palmer had also been the one to consummate the deal that got Bunny back onto commercial records, albeit with a small label having only limited distribution. By the end of 1941, Berigan had almost completely retired his various debts.

This business *modus operandi* also allowed Bunny some flexibility in his personal work schedule. Palmer may well have been cultivating opportunities for Berigan to have a work life away from his band. As we shall see, a golden opportunity would soon come his way that would require his services, but not those of his band, and with the assistance of Palmer, he was able to take advantage of it without fear of losing his band. I believe that if Bunny's health had not begun to disintegrate early in 1942, he would have had more and more opportunities to work in a much wider variety of musical settings, and could well have established an economic base as a trumpet soloist, independent of a constantly touring band, or of confining and stultifying studio and freelance recording work.

But in spite of all of the positive signs in Berigan's career as 1941 ended, there was still an elephant in the room: his chronic alcoholism, and the devastating effect it was now having on his severely damaged liver. Bunny's drinking, like that of any chronic alcoholic, had escalated steadily over the years. By late 1941, he simply needed more booze each day to function than he had needed previously. To those not acquainted with his needs in this regard, indeed, to those with whom he worked on a daily basis, his intake of alcohol was shockingly large. In Bunny's view, he was controlling his drinking, taking just enough so that he could function. Although ominous signs were beginning to appear concerning his health, he put a good face on them, and told anyone who would listen that this band would soon be the best he ever led.

After the November 24 recording date, the Berigan band played a few scattered one-nighters, then landed a one-night gig at the Pennsylvania Hotel Roof in New York City on December 5. It was Bunny's first return to the Penn since his successful run there in the spring and early summer of 1937, when he was building his name as a bandleader. Vocalist Mickey Irons recalled that gig rather wistfully:

> That was my last date with the band. Glenn Miller's band was occupying the Café Rouge room and we played on the Roof. By that time, Bunny's drinking was definitely interfering with jobs or the lack of them. He spent a lot of time in his hotel room, alone. Donna would only travel with us occasionally. He was going through at least a dozen bottles of Calvert's Special a week! The band-boy had the job of filling a Coke bottle with the stuff and it would be passed along the sax section to the piano, where it stood within easy reach of Bunny throughout the set. I wonder who he thought he was kidding? I'd gotten my draft notice and I thought I'd be going into the service pretty soon, so I said goodbye to Bunny and the rest of the guys.[48]

In the wake of the departure of Mickey Irons, Bunny found himself in need of a male vocalist. It is not known if Lynne Richards remained with the Berigan band for very long after the November 24 recording session, but probably by the time Irons left, Bunny had both a new male *and female* vocalist, and they were married to each other. Danny Richards recalled how he came to join the Berigan band for the third time:

> Kay (Little) and I had gotten married while we were working with the old Berigan band under Pee Wee Erwin. *(sic)* By that time, very few of Bunny's former musicians were still with Pee Wee, and in early December 1941, we got a call from Don Palmer asking us both if we would consider rejoining Bunny. We said OK and joined the band in Trenton, New Jersey, while they were on a short layoff. I fronted the band a couple of times when Bunny was 'sick,' and some of the men suggested I take it over. Bunny seemed less sure of himself than before when I was with the band in 1939 and 40-41, and he now would break out in a heavy sweat when working hard on the bandstand.[49]

In spite of the confusion and anxiety caused by the Japanese attack on Pearl Harbor on December 7, 1941, the balance of that month was fairly busy for the Berigan band: December 6, at the Elk's Club, Heampstead, New York; December 7, at the Tic-Toc Club in Boston. (Here is how that gig was advertised: "In Person: Bunny Berigan and his orchestra—Sunday only! December 7. First show at 2 o'clock, continuous all day. Six vaudeville acts, Joe Neville's ork. No Cover. Tic-Toc, 245 Tremont—opposite the Met Theatre."[50])

From there they played a two-or three-day engagement at the Astor Theater, Reading, Pennsylvania; then a one-nighter at the Moose Lodge in Lancaster, Pennsylvania, on the 12th; then a gig at the Foot Guard Armory in Hartford, Connecticut, opposite Louis Prima's band. Young Jack Sperling's competitive instincts were aroused on that date: "I particularly remember that date. Louis Prima's drummer was Jimmy Vincent, and on one number Louis gave him a long drum solo which had the kids yelling for more. I kept begging Bunny to let me do my specialty, but he said no."[51] Nevertheless, this engagement was a rousing success: "A last minute switch threw a scheduled 'Salute to the Troops' Ball from the State Armory in Hartford, Connecticut, to the antiquated Foot Guard Armory on Saturday night (13th). Approximately 3,500 persons attended the affair. Music was provided by Bunny Berigan and Louis Prima."[52]

After this series of dates, it appears that MCA resorted once again to the band-booking dartboard to fill in dates for the Berigan ensemble: December 19, Sanford Armory, Sanford, North Carolina; the 20th, Cherokee Country Club, Knoxville, Tennessee; the 25th, Christmas night, at Waldamere Park, Erie, Pennsylvania; then a backbreaking jump of 450 miles on December 26 to Hotel Du Pont, Wilmington, Delaware; and finally a return to the Pennsylvania Roof in Manhattan on the 27th.

It was at this engagement that two of Bunny's idolaters came to visit. Trumpeter John Best, whose playing always reflected his admiration for Berigan, (hear his great solo on Glenn Miller's classic recording of "Star Dust"), remembered: "Bobby Hackett and I were with Glenn Miller at the Pennsylvania Hotel, and Bunny had his band up on the Penn Roof playing for a private party. Bobby said 'Let's go up and hear Bunny during our intermission.' So we did, and Bunny came over and spoke to us. We were amazed. Bunny looked terrible to me; his eyes could hardly focus. Bunny cracked: 'There's a rumor goin' around that I'm no longer alive. Ain't I the damnest looking ghost you ever saw?' I'll never forget that."[53] I wonder if John and Bobby asked Bunny where he had been over the previous several weeks, or where he was going in the next few days?

There were still more road dates to complete before the end of the year. December 28, Newark, New Jersey; the 29th, Scott High School, Coatsville, Pennsylvania; Milford Armory, Milford, Delaware on the 30th; and finally, after travelling overnight some 300 miles in the winter into the mountains of Pennsylvania, December 31, 1941, at the Jaffa Mosque Masonic Temple, Altoona, Pennsylvania.[54]

Notes

[1] *Down Beat:* August 15, 1941, cited in the White materials.

[2] *Variety:* August 6, 1941, cited in the White materials.

[3] White materials: July 30, 1941.

[4] *Trenton Magazine:* June 1967, cited in the White materials: July 30, 1941.

[5] White materials: July 30, 1941.

[6] *This Horn for Hire, the Career and Life of Pee Wee Erwin,* as told to Warren W. Vaché, Scarecrow Press and the Institute of Jazz Studies, Rutgers University (1987), 185.

[7] *Music and Rhythm:* August 1941, cited in the White materials: July 29, 1941.

[8] *Ibid.*

[9] *Ibid.*

[10] White materials: July 31, 1941.

[11] *Ibid.*

[12] *Ibid.*

[13] Gene Kutch's diary was obtained from Kutch by Robert Dupuis, who turned over a copy to Bozy White.

[14] White materials: August 1, 1941.

[15] White materials: August 2, 1941.

[16] There were two ballrooms at Buckeye Lake: the Crystal, where the Berigan band played, and the Pier. Apparently for the 1941 season, Buckeye Lake's management referred to the Crystal as the Danceteria.

[17] *Down Beat:* September 1, 1941, cited in the White materials.

[18] Saxophonist/singer Gordon Lee "Tex" Beneke was born on February 12, 1914, in Ft. Worth, Texas. He is remembered most for the work he did with the Glenn Miller band from 1938–1942. Miller featured his singing prominently, mostly on rhythm tunes and novelties, and as a result, he became well known to the public. After military service in World War II, Beneke led bands off and on for the next fifty years, always highlighting his good-natured singing. He died on May 30, 2000, in Costa Mesa, California.

[19] White materials: August 2, 1941.

[20] *Ibid.*

[21] *Down Beat:* September 1, 1941, cited in the White materials.

[22] *Ibid.*

[23] *Ibid.*

[24] White materials: September 4, 1941.

[25] White materials: September 7, 1941.

[26] Dupuis: 251.

[27] White materials: September 7, 1941.

[28] Interview of Jack Sperling by Robert Dupuis; Dupuis archive, UW–Madison.

[29] *Ibid.*

[30] *Jacksonville Journal:* September 10, 1941, cited in the White materials.

[31] White materials: September 10, 1941.

[32] Dupuis: 235

[33] *Ibid.*

[34] White materials: September 28, 1941.

[35] White materials: October 2, 1941.

[36] *Down Beat:* November 1, 1941, cited in the White materials.

[37] The information from the October 15, 1941, *Hopewell Herald* provided by Carl A. Hallstrom.

[38] *Variety:* November 12, 1941, cited in the White materials.

[39] I must thank Perry Huntoon for providing me with a dub of the "Pepsi-Cola Hits the Spot" recording.

[40] White materials: November 4, 1941.

[41] Dupuis: 236.

[42] *Fox Lake Representative:* November 20, 1941, cited in the White materials. The marker on the grave of William Patrick Berigan states that he was born in 1872.

[43] *Billboard:* November 29, 1941, cited in the White materials.

[44] White materials: November 14, 1941.

[45] White materials: November 24, 1941.

[46] *Ibid.* The White materials state that the identification of Edgar Sampson as arranger of "I Got It Bad" was verified by Gene Kutch, Ed Lange, and George Quinty.

[47] A similar four-saxophone voicing (with alto saxophonist Hank Freeman playing the baritone sax) was used to great effect by Artie Shaw's swinging 1939 band. "Serenade to a Savage," "Them There Eyes," "My Blue Heaven," "St. Louis Blues," "El Rancho Grande," and "Shadows" are some examples. Duke Ellington had used variations on this

blend of saxophone sounds throughout the 1930s, before the arrival of the fifth saxophone player in his band, tenor saxophonist Ben Webster.

[48] White materials: December 5, 1941.

[49] White materials: mid-December 1941.

[50] *Boston Daily Record:* December 5–6, 1941, cited in the White materials.

[51] White materials: December 13, 1941.

[52] *Variety:* December 17, 1941, cited in the White materials.

[53] Dupuis: 283, from an interview of John Best by Norm Krusinski, ca. 1987. Norm Krusinski was an avid Berigan fan and collected much Berigan memorabilia. This memorabilia is now a part of a Berigan collection at the Mills Music Library at the University of Wisconsin at Madison.

[54] White materials: December 27, 1941.

Chapter 24
No Exit

On the first of January 1942, an exhausted Bunny Berigan entrained at Grand Central Terminal heading for Hollywood. He arrived at Union Station in Los Angeles on January 4. The next day, he reported to the soundstage at the RKO Studio to begin work on the soundtrack for the feature film then in production called *Syncopation*. *Down Beat* reported the particulars:

> Headline: Bunny Gets the Call—When You hear Jackie Cooper apparently playing cornet in the new RKO film, *Syncopation*,[1] that will actually be Bunny Berigan's horn you'll hear pouring out golden notes. Bunny has been signed by producer William Dieterle to record the soundtrack, which will supply music for the Cooper scenes. He reported for work on January 5. Also in the picture is Rex Stewart, who enacts a role somewhat reminiscent of the great forerunner of today's hot trumpet men, Buddy Bolden. Stewart, a member of the Duke Ellington orchestra, also recorded the music to go with his impersonation. Said Leith Stevens musical director of *Syncopation* concerning Bunny Berigan: 'We selected Bunny, not only because we believe him to be one of the best in the country, but also because his musical style seemed to fit with the character played by Jackie Cooper. Cooper does not represent any one musician, but is a composite of several great trumpet players.'[2]

While Bunny was in Hollywood, Don Palmer stayed with the Berigan band in the east. He reassured the band's members that Bunny would return in a few weeks and that MCA had lined up a lot of work for them. The band kept in trim by playing a few dates while Bunny was gone, being led on them by Danny Richards. However, audiences were not interested in the Bunny Berigan band without Bunny. This experience immediately demonstrated to the sidemen and everyone else connected with the band that even though the musicians were the same, and the quality of their performances was pretty much the same as when Bunny fronted, without Bunny the band had little or no identity, and held scant appeal for audiences. Berigan's sidemen decided that it was in their best interest to wait for their charismatic leader to return. There were no defections during the month Bunny was away.

Meanwhile, Bunny began his work in Hollywood on the soundtrack of the film *Syncopation*. Many musicians who had met Berigan previously but had not seen him recently were shocked at his shrunken physical appearance and apparent lack of strength and stamina. Pianist Stan Wrightsman worked on the film with him: "Bunny was brought out by MCA and was paid $1,500 for 15 days

451

work. He certainly was in poor shape and had lost an awful lot of weight, which I'm sure had sapped his stamina. He just couldn't get through the long parts, so he was told to start low and work up to the high notes. He just hadn't got it, though, and almost all the parts had to be fixed up so they could get enough soundtrack to use. The men from the small band were freelancers around Hollywood and hired to do the small band sequences only."[3]

One of Bunny's former first trumpeters, Johnny Napton, also encountered Berigan under rather strange circumstances: "I was working with Jan Savitt on the west coast and Bunny got me out of bed one morning at 5 a.m. to ask if he could borrow my horn! He explained that his had gotten mislaid somehow and he needed one for his job at RKO that morning. He looked terrible, as sick as hell!"[4] We do not know if Bunny was drinking more to cope with the challenges of the work he was being asked to do, or drinking less to try to be less under the influence of alcohol, thus triggering the DTs. Or, was the cirrhosis shutting down his liver function, causing him to look and feel progressively worse?

What is certain however is that Berigan was outside his zone of security, and away from his support group (Palmer and his band), and when that happened, his intake of alcohol usually increased. *Down Beat* featured an article about what Bunny was required to do to earn the $100 a day he was being paid:

> Headline: Trumpeters Sweat in Studio as they 'Make Up Music': In a big barn-like soundstage at RKO, Bunny Berigan and George Thow are sitting side by side, day after day, performing one of the most unusual jobs ever tossed at a musician. Under the direction of Leith Stevens,[5] they are 'dubbing' the trumpet solos which play an important part in RKO's cavalcade of jazz, *Syncopation.* In most work of this kind, the soundtrack is recorded first and the actors are photographed while they listen to a playback and synchronize their actions to the music. But in this case, the picture was completed first and now the trumpeters have to watch the picture and improvise passages that will fit the action on the screen, even to the finger movements of the actors on the valves on the instruments in their hands. Berigan and Thow, who do the sound for two characters in the picture who are supposed to be trumpet players, have no orchestra nor accompaniment to back them up while working in many cases, though they have to add the trumpet solos to music which has already been recorded. They listen to the music through earphones and record the trumpet solos, which will be mixed with the original soundtrack.[6]

Although Berigan started the project in fair condition, as the demands and frustration of his work assignment increased, so apparently did his intake of alcohol. Consequently, his physical condition deteriorated, as did his ability to play the trumpet well. Bassist Budd Hatch also worked on this project with Bunny: "I had never worked with Bunny before, in fact I'd never even met him. The men in the small band were used only in the sequences seen on the screen as a small band. The rest of the score was performed by the regular RKO studio orchestra. Bunny played OK when he first arrived, but he drank more and more as the days went by and just couldn't handle the long parts. George Thow did a lot of the work originally assigned to Bunny."[7] Thow, who had replaced Bunny in the Dorsey Brothers Orchestra in 1934, recalled how the project was eventually completed:

> Dave Torbett, who was the arranger, said that Rex Stewart was 'inadequate,' can you imagine? So Bunny was hired to do all the featured trumpet spots, even though he was in pretty bad shape when he reported to the studio, and as his condition became more apparent to Leith Stevens, I was assigned much more of the work. I was originally scheduled to record parts played by the little colored boy on the screen. Subsequently, I was delegated to do parts played on the screen by Jackie Cooper. In the end, I did most of the trumpet playing in the movie, with the exception of a high-note sequence done by Bunny and, later, doctored up by Gene La Freniere, who was under contract to RKO. Bunny wasn't fired and was paid in full.[8]

Trumpeter Gene La Freniere's recollection adds a bit more clarity, perhaps: RKO had no regular studio orchestra at that time, but I was first call on trumpet and did plenty of free-lance work. I was called by the studio to remake some of Bunny's parts, even though he was still around.[9]

I have recently acquired a copy of *Syncopation,* and have been able to listen to the soundtrack carefully and repeatedly, and draw some conclusions as to how much of Berigan's trumpet playing is a part of the finished film. Despite the comments above by musicians who worked on the soundtrack with Bunny, I am of the opinion that a good bit of his playing is there, and what is there is of high quality. The sequences listed in appendix 6 sound very much like Berigan's playing, and if they are not, whoever played them was doing a superb impersonation of Bunny.

When Berigan was not on the soundstage at RKO, he found many friends with whom to share his time. One of these was Ray Linn, the young trumpet player with whom he had worked during the Tommy Dorsey interlude in 1940. Linn recalled a typically Beriganesque episode:

> I remember the last time I saw Bunny. He was in Hollywood working on the soundtrack of a movie at RKO studios and I was with Woody Herman's band making a movie at Universal Studios. Tommy Dorsey was playing at the Hollywood Palladium and most of his musicians stayed at the Plaza Hotel, a very swinging joint situated just a few steps from Hollywood Boulevard on Vine Street. All the musicians stayed there. I say 'stayed,' because very few actually ever slept there! Joey Bushkin and Chuck Peterson from Tommy's band came up to my room with Bunny, who had somehow learned that I was the proud possessor of a brand new .38 super Colt automatic pistol. Despite the fact that it was about 3 a.m., showing the gun to Bunny and allowing him to handle it wasn't enough for him. He actually wanted to fire it! He refused to leave with the other two guys until I placed a cartridge in the chamber and led him into the bathroom. We both stepped into the empty bathtub and I opened the window. While I held his wrist steady, he fired the lone round straight upwards into the early morning air. Fortunately, the street below was deserted, so I guess no one in the hotel

would have any idea where the shot came from. We heard some voices out in the hallway immediately after the shot, but I guess our little caper went totally undetected. I was only 21 then, so possibly might have been excused such an act, but Bunny was about 33 and should have been the steadying influence. But the expression on his face after pulling the trigger was the happiest smile I ever saw! It was the smile of a happy schoolboy. I guess he never did really grow up.[10]

Bunny also spent weekends visiting bands playing in the Manhattan Beach–Redondo Beach areas, sometimes sitting in. Although his body was collapsing from the inside, and his ability to perform on trumpet was erratic, his love of playing and the excitement of jazz were still very much a part of his makeup.

As one would expect, Bunny went to visit Tommy Dorsey and his band at the Palladium. Joe Bushkin, who was still TD's pianist, vividly recalled what happened:

We were playing a Sunday matinee at the Palladium. The place was jammed with people, and we look out in the audience, and there's Bunny standing there. Tommy stopped the band in the middle of the tune. He said: 'Ladies and gentlemen, a great personal friend and a wonderful musician is with us today—Bunny Berigan!' The audience went up in smoke, really excited. Tommy says, 'Come on up and play something Bunny.' Bunny's already got his afternoon 'load' on and he says, 'I haven't got my mouthpiece with me.' Ziggy Elman offered Bunny his trumpet, and we were going to do 'I Can't Get Started.' He just started to play it, and I don't know if it was Ziggy's mouthpiece or what the hell it was, but he was in trouble. Bunny couldn't get through it. It absolutely tore us up, man![11]

This incident had to have occurred before January 19, because that was the date Joe Bushkin left the Tommy Dorsey band to go into the army.[12]

Meanwhile, back in the east, Danny Richards was fronting the Berigan band on Saturdays and Sundays at the El Rancho Club in Chester, Pennsylvania, just south of Philadelphia. Rumors of all kinds were filtering back to the band about Bunny in Hollywood. This bit of "information" appeared in *Variety* on January 21, 1942:

Bunny Berigan's band is to join its leader in California on February 13, to open a four weeks stay at the Casa Manana, Culver City. Film work and four weeks at the Casa Manana is expected to finally erase all the debts Berigan had when he returned to leadership last year. He picked up the baton more than $14,000 in the red to AFM, hotels, etc., but under the direction of Harry Moss, MCA executive, who has been handling his affairs, the debt has been whittled down to little more than $3,000. His current outfit is his second, his first having walked out en masse on him about six months ago, because of wages.[13]

Billboard reported more of the same: "Bunny Berigan will remain in California after completing work on 'Young Man With A Horn' *(sic)* picture. His band will go out there to join him at Casa Manana, opening February 13."[14] Then, unceremoniously, this appeared in *Variety*: "Jack Teagarden's band goes into the Casa Manana, Culver City on February 13, in place of Bunny Berigan. Berigan may fulfill his contract later."[15] Had MCA really been trying to get Bunny the gig at the Casa Manana, or was this simply a ruse to keep his underemployed band members from quitting as a group, or going to another leader? Whatever the case, Berigan's band members, with Don Palmer's constant reassurance, had waited for him to return.

Berigan completed his work in California by the end of January and rejoined his band in Cincinnati, Ohio, for a two-night engagement at the University of Cincinnati on February 6–7. Evidently he was not happy with the sound of the band upon his return because he rehearsed them for four hours at some time during this engagement. It was at this gig that the "permanent" replacement for tenor saxophonist Weebee Joustra, Neal Smith, joined the Berigan band. Joustra and Bunny had come to a parting of the ways as a result of Bunny asking the band members to sign a photo for a fan, and Joustra refusing.[16] This had happened shortly before the November 24 recording date, and after Joustra left in early December, Red Lange took over the jazz tenor and clarinet solos, and Bunny had used a series of subs to cover Joustra's chair.

Tenor saxophonist Neal Smith remembered the scene when he joined Bunny:

> I joined Bunny Berigan in Cincinnati, Ohio. The band's arrangements were being written mainly by Gene Kutch, with a few by Van Alexander, as well as the things from his old book. Bunny could still play with fire and inspiration some nights. When he was ON, he was magnificent. There was a glorious sound from that horn, low, middle or high registers, but he always seemed to need encouragement. He was a tired man by then—a worn out shell at 33—but he was always a gentleman and very kind to my wife and me. I was proud to have known him and to have played with him.[17]

From Cincinnati, Bunny returned to the Aragon Ballroom in Cleveland, where he had always been received warmly, for a one-nighter on February 8. The next day, he rehearsed the men once again, for an upcoming theater engagement. They then moved on to a one-nighter at the Aragon Ballroom in Pittsburgh on February 10. Evidently Bunny and the band pleased the Pittsburgh dancers: "Bunny Berigan has been top grosser for traveling bands at the Aragon Ballroom here (Pittsburgh) so far this season. The old Mose Temple Auditorium has been converted into the Aragon Ballroom last fall and has been conducting three public dances per week and renting the room out on other nights. Berigan is due to return soon."[18] The band then traveled to Olean, New York, where they played three shows at the Palace Theater on February 11. After this, they returned to northeast Ohio, to play a dance date at the Nu-Elms Ballroom in Youngstown, Ohio, on the 12th. Just before the gig, new sideman Neal Smith attempted to have a conversation with Berigan: "That was a very snowy day and I got the chance to talk to Bunny before the job. I tried to sound him out about his drinking, his general health and his future—to try to get close to the man inside the man so to speak. He just looked at me in a strange kind of way and said, 'Don't you worry about me, Neal, I just *know*.' But he wouldn't elaborate and left me guessing whether he was making some kind of prediction or not."[19]

Gault, Ontario was the next stop, where the band played at the Highlands Hotel on the 13th. Bunny's fixation with shooting expressed itself again, in a typically juvenile way. Jack Sperling remembered: "We arrived in Gault very early in the morning and we sent the band-boy off to look for food and coffee while we did a little sightseeing. There was a church in the square in the middle of the town and the clock in the church-tower was lit up. Bunny had brought along his air rifle and he tried to shoot out the light in the clock tower."[20] The bedraggled musicians returned once again to northeast Ohio, this time to the Aragon Ballroom in Cleveland, where they played a Valentine's Day dance on February 14. They remained in Cleveland the next two days, staying at the Alberton Hotel, rehearsing for about three hours each day.[21]

On February 17, Bunny and company played a dance date at the Rainbow Gardens Ballroom in Fremont, Ohio. The gig, a policeman's ball, ran from 10:00 p.m. to 3:00 a.m. Kutch's diary contained this cryptic entry for that date: "What a Ball! Left for Columbus, Ohio, 3:00 a.m."[22] In Columbus, the band had an off day on the 18th, resting at the Chittenden Hotel. They left Columbus at 7:30 a.m. on the 19th for Baltimore, where they arrived at 7:30 p.m. (approximately 430 miles on 1942 roads in the winter) for a gig at the Lord Baltimore Hotel. This was a real sweet job—for the Clothing Manufacturing Association, from 10:00 p.m. to 5:00 a.m., including playing for a floor show! An exhausted Berigan went on to New York from there, with his musicians going to their homes, most of which were in Trenton, New Jersey, for a short hiatus.

A somewhat refreshed Berigan band resumed activity on February 23 at the Totem Pole Ballroom, Auburndale, Massachusetts, where they enjoyed an engagement of six days, closing on the 28th. While at the Totem Pole, the band broadcast over station WAAB, on the 25th and 26th. Business was booming at the Totem Pole: Gene Kutch: "The boys in the band stayed at the Lorraine Hotel in Boston. It was a great engagement. On our last night, we attracted a crowd of about 3,000 customers. Lawrence Welk replaced us."[23] *Variety* reported on Bunny's success at the Totem Pole: "Bunny Berigan at the Totem Pole, Auburndale, Massachusetts, Feb. 23–28, is always a favorite here with 12,200 dancers at the usual $1.45 cents per couple for a fine gross of $8,845. Turned in the heaviest Saturday (February 28) ($3,000) in weeks."[24] Bunny had some stiff competition while he was in Boston. On February 28, the Raymor-Playmor twin ballrooms were presenting Stan Kenton and Will Bradley.

After the Totem Pole gig, the band played a one-nighter in New Britain, Connecticut, and then took another few days off. During the month of February, after Bunny rejoined his band, they had played engagements on 17 of 23 dates. On one of those dates, they had played three shows. On three of the six "off dates," the band rehearsed. On only three of the off dates had the band actually rested. For whatever reasons, MCA was now finding more work for the Berigan band. Clearly, Bunny Berigan was on the comeback trail in early 1942.

During the brief respite at the beginning of March, Bunny temporarily replaced female vocalist Kay Little with Nita Sharon. This replacement applied only to the band's road engagements. Ms. Little would record with Bunny soon on a previously set date. Bunny was not displeased with the singing of Kay Little, who was also Mrs. Danny Richards. George Quinty provided the background details: "I talked Bunny into hiring Nita Sharon as a temporary replacement for Kay Little, who had discovered she was pregnant and wanted to go home to her folks for awhile. I knew Nita, who had been working in Cleveland, so I got hold of Kutchie to play for an audition for her. She got the job, but she didn't last very long."[25]

Another incident occurred during Bunny's brief time away from his band. There are conflicting reports as to what actually happened. Here are several:

> Bunny Berigan was scheduled for a spot on the Eddie Cantor NBC Ipana-Sal Hepatica program last week (March 4), but was canceled during the dress rehearsal when it was found that the material on hand ran far beyond the show's 30 minutes. Bunny was paid his $250 salary he was to have gotten as a soloist, his band laying off that evening. The trumpeter's failure to appear on the show brought rumors among musicians that he had been on his bad behavior. MCA's Harry Moss emphatically denied the reports while explaining Bunny's absence.[26]

Saxophonist Artie Manners added his remembrance: "I hadn't seen Bunny since he worked with us at CBS. Then one day in spring 1942, I went to do the Eddie Cantor show and Bunny was to be a guest star. We were pleased to see each other of course, although it took everything I had not to show my shock and dismay at the way he looked! He really looked terrible and it made me feel awful. He never showed up for the program anyway."[27] Other musicians on the scene also had memories of this event. Artie Foster and Larry Tise recalled: "We were working with the Cookie Fairchild orchestra on the Eddie Cantor show. Bunny came to the rehearsal in extra bad shape and played so badly that the program director decided to cut his solo out of the show. We were all upset to see how much he had gone downhill, feeling that he was hurting himself, trying to play in that condition."[28] Sam Shoobe (bass) commented: "I had worked with Bunny a number of times before and he was a big man, six feet tall or more. When I saw him at the Eddie Cantor rehearsal, I could not believe it! He'd lost so much weight and looked and played so bad."[29]

Another supposed witness to at least part of this event was Bunny's former drummer, Johnny Blowers. Here is his recollection, summoned many years after the fact, probably in the early 1990s:

> I was with CBS in the early 1940s, and was doing a children's show. During a break, I was sitting in the hall reading the Sunday *Times* with my legs crossed, and all at once I felt somebody kick my foot. I looked up, and it was Bunny Berigan. It was frightening. The Bunny I knew had always been big and strong. He

looked like a football player, and he was a good-looking man. What I was seeing now was enough to make me cry. He was so thin he looked like my little finger, and when he spoke it was as though he could hardly make the effort. We exchanged greetings and then I asked him what he was doing there at nine o'clock in the morning. 'I'm doing a guest shot on the Major Bowes program,' he said. 'How about having a drink with me?' I reminded him that I did not drink any more, but went with him to the men's room, where he pulled out a pint of scotch and drank it down. He drained the bottle dry. That was the last time I saw him alive.[30]

Since March 4, 1942, was a Wednesday, not a Sunday, the Eddie Cantor show was on NBC, not CBS, and there is no evidence that Bunny appeared on the Major Bowes show at this time, one wonders where and when Johnny Blowers encountered Berigan.

The Berigan band had more one-nighters lined up. They regrouped on March 6 for a dance date at the NRC Ballroom, Nashua, New Hampshire, and then went to Portland, Maine, for a gig at Picker Gardens on the 7th. The next night, they played at Hamilton Park, Waterbury, Connecticut. Red Lange drove Bunny from one gig to another on occasion during that winter: "On one of those long, cold over-night jumps, I was driving and Bunny was asleep in the front seat with his coon-skin cap and his overcoat collar up over his neck. We were stopped by a traffic cop for speeding and he asked, 'What's wrong with him?' I told him it was Bunny Berigan, but he didn't believe me. So I woke Bunny up—with great difficulty—and the cop, who was 'hep,' was so happy at meeting Bunny that he let us go without a ticket!"[31] The band was off on March 9, but gathered in New York on the 10th for one of Bunny's customary pre-recording session rehearsals. This one lasted three hours and took place at Haven Studios. The next day, they again entered the World Recording Studios, 711 Fifth Avenue, and cut four more records for the Elite Label.

The personnel in the studio that day with Bunny were: Kenny Davis (lead), Bob Mansell, Fred Norton, trumpets; Max Smith, Charlie Stout, trombones; George Quinty (lead alto), Walt Mellor (alto and baritone), Red Lange, Neal Smith (tenors), saxophones; Gene Kutch, piano; Tony Espen, bass; Jack Sperling, drums; Danny Richards, Kay Little, vocals. Danny Richards, after waiting for more than three years to record with Bunny Berigan, would finally get his chance. Kay Little would also record with the band, even though Nita Sharon probably continued working on the road with Berigan temporarily.

The first tune they recorded was Hoagy Carmichael's fine ballad "Skylark," with a lyric by Johnny Mercer.[32] Bunny had finally reached the point where he was recording at least some of the "A" material in the current pop song marketplace. Gene Kutch wrote the arrangement, and it is excellent. The performance starts off with the reeds (Mellor on baritone) laying down rich chords over which the open brass play a simple fanfare. After this dramatic eight-bar introduction, which is really a modulation into the first chorus, the brass start the exposition of the melody, but Bunny, on his warm open trumpet, finishes their

No Exit

statement, an effective touch. A tasty modulation brings Danny Richards to the microphone. He was an exceptionally fine singer, with a silky baritone voice. Here, he handles the poetic lyric with relaxed aplomb. It is obvious why Richards was popular with audiences; he had a great voice, and he knew how to use it to sell a lyric very subtly, yet very persuasively. Kutch's use of the saxophones behind Richards's singing on the main strain of the melody, and then of the tightly muted brass on the bridge, is splendidly colorful and very musical. "Kutchie," as he was known in the band, like a number of others before him, had developed into a fine arranger while he was in the employ of Bunny Berigan. After the vocal chorus, the band plays a bit and then Kutch sets up the dramatic finish perfectly: the open brass move into their upper register, and then Mr. Trumpet *arrives.* In spite of all of the stories of Bunny's shrunken body, and of his excessive drinking, of the grief that laid him low after his father died, and of the exhaustion he must have felt from almost nonstop touring, *this man could still play the trumpet superbly well!* Like a veteran heavyweight boxer, he does not throw his knockout punch at the opening bell. Instead, he first moves around in his capacious middle register, the golden tones tumbling out of the bell of his trumpet, toying with the listener. And then, lightning strikes. After a dramatic pause, he leaps into his high register playing a coda that no other trumpeter could have ever played more beautifully or passionately, capping it with a ringing high F on his trumpet (concert E flat). It is a thrilling musical moment, and it is quintessential Berigan.

Gene Kutch's arrangement of "Skylark" employed a couple of delightful modulations taking the music from one key to another. Modulations were one of the glories of the music of the great bands of the swing era. All arrangers used them, but some were more creative than others. The modulations written by Jerry Gray, for example, tended to be short and direct, but always very effective and musical. Eddie Sauter's modulations tended to be longer, with considerably more ambiguity about where he was taking the music, but were equally rewarding. In very many swing era arrangements containing a vocal chorus, there is a modulation from the first chorus, which usually was the band's chorus, to the second or vocalist's chorus.

I have always appreciated these changes of key, but for a long time did not really understand why they were so valuable a musical device. Then I stumbled upon this startlingly brilliant explanation given by the composer Darius Milhaud to a young pianist who was studying with him named Dave Brubeck.[33]

At my lessons with Milhaud, he would play through my compositions and make suggestions. One piece was a sonata. I thought the second theme was fine. But he said, 'put a flat in front of every note in that theme.' I did, and it was transformed, so that when the piece returned to the first theme there was a modulation. He always said that modulation was the greatest thing in music—that it could lift your spirit...or bring it down. Then he said something I've never forgotten: 'The reason I don't like twelve-tone music is that you're never someplace. Therefore you can never go someplace. Beethoven loved modulation. So did Brahms. They're always taking us to a new place."[34]

(Note: To oversimplify, twelve-tone composition uses all twelve notes in the chromatic scale in such a way as to prevent the emphasis of any one tone, and as a result, the music avoids being in any one key.)

"My Little Cousin" was composed by Arthur Schwartz and a number of others, and was arranged for the Berigan band by Van Alexander. This rendition swings, and spots Bunny punching out the melody in the first chorus and then playing lead trumpet in different places after the vocal chorus. Kay Little, sounding somewhat like Connie Haines who was then being featured by Tommy Dorsey, and perhaps a bit like Louise Tobin, sings the lyric enthusiastically and well. The tiny tenor sax spot right after the vocal is played by Red Lange. One wishes that Bunny had allotted him more solo space—he was a capable jazz player. But on these records the arrangements basically feature the Berigan trumpet. Bunny then leads the brass in a very exciting way until he glisses on into his solo. Here he is in Ziggy Elman territory, playing with just the right Jewish flavor before he works his way up to the high note finish.

"Somebody Else Is Taking My Place" was composed by Russ Morgan, Dick Howard, and Bob Ellsworth in 1937, but was resurrected as a World War II pop hit exploiting the separations that were occurring throughout the nation as young men went off to war. Here it is cast in a brisk-tempo dance arrangement by Gene Kutch, which Bunny and the Berigan band play very well. Once again, Mr. B. states the melody in the first chorus on open trumpet. Kutch's brass voicings are very similar to those also being used then by Benny Goodman's young pianist and arranger, Mel Powell.[35] Berigan plays the modulation into Kay Little's vocal, again on open trumpet. She sings with gusto here, displaying good range and pitch control. Bunny leads the brass after the vocal, and Red Lange again pops out of the ensemble briefly before Bunny and the brass wrap things up brightly.

Danny Richards returns to sing Irving Berlin's "Me and My Melinda." Berigan's exposition of the melody shows him once again painting his musical picture with broad strokes. Red Lange, who wrote this rhythmic chart, allowed himself a few bars leading the saxophones with his tenor, and later a short solo. After the vocal chorus, Bunny follows Lange with a few solo bars before he soars off at the end.

Berigan had every reason to be very happy with this recording session. He had played wonderfully, his band sounded tight and swinging, and his vocalists both did their jobs very well. The arrangements his band played were good, with Kutch's chart on "Skylark" being excellent. The tunes, with the exception of "Skylark," were ordinary items then being featured by almost all dance bands, and as such were grist for the pop record market. "Skylark" was also very popular then, but it is clearly a cut above the run-of-the-mill pop tunes that then formed the core of most bands' repertoires. I think that Eli Oberstein was also probably quite pleased with the recordings Bunny and company made that day. This recording session was the best Bunny had had in three years. These recordings, as issued on the Elite label, were on the market by mid-April. (Note: Some releases, including those appearing by license to the Firestone Tire and Rubber Company on their Air Chief Philharmonic label, incorrectly attribute the vocals done by Kay Little on the March 11, 1942, Berigan recordings to Nita Sharon.)

The band had the next day, March 12, off, then reconvened in Wilmington, Delaware at a place called The Black Cat. This, by all accounts, was not a good gig. Gene Kutch: "We played from 9 p.m. to around 1 a.m. the next morning. It was a lousy place with a very small, cramped bandstand."[36] Bob Bierman, a jazz record collector, recounted: "I saw the band at that small roadhouse on the outskirts of Wilmington, Delaware. Bunny did very little playing that night so I assumed he was feeling bad. But the crowd kept asking for 'I Can't Get Started,' which he was reluctant to play. But finally he gave in, and it was pathetic."[37]

George Quinty had observed Berigan's behavior for about seven months by this time and had come to some conclusions:

Bunny never complained. He stayed optimistic, but there were times when you knew he was in pain. He'd press his hand on his side or hold his back. Once he showed us this hard lump on his liver. Don Palmer said that it was hardening. But he'd sit on that Greyhound bus and smile as though nothing were wrong. I never saw him when he couldn't play. I never saw him when he could not make a job because he was drunk. I did see him when he should not have made a job because he was sick. He made and played every job—even when he was in a lot of pain.[38]

Berigan and the band then moved on to a dance date at the Brookline Country Club, near Philadelphia, on March 14. It was on this gig that they had the kind of dancing-in-the-dark experience that most bands can live without:

Bunny broadcasts in 'blackout' achieving a unique distinction among American bandsmen which is all too familiar to their British brothers. The Berigan band was playing the Brookline Country Club near Philadelphia, with a broadcast scheduled from the spot for 12:05 to 12:45 a.m. over WCAU. Two minutes before they were to go on the air, the lights went out. This was not due to any air-raid drill or test blackout, just a break in the power supply. The lines to the radio station were open and so the broadcast had to go on just as if the men could read their music. For 20 minutes Bunny and his boys played from memory, while the Haverford township police carried the torch for 1,200 dancers, playing flashlights over the crowd at intervals to keep the place from going completely dark. The dancers thought the whole thing was part of the show, according to the manager of the Brookline, and took the blackout as just so much fun, averting panic and trouble for everybody but Bunny Berigan and his enforcedly faking musicians.[39]

This engagement was yet another successful one for Bunny, despite the blackout. This blurb from *Billboard* puts his success on the road into perspective: "The Brookline Country Club was taken over by two promoters and the spot first started booking bands in September 1941. It's outside of Philadelphia and the first 52 dances grossed $39,930, averaging only $768 per date—not much of a profit, but it is beginning to make a bit more on most bands. The biggest was Tommy Dorsey with $2,425 on October 2, 1941; Bunny Berigan (March 14, 1942) was better than average at $980. Van Alexander was the low, with only $140 (October 9, 1941)."[40]

Berigan's band of vagabond musicians kept moving and kept working hard. Their next date was at the Holyoke Theater, Holyoke, Massachusetts, on March 15. Gene Kutch, with the assistance of his diary, later remembered what the band's activities were during those few days in mid-March: "That was a hectic weekend. We'd driven from Wilmington, Delaware, to Philadelphia, where we played from 9 p.m. to 1 a.m., including a 45 minutes broadcast over station WCAU. We drove back to New York after finishing work and left again around 5.30 a.m. for Holyoke, arriving there at 11.30 a.m. We played five shows at the theatre, one of which included a half-hour broadcast over a local radio station. We shared the bill with the John Kirby band."[41] The next night, they played at Fort Slocum, New Rochelle, New York, gratis. March 17 was an off day in New York, but the next day Bunny rehearsed the band at Haven Studio. They then moved west to Pittsburgh, where they played two nights, the 19th and 20th, at the William Penn Hotel. Kutch again provided some background: "We stayed at the Fort Pitt Hotel and played the Military Ball at the William Penn Hotel, along with the bands of Ted Weems, Sammy Watkins, and Rusty Williams. After the job, we left around 3 a.m. to drive to Bowling Green, Ohio."[42] While playing at what was then Bowling Green College (later State University), a number of photographs were taken. They clearly indicate that Kay Little was the girl vocalist on that date. The personnel was the same as the March 11 recording date, except trombonist Frank Webb had replaced Charlie Stout.

The next day, March 22, the Berigan band played three shows at the Majestic Theater, Harnell, New York. In the audience for one of those shows was young Charles Champlin, later to gain fame as a journalist with Time-Life magazines, and the *Los Angeles Times:* "I saw Bunny on my 16th birthday at the theatre. He looked terrible but played wonderfully to a standing room crowd in the boondocks of western New York State."[43] After that gig, they had the next day, Monday, March 22, off. Then they returned to Pittsburgh for a one-nighter at the Aragon Ballroom on the 23rd, after which there were a couple more off days. They resumed their tour in Ann Arbor, Michigan on the 27th, playing at Union Ballroom on the campus of the University of Michigan for the annual "Slide Rule Ball" held for the university's engineering students. Their next one-nighter was at the I.M.A. Auditorium in Flint, Michigan. En route, there was a highway mishap. As a result, a trumpet player by the name of Pat Marr found himself suddenly playing with Bunny Berigan: "The Berigan band was driving to Flint to play the I.M.A., where all the bands played, when they were involved in an auto accident outside of Port Huron, Michigan. Four bandsmen were hurt and Bunny had to use subs, one of which was me. I was about 16 years old then."[44] The next night they played in Toledo, Ohio at the Trianon Ballroom. Evidently one of the musicians injured in the auto collision was unable to return to work with the band because Bunny hired a new trumpeter in Toledo, Clair

Perrault: "I was very young (probably 18) when I joined Bunny. I think it was at Toledo, Ohio. Red Lange was on tenor sax, Frank Webb on one trombone and Kutch and Espen in the rhythm section."[45] Perrault played second trumpet in the section. That means that lead trumpeter Kenny Davis was not replaced, and that either Bob Mansell or Fred Norton was.

In spite of the tension and anxiety this series of events had caused, and his deteriorating health, Bunny was still able to play magnificently. Jack Sperling recalled the Toledo date very well: "Bunny played at his very best that night. As he said, 'When you play a musical instrument, you tell a story, one that the people out there can understand. You play to the very best of your ability. You close your eyes, just like you were telling it from a story book.' We heard later that our band had outdrawn Tommy Dorsey, who was playing at the Rainbow Gardens in nearby Fremont, Ohio."[46] After this gig, the band had two days off.

The month of March had been a very successful one for Bunny and the band. They were playing well, working regularly and making money on the road, and made four good records. MCA was now promoting him in all advertisements as "The Miracle Man of Music."

On April Fool's Day, MCA treated Bunny and his bandsmen to one of their patented "tricks." Gene Kutch remembered it: "We stayed at the Waldorf Hotel in Toledo, Ohio, and drove from there to Toronto and played at the Palais Royal (on April 1) before driving all the way back to Toledo in the early hours of Thursday morning. After going to church, we left again at midnight on Friday (April 3) and drove to Cincinnati, arriving about 9 a.m. and checking in at the Fountain Square Hotel there."[47] At Castle Farms just outside Cincinnati, the band played from 9:30 p.m. to 2:30 a.m., and played for a floor show in addition to their normal program of dance music. The next night found them at a dance date at the Crystal Beach Park Pavilion, Vermillion, Ohio. From there, they went to Detroit to play at the Graystone Ballroom, opposite a black band called the Alabama State Collegians, a name Erskine Hawkins's band had in its earliest days.

It was after this gig that Danny Richards, surely the most popular performer in the band after Bunny, was forced to leave. He recalled the details, and provided a very concise summary of his three-year association with Berigan: "I had my Army physical on April 7th and was inducted into the Army on April 9th. Kay stayed with the band for a little while after I left. Bunny was a grand guy. And I believe I'm well qualified to say this because I knew him at his best and at his worst, and his worst was not as bad as everybody has been led to believe."[48]

It was at this time that the band's personnel, which had been so remarkably stable for many months, began to undergo a few changes. The ever-increasing draft of young men into military service during World War II was beginning to catch up with some of the musicians in the Berigan band, and the inevitable movement of musicians from band to band was also having its effect. Trumpeter Charlie Mitchell joined the band shortly before Danny Richards left, and tenor saxist Red Lange turned in his notice. He wanted to get off the road, and return to his duties as a member of the house band at the Trianon Ballroom in Toledo, Ohio, his home town. He left after the band played a gig in Norwalk, Ohio on April 6.

Despite these losses, Bunny forged ahead. After a travel day on April 7, the band played at the Maryland Theater, Cumberland, Maryland, on April 8. Kutch's diary explains what happened during this couple of days: "We checked into the Cumberland Hotel and then played four shows at the Maryland Theatre. We left after the last show and drove to Wooster, Ohio, arriving at 6 a.m. on Friday and checked into the Ohio Hotel there."[49] At Wooster, the band played at the College of Wooster on the 10th, then drove to Saginaw, Michigan for a one-nighter the next night. It was after this gig that an exhausted Red Lange departed: "I left the band after a date in Saginaw, Michigan. The band played for the Knights of Columbus Ball opposite Leroy Smith, and after we finished the job, I left for Toledo."[50] Lange was replaced by Eddie Swift. After this gig, the band moved on to Youngstown, Ohio, (a trip of approximately 350 miles) to begin an engagement at the Nu-Elms Ballroom there.

Perhaps Bunny (or Palmer) told MCA that he and the band were now exhausted by the grueling travel of the previous two months, and needed to settle down somewhere for a while to recuperate. Whatever happened, MCA's plan was to use the Nu-Elms Ballroom in Youngstown as the Berigan band's base of operations for a week or so, doing one-nighters into the surrounding territory. The band opened at the Nu-Elms on Sunday, April 12, playing an afternoon session at 3:30 and an evening session at 8:30. It appears that during the afternoon session the band was broadcast. One tune was recorded: "I'm Confessin'". Based on the sound of the brass voicings used throughout this arrangement, which are identical to those in Gene Kutch's arrangement of "Somebody Else Is Taking My Place," I think this chart was written by Kutch. Bunny has three separate solos, each on open trumpet, and they are excellent. This is the last known recording of Bunny Berigan.

The next night, the band played a dance date at Cole Auditorium in Norwalk, Ohio for the benefit of the Norwalk Police Department. They returned to the Nu-Elms for the evening of April 14. What happened the next day is not known, but they may well have played another one-nighter near Youngstown. They were at the Nu-Elms again on April 16 (Thursday) and on the 19th (Sunday), which was their last night there. Between these dates, they played at Granville College, Granville, Ohio on the 17th, and at Grove City College, Grove City, Pennsylvania, on the 18th. It appears that Kay Little left the band permanently in Youngstown, and new girl vocalist, Doris Bell, joined.

There was now great concern in the band about Bunny's rapidly failing health. George Quinty remembered the time the band was in Youngstown:

> We stayed at the Palace Hotel, and I remember Ella Fitzgerald coming in to hear Bunny, also the entire Henry Busse band. Busse offered me a job with his band, and when I told Bunny, he said, 'Take it George, get some more experience and a reputation.' I guess we all had realized that Bunny was a sick man by then, but

we never dreamed that he might die soon, even though he looked haggard and his clothes were hanging on him. I don't think Donna made things any easier for him either, the way she treated him. One day, my wife, Helen, asked him, 'Bunny, what are you trying to do to yourself? A guy who's so handsome and plays so beautifully.' And all that Bunny replied was, 'Ask Jimmy Petrillo about that.' He loved his daughters and at the slightest excuse would bring out their photos that he always carried in his wallet. He was always so calm, nothing seemed to upset him. He used to tell me I was the only musician he'd ever met who did not drink or smoke. He was a strict Catholic and used to often go to Mass, but I think there was something wrong between Donna and him. It was ironic, really, because Don Palmer used to call her a lush. She'd call him up at any hour of day or night to get him to bring her some booze. He reckoned she made Bunny worse. His playing at the Elms was pretty bad.[51]

Sick or not, Bunny had to make the next one-nighter, which was on April 21 at the Aragon Ballroom in Pittsburgh. It is unclear whether he played all, a part, or none of this job. Gene Kutch, probably with the assistance of his diary, recalled that Claude Thornhill, who was also playing in Pittsburgh with his band on that date, came to the Aragon and played a set or two to help Bunny out. After the Aragon gig, Bunny had to be taken to Allegheny General Hospital, 320 East North Avenue, in Pittsburgh. The acute ailments that put him in the hospital then were complete exhaustion, malnutrition, and pneumonia. These health challenges were in addition to his chronic alcoholism and advanced cirrhosis of the liver. His profoundly damaged liver had caused portal hypertension to occur. Attempts by his body to establish a better, collateral flow of blood between the portal and systemic circulations had resulted in enlarged veins at the points of connection, mainly the esophagus and the intestine. His blood pressure, no doubt elevated by his playing the trumpet, had caused these thin-walled veins (varices) to rupture.[52] Bunny's pneumonia had undoubtedly been caused by him aspirating the blood that was seeping through the ruptured veins in his esophagus. The internal mechanism that would cause Bunny Berigan's death had now started.

Nevertheless, his band had to move on to honor the engagements MCA had booked.

Bunny Berigan is in Allegheny State Hospital in Pittsburgh recovering from an attack of pneumonia. He played that city with his band on Tuesday (21st), thereafter being hospitalized. His outfit went on without him to Andy Perry's Empire Ballroom in Allentown, Pennsylvania, the next night. The group opened a stay at the Summit in Baltimore the next night (Thursday), where Bunny will rejoin the band when he is sufficiently recovered.[53]

While he was hospitalized, MCA arranged for the Berigan band to be led by vocalist Sonny Skylar, who had been preparing to go on the road with his own band after singing with Vincent Lopez's band for some time previously.

At the same time, the various ramifications on the home-front caused by World War II were beginning to be felt. "Transportation difficulties are the major source of conversation around band agencies at the moment...and major source of gloom. Last week's announcement of gasoline rationing to begin next month was another blow to already reeling one-nighter bands."[54] This development was but one of many that would eventually cause the demise of the big band era.

The Berigan band had been booked into a two-week stand at the Summit Club, near Pimlico Racetrack, in Baltimore, to commence on April 23. They followed the McFarland Twins Orchestra into that venue. It was probably at that location that Sonny Skylar and his girl vocalist Jeanne D'Arcy joined the Berigan troupe. As the days passed while the band was there without Bunny, disturbing reports began to filter out of Pittsburgh that he was much sicker than anyone had thought. An air of uncertainty came over the Berigan bandsmen. A number of sidemen, seeking more stable incomes, gave notice to Don Palmer. Among those who would soon depart were drummer Jack Sperling, first trumpeter Kenny Davis, another trumpeter, and saxist Walt Mellor. Charlie Mitchell, who had joined a few weeks before, took over the first trumpet duties. The other new trumpeter was Dick Kemp, who played second. The new saxist was Bernie Scherr, and the new drummer was Charlie DeBona.[55] When news of these impending personnel changes reached Bunny in Pittsburgh, he was deeply disturbed, no doubt because he remembered that shortly after his hospitalization at the end of 1939, he was forced to give up his band. But in the two and a half years since that previous hospitalization, much more damage had been done to his liver by cirrhosis. Despite the grave warnings of the physicians at Allegheny General Hospital that if he resumed playing the trumpet he would literally be killing himself, Berigan resolved to rejoin his band as soon as possible. MCA was also concerned about Bunny being away from his band because the Bunny Berigan band without Bunny Berigan was just another band, and they were having a hard enough time booking name road bands with their name leaders present. Berigan's seventeen-day absence from his band had caused doubts about his ability to keep the group together. The fact that Berigan was now literally dying did not appear to make much difference either to him or to MCA.

There has been considerable confusion concerning Berigan's obviously premature departure from Allegheny General Hospital, which happened on either May 7 or 8. It is likely that he rejoined his band at the Summit on May 8. Some sources say that Bunny was ordered out of the hospital by Harry Moss of MCA, who thought that Bunny's latest health problem was simply that he was drinking too much. There is no evidence to support this however. No source that I have seen has stated that Bunny himself wanted to rejoin his band at the earliest possible time to prevent its dissolution, notwithstanding his life-threatening cirrhosis. But I think that was exactly his thought process as he left the hospital and rejoined his band. Berigan's stubbornness has seldom been noted, much less discussed, as a reason why he behaved the way he did throughout his life.

When his musicians saw him upon his return, they were shocked. Gene Kutch recalled: Bunny was yellow, really ill. We had to lift him on to the bandstand at the Summit and prop him against the piano. He could hardly get a sound out of the trumpet.[56] Jack Sperling added more details:

> Sonny Skylar and Jeanne D'Arcy fronted for the first part of the Summit engagement, when I gave Don Palmer my notice. I didn't leave until after Bunny had gotten out of the hospital and was back to finish the date. I noticed that he spat some blood into his handkerchief after each number, but he didn't complain. On my last night, my father came down to help me load my drums into the car and Bunny came out of the club to say goodbye and suddenly fell down the steps. My dad and I helped him to his feet and he said that his legs had just given way under him. Bunny rarely told me how to play. But on occasion, when I got carried away, he would say: 'Just keep it walking Jackie—keep the wood on the skin.' He was very particular about tempo however. I saw him again in New York a week or so later and his skin had gone yellow. He really looked awful.[57]

Drummer Charlie DeBona replaced Jack Sperling.

> I joined the band in Baltimore. Jack Sperling had just left, Dick Kemp was new in the trumpet section, and saxist Bernie Scherr was another newcomer. Dick Kemp used to copy all of Bunny's solos just in case he couldn't make it. Donna used to ask me to keep an eye on Bunny and try to persuade him to go for afternoon walks. Unfortunately, when we did, he'd be bound to meet some old acquaintance who would invite him for a drink and that was the end of the walk! I remember he was jaundiced at that time, showing that drink had gotten to his liver.[58]

Clearly, Bunny Berigan was in no condition to be playing his trumpet or leading a band on the road. Nevertheless, he continued to do both. He also continued drinking.

While Bunny had been hospitalized, Don Palmer took control of his trumpet. He noticed that its mouthpiece looked strange, with a groove cut into the bottom of it. Gene Kutch recalled what then happened:

> Bunny had this old unplated brass mouthpiece that he had had someone specifically put a groove in. It was on the bottom part, kinda like a grip. Don Palmer took it and had someone smooth out that groove. When Bunny came back he picks it up and says, 'Who the hell has been screwing around with my horn?' And Don says, 'I thought it was just a dent.' Bunny says, 'Goddammit, don't do something like that on your own. Next time ask!' I guess that's only the second time I ever saw Bunny get mad. But not having his favorite mouthpiece did not help him.[59]

The Summit engagement, which had been extended for a week after Bunny rejoined his band, had been a harrowing experience for everyone connected with it. It ended on May 13.

The next day, they played a U.S.O. benefit at the army base at Aberdeen, Maryland, followed by another performance before a military audience at the U.S. Naval Station, Bay Ridge, Maryland, the day after that. Quinty recalled how Bunny husbanded his energies on that date: "That was one of the many free jobs we played for the U.S.O., and I asked if I could take my wife and two kids along. That night I was featured on a tune called 'Solid, Jack!' which had been Jackie Sperling's drum speciality, and Bunny let me take eight or nine solo choruses! Those two thousand sailors really loved it, and didn't they cheer when Bunny went into 'I Can't Get Started'! I never saw such magnetism in any other man!"[60]

Quinty also recalled some "scuttlebutt" that was going around the Berigan band then:

Although he'd only been out of hospital a short while, Bunny always acceded to requests for 'I Can't Get Started' and held that last note so big and full! I'd never heard him play it better. On that date, Don Palmer told us that the band had a chance to enlist in the Navy as a complete unit, with each member being made a Petty Officer and Bunny a Chief Petty Officer. We all agreed to take physicals, which everybody passed except Bunny. The boys didn't want the band to break up, so we decided not to enlist but we did play the Naval Base, where we were invited to eat in the Officers' Mess. The top brass all wanted to hear Bunny.[61]

On Saturday, May 16, they returned to New York for a one-nighter at Manhattan Center. While he was there, Bunny was seen by a musician friend:

My wife and I were sitting in a little restaurant on Seventh Avenue, just across from the Taft Hotel. Suddenly, my wife exclaimed, 'Oh, look, there's Bunny.' I had just returned from a date in Buffalo and I'd heard about his work on the movie and wanted to ask him about it. So I ran out into the street, calling, 'Hey, Bunny!' He was up ahead on the sidewalk with a couple of guys and he stopped and turned around. When I saw him, I got such a shock. His eyes were sunken in and discolored. His skin was tight and blotchy. We talked for a while and he told me he had a date coming up in Boston.[62]

While Bunny was in New York, he was able to visit his daughters. Patricia Berigan remembered that visit vividly:

Jo and I were brought to the hotel to see Daddy after he got out of the hospital about a month before he died. We knew he'd been in the hospital, and we knew he was very ill. We were taken for an afternoon's visit but were told we could only stay a little while because he was so tired and weak. I remember so distinctly how very jaundiced he looked—although of course I didn't know that word. I asked, 'Why are you so yellow, Daddy?' He said he was going to be OK. It was at that time that he told me, 'Just in case, if anything should happen to me, your Mom can't take care of you guys. You're going to have to do it. I want you to take care of your sister for me.' And that was the last time I saw my Daddy.[63]

Bunny and the band opened at the Tic-Toc Club in Boston the next evening, May 17, for a week's stand. They were part of a review that included six vaudeville acts, and probably numerous shows each day.[64] While he was at the Tic-Toc, another old friend, trumpeter Henry "Red" Allen, came to see Bunny. He too was distressed by Berigan's shrunken appearance and weakness. Bunny was "...too weak to stand up for a whole set, taking most of his solos sitting down. Allen begged him not to take the band on to Virginia, but Berigan insisted that he would soon be fine again."[65] During this gig, however, Bunny's playing was apparently very good. Kutch recalled: "We get to Boston and Bunny's playing his ass off. He sounds great! But by now, he's guzzling like mad. We're bringing him food and he thanks us, but he just isn't interested; he hardly eats anything. He's going on nervous energy now."[66] All the while, Bunny kept spitting blood into a handkerchief after he played his trumpet.

During at least a part of the Tic-Toc engagement, Donna was with Bunny. He had had little contact with her since the band's residency at the Roosevelt Hotel in Jacksonville, Florida, the previous September. As usual, her presence did not help him. By this late date, all pretenses had been dropped. Their marriage was over. But, in the wake of Bunny's hospitalization in Pittsburgh, Donna perhaps was now genuinely concerned that this latest illness was one from which he might not recover. He was, after all, her sole means of support. So she was there ostensibly to try to help him limit his drinking. But, as on most previous occasions when she was supposed to be doing this, the net result was that Bunny drank more. That happened this time too. After a number of heated arguments with him, she left Boston and probably returned to New York.

Where she might have been living in New York is not clear. It is most unlikely that Bunny and Donna were living together then. Indeed, they probably had not been living together for quite a while. Bob Davis, who for a time was married to Joyce Berigan, related this bit of information to one of the White researchers: "My wife, Joyce, told me that Bunny and Donna were more or less separated at that time and that she was living at another hotel."[67] Donna later (much later, in the 1980s) told Robert Dupuis that after Bunny's funeral and burial in Fox Lake, "I went back to an apartment in Harlem with the kids."[68] One of Bunny's obituaries stated that the Berigan daughters were "attending a Long Island school."[69] Harlem, needless to say, is not on Long Island. Although the Berigan girls remained with Donna for a short time after Bunny's death, soon thereafter, they were moved to the Riverdale section of the Bronx, where they were in fact raised by Darrell McArthur, Donna's brother, and his wife Joyce.[70] These facts and factual discrepancies, along with Donna's own alcoholism, make her various statements about what happened during the last days of Bunny's life suspect. One also wonders about the relationship Donna had prior to Bunny's death with the pianist George Zack. Donna married Zack a couple of years after Bunny's death. She spent at least part of the day Berigan died with George Zack.[71] Against this background, Bunny's statement to his daughter Patricia when he saw her for the last time takes on a deeper meaning, and was confirmed by events that later occurred involving Donna's legal rights as mother of the Berigan girls.

Gene Kutch's recollection of Bunny's good playing in Boston was corroborated by *Down Beat:* "Bunny Berigan Back—Blowing 'Em Big: Boston— Bunny Berigan, completely recovered from the pneumonia that kept him in a Pittsburgh hospital bed while Sonny Skylar fronted his band at the Summit Inn, Baltimore, has been playing some one nighters in this territory. The Bunn (sic) looked pretty hale and is playing his head off."[72]

The Berigan band left Boston on Sunday May 24, and headed to the Palomar Ballroom in Norfolk, Virginia for a three-night stand, May 25–27. At this location, a fan named Jack Pyle was in the audience on one of the nights. Here is what he later recalled:

> I saw the band at the Palomar in Norfolk and they had a girl vocalist called Doris Bell, who got a wire that said that her boyfriend had been killed in the service. Doc Pugh, the band-boy, tried to console her and impress upon her that 'the show must go on.' I had gone out front to watch the band, when, after about an hour or so, Bunny walked over to the microphone and beckoned for attention. 'Ladies and gentlemen,' he began, 'I've had a lot of requests this evening to play our theme song, 'I Can't Get Started.' Well, you'll have to pardon me, but I just got out of the hospital a few weeks ago and I'm not feeling up to par. Now, I'll tell you what I'll do. I'll *try* to play it for you, but remember, if I miss, it's your fault!' Bunny didn't miss. He played it as I never heard it played before. You could see he was really working. He went through the entire arrangement with flawless precision. When he pointed his horn toward the sky and hit a perfect F sharp (sic) above high C, the crowd rose to its feet in a tremendous round of applause which lasted five minutes![73]

On May 28, the Bunny and his band traveled to play at Milford Academy, Milford, Connecticut. Marshal Robbins, son of music publisher Jack Robbins, was at that dance: "I was attending Milford College and Bunny Berigan was booked to play the end-of-term prom. He looked very sickly, but even though he was drinking heavily, he played pretty well."[74] Trombonist Max Smith, who had spent most of the previous two years working with Berigan, recalled the general attitude around the Berigan band then about Bunny's health: "None of us in the band had any idea of how ill Bunny was. Some nights he was very weak and would just stand and lean against the piano, not playing much at all. But we'd seen him 'sick' before and when he'd stop drinking for a few days, he'd start to look like a new man. No drinks for a week and the yellow color in his skin would change and his eyes would also clear up. So we assumed it would happen this time."[75]

After the Milford job, the band drove to Scranton, Pennsylvania, for a dance date at the University of Scranton, on May 29. At this gig, Bunny headed a student committee to pick the University May Queen.[76] This job was a warm-up for a really good gig the next night, Saturday May 30, at one of the best venues for a big band, the Sunnybrook Ballroom in Pottstown, Pennsylvania. Here is some information about the Sunnybrook Ballroom in particular, and what was happening to the dance band business in general as the effects of World War II continued to be felt in the United States in mid-1942:

> Ray Hartstine's Sunnybrook Ballroom, Pottstown, top Saturday night spot for traveling bands in Eastern Pennsylvanian territory, faces the prospect of a shutdown because of gas rationing. Hartstine has opened the spot for the past eleven years and says it has depended for 98% of its patronage on private autos, with dancers coming from a radius of 50 miles or more. Sunnybrook is one of the choicest one-nighter bookings and buys most of its bands from MCA and is usually booked four to six weeks ahead. The ballroom has been in the enviable position of almost always getting first call on available names. Being an extra-large ballroom, it gave top names a chance to run a percentage. The spot had to close in mid-July (1942). July 4, usually the biggest dance of the year, drew only 175 with a 70 cents gate, for a gross of less than $125. Later, in October 1942, the spot attempted a comeback with name bands once a week. Hartstine was in the construction business before becoming a ballroom operator. It is said that he got Sunnybrook (capacity of between five and six thousand) when, after he built it, its owners could not pay for his work. It is one of the biggest spots in the east.[77]

The distance from Scranton to Pottstown, Pennsylvania, is approximately 110 miles. Compared with many jumps MCA had required the Berigan band to make between one-nighters, this one was rather short. No one had the slightest concern about making the trip from Scranton to Pottstown. After the Scranton dance, the band probably checked into a hotel and got some much needed sleep. They likely spent a good part of the next day relaxing, assuming the bus ride to Pottstown would easily be accomplished in a couple of hours, at most. Some time during the day, Bunny and trumpeter Charlie Mitchell drove to Pottstown in Mitchell's car, with a couple of other band members. They had encountered no problems. It had been an easy drive. George Quinty filled in the details:

> Bunny played Ray Hartstine's Sunnybrook Ballroom every Memorial Day and still held the attendance record there. Bunny decided to ride in Charlie Mitchell's Lincoln instead of the bus, which was driven by a Hungarian guy from Jersey City. The weather was terrible and somewhere along the way we got diverted by a traffic cop, because of an accident up ahead. We'd left in the early afternoon and when it was getting dark, someone asked Don Palmer if we ought to be near our destination. He got our driver to stop at the next traffic light and get directions from a policeman. It turned out that we were going in the wrong direction! Don attempted to charter an airplane at a nearby airfield, but had no luck as everything was grounded due to the bad weather. He told the driver to step on it and arranged for a police escort with flashing red lights and screaming sirens! But it was around 11.30 p.m. when we finally got to Pottstown and the place was closed and deserted. Charlie Mitchell was waiting for us, but Bunny had gone back to New York. Charlie said Bunny was broken-hearted and had sat in the car, killing two fifths of whisky, while he waited for us to turn up. The guys in the band were all upset about missing the job, especially as we were due on the air for a half-hour broadcast over CBS. I believe that more than two thousand people were giv-

en their money back. It was a terrible blow for Bunny, possibly the last straw, I guess.[78]

Berigan had attempted to mollify the large crowd at the Sunnybrook by staging an impromptu jam session with the few musicians who were there with him, but it did not work. Don Palmer learned from Charlie Mitchell that after this, Bunny went outside and started to vomit blood. Once again, he had been the innocent victim of the vicissitudes of being the leader of a touring dance band. When this type of situation had happened previously, it had cost him dearly. As he rode back to New York that night, he undoubtedly wondered and worried about how this latest fiasco would play out. He also had to be worried about his physical condition. No amount of denial could alter the fact that from somewhere inside his body, he was now bleeding more profusely. This could not go on much longer.

The abortive engagement at the Sunnybrook Ballroom was the last time that Bunny Berigan ever played his trumpet.

The next night, Sunday, May 31, Bunny and the band were scheduled to play at Manhattan Center in New York, the site of previous triumphs. The band showed up, as did a good crowd, but Bunny didn't. He had sequestered himself in a transient room at the Van Cortlandt Hotel, 142 West Forty-ninth Street. He had no permanent residence in New York City since he lost both his home in Rego Park, Queens, and his apartment on Central Park West as a result of the financial debacle that swamped him in 1939. He no doubt had met with Don Palmer during that day, and Palmer saw that Bunny was now facing a life-threatening health crisis.

Palmer had to somehow figure out how to cover the gig that night, so there would not be another disastrous cancellation. He probably also consulted Harry Moss at MCA, who likely contacted Benny Goodman, who was then playing at the Hotel New Yorker, which is next door to Manhattan Center. When the gravity of Bunny's health situation was explained to Goodman by Moss and Palmer, he agreed to try to save the gig for the leaderless Berigan band. In addition to doing that, BG was also involved in trying to work out an interim solution for the problem of who might lead the Berigan band while Bunny recuperated. George Quinty remembered what transpired:

> Don Palmer went on the stage to announce that Bunny was being hospitalized. The crowd was getting restless and he said, 'Benny Goodman has agreed to come down and play with the band.' We played a couple of ballads to cover Bunny's absence, arrangements that didn't feature him much, and shortly after, Benny Goodman arrived, accompanied by some of his musicians, including Lou McGarity, Mel Powell and Vido Musso. During an intermission, Don Palmer was talking to Musso and suggesting he should leave Goodman, temporarily, to front our band until Bunny was fit again. 'Yeah, man, Bunny hasta get well,' said Vido, in his thick Italian accent. 'I'll tell ya what I'ma gonna do. I'ma gonna leada da band for a hundred dollars a week. That's two hundred less than I'ma gettin' with Benny!'[79]

Berigan's severe internal bleeding had no doubt continued through the day of May 31 and into the night. He called Don Palmer at around 7:00 a.m. on Monday, June 1, and informed him that the bleeding was not abating. Palmer immediately took him to New York Polyclinic Hospital, 345 West Fiftieth Street,[80] near the Van Cortlandt Hotel. Throughout the day of June 1, Bunny's condition worsened. The internal bleeding that had begun some time before he entered the hospital in Pittsburgh, which had been aggravated by his playing the trumpet after that hospitalization, was now unable to be checked. Berigan's chronic cirrhosis had caused his liver to swell and become hard, resulting in the portal hypertension that in turn had caused the veins in his esophagus and intestine to burst. A number of musicians, including fellow trumpeter Billy Butterfield, came to visit Bunny in the hospital on June 1, and asked if they could donate blood to save him. They were told that would not help him because he would continue to hemorrhage whatever blood was in his body. Consequently, he was now in the final stages of bleeding to death. Bunny Berigan died at 3:30 a.m. on Tuesday, June 2, 1942. He had lived exactly thirty-three years and seven months.

Notes

[1] For detailed information about the film *Syncopation,* see appendix six.

[2] *Down Beat:* January 15, 1942, cited in the White materials.

[3] White materials: January 5, 1942.

[4] *Ibid.*

[5] Leith Stevens (1909–1970) was born in Mt. Moriah, Missouri. He was a child prodigy as a pianist. He began working for CBS radio in New York in the mid-1930s, basically as a conductor on many radio programs, including the *Saturday Night Swing Club,* where he met Bunny Berigan. He went to Hollywood in 1940 to work in films as a composer, and spent the rest of his career there. His most notable work is the score for the film *The Wild One,* made by Columbia Pictures in 1953. In it is the exquisite "Blues for Brando," (later recorded by a group that was essentially Shorty Rogers and His Giants) dedicated to that film's jazz-loving star, Marlon Brando. Stevens died in Los Angeles as the result of a myocardial infarction caused by his being told that his wife had just been killed in an automobile accident.

[6] *Down Beat:* February 1, 1942, cited in the White materials.

[7] White materials: January 5, 1942.

[8] *Ibid.*

[9] *Ibid.*

[10] White materials: January 11, 1942.

[11] Dupuis: 238.

[12] *Metronome:* February 1942, cited in the White materials.

[13] *Variety:* January 21, 1942, cited in the White materials.

[14] *Billboard:* January 24, 1942, cited in the White materials.

[15] *Variety:* January 28, 1942, cited in the White materials.

[16] White materials: November 23, 1941.

[17] White materials: February 6, 1942.

---

[18] *Billboard:* March 14, 1942, cited in the White materials.

[19] White materials: February 12, 1942.

[20] White materials: February 13, 1942.

[21] White materials: February 14, 1942.

[22] White materials: February 17, 1942.

[23] White materials: February 28, 1942.

[24] *Variety:* March 4, 1942, cited in the White materials:

[25] White materials: March 1, 1942.

[26] *Variety:* March 11, 1942, cited in the White materials.

[27] White materials: March 4, 1942.

[28] *Ibid.*

[29] *Ibid.*

[30] Blowers: 43.

[31] White materials: March 7, 1942

[32] John Herndon "Johnny" Mercer was born on November 18, 1909, in Savannah, Georgia. Although Mercer had considerable success in his career as a singer and composer of music, it was his great talent as a lyricist that gained him most renown. Mercer was drawn to jazz as a youngster, and he soon absorbed the rhythms and feeling of jazz, and was able to imbue the lyrics he wrote with a strong jazz flavor. He was also a master of vernacular language, and used this in combination with his southern sensibilities and poetic wit, to create dozens of lyrics for some of the best American popular songs. He worked with most of the greatest composers of the golden age of American popular song from the 1930s into the 1960s. Among his most memorable lyrics: "Jeepers Creepers," "Day In, Day Out," "Fools Rush In," "Dearly Beloved," "Dream," "Laura," "Autumn Leaves," "One For My Baby," "I Wanna Be Around," and "Moon River." Johnny Mercer died on June 25, 1976, in Bel Air, California.

[33] Pianist David Warren Brubeck was born on December 6, 1920, in Concord, California. Dave Brubeck has had a long and successful career as a jazz pianist and composer.

[34] *Take Five—The Public and Private Lives of Paul Desmond,* by Doug Ramsey, Parkside Publications Inc. (2005), 89.

[35] Melvin Epstein, known professionally as Mel Powell, was born on February 12, 1923 in the Bronx, New York. Powell was a child prodigy on piano, and began his professional career as a teenager. His first big break came when he was hired by Benny Goodman in 1941. With Goodman Powell played piano and also began working as an arranger and composer of jazz originals. From Goodman Powell went to Glenn Miller's army air force band during World War II, where his reputation grew substantially. After World War II, Powell worked with Goodman again, and then in Hollywood for a few years. He studied with composer Paul Hindemith from 1948–1952, and from the early 1950s became much less involved in jazz. Powell returned on occasion to playing jazz in the late 1980s. He was a long-time admirer of Berigan's playing, once said this to the writer Gene Lees: "Wit. Caprice. Bunny Berigan playing 'I Can't Get Started,' if you happen to like that, which I do." See *Arranging the Score: Portraits of the Great Arrangers,* (2000), Cassell (2002), 255. Mel Powell died on April 24, 1998, in Sherman Oaks, California.

[36] White materials: March 13, 1942.

[37] *Ibid.*

[38] Dupuis: 258.

[39] *Metronome:* April 1942, cited in the White materials.

[40] *Billboard:* October 3, 1942, cited in the White materials: March 14, 1942.

[41] White materials: March 15, 1942.

[42] White materials: March 20, 1942.

[43] White materials: March 22, 1942.

[44] White materials: March 28, 1942.

[45] White materials: March 29, 1942.

[46] *Ibid.*

[47] White materials: April 1, 1942.

[48] White materials: April 6, 1942.

[49] White materials: April 8, 1942.

[50] White materials: April 11, 1942.

[51] White materials: April 19, 1942.

[52] *Jazz and Death:* 106–107.

[53] *Variety:* April 29, 1942, cited in the White materials.

[54] *Variety:* April 22, 1942, cited in the White materials.

[55] White materials: April 23, 1942.

[56] White materials: May 8, 1942

[57] *Ibid.* Jack Sperling's comments about Berigan's instructions to him are in the interview Robert Dupuis did with Sperling. Dupuis archive, UW–Madison.

[58] *Ibid.*

[59] Dupuis: 259.

[60] White materials: May 15, 1942.

[61] White materials: May 27, 1942.

[62] White materials: May 16, 1942. The identity of this musician is not revealed in the White materials.

[63] Dupuis: 258.

[64] White materials: May 17, 1942.

[65] *Giants of Jazz:* 26.

[66] Dupuis: 259.

[67] White materials: June 2, 1942

[68] Dupuis: 264.

[69] *Boston Record American,* June 2, 1942.

[70] This fact was initially revealed to me by Berigan biographer Robert Dupuis in a conversation that took place in early 2008.

[71] Dupuis: 262.

[72] *Down Beat:* June 1, 1942, cited in the White materials.

[73] White materials: May 27, 1942.

[74] White materials: May 28, 1942.

[75] *Ibid.*

[76] White materials: May 29, 1942.

[77] This is a consolidation of information that appeared in *Billboard,* May 23, 1942; July 18, 1942; and October 10, 1942; as well as information that appeared in the July 29, 1942, issue of *Variety.* Cited in the White materials: May 30, 1942.

[78] *Ibid.*

[79] White materials: May 31, 1942.

[80] White materials: June 1, 1942. The address contained in the White materials for "Polyclinic Hospital" is 345 West Fifteenth Street, which is incorrect. The Polyclinic Hospital to which Berigan was taken was New York Polyclinic Hospital, located at 345 West Fiftieth Street, not far from the Van Cortland Hotel. The building in which Bunny Beri-

gan died remains standing as of the summer of 2011. It is now the site of Grenadier Po-lyclinic, which is a part of the New York City Free Clinic. This Polyclinic Hospital is not to be confused with the Polyclinic Hospital, now known as Stuyvesant Polyclinic Hospit-al, which was in 1942 (as it is today) located at 137 Second Avenue. Among the many notables who died there were: O.Henry (1910), Rudolph Valentino (1926), and Langston Hughes (1967). Marilyn Monroe had gall bladder surgery there in 1961, and recuperated there for several days.

Chapter 25
The Legend Begins

The inaccuracies, contradictions, and exaggerations that had been a part of Bunny Berigan's life continued after his death. And so the distorted picture of him that had existed while he lived began to be embellished further after he died. Many people had wanted a piece of Berigan while he was alive. Now that he was dead, most of those people, and many more who knew little or almost nothing about him, rushed forward to give their recollections and express their opinions.

In reviewing Bunny Berigan's death certificate, which contains information provided by Donna, who signed it, several errors appear. Bunny's mother is identified as Mayme "Slitzenberger" instead of the correct Schlitzberg. One would think that Donna, after eleven years of marriage to Bunny, and after spending many months living with Mayme over those years in Fox Lake in close contact with the Schlitzberg family, would have known Mayme's family name. Donna also reported that Bunny resided in New York City for fifteen years when in reality he lived there for about twelve and a half years. Finally, it appears that Donna, perhaps to avoid embarrassment, stated that she resided with Bunny at the Van Cortlandt Hotel, which is almost certainly not true. Clearly, Donna had gone to New York Polyclinic Hospital sometime during the day of June 2, 1942, to provide the hospital staff with the information that was required to complete Bunny's death certificate. In light of the fact that she had spent at least some part of that day drinking with George Zack (see below), one wonders what condition she was in when she arrived at the hospital. On the other hand, Donna never really appeared to have been completely in touch with what was going on in Bunny's life at any time while he was alive, so why should she be expected know all of the details after he died.

It should also be noted that Bunny Berigan's death certificate does not contain information about the medical causes of his death. That information was recorded in a separate document called a "confidential medical report," referred to in item 22 of his death certificate. I have obtained a copy of that report. It does not contain any surprises. John H. Burke, M.D., who signed the death certificate, stated the following conclusions, based on "laboratory tests and clinical findings," the principal cause of death was "frank hemhorrage, edema, hematoemesis secondary to obstructive portal cirrhosis." In layman's language, he died from extreme internal bleeding, an excess buildup of blood internally, vomiting of blood. The "contributory cause of death" was "portal liver cirrhosis, intestinal varices." Berigan bled internally from varices (swollen and ruptured blood vessels) in the portal vein (which passes through the liver) and the intestine, until he died. Bunny Berigan's death was neither pleasant nor peaceful.

The obituary that appeared in the New York *Times* was fairly accurate:

Bernard (Bunny) Berigan, 33 year old orchestra leader and trumpet player, died early yesterday morning in the Polyclinic Hospital, where he was taken on Monday. He was stricken Sunday night at the Van Cortland Hotel, 142 West Forty-ninth Street, where he made his home. The orchestra leader, who became well-known by his distinctive trumpet playing during the jitterbug era, first became ill on April 20, while on tour in Pennsylvania. After spending two weeks in a Pittsburgh hospital, he was warned against playing his trumpet. His final collapse was attributed to his insistence on playing the instrument that won him his success as a soloist in a number of famous name bands before organizing his own band. Don Palmer, manager of the Bunny Berigan band, said that in compliance with Mr. Berigan's wish, his band will be kept intact under the Berigan name, that Mrs. Donna Berigan, his widow, will maintain his financial interest in it and that Vido Musso, saxophonist in the band, will be the new leader. The band left last night to fill out-of-town engagements. Mr. Berigan was born at Fox Lake, Wisconsin, and earned his living playing the violin and trumpet from the time he was fourteen. He had appeared as a featured soloist with Rudy Vallee, Tommy Dorsey, Abe Lyman, Benny Goodman and Paul Whiteman. His best known recording, which became his theme song, was 'I Can't Get Started With You.' Since organizing his own orchestra five years ago, Mr. Berigan played his trumpet in nearly every number and directed the orchestra at the same time. Besides his widow, he leaves two daughters, Patricia, aged ten, and Joyce, five; his mother, Mrs. Mame Berigan, and a brother, Don Berigan, both of Fox Lake. The body will lie in state at Stafford's Funeral Parlor, 307 West Fifty-first Street, until 11 a.m. today, when a funeral service will be held at St. Malachy's Church, West Forty-ninth Street, between Seventh and Eighth Avenues. Burial will be at Fox Lake.[1]

The one that appeared in the Boston *Record American* was less so:

Bunny Berigan's sweet and hot trumpet was stilled today. The 33-year-old bandleader died at Polyclinic Hospital of an intestinal disturbance, which he had been warned would be aggravated if he did not lay aside the trumpet. He chose to play to the end. Berigan, according to his manager, was treated at a hospital for a serious stomach ailment in April and May and was warned upon his discharge not to play his trumpet again. However, he continued to play and on Sunday night was stricken at his hotel suite and taken to the hospital by his wife, Donna, and the family physician. Booked to play at Manhattan Center that night, Berigan was substituted by Benny Goodman. Before he died, Berigan stipulated that his band keep functioning with Vido Musso as leader and that Mrs. Berigan retain a financial interest. In addition to Mrs. Berigan, he is survived by two daughters, Patricia, 10, and Joyce, 5, both attending a Long Island school, his mother, Mrs. Mame Berigan, and a brother, Don, both of Fox Lake, Wisconsin. A high requiem mass will be celebrated at St. Malachy's Catholic Church (the Actors' Church), tomorrow at 11 a.m. and interment will be at Fox Lake.[2]

The trade papers, for whom Bunny had been a source for so many stories while he lived, now reported their versions of his life, which seem to have more that a little (mis)information provided by the MCA publicity department. From *Variety*:

Bunny Berigan, one of the most respected trumpet players in the music business, died early yesterday (Tuesday) morning in Polyclinic Hospital, New York City. He was admitted to that institute the previous afternoon after suffering a hemorrhage, during which he had lost a considerable amount of blood. He was 31. His private life is ascribed as contributing to his early demise, for he died of the same causes as that other great trumpeter, Bix Beiderbecke. Berigan's last date with his band was at the University of Scranton, Scranton, Pa., last Friday (29th). On Saturday night, he was scheduled to perform at Ray Hartenstine's (sic) Sunnybrook Ballroom, Pottstown, PA but dancers were refunded admissions when most of the band did not arrive until midnight, because of mechanical trouble with the bus they were riding. Berigan, traveling by private car, was at the dancery on time and staged an impromptu jam session with several others of his men who arrived on time. Sunday night (May 31), he was to have played at Manhattan Center, New York, but he had by that time become ill and his band worked without him, while Benny Goodman batoned and helped out with his sextet. Berigan's last sideman connection was with Tommy Dorsey, whom he left two years ago to form another band of his own. This was handled by Harry Moss, of the Music Corporation of America. To Moss goes all the credit for keeping Berigan in the running since he directed all of the leader's activities, saw to it that he worked almost without a day off and supervised the financial end of the outfit to the extent that Berigan's total debts, which at the time he left Dorsey were about $15,000, had been cut to almost nothing at the time of his death. Berigan's band will be kept intact by Moss if possible, with a new leader installed. Moss is also huddling at the moment with Benny Goodman, Tommy Dorsey and other well known batoneer friends of Berigan to set up some sort of trust fund for Berigan's wife, Donna, and his two children, Joyce and Pat, who survive, along with Berigan's mother and brother. The leader was gravely ill only about four weeks ago. He spent more than a week in Allegheny State Hospital, Pittsburgh, with a siege of pneumonia.[3]

From *Melody Maker*:

Headline: Bunny Berigan Died—Aged 31. *The Melody Maker* deeply regrets to report that Bunny Berigan, Famous White American trumpet ace has just died in the Polytechnic Hospital, New York at the early age of 31. Bunny had been ill for some time with pneumonia but insisted on carrying on with his work. Finally a severe hemorrhage sent him to the hospital on May 31, but by then it was too late, and his condition gradually worsened. His last date with his band was at Sunnybrook Ballroom, Pennsylvania, when he took part in an impromptu jam session with several of his boys, when a number of the orchestra failed to arrive owing to a mechanical breakdown. On Sunday (May 31) he was to have played a big date at Manhattan Center, N.Y. but he was in the hospital then and Benny Goodman sportingly batoned the Berigan outfit, and helped out the programme with the BG Sextet. Bunny Berigan was born in Green Bay, Wisconsin in 1911.

He started his musical career as a concert violinist, but the jazz bug soon bit him and we find him in 1928 playing at the Hofbrau, NYC, with Frank Cornwell's Orchestra. His playing here soon attracted notice, and he was quickly signed up by Hal Kemp. After a season at the Taft Hotel, New York, he came to England with that outfit in 1930. His grand modern style trumpet playing soon established him as a London favourite. Back in New York in 1931 he embarked on a free-lance career, playing and recording with Paul Whiteman, Rudy Vallee, Freddie Rich, Frankie Trumbauer and Bud Freeman; finally signing up with the all-star Dorsey Bros ork. He left there in 1933 to join Benny Goodman, but his rather volatile temperament clashed with that of the leader and he left again after 18 months to form his own band which for a time looked like being a huge success at the Hotel Pennsylvania, NY. Debts, union troubles and squabbles with the band all had a say in the matter though and Bunny packed up leading in 1938 to take on another spell of free-lancing, during which time he played in the CBS house band and led several sessions in the famous Saturday Night Swing Club series. Berigan was always a 'come-back-for-more' guy and early in 1939 he made another attempt to get a big orchestra going but this effort was even more disastrous and in the autumn he was glad to join the Tommy Dorsey band as first trumpet in an effort to clear up debts to the tune of $15,000. This time, The Music Corporation of America handled his affairs, and things were on the up-and-up with him for some time. Although without a resident job, the band was in great demand for one-night stands, etc., and Bunny was just paying off the last of his debts when ill-health (the results of years of worry) over-took him. The rest you know.[4]

Even Bunny's hometown newspaper had difficulty accurately reporting the facts:

This community was shocked Tuesday to learn of the sudden death of Bunny Berigan, famous musician, at New York on Monday night. Death was due to a throat infection that proved fatal. Funeral services were held at New York and the body was shipped here, where it was at the Tims Funeral Home over Friday night for burial here Saturday morning. Bernard Berigan was the son of Mr. and Mrs. William Berigan of this city. He was born November 2, 1908. He attended the Fox Lake public schools and then finished his education at Wisconsin High School in Madison, where he played with orchestras and his superlative trumpet playing soon attracted notice. After leaving Madison, he played trumpet in such renowned orchestras as Paul Whiteman, Benny Goodman, Hal Kemp and Ted Lyon. He later conducted his own orchestra for three and a half years, which was among the prominent orchestras on the air. He then played with Tommy Dorsey for a year or so and at the time of his death was again conducting his own orchestra over the air. While his orchestra has never played in Fox Lake, Bunny has played with visiting orchestras here and many local people have heard him in person and over the air. He leaves to mourn his untimely demise, his mother, Mrs. Mame Berigan, one brother, Donald of Fox Lake, his wife and two children. He was located in New York for the past 15 years.[5]

Other obituaries appeared in newspapers across the country. Many were edited versions of the one that appeared in the *New York Times*.

Available information indicates that only Tommy Dorsey and Don Palmer were with Bunny Berigan at the time of his death. Nothing has come to light indicating that Lee Wiley visited Bunny in the hospital, or attended his wake or funeral. Donna was not with Bunny when he died. She related much later to Robert Dupuis the following concerning the last time she saw Bunny:

> They were having a heated argument, Bunny and the priest. Bunny was saying he wasn't a Catholic. At one point he became a Christian Scientist so as to convince people that he wasn't a drinker like they said he was. I told the priest that he wasn't a Christian Scientist, that he had been brought up a Catholic, and so was I. So later the priest told me, 'There's nothing more you can do for him tonight. You go home, and if anything happens, we'll call you.' I wanted to stay with him because he looked so bad, and they didn't seem to think that he was going to make it. I was upset because they sent me home. I went back to the hotel and sat on the couch. Nobody called. I had the radio on and all of a sudden I heard, 'Bunny Berigan just passed away.' It was about four o'clock in the morning. I figured I'd get some calls, but nobody called—not Harry Moss, or Benny Goodman, or Tommy Dorsey—nobody. Finally, about six-thirty in the morning I heard a knock at the door and it was George Zack, the piano player. He said, 'Where's everybody? You mean nobody's here! It's been announced on the radio; they know where you are.' So he sat with me, went down and got some coffee and something to eat and brought up a drink too. He thought I'd appreciate that, which I did. My girlfriend Kay Altpeter called me and came over.[6]

Many years before making this statement, Donna recalled the same events to one of the White researchers:

> I heard the news of Bunny's death on an early morning radio broadcast and I just sat there, stunned with disbelief. In fact, I was still in a daze a couple of years later. Harry Moss from MCA called round later to ask if I'd heard the news, and said something about me having to go back to work. What could I do for a living? The only occupation I'd known was dancing, and I hadn't done any of that for ten years! And there wasn't any money. Bunny left none and all I had when he died was a couple of dollars in my purse. There was no insurance neither, because Bunny's auditor had allowed the policy to lapse. Some souvenir hunters had stolen his pen, his cuff-links and his tie clasp. I don't know what happened to his trumpet, which had a specially built mouthpiece. At about six o'clock in the evening, there was a knock at the door. It was George Zack, a piano player friend of Bunny's. He was the only one who showed up to pay his respects.[7]

The White researcher who interviewed Donna, Bob Wilson, also reported that when Donna made these statements, she was married to George Zack, who was present at the interview. Donna's recollections seemed to always be refracted through the prism of her self-made victimhood. As an alcoholic, she very often lived in world of fantasy and denial.

On June 2, Bunny's body was removed from Polyclinic Hospital to Stafford's Funeral Parlor. There it was prepared and put on display. It remained there until the following morning, when a funeral service was held. Those who came to Stafford's Funeral Parlor to pay their respects included Georgie Auld, the young saxophonist whose career Bunny had launched: "I loved that guy. When he died, I went to the funeral parlor before they had him gussied up, took out my comb, and combed his moustache. He was like—like my godfather."[8]

Not much more information is extant concerning Bunny's wake. It is very likely that his wake, funeral at St. Malachy's Church[9] in New York, and the transportation of his body (and Donna) back to Fox Lake, were orchestrated by Tommy Dorsey, possibly with the assistance of MCA. That would explain Ziggy Elman, then still being featured as TD's trumpet soloist, and a number of MCA's top bandleaders, being tapped as pall-bearers. Elman remembered "It was an honor for me to be asked to be a pall-bearer at the funeral service, as all the others were bandleaders like Sammy Kaye, Charlie Spivak and GuyLombardo."[10] If Tommy Dorsey did not pay all of the expenses for these things (and for Bunny's hospitalization) himself completely, he certainly contributed to all such payments and facilitated the gathering of funds for them from other contributors.[11] Based on all available evidence, Tommy Dorsey loved Bunny Berigan in very much the same manner that he loved his brother Jimmy, that is to say with a complete awareness of his many pecadilloes, most of which he overlooked most of the time. Donna harbored a visceral hatred of Tommy Dorsey from the 1930s until the day she died, and never missed an opportunity to either vilify him or criticize his motives. When she was in Fox Lake for Bunny's funeral and burial, she expressed some of this rancor to Loretta Berigan, Bunny's brother's wife: "I think she felt the most animosity toward Tommy Dorsey. She thought he had been taking money from Bunny's wages when he was with Tommy the second time. And apparently she and Tommy had had some confrontations. Donna told me that Tommy had called her 'a whore, a tramp, and a no-good bum.'"[12]

Bunny's body was transported from New York to Fox Lake by train on June 4, accompanied only by Donna. Tommy Dorsey was with his band at the Astor Roof in New York, and Don Palmer had rejoined the remnants of the eponymous Berigan band on the road. The train arrived in Fox Lake at about 7:00 p.m. on June 4. Ray Groose (or Grosse),[13] one of Bunny's musical associates from the early days, recalled that evening: "The funeral train carrying Bunny's body was one half passenger and one half freight and had to be switched at Beaver Dam. We (Groose and his wife and possibly other friends and/or relatives) picked up Donna at Beaver Dam and she rode to Fox Lake with us in the auto. Paul Whiteman had sent a large white orchid display, which was stolen en route. Tommy Dorsey sent a spray of purple orchids which did arrive. Bunny looked pretty good in the open coffin. The body was at a funeral parlor and then taken to the cemetery for the service, which was attended mostly by family and relatives."[14]

Loretta Berigan shared a room with Donna while she was in Fox Lake for the final rites.

We stayed at Dais and Harry Timm's home.[15] She was Mayme's second oldest sister, Theresa. Bunny was laid out there. Don was drunk through the entire thing. Donna was practically incoherent with grief, and she was drinking quite a bit too. We talked about many things, and Donna really poured her heart out. She was bitter about how they forced Bunny to work when he was too ill. She mentioned Harry Moss and James Petrillo. She was angry at them, as she had been with Arthur Michaud in some of the letters that Mayme had let me read earlier. Donna was quite a letter writer. She was concerned about money and how she would support the kids and herself. She said Don Palmer had helped Bunny pay back a lot of what he owed, but she was worried about what would happen with the remaining debts.[16]

An accepted part of the Berigan legend is that Bunny's funeral expenses in Fox Lake were never paid. This story was given credence because Bunny was laid to rest in St. Mary's Cemetery, about four miles south of Fox Lake, without a grave marker.[17] There is evidence however that this is not true. In the 1980s, Robert Dupuis interviewed Orville Kratz, who was the funeral director who handled the funeral arrangements in Fox Lake for Bunny Berigan.

The body was shipped from New York to the Fox Lake depot, where I met it. I remember there was a young man who hopped off of the train who was a fan of Bunny's. Bunny's mother—I admired her a lot—came to me and said, 'First my husband and now Bunny.' She knew that Bunny had assumed the responsibility for paying for his dad's funeral but that it hadn't been paid yet. I told her not to worry about it. She was grief-stricken. We had the service and the burial. Not long after that she came into our office—at that time our whole operation was in just a small corner of Jack Schlitzberg's furniture store—and told me about an insurance policy that had turned up. Somehow Bunny had this one that he hadn't converted the beneficiary from his mother's name to his wife's. Mayme came in and said, 'I want to pay for Bill's and Bunny's funerals.' That was a godsend for us; at that time every penny we could get a hold of was like a million dollars. I was very appreciative, and took off something like $125 from the bill. I always said 'There's one lady who won't be buried as a pauper.' Tommy Dorsey called us and said that the expenses in New York were all paid for, plus the transportation to Fox Lake. But Mayme paid us for the services here with that insurance policy.[18]

This story is unverified, of course, and now unverifiable, but in some respects it is believable. It is very probable that Mayme paid Orville Kratz for the services he had rendered for a number of reasons. First, from all reports, she was a very honorable person who was widely respected in the community where she spent almost all of her life. Second, it would have been very awkward for Jack Schlitzberg's sister to have an unpaid bill with Jack Schlitzberg's tenant, especially in a small town like Fox Lake. I think it likely that when Mayme's brother realized what the situation was, he went to her and offered either to give or loan her the money to pay Kratz. She then could have gone to Kratz with the money and a little white lie, and everyone would feel better. Given Bunny's ways, the story about the insurance policy, though possible, seems less likely.

Donna was the beneficiary of much sympathy in the period after Bunny's death, especially from those who did not know her. She was widely regarded as the young mother of two growing children who had been tragically widowed as the result of Bunny's ungoverned drinking, irresponsibility, and other dissolute ways. The truth was far more complicated. As we have seen, Bunny's drinking in the last five years of his life was heavy by all objective standards, but rarely did it render him unable to appear with his band, and play acceptably. The various illnesses that were caused by Bunny's chronic alcoholism, paramount of which was the cirrhosis that eventually killed him, sometimes caused him not to be able to play up to his full potential. What's more, whenever Bunny attempted to stop drinking entirely, and consequently began to suffer from delirium tremens, his ability to play the trumpet was also negatively affected. Still, unless he was hospitalized, he almost always appeared wherever and whenever MCA told him to appear, played in at least an acceptable professional manner and frequently brilliantly, pleased audiences, and otherwise behaved as the responsible leader of his band. And on the very few occasions when he did not appear where he was supposed to, it was not his fault. Within the context of his severe alcoholism, and the grueling schedule set for him by MCA, Bunny Berigan functioned remarkably well as a bandleader and trumpet virtuoso. Indeed, in the face of mortal illness, he continued performing before audiences on the road until only three days before he died.

The other factors that contributed to Bunny's popularity as a musician and bandleader while he lived, most notably his immense talent as a trumpet soloist whose playing communicated immediately and strongly with his audiences, and his gentle, humorous personality, continued to cause people to think well of him after he died. Also, the person who was probably his best and closest friend, Tommy Dorsey, acted as the catalyst for the numerous charitable works that were begun shortly after he died for the benefit of Donna and the girls. Finally, the much maligned (often with good reason) Harry Moss, who directed the activities of the last two Berigan bands for MCA, seems to have assisted TD in soliciting funds for the Berigan family trust from numerous MCA bandleaders, who then asked others for donations.

At the week's end it began to look as if Berigan's widow and two young children will be amply provided for. Tommy Dorsey has added Berigan's name to his weekly payroll, the understanding being that Berigan's family will receive union scale on every job the Dorsey band plays from now on. Bob Weitman, general manager of the Paramount Theatre here, Robert K. Christenberry, head of Hotel Astor here, and William P. Farnsworth, attorney, will administer a trust fund, contributions to which have been coming in as a result of wires sent to bandleaders and publishers by Dorsey, Benny Goodman and Fred Waring. Similar communications have been sent to ballroom ops., hotel execs., and other location managers by Harry Moss, Mike Nidorf and Willard Alexander of MCA, GAC and William Morris, respectively. Weitman, Christenberry and Farnsworth hope to secure enough coin to assure the support of Mrs. Berigan and the children at least until such time as the kids are able to take over the burden themselves.[19]

Bunny Berigan's friends have started a trust fund for the support of his children. It's an idea instigated by Tommy Dorsey, whose lawyer, William P. Farnsworth is one of the fund's trustees. The other trustees are Bob Weitman, manager of the Paramount, Bob Christenberry manager of the Astor Hotel and Harry Moss of MCA. All who would like to contribute to the Trust Fund can do so by sending contributions of any size to Wm. P. Farnsworth, 70 West Fortieth Street, NYC. Checks and money orders should be made payable to the 'Bunny Berigan Trust Fund.'[20]

When the news of Bunny Berigan's death was made public here last week, Benny Goodman, Tommy Dorsey, and Fred Waring immediately took steps to establish a trust fund for Bunny's widow and two children. Berigan died penniless. The three leaders sent telegrams to all the nation's prominent dance band leaders, asking them to contribute to the fund. They were asked to send their contributions to 'The Bunny Berigan Trust Fund,' c/o William P. Farnsworth, Trustee, 70 West Fortieth Street, New York City.[21]

These actions by Bunny's friends and associates in the music business were admirable. But, as everyone knows, acts of charity that are widely publicized somehow lose the patina of altruism. Everyone who participated in this public outpouring of support for Bunny's widow and children was the beneficiary of at least some goodwill in their own business enterprises as a result. Still, a number of people did actually solicit quite a bit of money for this fund. In 1942, Howard Lanin was a Philadelphia orchestra leader. In 1930 he was one of the first contractors to employ Bunny in New York. He recalled, "I was contacted by Fred Waring or his office and asked to give money to help pay for shipping Bunny Berigan's body back to Fox Lake. I kicked in $50 and I know others did also."[22] Pianist Paul Mertz reflected: I knew Bunny, used to see him a lot at Plunkett's and might have recorded with him on some commercial records. I saw the musical *Everybody's Welcome*; boy was the band FINE! By the time Bunny died I had moved to the West Coast, but I got request for funds from the East on the letterhead of Fred Waring. I doubt Bunny had any connection with Waring, but I guess his name was big then. I donated and I know others got the same letter and did the same.[23]

Soon after Bunny's death, Harry James also gave money to Donna, as this blurb reveals: "Dance for Mrs. Berigan was held at the Hollywood Palladium on June 20. Harry James and his orchestra donated their services and all receipts will go to Mrs. Berigan. Admission was fifty cents."[24]

There was also some indication in the obituaries that money derived from the operation of the Bunny Berigan ghost band, one of the first of these somewhat ambiguous enterprises, was to go to the Berigan family trust fund. Whether this actually happened is not known. But it is safe to say that an amount of money was gathered from a number of sources for this trust fund and/or for Donna in the months after Bunny's death, and it was used for the support of Donna and the girls for a substantial period of time. Disbursements from the trust fund as a matter of necessity had to be made to Donna because her daughters were still minors. Her stewardship of those funds was called into question in the period after Bunny's death and before her marriage to George Zack.

In the meantime, Bunny's other family, the one he had lived with day to day on the road, the now leaderless Bunny Berigan band, was still working. Due to Bunny's recent success, the band's engagement book was relatively full for the next several weeks, at least. They had traveled to Virginia to play a gig at the Episcopal School in Alexandria on June 2. Lead alto saxophonist George Quinty, who was one of the older and more mature members of the band, probably led the band on this job. Don Palmer had stayed in New York for Bunny's wake and funeral. Quinty later recalled what occurred that night: "We only learned of Bunny's death on that date. Charlie Mitchell was fighting back the tears as he tried to play 'I Can't Get Started'. He and Bunny were very close friends from 'way back.' He and Max 'Smitty' Smith had both known Bunny a long time and played with him on many dates. That night was like a wake. We were all only going through the motions, our thoughts being elsewhere."[25] Nevertheless, there were more one-nighters for the band to play. On June 3, they were at the Dreamland Ballroom at Conneaut Lake Park, a few miles west of Meadville, Pennsylvania. From there, it was on to Akron, Ohio on June 4, and then to Pittsburgh, and a gig at the Syria Mosque on the 5th. On all of these dates, the band merely appeared and played, without a "name" leader. MCA was taking care of that back in New York. Evidently the morbid curiosity of those who came out to see the band on those couple of dates was enough of a box office draw to prevent their cancellation.

Tenor saxophonist Vido Musso joined the band at Coney Island, Cincinnati, Ohio on Saturday June 6, 1942. Here is how the local press reported that event:

> Headline Vido Musso To Lead Bunny Berigan Ork: Vido Musso has left his high-paid tenor sax berth with Benny Goodman to take over leadership of the late Bunny Berigan's outfit tonight (6th) at Coney Island Park, Cincinnati. Hundreds of Greater Cincinnatians last night paid an unusual tribute to the memory of Bunny Berigan, noted young bandleader who died last Tuesday. They turned out in force to dance to the music of his orchestra, baton in the hand of Vido Musso, loaned by Benny Goodman to direct the band. During the course of the evening, there was an interlude that might have been termed a sort of memorial service, during which the band played some of Berigan's own compositions. Musso, playing his tenor saxophone, and Kay Little, attractive vocal soloist, scored repeatedly with solo offerings.[26]

It is far from certain that Kay Little, who was expecting a baby and whose husband, Danny Richards, was in the military, was still with the Berigan ghost band in June of 1942. We have seen that for the sake of expediency, MCA sometimes allowed one vocalist to be passed off as the one whose name appeared in MCA's advance publicity for the band, even if that vocalist was someone else. Nevertheless, Ms. Little, who was an audience-pleasing vocalist, may well have worked with the Berigan ghost band for awhile. The Coney Island engagement lasted until June 11.

The band then went on to a job at Jefferson Beach, near Detroit, which lasted from June 12 to the 15th, and from there, to a string of gigs in Ohio. And so it went. At some point, MCA and Musso dropped the Berigan name from the band's billing, probably after they realized that the public would accept Musso as a name bandleader. One-nighter business in the summer of 1942 was the best it had been in sixteen years, despite the various problems that by then were being caused by the draft of young men into military service and various World War II home front disruptions, including gas rationing.[27] The strong upturn in the U.S. economy caused by war industries gearing up was undoubtedly the reason for this. The band's personnel gradually changed, and Musso gradually dispensed with the Berigan library, which then vanished almost immediately, except for a few charts that were taken by sidemen as mementos.[28]

In spite of the increased demand for big bands in mid-1942, the overall effects of World War II on civilian life in the United States were making it increasingly difficult to keep big bands on the road. "Musical instrument manufacturing was cut back due to restrictions on the use of precious metals, and there was a ban on juke box manufacturing. In May, 1942, record production was slashed by one-third because of shellac shortages. By August, gas rationing was reduced to two gallons per week, and bands had to travel by train or car—no buses."[29] Faced with all of these challenges, plus the ordinary headaches of leading a big band on the road, Musso broke up the band at the end of September.

Presumably, Musso's time as the leader of a touring band had been profitable for him. He led the band through the summer months that were always more lucrative for road bands than the colder months, when inclement weather could make travel for both the bands and their audiences difficult and sometimes hazardous. Vido Musso returned to life as a high-profile sideman, joining Woody Herman. He then served briefly in the U.S. Marine Corps and was employed for a time in a defense plant. After World War II, he sometimes worked as a sideman, most notably with Stan Kenton, but more often as a leader of bands of various size in the Los Angeles area. He also appeared in several films, looking good and playing well. Musso, who was frequently the butt of musicians' jokes because of the way he sometimes misused the English language, was careful with his money, invested in real estate in California after World War II, and lived comfortably until his death on January 9, 1982, in Rancho Mirage, California, at age sixty-nine.

In its September 1, 1942, issue, *Down Beat* ran a lengthy interview with Don Palmer. Here it is:

Large headline: 'Manager Nails Berigan Lies' Bunny paid off $15,000 In Year, No Irresponsible Drunkard Could Do That!

New York—'Take it from me, those stories you hear about Bunny Berigan drinking himself to death are so much hot air. They couldn't be more wrong.' Don Palmer, who road-managed the Berigan crew during the year before the trumpet player's death, made this claim in an exclusive interview with *Down Beat*. Although Don was approached by a national slick magazine for a story just after Bunny died, he was too broken up at the time to give out with the straight account and felt, too, that musicdom's newspaper rightfully had first claim on it. 'If ever a guy put his whole heart and soul into making an organization click, that guy was Bunny Berigan,' Don went on. 'That's why these false rumors bother me and the rest of Bunny's real friends so much. It's just not fair that the thousands of kids all over the country, who thought of him as a great musician and someone to model their music life on, should be disillusioned by lies and gossip spread by squares who never even knew Bunny. More important, it isn't right that the memory of one of the greatest jazzmen should be defamed and that he should have a completely inaccurate picture of his last days to confuse jazz historians.'

He Was Not a Lush
'I'm not going to tell you that Bunny didn't take a drink while I was with him because that wouldn't be true. But he was far from being the irresponsible drunkard that they've made him out. And you don't have to take my word for that, either. Just look up the records. During the last twelve months, there wasn't one complaint sent into Harry Moss of MCA who handled the band's account. Just the opposite was true. Not only did Bunny break attendance records set up by bands like Gray Gordon, Will Osborne and Russ Morgan, but bookers all over the country sent in enthusiastic accounts to the New York office about the band and his behavior. Even then, they'd heard the stories about Bunny and were almost surprised to see him reach the band stand sober and on time. But to really prove what I am telling you, here is a story that not many people know and that shows just what a real guy Bunny was. When Harry Moss took the band over on July 28, 1941, Bunny was twenty thousand dollars in debt. At the time of his death, he was less than five thousand dollars in debt. Does that sound as though he hadn't been working hard and plugging to get places? He traveled all over the country and did two hundred one-nighters in a year's time. No screwball drunk could do that. Bunny had one big idea and that was to produce the best band in the business. Nothing else mattered. We knew that he was working too hard and told him so. Once when he had just been released from the hospital, the doctors told him that he shouldn't work for at least three months. A few days later he was back with the band again, playing harder than ever.'

Refused to Rest
'I tried to get him to take a lay-off and let the band use his name while he rested, and take enough of a cut to keep him going, but he wouldn't listen to me. We nearly had a fight one night when he was ill and I tried to keep him from working. Another time, Harry Moss flew to Norfolk to get him to quit, but without success. Trouble was that Bunny's health was undetermined from years of fast living that went way back to the time when Hal Kemp brought him into the music business. Bunny was never the kind of person who took things easily. He worked hard and played just as hard. He didn't know how to relax. Besides that, his dad died not long before Bunny did and that didn't help matters any.'

Cut Too Few Records
'One of my biggest regrets,' Don said, 'is that Bunny didn't make more records during his last days. Then everyone could see how well he was playing, in spite of feeling tough a lot of the time. The last sides that he cut were for Elite Records, during the latter part of April, 1942. The titles were 'My Little Cousin'; 'Skylark'; 'Me and My Melinda'; and 'Somebody Else Is Taking My Place'. They should be released shortly in a Memorial Album. I'm glad I can say that Bunny died happily. Vido Musso, who took over the band, Tommy Dorsey and I were at his bed-side. One of his last wishes was that the band should stay together and go places. I don't have to tell you that we're going to do just that. A lot of people have written in to me asking what happened to Bunny's trumpet. I have it and the mouthpiece that he used for his 'I Can't Get Started' number. I intend to hold on to them for the time being; perhaps later they'll be placed in jazz historical collection.'

TD Was a Pal!
'I want to say that a lot of credit should be given to Harry Moss for the fine job he did after he took over the band and for the personal interest he took in Bunny. Tommy Dorsey also did everything that he could for Bunny, and gave his family a wonderful lift after his death. Maybe this article will do something to clear up the confusion about Bunny's death. The whole musical world should know what a loss they've suffered and that the most wonderful musician who ever lived spent his last days in the best of show tradition, working to do the stuff he loved in the best way that he possibly could."[30]

   Based on the available evidence, much though not all of what Palmer stated in this interview was correct. Unlike other commentators, I do not think this tribute by Palmer to Bunny was being made insincerely or with ulterior motives. By the time this "interview" appeared, Bunny's band had evolved into the Vido Musso band. Therefore, publicity for Bunny Berigan would not have benefited the Musso band, MCA, or Palmer. Although some of the numbers that Palmer cited may be exaggerations,[31] Palmer's points that (1) Bunny worked very hard and was very responsible during the last months of his life, and (2) as a result paid off a lot of his debts, are nevertheless valid.
   At least one assertion made by Palmer seems to be a great exaggeration however—that Bunny was $15,000 in debt when Harry Moss took over the administration of Berigan's finances. Moss took on this responsibility in April of 1941.[32] At that time, it was reported that Bunny had been able to "whittle down most of (his previous) debt," but was going in the hole again by not paying his sidemen fully because MCA for whatever reason was not providing the band with enough work to balance its finances. When the "band mutiny" later occurred, in July of 1941, Bunny owed his musicians approximately $900, and he also owed MCA for the hotel bill he had skipped out on in Trenton, New Jersey.[33] If this is added to what was left of his previous debt, the total would have been nowhere near $15,000. A figure of $1,500 seems more probable. Indeed, it had been reported in the November 12, 1941, issue of *Variety* that Bunny was

then almost debt-free "except for a small amount of government taxes." It appears certain from the way the final Berigan band was being operated, with the sidemen being paid only when they played without fixed weekly salaries, that Bunny was incurring no new debt as a result of operating that band. Thus the debt Bunny was paying down or off during the last six months of his life probably was $1,000 or less.

I do believe however that MCA would have paid the Sunnybrook Ballroom management for the missed Berigan date on May 30, to preserve goodwill with that very lucrative venue. (That fiasco seems to have been the fault of Don Palmer, who some sidemen reported had fallen asleep on the band bus while it sped *away* from the Sunnybrook Ballroom on the afternoon of May 30.) MCA then probably recouped this loss from whatever income would have gone to Bunny's heirs from the operations of the Berigan ghost band immediately after his death. This loss would probably have been in the $500 range however. It is extremely likely that without the Sunnybrook debacle, Bunny would have been debt-free at the time of his death. Thus, the thought of having to pay for someone else's negligence yet again, which he did indeed do after his death, undoubtedly had upset Bunny greatly in the final hours of his life.

Meanwhile, Donna, described by her sister-in-law Loretta as "quite a letter writer," began to correspond with various people about her recently departed husband. A letter from her caught up with Danny Richards somewhere while he was on active duty with the army. "I received a letter from Donna telling me of his death, and letting me know how highly Bunny thought of me. Let me tell you, boy, the tears flowed that day. I can't begin to tell you how I felt."[34] Joe Bushkin was in the army air force stationed at March Field, in California on June 3, 1942. "I went to the day room to pick up the *L. A. Times*, and it said, 'Bunny Berigan dead at 33.' I just threw up. It seemed a perfectly natural reaction for me. I got a beautiful letter from Jo Stafford describing the wake they had in New York. My dad sent Donna a hundred dollars for me."[35] Mike Zirpolo Sr., who had seen Bunny at the peak of his powers in 1938, was boarding a troop train in Newark, New Jersey with fellow army privates when he picked up a *New York Times*. "I was completely stunned. I had no idea that Bunny Berigan had any health problems. It was simply unimaginable to me that the powerful, young, god-like man I had seen in 1938 was dead by 1942. That news was deeply disturbing to me."[36]

Donna's own alcoholism apparently worsened after Bunny's death. In spite of the assistance she was receiving from the trust fund set up by Bunny's friends and associates in the music business, she "...was unable to shoulder the financial and other responsibilities of raising (her) children, and shortly after her daughters witnessed her being taken by ambulance to Belleview Hospital for detoxification, their temporary custody was awarded to Darrell and Joyce McArthur."[37] Bob Davis, Joyce Berigan's second husband, made this statement to one of the White research team: "After Bunny's death there was a big family feud. Apparently Darrell McArthur, Donna's brother, hated Bunny with a passion, and went to court later to try to get the two kids away from Donna. The court set up the estate, with Donna getting one third and each child getting a third."[38]

There was far more to it than that. After Donna was taken to the hospital, the girls (Pat was then ten and Joyce six) were literally left with nowhere to go. A policeman who was on the scene asked Pat if she was Bunny Berigan's daughter. Pat said yes and asked him to call her uncle and aunt, Darrell and Joyce McArthur, who lived in the Riverdale section of the Bronx, then a lovely residential area. The girls then went to live with the McArthurs temporarily. When Donna was released from the hospital, she took them back, and for a short time she and they lived with Rollo Laylan and his wife. This living arrangement did not work out, and it was then that Darrell McArthur took whatever legal steps were necessary to obtain legal custody of Pat and Jo.

Shortly after this, Donna married pianist George Zack, who was also an alcoholic, and continued drinking. Her daughters were then raised by her brother and sister-in-law, and continued to live with them until they married. Patricia Berigan, reflecting on all of this many years later, was very grateful to her uncle and aunt for providing her and Joyce a stable home. Although she had fond memories of Darrell and Joyce, she also recognized that there had been emotional damage from the chaotic years before. "The way we were bounced around with so many different adults in charge, it was hard to develop a value system of our own that would serve us. It was not a textbook childhood."[39]

The estate/trust fund continued for some time:

Headline: Auld Disc Aids Berigan Fund: New York—The Bunny Berigan fund is being given a boost with a share of the royalties of the recording of 'I Can't Get Started,' recently (May 22, 1944) cut for Apollo by Georgie Auld's band. Jazzsters will remember that Auld was one of the stars of the original Berigan recording. The Berigan fund was created at the time of trumpet player's death on June 2, 1942, to undertake the education of his two children. At the present time the fund is depleted. Contributions may be addressed to Harry Moss, 745 Fifth Avenue, New York City.[40]

The funds for the support of the two children of the late Bunny Berigan, which Harry Moss has ably administered for three years, is running low. Send contributions to Harry Moss at the Lincoln in New York, or to Bob Christenberry at the Astor, or Bob Weitman at the Paramount, all in Manhattan.[41]

Neither of these articles mentioned Donna, indicating that the change of custody of the Berigan girls had taken place before mid-1944.

Trumpeter Billy Butterfield,[42] whom I have always considered to have been one of Bunny's musical heirs, while leading his own band in the mid-1940s, received a steady stream of requests to play Bunny's theme song. "Inspired by the number of requests to play the number, trumpeter Billy Butterfield has recorded Bunny Berigan's theme song 'I Can't Get Started' for Capitol. Dedicated to Bunny, royalties will be given to the fund started and maintained by musicians for the Berigan family." [43] Butterfield was a man who had a deeply ironic sense of humor. He recalled that particular matter in a way that would have brought a smile of recognition to the face of Bunny Berigan. After that recording was made "...unfortunately, my own band collapsed, and General Artists, my agents, seized whatever money or royalties there were to pay uncollected commissions."[44]

As the 1940s ended and the 1950s began, both pop music and jazz continued to move away from the format in which big band jazz had flourished. The big band era had effectively ended in the mid to late 1940s. Starting in the late 1930s, MCA began to concentrate its energies first in the movie business, and later in television. As the '40s progressed, MCA's clients were increasingly no longer bandleaders, but movie stars, writers, and others connected with that part of the entertainment business. MCA's business plan for presenting live bands in every possible venue in the United States had been based on very low Depression-era costs. The onset of World War II and the inflation thereafter changed that. Consequently operating big bands on the road went from being an extremely risky business for bandleaders, to being nearly cost prohibitive for them. MCA's business plan was also based on radio being the principal mass medium to promote their bands. As television replaced radio as the major source of home entertainment in the late 1940s and early 1950s, the promotional push that had been provided to bands by radio did not continue with television. If people could see a band at home in their living room on television for free, why would they want to stand the expense and inconvenience of going out to hear and see a band? Demand for dance bands on the road plummeted as a result. Many of the hundreds of musicians who had received invaluable training as sidemen in touring big bands began to work either as jazz musicians with small groups (when they could find work), or settled in New York or Hollywood, where they could use their skills providing the background music for radio and TV shows, commercial recordings, and movies. Many more returned to their home towns, where they worked part-time as musicians if they could, and took day jobs to earn a living.

As the music scene changed during and immediately after World War II, the recordings of Bunny Berigan gradually disappeared from the market. His last recordings, made for Eli Oberstein's small Elite label, had limited distribution from the beginning. The shellac shortage caused by World War II further limited their distribution. The classic Victor recording of "I Can't Get Started," in its abridged form on a ten-inch 78 rpm shellac disc that could be played on jukeboxes, remained available throughout the remainder of the 78 era. Aside from the album of 78s Victor issued in 1944 (P-134) entitled *Bunny Berigan— Memorial Album*, few of Bunny's other recordings were commercially available then.[45] And with Berigan himself no longer on the scene appearing around the country, on radio, or on film, his name receded from public awareness. From the standpoint of the current hit/pop music business where Bunny had always been required to work, his music became a thing of the past.

As the format of commercial recordings changed from brittle shellac 78s to vinyl 33-1/3 rpm LPs throughout the 1950s, the commercial recordings of Bunny Berigan and His Orchestra remained somewhat rare. There was an early 45 rpm disc bearing "I Can't Get Started"/"Frankie and Johnny" (RCA Victor 47-2956), circa 1949, and the same titles in RCA's "Gold Standard" series a few years later (447-0075). More significantly, *Bunny Berigan Plays Again* (RCA Victor LPT-1003), a twelve-inch "Collectors Issue" LP, including the full-length version of "I Can't Get Started," was released in 1951. There was also a ten-inch Elite LP titled *Bunny Berigan's Last Recordings,* made in 1954, along with a single 45 EP of the same name. In 1956, Epic released a twelve-inch LP, *Take It, Bunny* (LG-3109), which contained a number of his pre-Victor recordings. The same tunes were also available as three separate EPs. RCA added a four song "Gold Standard" EP, with a color or colorized picture of Bunny (EPA-5003). In 1960, Epic did another twelve-inch LP of pre-Victor sides, *Bunny Berigan & His Boys.*[46]

LP releases of recordings made by Benny Goodman and Tommy Dorsey during the times when Bunny was recording with them also trickled into the marketplace during the 1950s. Jazz cornetist Ruby Braff recorded a *Hi-Fi Salute to Bunny,* RCA Victor LPM-1510, which was released in 1957. Shortly after that, possibly in response to the sales of the Braff disc, RCA Victor issued LPM 2078, *Bunny Berigan and His Orchestra—Great Dance Bands of the '30s and '40s.* This LP contained twelve sides, including many of Berigan's best RCA Victor performances. The success of that record brought about the second RCA LP release of Berigan recordings entitled *Bunny,* in 1960. This LP (CAL-550) was issued on the budget-priced Camden label, and contained a dozen more excellent Berigan/Victor recordings. From then until 1972, there were no more significant releases of the recordings of Bunny Berigan and His Orchestra. In 1972, RCA Victor issued sixteen more Berigan/Victor recordings on LPV-581 as a part of its "Vintage" series. This LP contained all of the "Beiderbecke Suite" recordings, and some intelligent (though not totally accurate) liner notes by Dan Morgenstern, who was then the editor of *Down Beat.* Although this album was labeled as "Volume 1," no Volume 2 was ever issued.

The 1970s also saw the first hints that the huge Berigan research project that eventually would become what has been referred to herein as the "White materials" was nearing completion, under the direction of Cedric "Bozy" White. This information was first disclosed on the back of the dust jackets for various LPs issued on the Shoestring label, which was operated by Mr. White. These LPs contained many airchecks, a few Berigan oddities like some of the demonstration recordings Bunny made in 1939, and the two Norge transcriptions he made in 1937. Also in the 1970s, various *Thesaurus* transcription recordings by the Berigan band began to appear on LP.

As the 1970s turned into the '80s, RCA issued on LP all of Bunny's commercial recordings for the Victor label as a part of their excellent Bluebird "Complete" series. These sets were well produced with good sound, and liner notes. From approximately 1970 until the end of the LP era in approximately 1990, many other Berigan recordings were issued in that format from both the pre-Victor and Victor years. The 1990s saw the issuance of most of Bunny's commercial recordings as a leader on the French "Classics" label in the then new digital compact disc format. This decade also was when almost all of the Berigan/*Thesaurus* recordings were issued on CD. As the new millennium began, more Berigan CDs hit the market, most notably the multidisc set of Bunny's work as a sideman in the early 1930s on the Mosaic label. As this is written, there are more recordings by Bunny Berigan available in the marketplace (including Internet downloads) than at any previous time. Nevertheless, the dozens of aircheck recordings Bunny made in the period 1939–1942 (see appendix 3) remain largely unissued.

In the 1970s, two notable Hollywood films included the music of Bunny Berigan. *Save the Tiger* (Paramount, 1973), starring Jack Lemmon and Jack Gilford, set in the early 1970s, begins with a lonesome sounding trumpet (not Berigan) playing "I Can't Get Started," and ends with most of Bunny's classic Victor recording being played behind the closing credits. In one scene, "I Can't Get Started" (again not played by Berigan) is playing on Lemmon's car stereo while he drives through a desolate section of downtown Los Angeles. Later, in a marijuana-induced stream-of-consciousness recitation of the names of "famous people" with a young woman less than half his age, Lemmon includes the name Bunny Berigan.

The classic film *Chinatown* (Paramount, 1974), starring Jack Nicholson and Faye Dunaway, is set in Los Angeles in 1937. The exquisite music behind the main title at the opening of the film, immediately evokes that time. It includes a Beriganesque trumpet solo expertly played by Hollywood studio veteran Uan Rasey. This "Love Theme from Chinatown," reappears throughout the film. A few bars of Berigan's Victor recording of "I Can't Get Started" is heard during a scene where Nicholson is trying to figure out why precious Los Angeles water is being pumped into the Pacific Ocean.

It was not mere coincidence that the music of Bunny Berigan was heard in these two Paramount films from the 1970s. Robert Evans, the producer of *Chinatown* and a major player at Paramount then, loved Bunny Berigan's "I Can't Get Started."[47] Berigan's music can also be heard on the soundtrack to the TV movie *Tales from the Hollywood Hills: Natica Jackson* (1987), and the film *Brick* (2005). In the fall of 2010, Berigan's recording of "Heigh-Ho" was used that the background music on a television ad for Levi's jeans. It can be said with assurance that Bunny Berigan's music, especially "I Can't Get Started," has become interwoven in the fabric of American popular culture.

Berigan also was mentioned on numerous occasions and sometimes figured in the story line of the eponymous comic strip *Crankshaft*, which debuted in 1987.

Robert Dupuis published his biography of Bunny Berigan in 1993. Various writings by jazz trumpeter Richard M. Sudhalter about Berigan's music began to appear in the 1980s, and continued into 2002, when illness forced him to stop. After Bozy White's death in 2004, the materials about Bunny that he had been gathering with others since 1949 passed into the hands of Perry Huntoon, who with others has been preparing them to be published.

Among the hundreds of aircheck recordings of vintage jazz made by expert audio engineer William Alcott "Bill" Savory (1916–2004) in the late 1930s, which in 2010 were turned over by Savory's son to the National Jazz Museum in Harlem, are yet more recordings made by Bunny Berigan. When some of these recordings were played in a program at the museum in the fall of 2010 featuring the music of great jazz trumpeters from the late 1930s, there was a fervid audience response.

Bunny's mother, Mary Catherine Schlitzberg Berigan, died on May 26, 1944 of liver and intestinal cancer. She was sixty-nine years old.[48] Bunny's brother Don died on May 21, 1983, just short of his seventy-eighth birthday.[49] Bunny's daughters, Patricia and Joyce, grew up in the custody of their uncle and aunt, Darrell and Joyce McArthur, married, and eventually produced nine sons between them. Knowing Bunny's fondness for children and family life, one can easily imagine the delight he would have taken in this large brood of grandsons. Patricia Berigan Slavin died on December 8, 1998, in Kansas City, Missouri, aged sixty-six. Donna divorced George Zack in 1958, and married for a third time, to Bernard Burmeister. She died on March 15, 1986, in Kansas City, Missouri, the result of chronic emphysema.[50] She was almost seventy-four at the time of her death. Lee Wiley died on December 11, 1975 in New York City at age sixty-seven, a victim of colon cancer. Bunny's youngest daughter, Joyce Berigan (Bryden) Hansen, passed away on July 4, 2011, at age seventy-five, in Madison, Wisconsin.

Despite the many inaccuracies, contradictions, and exaggerations that have been told and retold through the years about Bunny Berigan, about this there is no doubt: he was a superb musician and a great jazz trumpeter. It is his music that, while he lived and since his death, was, is, and forever will be his greatest triumph. After all of the anguish he suffered in his life, after all of the hype and misinformation about him generated by MCA and the other business entities that profited from his talent and hard work faded, indeed after his own charismatic persona disappeared into the mists of the past, what has remained is his music. His music continues to speak to people on many levels. That has been more than enough for me.

Notes

1 *New York Times:* June 3, 1942.
2 *Boston Record American:* June 2, 1942, cited in the White materials.
3 *Variety:* June 3, 1942, cited in the White materials.
4 *Melody Maker:* July 11, 1942, cited in the White materials.
5 *Fox Lake Representative:* June 5, 1942, cited in the White materials.

[6] Dupuis: 262.

[7] White materials: June 2, 1942.

[8] *Traps, the Drum Wonder:* 40.

[9] Located at 239 West Forty-ninth Street, between Broadway and Eighth Avenue, St. Malachy's Catholic Church was at its height as "the actors' church" in the period from the 1920s to the 1950s. Among those who worshipped there frequently, in addition to Bunny Berigan, were George M. Cohan, Spencer Tracy, Perry Como, Irene Dunne, Hildegarde, Florence Henderson, Elaine Stritch, Rosalind Russell, Abbott and Costello, Danny Thomas, Bob and Dolores Hope, Fred Allen, Don Ameche, Pat O'Brien, Ray Bolger, Lillian Gish, and Jimmy Durante. It remains a vital part of Manhattan's theater district community, and is the spiritual home of many entertainers today, including Chita Rivera, and Antonio Banderas.

[10] White materials: June 3, 1942.

[11] Dupuis: 265. See also *Down Beat:* July 1, 1942, and *Metronome:* July 1942.

[12] Dupuis: 264.

[13] Ray Groose's name was spelled "Grosse" in the *Fox Lake Representative* picture/caption that appeared on October 8, 1950, when a red granite headstone was placed on Berigan's grave. Groose was among a group of Bunny's early musical associates and others who raised the money to place the headstone. Since Groose was interviewed by the various White researchers over the years, and his name is spelled "Groose" in the White materials. I will assume that that spelling is correct.

[14] White materials: June 4, 1942.

[15] The home where Bunny's body lay in Fox Lake still stands, and is very near to the small Fox Lake railroad station.

[16] Dupuis: 264.

[17] This situation was rectified in 1950 when a group of Bunny's friends, musical associates, and fans gathered the funds necessary to place a red granite headstone on his grave. See note 13 above.

[18] Dupuis: 265.

[19] *Billboard:* June 13, 1942, cited in the White materials.

[20] *Metronome:* July 1942, cited in the White materials.

[21] *Down Beat:* June 15, 1942, cited in the White materials.

[22] White materials: June 6, 1942.

[23] *Ibid.*

[24] *Metronome:* July 1942, cited in the White materials.

[25] White materials: June 2, 1942.

[26] *Cincinnati Enquirer:* June 7, 1942, cited in the White materials.

[27] *Billboard:* October 3, 1942, cited in the White materials.

[28] Dupuis: 273.

[29] *Out of the Cool—Gil Evans, His Life and Music,* by Stephanie Stein Crease, A Cappella Books, (2002), 94–95.

[30] *Down Beat:* September 1, 1942, cited in the White materials.

[31] Robert Dupuis correctly states in his Berigan biography the number of dates played by the so-called kids' band: 167. This number is still evidence of the backbreaking schedule Bunny maintained during the last months of his life.

[32] *Billboard:* May 3, 1941.

[33] *Variety:* August 6, 1941.

[34] Dupuis: 266.

[35] *Ibid.*

[36] Told many times over the years by my father to me, usually after listening to a particularly brilliant Berigan solo on a recording.

[37] Dupuis: 293.

[38] White materials: June 5, 1942.

[39] Information regarding the change of custody of Pat and Joyce Berigan from Donna to Darrell and Joyce McArthur was provided by Patricia Berigan to Robert Dupuis; Dupuis archive, UW–Madison.

[40] *Down Beat:* June 15, 1944, cited in the White materials.

[41] *Down Beat:* January 1, 1947, cited in the White materials.

[42] Trumpeter Charles William "Billy" Butterfield was born in Middletown, Ohio, on January 14, 1917. His name band career began in 1937 with the Bob Crosby band. His warm-toned trumpet was featured on a number of Crosby recordings, most notable of which was an instrumental written for him by the Crosby band's bassist/arranger Bob Haggart entitled "I'm Free." This tune was given a lyric by Johnny Burke, and found lasting acceptance as the song "What's New?" After World War II, Butterfield led a good big band for a couple of years, but the swing era was over by then and he left bandleading deeply in debt. Possessing many of the same skills as Bunny Berigan, Butterfield commenced a long and lucrative career in the broadcast and recording studios of New York in the late 1940s. During the next thirty years, Butterfield also made many recordings under his own name. He also joined, toured, and recorded with the band co-led by his old Crosby band associates trumpeter Yank Lawson and bassist Bob Haggart called the World's Greatest Jazzband, in the late 1960s. All of the recordings Butterfield made in those years reveal that he maintained his skills as a jazz soloist well into the 1980s. From the 1970s into the 1980s, Butterfield appeared at jazz festivals in the United States and Europe. He died of cancer on March 18, 1988, in North Palm Beach, Florida.

[43] *Metronome:* December 1947, cited in the White materials.

[44] Billy Butterfield to Robert Dupuis, May 7, 1987, cited in Dupuis: 267.

[45] Victor released P-134, the *Bunny Berigan Memorial Album* of 78s in 1944. A 45 rpm issue of "I Can't Get Started"/"Frankie and Johnny," RCA Victor 47-2956, was issued circa 1949. *Bunny Berigan Plays Again,* RCA Victor LPT-1003, was issued in the early 1950s, as was a twelve-inch "Collector's Issue" LP. Berigan's recordings for the Elite label appeared on a ten-inch 33 rpm disc for the first time in 1954.

[46] This discographical information was provided by Christopher Popa.

[47] Liner notes for the original motion picture soundtrack for *Chinatown,* Varese Sarabande VSD-5677 (1995, MCA Records), by Kevin Mulhall. This soundtrack was originally issued in 1974 by ABC Records, Inc. Jerry Goldsmith composed the score, which was superbly arranged by Arthur Morton.

[48] Dupuis: 293.

[49] *Ibid:* 294.

[50] *Ibid.*

Appendix One
Aircheck Recordings by Bunny Berigan and His Orchestra, 1937–1938*

March 7, 1937—Norge Radio Show transcriptions: (Program #5) "There's a Small Hotel"; "Stompin' at the Savoy"; (Program # 37) "Organ Grinder's Swing"; "You Turned the Tables on Me" (vocal Carol McKay).

April 17, 1937—*Saturday Night Swing Club* broadcast, CBS radio network: Bunny Berigan appeared as a soloist on this network radio show, performing with Leith Stevens and the CBS Orchestra. He was featured on "Careless Love," "The Blue Room," and "Swanee River."

May 1, 1937—WABC–New York, 11:05 p.m.–11:30 p.m., from the Madhattan Room of Hotel Pennsylvania, New York City: introduction and theme; "You Can't Run Away from Love" (vocal Carol McKay); "The You and Me That Used to Be" (vocal Ford Leary). Note: On all of the broadcasts referred to from the Madhattan Room, the Berigan band also played a number of tunes that for some reason were not recorded.

May 5, 1937—WABC–New York, 11:05 p.m.–11:30 p.m., from the Madhattan Room of Hotel Pennsylvania, New York City, Bert Parks, announcer: (joined in progress) "The You and Me That Used to Be" (vocal Ford Leary); "Swanee River"; "Big John Special"; theme and closing.

May 8, 1937—WABC–New York, 11:05 p.m.–11:30 p.m., from the Madhattan Room of Hotel Pennsylvania, New York City: "You Showed Me the Way" (vocal Carol McKay); "Summer Night" (CM); "King Porter Stomp."

May 9, 1937—*Fun in Swingtime* radio show, 6:30 p.m.–7:00 p.m., WOR studios, New York City: "Melody in F"; "It's Swell of You" (vocal Carol McKay); "'Cause My Baby Says It's So" (vocal Bunny Berigan); "Black Bottom."

May 12, 1937—WABC–New York, 11:00 p.m.–11:30 p.m., from the Madhattan Room of Hotel Pennsylvania, New York City, Ken Roberts, announcer: "They All Laughed" (vocal Carol McKay); "Mahogany Hall Stomp"; theme and closing.

May 13, 1937—WOR–New York, 12:00 midnight–12:30 a.m., from the Madhattan Room of Hotel Pennsylvania, New York City, Howard Doyle, announcer: "Mr. Ghost Goes to Town," "Royal Garden Blues," theme and closing.

May 29, 1937—WABC-New York, 7:00 p.m. to 7:30 p.m. CBS's *Saturday Night Swing Club* presented Bunny Berigan and His Orchestra as a part of its show via a live feed from the Hotel Pennsylvania. The tune that was included as a part of the *SNSC* show was "You Can't Run Away from Love Tonight," without the vocal chorus.

June 11, 1937—WABC–New York, 11:15 p.m.–???, from the Roof Garden of Hotel Pennsylvania, New York City: "Swanee River" (extended version); "Frankie and Johnny" (incomplete).

June 12, 1937—WABC–New York, 11:00 p.m.–11:30 p.m., from the Roof Garden of Hotel Pennsylvania, New York City: "Rose Room," and "Peckin'". CBS's *Saturday Night Swing Club* celebrated its first anniversary with a special show that started at midnight and ran until 1:30 a.m. on June 13. At some point in this broadcast, Bunny Berigan and His Orchestra were featured on one tune, "Am I Blue?" via a live feed from the Pennsylvania Roof.

June 13, 1937—WJZ–New York (NBC Blue), 2:00 p.m.–3:00 p.m. Bunny Berigan and His Orchestra were featured on NBC's RCA *Magic Key of Radio* program to promote a few of their new Victor records. They came on with a few bars of his theme, and then played "You Can't Run Away from Love Tonight" (vocal Ruth Bradley) and "Swanee River." The announcer for this program was Ben Grauer.

June 26, 1937—WABC-New York, 11:00 p.m.–11:30 p.m., from the Roof Garden of Hotel Pennsylvania, New York City: theme; "Peckin'"; "The First Time I Saw You" (vocal Ruth Bradley); "The Goona Goo" (vocal Bunny Berigan); "All Dark People Are Light on Their Feet" (vocal Ruth Bradley?); "When Two People Love Each Other" (RB); "Am I Blue?"; "Wake Up and Live" (RB); "Royal Garden Blues."

June 29, 1937—WABC–New York, 11:00 p.m.–11:30 p.m., from the Roof Garden of Hotel Pennsylvania, New York City; Bert Parks, announcer: "Dark Eyes"; "Wang Wang Blues"; "You're Gonna Wake Up Someday" (vocal Ruth Bradley); "The Man in the Moon" (RB); "Kiss Me Again"; "Poor Robinson Crusoe" (RB); "They All Laughed" (RB); "Louise"; "You Can't Run Away from Love Tonight" (RB); "Swanee River."

July 3, 1937—WABC–New York, 11:00 p.m.–11:30 p.m., from the Roof Garden of Hotel Pennsylvania, New York City: "Black Bottom"; "So Rare" (vocal

Ruth Bradley); "If I Had You"; "The Lady From Fifth Avenue" (RB); "All Dark People Are Light on Their Feet"; "Toodle-Oo"; "I'm Happy Darling, Dancing with You" (RB); "'Cause My Baby Says It's So" (vocal Bunny Berigan); "All God's Chillun Got Rhythm" (RB); "Mahogany Hall Stomp."

July 4, 1937—*Fun in Swingtime* radio show, WOR studios, 6:30 p.m.–7:00 p.m., New York City: "It Looks like Rain in Cherry Blossom Lane" (vocal Ruth Bradley); "They All Laughed" (RB); "Dark Eyes."

Juyl 6, 1937—WABC-New York, 11:05 p.m.–11:30 p.m., from the Roof Garden of Hotel Pennsylvania: theme (partial); "The You and Me That Used to Be" (vocal Ruth Bradley); "Who'll Be the One This Summer?" (RB); "You Can't Run Away from Love Tonight" (RB); "The Prisoner's Song"; "Poor Robinson Crusoe" (RB); "Love Is a Merry-Go-Round" (RB); "Swanee River"; "The Image of You" (RB); "Louise."

July 13, 1937—WABC-New York, 11:05 p.m.–11:30 p.m., from Pavilion Royal, Valley Stream, Long Island, New York: "Mother Goose" (vocal Ruth Bradley); "Swanee River"; "It Looks like Rain in Cherry Blossom Lane" (RB); "If I Had My Way"; "Rockin' Chair Swing"; "The Prisoner's Song"; "The Lady from Fifth Avenue" (RB); "Rose Room"; "I'm Happy Darling, Dancing with You" (RB); theme and closing.

July 16, 1937—NBC radio network shortwave broadcast to Great Britain via the BBC, 2:00 p.m.–3:00 p.m.?? Eastern time. It is not known from where this broadcast originated, but the NBC series of shortwave broadcasts to Great Britain entitled *America Dances* usually emanated from the NBC studios in Radio City. "Frankie and Johnny"; "'Cause My Baby Says It's So" (probably with a vocal by Bunny Berigan); "Mahogany Hall Stomp." The bands of Tommy Dorsey and Guy Lombardo also played on this broadcast.

July 17, 1937—WABC–New York, 11:05 p.m.–11:30 p.m., from Pavilion Royal, Valley Stream Long Island, New York: "Trees"; "It Looks like Rain in Cherry Blossom Lane" (vocal Ruth Bradley); "If I Had You"; "Rockin' Chair Swing"; "The Lady From Fifth Avenue" (RB); "I'm Happy Darling, Dancing with You" (RB); "The Prisoner's Song."

July 20, 1937—WABC–New York, 11:05 p.m.–11:30 p.m., from Pavilion Royal, Valley Stream Long Island, New York: "The Image of You" (vocal Ruth Bradley); "Frankie and Johnny"; "How Deep Is the Ocean?"; "I Can't Get Started" (vocal Bunny Berigan?); "'Cause My Baby Says It's So" (RB); "Never in a Million Years" (RB); "Swanee River"; "The Morning After" (RB); "The Prisoner's Song."

July 24, 1937—WABC–New York, 11:05 p.m.–11:30 p.m., from Pavilion Royal, Valley Stream Long Island, New York: "Black Bottom"; "Easy Living" (vocal Ruth Bradley); "The Ubangi Man"; "The Lady from Fifth Avenue" (RB); "Russian Lullaby"; "Strangers in the Dark" (RB); "Satan Takes a Holiday"; "Rockin' Chair Swing"; "Poor Robinson Crusoe" (RB); theme and closing.

August 3, 1937—WABC–New York, 11:05 p.m.–11:30 p.m., from Pavilion Royal, Valley Stream Long Island, New York: "Black Bottom"; "When Two Love Each Other" (vocal Gail Reese); "The Lady from Fifth Avenue" (GR); "Gone With the Wind"; "Royal Garden Blues"; "Poor Robinson Crusoe" (GR); "Satan Takes a Holiday"; "Love Is a Merry-Go-Round" (GR); "Yes, We Have No Bananas"; theme and closing.

August 10, 1937—WABC–New York, 11:05 p.m.–11:30 p.m., from Pavilion Royal, Valley Stream Long Island, New York: theme and introduction; "Mahogany Hall Stomp"; "A Little Bit Later On"; "Roses in December" (vocal Gail Reese); "Russian Lullaby"; "I'm Feeling like a Million" (GR); "Poor Robinson Crusoe" (GR??); "You Can't Run Away from Love Tonight" (GR); "Frankie and Johnny"; "The Lady from Fifth Avenue" (GR); theme and closing.

August 17, 1937—WABC–New York, 11:05 p.m.–11:30 p.m., from Pavilion Royal, Valley Stream Long Island, New York: theme and introduction; "Black Bottom"; "Sailboat in the Moonlight" (vocal Gail Reese??); "You Can't Run Away From Love Tonight" (GR); "Roses in December" (GR); "Swanee River"; "Let 'Er Go" (GR); "'Tain't So Honey, 'Tain't So"; "Stop, You're Breaking My Heart" (GR); "Mahogany Hall Stomp"; theme and closing.

August 21, 1937—WABC–New York, 11:05 p.m.–11:30 p.m., from Pavilion Royal, Valley Stream Long Island, New York: theme and introduction; "You Can't Run Away from Love Tonight" (vocal Gail Reese); "Yours and Mine"; "Thou Swell"; "A Message from the Man in the Moon" (GR); "Russian Lullaby"; "That Old Feeling" (GR); "'Cause My Baby Says It's So" (vocal Bunny Berigan); "I'm Feeling like a Million" (GR); "Yes, We Have No Bananas"; theme and closing.

October 7, 1937—*Fun in Swingtime* radio show, WOR studios 6:30 p.m.–7:00 p.m., New York City: "A Study in Brown"; "Caravan"; "Posin'" (with Tim and Irene); "A Sailboat in the Moonlight" (vocal Gail Reese??); "Kiss Me Again"; theme and closing.

October 10, 1937—Martin Block's *WNEW Swing Concert,* 11:30 p.m.–12:30 a.m., unknown studio location, New York City. Bunny Berigan played solos on the following tunes, accompanied by the WNEW House Orchestra: "Black Bottom"; "The Ubangi Man"; "Honeysuckle Rose"; and "Russian Lullaby."

October 14, 1937—*Martin Block's Make Believe Ballroom,* WNEW–New York, 6:00 p.m-6:30 p.m.; unknown studio location New York City. Bunny Berigan and His Orchestra performed the following: "A Study in Brown"; "Why Talk about Love?" (vocal Gail Reese); "Let 'Er Go" (GR); "That Old Feeling" (GR); "Frankie and Johnny"; "I Want a New Romance"; (GR); "Caravan"; "The Prisoner's Song."

November 13, 1937—WABC–New York, 11:00 p.m–11:30 p.m., from Valley Dale Ballroom, Columbus, Ohio: "Peg O' My Heart"; "So Many Memories" (vocal Gail Reese); "Can't Help Lovin' That Man"; "Miles Apart" (GR); "Sweet Varsity Sue" (GR); "I'd Love to Play a Love Scene" (GR); "No One Else But You"; "A Strange Loneliness" (GR); "The Prisoner's Song"; theme and closing.

March 10, 1038—WABC–New York, 11:30 p.m.–midnight, location unknown. "Back in Your Own Back Yard"; "A Serenade to the Stars" (vocal Gail Reese); "Heigh-Ho" (GR); "Goodnight Angel" (GR); "In a Little Spanish Town"; "Thanks for the Memory"; "'Tain't So Honey, 'Tain't So"; "The One I Love" (GR); "The Prisoner's Song."

April 1, 1938—WABC-New York, 8:30 p.m.–9:00 p.m., *Paul Whiteman in Concert*; unknown location in New York City. Bunny Berigan played a solo on "Dark Eyes" accompanied by Paul Whiteman's orchestra.

Spring 1938—unknown date and location: "Wacky Dust" (vocal Ruth Gaylor); "Moten Swing." These two titles probably were recorded at different times. "Moten Swing," though only a fragment, still clocks in at 4:33, and features some exceptional Berigan and a trombone solo by Sonny Lee. Vocalist Ruth Gaylor joined the Berigan band on approximately April 15, 1938. Sonny Lee departed on approximately the same date.

June 26, 1938—WJZ–New York, 2:00 p.m.–3:00 p.m. Bunny Berigan and His Orchestra were featured on NBC's *RCA Magic Key of Radio* program to promote a few of their new Victor records. They came on with a few bars of the theme, then played "Somewhere with Somebody Else" (vocal Dick Wharton), and "The Prisoner's Song."

July 23, 1938—via CBS to Great Britain, from the Marine Ballroom on the Steel Pier, Atlantic City, New Jersey. Since this broadcast was heard in England at 10:30 p.m., it originated some five hours earlier (Eastern time) from the Steel Pier. Theme and introduction; "Shanghai Shuffle"; "Somewhere with Somebody Else" (vocal??, probably Ruth Gaylor); "My Melancholy Baby"; "Flat Foot Floogie" (vocal Bunny Berigan?); "Wacky Dust"; "Devil's Holiday"; theme and closing.

Circa September 24, 1938, Bunny Berigan appeared on CBS's *Saturday Night Swing Club* and played "Dark Eyes," accompanied by the CBS House Orchestra.

October 5, 1938—WABC–New York, 11:30 p.m.–midnight, from Roseland Ballroom, New York City: "Gangbusters' Holiday"; "There's Something about an Old Love" (vocal Dick Wharton); "Royal Garden Blues"; "Small Fry" (vocal Jayne Dover); "The Wearin' of the Green"; "Now It Can Be Told" (DW); "Wacky Dust" (JD); "The Prisoner's Song."

October 12, 1938—WABC–New York, 11:30 p.m.–midnight, from Roseland Ballroom, New York City: "Black Bottom"; "Change Partners" (vocal Dick Wharton); "Sugar Foot Stomp"; "Livery Stable Blues"; "One O'Clock Jump"; "So Help Me" (DW); "Wacky Dust" (vocal Jayne Dover); "Anything Goes"; theme and closing.

December 1, 1938—WNEW–New York, unknown time in the evening. Berigan appeared on a jam session broadcast organized by radio personality Martin Block. An aircheck of this broadcast is among the numerous Berigan performances that are a part of the "Savory Recordings" (see below) now owned by the National Jazz Museum in Harlem. It is in excellent fidelity and presents Bunny in an informal setting with the following musicians: guitarist Slim Gaillard and bassist Slam Stewart, then performing together as *Slim and Slam;* tenor saxophonist Joe Thomas and trombonist Trummy Young, then with Jimmie Lunceford; clarinetist Buster Bailey and pianist Billy Kyle, then with John Kirby; and drummer Slick Jones, then with Fats Waller. Among the tunes recorded: an ad-lib "Blues," "I Got Rhythm," and a marvelous rendering of "I Can't Get Started," which is notable for Berigan's very relaxed vocal chorus.[1]

Notes

* A few airchecks of performances by Bunny Berigan without his band are included in this appendix. Most information contained in appendix 1 was derived from the White materials. The Berigan airchecks from his band's broadcasts from the Paradise Restaurant in New York City in the spring of 1938 are contained as a group in appendix 2.

Note: In August of 2010, it was announced by the National Jazz Museum in Harlem that approximately one hundred hours of off-the-air recordings of radio broadcasts by many of the greatest jazz musicians playing in the years 1935–1940, including Bunny Berigan, made by Bill Savory, a professional sound engineer, had recently been acquired by the museum. Attempts to obtain information as to which among these recordings were made by Berigan, what songs were played, and the dates and places where the broadcasts originated, (except for the above-described December 1, 1938 aircheck), have been largely unsuccessful, presumably because this information is still being gathered and organized. The National Jazz Museum in Harlem, through its director, Loren Schoenberg, has stated its intention to make these recordings and all information about them available to the public.

---

[1] I must thank the Director of the National Jazz Museum in Harlem, Loren Schoenberg, for playing some excerpts of the Savory/Berigan recordings now owned by the Museum for me when I visited him there on April 22, 2011.

Appendix Two
Bunny Berigan and His Orchestra
at the Paradise Restaurant

Bunny Berigan and His Orchestra opened at the Paradise Restaurant, Broadway and Forty-ninth Street, New York City on Sunday, March 20, 1938. During the band's stay there, they broadcast frequently over WOR–New York and the Mutual Network. Some of the Berigan band's finest playing during this engagement was captured on airchecks. Below is a listing of some of the tunes that were played during this engagement. The vast majority of these titles have been recorded as airchecks; those marked with an asterisk (*) were not. The Mutual announcers who hosted these broadcasts were Sidney Walton, Jerry Lawrence, and Herbert Morrison. (Herbert "Herb" Morrison [1905–1989] was the announcer who was working with a Pathgrams newsreel crew for WLS–Chicago at Lakehurst, New Jersey, on May 10, 1937, covering the arrival of the German zeppelin *Hindenburg*. His emotional account of the fiery crash of the *Hindenburg* is a milestone of news reporting.)

Sunday, March 27, 1938, 11:30 p.m.– midnight: introduction and theme; "Back in Your Own Back Yard"; "Down Stream," vocal, Gail Reese; "Rose Room"; "Sweet as a Song" (GR); "Let 'Er Go" (as an instrumental); "'Round My Old Deserted Farm" (GR); "How'd Ya Like to Love Me?" (GR); "Louisiana" (arrangement Lippman); theme and closing.

Sunday, April 3, 1938, midnight–12:30 a.m.: introduction and theme; "Have You Ever Been in Heaven?" (GR); "I Dance Alone" (GR);* "Peg O' My Heart"; Azure";* "Royal Garden Blues"; "An Old Straw Hat" (GR)";* "It's Wonderful" (GR); "Caravan";* "Frankie and Johnnie"; theme and closing.

Friday, April 8, 1938, 11:30–midnight: "It's Wonderful" (GR); "Swanee River"; "'Round My Old Deserted Farm" (GR); "Devil's Holiday"; "An Old Straw Hat" (GR); "Am I Blue?"; "Whistle While You Work"(GR); "Let 'Er Go" (as an instrumental/partial); theme and closing.

Sunday, April 10, 1938, midnight–12:30 a.m.: "You Took the Words Right Out of My Heart" (GR); "Kiss Me Again"; "Sweet Varsity Sue" (GR); unknown title, vocal Gail Reese; "The Prisoner's Song" (incomplete). At some point in this broadcast, "Shanghai Shuffle" was played.

Saturday, April 16, 1938, 10:30 p.m.–11:00 p.m. (Herb Morrison, announcer): "Star Dust," vocal Dick Wharton; unknown title, vocal Ruth Gaylor; "A Study in Brown" (incomplete); segue into theme and closing.

Sunday, April 24, 1938, midnight–12:30 a.m.: "I'll Always Be in Love with You"; "'Round My Old Deserted Farm" (RG);* "Shanghai Shuffle"; "Moonshine over Kentucky" (RG)*.

Tuesday, May 3, 1938, WMCA, 10:30–11:00 p.m. (Herb Morrison, announcer): "Moonshine over Kentucky" (RG); "Down Stream" (RG); "Heigh-Ho" (RG); "Trees"; "Black Bottom" (interpolating "The Peanut Vendor" and "Christopher Columbus"); theme and closing.

Many of these titles can be found on Jazz Hour CD JH-1022.

Appendix Three
1938 *Thesaurus* Radio Transcription Recordings
by Bunny Berigan and His Orchestra

Recorded on June 27, 1938, in New York City. (See note below.) Personnel: Bunny Berigan, leader/trumpet; Steve Lipkins, Irving Goodman, trumpets; Nat Lobovsky and Ray Conniff, trombones; Mike Doty, Joe Dixon, Georgie Auld, Clyde Rounds, saxophones/clarinets; Joe Bushkin, piano; Dick Wharton, guitar; Hank Wayland, bass; Johnny Blowers, drums. (I) = instrumental; (RG) = vocal by Ruth Gaylor (listed as "Elsie Wright" on the *Thesaurus* issues); (BM&b) = vocal by Bernie Mackey (as "Burt Victor") and band; (DW) = vocal by Dick Wharton (as "Bob Brown").

Thesaurus transcriptions were leased to radio stations, and the names of the performers who recorded them (which were often pseudonyms) were not used when the discs were played on radio. Each tune was recorded in one take, and very often, vocals were excised from arrangements that had been written specifically to present a vocal chorus. Considering the conditions under which these recordings were made, it is remarkable that the quality of the performances is as high as it is. Indeed, many of Bunny Berigan's *Thesaurus* transcription recordings contain performances that are superior to those on the commercial records he made for RCA Victor.

"Now It Can Be Told"	(I)	1:58
"My Walking Stick"	(RG)	3:20
"Wacky Dust"	(I)	2:42
"And So Forth"	(I)	2:10
"Flat Foot Floogie"	(BM&b)	3:43
"Ten Easy Lessons"	(RG)	3:10
"I Got a Guy"	(I)	2:04
"Tonight Will Live"	(I)	1:50
"Cowboy from Brooklyn"	(I)	1:57
"Easy to Find and Hard to Lose"	(DW)	3:13
"Don't Wake Up My Heart"	(DW)	2:47
"Frankie and Johnnie"	(I)	2:45
"The Pied Piper"	(RG)	3:28
"I Never Knew"	(I)	2:20
"Shanghai Shuffle"	(I)	3:38

"Devil's Holiday"	(I)	2:38
"The Wearin' of the Green"	(I)	3:29
"Sunday"	(I)	2:23
"I'll Always Be in Love with You"	(I)	3:29
"Black Bottom"	(I)	2:54

Notes on the June 27, 1938, recordings:

1) Irving Berlin's "My Walking Stick" had been recorded on Victor by Tommy Dorsey (April 27, 1938) with a vocal by Edythe Wright, so Bunny was unable to record it for Victor. That is too bad, because this arrangement, with solos by Dixon, Conniff, and Auld, is excellent. In this version, Bunny, using his kazoo mute, gives new meaning to the term "dirty" trumpet. Based on the use of the reeds and trombones, I would say that this is almost certainly a Lippman chart.

2) "Flat Foot Floogie" was a current pop composed by the absolutely wild Slim Gaillard, the fine bassist Slam Stewart (then performing together as "Slim and Slam"), and Bud Green. Bunny was aced out on this by Benny Goodman, who had a good recording of it (with a tasty Harry James trumpet solo) on Victor (May 31, 1938). In this version, Bernard N. "Bernie" Mackey, who had subbed for an ailing Robert "Little Gate" Walker as the Berigan band's equipment manager/truck driver earlier in the year, then remained as Little Gate's assistant when he returned, was tapped to sing the jivey lyric. Although this all seems rather improbable, Mackey was then studying guitar, and later joined the Ink Spots playing guitar and singing, so he no doubt had some singing experience. Bunny contributes an exuberant trumpet solo; Bushkin, Conniff, Auld, and Dixon also solo. Clocking in at 3:43, this performance hints at what the Berigan band would do in front of audiences, by extending arrangements to allow for more solos. There is no indication anywhere as to who wrote this chart, though I suspect it was one of Andy Phillips's first arrangements for the Berigan band.

3) "Shanghai Shuffle" was arranged by Fletcher Henderson, and is the same arrangement that he recorded with his own band for Decca on September 11, 1934. The soloists are Auld, Dixon on clarinet, Bunny's splendid trumpet, and Dixon again, but on alto sax.

4) "I Got a Guy" and "Tonight Will Live" both dispense with the vocal chorus. These are good examples of how good rather lightweight pop tunes could sound when played by Bunny and his boys, without a vocal chorus to weigh down the performance.

5) "Cowboy from Brooklyn" was composed by the great Harry Warren.[1] (The lyric by Johnny Mercer was not sung in this performance.) This simple rhythmic novelty tune from the film of the same name starring Dick Powell *could and*

should have been recorded by the Berigan band, *with a vocal.* This sort of material was not suited to Berigan's male vocalist Dick Wharton, though Ruthie Gaylor could have made it work as a "cowgirl." Joe Bushkin, who occasionally sang novelties, also could have made it work. It would have been an attractive recording. The minimalist arrangement, probably by Andy Phillips, is straightforward and swinging, and with a bit of sprucing up, would have set off the vocal quite nicely. As discussed in the text, Victor's executives were oblivious, probably because Tommy Dorsey had already recorded the tune. This performance contains a rather awkward pause, which occurs at the point where the vocal chorus was excised, after which there is a brief but marvelous tenor saxophone solo by Georgie Auld.

6) "Devil's Holiday" was arranged by Benny Carter, and is the same arrangement he recorded with his own band for Columbia (Parlophone) on October 16, 1933. Auld leads off on tenor saxophone with Bunny's impassioned trumpet lead and Blowers's backbeats behind him. Dixon plays an agile clarinet solo, followed by Bunny. (Hear the exceptional saxophone section passages along the way, a Carter trademark.)

7) "Easy to Find, Hard to Lose" spots another good dance arrangement, probably by Andy Phillips, with Bunny setting forth the melody using a Harmon mute. Dick Wharton sings the lyric. Listen to Bunny scale the heights after the vocal! Other soloists were Auld and Lobovsky.

8) "The Wearin' of the Green" is performed well by Bunny and the band here, but not as well as the Victor recording, which is definitive.

9) Likewise, "The Pied Piper" gets a good presentation here, quite different from the Victor record, but slightly less exciting than that performance.

10) "Sunday" is likely a Lippman arrangement featuring solos by Bunny, Bushkin, and Dixon. It is taken at a brisk tempo and is an excellent example of how this band could interpret a good song cast in a fine arrangement. Lippman was clearly influenced by Fletcher Henderson here—listen to the clarinets in the final chorus. This performance swings all the way.

11) "Frankie and Johnnie" was a staple of the Berigan repertoire, and the band never performed it any better than it does here. The soloists in this rollicking performance are Berigan, Auld, Dixon, Wayland, and Blowers. Bunny's trumpet lead lights up the last chorus.

12) "Don't Wake Up My Heart" was another current pop tune from 1938. Auld and Lobovsky play solos in the first chorus, along with Bunny once again using a Harmon mute. I'd say that this is a Lippman arrangement because of his dep-

loyment of the reeds. Wharton sings and then the band ushers in Mr. B. for a few final thoughts.

13) "I'll Always Be in Love with You" was arranged by Fletcher Henderson, and is the same arrangement he recorded for Victor with his own band on April 9, 1936. This arrangement was also recorded for Victor by Benny Goodman on December 15, 1938. (BG by then evidently had enough power at Victor to record this tune for that label even though the Henderson disc may still have been on the market.) Soloists here are Auld, Dixon, an ultrawarm Berigan, Bushkin, and Conniff. One wonders why Bunny didn't record this for Victor. He was obviously playing it months before the Goodman recording was made. Victor's executives may well have nixed any such idea in deference to the Henderson disc.

14) "I Never Knew (I Could Love Anybody)" is taken at fast tempo. This arrangement features a solo by Conniff, then a splendid soli chorus by the saxophones, a brass fanfare, rocking Auld, then a Berigan-led finale.

15) "Black Bottom" is another Berigan standard, which could be expanded and contracted to accommodate time constraints. Here, we have two minutes and fifty-five seconds of swing spotting a sweeping solo by Bunny, with Auld and Conniff also contributing bracing solos.

Recorded on August 8–9, 1938, in New York City: Personnel as above except Bernard "Buddy" Rich replaces Blowers on drums.

"Small Fry"	(RG)	3:41
"So Help Me"	(DW)	2:52
"My Best Wishes"	(I)	2:32
"Will You Remember Tonight Tomorrow?"	(I)	2:08
"Hi Yo, Silver"	(RG&b)	2:03
"There's Something about an Old Love"	(DW)	3:17
"Where in the World?"	(DW)	3:18
"Meet the Beat of My Heart"	(I)	2:05
"I Used to Be Color Blind"	(I)	3:22
"Change Partners"	(I)	2:34
"Night Filled with Music"	(I)	2:48
"There's a Brand New Picture in My Picture Frame"	(I)	2:01
"Sing You Sinners"	(I)	2:27

"Peg O' My Heart"	(I)	2:56
"'Tain't So Honey, 'Tain't So"	(I)	3:13
"Mahogany Hall Stomp"	(I)	2:16

Almost all of these titles can be found on Jazz Classics CD-JZCL 5016 entitled *Bunny Berigan and the Rhythm Makers.*

Notes on the August 8–9, 1938 recordings:

1) "There's Something about an Old Love" was arranged by Andy Phillips, who by this time was writing most arrangements on current pop tunes for the Berigan band. It is cast in an especially musical setting.

2) "Small Fry" was brand new when this recording was made. This novelty tune was composed by Frank Loesser and Hoagy Carmichael for the film *Sing You Sinners* and it gets a good swinging treatment here.

3) "Change Partners" is one of Irving Berlin's most sensuous ballads. This arrangement, which I think was written by Joe Lippman, later featured a vocal chorus, which sung by Danny Richards, the best male vocalist ever to work with Berigan, would have made a wonderful record. Bunny's lovely open trumpet is the highlight of this performance.

4) "Sing You Sinners" was arranged by Fletcher Henderson, and is the same arrangement he recorded on Vocalion with his own band on October 25, 1937. Just so that everyone is confused, this tune was composed by Sam Coslow for the 1930 film *Honey,* and has absolutely no connection with the 1938 film entitled *Sing You Sinners.*

5) Along with "The Wearin' of the Green," "Peg O' My Heart" is another of the "Irish" tunes Bunny had in his book at this time. It was reported in *Billboard* in the spring of 1938 that "Bunny Berigan has been signed by Jack Robbins to make swing arrangements of Irish ballads and folk songs. He is giving his swing style the once-over and has arranger Willard Robison to inject his 'Deep River' rhythm."[2] This rendition of "Peg O' My Heart" is brimming with spirit and is the best of Bunny's recordings of it. In spite of the above-cited comment about Willard Robison, I think he had nothing to do with this arrangement. I'd say it was written by Joe Lippman.

There is some confusion as to where some of the 1938 Berigan *Thesaurus* transcriptions were made. One musician who was a member of Bunny's band when the 1938 sessions were recorded (Joe Dixon) suggested that one of those sessions was made at RCA Victor's "church studio" in Camden, New Jersey. I am of the opinion that this is very unlikely based on the itinerary of the Berigan band on the dates before and after the two 1938 Berigan/*Thesaurus* sessions. I also offer the following information which is contained in *Benny Goodman, The Record of a Legend,* by D. Russell Connor, Let's Dance Corp. (1984), page 63: "In early 1935, the National Broadcasting Company inaugurated its *Thesaurus* electrical transcription service. Its discs were 16" lateral cut 331/3 rpm plastic ETs, distributed on a lease basis to subscribing stations. ...All of the *Thesaurus* ETs were recorded in New York City and pressed in Camden, New Jersey."

Notes

[1] Harry Warren was born Salvatore Antonio Guaragna on December 24, 1893 in Brooklyn, New York. Although he did work for a short time in the Broadway theater, his greatest songs were composed for Hollywood films from the 1930s into the 1950s. The number of hits and standards composed by Harry Warren is staggering. A few choice examples include "Forty-Second Street," "The Boulevard of Broken Dreams," "Lullaby of Broadway," "September in the Rain," "Chatanooga Choo-Choo," "At Last," "I Had the Craziest Dream," "Serenade in Blue," "There Will Never Be Another You," "The More I See You," "That's Amore," "An Affair to Remember." Harry Warren died on September 22, 1981, in Los Angeles, California.

[2] *Billboard:* April 30 and May 7, 1938, as cited in the White materials: April 30, 1938.

Appendix Four
Aircheck Recordings by Bunny Berigan and His Orchestra, 1939–1942

The following are recordings of broadcasts by Bunny Berigan and His Orchestra. The vast majority of these aircheck recordings have never ever been issued commercially.

Note: The aircheck recordings of "Hold Tight" (January 21, 1939), and "Old Man Mose" (January 28, 1939), which have been issued numerous times as being by Bunny Berigan and His Orchestra, are *not* recordings by the Berigan band, nor do they feature the solos of Bunny Berigan. They are probably from the *Saturday Night Swing Club* broadcasts made on those dates, and feature the CBS house band. I discern the distinctive first alto saxophone sound of Nuncio "Toots" Mondello on these recordings, and he was a member of the CBS band at that time.

March 19, 1939—Hotel New Yorker, New York City; WABC–New York, 10:00 p.m.–11:30 p.m.: "Trees"; "I Have Eyes" (vocal Kathleen Lane); "Gangbusters' Holiday"; "I Cried for You" (KL); "A Room with a View" (vocal Danny Richards); "Little Gate's Special"; theme and closing.

Ca. April 9, 1939—Trianon Ballroom, Cleveland, Ohio; WCLE–Cleveland, 11:00 p.m.–11:30 p.m.: "Familiar Moe";* "Trees"; I Want My Share of Love" (KL); "This Night" (DR); "Black Bottom"; "I Cried for You" (KL); "Little Gate's Special"; "I Can't Forget You." (*"Familiar Moe," an original composition /arrangement by Ray Conniff, which is a clever concoction blending the riff tune "Time Out," composed Edgar Battle and Eddie Durham, and arranged by Durham for the early Count Basie band, and the chords behind the trombone solo [played many times by Conniff] in Joe Lippman's arrangement for the Berigan band on "A Study in Brown." It is the antecedent for his marvelous study in chromaticism "Prelude in C Sharp Major," which was recorded by Artie Shaw in December of 1940.)

Circa June 22, 1939—Westwood Symphony Gardens, Dearborn, Michigan; WWJ–Detroit, 12:00 midnight–12:30 a.m.: theme, with opening announcements; "My Melancholy Baby"; "I Can't Get Started" (incomplete with announcements); "Sobbin' Blues"; "Deep Purple" (DR); "The Lady's in Love with You" (vocal Wendy Bishop); "Savoy Jump"; "'Deed I Do"; "If You Ever

Change Your Mind" (WB, incomplete); "Deep Purple" (DR); "'Tain't So Honey, 'Tain't So"; "Patty Cake, Patty Cake" (WB); "The Masquerade is Over" (DR).

June 25, 1939—Valley Dale Ballroom, Columbus, Ohio; WABC–New York, 12:00 midnight–12:30 a.m.: theme (incomplete); "St Louis Blues"; "That Sentimental Sandwich" (DR); "If You Ever Change Your Mind"; (vocal Ellen Kaye [Kayler]); "Little Gate's Special"; "Deep Purple" (DR); "Patty Cake, Patty Cake" (EK); "Savoy Jump"; theme (incomplete).

July 11, 1939—Panther Room of Hotel Sherman, Chicago, Illinois; WMAQ–Chicago, 11:00 p.m.–11:30 p.m.: "Heaven Can Wait"; "The Lady's in Love with You" (EK); "The Lamp Is Low" (DR).

July 21, 1939—Panther Room of Hotel Sherman, Chicago; WENR–Chicago, 11:00–11:30 p.m.: "St. Louis Blues"; "Azure"; "Our Love" (DR); "Savoy Jump"; "And the Angels Sing" (DR); "That Sentimental Sandwich" (DR); "Symphony in Riffs."

July 23, 1939—Panther Room of Hotel Sherman, Chicago; WENR–Chicago, 11:00 p.m.–11:30 p.m.: "Perisphere Hop"; "The Day We Meet Again" (DR); "In The Middle of a Dream" (DR); "Moten Swing"; "Blue Evening" (DR); "Don't Worry 'Bout Me" (DR); "Especially for You"; "Trylon Trot."

July 25, 1939—Panther Room of Hotel Sherman, Chicago; WENR–Chicago, 12:30 a.m.–1:00 a.m: "Shanghai Shuffle"; "White Sails"; "The Day We Meet Again" (DR); "There'll Be Some Changes Made"; "I Poured My Heart into a Song" (DR); "Especially for You"; "Blue Evening; (DR); "Sugar Foot Stomp"; theme (incomplete).

July 27, 1939—Panther Room of Hotel Sherman, Chicago; WENR–Chicago, 11:00 p.m.–11:30 p.m.: "St. Louis Blues"; "The Lamp Is Low"; "My Heart Has Wings" (DR); "'Deed I Do"; (vocal Bunny Berigan); "Jelly Roll Blues"; "Rendezvous Time in Paree" (DR); "White Sails"; "Devil's Holiday"; theme (incomplete).

July 28, 1939—Panther Room of Hotel Sherman, Chicago; WENR–Chicago, 11:00 p.m.–11:30 p.m.: "'Tain't So Honey, 'Tain't So"; "Moon Love"; "I Poured My Heart into a Song" (DR); "Sobbin' Blues"; "Azure"; "In the Middle of a Dream" (DR); "Especially for You"; theme (incomplete).

July 29, 1939—Panther Room of Hotel Sherman, Chicago; WENR–Chicago, 11:00 p.m.–11:30 p.m.: "Trylon Trot"; "Azure"; "Don't Worry 'Bout Me" (DR);

"Shanghai Shuffle"; "The Lady's in Love with You" (vocal Joe Bushkin); "Wacky Dust"; "The Day We Meet Again" (DR); theme (incomplete).

July 30, 1939—Panther Room of Hotel Sherman, Chicago; WENR–Chicago, 11:00 p.m.–11:30 p.m.: "Black Bottom"; "Especially for You"; "My Heart Has Wings" (DR); "I Can't Get Started" (vocal Bunny Berigan); "The Lamp Is Low"; "Blue Evening" (DR); "The Wearin' of the Green"; theme (incomplete).

The following titles were also recorded while the Berigan band was at Hotel Sherman in 1939. The dates are unknown; some may be from the above-cited broadcasts, some from other dates. "Livery Stable Blues";* "'Deed I Do"; "Savoy Jump"; "I Can't Get Started" (vocal Berigan, incomplete, with announcements); "Sugar Foot Stomp"; "Panama"; "Easy to Blame the Weather" (DR); "Our Love"; "Jazz Me Blues"; and "The Prisoner's Song." Any of these titles that duplicate ones previously cited may be different performances of the same song. (*Berigan's two chorus solo on "Livery Stable Blues" is magnificent. The first twelve bars have him playing in his middle and low registers, setting up what is to come. The second twelve bars, including room-shaking high notes, demonstrate a supreme level of virtuoso instrumental command and a musical imagination of almost frightening intensity.)

September 20, 1939—Totem Pole Ballroom, Norumbega Park, Auburndale, Massachusetts; WOR–New York, 8:00 p.m.–8:30 p.m.: theme (incomplete); "Don't Worry 'Bout Me" (DR); "Ay-Ay-Ay"; "Our Love" (DR); "Begin the Beguine"; "'Deed I Do" (incomplete); "On the Alamo" (incomplete).

September 26, 1939—Manhattan Center, New York City; WNEW–New York, 8:00 p.m.–8:30 p.m.: theme (incomplete with announcements); "Ay-Ay-Ay"; "I Poured My Heart into a Song" (DR); "Caravan"; "Swingin' and Jumpin'"; "Little Gate's Special"; theme (incomplete with announcements).

October 16, 1939—Mardi Gras Casino, New York World's Fair, New York City; WEEI–Boston, 11:30 p.m.–midnight: "Ay-Ay-Ay"; "My Heart Has Wings" (DR); "Caravan"; "Russian Lullaby"; "Begin the Beguine"; "I Poured My Heart into a Song" (DR); "Royal Garden Blues"; theme (incomplete).

October 23, 1939 – Southland Club, Boston; WJZ–Boston, 10:00 p.m.–10:30 p.m.: "Ay-Ay-Ay"; "Over the Rainbow: (vocal Kay Doyle); "Swingin' and Jumpin'"; "What's New?" (DR); "St. Louis Blues" (vocal Al Jennings); "The Jumpin' Jive" (KD); "I Poured My Heart into a Song" (DR); theme (incomplete).

January 22, 1940—Marionette Room of Hotel Brunswick, Boston; WEEI–Boston, midnight–12:30 a.m.: "Peg O' My Heart"; "Last Night" (DR); "Careless"; "Coquette"; "You're a Lucky Guy"; "Azure"; "Faithful Forever" (DR); "'Tain't So Honey, 'Tain't So"; theme (incomplete).

January 24, 1940—Marionette Room of Hotel Brunswick, Boston; WEEI–Boston, midnight–12:30 a.m.: "In the Mood"; "After All" (DR); "Would Ya Mind?"; "Ay-Ay-Ay"; "Faithful Forever" (DR); "Jelly Roll Blues"; "The Prisoner's Song"; theme (incomplete).

October 14, 1940—Dancing Campus, New York World's Fair, New York City; WEAF or WJZ, time unknown: theme (with announcements); "Swingin' on the Campus"; "Maybe" (DR); "Rum Boogie" (vocal Kathleen Lane); "There I Go" (DR); "Tuxedo Junction"; "A Million Dreams Ago" (KL); "Marcheta"; theme (incomplete).

January 19, 1941—Valley Dale Ballroom, Columbus. While the Berigan band played this engagement, someone made a few homemade recordings. They are: "Lover Come Back to Me"; an unknown ballad; "Swanee River"; "The Nearness of You" (DR).

April 22, 1941—Carnegie Hall, New York City. Bunny Berigan appeared without his band as a part of a large review entitled *A Café Society Concert—Jazz and Classics*. He played on "One O'Clock Jump" and "Blues." The concert was not broadcast but some or all of it was recorded.

November 4, 1941—Possibly World Recording Studios, New York City. This is not an aircheck, but rather a promotional recording date, which was sponsored by Pepsi-Cola. The tunes recorded were jingles promoting Pepsi-Cola: "Pepsi-Cola Hits the Spot"; and "Get Hep with Pepsi-Cola."

April 12, 1942 – Nu-Elms Ballroom, Youngstown, Ohio, time and station unknown: "I'm Confessin'." This is the last known recording made by Bunny Berigan.

Appendix Five
Studio Talk

The following is a transcript of the discussion in the recording studio after a rejected take of "Find Me a Primitive Man," April 11, 1940. By the time this exchange took place shortly after midnight, Bunny Berigan had been in recording studios for the previous fifteen hours, with two short breaks for lunch and dinner. This recording session with Lee Wiley, which had produced three usable masters among numerous rejected takes and breakdowns, was entering hour five.

A take of "Find Me a Primitive Man" ends. Laughter.

Lee Wiley: Well, that was perfect all except the end, I think, and that don't upset me that much...Wasn't it?

Berigan begins humming the melody of "Find Me a Primitive Man," perfectly on pitch.

LW: Well, what was wrong with that? That's what I'm trying to figure out.

Berigan continues humming. There is silence otherwise. Breaking the pregnant pause...

Joe Bushkin (piano): Well, it was OK except for the ending.

Berigan continues humming, and then...to Wiley:

BB: You didn't, you don't do what (we rehearsed)...

LW: (defensively to Bushkin) ...You didn't change the chord...

BB: (to Wiley)...*You* don't change the chord...

LW: (peevishly)...Well, it doesn't matter what I do. I can do anything...

JB: Well, I got to know what you're doing...

LW: (now conciliatory, to Bushkin)...Darling, I started out and the reason I didn't change is that you didn't give me a chord. You only played one chord with me...

JB: I played two chords...

BB: (softly to Wiley)...Uh, you just didn't sing the last note. That was all that was wrong. Know what I mean?

LW: I didn't because he didn't change the chord.

BB: No, he played the same as he always played.

LW: (in her most sheepish, babylike voice to Berigan)…Well, if he did, I would have sung it. (Then more defensively, to Bushkin)…I've been doing that all my life, I don't know why I wouldn't have done it there…*You didn't change in the right places*…

BB: (Now agitated, to the recording supervisor) …Put on some more wax! Put on some more wax!

Sid Weiss (bass): Well, let's make this one.

George Wettling (drums) starts drumming on his high-hat cymbals.

Berigan resumes humming…and a new take begins.

Appendix Six
Information Regarding the Film *Syncopation*

Produced by RKO-Radio Pictures; William Dieterle, Director/Producer. Filmed in black and white; running time, 90 minutes. Released on May 22, 1942. From an original story *The Band Played On,* by Valentine Davies.
Cast:

Jackie Cooper	—	Johnny
Bonita Granville	—	Kit Latimer
Adolphe Menjou	—	George Latimer
Todd Duncan	—	Reggie/Rex Tearbone
George Bancroft	—	Mr. Porter
Rex Stewart	—	King Jeffers (no screen credit)

Connie Boswell appears toward the end of the film and sings "Under a Falling Star."

Music supervision was by Leith Stevens. The musicians whose playing is heard on the soundtrack in the numerous traditional jazz band and solo piano sequences that appear during the film (except for the All-Star epilogue), including Bunny Berigan, receive no screen credit.

The epilogue contains the following musicians, who were selected as "The All-American Dance Band" by the readers of the *Saturday Evening Post* magazine: Benny Goodman, clarinet; Jack Jenney (erroneously billed as "Jenny"), trombone; Harry James, trumpet; Charlie Barnet, tenor saxophone; Alvino Rey, guitar; Joe Venuti, violin; Gene Krupa, drums. Each of them appears and is plainly identified onscreen. Eddie Duchin was selected as pianist, but did not appear in the film or play on the soundtrack. The piano parts for the epilogue were played by Howard Smith; the bass parts by Bob Haggart. Neither appeared onscreen or received any screen credit. The epilogue sequences were filmed and the soundtrack for it was recorded at the Fox-Movietone studios in Manhattan in February 1942.

I am of the opinion that Bunny Berigan's trumpet can be heard in the following sequences:
—When Reggie plays with King Jeffers.
—When Kit is listening to a record on her birthday.
—When Rex Tearbone is playing trumpet on closing night in a club on Basin Street.

—When Reggie/Rex is playing in a club in Chicago.
—When Reggie/Rex is playing to a star to console Kit.
—When Johnny sits-in with Rex for an all-night jam session.
—When Johnny plays at the Club Grandioso.
—When Johnny and his band members learn they have been booked into the Star Room.
—When Kit and Johnny dance to the music of a phonograph record.
—When Johnny's band is playing at the Jive Club.
—At the beginning of the closing credits.

General Index

Name Index

About the Author

Michael P. Zirpolo is a practicing lawyer in Canton, Ohio. He has written numerous articles and given many lectures in the last fifteen years on jazz musicians from the swing era, including Duke Ellington (and his sidemen Sonny Greer and Russell Procope), Artie Shaw, Roy Eldridge, Tommy Dorsey, Gene Krupa, and Bunny Berigan. He has written criticisms of reissues of classic jazz recordings and of books about the music and musicians of the swing era. He has also written about the development of swing and the contributions to that development made by Louis Armstrong and Bix Beiderbecke. He is a longtime collector of jazz recordings from the 1920s to the 1980s, and has developed considerable skill in the art of digitally remastering vintage recordings. He is frequently consulted by writers and collectors of vintage jazz recordings from around the globe with questions about the music, recordings, and musicians of the swing era, and has appeared on radio and television discussing classic jazz. In addition to jazz and American popular song, he is a devotee of long form music. He can be contacted at: mzirpolo@neo.rr.com